INTERNATIONAL
INVESTMENTS PROTECTION

INTERNATIONAL INVESTMENTS PROTECTION

Comparative Law Analysis of
Bilateral and Multilateral Interstate Conventions,
Doctrinal Texts and Arbitral Jurisprudence
concerning Foreign Investments

Jan SCHOKKAERT, j.d.
Yvon HECKSCHER, j.d.

FOREWORD BY
Filip REYNTJENS
Professor of Law and Politics
University of Antwerp

*Work published with the support of the
Antwerp University Institute for Development
Policy and Management (IOB)
Antwerp, Belgium*

BRUXELLES
2 0 0 9

ISBN 978-2-8027-2628-9

D / 2009 / 0023 / 27

© 2009 Etablissements Emile Bruylant, S.A.
Rue de la Régence 67, 1000 Bruxelles.

Tous droits, même de reproduction d'extraits, de reproduction photomécanique ou de traduction, réservés.
IMPRIMÉ EN BELGIQUE

ACKNOWLEDGMENTS

This Work is the result of close cooperation between the authors in the area of law and linguistics as well as in the technologies which modern composition of any work of letters now requires. Each author contributed his knowledge of the law on the subject and critiqued the other unrelentingly, the aim being a melding of the authors' occasionally greater experience with any one of the subjects treated and the correct presentation of the results of this critique in a language that is now frequently seen as the lingua franca of the investment world.

The authors owe a significant debt of gratitude to Dr. Filip REYNTJENS, Professor of Law and Politics, University of Antwerp, Belgium, whose encouragement and guidance on a broad swath of subjects encompassed by this Work have in no small measure made it possible. Our thanks also to Mr. ERKENS and Mr. COLIN, of the Law Library of the Belgian Ministry of Foreign Affairs for their assistance in the selection of the bibliography we have drawn upon.

The presentation also required a significant reliance on electronic composition technology and computer literacy. Our acknowledgments of a debt that will be difficult to repay goes to Gisèle Dominique HECKSCHER, MBA in Information Sciences, University of Oakland, for her willingness to help guide our steps and improve composition through the best use of composition technology and word processing programs, as well as to Ken EDWARDS, computer technician, for helping us keep our computers and word processing programs and equipment in optimal condition throughout the many months that the composition, review and proofing of this Work required. Without naming several others, who engaged us in discussions of the many topics addressed in this Work and helped us refine our analysis so that it will be presented in a form that provides the maximum assistance to our readers, we wish to express our gratitude to them.

Not all topics have been addressed in the same depth, mostly because as we developed our composition, we came to the conclusion that, had we given to all topics an equal amount of attention, the physical size of the Work might have deterred many of our readers who are already professionals in their own right. We shall be grateful to all our readers for any comments, questions or critiques they may be willing to communicate to help us improve a Work that, in essence, is in the flux of ever changing circumstances in the international investment world.

ADVICE TO READERS

This Work contains numerous citations from the works of authors whose comments we have used to illustrate our remarks. We have striven to reproduce in the English language as faithfully as possible the presumed meaning and intentions of the authors cited but we admit that verbatim translations sometimes obscure such meaning. Hence, somewhat in free style, we have translated idiomatic uses proper to a particular language, such as French, Dutch, German into a form which, idiomatically in English, will most closely resemble what the authors of this work think was intended in the original text. At the bottom of each page where a citation is listed for reference, the original title of the work cited has been provided so the reader may more easily verify the fidelity of our translations. We offer our most sincere apologies if, on occasion, we may have diverged, misinterpreted, gone beyond or fallen short of the original author's meaning and invite all our readers, should any of them be of that opinion, to alert us to any such divergence or misinterpretation.

The Work includes a Bibliography with categories of Authors, Other Authorities, Table of Cases, and a Table of Websites. It contains also an extensive word index. To our knowledge, no such index exists in the legal or technical literature relating to international investment conventions. This Work does not aspire to cover all forms of and all locations of international investment. Its focus is on private foreign investment in less developed countries, sometimes referred to as the less industrialized world. No significant attempt has been made to analyse investments between countries of the industialised world. Nonetheless. it should be of substantial value in expediting a reader's research of any one particular topic regarding conventional protection of international investments in second and third world locations.

For the moment, we believe the present Work constitutes an important step in alerting jurists, legislative aides, prospective investors and their counsellors to problems and suggesting solutions to them in the field of conventional protection of international investments, which, in the past, all too often have proven to be a literal minefield for the underinformed.

The authors

TABLE OF CONTENTS
*(References are to page number (right),
paragraph number (left))*

	PAGES
ACKNOWLEDGMENTS	VII
ADVICE TO READERS	IX
FOREWORD	1
CHAPTER I. – INTRODUCTION	5
1.1. – *Investment Doctrinally Defined*	5
1.2. – *Elements of "Investments"*	6
1.3. – *Direct or Indirect Investments*	7
1.4. – *"New Investment forms"*	11
1.5. – *International Investments*	13
1.6. – *Limited review*	18
CHAPTER II. – DIPLOMATIC PROTECTION FOR INTERNATIONAL INVESTMENTS AND INVESTORS	19
2.1. – *Entitlement to diplomatic Protection*	19
2.2. – *Duty to accept protection*	20
2.3. – *Waiver of indemnification*	22
2.4. – *Diplomatic Protection is available to Nationals only*	23
2.5. – *Effect of "control"*	24
2.6. – *Direct Filing of Claims by Claimant, e.g. through local Tribunals*	25
2.7. – *Only States may file in international judiciary Tribunals*	26
2.8. – *Procedure for filing individual Claims*	28

	PAGES
2.9. – *Violation of local Law disqualifies diplomatic Protection*	30
2.10. – *Exhaustion of Local Remedies – A Prerequisite*	31
CHAPTER III. – NATIONAL PROTECTION OF INTERNATIONAL INVESTMENTS	35
3.1. – *Origins of national protection*	35
3.2. – *Linking investments with economic growth and development*	35
3.3. – *Analysis of investment codes*	37
3.4. – *Need for conventional protection*	62
CHAPTER IV. – CONVENTION BASED INVESTMENT PROTECTION	65
4.1. – *Need for Convention based Investment Protection*	65
4.2. – *Scholars' Diversity of Opinion regarding BIT's*	66
4.3. – *Economic Impact of BIT's*	68
4.4. – *Inadequacy and Inconsistency of Information*	71
4.5. – *International investors' expectations*	74
4.6. – *Bilateralism vs. Multilateralism*	75
CHAPTER V. – MULTILATERAL PROTECTION CONVENTIONS	77
5.1. – *Premise of Multilateral Conventions*	77
5.2. – *Organisation for Economic Cooperation and Development (OECD)*	78
5.3. – *Consolidated text – M.A.I.*	79
5.4. – *The Cotonou Convention*	81
5.5. – *North American Free Trade Agreement (NAFTA)*	85
5.6. – *Protocol of Colonia – Mercosur*	91
5.7. – *Investment Agreement of the Organisation of the Islamic Conference*	94
5.8. – *ASEAN Agreement – Association of Southeast Asian Nations*	99
CHAPTER VI. – MODEL CONVENTIONS	103
6.1. – *Advantages of standard Text*	103

	Pages
6.2. – *Issues*	105
6.3. – *Models*	106

Chapter VII. – Protected investors-nationality 219

7.1. – *Nationals and Citizens*	219
7.2. – *Protection for Individuals*	220
7.3. – *Effect of Changes in an individual Investor's Nationality*	222
7.4. – *Nationality to be more than "theoretical"*	230
7.5. – *Pros and contras of "effective nationality"*	233
7.6. – *Protection for Legal Persons – Nationality of Corporations and other "non-physical" Persons*	236
7.7. – *ICSID View on Nationality*	250
7.8. – *Multinationals and transnationals*	254

Chapter VIII. – Control 257

8.1. – *Control Theory*	257
8.2. – *Antecedents of "Control"*	260
8.3. – *Barcelona Traction Triangulation*	262
8.4. – *BIT's triangulation "link" between States*	264
8.5. – *Need to define "control" in BIT's*	267
8.6. – *Notion of Control in Washington Convention (ICSID)*	273
8.7. – *Impracticability of Uniform Regulation*	289

Chapter IX. – Protected investments definitions 293

9.1. – *Doctrinal Definition of Investments*	293
9.2. – *Conventional Definition of Investments*	294

Chapter X. – Promotion & admittal of investments 315

10.1. – *No Right to foreign Establishment*	315

	Pages
10.2. – *State is Sovereign*	316
10.3. – *Approval Process*	317
10.4. – *Formula for Approval*	318
10.5. – *Risk of arbitrary Change in Law*	319
10.6. – *US Formula*	320
10.7. – *Developing Countries' formula*	322
10.8. – *ICSID Amco/Indonesia Case*	322
CHAPTER XI. – "Fair and equitable treatment"	327
11.1. – *No absolute Right to Invest*	327
11.2. – *Character of "fair and equitable" treatment obligation*	328
11.3. – *Fair and Equitable Treatment obligation under Customary International Law*	329
11.4. – *Content of fair treatment obligation*	331
11.5. – *Other Standards of Treatment*	333
11.6. – *Specific reference to international law*	336
11.7. – *Conventional provisions on fair and equitable treatment*	339
11.8. – *Jurisprudence on treatment of foreign investments*	350
11.9. – *Conclusion*	354
CHAPTER XII. – Environment	355
12.1. – *Protection of the environment*	355
12.2. – *NAFTA Link between environment protection with investment promotion*	356
12.3. – *Canadian BIT's environmental position*	357
12.4. – *USA Formula*	358
12.5. – *Organisation for economic Co-operation and Development (OECD)*	359
12.6. – *European BIT's Clauses relating to the environment*	360

	Pages
12.7. – *Arbitral jurisprudence*	362
CHAPTER XIII. – EXPROPRIATIONS AND NATIONALISATIONS	365
13.1. – *Respect for Property Rights*	365
13.2. – *States' fundamental right to take private property*	367
13.3. – *Forms of Deprivation of private Property Rights*	368
13.4. – *Definitions of Forms of Deprivation*	368
13.5. – *Indirect privative measures*	371
13.6. – *International Law Principles*	373
13.7. – *Jurisprudence*	392
13.8. – *Valuation issues*	402
13.9. – *BIT Expropriation and Nationalisation Clauses*	408
13.10. – *Interest*	414
13.11. – *War Damages Specific Indemnification*	418
CHAPTER XIV. – TRANSFERS & SUBROGATIONS	423
14.1. – *Transfers relating to investments*	423
14.2. – *Conventional rules on Transfers*	424
14.3. – *Subrogation*	431
CHAPTER XV. – APPLICABLE LAW ON INVESTMENTS	449
15.1. – *Basic principle : application of Domestic Law*	449
15.2. – *Host States' position*	450
15.3. – *Need for international rules*	451
15.4. – *State Contracts*	455
CHAPTER XVI. – JURIDICTION SETTLEMENT OF INVESTMENT DISPUTES THROUGH ARBITRATION	491
16.1. – *Elements of international investment dispute resolution*	491

XVIII   INTERNATIONAL INVESTMENTS PROTECTION

	Pages
16.2. – *What constitutes international arbitration*	494
16.3. – *Types of arbitration*	497
16.4. – *Advantages and disadvantages of arbitration*	499
16.5. – *BITs Reference to International Arbitration Institutions*	507
16.6. – *The ICC International Court of Arbitration*	509
16.7. – *OHADA's Common Court of Justice and Arbitration (CCJA)*	517
16.8. – *ICSID The International Centre for Settlement of Investment Disputes*	520
16.9. – *London Court of International Arbitration (LCIA)*	553
16.10. – *Sui generis United States Court : United States Court of International Trade (USCIT)*	564
16.11. – *Applicable Law on Investment Disputes*	592
16.12. – *Examples of arbitration clauses to be inserted in State Contracts*	599
16.13. – *Investment disputes resolution system and arbitration clauses in BIT's*	600
CHAPTER XVII. – Inter-state disputes regarding BIT's' interpretation	603
17.1. – *Common Interpretation of the Washington Convention*	603
17.2. – *Common interpretation problems of BIT's*	603
17.3. – *Classical Settlement Formula*	605
17.4. – *Some countries deviate from the classical formula*	607
17.5. – *Interpretation Problems*	615
CHAPTER XVIII. – Scope of bilateral investment treaties	619
18.1. – *Objective and personal scope of BIT's*	619
18.2. – *Geographic Scope*	619
18.3. – *Temporal scope*	621
CHAPTER XIX. – Future expectations	627
19.1. – *Economic Value*	627

	PAGES
19.2. – *Bringing the model conventions and BIT's up to date*	628
19.3. – *Changing Circumstances*	628

APPENDIX I. – BURUNDI CASE NOTES 631

RESTRICTIONS ON STATE SOVEREIGNTY – JUS STANDI OF SHAREHOLDERS ... 631

    APP. I.1. – *ICSID case : "Goetz v. Burundi"* 631

    APP. I.2. – *Case Background – Factual Findings* 632

    APP. I.3. – *Applicable provisions of the model convention and actual BIT's*   633

    APP. I.4. – *Comparative Definitions of Property privative Measures* 634

    APP. I.5. – *De iure vs. de facto ("Creeping") Deprivation* 636

    APP. I.6. – *Application to Goetz v. Burundi* 638

    APP. I.7. – *Do shareholders have "ius standi"?* 639

    APP. I.8. – *The deprivation must be illegal* 643

    APP. I.9. – *The valuation issue* 645

    APP. I.10. – *Interest* 646

    APP. I.11. – *Duty to respect national and international law* 646

    APP. I.12. – *Does the Burundi case set a precedent?* 647

APPENDIX II. – ZAIRE CASE NOTES 649

INVESTMENTS IN THE DEMOCRATIC REPUBLIC OF CONGO (FORMERLY KNOWN AS ZAIRE) 649

    APP. II.1. – *Background* 649

    APP. II.2. – *Indemnification of "Zairianised" assets – Valuation of Assets*   650

    APP. II.3. – *National Protection of international investments in the DRC* .. 651

ANNEX. – NORWEGIAN MODEL CONVENTION 661

TABLE OF AUTHORITIES. – BIBLIOGRAPHY 681

    I. – *Books* 681

	Pages
II. – *Citations of legal reviews (with footnote references)*	683
III. – *Websites*	689
IV. – *Cases*	690
Index	693

FOREWORD

Ideals of "self-reliance" and "independence" from assistance and support given by States and other sources have long been part of political discourse. For some, such ideals may have historical, moral and even philosophical dimensions, but in economic circles they have been abandoned. The complexity and interwoven nature of issues and interests in the world of national and international relations have made these ideals obsolete. In today's world economy, businesses and States have become dependent on actors that are active across the globe.

Interdependence and economic interaction are now acknowledged realities in the international investment world. Developing countries have come to realise that investments from abroad provide crucial levers. When capital is in short supply, or virtually inexistent, they see foreign equity as a possible solution for important national challenges, such as unemployment and foreign currency shortfalls. Such influx may help their balance of payments, because companies with a substantial international presence often establish subsidiaries in developing and other countries. These subsidiaries are instrumental in increasing commercial exchanges and procuring, through their exports, new foreign currency sources.

A policy of promotion and facilitation of foreign investment is adopted by less or least developed countries (LDC's) and developed countries alike. Nonetheless, the need is the greatest in LDC's, although capital injection is not the sole factor of economic growth. Technology transfer has an even greater impact on LDC's, but it rests to an even greater degree on the collaboration of foreign businesses.

Unfortunately, when venturing in LDC's, investors have often encountered an unfavourable environment, including measures privative of property through nationalisations by local authorities. While, in recent years, the frequency of these measures has decreased, this risk has not disappeared.

Therefore, protection of international investment has remained a major concern in economic circles. Sometimes, formal contracts may be negotiated between a foreign investor and the host State, but these vehicles for the integrity of foreign capital have often not been respected by host States. They are tempted to adopt a purely nationalistic approach and pretend that their national legislation provides sufficient guarantees for foreign investments. Experience has shown, however, that protection through an international convention is by far the better solution. States whose nationals wish to invest abroad have taken into account the recommendations of various international bodies by adopting a policy of negotiating a number of Bilateral Investment Treaties (BIT's) with LDC's for the mutual protection of each party. Host States in Africa and Asia have yielded to this trend and abandoned their reluctance, having come to the realisation that such treaties can and do attract and give direction to foreign investors.

A rather impressive network of BIT's has emerged worldwide from this convergence of interests. The authors, Jan SCHOKKAERT, J.D., honorary Executive Director of Administration of the Belgian Ministry of Foreign Affairs, where he used to be responsible for the drafting and negotiation of BIT's, and Yvon HECKSCHER, J.D., an international lawyer now living in California, have collaborated in the writing of this book, which sheds light on the complex subject of the law and practice applicable to BIT's.

The publication of this work is timely. International arbitral jurisprudence has recently made enormous progress. In its early years, the International Centre for the Settlement of International Disputes (ICSID), created by the Multilateral Washington Convention (1965) was not very successful, but today investors and States alike have found their way to this institution. A large number of innovative decisions have been rendered with increasing frequency. The authors provide legal commentaries and analyses of important decisional milestones that will, in the future, be of significant value for the drafting of new BIT texts.

The international practice of both investor and host States has also markedly evolved. The preparation of rules for fair and equitable treatment, extended to foreign investors, has been largely completed. Arbitral procedures for the settlement of disputes relating to international investments have been revised and perfected. The investors' right to designate arbitration institutions of their choice, such as ICSID or the International Chamber of Commerce, is now firmly anchored in the law and is no longer subject to States' challenges. In addition, the States' anticipatory consent to the filing by investors of arbitration proceedings has become the norm and will substantially augment the legal security of investments.

The authors have made numerous suggestions that will be of value in the development of future BIT's and State Contracts. I am particularly pleased that contacts and exchanges with the University of Antwerp's Institute of Development Policy and Management (IOB) have contributed to the research and publication of this work. It will increase the skills of both investors and States, be they industrialised or in transition, when concluding conventional instruments regarding the legal status of foreign investments.

Filip REYNTJENS
Professor of Law and Politics
Institute of Development Policy
and Management
University of Antwerp

CHAPTER I
INTRODUCTION

1.1. – Investment Doctrinally Defined

A broad definition of investment is intended to cover any contribution in money or in kind in specific sectors of an established economy, such as industry and associated activities. Doctrine generally defines "investments", when made from a private source and for an economic purpose, as all contributions of capital or goods in a business enterprise, with the intent that they shall yield productivity and profit. Thus contributions made from a public source, such as a government agency, an international organisation, or a non-governmental organisation, whose purpose is political, charitable, or otherwise non-economic and not designed to be lucrative or self-beneficial, are not "investments" within the scope of the doctrine or its generalised counterpart, and, notwithstanding possible analogies, are not addressed in this work.

The doctrinal definition is inadequate to convey a full list of the conditions that will, when met, qualify as "investment" any and all types of economic activity in modern society. Arbitral jurisprudence, in particular, has expanded the *general* notion of investment, requiring a deeper scrutiny in order to update the definition of the term, as it is more currently understood.

Economists have traditionally defined "investment" as any acquisition of capital goods for the purpose of obtaining a return or a desirable use. Their basic premise is that private investments are made to produce profit, not welfare[1]. This

---

[1] *Répertoire de droit international*, Dalloz, Paris, 1969, p. 190.

definition also falters, when a modern look is given to activities going beyond the traditional economic view. Here again, arbitral jurisprudence helps fill the gap.

Many arbitral awards echo the notion that it is impossible adequately to define "investments". It is better, they say, just to verify whether a given activity meets the principal elements that characterise what is generally understood to mean "investment". Thus, any review of the law and contract practice for the protection of private foreign investments must be matched to activities that include these elements. Such investments are made abroad by individuals and corporations or other forms of business entity created under local corporate law and, of course, do not include public projects, though such projects may, on occasion subcontract their realisation in whole or in part to private investors.

To simplify these definitional distinctions, we have chosen to define foreign investments as private placements and contributions of cash and other capital in enterprises active in the economies of foreign States only, that is, States other than those of the investors.

1.2. – Elements of "Investments"

This work addresses opportunities and problems presented by investments abroad. "Abroad", as used herein, refers to a jurisdictional location other than that to which an investor is deemed to have allegiance, that is, of which an investor has the nationality.

To qualify as an "investment" project in this review, the project must first be given an *infusion of assets*. This may take the form of money, goods or services but they must be contributed to the intended project. A mere infusion of ideas, a critique, an analysis, a research study, unless accompanied by other circumstances, are not investments addressed in this review.

Second, the project must have a given *duration*. Expectations of the duration may sometimes not be met and the project may suffer a breakdown, in actuality, the project may be aborted prior to its intended duration, fail to meet expectations, but, clearly, at the outset, there must have been an expectation of the project's duration or the project fails the test.

The third required feature is the expectation of regular or ultimate *profits or return*. In actuality, the project may never yield a profit, might even produce a loss. Normally, singularity of return, such as a one-time pay-off, would not meet this requirement, though special circumstances may otherwise confound the critic.

The fourth feature of the project is, self-evidently, *risk*. Frequently, risk is assumed by both sides of a transaction. Each side is, or should be, aware that certainty of benefit is relative. Each side then seeks ways to minimise the risk to its side through appropriate studies, analyses and comparisons, which they then attempt to buttress with legal constraints, worded as strongly as each side will tolerate in respect of the other and known to be supported by an international system of impartial decisional authority and enforcement. There is no unanimity among experts as to whether, to qualify as a direct investment, all of these four elements must be present contemporaneously. To understand what "investments" are, within the scope of this work, it is necessary to understand the constraints, namely international treaties and the State contracts, which are subsumed under the general concept of international investment "Conventions".

1.3. – DIRECT OR INDIRECT INVESTMENTS

1.3.1. – *Direct Investments*

The Organisation for Economic Cooperation and Development (OECD) benchmark definition of foreign direct investment ("Benchmark Definition") and the International Monetary Fund's Balance of Payments Compilation Guide ("BOCG") describe direct investments as follows:

> "Direct investment is the category of international investment that reflects the objectives of an entity resident in one economy obtaining a lasting interest in an enterprise residing in another economy."[2]

Doctrinally direct investments have been defined as follows:

> "An investment is deemed 'direct' when capital contributions are at stake, which are placed at the disposal of a commercial or industrial enterprise by the owner of the capital contributed, usually the investor. The investor then actively assures the management of the target enterprise, whose financial liabilities he may generally guarantee."[3]

Some authors require that the direct investor must in any case assume control over the company in which he has invested:

> "Investment is effected in the majority of cases by means of a financial participation. A fundamental distinction must always be made according to whether or not this financial participation assures the investor effective control of the enterprise. If it does, there is a case of direct investment."[4]

This position is debatable. Not infrequently two or more physical persons (f.ex. family related members) make an investment in a business and designate that one of them be the manager assuming the control of the enterprise. All members of the family investing directly capital for the creation of an enterprise are direct investors. The determining factor for the direct character of an investment is the way capital is contributed.

---

[2] IMF Committee on balance of payments Statistics and OECD workshop on international investment statistics, DITEG# 3: Indirect investment, defining the Scope of the Direct Investment Relationship, prepared by Marie MONTANJEES, IMF Statistics department, April 2004, p. 2.

[3] SCHOKKAERT, Jan, "La pratique conventionnelle européenne en matière de protection juridique des investissements privés, effectué à l'étranger", *Revue de droit international et de droit comparé*, Bruylant, Brussels, June 2003, p. 328.

[4] CARREAU, Jean, *Droit international économique*, Paris, Librairie générale de droit et de jurisprudence, LGDJ, 1980, p. 457.

The positive impact of direct investment on economic growth can hardly be denied. Governments worldwide promote direct investment:

> "One thing is certain: all countries and regions find it increasingly difficult to stay competitive without international trade and foreign direct investment (FDI) which sustain growth and bring at least four things of value: financial capital, management skills, technology, and access to export markets-and therefore enhance a country's and its regions' competitiveness in the global marketplace."[5]

It would be wrong to think that promotion of national and international investments is only what less developing countries (LDC's) do. Industrially developed countries (DC's) are also aware of the importance of stimulating direct investment. In most European countries, laws and regulations have been adopted for that very purpose.

1.3.2. – Indirect Investments

Investments may also be made indirectly. An investment is deemed indirect when it only consists either of the acquisition of shares of stock and other types of holding representing equity parts of the capital of an enterprise, or of debenture bonds, or even the more modern derivatives, basically for speculative purposes. They are alternatively called "portfolio investments".

Some authors believe that only the direct contribution of capital to an enterprise can be considered as an "investment", whereas portfolio investments cannot because they do not create an added value to the economic development of an enterprise:

> "Direct investment means the investment of money, goods or services, in a project for entrepreneurial commitment, especially establishing subsidiary companies or taking-over enterprises, capitalising branches and plans (endowments). Such investments are characterised

---

[5] OGUTÇU, Mehmet, "Foreign direct investment and regional ndevelopment", *The journal of world investment*, June 2003, Genève, p. 493.

by their direct use for a specific project (not through the capital market) amortisation and profit dependent upon the success of the project (entrepreneurial risk), long-term or unlimited period and an enduring entrepreneurial commitment to the project accompanying the investment. This is in contrast with "portfolio investments" which are placed through the capital market without entrepreneurial commitment, are relatively short term and made only for the sake of capital yield."[6]

Admittedly, most stock market operations are purely speculative. The occasional investor buying bonds, shares, etc. is only interested in making a profit by speculating on the chance of a rise in the value of such papers.

It would also be wrong to infer that stock exchange transactions never produce an economic added value. A merger typically looks to results of added value, as when the dominant partner aims to control and manage all industrial activity of the other.

Likewise, when an enterprise issues bonds, the buyers may be considered as investors bringing in needed capital. It is therefore illogical to exclude their investment – which are equally deserving of protection – merely because theirs may be called "indirect".

Nonetheless, it is generally admitted, doctrinally, that certain conditions ought to be met before a given economic event may be considered an "investment". This view principally lays down three elements: (1) an asset, usually a capital infusion; (2) duration, in the sense the investment must have a specific time dimension; and (3) risk, in that the investment's yield must have some relation to the rate of growth and quality of operation of the enterprise. As said above a fourth element "return and profit" is uncertain. These elements are present in both direct and indirect investments.

Indirect investments are capital, they have a maturity date and they could become valueless if the enterprise fails. In our

---

[6] OGUÇU, Mehmet, *op. cit.*, p. 493.

view, on that score alone, they meet the criteria for conventional protection[7].

1.4. – "New Investment forms"

1.4.1. – *Ordinary Forms*

In this review of foreign investment protection, the term "new investment forms" is used to define generically as international investments those in which the foreign investors do not necessarily have a determinable capital interest, majority or minority. These new forms, which we opt, paradoxically, to call "ordinary" because other "new" forms have arisen which do not fit the mold, include:

- Joint ventures where the foreign associates effectively controls at least 50% of the capital,
- various kinds of international agreements which, at least for the foreign enterprise, in whole or in part, are in the nature of an investment.

These new forms are therefore best categorised as recent denizens of a gray area, half-way between the two classical types of international activity, namely strictly export or strictly directly invested and dependent foreign branches.

In Oman's typology[8], new forms of investment are as follows:

- joint ventures, in which two enterprises (one of which is foreign, the other domestic) each hold a share in the capital, run the same risks, share the proceeds and both contribute technology;

---

[7] Some authors seem to prefer to limit the scope of the term "investment". They look on it as a phenomenon of "development cooperation" and claim that only capital infusions and financial operations contributing to the growth of the host State deserve the right to be deemed "investments" deserving the protection of conventions. There is no unanimity on whether such contribution should be a condition to protection.

[8] OMAN, Charles, *Les nouvelles formes d'investissement*, Paris, OCDE, 1984, p. 12 (New forms of investment, Organisation for economic cooperation and development).

- Licensing, by means of which the foreign owner of the licence (for the use of a patent) delivers to the domestic company its technology and its "know how"; payment for this contribution may be in the form of a share in the capital of the company established on foreign territory or through the conclusion of an agreement for the sale of products at a favourable price (buy-back and lease-back agreements);
- Management contracts by which the foreign investor undertakes to complete a project or manage an enterprise in a developing country;
- "Turnkey" contracts requiring the investor to install an integrated manufacturing unit or carry out infrastructure projects in the host country, along with technology transfer, etc.
- International Dealership Contracts, between a foreign investor and a host country dealer; the local dealer often receives raw materials for the production of "finished products" which are then to be "commercialised" by the foreign investor.

1.4.2. – *Latest New Forms*

Outsourcing could be added to Oman's typology. Outsourcing is ordinarily (but not necessarily) not a joint venture, not a licensing, nor a dealership but involves contracting with a local entity to supply a workforce and premises necessary to produce goods or services sold world-wide ("commercialised") by the investor or its subsidiaries. Outsourcing is not properly a "turnkey" contract either because turnkeys are usually of the kind that allows the recipient to market the goods he produces in the turnkey plant; for example, the American Bechtel Corporation delivering a "turnkey" petroleum refining plant but not participating in the distribution of petroleum which is given to BP or Shell. Likewise management contracts are not the same as outsourcing contracts. However, outsourcing may, as an incentive for either party, take the form of a joint venture and may, for the legal protection of a patent, involve a licence.

All of these are merely examples of contracts and specific operations which could be called investments "new form". Few have so far been tested in arbitration tribunals. We can expect human imagination and trade needs to spawn further unorthodox forms of foreign investments. It is perhaps easy to be overwhelmed by the plethora of diverse vehicles for foreign direct investments but it is, as we hope to show, still possible to derive some general observations and, eventually, some principles that may be applicable to all forms of foreign investments.

1.5. – INTERNATIONAL INVESTMENTS

Besides distinguishing between direct and indirect investments, distinctions exist between investments made in the country of the investor and those made abroad by a national investor. Different rules apply to investments made nationally and those which involve more than one nation, i.e. are "international." These distinctions are in large part based on the law that governs national and international investments. National investments for any one Nation are usually governed by national investment and other civil and corporation codes and jurisprudence. International investments are affected by national investment codes but are governed also by international common law, international conventions and jurisprudence and occasionally by doctrinal texts.

1.5.1. – *Purpose*

From a purely economic viewpoint, investments made by national investors should have the same effect on economic development as investments made by international investors. Nonetheless, some countries attach more importance to investments made by foreigners. The issue here is "availability". In the less developed countries (LDC), available capital, skilled workers, modern or sophisticated infrastructure, a complex and educated judiciary, a non-corrupt public administrative sector are often insufficient. Without a doubt, many of those countries follow an active and alluring policy for the encouragement of foreign investment.

1.5.2. – *"International" defined*

An investment made by an individual in the territory of a State may be seen as an "international" investment when this person's nationality is not of that State. When using this definition, there is a risk of overstating the scope of international investment. Conceivably, a permanent resident, not a citizen of a State may make minor investments locally and have no other foreign ties than his nationality. His local investment may then only with difficulty be called an "international investment" within the scope of this Work.

A problem could also arise when such an individual has multiple nationalities. This topic and other problems arising from nationality are dealt with more extensively in Chapter VII of this Work. International law generally holds that each State has the right to define in its own legislation how such an individual's nationality will be determined for the purpose of the proposed investment.

1.5.3. – *Corporate Nationality*

Investments made by a corporation have an international character when these corporations have the nationality of one State and when they realise investment projects in the territory of a foreign State. In the interpretation of any individual bilateral investment treaty, it may sometimes be difficult to determine the nationality of a foreign investor, because the attitude taken by the Contracting parties, and the wording of their agreement are not uniform.

In many European countries, prevailing opinion is that a corporation, or other business entity with status as a legal person, has the nationality of the country in whose territory its place of principal business is set. It is generally understood that the principal place of business is where upper management functions are exercised :

> "The principal place of business of a corporation is deemed to be where its administration principally resides, the place where it has established its general books of account, where its keeps its archives, where its general meetings are held, in a word, where the managerial activity is concentrated, the centre of its interests and of its corporate affairs." [9]

There are other traditional tests to determine or deny corporate nationality. For instance, the place where a corporation's resources are exploited has, per se, no bearing at all on the nationality of a corporation. Sometimes the nationality of a corporation is determined on the basis of control i.e. if a majority of individual foreign shareholders, with a same nationality, control the corporation, this corporation acquires the nationality of these shareholders.

This may cause some difficulties.

J. Schokkaert has commented :

> "We could expect other difficulties, when the nationality of a corporation is to be determined on the basis of control. As everyone knows, transferring shares of stock from one individual to another is not a problem and occurs daily. As a result, there is constant change in the composition of the company's capital. If the control theory is to be applied, frequent changes in the nationality of the company would result. These changes are incompatible with the need to assure the constancy of the legal status of the company. As an example, problems would arise in determining which diplomatic protection the company should enjoy." [10]

This general topic is addressed in further detail in Chapters VII and VIII of this work.

---

[9] Le *Répertoire pratique de droit belge*, Brussels, Bruylant, 2007, n° 34 Corporations.

[10] SCHOKKAERT, Jan, "Verdragsrechtelijke schadeloosstelling van in het buitenland benadeelde particuliere bezittingen", *Rechtskundig weekblad*, 1974, n° 36, p. 2262 ("Conventional Indemnification of private assets, affected on foreign territory" – *Legal weekly*).

1.5.4. – *International character of investments*

Be that as it may, traditional nationality principles have played, and for the immediately foreseeable future, will continue to play an important role in the use and administration of Bilateral Investments Treaties (BITs) and State Contracts. Nationality may be increasingly difficult to determine, but, for the time being, they remain relevant and material. In the past, at least, traditional nationality principles had usually sufficed to confer at least an international character to an investment. CARREAU does not agree and uses the following additional criteria:

> "In order to determine whether a private investment is of an international character, it is usually insufficient merely to apply the criteria applicable to individuals and corporations in the operation of the business. With respect to individuals, the real criterion seems to be their place of residence. With respect to corporations, the control criterion governs. Those are the elements defining in most cases the scope of application of national regulation." [11]

A literal application of these additional criteria could bring about practical difficulties not easily resolved. Thus, as we have seen, an investor, who is "domiciled" in a particular country but has a residence in another for several years, could well be deemed a "national investor" in the country of his residence. This could be a disadvantage to him, since, under these circumstances, he could be excluded from the specific benefits conferred upon foreign investors by the country of his domicile. Laying the problems of corporate nationality aside for a moment, it is probably true that a physical person is more amenable to a determination of nationality, though by no means indisputably as some of the cases cited in this Work will illustrate.

---

[11] CARREAU, Jean, *op. cit.*, p. 458, see footnote 4.

1.5.5. – *Domicile and residence*

In practical terms, the domicile of an individual is the place where the centre of his interests is, where he can be sued judicially and where his name is entered on the civil status registers :

> "The domicile is the place where the individual is tied to the rights he claims to have and the duties to which he is subject, and where he can be reached because he is present there or is deemed to be [12]."

The legal distinctions between residence and domicile have been diversely argued, hitherto with significant effect on the individual's rights and obligations, but more recently with increasing irrelevance. Thus,

> "Residence is the factual (not legal) place of establishment of a person during a certain period of time, so long as he does not have the intent to assert his rights in that place or carry out his obligations there. Registration in the population registries of the place of residence is not obligatory." [13]

This is a common perception but in some countries, residence and domicile are or have become extremely fluid concepts. A resident of, say, California might well be officially registered in the Civil Status Registry of, say, Antwerp, Belgium, or Guadalajara, Mexico, and therefore deemed to be "domiciled" in Antwerp or Guadalajara, but, nonetheless, will be able to assert his rights and carry out his obligations in California, whenever he happens to be there. Many Mexicans, for instance, lawful residents in California, travel each year back to Mexico to vote in local elections, may well maintain a house in both countries but spend most of the year in California and assert all of the rights and are subject to all of the obligations of California residents.

Clearly, though spelled identically in English and French, and similarly in Spanish, the terms "domicile" and "resi-

---

[12] Comité européen de coopération juridique, Conseil de l'Europe, "Questionnaire relatif à la notion de résidence, et à la notion de domicile", Paris, 1975, p. 3.

[13] DILLEMANS, Roger, *Wegwijs recht*, Leuven, Davidsfonds, 2000, p. 25.

dence", "domicilio" and "residencia" do not have the same dimensions of meaning in different countries.

An investor with residence abroad may ask that he be entered in the "Register of Immatriculation" of the Embassy or Consulate within the country of residence but this registration is not mandatory and does not determine "domicile" and its attendant nationality characterisation.

Nationality problems affecting companies may even be more complex. The extreme globalisation of economies brings about constant changes in the composition of its shareholders. Majority investment, and therefore control, often change. As a result, a corporation that may be subject to the legal system of a specific State, may find itself as subject concurrently to the legal system of another, or, sometimes subject to that of one State and sometimes to that of another.

1.6. – LIMITED REVIEW

This Work, therefore, reviews the legal and conventional protection available for investments, made abroad by individuals or corporations, that are most common and regarding which there is a track record of jurisprudence, so long as they are in the form of placements or contributions of capital, know how, management etc., or in the form of cash or equivalent in enterprises active in the economies of foreign States. In summary, foreign investments are participations in a foreign country's existing or potential industry made for the purpose of production and profit.

CHAPTER II

DIPLOMATIC PROTECTION FOR INTERNATIONAL INVESTMENTS AND INVESTORS

2.1. – ENTITLEMENT TO DIPLOMATIC PROTECTION

All individuals and corporations, including investors, owners of assets and interests who may be affected by measures taken by the foreign State may ask for assistance from and protection by the State of which they are nationals. In the Commission for International Law (CIL), this protection has been defined as follows:

> "Diplomatic protection is any action used by one State against another by reason of the prejudice inflicted on a person who is a national of the first State, or his assets, by an act or omission to act, deemed illegal internationally, and attributable to the second State."[14]

The jurisdiction of a State to intervene in the action of other States in order to defend their nationals' rights and interests has been confirmed in international treaties:

> "The function of a diplomatic mission includes:
> (a) representing the State in regards to the host State;
> (b) the defense of State interests through its envoy to the host State within the limits of international law (Article 3.1 Treaty of Vienna, dated 18 April 1961, regarding diplomatic relations)...
>
> Consular activities include:
> (a) defence on the territory of the State of residence of the interests of the delegating State and its nationals, whether individuals or corporations, within the limits of international law (Article 5a of the Treaty of Vienna, dated 24 April 1963, regarding consular relations)."

---

[14] Commission du droit international (CDI) de l'Organisation des Nations Unies, *Rapport "2000"*, New York, 2000, p. 425.

It would be an error to think that individuals and companies have an absolute and unconditional right to diplomatic or consular protection:

> "The State shall be deemed its own master in deciding if it will grant its protection, to what extent it will do so and when it shall cease. In this connection, it has a discretionary power whose scope depends of considerations political in nature and different from those surrounding individual cases." [15]

It can happen, for instance, that an Ambassador is recalled in the face of a political conflict. The recalling State can thus postpone the execution of an important bilateral convention. When nationals of that State, for instance, request assistance from State authorities (f.i. for indemnification of damages to their personal interests), the latter may refuse or postpone action till further order to do so.

2.2. – Duty to accept protection

Quite another matter is whether a State can force its representative to grant diplomatic protection, if its nationals do not file any request for it. Thus, is an individual required formally to file a request in order to justify intervention or should he be obliged to accept intervention, even when he opposes it for his own specific reasons?

Should the foreign investor have entered into an investment contract in a specific sector (e.g. oil) and the measures taken by the host have caused an expropriation in another sector, where the investor has a less important interest, it is not unlikely that he will not seek diplomatic protection for the expropriation. He is perhaps motivated by a fear that his request will aggravate the host State and thereby work to his detriment in the main sector that he exploits. There is no

---

[15] *Barcelona Traction, Light and Power Company, Limited, Judgment International Court of Justice (ICJ), Reports,* 1970, p. 45.

unanimity of view whether diplomatic or consular protection will then be forced on such investor:

> "Certain States, like the Soviet Union, believe that a consular official is a State official, submitted to the power of the sending State he represents, and that, therefore, this official has the right to intervene, even if the nationals of the sending State oppose it. To a certain extent, France shares that opinion, in as much as French merchants have been forced to register in the Registers of the Diplomatic Mission they depend from. By reason of this registration, they will find themselves under the mandatory protection of consular and diplomatic officials. Other States, such as the USA, the UK and Belgium hold to the opinion that consular protection cannot be imposed, given that such an imposition runs counter to the sovereignty of the host State and to personal civil rights." [16]

There is no formal link between, on the one hand, inscription in the registers of diplomatic missions, and, on the other, the obligation of a dependent national to accept the protection. When riots occurred in Zaire (1991), Belgian authorities took measures for the repatriation of Belgians residing in the territory of Zaire. However, many of them, though registered in the Embassy's or consular registries, refused the aid offered and decided to stay in the country.

The sending State should take into account public interest and prioritise it over individual interests. If measures privative of property are taken abroad, the sending State will undertake a global action of protection and defense in favour of a group of nationals damaged by the measures. The mere fact that some affected individuals wish to reject the State's intervention for their benefit will not lead the State to abstain from such intervention. That should be the general rule but different States have different policies. Thus, a State may take a pragmatic approach, undeterred by strict considerations of principle, and extend protection to those interests who may *best* have supported the then Administration polit-

---

[16] VRANKEN, André, *Hedendaags consulair recht*, Lier, Uitgeverij Cockaert, 1989, p. 146.

ically during the last elections. The State's administration may then be ready to suspend such protection when such interests object, even if other interests which may be of lesser importance or be of a different political persuasion, may suffer by reason of such suspension. A diplomatic corps that is impervious to political winds at home is the exception, not the rule.

Should a sending State negotiate a global indemnification agreement with an expropriating State, none of the sending State's nationals, affected by the expropriation, will be excluded from the benefits of such an agreement. Thus, even if a person refuses the benefits of such intervention, if he has been injured, he nonetheless keeps the status of rightful claimant within the framework of the agreement, notwithstanding his former opposition to it for his own personal or economic reasons.

This does not necessarily mean that such an individual will be forced to accept the indemnity to be paid him on the basis of the indemnification agreement. In most countries, these agreements are submitted for approval by Parliament, or equivalent Congress and after its consent, their validity is no longer open to question. Should an injured person decide not to accept the terms of the negotiated agreement, he could abstain from filing a request for indemnity and can thereby exclude himself from the application of the agreement.

This system was followed in European countries for the implementation of indemnification agreements concerning nationalisation measures in the past.

2.3. – WAIVER OF INDEMNIFICATION

Such an abstention implies also a renunciation of indemnification. Contracting States generally insert in their agreements a provision by virtue of which the expropriating State will, in such cases, be relieved from any liability and will not be required to pay any complementary indemnity. In that case, one of the Contracting States commits itself to the other not to support claims for indemnification filed after the entry into force of the indemnification agreement.

For example, we refer to the indemnification agreement between the Kingdoms of Morocco and Belgium, signed in Rabat on 18 October 1967 (Belgian Federal Register, 17 June 1991):

> "This agreement will have a liberating effect on the Government of the Kingdom of Morocco, in relation to the claims covered by articles 1 and 2 above, whether they originate from the Kingdom of Belgium or from individuals or corporations mentioned in those articles."

Starting from the date of signature of the agreement, Belgium agreed, for as long as Morocco carried out the obligations imposed upon it by virtue of the agreement, to provide no further support to posterior claims of its nationals regarding the properties, the rights and interests covered by the agreement and filed with the Moroccan Government or arbitral or judicial tribunals (***Article 8** of Agreement*).

2.4. – DIPLOMATIC PROTECTION IS AVAILABLE TO NATIONALS ONLY

Within the limits set forth by international law, States place conditions in the extension of diplomatic protection. One of these conditions is that the party seeking protection be a national of the State whose protection he invokes. The applicant must be a citizen of the sending State:

> "This right is necessarily limited to intervention on behalf of its own nationals because, in the absence of a special agreement, it is the bond of nationality between the State and the individual which alone confers upon the State the right of diplomatic protection, and it is a part of the function of diplomatic protection that the right to take up a claim and to ensure respect for the rules of international law must be envisaged."[17]

---

[17] *Panevezys/Saldutiskis Railway Case*, Permanent Court of International Justice (PCIJ), Judgment of 28 February 1939, série A/B, *Fascicule*, n° 75, p. 16.

It is however quite possible to deviate, by means of a convention (in the absence of a special agreement) to the basic principle which both international law and international jurisprudence acknowledge. Within the European Union, for example, it has been agreed that, in exceptional cases, a member State shall be able to grant consular assistance to a citizen of another member State. This would be allowed when the other member State does not have a diplomatic or consular office in the host State.

2.5. – Effect of "control"

Underlying most negotiations of investment agreements between developed countries and LDC's runs a strong concern, on the part of the host States, many of which have only recently shaken off the yoke of colonisation, that their sovereignty be solemnly respected. At the same time, among foreign investors, runs an equally strong concern that they shall be treated without discrimination in favor of national enterprises. International arbitration is the lodestone most foreign investors rely on to reduce the risk of discriminatory treatment.

Many investors have, for instance, expressed concern that, where national legislation in a host State requires the foreign investments to be incorporated locally, and thereby acquire, on the face of the record, the nationality of the host State, the basic principle that international arbitration will not apply to disputes between a State and its nationals will work to their disadvantage. Although resisted by host States as proscribed interferences with their sovereignty, realism has prevailed in most instances and, as a counterbalance to the host States' insistence that the investments on their territory be tied to local laws by requiring them to be locally incorporated, host States have allowed that where a local company, established with the foreign investor's resources, is controlled by a foreign entity, that investor's local company will likewise be considered to be foreign. This concession has ramifications and unintended consequences to the availability and finality of diplomatic protection, which have given rise to disagreements and resulting litigation. This topic is addressed in greater detail in Chapter VIII.

2.6. – Direct Filing of Claims by Claimant, e.g. through local Tribunals

May any person who has sustained damages by reason of the action of the host State file a claim directly with the host State's authorities regarding an investment dispute?

The answer to this question is not so simple. First of all, it is possible that no bilateral agreement has actually been concluded between the States involved, but if there is, then, insofar as purely administrative measures are concerned, chances are it will not improbably encounter difficulties along the way. According to principles of international law, confirmed by international conventions, diplomatic and consular offices are the means by which a State and its national may be represented in the foreign forum. Hence the forum's authorities will often reject individual claims filed directly with them.

On the other hand, it is quite possible that an individual will have the possibility to file a judicial procedure in the local tribunals or courts. Some States, however, balk at submitting their sovereign powers to their own local tribunals, believing that the legislative, and not the judiciary, is the ultimate authority:

> "The immunity of jurisdiction and execution very often sets hurdles to the procedure which arises from the contractual relations between a private party and a State. Indisputably the execution of court orders or arbitral awards during the last thirty years has followed an encouraging evolution towards the fall of the traditional privilege granted to States. However, the process of seizure and realisation of the goods owned by a State remain often problematic. International

treaties, national laws and – mainly-case law are far from being homogeneous.[18]"

The sending State has no right of intervention in such procedures, even if filed by one of its nationals. The sending State has only the right to verify that its nationals are not discriminated against and that they are given access to the judicial process equally with nationals of the host State and third States.

2.7. – ONLY STATES MAY FILE IN INTERNATIONAL JUDICIARY TRIBUNALS

Insofar as international judiciary tribunals are concerned individuals could not file a claim because only states may file in those venues. An individual, for example, could not file a procedure with the International Court of Justice (ICJ) in the Hague. However, a State may, with respect to its own nationals, use its access rights to facilitate the prosecution of its nationals' claims :

> "On the level of international law, the State may substitute itself to private parties on the basis that the State itself has been damaged by its nationals' losses. The same rule applies to international tribunals, in the sense that private persons cannot be parties to a process in those venues. The State then makes its nationals' cause its own and assumes the defense of its nationals' interests."[19]

According to international jurisprudence, in this kind of case, the State does not actually intervene in the name of its nationals but merely relies on one of its own rights, that is, to require that international law be respected not only in interstate relations but also in relations between a State and the nationals of another State :

---

[18] KNOEPFLER, François, "L'immunité d'éxécution contre les Etats", *Revue de l'arbitrage*, Paris, July 2003, n° 3, p. 1018 ("States' immunity from execution", *Arbitration Review*, Paris, July 2003).

[19] SCHOKKAERT, Jan, "Pratique contractuelle de la Belgique en matière d'indemnisation des avoirs privés lésés à l'étranger", *Revue belge de droit international (RBDI)*, Université de Bruxelles, septembre 1974, p. 435.

> "Diplomatic protection and international judicial protection constitute a measure of defense of State rights.
>
> As has been said and repeated in the Permanent Court of international Justice: 'by assuming the position of one of its nationals, and by setting diplomatic or international justice action in motion in his favour, the State, in fact, is making a claim in its own right, namely the right to have international law respected in the name of one of its citizens'." [20]

International conventions are the means by which States may be allowed to deviate from this rule of international law. The prototype of such a convention, favouring international investors, is the Washington Convention, signed on 18 March 1965, for the Settlement of International Disputes between states and nationals of other states (Convention creating ICSID: International Centre for the settlement of Investment Disputes – see *infra*).

Originally, States were most reluctant to adhere to the Convention but since then a large number of arbitration procedures have been filed at the Centre. The principal condition for access to the Centre is adherence by the Contracting States.

Some authors believe that the State's consent must be given for each investment dispute:

> "It is, first of all, the recognition that a party that is not a State, in other words, the investor himself, will be able, in his own name and without the need for joining his own State to his request for arbitration directly to address an international tribunal. The States which signed the Convention, conceded this principle, but only the principle. No signatory State is obliged to resort to the facilities provided for by the Convention nor to agree that they shall resort to them, and no foreign investor may initiate a procedure against a signatory State without the consent of that State." [21]

This specific issue is examined further, extensively, below.

---

[20] SCHOKKAERT, Jan, *op. cit.*, pp. 435 et 436, footnote 19.
[21] SCHOKKAERT, Jan, *op. cit.*, pp. 435 et 436, footnote 19.

2.8. – Procedure for filing individual Claims

Claimants desiring official support against a foreign State must first submit a request for intervention to their local Department of State or Ministry of Foreign Affairs. The appropriate Secretary or Minister may then instruct the diplomatic missions or consular representations concerned. The efficacy of the official protection will be a function of the legal basis asserted as justification for the steps to be taken. In the event no bilateral agreement protecting international investments exists between the sending State and the host State, official support might follow from principles of international law only.

For example, all agreements providing for claimants' indemnification for goods and other interests affected by an Eastern European State's nationalisation measures occurring after the Second World War used international law as their legal basis. These agreements imposed on the expropriating State the burden of paying indemnities to former owners. This burden has been questioned only on very rare occasions:

> "In the event that this or that State which effected nationalisation undertook an obligation to pay compensation to the nationals of another State in a bilateral treaty with that State, it was done not because the State was obliged to do so under the regulation of international law, but voluntarily, and neither does the number of such bilateral treaties tend to constitute an international customary law, be it only in *'statu nascendi'*." [22]

This is an isolated position, at odds with common sense. A State's international obligation to indemnify an affected investor and to repair the damages he has sustained is also confirmed by several other important decisions, such as that of the International Court of Justice. Countries of the old East bloc and certain African States would never have agreed to indemnification accords if they had not been convinced

---

[22] LILLICH, Richard and Weston BURNS, *International Claims: Their settlement by lump sum agreements*, Charlottesville, University Press of Virginia, 1975, p. 248.

that this obligation was based on the rules and principles of international law.

It should be quite obvious that negotiations on this issue and the indemnification procedures selected are made easier when they are supported not only by principles but also by existing international agreements. International investors would be well advised, before initiating their investments, to conclude specific investment accord with the host State (cfr *infra* : State Contracts).

Should this advice be followed, it would be necessary to include in this accord a clause specifying that applicable law includes also international law (including international agreements and treaties). Failing such a clause, the contracting States will surely want to argue an exclusive application of their own national law. When the accord contains an applicable law clause, a solid legal basis exists to compel the host State to treat the foreign investor fairly :

> "It is not necessary here to analyse these clauses in detail in order to appreciate how international law meshes with local law or with general legal principles. It should be enough to see that these clauses, to the extent they place local law under the control of international law, withhold from the host State the opportunity to modify the latter in order to affect the signed accord. Any unilateral modification adopted legislatively or otherwise will be denied by the arbitral tribunal if it appears to be contrary to the principle of *'pacta sunt servanda'*, flowing from international law. A contract containing such a clause is one that the State has concluded outside of its own legal regimen. Hence, it belongs then to the legal regimen of international law." [23]

Nothing prevents a reference to national law from being made in a State Contract, so long as the contract also provides for the application of international law. Such a clause will give the foreign investor greater guarantees than that stating that just and equitable treatment will be provided.

---

[23] LEBEN, Charles, "L'évolution de la notion de Contrat d'Etat", *Revue de l'arbitrage*, Paris, 3/2003, p. 641.

2.9. – VIOLATION OF LOCAL LAW DISQUALIFIES DIPLOMATIC PROTECTION

Every investor residing in the territory of a foreign State is subject to the laws of that State to the same extent as a national of that State would be. The national of a State who has chosen to reside abroad, and who violates local investment law, cannot appeal to diplomatic or consular protection for his defence.

A special provision appears on this subject in the Congolese investment code:

> "Any foreign or national investor, who conducts a legal activity, whether allowed or not, will have the general benefit of general guarantees derived from this law." (Article I)

"*A contrario*", one may reason that investors who conduct an illegal activity are excluded from such guarantees. This would flow from the "clean hands" doctrine, which is also part of international law:

> "It appears that the national State has the right to endorse a claim of one of its nationals only if the latter has been operating legally, with 'clean hands' as is said in British jurisprudence.
>
> A demurrer to a claimant's demand shall therefore be sustained if it is shown that he has violated local law or has demonstrated an activity contrary to international law.[24]"

This rule is applied in all legal systems. Judicial decisions applying this principle are many. Examples may also be found in the jurisprudence of international courts. This applies of course also to legislation specific to investments. In the event false documents are submitted for the purpose of obtaining an investment permit (agreement), any State protection *to* which the submitting party might otherwise be entitled becomes void. Moreover, this principle also applies

---

[24] DELBEZ. Louis, *Les principes généraux du contentieux international*, Paris, Librairie générale de droit et de jurisprudence, LGDJ/Paris, 1962, p. 196 (General Principles in International Litigation).

to the violation of ordinary laws and the same consequences follow. That would, for example, be the case if fraudulent acts, such as concealment of important elements of the submittal, violations of local tax law, etc., were committed during the negotiation of agreements. Thus, in general, violations of the law render unavailable diplomatic and consular protection.

2.10. – Exhaustion of Local Remedies – A Prerequisite

There is a difference, at the international level at least, between diplomatic support and diplomatic protection. The latter is usually exercised through the action of international tribunals, such as the International Court of Justice (ICJ).

When minor damages, incurred or threatened, to their nationals, are alleged, States usually offer them the support of their diplomatic and consular missions. These organisms have been given the task of protecting their nationals from the action or threat of foreign authorities affecting, for instance, their economic interests, and in particular, when the action or threat is alleged to be discriminatory. However, this protection may also be for something as simple as the refusal to issue or renew, without justification, a visa.

On the other hand, more forcible diplomatic protection occurs when the State of such nationals files a judicial action, in an international court, against another State, alleged to have seriously harmed the interests of such nationals. In this case, the plaintiff State is authorized to assume that protection on behalf of its nationals. Decisions of the International Court of Justice show that the plaintiff State submits its claim in its own name, on the theory that its own interests have been harmed as a result of the illegal action of the respondent State:

> "The classic rule on this matter was well established in the 'Mayromatic Concessions' case, where the Permanent Court of Justice ruled

that 'by taking up the case of its subjects and by resorting to diplomatic action or international proceedings on his behalf, a State is in reality, asserting its own rights – its right to ensure, in the person of its subjects, respect for the rules of international law'."[25]

Action of this kind may only be imagined, when extremely important interests need protection. In such a case, the international rule as to 'exhaustion of remedies' always comes into play. Respecting such rule is viewed as a 'prequisite for the exercise of diplomatic protection'. The rationale for the rule is respect for the sovereignty of the State concerned. This State is offering to claimants the opportunity to settle their disputes and to find justice through the legal organisms and systems set up on its territory. Thus, it is logical that persons who claim to have been harmed must first see redress with the organisms a sovereign State has placed at their disposal before being allowed to take measures that shift their claims to the international level.

Exhaustion of local remedies implies the existence of a rule that the petitioner should use up all of the local administrative or judicial means at his disposal to obtain redress in the host country. The rule is not absolute : there are limits, which are reached when it may be shown that any such recourse could not possibly have a favourable outcome :

"If it can be established[26] that the legal system does not provide for an appropriate remedy to redress the violation occurred, be it that no adequate system of judicial protection exists at all, that no adequate remedy exists for the specific violation or that for other legal or factual reasons an abstractly existing remedy is not available to the individual in the specific circumstances of the case, the alien is not expected to exhaust the local remedies. Mere doubts about the effectiveness of local remedies, however, do not absolve the author from pursuing such remedies."

The failing State could therefore be faulted for its breach of its duty to afford due process to foreign claimants. That

---

[25] *International Law Association*, Report Toronto Conference 2006, p. 355.
[26] *International Law Association*, op. cit., p. 365, see footnote 25.

breach allows the claimants to bypass the rule. It is no doubt safer to anticipate the problem. As is usual in international common law, the parties' written agreement can expressly provide for situations of this type. We would recommend a simple clause stating that the "exhaustion of local remedies" rule is inapplicable to transactions under the agreement. Foreign investors have a stake in having such a clause included in the BIT between their home State and the host State. (cfr infra subtitle 16.8.5.1)

As a matter of historical interest, the "exhaustion of local remedies" rule has long been a part of international law and may be seen as beneficial to foreign claimants, for it means that, despite their alienage, there are jurisdictionally approved, local means to settle disputes stemming from host State acts that may have harmed them.

CHAPTER III

NATIONAL PROTECTION OF INTERNATIONAL INVESTMENTS

3.1. – Origins of national protection

Few doubt that investments made by State nationals or by foreign individuals or corporations are of great importance for State economies. Many economists and scientists have long considered investment as one of the most important economic activities.

During the period following the Second World War, many new States, mostly in Africa and Asia, have made their début on the world stage. As soon as they became independent, they displayed a major interest in promoting investments. Lacking the necessary local capital, these States have wanted to encourage foreign investors to invest on their territories. To achieve this goal, the less developed countries (LDC's) have passed specific legislation, generally going under the name of "investment codes". This legislation provided for fiscal and other advantages as well as protection clauses favouring national and foreign investors.

3.2. – Linking investments with economic growth and development

LDC's, therefore, are by and large convinced that investments represent an important element of their growth and economic development. The following quotation highlights this conviction:

> "Investments have been found to be a top notch factor in the promotion of economic growth and development contributing to an

enlargement of economic horizons. Economic growth itself posits major structural changes and corresponding modifications of States' institutional and social physiognomies...

No investment, no growth seems to be a *sine qua non* equation. Thus made clear for all to see, the driving need is for Governments to formulate and carry out an economic strategy with sufficient allure to compete successfully with other national players in the world capital market.[27]"

An in-depth international study[28] led to the conclusion that private investments primarily contribute the most to economic development.

It has been verified that development measured by the growth of the GDP depends mainly on the level of the investment. The following table shows the relationship between the GDI (Gross Domestic Investment) and the growth of the GDP:

Relationship between Investment and Growth

GDI = Gross Domestic Investment	GDP = Gross Domestic Product
GDI < 18% of the GDP	GDP growth < 3%
GDI = 20% of the GDP	GDP growth is between 3 and 5%
GDI = 30% of the GDP	GDP growth = 8%

The following chart from an international study shows clearly that (a) the link between Investment and Growth is strong, (b) public investment is relatively constant (between 8 and 9% of GDP) in all growth situation (due to budget deficit constraint), and (c) the economic development is mostly linked to the level of private investment.

However in countries like Rwanda where Agriculture provides 40% of the GDP, the growth of output is also linked to other factors not related to capital inputs, such as agriculture work, rain and price structure of agriculture products.

---

[27] *Code des investissements congolais*, Loi n° 004/2002, 21 février 2002, *Journal officiel* n° 6, 15 mars 2002, Exposé des motifs, p. 1.

[28] *Paths out of Poverty*, International Finance Corporation, Washington DC, 2000, p. 5.

Private Investment and Growth

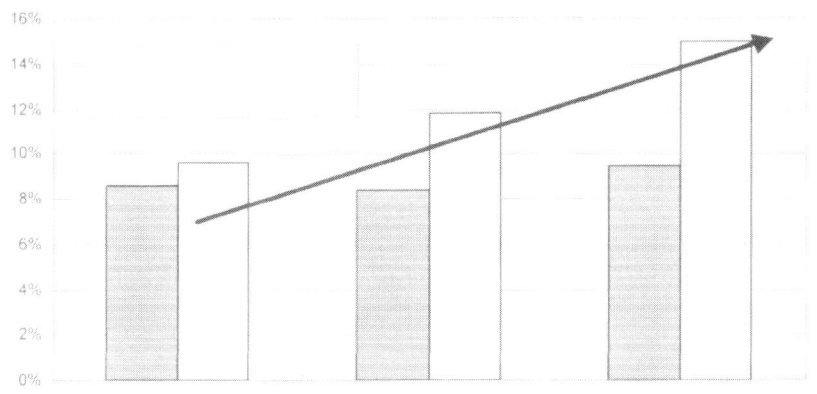

3.3. – ANALYSIS OF INVESTMENT CODES

There are many investment codes in the world, particularly in African and Asian LDC's. These laws have common characteristics but there are of course some differences. Here are a few examples:

3.3.1. – *Congo (RDC)*

Law no. 009/2002 dated 21 February 2002, affecting the Investment Code and published in *Official Journal,* no. 6 dated 15 March 2002, establishes a national agency for the promotion of investments (ANAPI). Its objective was to determine the conditions and advantages as well as the general regulations applicable to direct, national or foreign investments made in the Democratic Republic of the Congo in economic sectors not expressly reserved to the State.

3.3.1.1. *Definitions*

Foreign investors are defined as follows:

"Any physical person who does not have Congolese nationality or having the Congolese nationality but residing abroad and any public or private moral person having its social seat outside of Congolese territory and having made a direct investment in the Democratic Republic of the Congo." (article 2)

The law logically limits itself to direct investments: it is the category of investments that could mostly contribute to the Congo's economic growth and development. However, as a consequence, the States of the investors will have to obtain, by conventional means, protection guarantees for triangular investments and portfolio investments.

Insofar as corporations are concerned, the definition corresponds to the current norm in Europe and other countries. The seat theory is followed.

Regarding individuals, the introduction of a particular notion of nationality may cause confusion. On the basis of his residence abroad, a physical person of Congolese nationality is considered "a foreign investor". The double nationality issue may arise here since the Congo and the State of residence of the Congolese investor may apply different criteria for the acquisition of nationality by individuals. Here again, co-contracting States with the Congo have to set up a conventional formula for removing the confusion.

3.3.1.2. *Admittal of foreign investments*

Foreign investors desirous of obtaining the benefits of the law's provisions must submit an agreement request with ANAPI.

Appropriate Ministries then review and eventually approve the request. Important economic sectors fall outside the code's field of application: mines and petroleum, banks, insurance and reinsurance, weapons production and related activities, explosives, assembly of military or paramilitary, security services, commercial activities. These areas of economic activity are subject to special laws.

The delivery of an investment licence is subject to meeting certain conditions. Most of these conditions may be justified from economic (minimum investment amount of US dollars

200,000) and environmental viewpoints. One condition, however, may give rise to misunderstandings : the investor must be an economic entity under Congolese law. Obviously, there is here a confusion between the investor (having foreign nationality) and the investment whose legal form must be corporate.

3.3.1.3. *Benefits*

Through the Investment Project Agreement, which requires them to conform to the rules of the Investment Code,[29] the State grants various customs and fiscal benefits to investors :

3.3.1.3.1. *Customs Benefits*

- Other than the administrative duty of 5%, the full waiver, for public utility investments, of import duties and imposts on the importation of machines, new tools and materials, original spare parts not exceeding 10% of the CIF value of such products;
- Total waiver, with respect to all other investments, of import duties and taxes for machines, new tools and materials, original spare parts not exceeding 10% of the value of such products. The administrative fee of 5% remains applicable;
- Waiver of export duties and taxes for all or part of finished, processed or semi-processed products subject to conditions favourable to the balance of payments.

3.3.1.3.2. *Fiscal Benefits*

- Total waiver of the professional tax on income based on the general proceeds of the approved investment;
- Waiver of the real estate tax (on real estate and buildings);
- Waiver of the proportional tax at the time of incoporation or capital increase of limited liability companies (SARL's);

---

[29] Http ://www.anapi.org/8_raisons.html.

- PME/PMI (small and medium enterprises/small and medium industries) also benefit from :
  - The discretion to calculate depreciation regressively;
  - A deduction from taxable income of training and education of personnel, protection and preservation of the environment;
- Waiver of registration fees of the new Commercial Registry.

All these benefits are granted for a period of 3 to 5 years, according to the economic region involved where the enterprise is to be located and runs from the time the goods and services are first marketed by the enterprise which produced them.

3.3.1.4. *Treatment of investors*

The new law pays homage to the principle of equal treatment of domestic and foreign investors. However according to international law, the level of protection given domestic investors should not necessarily be the maximum that foreign investors should enjoy. Domestic investors may have benefits not equal to the minimum afforded international investments. Foreign investors should be entitled to ask for a more favourable treatment and protection. Domestic norms of protection should not limit norms applicable to foreign investors :

> "The important thing from the point of view of international law is not the equality of nationals and foreigners : it is the recognition and respect for principles of international law. Should a State, for any reason, disregard them in relation with its own subjects, its international duty to observe them in relation to foreigners subsists, unaffected.[30]"

Fortunately, Congolese authorities have taken the primacy of international law into account. Hence, article 23 of the Code specifying that :

---

[30] FRIEDMAN, Samy, *Expropriation in international law*, London, Stevens and Sons, 1953, p. 130.

> "Physical and moral persons of foreign nationality shall be entitled to treatment identical to treatment granted to physical and moral persons of Congolese nationality."

has been amended to read:

> "The Democratic Republic of the Congo is committed to ensuring a fair and equitable treatment in conformity with international law to investors and investments made on its territory and to see to it that the enjoyment of such right shall not be hindered in law or in fact."

The law furthermore specifies its application and the securing of specific benefits depends of the "licit" character of the investment ("All investors, whether domestic or foreign, who conduct a licit activity"). Investors who might, when they first made their investments, have infringed on local legislation and have conducted inadmissible activities (whether punishable or not) are denied protection from Congolese authorities' decisions. Investors who received a licence ("*Agrément*") for making an investment and who, under the cover of this licence, actually conducted illicit operations (f.i. illicit banking activities) are placing themselves outside of the umbrella of the code. This principle is generally admitted and was already applicable under Roman Law: "*nullum commodum capere de sua propria iniuria potest et ex delicto non oritur actio*", that is, no one may benefit from his own illicit activity nor file an action originating in delictual activity.

3.3.1.5. *Individual property right*

The Investment Code recognises individual property rights and grants a few guarantees in the event that measures depriving owners of their property are taken against investments:

> "Individual or collective property rights acquired by an investor are guaranteed by the RDC Constitution. An investment may not, directly or indirectly, in whole or in part, be nationalised or expropriated by a new law and/or decision of a local authority with the same effect, except for a public use and provided just and equitable compensatory indemnity is awarded.

> The indemnity is deemed just, if it is based on the market value of the nationalised or expropriated asset : this value must be determined in adversary fashion immediately upon such expropriation or nationalisation, or before the decision to expropriate or nationalise is publicly announced." (article 26)

In many countries, the market value is used as the norm in order to fix the amount of the indemnity but this value is naturally subject to fluctuations. It is impossible to determine exactly the moment on which a decision of nationalization becomes public. Where investments in a local company are concerned, assuming its stock is quoted on a stock exchange, it may be assumed that rumours, however vague, about eventual measures of nationalisation, cause market value to go south immediately. Determining indemnity on the basis of "real value" should be the norm instead, for, then, investors would not be subject to seeing the market value of the nationalised assets reduced, and they would be able to prove a specific value on a date when nationalisation was still not yet considered ("*in tempore non suspecto*").

Pursuant to the investment code, the indemnity must be fixed "in adversary fashion." This means there is to be a direct contact between the expropriating State and the investor eventually with the assistance of competing experts. Clearly, an investor facing expropriation is always in a weak position. Nationalisation measures and like events only exceptionally affect few single investors. Usually, these measures have wide scope and affect groups of investors. In such cases, current practice is that negotiations are organised between the expropriating State and the State of the nationality of the affected investors.

With respect to delays, article 26 is not so clear. It would have been preferable to set the time during which the expropriating agency must act to indemnify the investors affected by that State's expropriation action. Neither does the text say whether interest on overdue payment will be earned. The "*dies a quo*" for the calculation of interest due could be the date of nationalisation. This date is certain, and in almost all countries, nationalisation measures are published in the official National Register.

3.3.1.6. *Settlement of Investment Disputes*

The best way to settle disputes regarding investment contracts or interpretation of the investment code or other Congolese laws, is negotiation. The notion of prior negotiation will be found in European and even world practice. Congolese legislators therefore have properly included this principle in their Code.

The code does provide for an alternative method, when no settlement through negotiations is achieved within three months after notification of the existence of a dispute to an opposing party. When this condition is met, then an arbitration proceeding may be filed. A choice between two arbitration institutions is made available: the International Centre for the Settlement of Investment Disputes (ICSID) in Washington or the International chamber of Commerce (ICC) in Paris.

A few years ago, the Congolese government tried to avoid the jurisdiction of ICSID. In its article 25, the ICSID Convention provides that its jurisdiction shall extend to any legal dispute between a Contracting State (or any constituent subdivision or agency of a contracting State designated to the Centre by that State) and a national of another Contracting State.

At that time, the intention was to find a way for arguing that the investor concerned could not be considered a national of another State. In order to achieve this goal, the Congolese authorities stressed the point that a Congolese company, even when it was in the hands of foreign majority shareholders, who could consequently manage and control the company, remained a "national of the Congolese State" and not that of another Contracting State.

A foreign investor, having made his investment by means of a Congolese company in which he had a majority participation, could not, as a consequence, (pursuant to the opinion of Congolese authorities) file an arbitration proceeding at ICSID, because of the application of **Article 25** of the Code.

In 1997, for instance, in American Manufacturing & Trading Corporation (AMT) v. Republic of Congo, the Congolese State was trying to avoid an arbitration procedure filed against it at ICSID.[31] The company in this case was the "Société industrielle zaïroise" (SINZA), 94 % of its shares being owned by AMT. Zaïre pointed out that ICSID had no jurisdiction and declared the arbitration proceeding ill filed. The main Zaire argument was that AMT could not act in the name of SINZA because the latter was a Zaire company and therefore not a national of "another State." SINZA had made the investment as a Zaire corporation and AMT held a majority of the stock of SINZA, but this circumstance did not give it the right to act in the name of the Zaire investor SINZA. A decision was rendered on 21 February 1998, Zaire's argumentation being rejected.

The Tribunal decided that AMT had invested in Zaire territory by virtue of its ownership in SINZA's capital, and, hence, qualified as an investor.

Zaire became very rapidly aware that its attitude regarding ICSID's jurisdiction sent the wrong signal to potential foreign investors. A special clause, based on ICSID jurisprudence was therefore inserted in the investment code:

> "If the investor has made his investment through an intermediary Congolese corporation which he controls, the parties agree that such a corporation, for the purposes of the ICSID convention, must be deemed a national of another Contracting State." (Article 38 *in fine*)

This was a very good decision and doctrinal writers welcomed Zaïre's change in position:

---

[31] GAILLARD Emmanuel, *La jurisprudence du CIRDI*, Paris, Editions A. Pedone, 2004, p. 425.

"This provision seems to be a remodeling of the new code made on the basis of a provision in the arbitration decision in the AMT affair (victim of the looting of its industrial facilities at Masina (SYNZA)). Thus, in order to avoid ICSID's jurisdiction, the Zaire Republic had claimed that the victim of the looting (SYNZA SPRL) being a corporation under Congolese law, the dispute did not confront a 'foreign investor' and a foreign State. The tribunal has instead decided that it had jurisdiction, in the manner claimed by the AMT Corporation which owned a majority of shares of stock. Basically, Zaire lost for not having sufficiently protected the foreign investor." [32]

It should be added that in 1998, the decision of the arbitration tribunal was motivated not only by the provisions of the bilateral investment agreement USA/Zaire but also by article 25 of the ICSID Convention. The above mentioned "jurisdiction" clause could be inserted in any bilateral agreement between States and, if possible, in any specific investment agreement between the investor and the host State (cfr. *infra* : State Contracts).

3.3.2. – *Egypt*

The Arab Republic of Egypt has published at the end of the last century "Law n° 8 of 1997 on investment guarantees and incentives." [33]

3.3.2.1. *Limited application*

The provisions of the law apply to all companies and establishments to be incorporated after the date of its enforcement regardless of the legal form governing them, for exercising their activities limited to the in the law indicated fields. The Council of Ministers may add other fields as deemed needed for the country.

3.3.2.2. *Settlement of Investment Disputes*

Article 7 of the law reads as follows :

---

[32] GAILLARD Emmanuel, *op. cit.*, pp. 425 and s., see footnote 31.
[33] www.gafinet.net.

"The investment disputes regarding the implementation of the provisions of this Law may be settled in the manner agreed upon with the investor. The parties concerned may also agree to settle such disputes within the framework of the agreements in force between the Arab Republic of Egypt and the country of the investor, or within the framework of the Convention for the Settlement of Disputes arising from investments between the States and nationals of other countries, which the Arab Republic of Egypt has adhered to by Law No. 90 of 1971, and pursuant to the conditions, terms and cases where such agreements do apply, or according to the provisions of Law No. 27 of 1994 concerning Arbitration of Civil and Commercial Issues. It may also be agreed to settle said disputes through arbitration before the Cairo Regional Center for International Commercial Arbitration."[34]

This provision does not include the anticipatory consent of parties required for the filing of an arbitration procedure. The terms "agreed upon with the investor" prove that the parties (i.e. the investor and the host State) must enter into an agreement on this topic. The text does not specify that the investor may choose the arbitration institution which will have jurisdiction to decide the dispute relating to the investment. In the event a BIT has been entered into between the State of the investor and the host State, providing for the investor's choice and the anticipatory consent to any arbitration procedure, there would be no problem.

As an exception to the general rule, according to which disputes may, at the investor's choice, submit to local tribunals having jurisdiction, the Law provides for recourse to an Egyptian arbitration tribunal. However, this law offers no legal security sufficient for foreign investors who, therefore, must instead contemplate entering into an investment agreement or otherwise ensure the application of a BIT between the States concerned.

3.3.2.3. *Investment guarantees*

"Companies and establishments may not be nationalized or confiscated. Companies and establishments may neither be sequestrated nor

---

[34] www.gafinet.net.

may their assets be subject to administrative attachment, seized, restrained, frozen, or expropriated." (Articles 8 and 9)

Evidently, this law offers insufficient guarantees for foreign investors. The text does not specify that any condition has to be met to enable the State to proceed to apply restrictive or privative measures to assets. This silence is not encouraging. There is in fact an abundant arbitral and judiciary jurisprudence that can prove that a State always has the right to nationalise if public interest is involved:

> "First of all, the State is the natural protector of the public and social interest of the Nation. Consequently, except when a State acts like a simple private party and in no way exercises its sovereign prerogatives, the State is entitled to affect or suppress, when public interest demands it, the situation or the relationship it has created by a precedent act, even if that act is the source of the commitments and obligations of the State. This is a consequence of the fundamental principle of the sovereignty of States to proceed to nationalise or expropriate private property, which applies equally to contractual rights previously granted by such States, even if such rights belong to foreigners. This principle today is clearly admitted in various national legal systems as well as in international law. For the latter, the principle has been incorporated in the resolutions of the General Assembly of the United Nations Organisation (see Resolution 1803/XVII dated 14 December 1962) as well as a good many international legal decisions." [35]

The result is that the Egyptian State will always be able to proceed to nationalise, if those principles of international law are respected. The State must prove that public interest is involved and furthermore must recognise the right to indemnification.

Egyptian law is therefore very much incomplete. As stated earlier, foreign investors shall have to contemplate a specific investment agreement and verify whether or not a BIT exists between the concerned States.

---

[35] GAILLARD, Emmanuel, *op. cit.*, p. 145, see footnote 31.

3.3.3. – *Rwanda*

Rwanda's code was first made to apply under Law 21/87 dated 5 August 1987, abrogated by Law 14/98 dated 18 December 1998 which created the Rwandan Office for the Promotion of Investments, and was supplemented by Law 26/2005 dated 17 December 2005 relating to investment and export promotion and facilitation. Here are some of its most important provisions:

3.3.3.1. *Definitions Article 2 of Law 26* [36]

A distinction was made between internal and external investments:

> "Capital means any investment in cash, plant, equipment, plant, machinery, buildings, spare parts, and other business assets other than goodwill which are necessary for operations of an investment enterprise but which are not consumed in its regular opérations."

> "Foreign capital means foreign currency, plant machinery, ordinary equipment, spare parts and other business assets, other than goodwill, imported in Rwanda for investment in order to increase production of goods and services in the country."

A similar distinction is made in the definition of investors:

> "Foreign investor" means a physical person, a business company or a partnership that invests a minimum financial capital equivalent to at least two hundred and fifty thousand American Dollars (US$ 250,000) in foreign capital in an investment enterprise to which this Law applies, and is:
>
> (a) a physical person, who has no Rwandan Nationality or the nationality of one of the member states of the Common Market of East and Southern Africa, abbreviated as COMESA;
>
> (b) a commercial company incorporated under the laws of any country other than Rwanda or one of the member states of Common Market of East and Southern Africa, COMESA;
>
> "Local investor" means a physical person, a business company or a partnership that invests a minimum capital of at least one hundred

---

[36] Http://www.ripa.org.

thousand American Dollars (US$ 100.000) in an investment enterprise to which this law applies and is:

(a) a physical person, who holds a Rwandan nationality or of one of the member States of the Common Market of East and Southern Africa, (COMESA);

(b) a company incorporated under Rwandan laws of which more than fifty percent (50%) of its shares are held by persons who hold Rwandan nationality or of nationality of one of the member States of COMESA;

(c) a commercial company incorporated under Rwandan laws but of which more than fifty percent (50%) of the shares are held by persons who do not hold Rwanda nationality or who do not hold nationality of one of the member states of the Common Market of East and Southern Africa (COMESA);

(d) a partnership, in which a partner holds the biggest number of shares and does not hold a Rwandan nationality or a nationality of one of the member states of the Common market of East and Southern Africa (COMESA).

3.3.3.2. *Nationality Issues*

In bilateral agreements for the protection of international investments (BIT's), investors are generally defined as a physical or moral person having the nationality of the other Contracting State, according to the legislation that other State applies for determination of nationality and the status of persons. The Rwandan code defines foreign investors as a moral or physical person having neither Rwandan nationality nor the nationality of one of the members States of the Common Market for Eastern and Southern Africa (COMESA).[37] According to the investment code, physical and moral persons having COMESA nationality are therefore not considered as foreign investors.

Furthermore, the "Control" theory is applied to moral persons. A commercial company incorporated under the Rwandan laws but of which more than fifty percent (50%) of the

---

[37] The COMESA member states are: Burundi, Egypt, Madagascar, Sudan, Commoros, Eritrea, Malawi, Swaziland, D.R.Congo, Ethiopia, Mauritius, Uganda, Djibouti, Kenya, Rwanda, Zambia, Libya, Seychelles, Zimbabwe.

shares are held by persons who do not hold Rwandan nationality or who do not hold nationality of one of the member states of COMESA, is considered as a foreign company.

This could lead to difficulties in the event a State did not apply the control theory. Applying Rwandan law would then lead to a *"contradictio in terminis."* An investor who has the nationality of that State, investing in Rwanda, might be making an investment in a company having the same nationality as the investor even though the investment is on foreign soil.

It is therefore indispensable that precautions be taken to ensure that the provisions of BIT's with Rwanda are properly carried out. It would be useful to specify that in disputes relating to investments the Rwanda Government and its Co-contracting Party shall respect the control clauses of the BIT's.

3.3.3.3. *Registration*

To obtain an investment licence, a foreign investor has to submit, in writing, an application for investment project registration, to the Rwanda Investment promotion Agency (RIPA).

Broad duties are imposed on persons holding a registration certificate, *inter alia*:

- to make a declaration of the profits of the investment as required by the tax laws;
- to permit the employees of RIPA, in the execution of their duties, access to the premises and records of the investment enterprise;
- to produce a detailed annual activity report etc.

The certificate of registration of investment may be revoked for important reasons, such as conviction of and imprisonment for a criminal offence.

3.3.3.4. *Incentives* [38]

The holder of a certificate of registration of an investment project is entitled to several advantages (article 30, Rwandan Investment Code) and may benefit from:

a) Fiscal incentives as provided in Law no. 8/97 dated 26 June 1997 relating to Direct Tax Code affecting miscellaneous profits and professional revenues;
b) Investment premiums up to 30% of the value of the capital invested during the first year of operations;
c) additional rebate on taxable revenue amounting to 50% of the costs of creation, research and product development;
d) full credit for expenses of necessary infrastructure on site for the enterprise's activities;
e) refund of all customs duties and taxes paid on imported raw materials in the event of exports made outside of free customs zones and Office assistance for access to foreign markets, incorporation and promotional and commercial Fairs;
f) waiver of all export taxes.

Further benefits are granted for investments made in free customs zones.

3.3.3.5. *Protection of Foreigners' Investments*

Applicable laws are not consistent. Article 30 of the Rwandan Law 26/2005 reads:

> "The Government has the responsibility of protecting the capital invested. It shall not acquire the rights of an investor on a registered investment enterprise over any activity that is included in the activities of the investment enterprise except due to public interest according to periods and procedures provided by law and in consideration of prior payment of adequate compensation, in foreign convertible currency, in a period not exceeding twelve (12) months from the date of

---

[38] This list is not complete. Verification of the benefits applicable on the date the investment is made is suggested.

acquisition, and such amount is freely repatriated to a country of the investor's choice without being subject to any form of tax whatsoever.

Investment enterprises shall not be separated on issues relating to law or internal regulations that govern business enterprises and industries."

Article 38 of law no. 14/98 reads as follows:

"The State may not acquire or take possession, by any means whatever, of the rights of an investor in a registered enterprise, or of a claim of interest of a right in property or an activity which is a part of the activities of such enterprise. In the event of a taking or acquisition by the State, an adequate compensation, in convertible currency, shall be paid within twelve months at the most and may be freely transferred to the country selected by the investor, without the payment of any tax or impost of any nature whatever. Enterprises belonging to investors may not be subject to discriminatory measures, whether by law, decree, regulation or decision regulating the activities of commercial and industrial enterprises."

Law 26/2005 (which did not abrogate law 14/98) does not contain the same guarantees of protection for investors. Law 14/98 mentions expressly "taking of possession or acquisition by the State" whereas Law 26/2006 states: "it shall not acquire the rights of an investor." Neither text includes any duty to pay interest and there is no system for the establishment of the value of the expropriated assets. Consequently, it is indispensable that the protection of foreign investment be governed by conventional means.

3.3.3.6. Settlement of investment disputes

Law n° 26/2005 contains the following provisions, which are in conformity with law n° 14/98:

Article 31: "Where disputes arise between a foreign investor and the Agency or the Government of Rwanda in respect of a registered investment enterprise, all possible efforts shall be made to settle the disputes amicably through negotiations."

Article 32: "Disputes that arise between a foreign investor and the Agency or the Government of Rwanda in respect of a registered business enterprise that are not settled through negotiations shall be submitted to an arbitrator in accordance with the following manner and after both parties have mutually agreed upon it :

1° in consultation with the Centre responsible for settling disputes between investors;

2° in accordance with bilateral or multilateral agreements for protection of investment activities, which the Government of Rwanda and the country from which the investor originates signed;

3° in accordance with any other international procedure of settling investment disputes, particularly the Convention of 18 March, 1965, concerning the Settlement of Disputes in matters of investment arising between States and foreigners on investing in a country concluded under the *aegis* of the International Bank for Reconstruction and Development and ratified by the Republic of Rwanda under the Decree-Law of 16, July 1979 approved by law n° 01/82 of 26 January 1982 approving decrees and laws."

Article 34 : In case parties to a dispute do not agree on the mode or forum for arbitration, the party aggrieved by the dispossession or acquisition of his or her property, or the amount and compensation payable, or in respect of any other matter relating to the investment enterprise, may sue to a competent Rwandan court for the decision to be rendered.

Foreign investors' rights in Rwanda are uncertain. The law first stresses that the dispute may be settled amiably. However, no time has been set within which this mode of resolution must be followed. There is no *"dies a quo"* for the filing of an arbitration procedure. The law does not provide for the anticipatory consent of the Rwandan State regarding the filing of an arbitration procedure. There is therefore a risk that arbitration will be rejected particularly if the investor is involved in an important dispute with the State.

Finally, the law provides that for certain types of disputes (modality or forum of arbitration, amount of compensation, any other matter) the parties may submit the dispute to Rwandan tribunal having jurisdiction but the law does not state the investor has any choice in the matter. It is to be expected that RIPA will want to choose the judiciary solution more often.

3.3.4. – Thaïland

In January 2002, the last "Investment Promotion Act" (n° 3-B.E.2544) was published. A board of investment (B.O.I.) has been reorganised and the Office of the Board of Investment has received the power to execute the Investment Act (IPA).[39]

3.3.4.1. *Applying for and granting of promotion benefits*

On this topic the IPA provides:

> "Section 16. The activities which are eligible for investment promotion by the Board are those which are important and beneficial to the economic and social development, and security of the country, activities which involve production for export, activities which have high content of capital, labour or service or activities which utilise agricultural produce or natural resources as raw materials, provided that in the opinion of the Board, they are non-existent in the Kingdom, or existent but inadequate, or use out-of-date production processes.
>
> The Board shall make an announcement designating the types and sizes of investment activity eligible for promotion and may stipulate therein to the conditions under which promotion is to be granted and may amend or abolish those conditions at any time.
>
> Section 17. A person who seeks to be a promoted person shall file to the Office and application for promotion in accordance with the rules, procedure and forms prescribed by the Secretary General, describing the investment project for which promotion is sought.
>
> The promoted person shall be a company, a foundation or a cooperative established in accordance with the respective law. Application for promotion prior to the formation of a company, a foundation, or a co-operative under paragraph two shall be made in accordance with the rules, procedure and forms prescribed by the Secretary general."

Investors must comply with strict requirements. The Board of Investment (BOI) is vested with great powers in that it can designate in which economic sectors investments may be made. It can set a minimum amount to be invested and determine the number and nationality of allowable stockhold-

---

[39] Http://www.boi.go.th/english/about/law_and regulations.asp.

NATIONAL PROTECTION OF INTERNATIONAL INVESTMENTS 55

ers. This implies that the BOI may also require a minimum number of Thai stockholders held to participate in the investment.

The law does not define what is meant by the term "investor" and does not refer to physical persons, providing only as follows in this regard :

> "The promoted person shall be a company, a foundation or a cooperative established in accordance with applicable law."

It could be concluded that foreign investments made on Thai territory must be made in the form of a local corporation. The Code also provides that the BOI may choose among investments which are susceptible of benefiting from legal investment privileges, namely, those which are "economically and technologically sound."

3.3.4.2. *Rights and Benefits*

The law facilitates getting a residence permit for foreigners who wish to investigate the possibilities of investments in Thailand and provides for the possibility of residence permits for personnel hired by the investor :

> "Subject to the law on immigration, only in so far as it is not otherwise provided herein, the Board shall have the power to grant permission to foreign nationals for entry into the Kingdom for the purpose of studying investment opportunities or performing any other act benefiting investment for such period of time to stay in the Kingdom as the Board may deem appropriate." (section 24)
>
> "Subject to the law on immigration, only in so far as it is not otherwise provided herein, a promoted person shall be grant permission to bring into the Kingdom foreign nationals who are skilled workers, experts, spouses..." (section 25)

The law uses the term "nationals", which normally includes both physical and moral persons. It would have been clearer, of course, if the terms "physical persons" and "moral persons" had been used. Investors must apply for a permit in order to acquire real estate according to their needs for the investment :

"A promoted person shall be permitted to own land in order to carry on the promoted activity to such an extent as the Board deems appropriate, even in excess of the permissible limit under other laws.

In the case where the promoted person who is a foreign national under the Land Code dissolves his promoted activity or transfers it to another person, he shall dispose of the land he has been permitted to own within one year of the date of dissolution or transfer, or the Director General of the Land Department shall have the power to dispose of it." (section 27)

The right to alienate real estate acquired by the investor, in the event the investment project ends or is transferred, is limited, since, if the investor does not alienate it within the year after such cessation or transfer, Thai authorities then have the right to dispose of it.

The Board may grant fiscal benefits to investors, such as exemption from payment of import duties, exemption of legal person income tax on the net profit derived from the promoted activity, deduction of annual loss from the net profits etc. An investor in a promoted activity, whose domicile is outside the Kingdom of Thaïland:

"shall be granted permission to take out or remit abroad money in foreign currency if it represents an investment capital which the promoted person brought into the Kingdom and dividends or other returns of such capital."

3.3.4.3. *Guarantees and protection*

"The State shall not nationalise the activity of the promoted person. The State shall not undertake a new activity in competition with the promoted person." (sections 43 and 44).

As already stated, this non-nationalisation commitment will not be respected, if public interest intervenes. This rudimentary legal provision does not protect foreign investors sufficiently. An eventual nationalization is always possible and, furthermore, indemnification problems could arise, inasmuch as the law contains no provision for indemnification nor for the calculation of indemnities that eventually become due.

3.3.5. – *Ukraine*

The law of Ukraine on the regime of foreign investment was published on 25 April 1996 and stipulates the terms and conditions for foreign investment, based on the aims, principles and provisions of the legislation of Ukraine.[40]

The provisions of this law have their own special characteristics distinguishing it from African and Asian investment codes.

3.3.5.1. *Investors*

Article 1 of the Foreign Investment law (FIL) reads as follows :

> "Terms used in this Law have the following meanings :
> 1) foreign investors – persons engaged in investment activity within the territory of Ukraine, namely : legal entities, established according to legislation other than Ukrainian legislation; natural persons who are foreigners, who are not Ukrainian permanent residents and who are legally and otherwise competent; foreign countries, international governmental and non-governmental organisations; other foreign participants in investment activity, who are recognised as such by the legislation of Ukraine;
> 2) foreign investments are stores of value which are invested by foreign investors in objects of investment in accordance with the legislation of Ukraine with the aim of obtaining profit or achieving social results;
> 3) entity with foreign investment – an entity (organisation) of any form of legal organisation established according to the legislation of Ukraine, where foreign investment is no less than 10 per cent of the Statutory Fund. An entity shall obtain the status of an entity with foreign investment on the date of inclusion of the foreign investment to the balance sheet of the entity."

The discretion to invest is offered to private foreign persons as well as to foreign countries and governmental and non-governmental organisations. Just as in Canada, physical persons who have gained the status of "permanent resident" are

---
[40] Http://www3.sympatico.ca/tem-ukraine/law_fir.htm.

deemed to be Ukrainian nationals. An exceptional provision, deviating from the usual practice, requires that corporations, established in accordance with Ukrainian law, and in which foreigners hold a participation greater than 10 % of the capital stock, shall enjoy a special status as "entities with foreign investment". This is really a very low percentage which is not tied to "control" as in many other countries.

3.3.5.2. *Investments*

Foreign investments may be made in different forms, such as stipulated in article 3 of the Foreign Investment Law (FIL):

1. ownership interest in entities which are being established jointly with Ukrainian legal entities and natural persons, or acquisition of shares of functioning entities;
2. the establishment of entities wholly owned by foreign investors, subsidiaries and branches of foreign legal entities or full acquisition of existing entities;
3. the acquisition, which is not prohibited by the laws of Ukraine, of movable property or real estate including buildings, apartments, premises, equipment, transportation facilities and other property, by direct acquisition of property and proprietary complexes or in the form of stocks, bonds and other securities;
4. the acquisition of the rights to use land and/or concessions for the use of natural resources in the territory of Ukraine by foreign investors, independently or jointly with Ukrainian legal entities or physical persons;
5. the acquisition of other property rights;
6. other kinds of investment, which are not prohibited by the laws of Ukraine, in particular, those based on agreements with agents of economic activity in Ukraine without establishing a legal entity.

In general, host States require that the foreign investment be made by incorporating locally. The FIL acknowledges expressly "joint ventures" and add *expressis verbis* that the purchase of shares in existing corporations is considered an investment. The acquisition of existing corporations is also deemed an investment.

It is also quite interesting that the primacy of international law is expressly acknowledged:

> "Activities connected with foreign investments in Ukraine shall be regulated by this law, other legislative acts of Ukraine and international agreements of Ukraine. If an international agreement of Ukraine provides rules other than that provided for by the legislation of Ukraine, the rules of the international agreement shall apply" (article 6)

3.3.5.3. *National treatment*

Foreign investors are entitled to national treatment "with the exceptions provided for by Ukrainian legislation and international agreements of Ukraine." This provision does not appear to be very favourable because it could imply that a Ukrainian law might grant specific privileges to national companies. On the other hand, it might well be that, by reason of an international agreement, some foreign investors enjoy a specific treatment more favourable than the national treatment. Consequently, conventional provisions should correct this situation and stipulate that investors are entitled to national treatment, to most favoured nation treatment and in any event to treatment in conformance with international law.

3.3.5.4. *Stabilisation clause*

A very interesting provision, not to be found anywhere else, is that creating a stabilisation clause:

> "In the event that subsequent special legislation of Ukraine concerning foreign investments shall change the terms and conditions of guarantees for the protection of foreign investments specified in the Section II of this law, upon request of the foreign investor, government guarantees for the protection of foreign investment stipulated by this law shall apply for a period of ten years from the date when such legislation came into force." (article 8)

This provision is very favourable to foreign investors, and countries which negotiate with Ukraine for the conclusion of a bilateral investment treaty would be well served to include this clause in their agreements.

3.3.5.5. *Guarantees against seizure and unlawful acts*

Foreign investments shall not be nationalised. State bodies may not seize foreign investments, with the exception of emergency measures in the event of natural disaster, accidents, epidemics, or epizootics. However, the legal value of this commitment is affected by other legal provisions which established an indemnification system in the event such commitments are not respected. The law provides that:

> "Decisions in respect of the seizure of foreign investments and the terms and conditions of compensation may be appealed in court."

It is regrettable, of course, that only local tribunals have jurisdiction on this topic and that investors cannot appeal to international arbitration (cfr *infra*, Settlement of Investment Disputes). On the other hand, principles of indemnification applicable in international law have been included in the law:

> "Foreign investors have the right to receive compensation for their losses, including lost profit and moral damage incurred as a result of actions, inaction or improper fulfillment by the State bodies of Ukraine or their officials of the responsibilities in relation to foreign investors or entities with foreign investment stipulated by the legislation, according tot the legislation of Ukraine."

On this topic also therefore, Ukrainian legislation is more progressive than that of other countries, because it covers moral damages as well as even *"lucrum cessans."* The valuation of damages is made on the basis of current market prices. A substantiated valuation, certified by an auditor or auditing company, is also acceptable. This last provision is also innovative and cannot be found in other legislations on foreign investment. Payment of interest is provided for:

> "From the moment of receiving entitlement for compensation and up to the moment of its payment, interest for the amount of compensation shall be accrued at the average interest rate, at which London banks provide credits to first-class banks on the European foreign

exchange market (London Inter-Bank Offered Rate – LIBOR)." (article 10)

3.3.5.6. *Benefits for Foreign Investment Entities (EFI)*

EFI's must be established in accordance with Ukrainian legislation. They are required to provide information necessary to verify whether their manner of operation confirms to applicable law:

> "Statutory documents of entities with foreign investments shall include information required by the legislation of Ukraine for the appropriate organisational and legal form of the entity and also information on the nationality of its founders (equity holders)." (article 17)

Contrary to other countries, Ukraine does not grant fiscal benefits to investors who must pay taxes in accordance with Ukrainian legislation. They are, however, entitled to customs privileges, in particular, a waiver of customs duties for assets imported for the needs of the enterprise.

3.3.5.7. *Settlement of Investment Disputes*

Article 26 reads as follows:

> "Disputes between foreign investors and the State on the issues of the State regulations of foreign investments and activity of entities with foreign investments should be considered in the courts of Ukraine unless another procedure is stipulated by the international agreements of Ukraine. All other disputes are subject for consideration in the courts and/or arbitration courts of Ukraine or with the consent of the parties in the arbitration courts abroad."

For all other investor/State disputes regarding the application of Ukrainian laws and regulations, local tribunals have jurisdiction. What "all other disputes" covers is not quite clear. It may cover disputes regarding indemnification for damages sustained as a result of privative or restrictive measures affecting property. On this topic, article 9 already provides for the jurisdiction of local tribunals and both articles 26 and 9 do not contradict each other. It is, however, quite certain that this filing of an arbitration procedure could only take place if this eventuality is provided for in an agreement entered into with Ukraine, or that the parties (investor/State) give mutual effect to such an agreement. Anticipatory consent does not appear in the legislation. Countries that may be interested in concluding an agreement with Ukraine should therefore see to it that anticipatory consent to arbitration and the investor's free choice of an international arbitration tribunal are provided for.

3.4. – NEED FOR CONVENTIONAL PROTECTION

There are literally hundreds of investment codes in the world. Every one of them contain provisions which are of benefit to foreign investors. Despite imperfections and gaps, these codes are without a doubt quite useful.

However, purely national protection of international investments by the host State does not suffice. There are several arguments justifying this position.

First, undeniably, investment codes are born and disappear quite quickly. Benefits and guarantees of protection granted and acknowledged in one law are often cancelled by a new law. On a national scale, there is no continuity in the protection and legal security of foreign investors.

Second, notoriously many investment codes are rudimentary and do not contain minimum guarantees.

Therefore, national protection only is insufficient. Most States wish to protect efficiently those of its nationals who reside abroad and will therefore try to enter into bilateral investment treaties (BIT's). Should there arise a conflict between domestic law and a treaty, it is generally accepted that the treaty has precedence. It is therefore clearly in the investor's interest to have protection rules taken out of a national or domestic context and to conclude a State Contract with the host State which clearly confirms the Treaty's precedence.

The entry into force of a BIT cannot of course entail the disenfranchisement of codes and rules of law of the host State granting important benefits to foreign investors. It is therefore recommended that appropriate clauses referring to national treatment be included in BIT's.

CHAPTER IV
CONVENTION BASED INVESTMENT PROTECTION

4.1. – NEED FOR CONVENTION BASED INVESTMENT PROTECTION

Neither national laws of the host State nor the sending State's diplomatic and consular facilities offer sufficient protection for international investments. Shifting investment safety from the protection of national laws to that of international law responds to a real need. Internationalising the promotion of investments and their protection, by specific bilateral treaties (BIT's) is a phenomenon which was first brought to the attention of international investors during the nineteen sixties. The European Organisation for Cooperation and Economic Development (OECD) in 1967 wrote the "Convention Proposal for the Protection of Foreign Investments", whose text was distributed among the States members of this organisation, incentivising them to conclude bilateral accords (BIT) of protection, inspired by the European model.

The usefulness of bilateral investment protection treaties is usually viewed as a given in international relations:

> "The use of conventions for the promotion of international investment – and more particularly from North to South – has experienced a spectacular development during recent years. This development shows that the world's hopes henceforth lie in the growth of private investment more than in public transfers. As a result, promotion of international investment has become an imperative. However, this promotion occurs by the interplay of bilateral agreements that countries which export capital enter into with countries which import capital."[41]

---

[41] JUILLARD, Patrick, "Les conventions bilatérales d'investissement conclues par la France : A la recherhce d'un droit perdu ?", *Droit et pratique du commerce international*, 1987, Tome 13, n° 1, p. 9.

Multilateral treaties, signed and ratified by a group of Nations, are addressed in Chapter V.

4.2. – Scholars' Diversity of Opinion regarding BIT's

The usefulness of BIT's is not acknowledged by all legal scholars. For instance, in his study "Belgian bilateral investment treaties as a means for promoting and protecting foreign investments", W. VAN DE VOORDE[42] claimed two critical considerations putting in doubt the beneficial effects of BIT's. Like other authors (SCHACHTER[43], SORNARAJAH[44]) he has doubts about the value added by BIT's for international protection of investments.

In his opinion, these agreements must instead be considered as conventions confirming simply the legal principles laid down in other acts (international treaties). According to him, they bring no new elements to the rules and principles of international law:

> "It has been said that many commitments in these BIT's must be seen as being part of a *'quid pro quo'*. These treaties are contractual arrangements and hence the product of negotiation, based on a variety of considerations. They do not necessarily declare existing or generally accepted obligations under international law. However, a thorough examination undertaken by SORNARAJAH has shown that there is not sufficient consistency in the terms of investment treaties to find in them support for any definite principle of international law."

This position is inconsistent with the facts and understates the value of BIT's in a fractious world. Given the binding character of the obligations taken by the contracting States in favour of the foreign investors, BIT's are undeniably use-

---

[42] VAN DE VOORDE, Willem, "Belgian bilateral investment treaties as a means for promoting and protecting foreign investments", *Studia diplomatica*, Editions' Royal Institute for international relations, Brussels, 1991, Volume XLIV, n° 1, p. 109.

[43] SCHACHTER, Oscar, "Compensation for expropriation", *American Journal of International Law*, 1984, p. 121.

[44] SORNARAJAH, M., "The International Law on foreign investment", Cambridge University Press, 2004, Part IV 'Bilateral investment treaties'.

ful. These agreements are approved by the contracting States' competent authorities and are thereby incorporated in the internal law of such States. Subsequently, when the contracting States proceed to ratify the agreements and exchange the documents confirming such ratification, the BIT's become instruments of international law. Moreover, they are creating new legal rules that are valid at the international level.

In this connection, it is worthwhile to mention the contractual obligations taken in the area of arbitration of conflicts relating to investments (cfr *infra*). No State is obliged to submit to arbitration disputes concerning investments made by foreign persons. By resorting to clauses provided for in BIT's, arbitration of such disputes has become a current practice.

Indisputable advantages flow therefrom. Consequently, we adopt the opinions of those who advocate such agreements and who argue that BIT's provide a leverage for the creation of rules of international law:

> "According to WEIL, when such treaties (BIT's) exist, the contractual obligations between the host State and the investor are transformed into true international obligation in the sense of public international law. These bilateral treaties for the protection of investments represent truly an internationalisation of contractual obligations undertaken by the host States."[45]

In most BIT's, it is stipulated that the investment contracts between the host State and a private investor are subject to the legal system of the interstate bilateral convention. Consequently the investor derives therefrom greater guarantees that the host State will respect its contractual obligations. In the event it does not, the way to arbitration is therefore open to the investor.

Actually, the fact is that international law has precedence over national law, so that the BIT's legal and practical scope does increase the possibilities of action for the defence of

---

[45] Charles LEBEN, *op. cit.*, p. 643, see footnote 23.

investments. If a national law is contrary to any provisions of a convention concerning the protection of investments, the latter will have precedence :

> "The question therefore, whether international and municipal law are two different realms of law, or whether municipal law is the order in the hierarchy of legal norms, becomes a matter of minor interest. What is important is that Permanent Court International of Justice maintain the overriding character of international law." [46]

National law should consequently yield to the application of international law. In particular circumstances some States nonetheless reject the general rule of precedence of international law.

4.3. – Economic Impact of BIT's

Van De Voorde mentions a second argument in support of moderation in the use of BIT's, namely that it is not possible to demonstrate the economic impact of bilateral agreements :

> "In fact, the few economic surveys of Belgian foreign investment that we have found, do not really give sufficient information to answer our question. They do, for instance, not mention the amount of money that is invested in foreign countries, nor the possible evolution of that amount over the years. As a result it is impossible to quantify the evolution of foreign direct investment as a result of the conclusion of bilateral investment treaties. Neither of the studies refers in its commentary to the favourable effects of bilateral investment treaties." [47]

This is not an isolated position. BIT's have met and still do meet with considerable criticism. Critics doubt whether such treaties can actually influence the flow of foreign direct investments in developing countries :

> "A long-standing rationale for the conclusion of investment treaties has been their purported usefulness in stimulating new investments flows between the signatory countries. In essence, there is a straight-

---

[46] *Barcelona Traction, Light and Power Company Limited*, op. cit., p. 31, see footnote 15.
[47] Van de Voorde, Willem, op. cit., p. 110, see footnote 42, *Studia Diplomatica*, op. cit., p. 110, see footnote 40.

forward expectation that the treaties will encourage new investments, which will, in turn, contribute to the economic development of the host State. Assuming that Foreign Direct Investment can contribute to economic development, it remains questionable whether BIT's play a major role in stimulating those desired FDI flows."[48]

We admit that the impact of BIT's on the volume of investments is hard to quantify. Structural reasons are the cause of the difficulty. Formerly, there existed no legal obligation to declare investments made abroad. Today, such legal obligation exists in many countries. Statistics are regularly published by the National Banks of developed countries.

In the host countries, on the other hand, there are generally no reliable statistics, not even in the countries where international investments are subject to a procedure of agreement. This does not mean that BIT's are not contributing to the increase of investments in developing countries (DC's). An analysis of the classic provisions of BIT's, however, allows their positive effect to be established, principally in the field of promotion (and, as a result, on the volume) of foreign investments : reduction of political risks, exclusion of discriminatory measures, arbitral settlement of disputes, creation of a favourable climate for investments etc. (cfr *infra*).

Even when national legislation for efficient protection of investments is in force, BIT's are still preferable :

> "Host countries, of course, could unilaterally provide all of these protections without concluding any special agreement or treaty. By concluding a BIT, however, a host State commits itself to these protections, as a matter of law, and consents to an enforcement mechanism intended to ensure that the commitment is honoured. In short, the principal contribution of the BIT is to stabilise the investment climate, thereby reducing risk to investors."[49]

---

[48] PETERSON, Luke, Eric, "*BIT's and Development policy making*", Winnipeg, Manitoba, International institute for sustainable development, 2003, n° 1, p. 9.
[49] VANDEVELDE, Kenneth, "The economics of bilateral investment treaties", *Harvard International Law Journal (HILJ)*, Cambridge, 2000, n° 121, p. 488.

The United Nations Commission on Trade and Development (UNCTAD) is convinced of the positive impact of BIT's on the growth of investments:

> "Nevertheless, BIT's appear to have positively affected investments flows: empirical research indicates that the conclusion of BIT's, following a two year-lag, is associated with modest increases in foreign direct investment." [50]

The positive impact of BIT's on decisions of candidate-investors is not in doubt. But we agree also that these bilateral conventions alone are not sufficient. Several other factors may have a decisive influence. It is not the existence of an isolated incentive, but the combination and coexistence of many outstanding factors which lead to the attainment of investment goals. In the United Nations organisation, this idea is accepted and emphasised:

> "The existence of bilateral agreements is but one among several other factors that affect the decision of an investor to engage in this or another developing country. If, at least, a developing country is unable to offer beneficial guarantees to the foreign investors, the existence of a bilateral convention in itself does in practice not suffice to attract an investment." [51]

This is a correct concept. Indeed, the DC's have realised that administrative facilities and fiscal and financial advantages are necessary in order to bring the foreign investors to a decision.

In sum, BIT's are necessary and useful, so that the rights and interests of foreign investors may rest on an adequate legal basis:

> "Apart from political and economic considerations the relevance of BIT's is much more derived from their legal significance. They are part of international treaty law, one of the main sources of public international law as reflected in article 38 of the Statute of the International Court of Justice. They are, embedded in the rules of customary international law, with which they are inter-related in two ways: firstly, the idea

---

[50] VANDEVELDE, Kenneth, *op. cit.*, p. 489, see footnote 49.
[51] *Centre des Nations Unies sur les sociétés transnationales*, New York, 1989, p. 324.

of concluding BIT's came into being due to shortcomings in the customary international law of investment protection; secondly, the practice of BIT making might influence the development of customary law."[52]

No doubt, the usual text of BIT's could be significantly improved (cfr *infra*). Furthermore, it is clear that the authorities concerned could take measures in order to make existing BIT's better known. Often, the signing of a convention for protection of investments is used only to provide greater publicity to official missions abroad but their content is not sufficiently distributed, neither to the investors concerned nor to the organisations defending their interests (Chambers of Commerce etc.).

As is sometimes said "unknown is unloved" (*"ignoti nulla cupido"*). It happens that rather small enterprises (multinationals excepted) are not able either to prepare their investments abroad adequately or to locate them in the best places, because they are not sufficiently informed about existing BIT's nor as to the content of local investment codes. Knowledge of the content of those codes is also important for BIT negotiators. Incorporating certain provisions of national law in BIT's is hardly to be excluded. For instance, the conventional definition of investment could, in some cases, be broadened by elements appearing in certain codes. In arbitral proceedings, differences between the conventional definition of investments and the concepts incorporated in codes have created problems for arbitrators.

4.4. – INADEQUACY AND INCONSISTENCY OF INFORMATION

The nomenclature used for bilateral investment protection treaties is varied. Mostly, the following terms are used: "promotion of investments", "protection of investments", "bilat-

---

[52] FÜRACKER, Mathias, "Relevance and structure of Bilateral Investment treaties", *German arbitration journal*, Petersberger schiedstage, march 2006, pag. 4.

eral convention of protection", "reciprocal protection" (China). Apart from a few exceptions, BITS' concluded by, for instance, the Belgo-Luxemburg Economic Union are entitled "Agreement between the Belgo-Luxemburg Economic Union (BLEU) and ... concerning the reciprocal encouragement and protection of investments."

Do these agreements work as in a one-way street or do the contracting parties benefit really equally by these legal instruments?

SALEM is convinced of their perfect reciprocity:

"Besides their bilateral form, these accords generally place a developing country in the presence of a developed country. An economic assessment would lead one to think that such accords limit themselves to the protection of investments sourced by the developed country and made in the developing country. But a strictly legal reading of these accords does not support this conclusion. That is so because all accords are based on the principle of identical reciprocity and thereby are called upon to govern also and equally investments going the other way."[53]

As SALEM admits this approach is purely legalistic. The parties have, in principle, the same rights and obligations. But without any doubt, the investment flow is going in a one-way direction, that is, towards the countries in development. Investments made by nationals of developing States on the territory of developed States do not exist or are in any case a great exception. From the legal viewpoint, the contracting parties are effectively on equal terms. It may be that each party may, for instance, file an arbitration procedure but in fact, since investments are overwhelmingly made by the more developed country, the filing, if any, will most likely be done by an investor from the developed country. Realistically, the term "reciprocal" could be deleted in the title of the agreements and the sense would not be affected, so long, of

---

[53] SALEM, Mahmoud, "Le development de la protection conventionelle des investissements à l'étranger", *Journal de droit international JDI*, Editions Techniques, Paris, juin 1981, n° 3, p. 582. (Development of conventional Protection for Foreign Investments International Law Journal, Paris, June 1981).

course, as the developing countries involved accept the change. It is only a political token which is there to stress the point that the contracting parties deal with each other as legally equal sovereigns.

In any case, there are serious doctrinal doubts about the reality of "criss-cross investment flows" between developed and developing countries. These doubts highlight that any alleged reciprocity is unreal. Prestige and the need for self-affirmation are, for the developing countries, the motivating factors for the terminology :

> "In practice, of course, the latter type (investment of developing country in developed country) of investment will be extremely rare and it is probably no exaggeration to suggest that reciprocity is to a large extent a matter of prestige rather than reality." [54]

Although the removal of the term "reciprocal" in the title of these agreements is not strictly necessary, we are rather in favour of the English formula "Agreement for the Promotion and Protection of Investment."

In the final analysis, within the doctrine, there is the question whether the term "reciprocity" is not precisely what capital exporting countries are doing to make such export really effective :

> "Is there any justification for the suggestion that a convention which deals exclusively with the protection of foreign investments looks one-sided ? Should such a convention contain a correlative obligation upon the States from which the investment flows to contribute or ensure the contribution of capital ?" [55]

The answer to that question should be negative. In the great majority of cases, BIT's do not apply to the investments of the Contracting Parties themselves but aim to promote *private investments*. In a legal sense, a State may com-

---

[54] MANN, F.A., "British treaties 'promotion and protection of investments'", *British yearbook of international law (BYIL)*, 1981, p. 241.

[55] LAUTERPACHT, Eli, "The drafting of treaties fort he protection of investment", *British Institution of International law and comparative law quarterly*, London, 1962, n° 3, p. 27.

mit some or all of its nationals within the scope of an international agreement. The approval of such an agreement by the appropriate authority (usually the legislative branch of Government) creates that commitment. Of course, when it makes that commitment, the State ought to be quite informed as to which of its nationals it commits and the precise nature of the commitment. Yet, in the matter of international investments, it does not actually know who the investors will be nor what capital will be invested. One could say that the capital exporting State's obligation to protect matches or flows from its obligation to promote.

4.5. – INTERNATIONAL INVESTORS' EXPECTATIONS

Investors who have the means to invest abroad face an array of obstacles to any plans they may have for such investment. In principle, anyone with a minimum of capital and access to a foreign market may find it attractive to establish a business in a foreign locale, leading him to believe it would be more successful than establishing the same kind of business in his home State or expanding one that he is already operating there. Hence, it is usually the prospect of a better yield on his investment that prompts him to look abroad rather than at home.

However, there may be many other reasons, not least access to a more advantageous source of supplies, the exploitation of local mineral resources, pre-empting competition from an equally interested competitor, becoming a supplier to allied industries, and a host of other personal and commercial motivations.

After having selected a foreign location, he will, of course, become aware of local restraints upon his freedom of action, consult with local government agencies regarding the nature of permits to be obtained and in general become acquainted with requirements placed on business of all kinds by the foreign locale. He will be interested in assuring himself that his capital investment will be safe, that he will be able to repatriate profits and/or capital without encountering further obstacles or discrimination, and that, in general, he will be treated as well as domestic businesses, and, if the locale has already welcomed foreign businesses, that he will be accorded at least the same benefits and inducements that such businesses received.

In the course of his enquiries, he most probably will become aware of the existence, or not, of treaties of friendship and commerce between his own nation and the foreign nation where he plans his investment, the friendlier the treaty, perhaps the greater his determination to invest.

4.6. – BILATERALISM VS. MULTILATERALISM

The conventional protection of international investments rests on the twin pillars of bilateral investment treaties (BIT's) and multilateral conventions. What should be the preference, among States, for one over the other depends on their national circumstances, their needs and their resources.

The advantages of bilateralism are more consistent than those of multilateralism. Bilateral negotiation parallels more closely the actual and specific nature of the economic relations between the Contracting States. Furthermore, with respect to the actual issue of protection of international investments, local opinion and political preferences of each State may differ substantially and can better be handled when an accommodation of such differences is attempted than when multiple players must match their skills.

As an example, some States prefer claims to be subject to the jurisdiction of local tribunals, whereas other States prefer arbitration. Chances of successful negotiations are certainly enhanced when two States face off across the table, knowing they must compromise, without a doubt more so than when a large group of States confront each other.

The failure of attempts by the Organisation for Economic Cooperation and Development (OECD) for the establishment of a "Multilateral Agreement on Investments" (MAI) may be taken as proof. On the other hand, the success so far of the North American Agreement of Free Trade (NAFTA) could well be due to the fact that not more three States were involved.

However, that does not mean that the multilateral approach is useless. The Cotonou Agreement (cf. *infra*) and its predecessors, between the European Union and African, Caribbean Sea and Pacific Ocean Nations are signal examples of succesfully concluded multilateral agreements. The adoption in multilateral agreements of rules of international law is useful. Some authors may well be justified in claiming that international law contains few precise rules governing property rights in invested capital:

> "The principal substantive difficulty rendering desirable the conclusion of treaties containing rules relating to the treatment of foreign investment is the lack of certainty in the rules of customary international law dealing with property matters."[56]

This is an additional argument in favour of both bilateral and multilateral investment protection treaties. Besides, a reference to international law in such treaties always gives them added weight.

When negotiating bilateral agreements, references to multilateral agreements help reinforce the "reciprocal" commitments of the Contracting Parties. Even provisions of multilateral agreements, such as the MAI, which was not ratified, should be considered for inclusion. Without a doubt, there is interaction between multilateral and bilateral agreements. That topic will be addressed in another Chapter.

---

[56] LAUTERPACHT, Eli, *op. cit.*, p. 19, see footnote 55.

CHAPTER V
MULTILATERAL PROTECTION CONVENTIONS

5.1. – Premise of Multilateral Conventions

Nations have entered into a large number of treaties or "conventions" with each other, covering many topics of international interest. Some such treaties have been signed and ratified by a group of Nations, thus elevating the treaties to "multilateral" status. A much larger number of treaties are of the kind termed "bilateral", as between two nations. This Work is intended to address multilateral conventions only accessorily, in terms *of their eventual impact on the redaction* of "Bilateral Investment Treaties" (BIT's).

Like many other conventions between States, multilateral conventions are not self-executory. To become effective tools for ensuring compliance, they need individual ratification by the States wishing to adhere to them. They wish to do so when they are convinced that collective action is the best path to achieve discrete elements of their political and economic strategies, when they discover they do not possess the know-how or personnel to help them devise measures appropriate to carry out their strategies, when they discover that, short of war, in which they fear to be the losing Parties, they do not have a forum where to initiate interaction with other nations, or, simply and inclusively, when they fear that, without forging alliances with other nations with parallel interests, their interests risk being ignored or grossly violated.

5.2. – ORGANISATION FOR ECONOMIC COOPERATION AND DEVELOPMENT (OECD)

OECD has really been innovative in the area of foreign investors' protection. The organisation's Council adopted a Resolution on 12 October 1967 to that effect. It may seem a bit strange that the title of the Resolution "Draft Convention on the Protection of Foreign Property" does not mention investments but instead implies assets or goods. However, the Resolution's preamble clearly shows that the intent of the Resolution is to provide for the protection of foreign investments:

> "Considering that the widest application of these principles (as recognised in matters relating to investment protection) in the national legislation and in international treaties will encourage investment abroad."

Commentaries to the Preamble note that the term "assets" includes, without limitation, the notion of investments.

The organisation's Council recommended that the convention draft be used in the preparation of bilateral treaties for the protection of foreign assets (investments). This recommendation has, by and large, been followed. In the very first BIT's, traces of this draft may still be found. Nonetheless, some of the draft's provisions are problematic. Relative to fair and equitable treatment of foreign investors, for instance, the Resolution states:

> "The grant to nationals of a member State of a treatment which is actually more favourable than that allowed under the present Convention will not be deemed discrimination against the nationals of another Party for the sole reason that the latter's nationals do not benefit from such treatment." (Article 1)

This provision does not, however, appear in individual bilateral treaties of protection. Most such treaties already include favourable treatment clauses as well as the commonly worded "most favoured nation" clause. Granting to a protected investor a treatment that is less favourable than that granted to a third party nation would effectively be a discriminatory measure.

The draft convention uses the term "seizure of assets" to mean, according to its authors, not only direct deprivations (expropriations and nationalisations) but also indirect deprivations. Bilateral Investments Treaties do not adopt this term. The terms "direct or indirect expropriation" are used instead, explicitly in the bilateral treaties which define "assets" as:

> "all goods, rights and interests withheld directly or indirectly, including interests which a shareholder of a corporation is deemed to have in the assets of such corporation." (article 9c)

It may also be a little surprising that the comments to the draft Convention, noting that "investments" are included, have not led to the incorporation, *in the text of the draft convention*, of corresponding definitional clauses. The fact is that, at a certain moment in its work, OECD wanted to deviate from the bilateral approach and believed that the time was ripe for the development of a multilateral convention on investments (MAI). In effect, OECD was abandoning the idea that a bilateral convention system was to be the approach recommended to member States for agreements protecting investors' rights.

5.3. – Consolidated text – M.A.I.

OECD's ambition was to create a multilateral system for international investors open to being signed and ratified by member States, members of the European Union, and to being adhered to by non-member States.

Negotiations proceeded from 1995 to 1998 but the project failed and, as a result, no agreement was reached on a final text. A so-called "consolidated" text has been drafted and distributed but has not yet been approved. A few countries from South America (Argentina, Brazil and Chile) and a few

Asian countries (China, Hong Kong) have participated in the working meetings of OECD on the issue, as observers, but, surprisingly, no African country participated at all.

The failure of the negotiations does not necessarily mean that the work done was wasted. Documents established by experts in the topic as well as the consolidated text (non approved by MAI) are still an extremely rich source of information about the ideas and procedural rules, and as such, may well have an influence on the content of future BIT's.

Some of MAI provisions appearing but rarely in European BiT's are listed below.

5.3.1. – *Transparency*

The MAI requires the Contracting States to promote transparency in their treaties:

> "Each Contracting State shall promptly publish, or otherwise make publicly available, its laws, regulations, procedures and administrative rulings and judicial decisions of general application as well as international agreements which may affect the operation of an Agreement. Where a Contracting Party establishes policies which are not expressed in laws or regulations or by other means listed in this paragraph but which may affect the operation of the Agreement, that Contracting Party shall promptly publish them or otherwise make them publicly available." [57]

European BIT's contain no such provision but should. It often happens that foreign investors are surprised and face national legal and regulatory requirements which were never made known to them and which could seriously affect the management of their investments.

5.3.2. – *Monopolies – State Enterprises – Concessions*

OECD experts believed it would be useful to include clauses providing for protection for monopolies, either of the host State, or of private parties, and suggested the following:

---

[57] Http://ec.europa.eu/development/Geographical/Cotonouintro_en_cfn.

"Nothing in this Agreement shall be construed to prevent a Contracting Party from maintaining, designating or eliminating a monopoly. Each Contracting State shall (endeavour to) accord non-discriminatory treatment when designating a monopoly. Each Contracting State shall ensure that any privately-owned monopoly that its national (or sub-national) governments (maintain or) designate, provides non-discriminatory treatment to investments of investors of another Contracting Party in its supply of monopoly goods or services in the relevant market."

No BIT contains such a clause. This is not unusual, in that public investments, and therefore also public monopolies, are excluded from the application of BIT's. Protection is extended by BIT's only to private investments. Should an investor of a State which is a party to a BIT make an investment on the territory of the host State and legally turn it into a monopoly, it is quite probable that he would welcome the opportunity, but the grant of the monopoly could be considered discriminatory by another investor and cause litigation to proliferate. In any event, BIT's are not intended to protect monopolies, be they private or publicly owned, nor in the protection of State enterprises.

European BIT's which mention "public law concessions" as an investment are not concerned with concessions operated by a public authority. What the BIT's mean is that concessions granted by a public agency, under the authority of a public law, to a private person are covered.

5.4. – The Cotonou Convention

Economic relations between the European Union and African, Caribbean Sea and Pacific Ocean countries (ACP) were governed by the Lomé Convention, which expired in the year 2000. A new Convention has been signed in Cotonou, on 23 June 2000, valid for 20 years expiring in 2020.

5.4.1. – *Promotion of investments*

The Cotonou Convention provides, in part, as follows, with respect to encouragement and promotion of investments :

> "The ACP States, the Community and its member States, within the scope of their respective competencies, recognising the importance of private investment in the promotion of their development cooperation and acknowledging the need to take steps to promote such investment shall :
> - implement measures to encourage participation in their development efforts by private investors who comply with the objectives and priorities of ACP-EC development cooperation and with the appropriate laws and regulations of their respective States;
> - take measures and actions which help to create and maintain a predictable and secure investment climate as well as enter into negotiations on agreements which will implement such climate." ... (article 75)

5.4.2. – *Economic development*

Contributing to the development of the host State appears to be, in this convention, a condition of the existence of an investment. The Contracting Parties evidently are free to require such a condition as an essential element of an investment. Legally, a commitment undertaken on this subject by European countries is very explicit. However, litigation can ensue when this element of the investment is mentioned only in the preamble of an international treaty, as seems to be the case for many a BIT. In some BIT's, there is no mention of it :

> "Recognising that the promotion and protection of such investments on the basis of a bilateral agreement will be conductive to the stimulation of individual business initiative to the benefit of both countries" (Agreement Australia/Argentine, 23 August 1995)

but in US bilateral investment treaties, there is always an acknowledgement of the fact that a private investment is a stimulant for economic development, thus :

"The Government of the United States of America and the Government of (Country), hereinafter the Parties :

- desiring to promote greater economic cooperation between them with respect to an investment by nationals and enterprise of one Party on the territory of the other Party,
- recognising that agreement on the treatment to be accorded such investments will stimulate the flow of private capital *and the economic development of the Parties...*"

However, the provision, couched in the form of a condition to investment in the host State, exists only in the Preamble and not in the body of the text.

Thus, it will be the arbitrators who will decide whether an investment may exist on the basis of its contribution, or not, to the economic development of the host State. The decisions of the ICSID do not offer a parallel. In the *Salini* case, the arbitrators based their decision on the Preamble of the BIT Morocco/Italy to conclude that there was in fact a lawful investment :

"Doctrinal texts generally consider that an investment is based upon capital supply, a certain duration to carry out the bargain and a participation in the risks of the operation. A reading of the Preamble of the BIT allows us to add a criterion of contribution to the economic development of the host State where the investment is made... Insofar as contribution of the bargain to the economic development of the State of Morocco, this can hardly be contested."[58]

Unfortunately, no substantive argument is to be found in this decision.

In the case of *Malaysian Historical Salvors Sdn v. Malaysia*[59], the arbitrators decided that contribution to the economic development of the host State was not necessary in order for an activity or a commitment to be deemed an "investment" :

"It would seem consistent with the objective of the convention that a contract, in order to be considered an investment within the meaning of the provision, should fulfill the following three conditions :

---

[58] GAILLARD, Emmanuel, *op. cit.*, p. 635, see footnote 31.
[59] Www.worldbank.org/icsid.

- the Contracting Party has made contributions to the host Country;
- those contributions had a certain duration;
- they involved some risk for the contributor.

On the other hand, it is not necessary that the investment contribute more specifically to the host country's economic development, something that is difficult to ascertain and that is implicitly covered by the other three criteria."

As a matter of fact, contribution to the economic development is not so much an element of the investment but is a consequence of it. This result from an investment should be evident. Every private investment abroad is in and of itself beneficial to the economic development of the host State.

5.4.3. – *Protection of investments*

In the field of investment protection, the Convention of Cotonou stipulates further:

"1. The ACP and the Community and its Member States, within the scope of their respective competencies, affirm the need to promote and protect either Party's investments on their respective territories, and in this context affirm the importance of concluding, in their mutual interest, investment promotion and protection agreements which could also provide the basis for insurance and guarantee schemes.

2. ...

3. The Parties also agree to introduce, within the economic partnership agreements, and while respecting the respective competence of the Community and said Member States, general principles on protection and promotion of investments, which will endorse the best results agreed in the competent international fora or bilaterally." (article 78)

Concluding that contribution to the economic development of the host State is not an absolute requirement is therefore hardly irrational. Economic benefits are, instead, a consequence of the contribution. The quoted text is ambiguous and lends itself to different interpretations. When countries enter into bilateral agreement of promotion and protection of investments, then, the introduction within the economic partnership agreements, general principles of protection and promotion of investments is superfluous.

5.5. – NORTH AMERICAN FREE TRADE AGREEMENT (NAFTA)

This treaty was signed on 7 October 1992 by the United States of America, Mexico and Canada. It is best known under the abbreviation NAFTA but is also referred to, in French speaking countries as ALENA. It came into force on 1 January 1994.

Chapter eleven deals with investments. The US and Canada have developed their bilateral investment treaty practice, in large measure, on the protection structure provided for in NAFTA.

5.5.1. – *NAFTA'S General Scope*

Most conventions and international treaties begin with an article setting forth the scope of the document. Contrary to this practice, bilateral treaties are mostly silent in this regard. To determine what their scope actually is, the various articles of the BIT's, specifying the Contracting States' obligations with respect to investors and their investments have to be looked at. Some BIT's state:

> "This agreement shall apply to all investments made by investors of either Contracting Party in the territory of the other Contracting party, accepted as such in accordance with its laws and regulations, whether made before or after the coming into force of this Agreement." (Treaty Belgium/India, dated 31 October 1997, article 2; Belgian Federal Register of 16 January 2001)

To the extent this provision does not specify that investors are protected against measures privative of property rights, for which damages may be awarded and which were taken by a Contracting State against investments made by nationals of the other Contracting State, this provision is inadequate.

NAFTA is quite clear on the subject (article 1101):

> "Scope and coverage:
> 1. This chapter applies to measures adopted or maintained by a Party relating to:

a) investors of another Party;

b) investments of investors of another party in the territory of the Party;

c) with respect to articles 1106 and 1114, all investments in the territory of the Party.

2.....

3. This chapter does not apply to measures adopted or maintained by a Party to the extent that they are covered by Chapter Fourteen (Financial services).

4. Nothing in this Chapter shall be construed to prevent a Party from providing a service or performing a function such as law enforcement, correctional services, income security or insurance, social security or insurance, social welfare, public education, public training, health and child care, in a manner that is not inconsistent with this Chapter."

This explicit language defining the Treaty's scope, as that for the protection of investments against measures officially taken against them, is a real improvement of the text usually found in most BIT's. It seems odd that very extensive provisions have been drafted for the definition of "investment" but nothing is said about the kind of measures against which protection is provided. A simple list, with the usual caveat that it is without limitation, would be helpful. It is, for instance, important to know whether the Contracting States are responsible internationally to investors for compensable measures taken by the Federal Government of a Contracting State, by regional authorities of even local administrative agencies.

Doctrinal texts recognise without hesitation that the State is responsible for acts committed by its agencies:

"Acts of an agency of the State, of a territorial public collectivity or any entity enabled to carry out a public power, where such agency, collectivity or entity acted in the exercise of such power, are deemed to be acts of the Contracting State according to international law, even if such agency, collectivity or other entity acted beyond its jurisdiction according to domestic law or violated regulations defining its allowed activity." [60]

---

[60] International Law Commission (UNO – New York), *"Yearbook of the International law commission (ILC)"*, 1975, vol. ii, page 61.

The drafters of NAFTA were well aware of the doctrine. Article 105 stated precisely that:

> "the Parties to this Agreement shall see to it that all necessary measures will be taken to carry out the provisions of the present Agreement, in particular with respect to their compliance by the State and Provincial Governments."

Arbitral decisions appears to hew closely to the doctrinal position. On this very topic, a decision of the International Centre for the Settlement of International Disputes (ICSID) is quite instructive. In an arbitration proceeding, filed under NAFTA, by the METALCLAD company against Mexico, the Tribunal decided that the Mexican State was responsible for acts committed by the Mexican Commune of Guadalcazar. This approach (State responsibility for acts of its agencies) is perfectly compliant with well settled international common law. The principle has been clearly enunciated in article 10 of the draft provisions regarding the responsibility of States adopted in 1975 by the United Nations. Although still under study, this principle may be considered as an exact representation of law currently in force.[61]

European BIT's provisions concerning scope of application could be improved with a clear reference to investments and the measures aiming adversely affecting them.

5.5.2. – *State judicial Acts*

Of equal importance is the issue of the application of NAFTA to State judicial acts and the State's responsibility for judicial decisions of its Courts and tribunals. The doctrine holds that such a responsibility conforms to international law:

> "During the course of this century, the responsibility of State for acts of its judiciary has gradually been acknowledged. Although independent of Government, a State's judicial power is not independent of the State: a judgment rendered by a judiciary authority issues from

---

[61] GAILLARD, Emmanuel, *op. cit.*, page 672, see footnote 31.

a State agency in the same way as a law passed by the State's legislature or a decision taken by the State's Executive Office."[62]

NAFTA's provisions are not quite as clear in this context as for the preceding example:

> "Measures (referred to in article 1101) include all legislation, regulation, procedures, requirements or practices." (article 201)

The use of the term "procedures" would allow for the inclusion of judicial acts. According to ICSID arbitration jurisprudence (*Loewen v. US*), the definition of the term "measures", in particular the reference to "procedures", is so broad that it is incompatible with the idea that judicial acts would be excluded from the application of article 1101.

The arbitrators decided:

> "The interpretation, adopted by the present Tribunal, of the term 'measures' is consistent with the interpretation given to it in international law, which includes judicial acts. Such an interpretation of the term 'measures' is consistent with the general principle of State responsibility. This principle applies equally to agencies dispensing judicial functions and to those with legislative or executive responsibilities."[63]

NAFTA's text regarding the scope of application of the Agreement protects investors better than that which generally appears in bilateral investment treaties. In order to avoid unnecessary discussion about the scope of the term "measures", an alternative formula, expressly stating that the Agreement applies to every measures contrary to international law and to obligations of the Contracting States under the terms of the Agreement, would be desirable. Article 1139 ("Definitions") should be similarly amended.

---

[62] Eduardo JIMENEZ DE ARÉCHAGA, "International law in the past Third of a century", Academy of International Law, The Hague, Netherlands, *Collected Courses*, 1978, p. 159-1.

[63] GAILLARD, Emmanuel, *op. cit.*, p. 654, see footnote 31.

5.5.3. – *Performance Requirements*

In bilateral investment treaties, the Contracting states' obligations with respect to the operation, management, maintenance, utilisation, enjoyment, sales or any other form of alienation are tied to the required national treatment. NAFTA offers a better protection for investors, in as much as the contracting States' duties and the rights of investors are mentioned *"expressis verbis"* :

> "1. No Party may impose or enforce any of the following requirements, or enforce any commitment or undertaking in connection with the establishment, acquisition, expansion, management, conduct or operation of an investment of an investor of a Party or of a non-Party in its territory :
>
> a) to export a given level or percentage of goods or services;
>
> b) to achieve a given level or percentage of domestic content;
>
> c) to purchase, use or accord a preference to goods produced or services provided in its territory, or to purchase goods or services from persons in its territory;
>
> d) to relate in any way the volume or value of imports to the volume or value of exports or to the amount of foreign exchange inflows associated with such investment;
>
> e) to restrict sales of goods or services in its territory that such investment produces or provides by relating such sales in any way to the volume or value of its exports or foreign exchange earnings;
>
> f) to transfer technology, a production process or other proprietary knowledge to a person in its territory, except when, the requirement is imposed or the commitment or undertaking is enforced by a court, administrative tribunal or competition authority to remedy an alleged violation of competition laws or to act in a manner not inconsistent with other provisions of the Agreement; or
>
> g) to act as the exclusive supplier of the goods it produces or services it provides to a specific region or world market." (article 1106)

These provisions stem from a good many abuses of which investors have been the victims. It is therefore quite useful that the Contracting States are expressly prohibited from committing such acts. In this connection, article 1107 provides that investors may not be compelled to name persons of a specific nationality (for example nationals of the host State) to executive position of the enterprise.

5.5.4. – *Denial of benefits*

NAFTA's article 1113 specifies:

> "1. ...
>
> 2. Subject to prior notification and consultation in accordance with articles 1803 (Notification and Provision of information) and 2006, a Party may deny the benefits of this chapter to an investor of another Party that is an enterprise of such Party and to investments of such investors if investors of a non-Party own or control the enterprise and the enterprise has no substantial business activities in the territory of the Party under whose law it is constituted or organised."

This is a specific provision designed to discourage "phantom companies" or sham corporations. It happens sometimes that foreign companies create branches in a foreign country solely for accounting purposes (money transfers to temporary accounts for speculation, transfers for fiscal avoidance only). For example, if an investing State company establishes a branch in Canada (which is a party to NAFTA) and controls this branch, a denial of benefits could ensue. If this branch conducts no or little business in Canada but focuses its activities on the making of investments in the U.S., the U.S. could deny the Agreement's benefits to the Canadian branch on the basis that the Canadian activities are inconsequential.

Considering that economic activities are increasingly internationalised, this provision may well be an overkill.

5.5.5. – *Confidentiality*

Decisions made by NAFTA authorities, and the hearings to which they refer, are confidential, unlike those made by arbitrators acting under the argis of ICSID or ICC. Fore many who might otherwise benefit from a greater transparency, this is unfortunate.

5.6. – Protocol of Colonia – Mercosur

On 26 March 1001, Argentina, Brazil, Paraguay and Uruguay entered into a treaty creating a common market: Mercado del Sur (MERCOSUR). These countries also signed, on 17 January 1994 the Protocol of Colonia. To date, none of these countries have ratified the Protocol. Hence, this Act is not yet in force.

It seems, however, that negotiations are running to amend the Protocol. Some of the member States believe that the duties to be assumed by virtue of the Protocol are too burdensome. They claim to seek a "lighter" version of the temporary text of the 1994 Protocol. Some of the Protocol's provisions differ from those appearing in European BIT's. It is probable that any new version of the Protocol will include the principles enunciated in the 1994 version.

5.6.1. – *Definitions*

Protected investors are defined as follows:

"The term 'investor' will be assigned to:

a) any natural person who is a citizen of one of the Contracting Parties, or is a permanent resident of a Contracting Party, in accordance with their own legislation. The provisions of this Agreement will not be applicable to the investment made by a natural person that is a citizen of a member State in the territory of another member State, if such person, by the time the investment is made, resides permanently in this last member State, unless it is proved that the resources for such investment is originated abroad;

b) any firm constituted under the laws and regulations of a Contracting party and whose headquarters are situated in the same member State;

c) any firm established in the State where the investment is made which is effectively controlled either directly or indirectly by firms or individuals as defined in 'a' or 'b' above." (**Article 1**)

In accordance with well established practice, it is the nationality of physical persons which governs to decide whether the proposed investor is one from one of the Contracting Parties. In this view, the status of a permanent resident on the territory of a Contracting Party does not include the possibility that such person shall be considered an investor of such Contracting Party. Problems could arise in the case of say, a European investor who obtained the status of permanent resident in Argentina. Should he invest in Uruguay, he might be a beneficiary of the Protocol of Colonia, as resident of Argentina, when it comes into force. He might be a beneficiary of European BIT's concluded with Argentina and Uruguay. However, there might now be a conflict with the BIT between the European State and Argentina if, as in the Belgium/Argentina BIT for example, that State's BIT provides that the protected investor is:

> "any physical who, according to person legislation of any of the Contracting Parties is deemed to be a citizen of such Party." (article 1)

The investor, in this case, could be engaging in what is called "protection shopping". Should the Uruguayan Government take any measure against such investor which would be contrary to the provisions of the agreement, *he could then invoke either the Protocol of Colonia, or the European BIT with Argentina, or maybe both.* Actually, the Protocol or the BIT may open the way to ICSID's arbitration for the settlement of disputes relating to investments. How ICSID would resolve the problem when confronted by contradictory definitions of the term "investor" in the two documents is an interesting question. It may be noted, in passing, that applicable law is not provided for in the Protocol (and may likewise be absent in the BIT). Ideally, the Protocol will never become effective but a revised text will be adopted, using the investor's nationality to help ensure that he will be protected.

5.6.2. – *Source of Investment*

Another part of the Protocol could create further difficulties:

"The provisions of this agreement will not be applicable to the investment made by a natural person that is a citizen of a member State, on the territory of another member State, if such person, by the time the investment is made, resides permanently in this last Member State, unless it is proved that the resources for such investment is originated abroad." (article 1)

The Argentine national who makes an investment in Uruguay, should he in some fashion become a permanent resident on Uruguayan territory while making this investment could lose his protection rights under the Uruguay/Argentina BIT. The text does not actually mention *"statute of resident"* but refers only to a factual situation *"resides permanently"* that may be difficult to prove. Besides, the Protocol provides that the Argentine investor might be able to preserve his protection rights if the financial resources for the investment stem from Argentina or another foreign country. Actual residence and origin of funds may be difficult to prove. When the Protocol is amended, this problem should be addressed.

5.6.3. – *Treatment of Investments*

The Protocol contains merely a reference to national treatment and to most favoured nation treatment. There is no reference to the minimum standard of international law while such reference is usually inserted in BIT's.

5.6.4. – *Settlement of Investment Disputes*

The Protocol provides in part :

"The investor may choose to have recourse to international arbitration :

a) to the International Centre for the Settlement of Investment Disputes (ICSID) established by the Convention on the Settlement of Investment Disputes between States and nationals of other States, signed in Washington on March 18, 1965, when each Member State of the present Protocol had agreed with...." (**Article 9**)

Neither the anticipatory consent of the arbitrating States nor the abandonment of the exhaustion of domestic remedies requirement have been expressly provided for. This could be a problem for investors. Furthermore,, the Protocol provides that the arbitrators must consider international law.

Neither does it contain a provision on applicable law. As a consequence, the text does not guarantee an efficient arbitration procedure.

5.7. – INVESTMENT AGREEMENT OF THE ORGANISATION OF THE ISLAMIC CONFERENCE

The "Agreement on Promotion, Protection and Guarantee of Investments among Member States of the Organisation of the Islamic Conference" was signed in Baghdad on 5 June 1981 and entered into force on 23 September 1986. This instrument contains several characteristic provisions differing from those normally to be found in international practice. The Preamble itself is typical, in that its emphasis is on resource utilisation and on economic and even social cooperation:

> "Endeavouring to avail of the economic resources and potentialities available therein and to mobilise and utilise them in the best possible manner, within the framework of close cooperation among Member States,
>
> Convinced that relations among the Islamic States in the field of investment are one of the major areas of economic cooperation among these States through which economic and social development therein can be fostered on the basis of common interest and mutual benefit,
>
> Anxious to provide and develop a favourable climate for investments, in which the economic resources of the Islamic countries could circulate between them so that optimum utilisation could be made of these resources in a way that will serve their development and raise the standard of living of their peoples."

5.7.1. – *Definitions*

In marked contrast with other international agreements, whether multilateral or bilateral, the Parties chose from the very first to define the term "capital":

> "All assets (including everything that can be evaluated in monetary terms) owned by a contracting party to this agreement or by its nationals, whether a natural person or a corporate body and present in the territories of another contracting party whether these were transferred to or earned in it, and whether these be movable, immovable, in cash, in kind, tangible as well as everything pertaining to these capitals and investments by way of rights or claims and shall include the net profits from such assets and the undivided shares and intangible rights." (article 1)

The actual investment is deemed a transfer of capital to the territory of one of the Contracting Parties and its utilisation in situ by the investor:

> "Investor: The Government of any Contracting Party or natural person or corporate body, who is a national of a Contracting Party, and which owns the capital and invests it in the territory of another Contracting Party."

The nationality of physical persons is determined on the basis of applicable legislation whereas that of moral persons is determined by the law of the place of incorporation. As in Canada and the United States, each Government is therefore deemed as a potential investor as if it were a physical or moral person. European BIT's do not use such a provision.

5.7.2. – *Treatment of Investments*

The provisions relating to this topic are not mandatory and do not specify strict duties and obligations. The context is promissory rather then firm obligations:

> "The Contracting Parties will endeavour to offer various incentives and facilities for attracting capitals and encouraging its investment in their territories such as commercial, financial, tax and currency incentives, especially during the early years of the investment projects, in accordance with the laws, regulations and priorities of the host State." (article 4)

Usual practice requires the inclusion of a "national treatment" clause in the protection agreements. It is not followed here but instead there is a provision declaring that, in principle, the Contracting Parties will attempt to grant investment facilities. There is no reference at all to minimum treatment as guaranteed by the principles and rules of international law. However, there is a most favoured nation (MFN) clause :

> "a treatment not less favourable than the treatment accorded to investors belonging to another State not party to this Agreement."

A further limitation to investment protection is included in this Convention, providing a prohibition against any act contrary to public order and morals.

> "The investor shall be bound by the laws and regulations in force in the host State and shall refrain from all acts that may disturb public order or morals or that may be prejudicial to the public interest. He is also to refrain from exercising restrictive practices and from trying to achieve gains through unlawful means."

5.7.3. – *Investment guarantees*

Article 10 of the Convention expressly provided that the host State, its organisms, its institutions and local authorities shall undertake no measures limiting the management powers of the investor :

> "The host State shall undertake not to adopt or permit the adoption of any measure itself or through one of its organs, institutions or local authorities, if such a measure may directly or indirectly affect the ownership of the investor's capital or investment by depriving him totally or partially of his ownership or of all or part of his basic rights or the exercise of his authority on the ownership, possession or utilisation of his capital, or of his actual control over the investment, its management, making use out of it, enjoying its utilities, the realisation of its benefits or guaranteeing its development and growth."

This text gives the impression that total security and protection exists but paragraph 2 of the same article throws it in doubt. Firstly, the host State's right to expropriate is confirmed :

> "It will be permissible to : expropriate the investment in the public interest in accordance with the law, without discrimination and on prompt payment of adequate and effective compensation to the inves-

tor in accordance with the laws of the host State regulating such compensation, provided that the investor shall have the right to contest the measure of expropriation in the competent court of the host State."

This provision is no surprise, since it merely confirms the States' sovereign right, under certain conditions and in accordance with international law. The problem is that the payment of compensation is subject to the application of a national law, whose scope is unknown, but even if it were known, such law could be amended before the promulgation of legislation approving the appropriation projects. The Convention does not provide when, that is, the date on which compensation must be paid, the use of the term "prompt" providing no guarantee. Furthermore, no provision is made for the payment of interest on the indemnification to be paid, interest being generally prohibited in the Muslim world on religious grounds. The fact that local tribunals have jurisdiction over litigation relating to compensation offers no additional protection.

On this general topic, the text of the Convention raises the risk that the security and protection initially promised may be jeopardised by "preventive measures" issued by competent authorities:

> "It will, however, be permissible to: adopt preventive measures issued in accordance with an order from a competent legal authority and the execution measures of the decision given by a competent judicial authority."

5.7.4. – *Compensation for damages*

Article 13 of the Convention reads as follows:

> "(1) The investor shall be entitled to compensation for any damage resulting from any action of a Contracting Party or one of its public or local authorities or its institutions in the following cases:
>
> (a) Violation of any of the rights or guarantees accorded to the investor under this Agreement;

(b) Breach of any of the international obligations or undertakings imposed on the contracting party and arising under the Agreement for the benefit of the investor or the non-performance of whatever is necessary for its execution whether the same is international or due to negligence;

(c) Non-execution of a judicial decision requiring enforcement directly connected with the investment;

(d) Causing, by other means or by an act or omission, damage tot the investor in violation of laws in force in the state where the investments exists.

(2) The compensation shall be equivalent to the damage suffered by the investor depending on the type of damage and its quantum."

This provision is unique in international practice relating to conventional investment protection. On the other hand, the provision has a particularly important effect in that it acknowledges, as a principle, that compensation is due for damages resulting from the violation of international obligations flowing from BIT's and from the non-execution of judicial decisions. Furthermore, the State's authorities assume international responsibility for acts committed by their local agencies and institutions.

5.7.5. – *Settlement of Investment Disputes*

This Convention allows investors in the host States to file a judicial procedure with local ribunals in the event such investors should have reason to complain about a measure taken against their investments, to contest the conformance of such measures to national laws, or to demand that certain measures to which the host States are committed in favour of the investors be effectively complied with.

As soon as the investor has initiated a judicial procedure, his choice is final and he may not thereafter initiate an arbitration procedure. He may, however, submit the dispute to a conciliation and arbitration procedure. During the first phase, in accordance to an agreement between him and the host State, the dispute may be submitted for conciliation, for which a special request is to be submitted to the Secretary General of the organisation.

In the event conciliation is not successful, each Party has the right to file for an arbitration procedure, a request therefore to be submitted to the other Party by the most diligent Party. Each party shall designate an arbitrator, both of them shall then select a third who shall be President of the tribunal. In the event a Part fails to designate an arbitrator, or, should the arbitrators of both Parties fail to designate a President, the Secretary General of the organisation shall do so.

An agency is to be created within the Organisation and it shall have jurisdiction for the resolution of disputes relating to investments.

5.8. – ASEAN Agreement – Association of Southeast Asian Nations

On 12 September 1996, in Djakarta an agreement was entered into:

> "Protocol to amend the Agreement among the Governments of Brunei Darussalam, the republic of Indonesia, Malaysia, the Republic of the Philippines, the republic of Singapore, and the Kingdom of Thaïland for the promotion and protection of Investments."

The Basic Agreement was entered into in Manila on 15 December 1987. Vienam became a member of the Basic Agreement, as modified by the above Protocol. The new title of the Agreement reads as follows: "The ASEAN Agreement for the Promotion and Protection of Investments."

5.8.1. – *Companies*

A combination of the seat and control theory is used:

> "The term 'company' of a Contracting Party shall mean a corporation, partnership or other business association, incorporated or constituted under the laws in force in the territory of any Contracting Party wherein the place of effective mangament is situated." (article 1)

5.8.2. – *Applicability or Scope*

Article II reads as follows:

> "This Agreement shall apply to investments brought into, derived from or directly connected with investments brought into the territory of any Contracting Party by nationals or companies of any other Contracting party and which are specifically approved in writing and registered by the host country and upon such conditions as it deems fit for the purposes of the Agreement."

The terms "brought in the territory" seem to indicate that reinvestments are not included under the Agreement. A further limitation on investments results from the requirement of a written approval, granted only:

> "upon such conditions as it deems fit for the purposes of this Agreement."

The goals of the Agreement are listed in the Preamble:

> "...the importance of sustaining economic growth and development in all Member States through joint efforts in liberalising trade and promoting intra-ASEAN trade and investment flows... Acknowledging the importance of investment as a source of finance for sustaining the pace of economic, industrial and technological development of the region."

The authorities therefore reserve the right to refuse approval to investments which do not meet national needs.

5.8.3. – *Treatment*

The Contracting States agree to grant to investors a fair and equitable treatment and an efficient protection. However, a nationalistic bias appears at the same time:

> "Each Contracting Party shall, in a manner consistent with its national objectives encourage and create favourable conditions in its territory for investments from the other Contracting Party. All investments to which this Agreement relates shall subject to this Agreement, be governed by the laws and regulations of the host country..."

A most favoured nation clause has been included but there is no national treatment clause, the latter being granted only under the terms of special agreements between the Contracting States. Furthermore, there is no reference to treatment guaranteed by international law.

5.8.4. – *Expropriation and compensation*

According to usual practice in this area, Contracting States have agreed that measures of expropriation or nationalisation may be taken only for reasons of public utility, on a non-discriminatory basis and against payment of compensation. The latter is calculated on the basis of the market value. However, another provision has been included which can hardly be favourable for investors:

> "The compensation shall be settled and paid without unreasonable delay. The national or company affected shall have the right, under the law of the Contracting party making the expropriation, to prompt review by a judicial body or some other independent authority of that Contracting party in accordance with principles set out in this paragraph."

As explained below, investment disputes may be submitted to arbitration, including international arbitration, but there is no provision that this privilege applies also to expropriation measures. It is therefore to be feared that, in such cases, investors will have to look to the local judiciary to enforce their rights. The control theory is not mentioned in the texts to determine the nationality of a corporation. On the other hand, protection of capital evidence of participation, whether majority or minority, is expressly provided for:

> "Where a Contracting Party expropriates the assets of a company which is incorporated or constituted under the law in force in its territory, and in which nationals or companies of another Contracting Party own shares, it shall apply the provisions of paragraph 1 of this article so as to ensure the compensation provided for in that Paragraph to such nationals or companies to the extend of their interest in the assets expropriated."

5.8.5. – *Arbitration of Investment Disputes*

For the resolution of disputes relating to their investments, investors may resort to a conciliation or an arbitration procedure :

> "If such a dispute cannot thus be settled within six months of its being raised, then either party can elect to submit the dispute for conciliation or arbitration and such election shall be binding on the other party. The dispute may be brought before the International Centre for Settlement of Investment Disputes (ICSID), the United Commission on International Trade Law (UNCITRAL), the regional centre for arbitration at Kuala Lumpur or any other regional centre for arbitration in ASEAN, whichever body the parties to the dispute mutually agree to appoint for the purposes of conducting the arbitration." (article X)

There is no reference to anticipatory consent. The risk exists that the parties will not agree on the identity of one or the other arbitration organisms. Besides, the formulation regarding UNCITRAL is incorrect because this Commission does not manage arbitration proceedings and does not handle files. This Commission has merely established a project for arbitration conventions which could serve as a basis for parties that wish to enter into a convention.

Should the parties agree on the selection of an arbitration organism, an arbitral tribunal, composed of three members, will be established. The Contracting States have therefore returned to this complex formula, abandoned generally by other countries, to appeal to the President of the Court of International Justice for the designation of arbitrators, in the event that the parties fail to do so.

CHAPTER VI
MODEL CONVENTIONS

6.1. – Advantages of standard Text

North American and most Western European countries have developed model convention texts to serve as bases for negotiating and concluding bilateral investment treaties with developing countries. The inspiration for the models was the OECD draft convention begun in 1976.

Before the Washington Convention on the settlement of investment disputes by arbitration was adopted, bilateral agreements between investing countries and host States were relatively few. The Washington Convention ushered a period of great activity in this regard, simplifying the task of negotiators by setting a standard individual bilateral agreements could uniformly follow and which would be ratified with less local opposition and controversy. Differences between model conventions nonetheless exist, reflecting the respective strengths of the parties' bargaining positions as well as the level of awareness, on the part of the negotiators, of the needs of their respective clients, investors and State authorities. For even greater assistance, many countries caused their own model forms of BIT's to be drafted, which could be used in negotiating actual BIT's with most any developing country. The resolution of litigation through arbitration helped drafters of model BIT's amend and augment earlier models. In this Chapter, some of the models will be reviewed.

During the last few decades, the text of model conventions has been adapted and amended several times. No claim is made that the system is the best that could have been devised nor even that, having been worked on for so many years, it cannot be supplanted or supplemented. What is claimed is that no model convention is worth the paper it is written on unless it contains a minimum standard of protection and guarantee measures. Each concluded BIT cannot be a carbon copy of the model, but the provisions of each new agreement have to be adapted to the specific circumstances existing on the territory of the host State.

The attitude many host States have adopted in the past with respect to foreign investors has not always been such as would generate confidence among prospective foreign investors. Hence, BIT's with some of these States could bear some changes, generally in the sense of strengthening the investors' protection clauses. For instance, the whole gamut of measures privative of property, taken in the past by newly independent States must be taken as a hard reminder for investors and their home States alike that the initial euphoria accompanying the signing of a BIT can quickly disappear in the wake of political and economic changes in the host country and that sanctions for the violation of BIT protection clauses by the host State must be clearly set out. The best time for including such sanctions is during the "honeymoon" period, when investments are about to be made and the spirit infusing negotiations is at its most favourable. Prudence is particularly called for in clauses dealing with corporate nationality and most favoured nations' rights.

The comments in this Chapter regarding various models are not intended to be exhaustive but cover discrete BIT topics only where the individual provision appearing in the country' BIT selected departs significantly from the norm. They also include reflections on the apparent policies of the countries selected, as expressed in specific cases involving such countries, either before legislation incorporating the BIT form was adopted or before such form was publicised. They serve merely to illustrate differences between the approaches various countries have taken for the protection of their investors abroad and to sensitise future investors to pitfalls which insufficiently close review of such countries' bilateral treaty text forms or policies in respect of foreign investments protection may reserve for them. For full details, consult the full, published, BIT text.[64]

Most countries in Western Europe and North America have developed model conventions serving as bases for the negotiation and conclusion of bilateral investment protection conventions with developing countries. The source of inspiration for the models was the OCDE-draft convention first made public in 1976 (cfr *supra*) but even as between Western countries sharing a basic common culture and roughly equal economic affluence, there are significant differences between such countries' models.

6.2. – ISSUES

The main issues at stake in most BIT's are definitions of terms used, the scope and procedures for the settlement of disputes. Among the definitions, those that are of the greatest interest to the negotiators are those relating to the nationality of investors, the nature of their investments, the determination and effect of control over the investment, fair treatment and the rights of persons affected by expropriation and nationalisation. These issues interact, a position taken on any one of them having an effect on the others.

The most obvious such interaction is that of nationality and control. Since BIT's are intended for defining the rights and obligations of nationals of one of the Contracting States vis-à-vis the other Contracting States, and exclude filings by nationals against their own State, nationality is a *sine qua non* concern in the sense that it is one of the gates a prospective litigant must pass through before he can submit a justiciable claim. In this regard, phenomena such as double nationality and third party control over the investment have

---

[64] Http://www.unctadxi.org/templates/DocSearch____779.aspx.

lent a significant complexity to the interpretation of the law as applied to individual circumstances.

Likewise, who can be a protected investor and what is a protected investment raise questions that the "Definitions" articles of BIT's strive to resolve. Questions relating to the venue or venues, and the choice, if any, of venues frame the litigation of disputes and constitute yet another gate a prospective litigant has to face before he is allowed to prove the core of the facts underlying his claim.

6.3. – Models

6.3.1. – Afro-Asiatic Model

The Asian-African Legal Consultative Committee (AALCC) has undertaken the task of preparation of the drafts of model negotiating texts for bilateral agreements on promotion and protection of investments. The Committee has worked up several models but only the so-called Model A will be addressed in this Work, because it is the most liberal and corresponds better to the BIT's which have been entered into by countries from this area.

6.3.1.1. *Definitions*

The definition of "investor" in this model is somewhat surprising. The provision reads as follows:

> "National in respect of each Contracting Party means a natural person who is a national or deemed to be a national of the Party under its Constitution or relevant law."

This text is ambiguous and should have been formalised. A citizen is the physical person having the nationality of the Contracting State, in accordance with its legislation. In some states of the US, the term "citizen" has also, in the doctrine and other texts, been somewhat loosely attributed to corporations also. Regarding corporations, a reference has been made to the "substantial interest and majority shareholding". The term "substantial interest" is still too vague.

6.3.1.2. *Promotion of investments*

A special commitment has been provided in this respect. The Contracting Parties have agreed to organising periodic consultations :

> "The contracting Parties shall periodically consult among themselves concerning investment opportunities within the territory of each other in various sectors such as industry, mining, communications, agriculture and forestry to determine where investments from one Contracting Party into the other may be most beneficial in the interest of both the parties."

European BIT's do not include such commitments.

6.3.1.3. *Most favoured Nation Treatment*

Foreign investors are entitled to the most favoured nation treatment as well as national treatment. However, no reference has been made to the application of rules of international law, a distinct negative for candidate investors.

6.3.1.4. *Nationalisation and Expropriation*

The norm is the domestic law's precedence. Compensation of damages sustained by privative property measures is settled in accordance with national legislation. First, the indemnification must be documented in an agreement between the investor and local authorities, in which the investor is the weaker party. Should an agreement not succeed, national judicial relief is then to be sought :

> "The determination of the compensation, in the absence of agreement being reached between the investor and the host State, shall be referred to an independent judicial or administrative tribunal or authority competent under the laws of the expropriating State or to arbitration in accordance with the provisions of any agreement between the investor and the host State."

Obviously, legal security is not assured by this alternative. The host State would not have given its prior consent to an arbitral procedure and, hence, when litigation regarding indemnification begins, the host State will want to avoid it and prefer the jurisdiction of local tribunals.

6.3.1.5. *Settlement of Investment Disputes*

A distinction is to be made between litigation stemming from a nationalisation or expropriation measure, as described above, and, generally, any and all litigation that concerns the investment.

Under the terms of this model, an international investor may, as his first recourse, file his litigation with the competent domestic tribunals. If he so wishes, he may request for a conciliation procedure, as foreseen in the Washington Convention. The parties may also select the conciliation procedure developed by UNCITRAL (Conciliation rules 1980).

Should the conciliation attempts not be successful, the parties may, as a last resort, have recourse to arbitration, either in accordance with the Washington Convention or in accordance with the UNCITRAL procedure (Arbitration rules 1976). A similar form of settlement is included in the revised, Model B, convention but the text is less favourable for the international investor, forcing him to exhaust first all means of internal recourse before filing any arbitration or conciliation procedure:

> "If any dispute or differences should arise between a contracting party which cannot be resolved within a period of... through negotiation, either party to the dispute may initiate proceedings for conciliation, or arbitration after the local remedies have been exhausted." (article 10ii)

In this model, international investors may not choose the arbitration institution. As a result, the host State is in a stronger position, as it is the State which at the end of the day decides whether the litigation will be submitted to ICSID or a tribunal following the rules of UNCITRAL. Thus, European nations who sign protection agreements with African or Asian countries, should try to have an arbitration clause included providing that investors shall have recourse to the arbitration institution of their choice. The anticipatory consent of the host State to arbitration should also be requested.

Furthermore, it will be opportune to reject any requirement that the dispute be first submitted to a local jurisdiction. Living with such a requirement could be very tiresome and costly. Besides, objective judicial decisions of this kind are not always guaranteed. However, if the investor is given the choice between local tribunals and arbitration, the problem disappears.

6.3.2. – *Australia*

For a long time, Australia was satisfied with Friendship Treaties for Commerce and Navigation (FCN Treaties). In general, there were fragmentary provisions which referred to the protection of investments. There were agreements guaranteeing equality with national treatment and with the most favoured nation.

Australia has not made its model convention public. Its text is most likely in the process of evolving. The most recent convention is that concluded on 23 August 2005 with Mexico, and which came into force on 21 July 2007. Though it may not be considered a model for Australia, this text then probably reflects the current Australian practice and has certain characteristics which distinguish it from European practice.

6.3.2.1. *Nationality*

Australia grants to foreign investors the same protection as that granted to investors who are Australia citizens and those who have permanent resident status. Australian agreements generally assimilate the rights of permanent residents and citizens.

"Investor of a Party means:

i) A company;

ii) A natural person who is a citizen or permanent resident of a Party, according to its laws." (Article 1, Australia Sri Lanka Agreement dated 12 November 2002, Australia/Poland agreement dated 7 May 1991)

> For the purposes of article 1 of the Agreement, the term 'citizen' include a permanent resident (that is, a natural person whose residence in a Contracting Party is not limited to time under its laws), if, in accordance with the laws, regulations and policies of the Contracting Party concerned, they are treated as citizens for economic purposes." (Protocol Agreement Australia/United Mexican States, 23 August 2005).

The absolute assimilation of citizens and permanent residents is of dubious value. Left as such, this formula can create problems, particularly if the permanent resident has the nationality of the other Contracting Party, or if he has double nationality, that of the host State and that of the other Contracting Party.

To avoid conflicts in the application of Australian agreements, special provisions have been included, based on a formula adopted by Canada for its BIT's:

> "National of a Contracting Party means a natural person who is a citizen or a permanent resident of a Contracting Party under its law or a company;
>
> This agreement shall not apply to a person who is a permanent resident but not a citizen of a Contracting Party where:
>
> a) the provisions of an investment protection agreement between the other Contracting Party and the country of which the person is a citizen have already been invoked in respect of the same matter; or
>
> b) the person is a citizen of the other Contracting party."

This provision already existed in an older agreement, with China dated 11 July 1988. The proper application of the provisions of a BIT is further compromised if each of the Contracting Parties have different definitions of the term 'Investors' in the sense that one of the Contracting Parties holds its citizens to be investors but the other so holds with respect to both its citizens and its residents.

In the Australia/Argentine Agreement, such a provision has been inserted:

> "Investor of a Contracting Party means:
> i) in respect of Australia: a natural person who is a citizen or permanent resident of Australia...
> ii) in respect of the Argentine Republic: a natural person who is a national of the Argentina republic in accordance with its laws on nationality." (article 1)

An *ad hoc* solution has been improvised in this BIT:

> "In respect of Australia, this Agreement shall not apply to a natural person who is a permanent resident but not a citizen of Australia where:
> a) the provisions of an Investment Protection Agreement between the Argentine Republic and the country of which the Person is a citizen have already been invoked in respect of the same matter, or
> b) the person is a citizen of the Argentine Republic.
>
> In respect of the Argentine Republic, this Agreement shall not apply to the investments made by citizens of Australia if such persons have, at the time of making the investment, been domiciled in the Argentine Republic for more than two years unless the investor can prove that the investment was admitted into its territory from abroad."

We would be concerned that this formula may cause difficulties in its application, particularly in Argentina. In substance, domicile is substituted for residence to determine whether an investor shall be deemed Australian or Argentine.

6.3.2.2. *Investments*

The Australia/Mexico Convention states that the term "investment":

> "means every kind of asset, owned or controlled, directly or indirectly, by investors of one Contracting Party admitted in accordance with the laws, regulations and policies of the Contracting party in whose territory the investment is made..." (**Article 1**)

Right from the start, we run into a provision which limits the scope of the concept "investment" to those "owned" or "controlled". If the investor has made an investment, direct or indirect, it appears under this convention that he must be the owner (impliedly 100% owner), or, if such is not the case, he must have control over the investment. When the investor is a corporation, it must have, in theory at least, 50% or more of the capital. However, as we have seen in earlier chapters of this work, the notion of control is not a simple as it looks. It is not only the number of shares held that is used to determine who controls a company but the corporation's system for allowing shares to be voted must also be considered as well as the corporation's by-laws and the sending State's laws regulating corporations.

A second problem, in fact quite restrictive, is that the investment must have been explicitly "admitted" by the host Contracting State, in accordance with its laws. In European BIT's, the definition of investment is not so restrictive.

In the Australia/Mexico BIT, there is something special, namely, a definition of what investment does *not* mean :

"Investment does not mean :
- a loan to an enterprise or a debt security of an enterprise where the original maturity of the loan or debt security is less than three years;
- claims to money that arise solely from :
    i) commercial contracts for the sale of goods or services by a national or enterprise in the territory of a Contracting party to an enterprise in the territory of another Contracting party;
    ii) the extension of credit in connection with a commercial transaction such as trade financing other than a loan."

6.3.2.3. *Control*

If a person has the power to block important decisions or changes in the structure of the corporation, it could be said such person controls the corporation. There is therefore a problem of proof, should an investor seek protection for his investment, based on the agreement requiring that he exercise control over the corporate investment.

In the BIT Australia/Sri Lanka, dated 12 November 2002 (entry into force on 14 March 2007), an attempt has been made to give the idea of control some additional content:

> "The question of ownership or control with respect to an investment shall depend on the factual circumstances of the particular case. The following facts, *inter alia*, shall be accepted as evidence of such ownership or control:
>
> a) a substantial direct or indirect participation in the capital of the legal entity which allows for effective control, such as, in particular, a direct or indirect participation of more than 50% of the capital or a majority shareholding; or
>
> b) direct or indirect control of voting rights allowing for:
>   i) the exercise of a decisive power over management and operations; or
>   ii) the exercise of a decisive power over the composition of the board of directors or af any other managing body.
>
> Where there is a doubt as to whether an investor exercises ownership or control, the investor shall be responsible for demonstrating that such ownership or control exists."

How an investor can prove that he has control over an enterprise poses a bit of a conundrum. In arbitral awards, records of the board of directors' meetings, showing extensive powers given to the individual in question, have been accepted as proof. In other cases, a distinction has been made between "technical" positions and management. A shareholder with less than 50% of shares, but appointed to be the General Director, has been viewed as exercising control over the corporation. The problem with this definition is that, in any case, minority shareholdings appear to be excluded entirely from the possibility of protection. European practice on the other hand expressly holds that all participations, majority or minority, benefit from the protection agreement.

6.3.2.4. *Treatment of Investors*

In the FCN Agreement with the U.S., which came into force in January 2005, there figured also a guarantee of minimum treatment, conforming to international law practice:

"**Minimum Standard of Treatment**

Article 11.5 requires a Party to treat covered investments in accordance with the 'customary international law minimum standard of treatment of aliens'."

Annex 11-A confirms the understanding of the Parties that "customary international law" is law that results from a general and consistent practice of countries that they follow from a sense of legal obligation. It also confirms that the customary international law minimum standard of treatment of aliens refers to all customary international law principles that protect the economic rights and interests of aliens.

Two important aspects of this customary international law minimum standard of treatment of aliens are :

"'fair and equitable treatment' – this includes a requirement that a country not deny justice to foreign investors in accordance with the principle of due process embodied in the principal legal systems of the world; and

'full protection and security' – this requires a country to provide a minimum level of safety to foreign investors and their investments."

However, the Australian Government, like the US (which views FCN treaties with great favour) came to the conclusion that FCN's did not provide sufficient guarantees of protection for investors :

"The FCN treaties employed by the United States (and by Australia) also had the following shortcomings :

i. The clause on expropriation was inadequate to deal with creeping expropriation;

ii. The arbitration clause was poorly drafted. This is probably because FCN treaties were originally developed at a time when arbitration was seldom used;

iii. FCN Treaties were also inadequate to resolve problems related to the doctrines of foreign sovereign immunity and acts of state." [65]

---

[65] KOHONA, Palitha, "Investment protection Agreements : An Australian perspective", *Journal of World Trade Law*, 1987, n° 79, p. 82.

Driven by nationalisation spirits running high in the former colonies and by the activities of OECD, recommending that specific agreements be concluded, Australian authorities decided to change their policies. This development had as consequence that there was movement towards the realisation of specific bilateral protection agreements (BIT's).

6.3.2.5. *Equality of treatment*

The classical formula, that is, granting to foreign investors treatment equal to that granted nationals or the most favoured nation, has been adopted by Australia. Yet, it is odd that the standard minimum treatment is in conformity with rules and principles of international law and appears in the FCN but not in the Australian BIT's. This may just be an inadvertent deviation from usual international practice.

6.3.2.6. *Settlement of Investment Disputes*

As to disputes between a Contracting State and an investor from another Contracting State, the Australia system provides for either a judicial or administrative procedure or recourse to international arbitration. To avoid jurisdictional conflicts, the choice of the investor is considered binding:

> "Where an investor has submitted a dispute to the aforementioned competent tribunal of the Contracting Party which has admitted the investment or to international arbitration in accordance with paragraph 3 of this article, this choice shall be final."

Investors have a wide choice between the various arbitration institutions: ICSID in Washington, D.C., or an arbitration tribunal *ad hoc*, established from case to case set up in accordance with the Arbitration Rules of the United Nations Commission on International Trade law (UNCITRAL), *or to any other arbitration institution*, or in accordance with any other arbitration rules, as may be mutually agreed between the parties to the dispute.

This very liberal formula has advantages when compared to the limited choice investors have under other BIT's which have them bound to accept ICSID or the Chamber of International Trade in Paris or Stockholm. There are arbitration tribunals well known on every continent. According to circumstances, it should be possible to file an arbitration proceeding in Europe, in Asia, in the United States or in Africa. According to the Australian formula, investors may, if they so wish, submit their dispute to the host State, to the tribunals having jurisdiction in such State but this would be rather exceptional at least in Europe. It is difficult to deny that most developed States are reluctant to allow the tribunals of the host States to decide a case:

> "Failing such consultations and negotiations for the resolution of a dispute, the United States prototype provides for the aggrieved foreign investor to resort to the administrative or judicial tribunals available in the host State... Although there is a reluctance (at times unjustified) by capital exporting countries to rely exclusively on the tribunals of the host State to resolve investment disputes in the case of IPA's concluded with LDC's, it is noted that this is an option made available to disputants in some of the IPA's concluded with China" [66]

Besides arbitration, investors may also submit the dispute to local competent tribunals or address a request for conciliation in writing to the ICSID Secretary General in Washington. The wide discretion given investors is a hallmark of Australian arbitration legislation which recognises that host States' tribunals evoke limited enthusiasm and therefore allow investors the double option of using such tribunals or have a direct recourse to international arbitration.[67]

6.3.2.7. *Disputes between private Investors of both Contracting Parties*

Neither in Europe, nor in Canada, nor in the US, have there been provisions for the settlement of disputes between

---

[66] KOHONA, Palitha, *op. cit.*, p. 100, see footnote 65.
[67] The China/Belgium BIT provides similar benefits to investors of either State.

private investors of one of the contracting Parties and *private* investors from another Contracting Party. People seem to be happy with the notion that physical persons, including foreigners and corporations, have access to the local courts as well as to arbitration procedure, which, in accordance with the codes of the country in question, apply in that country.

Australia has innovated in this regard, by adding to its Agreements provisions concerning eventual disputes between investors from different Contracting States. Settlement of disputes between investors of the Contracting Parties : A contracting Party shall in accordance with its laws and regulations :

"a) provide investors of the other Contracting Party who have made investments within its territory and personnel employed by them for activities associated with investments full access to its competent judicial or administrative bodies in order to afford means of asserting claims and enforcing rights in respect of disputes with its own investors;

b) permit its investors to select means of their choice to settle disputes relating to investments with the investors of the other Contracting party, including arbitration conducted in a third country; and

c) provide for the recognition and enforcement of any resulting judgments or awards." (article 14 Agreement Australia/Argentina; Agreement Australia/Sri Lanka and Agreement Australia/Poland)

This provision does not exist in the Australia/Mexico Agreement dated 23 August 2005. Perhaps the trend has broken but will re-assert itself in future Agreements.

6.3.3. – *Belgium*

Bilateral investment protection agreements concluded in the name of the Belgo-Luxemburg Economic Union (known by their short title "BLEU-conventions") follow a model whose content has been primarily determined by Belgian practice, subsuming the role of the Grand Duchy without the need to invoke any delegation of powers from the latter. For practical reasons, the term "Belgian conventional practice" is used in this study to include both Belgian and Luxemburg practice.

The Belgian model convention, in its actual form, was developed in 1995. Inspiration from other practices (U.S. Australia, Canada, etc.) would no doubt be valuable in future redaction of the model, drawing upon these countries' wide experience in the promotion of investments in developing countries. So far, however, the only modification of the Belgian model convention realised to date concerns the protection of labour and the environment.

6.3.3.1. *Compensation for losses*

Article 5 of the Belgian model convention states as follows:

> "The investors of one of the Contracting Parties, whose investments may have sustained damages owing to war or other armed conflict, revolution, state of national emergency, insurrection, on the territory of the other contracting Party, will be treated by the latter no less favourably than investors of the most favoured nation, insofar as restitutions, indemnifications, compensations or other indemnities are concerned."

This provision is only inserted exceptionally in Belgium's BIT's. Developing countries often oppose the inclusion of such clause. It would be better to delete the term "war" from the text of the Belgian model convention (cfr *infra*). The past has taught that the consequences of war are very complex and of a particular nature, so much so that specific peace treaties have to be concluded. The application of BIT's to war losses may often cause problems which are practically without any solution. This is the case in particular for arbitration. The important number of post-war claims and of related compensatory damages makes arbitration procedures on an individual level impossible to introduce. It would be necessary to open negotiations between affected States, possibly resulting in peaces treaties. In the very special circumstances accompanying the state of war and post-war, special legislation is usually enacted in order to settle the distribution of enemy assets:

> "With regard to the first (peace treaties) enemy property legislation was an instrument of economic warfare aimed at denying the enemy the advantages to be derived from the anonymity and separate personality of corporations. Hence the lifting of the (corporate) veil was regarded as justified *'ex necessitate'* and was extended to all entities which were tainted with enemy character, even the nationals of the State enacting the legislation. The provisions of the peace treaties had a very special function: to protect allied property, and to seize and pool enemy property with a view to covering reparation claims. Such provisions are basically different in their rationale from those normally applicable." [68]

Post-war situations are thus very complex, following the parallel existence of claims of a different nature: indemnification of war losses, confiscation of enemy property for payment of indemnities by compensation, restitution of goods fallen in the hands of the enemy, measures of eventual sequestration. Consequently, the application of BIT's for the settlement of war indemnification problems appears impossible or impractical. Considering the difficulties which will arise concerning the valuation of assets damaged by war events, it is easy to conclude that *"ad hoc"* conventional settlements are required. Protection and compensation are issues affecting not just investors but other interests as well.

6.3.3.2. *Settlement of Investment Disputes*

6.3.3.2.1. *Local Courts*

It is perhaps not absolutely necessary to mention that the investor may have recourse to local tribunals. An investor who would wish to submit the dispute to the judicial arena in the host State will normally be able to do so, in as much as very few local codes forbid foreigners from filing in the

---

[68] *Barcelona Traction, Light and Power Company Limited, op. cit.*, p. 41, see footnote 15.

local courts. The problem is that, since the defendant in such cases will be the host State, hence, should the investor wish to reserve that possibility, he should be able to do so but will have a stronger hand if the BIT specifically allows him to do so.

6.3.3.2.2. *Amiable Composition*

The investment dispute settlement system presumes, under the Belgian model, that the parties will take the necessary steps to work out an amiable compromise before filing any judicial or arbitration procedure. The more diligent party will send to its counterpart a written notice, together with a memorandum containing all the details of the dispute (**Article 12** of the model convention).

If an amiable compromise cannot be reached, investors may then decide to file with the domestic court having jurisdiction over the matter. However, he also has the right to submit the matter immediately to international arbitration, either institutionally or *ad hoc* according to the United Nations Commission for International Commercial Law (UNCITRAL rules). Should he choose an institution, an investor may select that of his choice. The State Contracting Parties will have given their anticipatory consent to arbitration, irrevocably. On the other hand, the investor's consent need not be anticipatory but need exist only when the arbitration procedure is filed. The anticipatory consent of each State carries with it an abandonment of any objection based on the exhaustion of administrative or judicial domestic remedies.

6.3.3.2.3. *Arbitration and Conciliation*

Many international arbitration institutions offer a conciliation or mediation procedure for the settlement of claims that would otherwise be headed for arbitration. ICSID in Washington, for example, includes a procedure for investors who wish to file a conciliation brief. The Centre prescribes as follows :

"The Conciliation Commission (hereinafter called the Commission) shall be constituted as soon as possible after registration or a request pursuant to article 28" (article 29 Convention).

"If the parties reach agreement, the Commission shall draw up a report noting the issues in dispute and recording that the parties have reached agreement. If at any stage of the proceedings, it appears to the Commission that there is no likelihood of agreement between the parties, it shall close the proceedings and shall draw up a report noting the submission of the dispute and recording the failure of the parties to reach agreement." (article 34 Convention)

The LCIA International dispute resolution Centre in London, offers, as an alternative to arbitration, a mediation procedure :

"In most jurisdictions, ADR (alternative dispute resolution) is taken to mean only the non-adjudicative dispute resolution options, of which mediation is the most frequently used.

In essence, mediation is a negotiated settlement, conducted and concluded with the assistance of a neutral third party. The process is voluntary and does not lead to a binding decision, enforceable in its own right." [69]

The Commercial Arbitration and Mediation Center for the Americas (CAMCA) has also stressed the point that mediation, as well as arbitration, are important means for the solution of commercial and investment disputes :

"It is well recognised that the availability of prompt, effective and economical means of dispute resolution is an important element in the orderly growth and encouragement of international investment and trade. Increasingly, arbitration and mediation, instead of litigation in national courts, have become the preferred means of resolving international commercial disputes. With respect to private disputes arising in the sphere of the North American Free Trade Agreement (NAFTA), **Article 2022** of NAFTA specifically provides for the encouragement and use of arbitration and other alternative dispute resolution tech-

---

[69] Private archives.

niques (ADR) as the desirable means of resolving such controversies"[70]

This system has been adopted in Belgium, the difference with other countries who have likewise adopted the system, being that investors under the Belgian model do not have the option of choosing between arbitration and conciliation. If an investor does not wish to use local courts, he may directly file for arbitration. Admittedly, the investor who first seeks conciliation but is unsuccessful has lost a great deal of time but the chances of success in conciliation are not to be underestimated. It is for the investor to choose the way he deems most likely to succeed.

In retrospect, the inclusion of an option allowing the investor to file his complaint with the local host State tribunals may not be wholly necessary. It is a rare host State that would forbid a foreign investor from filing locally. Where the host State is the defendant, the option may have some value.

6.3.3.2.4. *Arbitration settlement procedure*

Consent by the parties to settlement by arbitration does not automatically trigger an arbitration procedure. The ICSID procedure begins when the petition for arbitration by the Centre's Secretary is filed. Normally, the arbitration tribunal itself decides the jurisdiction issue. As an exception to this rule, the Secretary General has been granted an additional fragmentary and preliminary power to deny the Centre's jurisdiction :

> "The secretary general will register the request, unless he finds, on the basis of the information contained in the request, that the dispute is manifestly outside the jurisdiction of the Centre. Refusal to register will obviously occur only in extreme cases, e.g. where it is clear on the face of the request that the applicant is not a national of a Contracting State or that the intended respondent has not consented to arbi-

---

[70] Private archives.

tration. No recourse is available against a refusal by the secretary general to register a request."[71]

An international investor's interest would also be well served if the BIT acknowledges that he has the right to choose the arbitration institution of his preference. He can then decide for himself, either to have recourse to the local tribunals or to international arbitration. Should he choose international arbitration, he may then choose which one. The reference in article 12 to ICSID is obvious since ICSID's class is evidently international. Investors, however, must still understand that ICSID does not recognise the public insurer's subrogation of the rights of investors who have been indemnified.

6.3.3.2.5. *Environment and Labour*

The new provisions on these matters are based on the "North American Free Trade Agreement" (NAFTA) concluded on 17 December 1992, by the USA, Canada and Mexico and entered into force on 1 January 1994.

Article 1114 of the treaty reads as follows:

"1. Nothing in this Chapter shall be construed to prevent a Party from adopting, maintaining or enforcing any measure otherwise consistent with this chapter that it considers appropriate to ensure that an investment activity in its territory is undertaken in a manner sensitive to environmental concerns.

2. The Parties recognise that it is inappropriate to encourage investment by relaxing domestic health, safety or environmental measures. Accordingly, a Party should not waive or otherwise derogate from, or offer to waive or otherwise derogate from, such measures as an encouragement for the establishment, acquisition, expansion or retention in its territory of an investment of an investor. If a Party considers that another Party has offered such an encouragement, it may request consultations with the other Party and the two Parties shall consult with a view to avoiding any such encouragement."

---

[71] BROCHES, Aron, "The convention on the settlement of investment disputes: Some observations on Jurisdiction", *The Columbia journal of transnational law*, vol. 5, n° 1, 1966, p. 272.

On the basis of the NAFTA treaty, a specific agreement "North American Agreement on environmental cooperation"(NAAEC), has been concluded on 13 September 1993. It entered into force on 1 January 1994. Article 3 of this agreement reads as follows:

> "**Levels of protection**: Recognising the right of each Party to establish its own levels of domestic environment protection and environmental development policies and priorities, and to adopt or modify accordingly its environmental laws and regulations, each Party shall ensure that its laws and regulations provide for high levels of environmental protection and shall strive to continue to improve those laws and regulations."

These texts have been practically copied when inserted in the model Belgian convention. The same is true for the "North American Agreement on Labour Cooperation" (NAALC), which came into force also on 1 January 1994.

It could be said that provisions of the Belgian model convention are merely exhortatory, i.e. "soft law." Written confirmations that environmental protection agreements will be respected entail no serious additional legal constraint. Of course, the well known principle that *"pacta sunt servanda"* obligates the Contracting Parties to respect their commitments. New rules of the model convention regarding environmental protection and workers' basic rights have not yet been adopted in current Belgian practice. In several BIT's, these provisions simply don't exist (e.g. Belgium/Montenegro dated 4 March 2004, Belgium/Croatia dated 31 October 2001, BIT's Belgium/Uruguay dated 4 November 1991 etc.).

LDC's in general are not convinced that it is really necessary to include such provisions in the BIT's, possibly because they believe that matters relating to the environment and to labour should be dealt with by separate agreements.

6.3.3.2.6. *Eligible arbitration venues*

The Belgian list of eligible arbitration institutions could be broadened. In Europe, for example, mention should be made of the "London Court of International Arbitration" (LCIA). In keeping with a proper deference to African nations, it should also mention an African institution : "The Common Court of Arbitration and Justice (CCJA) of the Organisation for African Harmonisation of Business Rights (OHADA)."

In Asia, there are other arbitration organisations : "Hong Kong International Arbitration Centre", etc. It is appropriate that the Belgian Centre for Arbitration and Mediation (CEPINA) be recognised since it has acquired an international reputation in arbitration and mediation matters. Recently, a cooperation agreement has been concluded between CEPINA and the International Chamber of Commerce's arbitration court (CCI). It would be certainly in Belgian international investors' interest to add CEPINA to the list of eligible arbitration institutions.

6.3.4. – *Canada*

Canada began to negotiate "Foreign Investment Promotion and Protection Agreements" (FIPA's) in 1989. The legislation expressly acknowledges the twin goals of the agreements : for Canada, to establish a new bond for commercial policy expansion, and for the co-contracting State, placing an emphasis on the beneficial effect of investments on its economic development :

> "Enhancing Canada's investment opportunities is essential to Canada's ongoing international competitiveness. FIPA's provide important disciplines that help to open international markets and make them more secure for Canadian investors. This has attendant benefits for Canadian job creation, the encouragement of increased domestic economy efficiencies and opportunities to attract new investment and technology in support of Canadian competitiveness, economic growth and prosperity.
>
> From the perspective of developing countries investment has a positive impact on development. FIPA's are a positive and useful vehicle in that regard... Developing countries need and want the capital that investment brings and they want to ensure that investment flows pre-

dictably to their countries. FIPA's provide for that necessary signal of stability." [72]

The Canadian Minister for Foreign Commerce, Hon. David L. EMERSON, stressed the interest Canada has regarding its international commercial status, to enter into "Free Trade Agreements" and FIPA's, stating:

> "For example, Canada negotiated a Foreign Investment and Protection Agreement (FIPA) with India that will give Canadian and Indian investors the protection and stability they need to take advantage of opportunities in each others' market." [73]

Before 1989, the Canadian FIPA's were based on a convention draft prepared by OECD in 1967. From 1994 on, bilateral agreements were inspired from the text of a model convention serving as for Canada in negotiations with investment partners on bilateral investment rules. In accordance with usual practice, economic partners were selected based on the commercial and economic prospects offered by candidate co-contracting parties. The current model, as it is used today, dates from 2004 and, like its predecessor, is primarily based on the text of the North American Free Trade Agreement (NAFTA).

Compared to model conventions used in Europe, the Canadian model convention has some different characteristics which may interest the drafters of other model conventions. For example:

6.3.4.1. *Definitions*

The Canadian model convention lists 40 definitions, whereas most BIT's limit themselves to sketching a general notion of the nature of investments and protected investors. The agreements are expressly stated to apply to measures adopted and maintained by one of the Contracting Parties regarding investments and investors of the other Contracting

---

[72] Http://www.dfait-maeci.gc.ca/tna-nac/what_fipa-en.asp.
[73] Private archives.

Party. According to their definition, these measures include any and all legislation, regulation, procedure, requirements or practice. Although not expressly mentioned, the term "procedure" may be interpreted as including any judicial procedure.

This very useful provision is characteristic of the Canadian model, which explicitly includes in the notion of Government, Federal as well as provincial and local governments.

6.3.4.2. *Treatment*

Article 3 specifies:

> "The treatment accorded by a Party under paragraphs 1 and 2 means, with respect to a sub-national government, treatment no less favourable than the treatment accorded, in like circumstances, by that sub-national government to investors and to investments of investors, of the Party of which it forms a part."

This provision simply recognises the jurisdiction of Provinces and Communes regarding foreign investments made on their territories and the duty of "subnational" governments to afford to foreign investors a treatment at least equal to that afforded to local investors. This provision does not affect the international responsibility of the Federal State for compensable measures taken by a subnational government.

6.3.4.3. *Nationality*

The definition of "national" is unique and surprising:

> "'National' means a physical person who is a citizen or a permanent resident of a Party."

Thus, the same protection is granted to a foreign person who has gained the status of permanent resident. This provision is similar to that found in the Protocol of Colonia (not yet in force, see Chapter II) and can lead to difficulties when a permanent resident present in Canadian territory happens to have the nationality of the country which has a BIT with Canada. In such a case, the permanent resident could demand that both protection agreements be applied. Canada foresaw this difficulty and, in such a case, would require that the investor, permanent resident of Canada, waive his right to the application of the BIT with the State of which he is a national, before proceeding on the basis of the Canadian agreement.

If the permanent resident has two nationalities, that of the country of which he is a national and that of the country which has a BIT with Canada, similar difficulties arise. In this case also, precautionary measures have been taken. The BIT between Canada and Peru, dated 20 June 2007 states as follows:

> "Investor of a Party means:
> (i) in the case of Canada:
>   a) Canada or a State enterprise of Canada, or,
>   b) a national or an enterprise of Canada that seeks to make, is making or has made an investment, a natural person who is a dual citizen shall be deemed to be exclusively a citizen of the State of his or her dominant nationality, and
> (ii) in the case of the Republic of Peru:
>   a) a State enterprise of the Republic of Peru, or
>   b) a national or enterprise of the republic of Peru that seeks to make, is making or has made an investment; a natural person who is a dual citizen shall be deemed to be exclusively a citizen of the State of his or her dominant and effective citizenship."

This is indeed a useful provision but it does not solve all the problems. Eventually, arbitrators will have to evaluate what is the dominant nationality of an investor. It might have been better to specify criteria for this evaluation.

6.3.4.4. *Executive persons*

A distinction is made between executive positions (*CEO = Chief executive officer* etc.) and the board of directors:

> "Neither of the parties may require that any of its companies, to the extent it is an investment hereunder, appoint to executive positions persons of any predetermined nationality." (article 6)

This is laudable. Some countries, host to international investors, yield to a very nationalistic policy. The grant of an investment licence may be made subject to the duty to appoint to important positions persons of the host country's nationality. This is obviously incompatible with the need to entrust the management of an enterprise with people who possess the necessary ability, independently of their nationality.

Contrary to this principle, Canada has accepted that the board of directors of an enterprise be composed of people selected on the basis of their nationality:

> "A Party may require that the majority of the members of the board of directors, or of a committee of the board, of an enterprise which is an investment under the terms hereunder, be of a specified nationality or reside in the territory, provided such requirement does not substantially modify the ability of the investor to control his investment."

This is a direct transposition of the NAFTA text and has been used in the Canada/Peru BIT dated 16 June 2007. A Board of Directors is a management tool with very extensive powers. Important management decisions usually have to be pre-approved by the Board. It seems evident that a majority of Peruvians members in the Board of Directors of a Canadian investment on Peruvian territory will result in a modification of the control exercised by the Canadian investor over its Peruvian operations.

In the event the Canadian investor submits a dispute to arbitration, arguing that he has lost control over the enterprise because of the duty imposed by Peru to appoint a Peruvian majority of the Board members, he may have some difficulty in proving loss of control by reason of this duty. What will be important in such a case are the By-Laws of the Peruvian corporation, specifically whether important decisions are approved by individual vote for each member of the Board or whether reasonable conditions will constrain the voting, or even if the number of shares held by individual members will determine the issue.

This provision is of dubious validity. It would have been better to avoid any reference to nationality or residence.

6.3.4.5. *Performance requirements*

More than most any other country, Canada prizes investment protection agreements that help develop commercial relationships. Interventions by the State on whose territory investments have been made by foreigners have sometimes turned out to be hostile to the development and growth of such investments. **Article 7** therefore attempts to make it impossible for a Party to impose restrictive requirements regarding the investments, such as a duty to export a stated amount or percentage of the products produced, meeting a given amount or percentage of product content from national resources, the duty ro purchase products nationally manufactured etc.

European countries usually merely prohibit discriminatory measures, as in :

> "Neither contracting Party shall in any way impair by arbitrary or discriminatory measures the management, maintenance, use, enjoyment or disposal of investments in its territory of investors of the other Contracting State."

The Canadian text constitutes a more effective guarantee, since it contains a list of concrete measures that may not be taken because they hinder the enterprise's freedom of management.

6.3.4.6. *Monopolies and State enterprises*

European BIT's do not apply to monopolies or State enterprises. Only private investments are afforded the protection and security by the BIT's. The Canadian model convention authorises the creation of monopolies and the establishment of State enterprises, raising an issue of protectionism. However, article 8 does discipline a Party with respect to the activities of such enterprises. If they have regulatory, administrative authority, they may not act in a way that is inconsistent with that Party's duties under the Protection Agreement. This means that, for instance in the case of an expropriation measure, taken by such entities, the obligations imposed by the Agreement must be followed (indemnification etc.). Protectionism is not limited to LDC's.

6.3.4.7. *Multiple Reservations and Exceptions*

Persons or companies which invest in Canada or in a country that has a BIT with Canada should pay close attention to the provisions of such BIT's. It is rather striking that a very large number of reservations and exceptions, affecting the application of some of the provisions of the BIT's, appear in the Appendices to such agreements. Thus, provisions such as national content and the most favoured nation are nearly eviscerated by what is contained in the lists of exclusions and exceptions of Appendices. The same is true for exceptions on the basis of which Parties are exonerated from duties provided for in the Agreements, based on a very diverse set of reasons: health protection, conservation of depleting natural resources, preservation of the integrity and stability of the financial sector of either of the contracting Parties, etc.

6.3.4.8. *Transparency*

The Canadian model Agreement also provides:

> "A key factor in engendering a stable investment climate and attracting high quality long-term investment is the Parties' commitment to transparency in making their investment rules and regulations readily available and accessible to investors, be they domestic or foreign." [74]

As a matter of fact, many foreign investors are not well informed, neither when they invest nor afterwards, about legal

---

[74] Http://www.dfait-maeci.gc.ca/tna-nac/what_fipa-en.asp.

and regulatory provisions applicable to their investments. It is therefore very important that the BIT include a duty on the part of each Contracting Party to provide to the investor the text of all laws and regulations which affect the establishment of their investment on their respective territories. This is a verified need some European countries seem to ignore.

6.3.4.9. Settlement of Investment disputes

Compared to European BIT's, the Canadian model text is unique. Canada has established for itself a particular mechanism for the settlement of investment disputes. The rules of Canadian procedure complement those of ICSID, as follows:

> "In the conduct of the proceeding, the Tribunal shall apply any agreement between the parties on procedural matters, except as otherwise provided in the Convention or the Administrative and financial regulations." (Rule 20, Arbitration rules ICSID).

The following table compares some of the applicable rules of procedure to be followed when filing an arbitration request:

ICSID	CANADA
Notice of Intent to submit a claim to arbitration	
NIHIL	> The disputing investor shall deliver to the disputing Party written notice of its intent to submit a claim to arbitration, at least 90 days before the claim is submitted
Settlement of a claim through consultation	
NIHIL	> Before a disputing investor may submit a Claim to arbitration, the disputing Parties shall first hold consultations in an attempt to settle a claim amicably
Conditions precedent to submission of a claim to arbitration	
Written consent of the Parties to submit the dispute to arbitration	> 6 months have elapsed since the events (measures) giving rise to the claim and not more than 3 years after the date of the measures;

NIHIL	> The investor has delivered notice of the claim at least 90 days prior to submission of the claim;
NIHIL	> The investor waive his right to initiate or continue before any administrative tribunal or court, or other dispute settlement procedures;

Submission of claim to arbitration

Any contracting party or any national of a contracting State wishing to institute arbitration proceedings, shall address a request in writing to the Secretary general (article 36 convention). The request shall contain information concerning the issues in dispute, the identity of the parties, and their consent to arbitration	SAME FORMULA AS WITH ICSID

6.3.4.10. *Intervention of* "Amici Curiae"

In general terms, only the parties and their counsel have access to an arbitral procedure which concerns them. Persons or corporations which are neither plaintiffs nor defendants in an arbitral procedure have no justiciable interest in the proceeding or in the issues thereof. The same applies to judicial proceedings, except that, in some advanced, industrialised countries, interest in transparency has historically allowed the general public to have access, in an observational capacity, to trials and other hearings, whereas in arbitration, it has not. The rule of "no interest, no standing" applies. This rule is also followed in other international relations, such as diplomatic interventions in favour of nationals with interests to defend abroad. Such intervention is no longer possible from the moment the interested parties have decided to submit their disputes to judges having jurisdiction. A case found to be "sub judice" is not amenable to diplomatic protection.

In the last few years, however, a question has arisen regarding the interest that certain persons or groups of persons (for instance, non-governmental organisations (NGO's)) should or should not be able to intervene in a procedure in the capacity of "*amici curiae*" (Friends of the Court), without thereby becoming parties to the proceeding. With particular interests to defend (for instance environmental protection), these third parties often would like to gain access to the hearings and debates, have the right to submit memoranda, and have access to the evidence presented.

A. PRUIJNER, who favors such intervention, claims it would serve as the proverbial canary in the mines of conventional arbitration. It is interesting to see that ICSID has undergone an evolution towards accepting the intervention of "*amici curiae*."

6.3.4.10.1. "Amici Curiae" at *ICSID*

In 2002, in the case of *Aguas de Tunari v. Bolivia*, environmental organisations submitted to ICSID a request for authorisation of intervention:

> "The request for intervention as *amici curiae* was particularly extensive in that they involved the right to submit written memoranda, the right to attend the hearings, the right to present oral argument, thus the right of access to every aspect of the procedure. However, the wish for transparency expressed by the Friends of the Court went even further and concerned the general public that is why the tribunal was requested to open to the public all of the phases of the procedure."[75]

The arbitration tribunal rejected the request for intervention in its decision dated 21 October 2005. The main argument adopted by the Tribunal was that it did not have jurisdiction to allow third parties to intervene in an arbitration proceeding made available by the anticipatory and mutual consent of the two contracting parties:

---

[75] STERN, Brigitte, "Un petit pas de plus : l'installation de la société civile dans l'arbitrage CRDI entre Etat et investisseur", *Revue de l'arbitrage*, LITEC, Paris, n° 1/2007, page 10.

"The tribunal's unanimous opinion is that your core requests are beyond the power of the authority of the tribunal to grant. The interplay of the two treaties involved (Washington Convention, BIT Netherlands with Bolivia and the consensual nature of arbitration) places the control of the issues you raise with the parties, not the Tribunal. In particular, it is manifestly clear to the Tribunal that it does not, absent the agreement of the parties, have the power to join a non-party to the proceedings; to provide access to hearings to non parties and a fortiori, to the public generally; or to make the documents of the proceedings public." [76]

The ICSID procedure did not, at that time, use the "*Amici Curiae*" formula. Its *legal grounds were perfectly valid*. However, two subsequent decisions were favourable to the introduction of briefs of *amici curiae*. In Aguas Argentinas et Aguas de Santa Fe, access to the Tribunal's hearings had been refused on the basis of Rule 32 regarding oral proceedings and enumerating who could be present at the hearings:

"Unless either party objects, the Tribunal, after consultation with the Secretary general, may allow other persons, besides the parties, their agents, counsel and advocates, witnesses and experts during their testimony, and officers of the tribunal to attend…"

The Tribunal decided that this rule was now perfectly clear:

"Rule 32(2) is clear that no other persons, except those specifically named in the Rule, may attend hearings unless both claimant and respondent affirmatively agree to the attendance of those persons." (para 8)

Furthermore, the Tribunal accepted the submission of briefs by *amici curiae*, defining the role of such intervening parties:

"In such cases, a non-party to the dispute, as 'a friend' offers to provide the court or tribunal its special perspectives, arguments, or expertise on the dispute, usually in the form of a written *amicus curiae* brief or submission."

---

[76] Www.worldbank.org/icsid, ICSID cases.

The tribunal evidently had to find a basis for asserting jurisdiction, since, at the time, neither the Washington Convention nor any arbitration rule authorised or prohibited accepting briefs from *amici curiae*. They used **Article 44** of the Washington Convention :

> "Any arbitration proceeding shall be conducted in accordance with the provisions of this section and, except as the parties otherwise agree, in accordance with the arbitration rules in effect on the date on which the parties consented to arbitration. If any question arises which is not covered by this section or the arbitration rules or any rules by the parties, the Tribunal shall decide the question."

By deciding that it had jurisdiction to accept the filing of memoranda by *amici curiae*, the Tribunal established that the request for intervention had to be based on public interest :

> "The factor that gives this case particular public interest is that the investment dispute centers around the water distribution and sewage systems of a large metropolitan area... Those systems provide basic public services to millions of people and as a result may raise a variety of complex public and international law questions, including human rights considerations." (**para 19**)

According to the doctrine, accepting such requests for intervention also contribute to the transparency of arbitral awards :

> "The trend in favour of opening and increasing the transparency of arbitration relative to investments does not stop to merely informing the public *a posteriori* but extends to requesting that arbitral tribunals may, before issuing their awards, hear the contentions of certain interest groups acting as *amici curiae*, such as is done in US judiciary tradition as well as in International Court of Justice proceedings." [77]

6.3.4.10.2. "Amici curiae" *at the CIJ*

Article 62 of the Statute of the Court of International Justice (CIJ) reads as follows :

---

[77] GAILLARD, Emmanuel, *op. cit.*, page 618, see footnote 31.

"1. Should a State consider that it has an interest of a legal nature which may be affected by the decision in the case, it may submit a request tot the Court to be permitted to intervene.

2. It shall be for the Court to decide upon this request."

The evolution, within ICSID, towards accepting memoranda from amici curiae stems and finds its inspiration from the NAFTA treaty, where the three Contracting States displayed a willingness to accept this formula. The appropriate NAFTA commission made its position quite clear on the subject:

"No provision of the North American Free Trade Agreement stops a judge, should he find it appropriate, from accepting briefs submitted by a person or entity not a party to the ('third party') dispute."

Conventional international law and favourable arbitral awards have had a mutual influence. Driven by these two elements, ICSID has finally inserted a new clause in the Arbitration Regulation, entitled "Submissions of Non-disputing Parties":

"After consulting both parties, the Tribunal may allow a person or entity that is not a party to the dispute (in this rule called the 'non-disputing' party) to file a written submission with the Tribunal regarding a matter within the scope of the dispute. In determining whether to allow such a filing, the Tribunal shall consider, among other things, the extent to which:

a) the non-disputing party submission would assist the Tribunal in the determination of a factual or legal issue related to the proceeding by bringing a perspective, particular knowledge or insight that is different from that of the disputing parties;

b) the non-disputing party submission would address a matter within the scope of the dispute;

c) the non-disputing party has a significant interest in the proceeding.

The tribunal shall ensure that the non-disputing party submission does not disrupt the proceeding or unduly burden or unfairly prejudice either party, and that both parties are given an opportunity to present their observations on the non-disputing party submission" (Rule 37).

6.3.4.10.3. *Canadian formula* "Amici curiae" *Formula*

The Canadian Government has wanted to close off any further discussion regarding the acceptability or not of memoranda submitted by *amici curiae*. In its model convention and in Canadian BIT's which are based on the model, provisions formally authorising such briefs have been added. A distinction, however, has been made between, on the one hand, a Contacting State (if it is a non-disputing Party that is not a party to an investment dispute) to which the investor belongs (that is, the investor who disputes and makes a claim against the other Contracting Party), and on the other hand, any third person (non-disputing Party, meaning a Person of a party or non-Party).

For the Contracting State which is not a party to the dispute regarding an investment, it is specified that:

> "1. On written notice to the disputing parties (disputing investor and disputing Contracting State), the non-disputing Party may make submissions to a Tribunal on a question of interpretation of this Agreement.
>
> 2. The non-disputing Party shall have the right to attend any hearings held under this section, whether or not it makes submissions to the Tribunal." (article 35)

6.3.4.11. *Availability of Diplomatic Protection under the Canadian Model*

The latter provision can be very useful. According to the Washington Convention, when the State (not a party to the dispute) of the investor grants diplomatic protection, it may only do so in limited fashion:

> "No Contracting State shall give diplomatic protection, or bring an international claim, in respect of a dispute which one of its nationals and another Contracting State shall have consented to submit or shall have submitted to arbitration under this Convention, unless such other Contracting State shall have failed to abide by and comply with the award rendered in the dispute." (article 27)

An investor may therefore ask for diplomatic protection of the State to which he belongs only after the end of the arbitration proceeding, that is, when it becomes clear the host State does not comply with the arbitral award. During the arbitration procedure, the investor is not in a position to ask his State to support his case and that State will not be permitted to do so. In fact, however, because of the provision, investors who have filed for an arbitration proceeding may invite their State to file with the Tribunal briefs concerning the dispute and thereby in effect support its national on his request:

> "On written notice to the disputing parties (investor and host State) the non-disputing Party (State of the investor) may make submissions to a Tribunal on a question of interpretation of this agreement."

6.3.4.12. *Influence of the NAFTA "Free Trade Commission"*

One of the most significant improvements in the FIPA model, therefore, is the institutionalisation of the possibility for non-disputing individuals or organisations to seek leave from the Tribunal to make their views known on the matters at issue in the arbitration. Guidelines for the acceptance of such written *"amicus curiae"* submissions by a Tribunal have been established, similar to those procedures under domestic law, including a required assessment of the proposed submission's relevance and assistance in resolving the dispute. Greater transparency and a greater opportunity for submittal to the arbitrators of a wider panorama of views are gained. These provisions are based on the NAFTA Free Trade Commission declaration and were issued in October 2003, substantially in the following terms:

> "**Statement of the Free Trade Commission on non-disputing party participation**

A. Non-disputing party participation [78]

1. No provision of the North American Free Trade Agreement ('NAFTA') limits a Tribunal's discretion to accept written submissions from a person or entity that is not a disputing party (a 'non-disputing party').

2. Nothing in this statement by the Free Trade Commission ('the FTC') prejudices the rights of NAFTA Parties under Article 1128 of the NAFTA.

3. Considering that written submissions by non-disputing parties in arbitrations under Section B of Chapter 11 of NAFTA may affect the operation of the Chapter, and in the interests of fairness and the orderly conduct of arbitrations under Chapter 11, the FTC recommends that Chapter 11 Tribunals adopt the following procedures with respect to such submissions.

B. Procedures

1. Any non-disputing party that is a person of a Party, or that has a significant presence in the territory of a Party, that wishes to file a written submission with the Tribunal (the 'applicant'), will apply for leave from the Tribunal to file such a submission. The applicant will attach the submission to the application.

2. The application for leave to file a non-disputing party submission will :

(a) be made in writing, dated and signed by the person filing the application, and include the address and other contact details of the applicant;
(b) be no longer than 5 typed pages;
(c) describe the applicant, including, where relevant, its membership and legal status (e.g., company, trade association or other non-governmental organisation), its general objectives, the nature of its activities, and any parent organisation (including any organisation that directly or indirectly controls the applicant);
(d) disclose whether or not the applicant has any affiliation, direct or indirect, with any disputing party;
(e) identify any government, person or organisation that has provided any financial or other assistance in preparing the submission;
(f) specify the nature of the interest that the applicant has in the arbitration;

---

[78] Http://www.dfait-maeci.gc.ca/tna-nac/what_fipa-en.asp#.

(g) identify the specific issues of fact or law in the arbitration that the applicant has addressed in its written submission;

(h) explain, by reference to the factors specified in paragraph 6, why the Tribunal should accept the submission; and

(i) be made in a language of the arbitration.

3. The submission filed by a non-disputing party will:

(a) be dated and signed by the person filing the submission;

(b) be concise, and in no case longer than 20 typed pages, including any appendices;

(c) set out a precise statement supporting the applicant's position on the issues; and

(d) only address matters within the scope of the dispute.

4. The application for leave to file a non-disputing party submission and the submission will be served on all disputing parties and the Tribunal.

5. The Tribunal will set an appropriate date by which the disputing parties may comment on the application for leave to file a non-disputing party submission.

6. In determining whether to grant leave to file a non-disputing party submission, the Tribunal will consider, among other things, the extent to which:

(a) the non-disputing party submission would assist the Tribunal in the determination of a factual or legal issue related to the arbitration by bringing a perspective, particular knowledge or insight that is different from that of the disputing parties;

(b) the non-disputing party submission would address matters within the scope of the dispute;

(c) the non-disputing party has a significant interest in the arbitration; and

(d) there is a public interest in the subject-matter of the arbitration. ..."

This Canadian practice has not been particularly welcome by all Contracting States. In Europe, the need for greater transparency in the arbitration proceedings has not yet percolated in legal minds. According to the usual European practice, one of the advantages of arbitration, as compared to a judicial proceeding, is precisely its confidential character. Canada has attempting to revise certain BIT's in order to include transparency provisions but not always successfully:

"Like the US model investment treaty, the Canadian template mandates that arbitral documents be publicly disclosed, and that hearings be registered and open to the interested public. These provisions were introduced into the Canadian and US model investment agreements following widespread criticisms that arbitration launched under the investment chapter of the North American Free Trade agreement (NAFTA) were shielded from public view despite holding important public policy implications. Notably, however, when the US Government agreed to changes to its BIT's with certain EU member States, no transparency provisions were added to the dispute settlement provisions of those treaties. As such, arbitrations might continue to proceed without public disclosure or open hearings." [79]

6.3.5. – China

6.3.5.1. Definitions

The Chinese definition of the term "investment" corresponds to definitions generally used elsewhere. However, the definition of the term "investor" is very fragmentary:

> "Economic entities established in accordance in accordance with the laws of the People's Republic of China and domiciled in the territory of the People's Republic of China."

There is no word as to legal capacity nor corporate seat. In its BIT's, China adapts its policy sometimes to international practice and uses a more adequate definition. In the Netherlands/China BIT (26 November 2001), for example, the following improved definition appears:

> "Investor means economic entities, including corporations, associations, partnerships and other organisations, incorporated and constituted under the laws and regulations of either Contracting party and have their seats in that Contracting party, irrespective of whether or not for profit and whether their liabilities are limited or not."

The Netherlands have adopted the Chinese formula but in other BIT's, the parties have accepted that the other Con-

---

[79] Investment treaty news 27/4/2007 : www.iisd.org/investment/itn.

tracting Party provide its own definition. This is the case in the Belgium/China BIT (4 June 1984):

> "Investor means in respect of the Kingdom of Belgium or the Grand-Duchy of Luxemburg: ... the companies, i.e. any legal person constituted in accordance with the legislation of the Kingdom of Belgium or of the Grand-Duchy of Luxemburg and having its registered office in the territory of the Kingdom of Belgium or the Grand-Duchy of Luxemburg."

6.3.5.2. *Treatment of Investments*

The Chinese model convention provides that:

> "Investments and activities associated with investments of investors of either Contracting party shall be accorded fair and equitable treatment and shall enjoy protection in the territory of the other Contracting Party. The treatment may not be less favorable than that of investors of a third State."

In this regard, it can again be seen that China appears to be ready to diverge substantially from its model convention. For example, in the above BIT with the Netherlands, provisions are included for the beneficial treatment, be it national or for the most favoured nation. Furthermore, emphasis has been laid on the application of the most favoured nation rule:

> "If the provisions of law of either Contracting Party or obligations under international law existing at present or established hereafter between the Contracting parties in addition to the present Agreement contain a regulation, whether specific or general, entitling investments by investors of the other Contracting party to a treatment more favourable than is provided for by the present Agreement, such regulation shall, in the extent that it is more favourable, prevail over the present agreement."

It is not clear whether the investor has the choice of the most favourable law. It will be difficult to foresee the reaction when the investor decides to select the law which appears most favourable to him. Furthermore, there is not the least reference to international law.

6.3.5.3. *Expropriation*

The text of the Chinese model convention is very succinct and does not provide a sense of the current Chinese practice. Insofar as expropriation is concerned, analyzing recent BIT's give us a better idea. Differences between BIT's are striking. In the China/Czech Republic Bit (8 December 2005), the basis for valuing expropriated assets is the true value. This evaluation is subject to a request for revision :

> "The investor affected shall have the right to prompt review, by judicial or other independent authority of that Contracting party, of his or its case and the valuation of his or its investment in accordance with the principles set out in this article."

It is stipulated that the expropriation shall be carried out under domestic due process of law. There is therefore a risk that investors will have to submit to local tribunals for the solution of litigation regarding an expropriation measure. The text does not provide for arbitration. On the other hand, the Dutch formula in the said BIT provides for the market value as a basis for valuation. Although recourse to local tribunals is not expressly reserved, the BIT states that :

> "the expropriation is done in the public interest and under domestic legal procedures."

Arbitration is not provided for in this article and in the arbitration article itself, nothing is said about litigation regarding expropriation. As said above, there is therefore a risk that investors will only be able to have recourse to local tribunals for the settlement of disputes relating to indemnification of expropriated assets. As a general observation, applicable to the redaction of all BIT's, the arbitration article mostly says little or nothing about the formula to follow in order to have the valuation of indemnifications revised.

On the other hand, the article regarding the settlement of disputes between the host State and the investor usually states that "every litigation relating to an investment" may be submitted to arbitration. Hence, difficulties should be few.

Nonetheless, silence on the topic is not the best formula for legal security. Drafters of BIT's should insist on clarity and expressly mention in the arbitration articles that they apply to any and all disputes relating to the investment, including but not necessarily limited to any and all disputes relating to expropriation, "as provided for in article..." A possible alternative would be to mention in the expropriation articles that revision of indemnifications as well as any and all disputes relating to expropriation may be submitted to arbitration. The Chinese authorities were conscious of eventual problems in this regard since, in the arbitration article in their model convention, it is stated:

> "If a dispute involving the amount of compensation for expropriation cannot be settled within six months after resort to negotiations as specified in Paragraph 1 of this article, it may be submitted at the request of either party to an *ad hoc* arbitral tribunal."

A realisation of the problem is meritorious but the text then should have been improved. It is, in any event, surprising that the Chinese authorities have foreseen the problem in their model convention but ignore it in their BIT's.

6.3.5.4. *Settlement of Investment Disputes*

The Chinese model convention also grants a preference to amiable settlement for disputes relating to investments. Lacking such a settlement, the next step is recourse to local tribunals. For litigation relating to expropriation, once a tribunal has jurisdiction over the case, arbitration in the usual sense is excluded. Recourse is had, not to ICSID, but to *ad hoc* arbitration. Somewhat curiously, the General Secretary of ICSID has jurisdiction for nominating the arbitrators and the procedural ICSID rules are applicable to the *ad hoc* arbitration proceeding. Legal security is not guaranteed since there is no anticipatory consent to arbitration of any kind.

Here again, Chinese practice differs substantially from their model convention.

In the said BIT between China and the Czech Republic, it is provided that :

> "the People's Republic of China will require the investor concerned to go through the domestic administrative review procedures specified by the laws and regulations of that Contracting Party, before the submission of a dispute to international arbitration."

This is of course an inconvenient drag on the arbitration solution. The Netherlands have, however, reached an advantageous formula in the China/Netherlands BIT. There, the investor has the choice between local tribunals and ICSID arbitration or arbitration *ad hoc* according to the rules of UNCITRAL. The investor may even abandon his judicial proceeding, so long as he abandons the judicial procedure, before initiating an arbitration proceeding. Anticipatory consent is granted :

> "If the dispute has not been settled amicably within a period of six months, from the date either party to the dispute requested amicable settlement, each Contracting party gives its unconditional consent to submit the dispute at request of the investor concerned to ICSID...."

6.3.6. – *France*

For a long time, France did not use any convention model. The bilateral agreements text was prepared based on provisions of the model developed by the Organisation for Economic Cooperation and Development (OECD). The model currently used by France is dated 14 February 2006.

6.3.6.1. *"Protected Investments" defined*

The French apply the phrase *"ratione temporis"* to their bilateral agreements :

> "...would the conventional provisions apply only to investments made after the coming into force of the agreement or will they apply also to investments made prior thereto? The question is not about retroactivity : the Convention will govern, certainly, the effects of sit-

uations existing before the agreement's effectivity, but the effects that are to be covered are not past but future."[80]

Accordingly, the conventional rules do not apply with retroactive effect to the dates on which the investments were made. The question is whether, after the coming into force of the agreement, will the rules apply to investments made before such date. In other words, if an investment made before the date of entry into force has been expropriated, will the investor be able to benefit from the provisions of the Agreement?

In principle, international agreements take effect only from the date on which they are ratified by the Contracting Parties. If the latter wish that the agreement be applicable to investments prior to such date, and still existing on the date of the treaty, that wish should be expressly mentioned in the Agreement. As a general rule, Contracting States do include a provision relating to prior investments. France does include one such provision in its agreements:

> "It is agreed that such assets must be or have been invested in accordance with the legislation of the Contracting Party on the territory or in the maritime zone where the investment was made, before or after the coming into force of this Agreement."

There is therefore a limit in the protection, since it will be granted only on condition that the investments made, before or after the entry into force of the Agreement, shall have been made or be made in accordance with applicable legal norms. The text could bear a little more precision. It could mention that investments must conform to legislation in force at the time such investments were made, thus avoiding the possibility that investments made prior will not be affected by eventually multiple subsequent legislation.

In other protection agreements, another limitation appears, in that the provisions of the agreement are applicable to all

---

[80] JUILLARD, Patrick, *Droit et pratique du commerce international*, op. cit., p. 25, see footnote 41.

investment, regardless of the time when they were made, before or after the entry into force of the agreement, with the exception of provisions relating to settlement of disputes:

> "The present agreement will also apply to investments made before the entry into force of this agreement by investors one of the Contracting Parties on the territory of the other Contracting Party in accordance with the laws and regulations of the latter. However, the present agreement does not apply to disputes occurring prior to such entry into force." [81]

This provision also appears in the model convention with UGANDA (article 12), a less developed country:

> "Previous investments: This agreement shall also apply to investments made before its entry into force by investors of one Contracting party in the territory of the other Contracting Party in accordance with the latter's laws and regulations. It shall, however, not be applicable to claims arising out of disputes which occurred prior to its entry into force." [82]

After it had been decided that the protection agreement is applicable to all investments, including those made before its entry into force, it seemed inadvisable to exclude investors who made prior investments from the benefit of the agreement relating to disputes. Less developed countries may well prefer this limitation, in as much as they are naturally more interested in new investments than in those that are already existing.

6.3.6.2. *International responsibility*

A well known principle of international law is that of the international responsibility of States for their federated regions. To avoid disputes on this subject, it is nonetheless useful to mention expressly in the agreements of protection that States are responsible for measures taken by political subdivisions or organisms dependent on the State. Several

---

[81] Burkina Faso/Belgium BIT dated 19 May 2001, Federal Register dated, 07/01/2004.
[82] Convention UGANDA/BLEU, 1 february 2005, article 12.

arbitral awards, reference is made to a holding of the International Law Commission:

> "The conduct of any organism of the State is deemed to be an act of the State according to international law, in that this organism exercises legislative, executive, judiciary or other powers, no matter the position it occupies in the organisation of the State and no matter its nature as a central government organism of the State or territorial collectivity of such State." [83]

Article 2 of the model French convention states as follows:

> "for the application of the present Agreement, it is understood that the Contracting Parties are responsible for the acts or omissions of their public collectivities and, in particular, of their federated States, regions, local collectivities and any other entity over which the Contracting Party exercised oversight, or representation or responsibility of its international relations or sovereignty."

Anticipatory consent has also been provided for:

> "in the case where a dispute is such as to result in responsibility for the actions or omissions of public collectivities or organisms dependent upon one of the Contracting Parties, within the scope of article 2 of the present Agreement, such public collectivity or such organism shall give their consent unconditionally for the settlement of disputes relating to investments by ICSID, within the scope of article 25 of the Convention for the Settlement of Disputes between states and nationals of other States, signed in Washington D.C. on 18 March 1965."

6.3.6.3. *State Contract protection*

Frequently, specific investment agreements are signed between an investor and the State where the investment is to be made. These agreements are generally called State Contracts. In such contracts, the investor is seen as the weaker of the two parties, having a tendency to make concessions regarding the treatment of investments. To avoid that the provisions of a State Contract may be invoked in order to

---

[83] Commission du droit international (CDI) de l'organisation des Nations Unies, *Rapport de l'Assemblée générale*, 53° session, supplément n° 10, A 56/10, p. 87.

oppose arbitration, France has provided that provisions relating to the settlement of disputes shall be applicable regardless of the provisions of a State Contract :

> "The provisions of article 8 (settlement of disputes through arbitration) shall apply even if a specific commitment has been made waiving international arbitration or designating an arbitral institution different from that mentioned in article 8 of the present Agreement."
> (**Article 10**)

This is an interesting precaution, which is not to be found in other model conventions. France has therefore been innovative in its posture regarding model treaties.

6.3.6.4. *Settlement of Investment Disputes*

As previously stated, France did not, for a long time, use a model convention. Hence, we can review a few of France's most recent BIT's to evaluate the French practice for the settlement of international disputes.

It is immediately apparent that French practice has been very diverse. The most frequently used formula is very simple, however, and offers no optimal guarantees to French international investors. In principle, all disputes are settled amiably. In the event no amiable arrangement can be reached, then six months after notice to the other party, the dispute is to be submitted to ICSID :

> "If such a dispute has not been settled within a delay of six months from the date it was raised by one of the parties to the dispute, it will be submitted, on the request of one or the other of these parties to arbitration by the Centre for the Settlement of Investment Disputes (ICSID) created by the Convention for the Settlement of Investment Disputes between States and nationals of other States, which was opened for signature in Washington D.C. on 18 March 1965."
> (Article 8 – French Model Convention)

The French formula also has many flaws. The prior consent of Contracting States to arbitration is not foreseen. Investors do not have freedom of choice as to arbitration institutions. Such a settlement system has been adopted in the French

BIT's with Slovenia (11 February 1998), Cambodia (13 July 2000), Guatemala (27 May 1998) and Nicaragua (13 February 1998).

The French/Mexican BIT dated 12 November 1998 contains a very special formula for settlement of investment disputes which deviates substantially from general European practice. This BIT contains a definition of disputes that may be subject to the system for the settlement of disputes : "This article only applies to disputes between a Contracting Party and an investor of the other contracting Party concerning an alleged breach of an obligation of the former under this Agreement which causes loss or damage to the investor or its investment." (Article 9, para 1). This would include disputes arising from an alleged failure to meet obligations undertaken by one of the Contracting Parties and based on the BIT, so long as such failure caused a loss or damage to the investors. It is obvious that such a definition restricts substantially investors' access to arbitration.

The inclusion of a definition of the term "disputes" as used in the French Mexican formula should be avoided. It is preferable to be satisfied with a definition of the term "investments" and to refer to "disputes" relative to investments. However, if a definition of "disputes" were wanted in the BIT, then it would be better to follow the American example :

> "For purposes of this treaty, an investment dispute is a dispute between a Party and a national or company of the other Party arising out of or relating to an investment authorisation, an investment agreement or a breach of any right conferred, created or recognised by this treaty with respect to a covered investment." (**Article XI 1, The 1994 U.S. Model Convention**)

This is a much better text but it could yet be improved by a reference to rights arising from international law. That it does not is consistent with U.S. reluctance to commit to submission to the threat of enforcement by international bodies operating outside of ICSID.

The French Mexican formula implies that investors must show proof of a breach of an obligation and the existence of some damage. These two requirements for access to arbitration may lead to endless arguments. Should, for instance, the host State deny an investor's wish to expand his enterprise for environmental reasons, can there still be breach or damage?

The French/Mexican agreement contains yet another provision whose correct application may turn out to be a problem:

> "With respect to the submission of a claim to arbitration:
>
> a) an investor of one Contracting Part may not allege that the other Contracting Party has breached an obligation under this Agreement both [a la fois] in arbitration under this Article and in a proceeding before a competent court or administrative tribunal of the former Contracting Party, party to the dispute.
>
> b) likewise, where an enterprise of one Contracting Party, that is a juridical person, which an investor of the other Contracting Party owns or controls, alleges in proceedings, before a competent Court or administrative tribunal of the Contracting Party, party to the dispute, that the former Contracting Party has breached an obligation under this agreement, the investor not allege that breach in an arbitration procedure undertaken under this present article" (article 9.2.b).

In its entirety, the text of article 9 regarding the settlement of investment disputes offers no greater guarantees to investors than the model convention itself. There is, in fact, no anticipatoiry consent clause, a traditional staple of European BIT's:

> "To this end, each contracting Party agrees in advance and irrevocably to the settlement of any dispute by this type of arbitration. Such consent implies that both Parties waive the right to demand that all domestic and administrative or judiciary remedies be exhausted."

The France-Mexico BIT provides that the investor may choose an arbitration institution (ICSID, UNCITRAL, ICC). That is indeed progress compared to the model convention but, since the Contracting States have not given their anticipatory consent to arbitration, that choice is illusory.

Article 9,2 a) is not clear. Logically, it should lead to the conclusion that the investor may not, in parallel, file a judiciary and an arbitration procedure simultaneously, but would such action be actually possible anyway ? Filing a procedure with ICSID in parallel to that filed with a Court is not allowed. Should an investor choose an ICSID arbitration procedure, he may not simultaneously file in a domestic court :

> "The consent of the parties to arbitration within the scope of the present convention is, unless otherwise provided, deemed to be an abandonment of recourse to any other means." (Article 26, ICSID Convention).

Besides, were the investor to file simultaneously with an arbitration institution other than ISCSID (for instance, the ICC), the arbitration institution will certainly also reject his application on the basis that the matter is already "sub judice". Furthermore, inversely, the filing of a judiciary procedure simultaneously with an arbitration procedure would be fruitless, subject to demurrer, or its local equivalent, in that an arbitration had been initiated and local laws usually give precedence to arbitral proceedings.

To help ensure maximum guarantees to investors, we therefore recommend that the applicable agreement provide, in the event of a dispute, for the filing of either a judicial proceeding or an arbitration request, in the investor's discretion. The choice, once made, should be final. Any prior recourse to the judicial branch must herefore exclude a later filing in arbitration, and vice versa.

6.3.7. – *Germany*

The German model convention contains some surprising provisions as to the scope of protection for investors, the nature of the German preferred MFN clause, the interpretation of the BIT, amongst other matters of interest to investors.

6.3.7.1. *Definitions*

"Protected investors" are understood to mean not only commercial companies with legal entity but also *de facto* associations (without legal entity) such as non-profit-making associations. This implies that a syndicate, *not being a legal entity with legal personality*, having made investments abroad, (for instance : shares in a foreign company) could, if need be, ask for protection on the basis of a BIT concluded between Germany and a developing country. This is a dangerous path, one that may lead to dangerous consequences.

6.3.7.2. *MFN-clause*

The German formulation of the most favoured nation clause (MFN-clause) also departs from European practice, in this sense that reference is made to the notion of control. This notion is also used in Canada :

> "Investment of an investor of a Party means an investment owned or controlled directly or indirectly by an investor of such Party." (Agreement Canada/Peru : 20 June 2007)

There is no explicit mention of the influence of "control" on the nationality of a company, but only of the right to "good treatment" :

> "Neither Contracting State shall subject investments in its territory owned or controlled by the investors of the other contracting State to treatment less favourable than it accords to investments of any third State." (article 3)

This provision implies that minority participation may not ask for such special protection. There may be some doubt about the drafters' intent. In any case, it is not always easy to determine with certainty that a company is controlled or not by a foreign investor (majority participation or more than majority). In some arbitration proceedings, it was stressed that control or the lack of it must be found, not only on the basis of the percentages of shares held but considering any circumstance whatever demonstrating there is effective control :

> "Nonetheless, it must be true that the smaller the percentage of shares with voting rights held by foreigners, the more attention should be given to other elements affecting this question. As has been noted by an author, 'a tribunal... may regard any criterion based on management, voting rights, shareholding or any other reasonable theory as being reasonable for the purpose.'" [84]

The effect of control on the nationality of the corporation is not directly at issue but instead it comes into play in reference to fair treatment :

> "Neither Contracting State shall subject investments in its territory owned or controlled by the investors of the other contracting State to treatment less favourable than it accords to investments of any third State." (article 3)

6.3.7.3. *Special exclusion of transport Constraints*

In a Protocol, which shall be regarded as an integral part of the protection treaty, the following provision has been inserted :

> "Whenever goods or persons connected with an investment are to be transported, each Contracting party shall neither exclude nor hinder transport enterprises of the other Contracting State and shall issue permits as required to carry out such transport. This shall include the transport of :
>
> a) goods directly intended for an investment within the meaning of the Treaty or acquired in the territory of either Contracting State or of any third State by or on behalf of an enterprise in which assets within the meaning of the Treaty are invested;
>
> b) persons travelling in connection with an investment."

This is a very useful provision which could advantageously be inserted in other model conventions. It happens quite often that host States take measures which hinder the good management of investments. It would therefore be useful to

---

[84] GAILLARD, Emmanuel, *op. cit.*, p. 398, see footnote 31.

provide for a duty on the part of the contracting States not to hinder by any measure whatsoever the good management of investments.

6.3.7.4. *Performance requirements*

It would be even more useful for Germany to follow the example of the Canadian model treaty form, based on NAFTA and enumerate the commitments of contracting States on this topic expressly, that is by adding explicitly "Performance requirements" which may not be imposed on investors such as:

> "1. Neither Party may impose or enforce any of the following requirements, or enforce any commitment or undertaking, in connection with the establishment, acquisition, expansion, management, conduct or operation of investment of an investor of a Party or a non-Party in its territory:
>
> a) to export a given level or percentage of goods;
>
> b) to achieve a given level or percentage of domestic content;
>
> c) to purchase, use or accord a preference to goods produced or services provided in its territory, or to purchase goods or services from persons in its territory;
>
> d) to relate in any way the volume or value of imports to the volume or value of exports or to the amount of foreign exchange inflows associated with such investment;
>
> e) to restrict sales of goods or services in its territory that such investment produces or provides by relating such sales in any way to the volume or value of its exports or foreign exchange earnings;
>
> f) to transfer technology, a production process or other proprietary knowledge to a person in its territory, except when the requirement is imposed or the commitment or undertaking is enforced by a court, administrative tribunal or competent authority, to remedy an alleged violation of competition laws or to act in a manner not inconsistent with other provisions of this Agreement; or
>
> g) to supply exclusively from the territory of the Party the goods it produces or the services it provides to a specific regional market or to the world market. [85]

---

[85] Article 7 of the Canada/Peru BIT dated 20 June 2007: http://www.dfait-maeci.ge.ca/tna-nas/fipa_list-en.asp.

2. Whenever goods... with an investment." (cfr *supra*, p. 40)

It is rather unusual that the State which is generally considered as the pioneer in and guide for concluding bilateral protection conventions nonetheless uses a text that has so many substantial flaws.

6.3.7.5. *Settlement of Investment Disputes*

In the German model, in the event the dispute is not settled amiably, then within six months after it has arisen, investors may have recourse to arbitration. Except upon the parties' agreement to the contrary, it is submitted to ICSID. The German model convention contains no provision regarding the anticipatory agreement of the parties nor the exhaustion of means of recourse internally. Besides, there is no provision guaranteeing that investors may have recourse to the arbitration institution of their choice.

One can hope that German BIT's which are negotiated on the basis of that convention will nonetheless contain clauses that are favourable to investors. Besides, nothing should prevent investors from concluding a State contract with more favourable provisions.

For the settlement of investment disputes, the arbitral procedure of ICSID has been chosen. A distinction is made based on the membership of both or only one of the contracting States in ICSID. In the first case, the applicable clause reads as follows :

> "If the divergence cannot be settled within six months of the date when it has been raised by one of the parties in dispute, it shall, at the request of the investor of the other Contracting Party, be submitted to arbitration. Unless the parties in dispute agree otherwise, the divergence shall be submitted for arbitration under the convention of 18 March 1965 on the settlement of investment disputes between States and nationals of other States." (**Article 11.2**)

This provision has not been sufficiently developed. Following the German formula, the investor may ask for submitting the dispute to the arbitration of ICSID. However, the parties in dispute, the investor and the contracting State, may choose an institution other than ICSID.

Conceivably, the parties to the dispute may not reach agreement on the designation of the arbitration institute to decide on the dispute. Following the usual practice, each Contracting State to the BIT has given its advance consent to arbitration. The investor could, without explicit consent of the contracting State, choose freely an arbitration institute, ICSID or another institution, mentioned in the BIT. It is surprising that such clause has not been inserted in the German model convention. It should have been appropriate to leave to the investor the choice of calling on one of the mentioned institutions (ICSID, CCI, LCIA etc.).

The provision "the award shall be enforced in accordance with domestic law" (**Article 11.3**) is also vulnerable to criticism. This provision should be accompanied by a reference to international law. The application of the International Convention of New York is preferable to a mere reference to domestic law.

In the second hypothesis, when one of the Contracting States is not a member of the Washinton Convention, the eventual dispute will be submitted to an ordinary arbitration procedure. It is clearly stated that the nomination of arbitrators is done in conformity with the procedure provided for in article 10, concerning the solution of conflicts of interpretation. A special provision has been inserted for the case in which a contracting State, not a member of ICSID, should become a member of the convention of Washington, after the effective date of the BIT. In this case, the procedure of ICSID applies and, curiously, each contracting Party gives its advance consent to arbitration : "each Contracting Party herewith declares its acceptance of such a procedure". In the meanwhile, the members of the Washington Convention have created a special procedure (Additional facility rules) for the case in which only one contracting State is a member of ICSID. It is to be expected that in the meanwhile Germany shall have modified its position and that this special system will be followed.

6.3.7.6. *Interpretation of BIT's*

Conflicts concerning the interpretation of BIT's have been provided for in that they are to be submitted to an arbitral tribunal. The arbitrators are designated by the contracting States. The chairman of the tribunal is designated by the two nominated arbitrators. This classic formula is generally used in the European conventional practice. Nonetheless, the procedure for the nomination of arbitrators is rather complex, because it requires an approach to the President of the International court of Justice if the parties do not in fact make the required nominations. The procedure could be made more flexible if it provided for the most diligent party, in such a case, to call on the ICSID Secretary General.

6.3.8. – *India*

6.3.8.1. *Definitions*

Regarding moral persons, India deems investors to be Indian not only companies that are incorporated and established in accordance with Indian law but also companies established in a third country in accordance with the laws of such country, if at least fifty-one percent of their equity interest is owned by investors of one of the Contracting Parties.

The inconvenients and difficulties inherent to this formula are commented on further in Chapter VIII on "Control".

6.3.8.2. *Promotion and protection of investment*

Regarding investment protection, the Indian model convention states:

> "Each Contracting Party shall encourage and create favourable conditions for investors of the other Contracting party to make invest-

ments in its territory, and admit such investments in accordance with its laws and policy."

The term "policy" is rarely to be found in other countries' BIT's. It is rather vague and allows the host State to exclude investments in certain sectors of the economy. Other countries such as the USA and Canada include an Appendix to some of their BIT's containing a list of economic and industrial sectors where foreign investors are not admitted. In this formula, therefore, investors are warned beforehand. India could, on the contrary, put into place protectionist measures at any moment.

The text does not include any reference to international law principles and rules. Furthermore, there is no article concerning "particular contracts" or "State Contracts". There is therefore no "umbrella" clause possibility. In some BIT's, this lacuna has been partially filled as follows:

> "Other commitments: Each Contracting Party shall observe any obligation it may have entered into with regard to an investment of an investor of the other Contracting party. In relation to such obligations, dispute resolution under this article shall, however, only be applicable in the absence of normal local judicial remedies being available."

Such a provision certainly does not offer enough guarantees for investors. It impliedly waives arbitration since the host State evidently gives precedence to local tribunals and will always find some tribunal asserting jurisdiction over the matter. An article on "particular contracts" or "State Contracts" is therefore absolutely necessary. BIT negotiators would be well advised to demand the insertion of such a clause.

6.3.8.3. *Expropriation*

The valuation of expropriated assets is done on the basis of "genuine value". In the text relating to the settlement of disputes between investor and State, no mention is made of indemnification owed on account of expropriation. The only basis available is the term "any dispute" to support the conclusion that all litigation relating to an investment, including those relating to expropriated assets, may be submitted to arbitration. In any event, the expropriation article formally holds that the local tribunals have jurisdiction. It is therefore desirable to have included in the BIT an express clause stating that litigation concerning expropriated assets shall also be submitted to arbitration and, preferably, that the investor's choice shall determine this issue.

6.3.8.4. *Applicable law*

This article of the Indian model convention provides that investments are subject to the application of domestic law of each Contracting State. This is logical enough but the drafters have apparently forgotten the need to internationalise the transaction. Negotiators should try to insert in BIT's with India a clause stating that principles and rules of international law are also applicable.

6.3.9. – *Italy*

Italy's model treaty was first used in 2003. It differs from other European model conventions in several respects.

6.3.9.1. *Definitions*

Article 1 of the model reads as follows:

> "The term 'investor' shall mean any natural or legal person of a Contracting party investing in the territory of the other Contracting Party as well as any foreign subsidiaries, affiliates and branches, controlled in any way by the above natural and legal persons.
>
> The term 'legal person' with reference to either Contracting party, shall mean any entity having its head office in the territory of one of the Contracting parties and recognised by it, such as public institutions, corporations, partnerships, foundations and associations, regardless of wether their liability is limited or otherwise."

Similarly to the Netherlands and Switzerland, Italy has extended the notion of "investor" to include shareholders of one of the Contracting States holding evidence of participation in a corporation constituted in and established on the territory of a third State, so long as such corporation has made an investment on the other Contracting State. This definition is hardly better than that adopted by Switzerland and Sweden and suffers from the same ills and other observations made in relation to the BIT models of those countries.

Furthermore, all of these texts are contrary to the goal of the interstate agreement such as it is expressed in their Preambles :

> "Desiring to establish favourable conditions to enhance economic cooperation between the two Countries, and especially in regard to capital investments by investors of one Contracting Party in the territory of the other Contracting Party..."

The goal of these agreements is not to protect investments made in foreign territories, that is, territories of third party countries which are not parties to the applicable BIT. In fact, each Contracting Party considers as its "investor" a legal person having its "seat" in the territory of a non-Contracting State and holding the nationality of such State. This attitude does not fit well with international law. The foreign third State should take care to protect its own investors.

It is possible to elaborate a formula that, within the framework of a BIT, will protect triangular investments but the success or failure of such arrangement will depend on the consent of the State of the legal person controlled by investors of one of the Contracting states and who have made an investment on the territory of the other Contracting State. A joint action of the investor from a Contracting State and the foreign corporation controlled by this investor can be imagined but the organisms in charge of this corporation (Board, Executive Officers, etc.) should expressly consent to such action. Furthermore, it will, in actual practice, be necessary for the State of the foreign corporation also consent because it will be called on to defend the interests of all the shareholders of such corporation, and, in particular the shareholders who are nationals of such foreign State :

"All BIT's incorporating the notion of 'control' into their definitions refer to 'direct' and 'indirect' control or ownership. This method highlights an important aspect of these treaties – namely that they protect investment of nationals or companies of a contracting party, no matter how many corporate layers exist between the national or company and the investment. Consequently, more than one home country may exercise diplomatic protection (Vandevelde, 1992)"[86]

It does therefore matter, for a third State to be involved, that a link exist between the host State and investors of a corporation established under the laws of such third party State.

6.3.9.2. *Legal Treatment*

In connection with the "fair and equitable treatment" provisions, the Italian model has created the term "legal treatment":

> "Each Contracting Party shall create and maintain in its territory a legal framework capable of guaranteeing to investors the continuity *of legal treatment*, including compliance in good faith to all undertakings entered into with regard to each individual investor." (article II,4).

This provision refers to the national legislation of each of the Contracting States in connection with benefits granted to both national and foreign investors, as well as the respect due to the commitments made in regards of each individual investor. Like many other States, the standard of treatment is the national standard and the standard of the Most Favoured Nation. However, the concept of "investment" is broadened in the sense that the treatment of investors applies also to "activities connected with an investment". These activities have been defined as follows:

> "The term 'activities connected with an investment' shall include, *inter alia*, the organisation, control, operation, maintenance and disposal of companies, branches, agencies, offices or other organisations for the conduct of business, the access to the financial markets; the

---

[86] Http://www.unctad.org/en/docs/itëica 20065.

borrowing of funds, the purchase, sale and issue of shares and other securities and the purchase of foreign exchange for imports necessary to the conduct of business affairs; the marketing of goods and services; the procurement, sale and transport of raw and processed materials, energy, fuels and production means and the dissemination of commercial information."

This special provision is quite useful and allows for a much wider protection for investors.

6.3.9.3. *Expropriation*

The model includes a peculiar provision regarding the redemption of expropriated properties:

"If, after the expropriation, the expropriated investment does not serve the anticipated purpose, wholly or partially, the former owner or his/its assignee shall be entitled to repurchase it. The price of such expropriated investment shall be calculated with reference to the date on which the repurchasing takes place, adopting the same valuation criteria taken into account when calculating the compensation referred to in paragraph 3 of this article.

The just compensation shall be equivalent to the fair market value of the expropriated investment immediately prior to the moment in which the decision to nationalise or expropriate was announced or made public. Whenever there are difficulties in ascertaining the fair market value, it shall be determined according to the internationally acknowledged evaluation standards." (**Article V, para 3**).

One may wonder whether this provision will ever be called on in a practical context. It relates to one of the conditions of the model which must be met in order to lend a licit character to expropriation measures, in particular those taken for a public purpose. There may be difficulties of proof that an expropriation measure was in fact not taken in the public interest. Sometimes, the proof will be obvious. For example, should property have been expropriated for the construction of a motorway, and the authorities having jurisdiction over the project decide that the construction project must be cancelled, there ought to be little problem of proof. Actual circumstances will determine whether proof will be easy or not.

The Italian text is silent or incomplete as to the conditions of redemption. The basis for evaluation should be the market value, but it would have been helpful to stipulate that the market value is that in effect on the date of redemption. Furthermore, fairness dictates that there also be an indemnity for circumstances prior to the redemption which, eventually, may cause the redemption price to be less than the amount of indemnification received by the expropriated owner.

6.3.9.4. *Favourable treatment*

Investors are always entitled to receive the treatment which appears most favourable to them. If a national law of one of the Contracting Parties or an international agreement to which she is also a Party provides a more favourable treatment than that provided for in the BIT, investors may claim the most favourable treatment. Even if a "specific contract" has been entered into with an investor and provides for benefits greater than those provided for in the Italian BIT, the provisions of that "specific contract" will govern.

6.3.9.5. *Stabilisation clauses*

Even more important and special to the Italian model when compared to other models is the "stabilisation" clause protecting investors in the event of modifying investment legislation :

> "After the date when the investment has been made, any substantial modification in the legislation of the Contracting Party regulating directly or indirectly the investment shall not be applied retroactively and the investments made under this Agreement shall therefore be protected." (Article Xii, para 3)

6.3.9.6. *Settlement of Investment disputes*

The Italian model's settlement procedure has unique characteristics. Investors may choose between submittal of the dispute to the local tribunals that have jurisdiction; to an *ad hoc* arbitration tribunal acting according to UNCITRAL rules; or to IDSID created according to the rules of the Washington Convention. It is not absolutely certain that investors may submit their disputes to ICSID because of the added requirement that :

> "if or as soon as both Contracting Parties have acceded to it."

where "it" means the Washington Convention. The unique physiognomy of the Italian model is a result of its allowed choice of arbitration *ad hoc* :

> "In the event that such dispute cannot be settled as provided for in paragraph 1 of this article (consultations) within six months from the date of the written application for settlement, the investor in question may submit at his choice the dispute for settlement to :
> a) ...
> b) an *ad hoc* Arbitration Tribunal, in compliance with the arbitration regulation of the UN Commission on International Trade Law (UNCITRAL); the host Contracting party undertakes hereby to accept reference to said arbitration."

The anticipatory consent of the Contracting States is provided for *in expressis verbis*, a useful precaution but the innovative character of the Italian model is mostly the inclusion of a highly detailed UNCITRAL procedure, in line with the anticipatory selection of the Chamber of Commerce Paris/ Stockholm as the arbitration institution :

> "The arbitration Tribunal shall be composed of three arbitrators; if they are not nationals of either Contracting party, they shall be nationals of States having diplomatic relations with both Contracting Parties, appointed by the President of the Arbitration Institute of the Stockholm/Paris Chamber, in his capacity as Appointing Authority. The arbitration will take place in Stockholm/Paris, unless the two Parties in arbitration have agreed otherwise. When delivering its decision, the Arbitration Tribunal shall apply the provision contained in this Agreement, as well as the principles of international law recognised by the two Contracting Parties. Recognition and implementation of the arbitration decision in the territory of the Contracting parties shall be governed by their respective national legislation, in compliance with the relevant international Conventions they are parties to." (**Article X, para 4**)

It is rather interesting that a renowned arbitration institution has been anticipatorily chosen, which, in the event of a dispute, will be able to apply the UNCITRAL rules of arbitration and administer the management of the request for arbitration.

6.3.10. – *Netherlands*

The Dutch model convention form became law in 2004.

6.3.10.1. *Definitions*

In most BIT's, the term "investor" means physical persons (nationals, residents) and moral persons (corporations, companies, enterprises) but in the Dutch model, it is stated otherwise:

> "The term *'nationals'* shall comprise with regard to either Contracting Party:
> (i) natural persons having the nationality of that Contracting Party;
> (ii) legal persons constituted under the law of that Contracting Party;
> (iii) legal persons not constituted under the law of that Contracting Party but controlled, directly or indirectly, by natural persons as defined in (i) or by legal persons as defined in (ii)." (**Article 1**)

This formula has been used in recent bilateral agreements (f.i. the BIT with Cambodia dated 23 July 2007; the BIT with Bahrein dated 10 April 2007). However in the agreement dated 20 March 2007 with the Democratic and Popular Republic of Algeria, and that dated 10 June 2005 with Armenia, the Netherlands have returned to the classic and preferable definition, using "investors" as a generic term but making a distinction between physical persons (natural persons) and legal persons:

> "The term 'investors' shall comprise with regard to either contracting Party:
> (i) natural persons having the nationality of that Contracting State;
> (ii) legal persons constituted under the law of that contracting State;

(iii) legal persons not constituted under the law of that Contracting State but controlled, directly or indirectly in accordance with the law of one of the Contracting Parties and finally legal persons which are not constituted in accordance with the law of either contracting Party."

6.3.10.2. *Control*

As stated earlier, problems may arise for the last category of persons which are legal persons constituted in accordance with the law of a third party State, not a Contracting Party, but which are controlled by nationals or moral persons of one of the Contracting Parties. For clarification, the applicable portion of paragraph (iii) of the text could be amended to read:

> "Legal persons constituted under the law of a third State, not a Contracting Party, but controlled, directly or indirectly, by natural persons or legal persons of one of the Contracting Parties."

It is assumed 'control' in this subparagraph is that achieved either by investments made by nationals of one of the Contracting Parties into a third State, or inversely by nationals of the other Contracting State.

Including in BIT's a provision specific to the protection of shareholders is in response to a concern expressed by the International Court of Justice, namely, that, internationally, there are no norms of protection sufficient to protect shareholders:

> "Considering the important developments of the last century, the growth of foreign investments and the expansion of the international activities of corporations and considering the way in which the economic interests of States have proliferated, it may at first sight appear surprising that the evolution of law has not gone further and that no generally accepted rules have cristallised on the international plane..." [87]

BIT's specific norms on this topic were certainly progressive but there is a doubt that they sufficiently guaranteed the inter-

---

[87] *Bracelona Traction, Light and Power Company Limited*, op. cit., para 89/90, see footnote 15.

ests of shareholders in triangular investment situations. The Netherlands had entered into a BIT with Russia. A parent Dutch corporation had created a branch in Poland, which it controlled, and could thereby defend the interests of both the parent and the branch, should an expropriation occur. Poland, however, might very well invoke the principle of "*res inter alios acta*" and might want to defend, single handedly the interest of the Polish company. If there were a Poland/Russia BIT, joint protection could be considered, so long as there also were an agreement between Poland and the Netherlands.

There is yet another difficulty in the right of protection granted by way of convention to shareholders of a Contracting State of a corporation established on the territory of a third State. According to international law, the management organisms of a company are those that have jurisdiction over the interests of such company. A State may also grant its diplomatic protection to the company as such and not to its shareholders. Shareholders have their own rights as against the company of which they are shareholders and therefore can file lawsuits against such organisms. Without any specific norm, shareholders of a foreign company may not by themselves defend the interests of that company :

> "It is a basic characteristic of the corporate structure that the company alone, through its directors or management acting in its name, can take action in respect of matters that are of a corporate character. The underlying justification for this is that, in seeking to serve its own best interests, the company will serve those of the shareholder too. Ordinarily, no individual shareholder can take legal steps, either in the name of the company or in his own name... The shareholders' rights in relation to the company and its assets remain limited, this being, moreover, a corollary of the limited nature of their liability.
>
> A shareholder is bound to take account of the risk of reduced dividends, capital depreciation or even loss, resulting from ordinary commercial hazards or from prejudice caused to the company by illegal treatment of some kind." [88]

---

[88] *Electronica Sicula S.p.A (ELSI)*, Judgment International Court of Justice (I.C.J.), *Reports*, 1989, p. 84.

In our example, in the event of a Russian expropriation of the assets of the Polish company established on Russian territory, the parent Dutch company and the Dutch shareholders would probably not be able to defend the interests of the Polish company they controlled. The Polish Government as well as the Polish company could claim they preferred to protect the company located on Polish territory and that foreign shareholders did not have conventional 'just standi' because Poland was not a member of the Convention.

Besides, similar difficulties would arise in the event there were a dispute between Russia and the Polish company, controlled by Dutchmen. An arbitration procedure could not be filed by the Dutch investors-shareholders without the consent of the Dutch company and the government of Poland. To avoid interstate conflicts, a formula similar to the Belgium/China BIT should be included (cfr *infra* subtitle 8.5).

6.3.10.3. *Fair Treatment*

The usual treatment is guaranteed, the standard being the national standard and that of the most favoured nation. An additional provision, rarely found in other BIT's, reads as follows:

> "Each Contracting party shall observe any obligation it may have entered into with regard to investments of nationals of the other Contracting Party."

This is totally superfluous since by definition an obligation is to be met. Beyond that, the model provides as follows regarding the relationship between local investment law and BIT **Article 3.5**:

> "If the provisions of law of either Contracting Party or obligations under international law existing at present or established hereafter between the Contracting parties in addition to the present Agreement contain a regulation, whether general or specific, entitling investments by nationals of the other Contracting party to a treatment more favourable than is provided for by the present Agreement, such regu-

lation shall, to the extent that it is more favourable, prevail over the present Agreement."

This is a consolidation of the national standard of treatment, the Most Favoured Clause and international law obligations. Were investors to observe that a new law on investments were more favourable than the provisions of the BIT, they could demand the more favourable treatment under the national law. Were investors to observe that a new BIT with a third party country contained provisions more favorable than that under which the investors are operating, they could invoke the MFN clause to obtain the more favourable treatment.

Nonetheless, **Article 3.5** should not be deemed superfluous and useless. At the heart of the matter is the issue of proof. Whether the standard sought is the more favourable national treatment or the more favourable treatment of a third country's investors, the complaining investor must still prove the difference. His task is made easier by the presence of Article 3(5) because it allows him to refer to a legal text or the provisions of a specific agreement as his basis for comparison.

6.3.10.4. *Expropriation*

As previously stated, a Contracting State's right to expropriate is subject to the fulfillment of three conditions required under international law : a public interest must exist, the act of expropriation must not be discriminatory and fair compensation must be paid. The Dutch model addresses compensation as follows :

> "The measures are taken against just compensation. Such compensation shall represent the genuine value of the investments affected, shall include interest at a normal commercial rate until the date of payment and shall, in order to be effective for the claimants, be paid and made transferable, without delay, to the country designated by the claimants concerned and in the currency of the country of which

the claimants are nationals or in any freely convertible currency accepted by the claimants."

This provision bases the calculation of interest on the *"dies ad quem"* standard (i.e. the day until interest is to be paid) but is silent on the issue of *"dies a quo"*, i.e. the date on which interest begins to run. The following provision should be added :

"...shall include interest at a normal commercial rate from the date of expropriation to the date of payment."

6.3.10.5. *Subrogation*

Article 8 of the model reads :

"If the investments of a national of the one Contracting Party, are insured against non-commercial risks or otherwise give rise to payment of indemnification in respect of such investments under a system established by law, regulation or government contract, any subrogation of the insurer or re-insurer or Agency designated by the one Contracting party to the rights of the said national pursuant to the terms of such insurance or any other indemnity given shall be recognised by the other Contracting party."

This text is more adequate than that found in most other BIT's. Generally, other BIT's which provide for subrogation rights refer only to an insurance contract entered into by the investor with the State itself or a public agency of such State. The Dutch terminology : "if the investments are insured..." is silent on the identity of the insurer and therefore does not exclude a private insurer. This is quite valuable since the Washington Convention Centre does not acknowledge subrogation in favour of public insurers. The Dutch text, i.e. Article 8 of the model is more properly related to **Article 9** regarding disputes between the investor and the host State, under the terms of which investors must set the matter before the Washington Conference Arbitration Centre (ICSID) and has no other choice.

6.3.11. – *Norway*

The Norwegian model convention is one of the more recent ones and has a unique place in Europe, being structured more clearly on the US and Canadian models.

6.3.11.1. *Preamble*

With few exceptions, a genuine care for the protection of the environment within the framework of BIT's has not yet really surfaced. This is no doubt due to the notion that this question is better handled by specific agreements. However, Norway has demonstrated in the preamble of its model convention its preoccupation for the safety of a good environment :

> "Desiring to achieve these objectives in a manner consistent with the protection of health, safety, and the environment, and the promotion of internationally recognised labour rights."

In the body of the BIT's, it is stated that :

> "nothing in this Agreement shall be construed to prevent a Party from adopting or enforcing measures necessary for the protection of the environment."

6.3.11.2. *Application and Scope*

North American influence clearly shows in the provisions on this topic :

> "This Agreement applies to measures adopted or maintained by a Party, after the entry into force of this Agreement, relating to investors of the other Party or to investments of investors of the other Party."

As stated elsewhere, this formula has greater merit than the European formula. From a legal standpoint, the goal of BIT's is the protection of investors and investments against restrictive and compensable measures taken by the host State and its authorities. It would be useful to lend a conventional definition of investments but it is also desirable to state what is the object of the protection guaranteed by the BIT's. No European country, other than Norway, has provided in their BIT's an opening article entitled "Scope". Such a provision is not superfluous and should be included in all BIT's.

6.3.11.3. *Definitions*

Differing from normal European practice, a moral person must fill certain conditions before being considered as an "investor", in particular it must be:

> "established in accordance with, and recognised as a legal person by the law of a Party, and engaged in substantive business operations in the territory of that Party..."

Contrary to other countries, Norway specifies that, for an operation to qualify as an "investment", the following elements which are characteristic of investments must be present:

> "In order to qualify as an investment under this Agreement, an asset must have the characteristics of an investment, such as the commitment of capital or other resources, the expectation of gain or profit, or the assumption of risk."

6.3.11.4. *Treatment of Investments*

The most favoured nation treatment does not extend to the mechanisms provided for in the BIT for the solution of disputes relating to investments. This implies that a more favourable mechanism granted to a third State is not automatically applicable to an investor from the Contracting States, through the application of the most favoured nation clause.

There is a reference to international law:

> "Each party shall accord to investors of the other Party, and their investments treatment in accordance with customary international law, including fair and equitable treatment and full protection and security."

Regarding expropriation and nationalisation measures and indemnification, conformance with principles of international law is required.

6.3.11.5. *Performance Requirements*

The Contracting States agree not to require investors to comply with any limitation on their power to manage their investments, such as :

> "to export a given level of goods, to relate the volume of imports to the volume of exports, to restrict sales, to transfer technology etc."

There is, however, an exception in the case where public interest justifies measures of this kind but, in such a case, pre-existing investments shall not be affected by such measures.

6.3.11.6. *Key Personnel*

The Contracting States agree to grant residence permits to physical persons in the employment of investors and working in the enterprises which are located in the host State.

6.3.11.7. *Settlement of Investment Disputes*

Investments made before the entry into force of the BIT are covered but disputes that have arisen before such entry are excluded from the resolution mechanism provided for in the agreement. The arbitration tribunal which will eventually be established to decide a dispute between the host State and an investor must apply rules of interpretation of international law. Although there is no longer any reference to the Treaty of Vienna, it is clear that those are the applicable rules, augmented by the principles deriving from the jurisprudence of the International Court of Justice.

On the European level, an innovation in the model convention is the creation of a mixed Committee which has jurisdiction to interpret the provisions of the BIT and whose interpretation will be binding on the arbitration tribunal. The resolution mechanism for the settlement of Host State/Investor disputes includes special characteristics which differ from current international practice.

Legal investment disputes, based on a claim that the Contracting Party has breached an obligation under the Agreement may be submitted by the investor to the procedure provided for in the BIT, on condition that he has incurred loss or damage by the aforesaid breach. The first step in the procedure is for the parties to the dispute, the investor and the host State, to seek to resolve the dispute through consultation.

After failure of the parties' consultations, and after having exhausted any administrative remedies for a solution, the second step in the procedure is the submission of the dispute to a local court. The third step is the submission to arbitration of ICSID under the following conditions :

1° if agreement cannot be reached between the parties within 36 months from its submission to the court;

2° there is no other remedy available to provide effective redress of the dispute;

3° the investor has provided a clear and unequivocal waiver of any right to pursue the matter before local courts.

Although other European countries are totally silent on the topic, the Norwegian model convention provides that the arbitral Tribunal has the authority to accept and consider written *"amicus curiae"* submissions from a person or entity that is not a disputing party, provided that the Tribunal has determined that they are directly relevant to the factual and legal issues under consideration.

The Norwegian formula has a good number of defects. First, the obligation to have recourse to administratie authorities and then to local tribunals is a heavy burden. Were arbitration immediately available, the procedural costs could be lightened. The anticipatory consent of the parties to ICSID arbitration is provided for but investors do not have the choice and may not open a procedure before another arbitration tribunal.

6.3.11.8. *Subrogation*

As previously stated, difficulties can arise within the framework of an ICSID arbitration proceeding regarding the recognition of subrogation. The Norwegian model convention states:

> "If the investments of an investor are insured against non-commercial risks, any subrogation of the claims of the investor pursuant to this Agreement, shall be recognised by the other Party."

Investors do not necessarily have to be insured by a State organism but could enter into an insurance agreement with a private insurer. In such a case, ICSID could recognise the subrogation right. The legal aspect of subrogation is rather confused. The text does not expressly mention:

> "where a contracting party or its designated agency has guaranteed."

but does say:

> "if the investor's investments are insured".

The text therefore impliedly recognises ICSID's right to honour subrogation, avoiding problems in this regard. However, the text's Appendix C also states:

> "This annex applies to legal diputes between an insurer and a Contracting party, based on article 22 (subrogation) of this Agreement, provided that the insurer does not have legal standing under **Article 25(1)(1)** of the ICSID convention."

The Norwegian authorities therefore assume that ICSID will not recognise subrogation and provides for an *ad hoc* arbitration procedure in according with UNCITRAL rules. Besides, the notion of a "legal dispute between an insurer and a Contracting Party" is off the mark. Evidently, the Contracting Parties recognise subrogation conventionally. There could be a dispute between, on the one hand, an investor and his insurer, and, on the other, ICSID. This issue is rather complex and has been treated in greated depth in Chapter XIV entitled "Transfers and Subrogation."

6.3.11.9. *Joint Committee*

Other countries also provide for the creation of a mixed committee within the framework of their BIT's, composed of representatives of the Contracting Parties but no country other than Norway provides for a mixed commission given important and extensive powers. Considering the unusual character of the applicable text, it is quoted here *"in extenso"* :

> "The Joint Committee shall :
> i. supervise the implementation of this Agreement;
> ii. in accordance with Article [Disputes between the Parties], endeavour to resolve disputes that may arise regarding the interpretation or application of this Agreement;
> iii. review the possibility of further removal of barriers to investment;
> iv. where relevant, suggest to the Parties ways to enhance and promote investment action;
> v. review investments covered by this Agreement;
> vi. review case-law of investment arbitration tribunals relevant to the implementation of this Agreement;
> vii. oversee the further elaboration of this Agreement;
> viii. where relevant, discuss issues related to corporate social responsibility, the preservation of the environment, public health and safety, the goal of sustainable development, anticorruption, employment and human rights; and
> ix. consider any other matter that may affect the operation of this Agreement.
>
> Where appropriate, the Joint Committee may :
> i. decide to amend the Agreement, as set forth in Article [Amendments]; and
> ii. interpret this Agreement, hearing in mind that this competence shall not be used to undermine the amendment provisions of Article [Amendments]. The Joint Committee should refrain from adopting interpretations of provisions already established.

This formula deserves to be emulated by other countries. In particular, institutionalising the possibility of entering into negotiations with respect to amendment of the BIT would be ~~is~~ most interesting. That could be an opportunity to bring into play the evolving arbitration jurisprudence regarding BIT interpretation.

6.3.11.10. *Exceptions*

Norway is one of the very few European countries that lists as many exceptions to limit the application of its BIT's:

a) general exceptions: the Contracting Parties may, for instance, take measures to maintain public order and for the protection of environment;
b) prudential regulation: measures may be taken to ensure the integrity and stability of the financial system, or to enhance market competition;
c) security exceptions: any Party may take any action which it considers necessary for the protection of its essential security interests, relating to investment in defence and security sectors;
d) cultural exceptions: the provisions of the Agreement shall not apply to measures specifically designed to preserve and promote linguistic and cultural diversity.

6.3.12. – *Russia*

Russian policy will be examined on the basis of a number of BIT's. Differences with other European BIT's will be highlighted.

6.3.12.1. *Definitions*

The term "investment" in the Russian model is comparably defined as in other European practice except that indirect investments are not covered. Regarding moral persons, a combination of the seat theory and of the place of incorporation theory is applied exceptionally. Thus the Cyprus/Russian Federation BIT, dated 11 April 1997 reads as follows :

> "Investor shall mean any legal person constituted or incorporated in accordance with the legislation of that Contracting party and having its seat in its territory.."

In addition, the moral person must be authorised to make investments on the territory of the host State. Regarding physical persons, the concept of "residence" which used to appear in USSR agreements, has now been replaced by the notion of citisenship.

6.3.12.2. *Treatment*

The convention includes an agreement to give investors "fair and equitable treatment". The host State is to respect this obligation in the event treatment is at least equal to that provided national investors or those of a third State. Furthermore, any discriminatory measure is excluded.

The Egypt/Russian Federation agreement dated 23 September 1997, contains an important restriction in this regard. It is not contrary to the notion of "fair and equitable treatment" to exclude investors from some sectors :

> "Each of the Contracting Parties shall reserve the rights to determine the branches of the economy and spheres of activity, in which activity by foreign investors is excluded or restricted."

However, there is no reference to the application of international law, an important shortcoming. Negotiators would be well advised to try to include such a reference in their BIT's since it contributes to the internationalisation of rights and obligations provided for in the conventions.

6.3.12.3. *Expropriation*

Measures of expropriation or nationalization may be undertaken only when the following conditions of international law are met :

"public interest, due process of law, non-discriminatory, effective compensation."

The bases for the calculation of indemnification vary: real value, market value, actual value. In the Norway/Russian Federation BIT (1995), there is no other specification:

> "Such compensation shall amount to the value of the investments immediately before the date of expropriation and shall be paid without delay and shall after two months from the date of expropriation until the date of payment include interest at a commercial rate established on a market basis."

It is unfortunate that, although the *"dies a quo"* and the *"dies ad quem"* are specified for the payment of interest, none is stated for the payment of indemnification. The text of the Netherlands/Russian Federation BIT, dated 5 October 1989, has yet another, greater disadvantage, since it contains no such provision at all:

> "The measures are accompanied by provisions for the payment of just compensation. Such compensation shall represent the real value of the investments affected and shall, in order to be effective for the claimants, be paid and made freely transferable without delay, in any freely convertible currency accepted by the claimants."

It is obvious that the term "without undue delay" offers no guarantee whatsoever for investors. A statement as to *"dies a quo"* and *"dies ad quem"* is indispensable. Exceptionally, the Hungary/Russian Federation BIT dated 5 March 1995 states:

> "The investor whose investments were expropriated shall have the right, under the laws and regulations of the Contracting party making the expropriation, to prompt review, by a judicial or other independent authority of that Contracting Party, of his or its case and the valuation of his or its investment, in accordance with the principles set out in paragraph 1 of this article."

It is open to question whether investors will want to have recourse to local tribunals. As already stated above, there are some doubts as to the feasibility of appealing to any arbitration mechanism including that provided by the convention:

"any dispute which may arise between an investor of one Contracting Party and the other Contracting Party."

Actually, there are no details on this topic in Article 8 of the aforesaid agreement between Hungary and Russia. There are likewise no details regarding the submittal of either disputes submitted to arbitration regarding compensation for expropriated assets or other disputes, likewise submitted, regarding investments.

When the USSR was in existence, negotiators were conscious of this problem. Article 10 of the Germany/Russia BIT dated 13 June 1987 states as follows:

> "(1) Disputes relating to investments between one Contracting Party and an investor of the other Contracting party shall, as far as possible, be settled amicably between the parties to the dispute.
>
> (2) If a dispute relating to the amount of compensation or the method of its payment, in accordance with article 4 of this agreement, or to freedom of transfer, in accordance with article 5 of this Agreement, is not settled within six months from the time when a claim is made by one of the parties to the dispute, either party to the dispute shall be entitled to refer the matter to an international, arbitral tribunal.
>
> (3) The procedure provided for in paragraph 2 of this article shall apply also to the disputes relating to matters which the parties to the dispute have agreed to submit to arbitration."

Unfortunately, anticipatory consent to arbitration has not been provided expressly but, in any event, this text allows the investor to have recourse to arbitration for "any dispute" relating to an investment including "compensation disputes in case of expropriation". Fortunately, as will appear in the next paragraph, there are more recent BIT's where the German model has been followed.

6.3.12.4. *Settlement of Disputes*

Russia is not a member of ICSID Convention regarding the International Centre for the Setttlement of Investment Disputes. For conducting arbitration, the convention has recourse to arbitration *ad hoc* or to institutional arbitration.

Normally the Arbitration Institute of the Chamber of Commerce in Stockholm, has jurisdiction. Before introduction of an arbitration procedure, the parties to the dispute must try to settle it through negotiations. If there is no solution within six months, arbitration is possible. The host State's anticipatory consent to arbitration does not appear in the BIT's. The text of the aforesaid BIT with Hungary states as follows:

> "If the dispute between an investor of one Contracting Party and the other Contracting Party cannot be settled within a period of six months from the date it arose, the investor shall be entitled to submit the case to ...arbitration."

This is hardly the equivalent of anticipatory consent. Actually, such consent must be expressly mentioned in the document, thus:

> "Each Contracting Party hereby consents to the submission of disputes to arbitration."

Exceptionally, the Dutch/Russian Federation BIT dated 5 October 1989 does contain an anticipatory consent clause but the text has other disadvantages. It states as follows:

> "(1) all disputes between a Contracting Party and an investor of the other Contracting party concerning an investment of the latter shall if possible be settled amicably.
>
> (2) Disputes concerning the amount or procedure of payment of compensation (expropriation)... may be referred by the investor to international arbitration or conciliation.
>
> (3) Each Contracting party hereby consents to the submission of disputes as referred to in paragraph 2 of this article to international arbitration or conciliation."

This text lacks precision. A textual interpretation leads to the conclusion that only litigation relating to indemnification for expropriated assets are to be submitted to arbitration. It is difficult to believe that such was the intention of the Contracting Parties.

In two other BIT's (Cyprus/Russia and Egypt/Russia), a clearer and more adequate text has been inserted:

> "In case of any dispute between a Contracting Party and an investor of the other Contracting party, arising in connection with a capital investment, including disputes concerning the amount, the terms or the procedure for the payment of compensation..."

Any such litigation may therefore be submitted to arbitration. The text also states, for the case where the litigation cannot be resolved by negotiation, that it shall be passed for consideration, at the investor's choice to:

> "a) a competent court or arbitration court of the Contracting Party, on whose territory the capital investments have been carried out;
>
> b) an *ad hoc* arbitration court, in conformity with the Arbitration regulations of the United Nations Commission on international trade law (UNCITRAL)."

It is unfortunate that the text is silent as to the host State's anticipatory consent. Actually, the investor's choice of venue in the submittal to institutional arbitration or arbitration *ad hoc* does not suffice. If, when the dispute arises, the host State does not expressly give its consent, there will be no arbitration.

6.3.13. – *Sweden*

6.3.13.1. *Definitions*

Sweden has also included in its model convention a definition of "investor" much along the lines adopted by Switzerland. However, Sweden makes it a practice to include this definition verbatim in its BIT's.

Article 1 regarding definitions sets forth under subparagraph (2) the concept of "investor":

> "The term 'investor' of a Contracting Party shall mean:
> (a) any natural person who is a national of that Contracting Party in accordance with its law, and

(b) any legal person or other organisation organised in accordance with the law applicable in that Contracting State, and

(c) any legal person not organised under the law of that Contracting Party but controlled by an investor as defined under (a) and (b)."

Subparagraph (c) is somewhat more limited in scope than the corresponding provision in the Swiss model convention (see *infra*), reading:

> "legal entities established under the law of any country which are, directly or indirectly, controlled by nationals of that Contracting Party or by legal entities having their seat, together with real economic activities, in the territory of that Contracting Party."

According to UNCTAD experts, the aim is to include companies that have been established under the laws of a third State not party to the BIT, but controlled by nationals (physical and moral persons) of one of the Contracting Parties:

> "The incorporation of the notion of control into BIT's may be better understood in the light of the decision of the International Court of Justice (ICJ) in the *Barcelona Traction, Light and Power Co., Ltd.* Case. In this dispute, the Court held that a company has the nationality of the country in which it is incorporated and that only the latter has the right of diplomatic intervention on behalf of the enterprise. Thus, the ICJ held that the Belgian Government was not entitled to protect the Spanish interests of a company incorporated in Canada but owned principally by Belgians" (private archives).

The terminology used (in subparagraph (c)) is noteworthy. An investment made by an investor from one of the Contracting Parties, consisting of the purchase of shares or other securities of stock participation issued by a corporation established on the territory of the other Contracting Party is also to be deemed an indirect investment. The "link" between the investment and the investor is in that the investment happens to be located on the territory of one of the Contracting Parties and the investor is from the other Contracting Party.

Protection is extended to these indirect investments, without any specific clause relating thereto other than the BIT definition of "investment". Article 1 subparagraph (c) also covers the situation where the link established between investor and his investment involves three States. Two of them are Contracting Parties. There is a third State, not a Contracting Party, on whose territory an investor from one of the Contracting Parties had made an investment in a company which, in turn, made investments in the territory of the host, i.e. the other Contracting State. These so-called triangular transactions (cfr *infra*) are increasingly likely to occur. The terms, therefore, used for the definition of "investment" and "investor" must be adapted to fit the type of transaction considered. For example, the language:

> "Any legal person not organised under the law of that Contracting Party but controlled by an investor as defined under a) and b)"

could be replaced by:

> "Any legal person organised under the law of a third country controlled by an investor of one of the Contracting Parties."

As previously stated, it is assumed 'control' in the foregoing subparagraph is that achieved either by investments made by nationals of one of the Contracting Parties into a third State, or inversely by nationals of the other Contracting State.

From the above it is clear that, in its present condition, the Swedish formula is not failproof. Under it, the third country concerned could claim not to be bound by the BIT providing for the protection of triangular investments. The claim would be based on the principle of "res inter alios acta". The third country could invoke its proper right to extend diplomatic protection to its national, a company established on its territory. This result would obtain, even though this company is controlled by foreign investors. Should there be no BIT between the third State and the State of the controlling company, no rule exists to justify special protection for triangular investments:

> "It is essentially bilateral relations which have been concerned, relations in which the rights of both the State exercising diplomatic protection and the State in respect of which protection is sought have

had to be safeguarded. Here as elsewhere, a body of rules could only have developed with the consent of those concerned. The difficulties encountered have been reflected in the evolution of the law on the subject. Thus, in the present state of law, the protection of shareholders requires that recourse be had to treaty stipulations or special agreements directly concluded between the private investor and the State in which the investment is placed. States ever more frequently provide for such protection in both bilateral and multilateral relations, either by means of special instruments or within the framework of wider economic arrangements [89].

Obviously, some sort of interstate concurrence is required. Had there been, in the Barcelona Traction case a BIT between Spain and Belgium, and another BIT between Belgium and Canada, providing for the protection of triangular investments, on the basis of the control theory, there would probably have been no problems.

Interstate conflicts are to be avoided whenever possible. There is, however, another solution. The China/Belgium BIT [90] provides a formula providing for the protection of triangular investments by investors of the Contracting State of the controlling company, in the event that the third State (not a Contracting Party) refuses or neglects to exercise its protection to the company in the host State.

In this situation too, the "res inter alios acta" principle could be invoked but the arbitrators or judges could take the refusal to protect as an element in reaching their decision allowing the protection by the controlling company's State. [91]

6.3.13.2. *Expropriation*

In the definition of "investment" no reference is made to minority participations of investors from one of the Contracting Parties in a company situated on the territory of the other Contracting Party. To correct this hiatus, an amend-

---

[89] *Barcelona Traction Light and Power Cy Limited, op. cit.*, p. 47, see footnote 15.
[90] *Journal official belge*, 16/09/1986, p. 12517.
[91] Until now there have been no arbitral decisions in this matter.

ment similar to the Swiss model convention provision, rarely found elsewhere, could be used for the Swedish model:

> "Where a Contracting party expropriates the assets of a company or an enterprise in its territory in which investors of the other Contracting party have an investment, including through the ownership of shares, it shall ensure that the provisions of this article are applied to the extent necessary to guarantee prompt, adequate and effective compensation in respect of their investment to such investors of the other Contracting party." (**Article 4**)

6.3.13.3. *Settlement of Investment disputes*

The usual formula was adopted. However, differing from provisions appearing in most other BIT's, investors may choose between "conciliation and arbitration". The disadvantages of this choice have already been pointed out in an earlier chapter. On the other hand, Sweden has included a very useful provision regarding consent to arbitration, seldom seen elsewhere:

> "The consent given by each Contracting Party in paragraph (2) and the submission of a dispute by an investor under the said paragraph shall constitute the written consent and the written agreement of the parties to the dispute to its submission for settlement for the purposes of Chapter II of the Washington Convention (Centre's jurisdiction) and for the purpose of the Additional Facility Rules, Article 1 of the UNCITRAL Arbitration Rules and Article II of the New York Convention." (**Article 8 (5)**)

It is a good idea to make it clear that the anticipatory consent of the Contracting Parties conforms to the requirements of the Washington Convention.

6.3.14. – *Switzerland*

6.3.14.1. *Preamble*

Generally speaking, most States do not manifest much concern about the bonds between international investment and international commerce. Bilateral agreements are viewed as legal documents which are primarily beneficial for nationals of one State investing on the territory of another Contracting state. Switzerland, however, like Canada, seems to be convinced that interaction exists between international investments and international commerce:

> "Switzerland's network of treaties on trade and investment is remarkably dense, extended and dynamic for a country which, after all, is relatively small. Whereas statistics cannot establish accurately a direct relationship between these treaties and Switzerland's external economy, the robustness or the latter strongly suggests that this network contributes to create and to sustain a favourable trade environment" [92]

6.3.14.2. *Definitions*

There is no uniformity of definitions of the term "investor". Article 1 of the model Swiss convention reads as follows:

> "The term 'investor' refers with regard to either Contracting Party to
> a) natural persons who, according to the law of that Contracting Party, are considered to be its nationals;
> b) legal entities, including companies, corporations, business associations and other organisations, which are constituted or otherwise duly organised under the laws of that Contracting Party and have their seat, together with real economic activities, in the territory of that same Contracting party;
> c) legal entities established under the law of any country which are, directly or indirectly, controlled by nationals of that Contracting party or by legal entities having their seat, together with real economic activities, in the territory of that Contracting Party."

Actually, four theories about investors are revealed in this definition. The theories concern the "nationality" of a corporation, which as explained in another Chapter, are or have become so fluid as to be nearly meaningless, the theory of the "seat", the theory of the "place of incorporation" and the theory of "control". In a practical sense, however, this model

---
[92] LIEBESKIND, Jean-Christophe, "The legal framework of Swiss International Trade and Investments", Part II, Protection, *The Journal of World Investment and Trade*, Geneva, 2006, Vol. 7, n° 4, p. 491.

convention formula, or combination of formulae, is not always observed in Swiss BIT's. In a rather old treaty, with Malaysia, dated 9 June 1978, the term "investor" was replaced by the term "corporations":

> "The term 'corporations' means:
> a) insofar as the Swiss Confederation is concerned, collectivities, establishments or foundations endowed with a legal personality as well as limited joint companies and shareholding companies, as well as any other community of persons not so endowed but established in accordance with Swiss law or in which Swiss nationals have directly or indirectly a dominant interest..." (**Article 2** of the Swiss BIT)

In more recent treaties, there are no longer any references to "legal entities" that do not have a legal personality. Years after 1978, Switzerland has returned to the formula which is generally used in international practice, where corporate investors are so-called "moral" or non-physical persons, hence corporations that do have a legal "personality".

In some Swiss BIT's, both the "seat" and the "control" theories are used:

> "With respect to each of the Contracting Parties, the term 'investor' means:
> (a) physical persons who, in accordance with the respective Contracting Party, are considered to be its nationals;
> (b) moral persons established in accordance with the legislation of such Contracting Party and which have their seat on its territory, or moral persons who, directly or indirectly, are controlled by nationals of such Party or by moral persons established under the laws of such Party and which have their seat on its territory."
> (Article 1 of the Switzerland/Guatemala BIT dated 9 September 2002)

The text of paragraph (b) is not too clear, possibly incorrect. The words "moral persons established in accordance with the legislation of such Contracting Party and which have their seat on its territory" are repeated without any indication as to any difference in their interpretation. Furthermore, the words "moral persons who, directly or indirectly, are controlled by nationals of such Party" can apparently be interpreted only to refer to corporations established in a third State but do not otherwise unambiguously confirm this interpretation.

The flaws in the Guatemala/Switzerland BIT have been corrected in the Switzerland/Algeria BIT dated 30 November 2004 :

> "With respect to each of the Contracting Parties, the term 'investor' means :
> (a) physical persons who, in accordance with the legislation of such Contracting Party, are considered its nationals;
> (b) legal entities, including corporations, registered companies, personal companies and other organisations which have been created or organised in any other way in accordance with the laws of such Party, and which have their seat as well as substantial economic activities on the territory of such Party;
> (c) legal entities which have not been established in accordance with the legislation of such Party but which are effectively controlled by physical or moral persons respectively in accordance with subparagraphs (a) and (b) of this paragraph." (**Article 1**)

The text of subparagraph (c) is somewhat clearer than the corresponding text in the Switzerland/Guatemala Treaty. It is apparent that it does not refer to companies locally established in the territories of the Parties, but companies established in third party countries, such as one that is not a Contracting Party to the BIT. This would also result from the application of the text of the model convention form :

> "legal entities established under the laws of any country."

In a very recent BIT, entered into between Switzerland and the Republic of Azerbäidjan, a more simple formula has been used :

> "For each of the Contracting Parties, the term 'investor' means.... Moral persons established in conformity with the legislation of such Party." (Article 1)

Thus, no further reference is made about the control "element" to distinguish this concept from *"control theory"* as used in nationality provisions. In the Swiss BIT texts quoted, the term *"control element"* has been coined to serve to determine whether a company established on the territory of a third State, not a party to the BIT, could nonetheless benefit to the same extent from the BIT's protection, if investors from one of the Contracting Parties exercise control over such third party company.

6.3.14.3. *Control*

A clearer expression of the "control theory" is to be found in Article 8 of the Azeri BIT, regarding the settlement of disputes between one of the Contracting Parties and an investor from the other Contracting Party :

> "A Company registered or established in accordance with laws in force on the territory of one of the Contracting Parties, which, before the dispute arose, was controlled by investors of the other Contracting Party, will be deemed, in the sense of **Article 25(2)(b)** of the Washington Convention, a corporation of the other Contracting Party."

Normally, a local company, established in an LDC by an investor from a developed country may not file an arbitration request against the host State on the basis of the BIT binding both countries. This specific clause, provides that such company, because of the control exercised on it by an investor of the other Contracting Party, has its nationality changed for the purposes of the dispute's arbitration and obtains the nationality of the foreign investors. This makes it possible for arbitration to occur between the host State and the foreign investors' local company, controlled by them. The local company is thus endowed with a conventional nationality in order to facilitate its recourse to arbitration.

The Azeri formula has also been used in the BIT between Switzerland and Serbia/Montenegro dated 7 December 2005. There is reason to believe that this formula will become the *"quod plerumque fit"* in Swiss practice.

6.3.14.4. *Scope*

Changes have also been made in the scope of the Swiss BIT's. The present agreement is applicable to investments made on the territory of one of the Contracting Parties, which are held or controlled, directly or indirectly, by investors from the other Contracting Party. It applies to investments made before or after this Agreement's date of entry into force but does not apply to disputes relative to events which arose before such date (**Article 2** of Azeri and Serbian BIT's).

Previously, BIT's provided that they applied always, whether for investments made before the BIT's date but still operative on the date the BIT came into force, or for investments made after such date. A limitation has now been introduced, in the sense that, even though the new BIT still applied to previous investments, the provisions of the new BIT relative to disputes arising from such previous investments do not apply to disputes arising from such previous investments. As a result, such disputes may not be submitted to arbitration under the new system.

There is yet another limitation in the application of the BIT with Guatemala dated 9 September 2002:

> "The present agreement is applicable to investments made on the territory of a Contracting Party, in accordance with its laws and regulations, by investors from the other Contracting Party, before or after its entry into force. It is, however, not applicable to claims arising from events occurring prior to such date."

These limitations may have dubious practical value. There are other Swiss BIT's which have application to the Guatemala agreement and which contain no such limitations to investments made before or after the entry of such BIT into force.[93] It is already known that, in nearly all BIT's, there is an MFN clause, which an investor could invoke to support

---
[93] Article 6 of the Switzerland/Lithuania BIT dated 23 December 1992.

the application of the Guatemala BIT to claims arising from events prior to its entry into force. To avoid this possibly unintended consequence, the Contracting Parties should expressly agree that the MFN clause is not applicable to such claims.

Some of the consequences flowing from this distinction are taken up under the "Settlement of Disputes" paragraph of this part.

6.3.14.5. *Expropriation*

In the definition of "investments", no reference has been made to minority participations from investors of one of the Contracting Parties in a company on the territory of the host State. Switzerland has not included in its model an appropriate provision, seldom to be found in other model conventions :

> "When a Contracting Party expropriates the assets of a company or an enterprise in its territory in which investors of the other contracting Party have an investment, including through the ownership of shares, it shall ensure that the provisions oif this Article are applied to the extent necessary to guarantee prompt, adequate and effective compensation to such investors of the other contracting Party."
> (**Article 4**)

6.3.14.6. *Settlement of Investment disputes*

The Swiss model convention deviates in several respects from the classical formula as written in other model treaties. The provision for consent to arbitration is one of them that may be deemed flawed. It states :

> "If these consultations do not result in a solution within six months from the date of request for consultation and if the investor concerned give a written consent, the dispute shall be submitted to the International Centre for Settlement of Investment Disputes (ICSID)."
> Article 9 (2)

This provision is included in the Swiss/Lithuania BIT. However, it happens quite often that LDC's try to avoid arbitration procedures and refuse to consent. That is why Contracting States take precautionary measures and require that each of the contracting Parties give its consent anticipatorily to arbitration filed on behalf of the investor:

> "In the absence of an amicable settlement by direct agreement between the parties to the dispute or by conciliation through diplomatic channels within six months from the notification, the dispute shall be submitted, at the option of the investor, either to the competent jurisdiction of the State where the investment was made or to international arbitration:
>
> To this end, each Contracting Party agrees in advance and irrevocably to the settlement of any dispute by this type of arbitration. Such consent implies that both Parties waive he right to demand that all domestic administrative or judiciary remedies be exhausted." [94]

In negotiations based on the model, Swiss negotiators have realised the extent of the flaw. In several of their bilateral agreements, a provision has been included, saying:

> "Each of the contracting Parties gives its unconditional and irrevocable consent to the submission to international arbitration of any and all dispute relative to an investment." (Serbia/Montenegro, Azerbaîdjian, Algeria, Guatema BIT's)

6.3.14.7. *Diplomatic Protection under the Swiss Model*

When a BIT has been entered into between two Contracting States, the question is often asked whether the investor may still contact his own State and ask for diplomatic intervention. Whether he may or not depends on the modalities and the scope of diplomatic interventions.

In Swiss doctrine, a distinction is made between diplomatic support and diplomatic protection. Diplomatic protection, *"stricto sensu"* is the most extreme of the two, in that it may involve the filing of an arbitration request with an international judiciary tribunal:

---

[94] Article 12 Belgian model treaty.

> "Diplomatic protection is an international law customary institution by which a Sovereign state is entitled to claim that the violation of international law towards its nationals by another State be repaired... and unlike in the case of diplomatic support, there is a novation and the State is vested with the rights of its citizen, by which the State is asserting its own right. There is a substitution of a private person by a subject of international law."[95]

That is, of course, an exceptional occurrence as well as a political decision. States will not easily initiate such action and will do so only when public interest is involved. One example is the litigation between Belgium and Spain which was filed with the International Court of Justice in 1970.[96]

In this *last* case, Canada was unwilling to defend an important group of Belgian nationals from the taking of property by Spanish authorities. The Belgian State considered that protection was required under international law and started a judiciary procedure before the International Court of Justice, because it was convinced that public interest rather than purely personal interests of the investors was at stake.

Diplomatic support or help is a classic action in international relations. The State may give instructions to its diplomatic and consular posts to intervene in favour of its nationals in order to defend or protect their interests in the event they might be unduly harmed by the foreign State:

> "By diplomatic support, is meant here diplomatic protection '*lato sensu*' or informed diplomatic protection. As noted above, unlike in the case of diplomatic protection, in this case, the supporting state is not vested with all the rights of its citizen."[97]

The legitimacy of diplomatic support or help is generally recognised in international relations. In the non-judiciary phase, diplomatic support may occur, when a dispute arises

---

[95] LIEBESKIND, Jean-Christophe, *op. cit.*, p. 487, see footnote 92.
[96] *Barcelona Traction Light and Power Company Limited*, *op. cit.*, p. 3, see footnote 15.
[97] LIEBESKIND, Jean-Christophe, *op. cit.*, p. 474, see footnote 92.

between investors and the host State. This is confirmed in most model conventions and also in that of Switzerland :

> "For the purpose of solving disputes with respect to investments between a Contracting Party and an investor of the other Contracting Party... consultations will take place between the parties concerned." (article 8(1))

As soon as this dispute is submitted to international arbitration, both the diplomatic protection (*stricto sensu* – judicial action) and the diplomatic protection (*lato sensu* – diplomatic support) are excluded. According to a principle of generally accepted international law, diplomatic interventions are not allowed, once the matter has been submitted to a judge having jurisdiction. A judicial action by a Contracting State in favour of an investor or group of investors is likewise excluded, in as much as the Contracting States have acknowledged in the BIT the investor's right to have recourse to international arbitration :

> "If these consultations do not result in a solution within six months from the date of request for consultation and if the investor concerned gives a written consent, the dispute shall be submitted to the International Centre for the Settlement of Investment Disputes (ICSID), instituted by the Convention of Washington of March 18, 1965, for the settlement of disputes regarding investments between States and nationals of other States."

An investor therefore has the right to waive a direct action by his State and may himself file a procedure before an international arbitration body. In Swiss doctrine, this is called the "diagonal" provision :

> "The distinctive feature of Swiss bilateral investment treaty (BIT) dispute resolution mechanism as from the 1980's is that they contain not only horizontal (valid between States) but, in particular, diagonal arbitration clauses, thus enabling investors to claim directly against the host State. Therefore BIT's systematically distinguish disputes between State Parties, on the one hand, and between State party and investor, on the other hand."[98]

---

[98] LIEBESKIND, Jean-Christophe, *op. cit.*, p. 474, see footnote 92.

Differently from other countries, Switzerland expressly refers to diplomatic intervention:

> "Neither Contracting Party shall pursue through diplomatic channels a dispute submitted to the Centre, unless:
>
> The Secretary General of the Centre or a Commission of Conciliation or an arbitral tribunal decide that the dispute is beyond the jurisdiction of the Centre, or,
>
> The other Contracting Party does not abide by or comply with the award rendered by an arbitral tribunal." (Article 8(4))

The use of the term "diplomatic channels" shows that Switzerland is referring to diplomatic support. This support is possible as long as the dispute has not yet been submitted to arbitration and also afterwards, should the host State ordered to pay compensation fails to comply with the decision.

The Swiss provision may be compared to article 27 of the Washington Convention:

> "(1) No Contracting state shall give diplomatic protection, or bring an international claim, in respect of a dispute which one of its nationals and another Contracting state shall have consented to submit or shall have submitted to arbitration under this Convention, unless such other contracting State shall have failed to abide by and comply with the award rendered in such dispute.
>
> (2) Diplomatic protection, for the purpose of paragraph (1), shall not include informal diplomatic exchanges for the sole purpose of facilitating a settlement of the dispute."

It is appropriate to interpret this text correctly. Paragraph (2) only applies when paragraph (1) has been exhausted. As stated before, neither judicial action nor diplomatic support are possible during an arbitration procedure.

Diplomatic assistance will again become available when it appears that the State ordered to pay compensation does not respect the decision.

6.3.14.8. *Conciliation and arbitration*

In order not to add unnecessary weight to the settlement procedure, most Contracting States do not usually call on the conciliation procedure and prefer a direct recourse to arbitration. In the Swiss BIT's, investors have a choice between conciliation and arbitration:

> "Should the parties disagree on whether the conciliation or arbitration is the most appropriate procedure, the investor shall decide."

The main difference between the two procedures is evidently that conciliation's only result is a written statement by the conciliators that there has or there has not been a compromissory solution to the dispute:

> "If the parties reach agreement, the Commission shall draw up a report noting the issues in dispute and recording that the parties have reached agreement. If, at any stage of the proceedings, it appears to the Commission that there is no likelihood of agreement between the parties, it shall close the proceedings and shall draw up a report noting the submission of the dispute and recording the failure of the parties to reach agreement." (**Article 34** Washington Convention)

An arbitration procedure ends in the issuance of a decision, duly entered and recorded:

> "The award of the Tribunal shall be in writing and shall be signed by the members of the tribunal who voted for it... The award shall be binding on the parties and shall not be subject to any appeal or to any other remedy except those provided for in this Convention."

It is therefore understandable why most countries provide for arbitration only in their BIT's. Consultations conducted prior to the filing of a proceeding might not end up in a compromise and it will then be unlikely that a conciliation procedure will succeed where consultations did not. Should conciliation be attempted and fail, the parties must then also consider the possibility of having to file an arbitration procedure.

Investors who opt for a conciliation procedure before engaging in arbitration proper, will be aware of the risk inherent to their choice, because, if neither the consultations nor the conciliation succeed, the whole matter, including arbitration may be delayed years. Many would conclude that a tri-phasic process (consultation, conciliation, arbitration) may not be the best solution and that it may be far better to skip conciliation altogether.

6.3.15. – *United Kingdom of Greaty Britain and Northern Ireland*

6.3.15.1. *Definitions*

6.3.15.1.1. *Nationality*

The United Kingdom of Great Britain and Ireland (UK) is also using a model convention, for the design and negotiation of BIT's. A physical person has a natural existence. A company has exclusively a legal existence. A company is endowed with legal personality – i.e. the quality of being a person – on the ground of the law. The founders of a company conform to the law of their choice. By the choice of the applicable law, a company is incorporated in the legal system of the chosen State. The company is then deemed to receive the nationality of this State but we have seen that this "nationality" is quite different from that of an ordinary physical citizen.

Like the USA, China, Russia and some Latino-American countries, the UK applies the theory of incorporation for the determination of the nationality of a company. In the UK model convention, a company is first defined following the theory of its establishment (hereafter "incorporation"):

> "Companies means:
> in respect of the United Kingdom: corporations, firms and associations incorporated or constituted under the law in force in any part of the United Kingdom or in any territory to which this Agreement is extended in accordance with the provisions of **Article 12**" (**Article 1**, definitions)

The founders of a company may, however, conform to the law of their choice. By the choice of the applicable law, a company is incorporated in the legal system of the chosen

State. The company then acquires the nationality of the State of their choice:

> "Taking into account that the nationality of a company is always a creation of a legal system, it is clear that the most logical solution is the determination of the nationality of a company in conformity with the law under which the legal person came to exist. This is the point of view of English law..."[99]

Most European countries follow the "seat" theory: that is, the law of the country where the company has its "seat" is applicable on the company and gives it nationality even if most of its commercial activities may be conducted elsewhere.

6.3.15.1.2. *Applicable law*

An important gap in the text of the UK model convention is the absence of reference to the application of international law. Where just and equitable treatment, reserved to investors and investments of the other Contracting Party, is mentioned, a twofold criterion is considered: the protection given to national investors and the protection of the most favoured nation. As stressed above, this is insufficient because national investors often enjoy only a minimum protection. Since, pursuant to international law, national treatment does not constitute a maximum for foreign investors, the latter may claim a protection which is superior to the one benefiting nationals of a State.

The most favoured nation clause should normally be mentioned in a BIT, but it is not sufficient on itself, because it does not exclude the possibility that protection of third State investors may be inferior to the international law obligations of a guest State.

---

[99] *Collected Courses*, The Hague Academy, Publisher Nyhoff, Martinus, 1931, p. 523.

6.3.15.1.3. *Indirect investments*

In most BIT's, provision is made that indirect investments (shares, private bonds etc.) may also benefit from the protection guaranteed by the BIT's. Nevertheless, the UK has given a very limited definition of the term 'investment' and the word "indirect" has not been inserted in the text.

In case of nationalisation or expropriation, the indemnification of holders of shares of companies (indirect investment) is nevertheless provided for in a specific clause:

> "where a contracting Party expropriates the assets of a company which is incorporated or constituted under the law in force of any part of its own territory, and in which nationals or companies of the other contracting party own shares, it shall ensure that the provisions of paragraph (1) of this article are applied to the extent necessary to guarantee prompt, adequate and effective compensation in respect of their investment, to such nationals or companies of the other Contracting party, who are owners of those shares." (**Article 5(2)**)

The general character of this text may lead one to think that majority participations, as well as minority participations, are protected. The guarantee, of course, only covers the indemnification in case of an expropriation and does not include just and equitable treatment.

6.3.15.1.4. *Control*

The theory of control is also followed in the UK, as appears from **Article 8** of the model:

> "A company which is incorporated or constituted under the law in force in the territory of one Contracting Party and in which, before such a dispute arises, the majority of shares are owned by nationals or companies of the other Contracting Party, shall, in accordance with article 25(2)b of the Washington Convention, be treated for the purpose of this Convention as a company of the other Contracting Party."

The focus of this clause is on the theory of control. If an investment is made by a British investor by creating a company on the territory of the other Contracting State to the

BIT, the company in which this investor has a majority participation, will be considered "British".

Normally, such company, if established in the territory and according to the laws of the other Contracting Party, would have the nationality of the other Contracting party, but it is considered a British company since the majority of shares is in the hands of British shareholders who have control of the company. A rather unusual situation results from this fact, a particular instance of double nationality. Even having the nationality of the host State, the company is made to acquire, by application of the Washington Convention, the nationality of the investor's State. The focus of this clause is on the theory of control. If an investment is made by a British investor by creating a company on the territory of the other Contracting State to the BIT, the company in which this investor has a majority participation, will be considered "British."

Normally, such company would have the nationality of the other Contracting Party but it is considered British because it is in the hands of a British shareholder who has control.

6.3.15.1.5. *Settlement of Investment Disputes*

In **Article 7** of the British model, there is a reference to the International Centre for Settlement of Investment Disputes (ICSID) if a dispute is referred to international arbitration. The investor has apparently no other choice. But, in fact, there is also an alternative formula for the settlement of disputes between an investor and a Host State. Where the dispute is referred to international arbitration, the national or company and the Contracting Party concerned in the dispute may agree to refer the dispute, either to ICSID, the Court of Arbitration of the International Chamber of Commerce, or an international arbitrator or *ad hoc* arbitration to be appointed by a special agreement or establishment under the Arbitration Rules of the United Nations Commission on international trade law (UNCITRAL).

It is surprising, however, that the anticipatory consent to arbitration of the Contracting Party is not mentioned and that, on the contrary, this Contracting Party may refuse the above mentioned alternative formula. In that case, the dispute shall at the request in writing of the national or the company concerned, submitted to arbitration under the UNCITRAL rules.

It would seem to be better just to give the investor the absolute choice of venue, under any circumstance.

6.3.16. – United States of America

6.3.16.1. The 1994 Model US Convention

6.3.16.1.1. Definition of "company"

The United States of America first developed a text of model convention in 1981. This model has been reviewed and is now referred to as "The 1994 US prototype Bilateral Investment Treaty". The drafters realised that it was not suitable to work on the basis of a stereotype text. Based on the experience acquired during several years of working with developing countries, they adapted and amended their prototype. In case of need, or should the adverse party ask for it, US negotiators insert new provisions in their agreements. This was the case for the definition of protected legal persons, the text reading as follows:

> "Company means any entity constituted or organised under applicable law, whether or not for profit, and whether privately or governmentally owned or controlled and includes a corporation, trust, partnership, sole proprietorship, branch, joint venture, association, or other organisation."

This is a very broad definition and includes two elements not found in European practice: the application of the BIT to State enterprises and a reference to the theory of control.

In Europe, BIT's are concluded specifically for the encouragement and protection of direct private investments in developing countries. Investments made by European authorities in the framework of development cooperation, fall outside the application of BIT's.

6.3.16.1.2. *Control*

In the agreement USA/Zaïre, dated 3 August 1984 (entered into force on 28 July 1989), the term "controlled", which had been inserted in the model convention of 1981, was eliminated from the definition of "company". In fact, this modification did not exclude the application of the theory of control, which found a place in the document in the definition of "investment":

> "Investment means every kind of investment, owned or controlled directly or indirectly, including equity, debt, and service and investment contracts, and includes..." (**Article 1,C**).

As previously suggested, the use of the theory of control, as applied in the determination of companies that benefit from or are otherwise subject to BIT's is ambiguous. The commentary taken up in the "letter of submittal" (to be compared with the "exposé des motifs" annexed to a draft of law in a Continental European context). prepared by US. Department of State (equivalent to European Ministry of Foreign Affairs) reveals US intentions:

> "Definition of 'own or control'; the definition which is included in the USA model convention text, was omitted from the Zaïre text. The reason for normally including such a definition is to highlight the fact that investments which the treaty is meant to cover includes those made through subsidiaries of companies of a 'Contracting Party', wherever located, thus even in third countries." [100]

Critics of the "control theory" find support in this excerpt for their opinions regarding the wholesale application of control theory. In actual practice, the US approach would allow, say, a Western European subsidiary subject to the control of a US multinational enterprise, and sustaining damages relat-

---

[100] Letter of Submittal, Department of State, Washington 26 February 1986.

ing to an investment made on the territory of another Western European State, to be entitled to the protection of the United States.

Admittedly this definition has not been inserted in the US model convention of 1994, but this does not mean that it has been discarded or proscribed from eventual future use.

There are practical problems that could arise from this controversial definition (cfr *supra*, Netherlands, Sweden). First of all, such an approach runs counter to the mainstream of international law. Problems could arise, should the USA conclude a BIT including such definition with a country in which the subsidiary has invested and the country of the subsidiary (not bound by a BIT).

Investors from that country and the US would be involved in an embarrassing legal imbroglio, because the American enterprise could ask for protection on the basis of a BIT, for herself as well as for its subsidiary. However, it is not hard to conceive of situations where the latter company might prefer to be assisted only by authorities in its own country. As a consequence, there could be conflicting interests. In legal terminology, the convention between the USA and the third party country may be considered as a *"res inter alios acta"* by the subsidiary as well as by its country. Yet, neither the subsidiary's country nor the subsidiary may want to be bound by such conventions.

An exception to the control theory has been made to apply, *expressis verbis*, to the US model convention of 1994, Article XII as follows:

> "Each Party reserves the right to deny to a company of the other Party the benefits of this treaty if nationals of a third country own or control the company and: a) the denying Party does not maintain normal economic relations with the third country; or b) the company has no substantial business activities in the territory of the Party under whose laws it is constituted or organised." [101]

---

[101] Letter of submittal, see footnote 100.

This is not to say that all references to third party conventions are to be avoided. Thus, the US model contains a very positive reference to the Convention of New York, dated 10 June 1958, concerning the recognition and the implementation of foreign arbitral sentences (cfr *infra*).

Despite European criticism, US authorities seem to be convinced of the superiority of their conventional practice in the field of protection of investments:

> "Our treaties, which draw upon language used in the US/FCN-treaties (friendship, commerce, navigation) as well as European counterparts, are more comprehensive and far-reaching than European BIT's." (cfr letter of submittal)

6.3.16.1.3. *Settlement of Investment disputes*

The procedure for the settlement of litigation regarding investments as specified in the US model convention is favourable to international investors. In the litigation's first phase, investors are able to choose, either to submit the litigation to local tribunals in the host State or to file for any other procedure for the settlement of litigation, so long as it was agreed so to do before the dispute arose. If, within three months, none of the options have been used, investors will be able to submit the dispute either to ICSID or to an *ad hoc* arbitration tribunal, established in accordance with UNCITRAL rules. Each of the Contracting Parties will have given its anticipatory assent to the submittal of the dispute to ICSID. The validity of such assent rests on the fulfillment of two conditions:

- The Centre must find it has jurisdiction in accordance with **Article 25(2)b** of the Washington Convention;
- This assent is in writing, in accordance with the New York Convention dated 10 June 1958 regarding the execution of arbitral awards.

In fact, under the US model, States must already have concluded a bilateral protection convention. BIT's between the US and generally provide for the anticipatory consent to

ICSID arbitration and confirm that investors may choose the arbitration venue:

> "Each Party hereby consents to the submission of any investment dispute for settlement by binding arbitration in accordance with the choice of the national or company." (**Article 9.4**)

US authorities have clearly understood the usefulness of expressly stating in the BIT's that **Article 25(2)b** shall apply. In the interest of investors, third States are required to insert a specific provision in the bilateral convention:

> "For purposes of **Article 25(2)b** of the ICSID convention and this article, a company of a Party that, immediately before the occurrence of the event, or events, giving rise to an investment dispute, was a covered investment, shall be treated as a company of the other Party." (**Article IX (8)**)

6.3.16.2. *The US model convention of 2004*

6.3.16.2.1. *Need for a new prototype*

The United States of America developed a new text of model convention in 2004. The 1994 US prototype for bilateral investment treaties has been reviewed, in accordance with provisions of the NAFTA agreement.

International arbitral decisions introducing new ideas and developments in the protection of investments, had also an influence on the publication of a new prototype.

Specific provisions in BIT's (after 2004) are the expression of the new US policy regarding the publication of laws and decisions respecting international investments:

> "Each Party shall ensure that its:
>
> a) laws, regulations, procedures, and administrative rulings of general application; and
>
> b) adjudicatory decisions, respecting any matter covered by this Treaty are promptly published or otherwise made publicly available."

For the first time, the link between investment and the protection of environment was provided for in the text of the USA model convention:

> "The Parties recognize that it is inappropriate to encourage investments by weakening or reducing the protections afforded in domestic environmental laws... If a Party considers that the other Party has offered such an encouragement, it may request consultations with the other Party and the two parties shall consult with a view to avoiding any such encouragement."

Finally, a complex set of complementary rules regarding the settlement of investment disputes by ICSID-arbitration, has been inserted in the new prototype.

6.3.16.2.2. *Comparison of US BIT's*

There is little similarity between the old and the new US model conventions. Just like Canada, the US have used the model of the NAFTA Agreement of 1992 to amend and complete their 1994 version of the BIT model convention (see Appendix C). The latter still has value, because most of the US BIT's date from the previous era and those instruments will remain in force for yet many years. Actually, the only BIT based on the new model is the US/Uruguay Convention (BIT's), signed on 4 November 2005 and entered into force on 1 November 2006. It is to be expected that many US BIT's will be renegotiated in order to adapt them to the new model convention.

The parallel application of two types of BIT's could create problems. In some cases, precautionary measures have been taken (see *infra* : Performance Requirements).

In Europe, BIT's are concluded specifically for the encouragement and protection of direct private investments in developing countries. Investments made by European authorities in the framework of development cooperation, fall outside the application of BIT's.

6.3.16.2.3. *Definitions*

As opposed to European BIT's, which are limited to a few definitions, international investors, nationals, territory, revenues), the new US model convention contains an impressive number of definitions. Here are a few of the principal ones:

"nationals" means : "...for the United States a natural person who is a national of the United States as defined in Title III of the Immigration and Nationality act";

the term "legal person" (or "moral person," as used in Europe) does not appear in the new text and the following has been substituted :

"enterprise" means an entity constituted or organised under applicable law, whether or not for profit, and whether privately or governmentally owned or controlled, including a corporation, trust, partnership, sole proprietorship, joint venture, association, or similar organisation; and a branch of an enterprise.

The generic "enterprise" is the favoured term, presumably since most enterprises have a legal identity. Other innovations are as follows :

"enterprise of a Party" means an enterprise constituted or organised under the law of a Party and a branch located in the territory of a Party and carrying out business activities there;

"claimant" means an investor of a Party that is a party to an investment dispute with the other Party (host State);

"respondent" means the Party that is a party to an investment dispute (host State);

"non-disputing Party" means the Party (State of the investor) that is not a party to an investment dispute.

"Investment" means every asset that an investor owns or controls, directly or indirectly, that has the characteristics of an investment, including such characteristics as the commitment of capital or other resources, the expectation of gain or profit, or the assumption of risk;

The defined forms of investment are European-style :

"covered investment" means with respect to a Party, an investment in its territory of an investor of the other Party in existence as to the date of entry into force of this Treaty or established, acquired, or expanded thereafter.

6.3.16.2.4. *Scope and coverage*

As a general rule, BIT's specify that they apply to investments made on the territories of one of the Contracting Party by investors from the other Contracting Party. An important difference in the new US text is that it expressly states that the treaty applies to :

> "measures" taken or maintained by a Contracting State in regards to investments by investors of the other Contracting State.

The text is therefore aimed at legal, regulatory, procedural and judiciary measures, along the lines of NAFTA. Some experts see a limitation of the scope of the BIT :

> "To limit the scope of application of the BIT in this manner may have significant practical effects for determining the universe of measures that could be challenged for purposes of dispute settlement procedures. The issue was discussed in the initial disputes invoking the application of NAFTA's Chapter 11 on investor-State dispute settlement procedures. In several cases, such as Pope and Talbot and S.D. Meyers, Canada sought to have the arbitral tribunal decline jurisdiction on the basis that the measures challenged dealt with trade in goods and as such, were governed by chapters of NAFTA other than the investment chapter. Consequently the argument was that measures concerning trade in goods were not subject to arbitration under the investment provisions of Chapter 11." [102]

Actually, this is not a limitation, but rather an extension of the scope. Several of the BIT's provisions show that the agreement is applicable to conventional obligations (e.g. : fair and equitable treatment, transfer permissions) to which each of the Contracting Parties have committed in regards to investors of the other Contracting Party. Furthermore, the BIT also applies to "measures" taken by either of the contracting States. Very clear and complete details of the scope of application meet the concern of the US that such scope be fully circumscribed, in accordance with the Treaty of Vienna on the law of Treaties. It would therefore be useful to subsume the two notions in one article only and specify that the BIT applies to conventional commitments in regards to investors as well as to compensable measures undertaken by

---

[102] Bilateral Investment treaties, UNCTAD, www.Unctad.org/en/docs/iteïca 20065.

a Contracting State against investments by investors from the other Contracting State.

There is in fact a significant difference between mistreatment of an investor (f.i. refusal to authorise exports) and taking with respect to him measures which cause him direct damage (expropriation measures or their equivalent). Consequently, it would be useful to avoid any misunderstandings at all simply by being more precise.

A special US BIT's concern is that they apply to State enterprises :

> "an enterprise owned or controlled through ownership interests, by Contracting Party."

6.3.16.2.5. *Standard treatment*

As in practically all BIT's, the US BIT model refers to national treatment and to MFN treatment. The criterion used for measuring whether the treatment used with foreign investors is fair and equitable is therefore the treatment enjoyed by its own investors and those of third party countries. Conforming to the rules and principles of international common law is deemed to be the minimum standard :

> "Each Party shall accord to covered investments treatment in accordance with customary international law, including fair and equitable treatment and full protection and security." (**Article 5, 1**)

It is the limited application of national and MFN treatment that distinguishes US (and Canadian) practice from that of European States. In Appendices I, II and III of the US/Uruguay BIT, which are an integral part of the treaty, there is a stipulation that theses clauses do not apply to a large number of economic sectors. For instance, Uruguay excludes the application of the national treatment standard, the performance requirements and the prohibition against requiring nationals to be appointed to executive positions in the "commercial fishing" sector. In the "media and communications" sector, Uruguayan nationals only may be appointed to "senior management and Board of directors." Foreign investors on Uruguayan territory therefore should be most careful and verify what, as a result of these limiting clauses, is or is not open to foreign investment.

6.3.16.2.6. *Expropriation*

The usual provisions (f.i. public utilities, non-discrimination, legal procedure, compensation) are included. However, there is a special provision regarding the currency of compensation money. Usually, BIT's require that compensation be paid in the currency of the investor or any other convertible currency. **Article 6,4** states as follows:

> "If the market value is denominated in a currency that is *not freely usable*, the compensation referred to in paragraph 1c – converted into the currency of payment at the market rate of exchange prevailing on the date of payment-shall be no less than:
> a) the fair market value on the date of expropriation, converted into a freely usable currency at the market rate of exchange prevailing on that date, plus
> b) interest, at a commercially reasonable rate for that freely usable currency, accrued from the date of expropriation until the date of payment."

It is rather odd that the amount of indemnities that are due may be expressed in a non-convertible currency which, subsequently, is to be recalculated on the basis of a currency that is. In any event, the free transfer of indemnities seems assured.

6.3.16.2.7. *Performance requirements*

As previously stated, the parallel application of BIT's based on the US model and other BIT models could create problems. For example, Belgian investors who invest on Uruguayan territory may invoke the application of the UEBL/ Uruguay BIT dated 4 November 1991. In the event "performance requirements" are imposed by Uruguayan authorities, investors will be able to invoke the US/URUGUAY BIT which forbids such a requirement. In fact, such investors may demand that the MFN provision be used, a provision which does not exist in the UEBL/Uruguay convention. To avoid problems of this kind, Article 8 regarding "performance requirements" provides that this clause is also applicable to investors from a third State :

> "In addition, so as not to place US and Uruguayan investors at a competitive disadvantage,... (the limitations) that article 8 imposes upon performance requirements also apply to all investments in the territory of a Party, including those owned or controlled by host-country investors or by investors of a non-Party." (**Article 8**, BIT US/Uruguay)

The performance requirements relate to the prohibition against the imposition on foreign investors of various constraints such as a level of production or export, restrictions on sales or purchases, mandatory transfer of technology etc.

6.3.16.2.8. *Cases of non-application of the US model BIT*

It is striking that the model US convention contains a large number of provisions limiting the application of BIT's :

> "a Party may prevent a transfer through the equitable, non-discriminatory, and good faith application of its laws relating to :
>
> a) bankruptcy, insolvency, or the protection of the rights of creditors;
>
> b) issuing, trading, or dealing in securities, futures, options, or derivatives;
>
> c) criminal or penal offenses;
>
> d) financial reporting or record keeping of transfers when necessary to assist law enforcement or financial regulatory authorities; or
>
> e) ensuring compliance with orders or judgments in judicial or administrative proceedings.
>
> **Articles 3** (National treatment), **4** (most favoured nation), **8** (performance requirements) and **9** (Senior management and board of directors) do not apply to any existing non-conforming measure that is maintained by a Party in its Schedule to **Annex I** or **Annex III**;
>
> **Articles 3, 4, 8** and **9** do not apply to any measure that a Party maintains with respect to sectors, subsectors, or activities, as set out in its Schedule to Annex II;

a Party may deny the benefits of this Treaty to an investor of the other Party that is an enterprise of such other Party and to investments of that investor if persons of a non-Party own or control the enterprise...;

a Party may deny the benefits of this treaty to an investor of the other Party that is an enterprise of such other Party and to investments of that investor if the enterprise has no substantial activities in the territory of the other Party and persons of a non-Party, or of the denying Party, own or control the enterprise;

Notwithstanding any other provision of this Treaty, a Party shall not be prevented from adopting or maintaining measures relating to financial services for prudential reasons, including for the protection of the investors, depositors, policy holders, or persons to whom a fiduciary duty is owed by a financial services supplier, or to ensure the integrity and stability of the financial system..."

6.3.16.2.9. *Settlement of Investment Disputes*

BIT's usually provide that any dispute "relating to an investment" may be submitted to arbitration. The new US formula is more complex:

"In the event that a disputing party considers that an investment dispute cannot be settled by consultation and negotiation:

The claimant, on its own behalf, may submit to arbitration under this section a claim

i) that the respondent has breached:

(A) an obligation under articles 3 through 10,

(B) an investment authorisation, or

(C) an investment agreement;

and

ii) that the claimant has incurred loss or damage by reason of, or arising out of that breach..."

This is a more consistent provision, logistically, but it may be sometimes more difficult to prove that a causative link exists between "breach of obligation" and the damages sustained.

Under **Article 26**, an investor may submit a claim to arbitration under several potential mechanisms, the ICSID convention, the arbitration rules of UNCITRAL, or under any other mutually agreed arbitral institution. The rules of arbitration of each chosen institution will govern the arbitration, except to the extent modified by the BIT. As a matter of fact, an entire arbitration procedure has been provided for in the US BIT.

Normally, BIT's provide that when a dispute arises, the most diligent party must notify the other, by writing, accompanied by a memorandum. The request for arbitration may not be filed until at least 6 months have passed from the date of notification. This implies that the parties must try, for a period of 6 months, to reach an amiable arrangement. In the event no amiable arrangement has been reached, the arbitration procedure may begin.

As in European BIT's, US BIT's also require parties to seek an amiable arrangement:

> "In the event of an investment dispute, the claimant and the respondent should initially seek to resolve the dispute through consultation and negotiation,which may include the use of non-binding, third party procedures."

However, the date (DN) when the dispute first arose is not certain. The *"dies a quo"* must necessarily be the date on which the "claimant" has notified the "respondent" that a dispute existed. Unfortunately, there is no provision requiring a "written notification" but a "delay" requirement has nonetheless been provided for the submission of the claim:

> "Provided that six months have elapsed since the events giving rise to the claim, a claimant may submit a claim."

This formula is very vague. How the claimant must notify the respondent that a dispute has arisen is not stated. In actual practice, the dispatch of a written notification is therefore necessary.

On the other hand, a specific delay has been specified for the submission of a claim (SC):

> "at least 90 days before submitting any claim to arbitration under this section, a claimant shall deliver to the respondent a written notice

of its intention (NOI) to submit the claim to arbitration ('notice of intent')."

The problem is that the claimant may arbitrarily set the *"dies a quo"* with respect to the required notice time. Before officially notifying the respondent about the existence of a dispute, he could have discreet contacts designed to achieve an amiable arrangement. In this way he can set forward in time the commencement of the actual arbitration procedure. He can thereby influence the date (*dies a quo*) on which the 6 month delay and the 90 day delay begins to run.

In the European system, there is a formal obligation to give notice of the dispute, whereas the US formula is satisfied with the vague notion :

"that six months have elapsed since the events giving rise to the claim." (arise of the dispute : AD).

It would have been preferable to select explicitly for a *"dies a quo"* the date on which the measures or breaches of obligations to which reference is made in **Article 24** occurred. Here are the actual time spans within which notices are to be given :

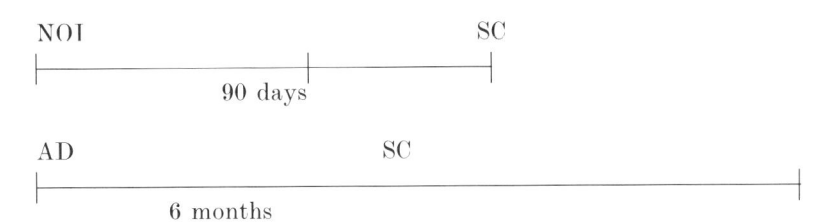

```
NOI                           SC
|—————————————————————————————|
         90 days

AD                SC
|—————————————————————————————————————————————|
         6 months
```

The request for arbitration must be filed within three years from the date the dispute arose, failing which the cause of action will be barred (PR).

```
AD                       PR
|————————————————————————————————————————|
         3 years
```

Article 26 of the model convention provides in this regard :

"if more than three years have elapsed from the date on which the claimant first acquired or should have required knowledge of the breach alleged under article 24..."

This formula is difficult to apply. The best formula is that which leaves to the claimant the discretion to set the starting date, that is, the date of which written notice has been sent by the claimant.

The arbitration tribunal must be constituted:

"within 75 days from the date that a claim is submitted to arbitration."

Here the *"dies a quo"* is a date certain. The date on which the notice was dispatched by the claimant does not count but the date:

"of notice of registration of the request to the parties by the Secretary General of ICSID."

If a tribunal has not been constituted within this delay, the Secretary general of ICSID, on the request of a disputing party, shall appoint, in his or her discretion, the arbitrator or arbitrators not yet appointed.

CHAPTER VII
PROTECTED INVESTORS-NATIONALITY

7.1. – Nationals and Citizens

According to immigration and other laws of some countries, a difference exists, as to physical persons, between the benefits and obligations of a "national" and a "citizen", the term "national" being generally interpreted more broadly than "citizen", to include persons who are not citizens but are nevertheless entitled to some form of protection by the State. For instance, in the United Kingdom, British citizenship is a branch of nationality, there co-existing a branch named "nationality (Overseas)", among other branches. United States citizens are deemed to be citizens of the United States of America as well of their State of birth or domicile. A U.S. national born in an American "territory" (i.e. not a "State") is not necessarily a U.S. citizen. Properly written international trade conventions will address the differences between nationals and citizens or subsume all categories or branches of nationality under the inclusive term "nationality".

A legal person is deemed a national of the State under whose laws it has been created. It is wholly fictional in the sense that it is a creation of the law merely to facilitate participation in its profits by its shareholders and limit their liability for losses. It does clearly not have all of the benefits and obligations of citizenship, although some legal texts have language identifying corporations established on their territory as "citizens" of that State. That language may be seen as misleading since the rights of physical "citizens" (e.g. voting, public welfare etc.) and their obligations (e.g. liability, conscription, etc.) are, in large measure, not co-extensive with the rights and liabilities of legal persons. That language, however, allows people, professional and lay alike, all too often to equate, when specific legislation is silent on the basic differences between them, the rights of physical and moral persons, leading them to inappropriate conclusions as to the treatment to be afforded to such persons. In arbitration, where fairness and equity are fundamental elements justifying its use, it is essential that these differences not be ignored.

For instance, under the laws of some States, insurance companies incorporated in another State are deemed to be "citizens" of the State where they operate and are required to file bonds for the payment of their obligations to residents of such State.[103] Under some fiscal laws, corporations are denied benefits granted physical citizens. Though the intention of such legislation may be laudable, it also serves to lend an aura of legitimacy to analogies in other matters between physical and moral persons. In subsequent chapters of this Work, it will become apparent that determining the nationality of a corporation is neither simple nor certain, no matter the intention of a corporation's founders may have been at the time of its founding and that such analogies blur the logic of the corporate fiction.

7.2. – Protection for Individuals

For physical persons, there are relatively few issues involving international protection. It is generally admitted that investors wishing to benefit from the rights and advantages of the BIT's, must have the nationality of a contracting State. The term "nationality" is not even explicitly mentioned in the text of the BIT's. There are exceptions to that rule. For instance, China and the Arab Republic Egypt have preferred to mention the term "nationality" in the text of their conventions for the designation of the Chinese and Egyptian investors. The condition of nationality may natu-

---

[103] *Republic Ins. Co. v. Cunningham*, Tex. Civ. App. 62 S.W.2d 339, 343.

rally be deduced from the definition of "protected investors". The terms "nationals" in English and "ressortissants" in French are used and refers to persons having the nationality of one of the Contracting States. In order to dispel any misunderstanding as to "nationals", "citizens" and "residents", the term "nationality" should, by preference, be mentioned explicitly in all BIT's.

The fact is that the term "nationality" is not frequently used in European conventional practice, at least insofar as the protection of investments is concerned. Only in the German BIT's, does the definition of the term "investors" refers more clearly to nationality:

> "Germans, within the meaning of the basic law (on nationality) of the Federal Republic of Germany."

This definition is alright as far as it goes but only brings on another layer of questions about who are "Germans" under the "basic law". There is a tendency, however, in recent European BIT's, to mention the term "nationality" expressly. Within OECD, the recommended text on this topic reads as follows:

> "Investor means: a natural person having the nationality of, or who is permanently residing in a Contracting Party, in accordance with the applicable law."

This recommendation has been followed in Italian BIT's:

> "The term 'natural person' with reference to either Contracting party, shall mean any individual having the nationality of that State in accordance with its laws." (BIT Italie/Nicaragua,20 avril 2004)

Likewise in the Netherlands:

> "The term 'national' shall comprise with regard to either Contracting Party the following subjects: natural persons having the nationality of that Contracting party in conformity with its Constitution and laws..." (BIT Netherlands/Costa Rica,21 may 1999)

7.3. – EFFECT OF CHANGES IN AN INDIVIDUAL INVESTOR'S NATIONALITY

7.3.1. – *Application to the individual's national authorities*

An investor, making investments in a developing country with which his country has concluded a BIT, will be able to ask his authorities for the protection guaranteed by the applicable BIT, for instance if his investment has been affected by measures privative or restrictive of property. The injured investor will thus have an interest in making an appeal to the competent offices of his country's State Department, Ministry of Foreign Affairs or other such agency in order to have his rights defended against action of the foreign authority concerned. Traditionally, the official steps, inviting the foreign authorities to respect the obligations provided for in the BIT's, are taken by the diplomatic and consular missions abroad of the investor's country.

As previously stressed, only persons with the nationality of the State whose diplomatic protection is sought, can have access to such right:

> "This right (of intervention) cannot be exercised (by a State) except in favour of its nationals because, in the absence of particular accords, it is the bond of nationality between the State and the individual which alone gives the State the right to exercise diplomatic protection." (C.P.J.I., 1939, n° 76, p. 16)

As already said, in the European Union, an exception to this rule has been provided for. This is in conformity with international law but it is worth recalling that, in the BIT's, no provision exists confirming this conventional exception. BIT's to be concluded in the future should mention this conventional exception explicitly. In this manner, host States would be barred from invoking the maxim *"res inter alios acta"* in order to refuse protection by a non-Contracting Party to investments made by investors of the other Contracting Party of the BIT.

7.3.2. – *Nationality Changes after Conclusion of BIT*

Problems could also arise in the case of a change of the nationality of an investor after making his investments abroad (marriage, naturalisation, abandonment, option, forfeiture). When a BIT is concluded with a developing country, each Contracting Party assumes obligations towards investors who are nationals of the other Contracting party. If an investor, within a short time after making his investment, having a nationality which entitles him to protection under the applicable BIT, then changes his nationality, losing his original nationality, he can no longer be considered a "national of the other Contracting Party" under that BIT. Under those conditions, the investor would no longer legally qualify for the protection provided for in the BIT concerned, unless an exception is provided for therein.

Provisions of some BIT's emphasise that protection of investments is guaranteed during ten years. Should an investor during that period acquire the nationality of a country which has not concluded a BIT with the developing country concerned, he will, despite the 10 year guarantee, no longer benefit from of assistance or help for his investments in the host State. Most BIT's do not contain any provision that could be of assistance in such a situation.

7.3.3. – *Double nationality*

Double or multiple nationality status may exist when the individual's acquisition of nationality is based on different legal systems. Thus, an investor with, say, U.S. nationality according to U.S. laws, might have a different nationality under the laws of other countries, say Mexico or Morocco. In Europe, Belgium, for instance, has recently relaxed its former intransigence regarding double nationality. Thus, starting in 2008[104], a Bel-

---

[104] This new rule was not applicable to Belgians who acquire the nationality of a State member of the Strasburg Convention of 6 May 1963. However, meanwhile Belgium has cancelled its adherence to this Convention.

gian national who voluntarily acquires another nationality no longer loses his Belgian nationality. Double nationality could happen anywhere, where nationality is based on the place of birth and national legislation does not as a rule forfeit a person's native nationality when he or she acquires the nationality of another country, although legislation in some States may require an individual to renounce his former nationality when he acquires that of such State voluntarily. A national's renunciation of nationality may be driven by motives which are inimical to a State's interest and, in these more modern times, it may therefore be resisted whereas previously it may have been welcomed or even compelled or virtually automatic.

An investor having double nationality status might therefore be excluded from the special protection granted to foreign investors, should one of his nationalities be that of the host State. The host State, which conferred upon him its own nationality status, could allow him only a purely national protection, often less favourable than that reserved for international investors.

To illustrate this situation, we can point to the BIT negotiated between the Kingdoms of Morocco and Belgium entered into on 13 April 1999 (ratified on 29 April 2002).

In this convention, an investor is defined as follows:

"Every physical person who, according to Belgian, Luxemburger or Moroccan legislation has respectively Belgian, Luxemburger or Moroccan nationality, and who makes an investment on the territory of another Contracting Party." (**Article 1.2a**)

Worldwide, quite a few persons have double nationalities. Belgium and Morocco provide an example. Belgian legislation, until 2008, regarding nationality required that whoever acquired a foreign nationality (f.i. by naturalisation) lost his Belgian nationality on the date of acquisition of the foreign nationality. On the other hand, Moroccan legislation does not impose this penalty and, hence, the Moroccan who acquires Belgian nationality keeps his nationality of origin, or so say Moroccan authorities.

This will have consequences in the application of the Belgium-Morocco BIT. A Moroccan who makes an investment on Moroccan territory and thereafter acquires Belgian nationality will be viewed as a Moroccan in Morocco and as Belgian in Belgium.

In the event of nationalisation or other expropriation of this Moroccan person's investment, its owner, were he to file for arbitration against the Kingdom of Morocco, will be met with a refusal by Morocco on the ground that he is a Moroccan citizen. Morocco will hold that the BIT does not apply to his case. With respect to ICSID, Moroccan authorities will demur to a request for arbitration on the basis of the fact that the applicant does not meet the requirement of being a "national of another State". Any steps taken from the Belgian side to protect the interests of "its investor" will be denied based on the Moroccan argument that Belgium does not have jurisdiction to represent the interests of a Moroccan national. This situation will change, starting in March 2008 when both Belgium and Morocco will recognise the double nationality, a further complication.

7.3.4. – *Dominant nationality*

Double nationality, *exists* where each nationality may be that of each of the two Contracting States, or where one of a person's nationalities is of a State which has no BIT with the other State, even though his other nationality may be one of the State with which the host state has a BIT. Any of these situations may cause practical problems which cannot be resolved if the two States adopt a strictly national attitude in the matter. The host State may claim the mere fact the double national has a nationality of a state with which the host state has no BIT, disqualifies the claimant. With respect to international claims, the doctrine as well as jurisprudence shows that persons who have double nationality may experience problems when claiming indemnification :

> "Even when the continuous nationality requirement has been met, problems have arisen when the otherwise eligible national also possessed the nationality of a foreign country, especially the nationality of the respondent State (which would otherwise be liable for indemnification)." [105]

This harsh and radical position has been softened in favour of claimants who would otherwise be entitled to indemnification. The need has been shown for the creation of a hierarchy of the two nationalities of the claimant, whereby the ranking nationality would be the principal or dominant nationality and the next in rank would be the other nationality, seen as the subsidiary nationality.

Internationally, this idea has led to the proposal of a new legal concept, namely, that of *effective and dominant nationality* :

> "Recently the doctrine of effective or dominant nationality has developed to mitigate the hardness of the traditional role, permitting the espousal of the claim of a dual national when such individual has a closer and more effective bond with the claimant State. The doctrine has received the endorsement of the United States Department of State, and there is reason to believe that the days of the traditional approach may be on the wane." [106]

British commissions in charge of vetting claims for indemnification of British assets nationalised in the old Eastern bloc countries have applied the new doctrine:

> "In cases where a person is of dual nationality, the general rules of international law must apply: claims for compensation for nationalised property belonging to him cannot be made against a State which lawfully also claims him as a citizen and the nationalising State must be free to decide with which State he has the strongest connections and which therefore will be competent to protect his interests." [107]

The expropriating State will of course want to keep payable indemnifications to a minimum and will oppose the

---
[105] LILLICH, Richard B and BURNS, H. Weston, *op. cit.*, p. 58, see footnote 22.
[106] LILLICH, Richard B and BURNS, H. Weston, *op. cit.*, p. 59, see footnote 22.
[107] *"Technical discussion on claim problems"*, Foreign Office, London, 1967, p. 65.

expansion of the group of indemnification claimants. We can expect that its decision will be rapidly taken and that the investor sustaining damage will be considered its own citizen and not the "national of another State". To come to an acceptable solution and avoid difficulties in concrete cases, applicable criteria should be established in the convention in order to determine which nationality will be the "dominant and effective" one. Thus, the BIT's should include provisions according to which one of the nationalities may be discarded by reference to the notion "dominant and effective nationality."

There is a precedent in the Belgian practice of nationalised assets indemnification:

> "It is agreed that persons of double Belgian and Egyptian nationalities are excluded from the application of this Agreement. In the event the Belgian national has a dual nationality that is not Egyptian, only persons will be deemed Belgian those who may be found to have the Belgian nationality as their effective and dominant nationality, for the purposes of this agreement."

Nothing has been provided for persons who have Belgian and Egyptian dual nationalities and the agreement does not apply to them. Obviously an exception could have been provided. It would have been preferable to determine what criteria will be used to determine the "dominant and effective nationality". It would therefore be useful to have BIT's include a clause regarding effective and dominant nationality, in order to resolve problems resulting from double nationality status. This concept is emerging in recent Canadian practice.

In older BIT's, the traditional clause read as follows:

> "...the term investor means with regard to either Contracting Party: any natural person possessing the citizenship of a Contracting Party in accordance with its laws." (BIT Canada/Poland, 22 November 1990, article 1 definitions)

On the other hand, in a more recent agreement, the following clause was adopted:

"a natural person who is a dual citizen shall be deemed to be exclusively a citizen of the State of his or her dominant and effective citizenship." (BIT Canada/Peru, 14 November 2006, article 1, definitions)

Hopefully, other States wil follow this example. However, when they do, they should also include criteria to be used to determine the dominant nationality of the claimant.

7.3.5. – *Criteria for dominant nationality*

Formulating the criteria for "effective and dominant nationality" is not all that easy. Many motivations may exist to influence the decision to change the nationality of the claimant : fiscal issues, marriage, tax evasion, adulthood options, residence permit entitlement, fraud etc. In many cases, obtaining a foreign nationality is purely speculative and has a specific purpose. In some cases, it is automatic, with little choice for the individual to avoid or refuse it. A dual nationality may be sometimes kept to gain or maintain advantages which may be bound to them such as lawful possession of two passports. Some have emotional or family ties to a former nationality and seek to regain it if legislation allows. Others still may wish to obtain the nationality of a country where special benefits or qualification are reserved for "nationals".

It is therefore appropriate to know what criteria, on the international level, should serve to help choose which of the two nationalities will be the one held to be "dominant and effective". The "*Nottebohm*" decision of 6 April 1955 in the International Court of Justice gives us a sense of the issue [108]. In that case, which involved Guatemala and Lichtenstein, it was decided that the Lichtenstein nationality, having been acquired by naturalisation, could not have been considered dominant and effective. At the time he filed his arbitration request for indemnification with Gua-

---

[108] *Nottebohm Case*, Judgment of 6 april 1955, *International Court of Justice (ICJ)*, Report 1955, p. 4.

temalan authorities, Nottebohm had Lichtenstein nationality. Before acquiring the Lichtenstein nationality, he was German. Since he maintained a domicile in Guatemala, the court held that he had not broken all bonds with his original nationality nor was he integrated in the Lichtenstein society. His request for indemnification of assets nationalised by Guatemala was rejected by the Court. It is possible that the rejection was as much due to the fiction of his Lichtensteiner nationality which the Court may have seen as a trick solely to gain the benefits of the Lichstensteiner nationality.

It is interesting to analyse how the Court formulated its reasons for upholding a demurrer to Nottebohm's claim. First, the court emphasised that the grant of nationality was an act of national jurisdiction. But, at the same time, it held that the determination of nationality is not automatically effective internationally and that Nottebohm's new nationality was not *"ipso facto"* binding on "third parties States":

> "However, international practice has many examples of acts done by a State while exercising its jurisdiction but which do not bind the international community, which are not to be imposed unquestioningly on other States or which can only be imposed under certain conditions that is, for instance, the case of a judgment delivered by a court of a State having jurisdiction and which is sought to be enforced in another State." [109]

Some States may refuse to acknowledge a claim of nationality in order to avoid or shirk responsibility for the acts or omissions of an individual. International acknowledgement of a particular nationality should not depend of rules of domestic law but on the basis of principles and criteria appurtenant to rules of international law. Whenever a decision must be taken about a person's nationality, internationally, that person's claims to a particular nationality should first be exam-

---

[109] *Nottebohm Case, op. cit.*, p. 21, see footnote 108.

ined on the basis of the real and effective bonds that person has with the country of which he claims to be a national.

7.4. – NATIONALITY TO BE MORE THAN "THEORETICAL"

The nationality of an individual is not just a theoretical concept, nor is it just form over substance. Ideally, – indeed some may say, traditionally, the "old-fashioned" way – nationality must be the legal expression of an individual's attachment to his motherland. Whether the "motherland" is the land of his birth and is distinguished from "fatherland", as the land of his father's birth, is an increasingly existential question with extra subjective overtones, some of which may be feigned. In theory therefore, it is only in that case that, based on outward appearances and an individual's pattern of conduct, his relationship to others of the same nationality, and a host of other convincing elements evidencing the dominance of one nationality over another, a person may be deemed an authentic national of a State and therefore may not be properly refused aid and assistance from the State to which he claims to belong. Clearly, to make this a requirement would ignore the fact that millions acquire a nationality by reason of an accident of birth rather than through conviction as to his "attachment to the motherland". For instance, a child born to an American diplomat in Austria acquires the US nationality, although Austrian law might also give him Austrian nationality. A child born to an American resident in Austria who is not a diplomat does not necessarily retain the nationality of his father when he reaches his majority. US laws then may allow him to "opt" for one or the other, hardly a failsafe proof of his "attachment" to the US or Austria. For all we know, he might be equally attached to both without thereby be vulnerable to being accused of unpatriotism by either.

Thus, using the criterion of a person's "attachment to the motherland" is a concept that may have been self-evident in the context of 19th and 20th century wars but has become increasingly diluted since then. Until that dilution is fully recognised, the fact remains, however, that, when a person with dual nationality is subject to the evaluation of international arbitration or of an international tribunal, priority will be given to a presumed "effective" nationality :

> "International arbitrators have decided in the same way many cases of dual nationality where the question was the dual national's entitlement to protection. They have made effective nationality a tenet of the law, so long as the facts supported it, that resting on a loftier bond between the individual in question and the State whose nationality is the ground for his claim. The circumstances considered are diverse and their importance vary from one case to the other : the individual's domicile is of great importance but also where his personal interests lie, his family links, his participation in public life, the love he has for the land he claims and demonstrates as well as that he imparts to his children." [110]

In international practice, there is a prevailing tendency to prefer a real and effective nationality :

> "The practice of certain States which refrain from exercising protection in favour of a naturalized person when, the latter has in fact, by its prolonged absence, severed his links with what was no longer for him anything but his nominal country, manifests the view of States that, in order to be capable of being invoked against another State, nationality must correspond with the factual situation" [111]

The Court reached its conclusion in the *Nottebohm* case on the ground that it was necessary to look into the real nationality of the individual to determine whether Lichtenstein did or did not have the right to submit an international indemnification claim in his favour :

> "Such being the character that nationality must show when it is invoked, so that the State which granted it may gain an entitlement

---

[110] *Nottebohm Case, op. cit*, p. 22, see footnote 108.
[111] *Nottebohm Case, op. cit.*, pp. 22 and 23, see footnote 108.

to extend its protection and to set in motion an international judicial proceeding, the Court must examine whether the nationality granted to Nottebohm through naturalization has that character, in other words, whether the factual bond between Nottebohm and Lichtenstein during the time preceding, surrounding and following his naturalisation, appears to be so sufficiently tight, so dominant in relation to the bonds that may exist between him and some other State, that it becomes possible to find that the nationality granted to him was 'effective' as the exact legal expression of a social bond, pre-existing and self-realising." [112]

This reasoning stands the usual legal approach on its head. Instead of looking to objective, demonstrable facts, the Court engages in a psychological evaluation of love, patriotism, interest in public life, etc, all of which are highly subjective, subject to each individual judge's social and political opinions and tendencies. An objective standard, more reliable in its factualism, would more logically measure an individual's material connections to the country he claims to be dominant in matters of nationality, where he makes a living, where his assets are concentrated, and last but not least, which is tied to him not so much by an act chosen by him (i.e. application for naturalisation) but by events over which he has little control (e.g. birth, military draft, territorial expansion), and which are measurable not so much by an individual's arguably self-serving affirmations but by facts on the ground.

Nonetheless, taking all of these factors into consideration, the judges decided that the Lichtensteiner nationality of Nottebohm was not "effective". Lichtenstein was told that the claimant had always resided in Guatemala, even after his naturalisation, and that Guatemala was the centre of his family and professional activities.

---

[112] *Nottebohm Case, op. cit.*, p. 24, see footnote 108.

7.5. – PROS AND CONTRAS OF "EFFECTIVE NATIONALITY"

Not all of the judges were in agreement with the contents of the decision and several dissenting opinions were filed. Helge Klaesstad pointed out that there were no international rules imposing residence status upon a person wishing to acquire a foreign nationality. On the other hand, she stated that several legislatures do impose residence requirements but that frequently exemptions therefrom are granted. This shows that residence is not a fundamental requirement.

According to Read, the decision was not acceptable because Guatemala had claimed that the naturalisation had not been lawfully granted and was contrary to Lichtensteiner legislation but had offered no proof thereof. Guatamela was therefore arguing falsely that Nottebohm's naturalisation had been granted contrary to generally accepted principles pertaining to naturalisation. He thought that the Court should not have based its decisions on those concepts in order to countenance the Guatemalan interpretation. The duty of the Court was to judge these cases on the basis of international law. The claim that the grant of naturalisation was not honest, because of the lack of bonds between Nottebohm and Lichtenstein should have been proven in the light of international rules.

Both Lichtenstein and Guatemala were in agreement that the state of international law on the subject could be derived from the text of the Treaty concerning conflicts of nationality law signed in The Hague on 12 April 1939 (Belgian Monitor of August 1939).

The **First Article** of this Treaty reads as follows:

> "Each State has jurisdiction to determine within the scope of its own legislation who are its nationals. This legislation must be acknowledged by other States so long as it conforms to international conventions, since international custom and legal principles are generally acknowledged in nationality matters."

Very curiously, both of the States in question were basing their arguments on the issue on the text of this treaty. Lichtenstein argued that it had jurisdiction to grant nationality status to Nottebohm. Guatemala claimed that, because no international convention existed between the two States and no customary law addressed the issue, only legal principles of a general nature could apply. According to the Guatemalan opinion, those principles were not part of the so-called "soft law" and in such opinion were therefore not binding on the States. Guatemala's argumentation is somewhat startling, since, even if "those" principles had been soft law, they would not as such have been binding.

Read notes that Guatemala contested the validity of the naturalisation, on the basis of an abuse of the country's laws and fraud, there being no bond whatever between Nottebohm and Liechtenstein :

> "An argument has been made during the course of the oral procedure. Thus it is evident that, in the opinion of the Government of Guatemala, there are no well established international principles relating to nationality but, instead, Lichtenstein's right to determine through its own legislation whether Mr. Nottebohm was one of its nationals and the Guatemalan obligation to be derived therefrom to acknowledge such legislation – including the right to oppose it – are limited not so much by rigid rules of international law but only by rules relating to the abuse of a country's laws and fraud." [113]

According to Read, there was presented no proof of abuse or fraud. He declared that the Court had rejected Lichtenstein's claim only because real bonds were absent between the interested individual and his "motherland Lichstenstein" (bond theory), without even examining in any depth whether the naturalisation law was effectively contrary to Lichtenstein law on nationality and generally admitted legal principles.

---

[113] *Nottebohm Case, op. cit.*, p. 40, see footnote 108.

It cannot be denied either that some States welcome registering on its rolls individuals who wish to become nationals of that State, bring significant assets with them, become valuable taxpayers and, at the risk of being a little bit crude about it, are given the opportunity to pay for the privilege of nationality when coupled with actual residence for an arbitrary number of years.

Just like Read, and for similar reasons, Guggenheim could not be in agreement with the decision. According to him, an enquiry ought to have been made to determine if the naturalisation conformed to Lichtenstein naturalisation law. The Court should not have passed judgment, as a Court of Appeals might, on the correct application of domestic law within the national judiciary system. But the Court should thoroughly examine whether the naturalisation proceeding was proper, this being a *sine qua non* condition allowing the referring the case to an international judge:

> "The international judge must be solely concerned with the domestic law and in particular that relating to nationality as an indispensable element of the claim standing before the court. The claimant therefore has the duty to prove that the naturalisation was a valid act, conforming to domestic law of the State concerned and the defense, if it contests the validity, has the burden of proving its invalidity." [114]

Still according to Guggenheim, Nottebohm's naturalisation was valid even under conventional international law. The Hague Treaty (cfr. *Supra*) does not say that, to be valid, a naturalisation requires effective and real bonds between the naturalised individual and the State which naturalised him. He does not deny the idea of an "effective and dominant nationality" but according to him it applies only in cases of dual nationality. Under this hypothesis, it would be necessary to decide which of the two States can grant diplomatic protection to the individual but this question does not arise in

---

[114] *Nottebohm Case, op. cit.*, p. 51, see footnote 108.

Nottebohm. He did have dual nationality. He lost his German nationality by reason of his naturalisation by Lichtenstein. What flows from this decision is that Nottebohm may no longer claim any diplomatic protection because he has become a "nationalityless" person. Yet, according to the Universal Declaration of Human Rights, every person has a right to have a nationality. From the non recognition of the Lichtensteiner nationality of Nottebohm flows the conclusion that his diplomatic protection is seriously compromised:

> "By revoking the right to protection, it becomes impossible to conduct an in depth examination of certain claims alleging a violation of rules of international law. If no other State is able to extend diplomatic protection – such as in this very case – claims made in the name of an individual whose nationality is contested or declared void on the international level, whilst he benefits from no other nationality, become moot." [115]

7.6. – Protection for Legal Persons – Nationality of Corporations and other "non-physical" persons

7.6.1. – *Essence of corporate nationality*

Different people have different opinions about the nature of corporate nationality. Clearly, corporate nationality is not the same as a physical person's nationality. The two share the name only of a distinguishing characteristic but, for most intents and purposes, the nationality of a corporation is not a nationality at all, when compared to the nationality of a physical person. Essentially, nationals are physical persons who have personal links with the State which has conferred nationality upon them, on the basis of birth, consanguinity, or affinity with other nationals of the same State, naturalisation etc., to which they may owe duties of conscription, voting, etc. and from which they are entitled to benefits such as social security,

---

[115] *Nottebohm Case, op. cit.*, p. 63, see footnote 108.

unemployment, medical, elections, etc. Clearly, corporate "nationality" shares no such links. Corporations are legal entities, often called "persons" by analogy to physical persons but having only economic, fiscal and legal links with the State of which they are determined to have the "nationality" :

> "In our opinion, the fact a legal person is deemed to have the nationality of a specific State does not mean anything more than this person is considered (often only for the purpose of a particular part of the law of that State) to be subject to the legal system of that State. This implies only that the laws of that State are applicable to such person and may exempt such person from the effect of discriminatory laws adopted by such State against 'foreign corporations' for the purpose of protecting certain national interests."[116]

Developing criteria to determine the nationality of a corporation can be just as complex, if not more so, than that of a physical person. Justification for conferring "nationality" on a corporation is based on an association of ideas that appear related but have, in fact, very little to do with each other. Thus, a corporation created under the laws of a State of the United States is deemed to have the "nationality" of the United States and such State, much as a person created (i.e. born) in the same locale will likewise have that nationality (*"ius soli"*). Obviously *"ius sanguinis"* will have no application and naturalisation is not, at least formally, available. On the other hand, a corporation may change its "nationality" when it changes the bases on which its nationality was determined upon its founding, a privilege not available to physical persons. Other than the dubious comparison of *"ius soli"*, the qualities of a physical person, by reason of which he or she has, acquires or loses nationality, have nothing in common with the qualities of a corporation, by reason of which it may have, acquire or lose its nationality.

---

[116] VAN BOXSOM, G., *Rechtsvergelijkende Studie over de nationaliteit van vennootschappen*, Brussels, Bruylant, 1994, p. 14.

7.6.2. – *Inherent ambiguity*

One could almost say that, when used with respect to a corporation, the term "nationality" is a misnomer, misleading the casual observer to draw quick and easy conclusions warranted with respect to physical persons but nonsensical with respect to corporations. Unfortunately, the term has acquired a patina of legality and no other noun, more representative of corporate qualities, benefits and obligations, has been coined.

Corporate domicile and residence are, for all practical purposes in a globalised world, so susceptible to manipulation as to become meaningless if not indeed deceptive. If the "control" criterion, so compelling to some for their categorisation of "investment", is transposed also to define nationality of a corporation, the fragmentation of shareholdings among physical shareholders of established but different nationalities leads to uncertainty in the nationality of the corporation, as shares change hands with increasing frequency on the stock markets of the world. If some of the shareholders are corporations, we are confronted by another tier of problems tied to control and nationality.

No doubt, in many cases, a majority of shareholders of like nationality can be identified, giving concerned government authorities a handle on the problem, but in an increasing number of cases, majority shareholdings are bought out by outsiders, who a few years later, may sell to yet another set or assemblage of sets of holders. Was Chrysler, when subject to Daimler-Benz control, a German company and will it, now that Daimler-Benz is getting rid of it, become again a U.S. company? Or did it simply go through its metamorphoses of nationality to become a national of one State for some purposes and of another State for other purposes?

Furthermore, in the cases of a myriad other companies, information regarding the nationality of its shareholders is not only difficult or impossible to obtain but, when obtainable, hopelessly out of date.

7.6.3. – *Character of corporate nationality*

There are quite a few controversial opinions around regarding the nationality of "legal persons". Some authors reject categorically the notion that there can be a nationality of such persons:

> "It's unusual to speak of the 'nationality' of legal persons and thus to import something that we predicate of natural persons into an area in which it can be applied by analogy only. Most of the effects of being an 'alien' or 'citizen' of the State are inapplicable in the field of corporations duties of allegiance or military service, the franchise and other political rights do not exist." [117]

However, even if the notion of "citizenship" for corporations is a misnomer, it clearly seems to some that it is appropriate to accept the idea that legal persons indeed have some kind of "nationality", if only to identify them with some jurisdiction to which they are more closely bound. Others disagree and raise the point that the term "nationality" is a term used in regards to corporations simply because no one has yet come up with other acceptable terminology that would better approximate what rights and obligations we mean when we speak of corporate "nationality". Some opponents of the use of nationality with respect to corporations use terminology such as "character" or "nature" of a legal person, but this does not appear to be a very useful, unambiguous alternative. In the US, for instance, with respect to physical persons, nationality and citizenship are nearly coterminous (there being some US nationals who are not citizens) but neither term fully describes the bundle of rights and obligations corporations established in a particular State may have. In the US, this problem is compounded by the fact the

---

[117] WOLFF, Joël M., *"Private International law"*, London, Clarendon Press Oxford, 1950, p. 308.

country is made of States which are at least supposedly "sovereign" in areas not pre-empted by the Federal Union. Hence, a corporation established in the State of California is a California corporation, not an "American" corporation, since it was not constituted under the federal laws, although common parlance may make it so and designate any corporation established under the laws of any of the 50 States of the Federal Union as an "American" national.

It is not necessarily suggested that there ought to be BIT's between everyone of the 50 US States and foreign countries, though certainly, in terms of size, territorially and economically, many US States match or surpass many foreign countries. It appears nearly axiomatic that an Idaho corporation should be able to claim the diplomatic protection of a US consulate or embassy solely by virtue of the fact that Idaho is a member State of the Federal Union.

Legal scholars should be imaginative enough to coin a word other than nationality for corporations. That alternative should inclusively describe the bundle of rights and obligations of corporations. Since these rights depend upon the legislation of the specific State where a corporation is created, it is not possible to homogenise this bundle of rights but only to note that, for purposes of deciding on a particular issue in arbitration, corporations created in a State of the U.S. has some rights and obligations which are common, or at least similar, and the differences otherwise may be ignored. Many corporate founders carefully choose the State in which they incorporate precisely because of these differences.

Either the imagination is lacking or the prospect of a wide ranging discussion about the coinage of an appropriate word is a deterrent enough to abstain when problems arise which can *grosso modo* be handled using terms in which experts in the field can instantly see nuances and are therefore disinclined to see the utility of any new coinage. Whatever the alternative term so chosen, or if none is, BIT's should be amended so that corporations and other forms of human associations are included expressis verbis among the beneficiaries of conventional as well as diplomatic and consular protection rather than have reliance placed on a common term covering disparate objects.

For instance, if it had not already been overused, the term "establishment" would come to mind since it is commonly said of a corporation whose origin consisted of documentation filed with the competent authorities of a particular State, that it was "established" in that State. Until a satisfactory word is coined, scholars and investors alike must use a term then which they may, with some degree of consistency throughout the venues they frequent, understand to mean something akin to the "nationality" of an individual but nonetheless avoiding inappropriate analogies.

In order to establish the idiosynchrasy of a corporate "nationality" (if no other term can be found) and delineate what the rights and duties of a corporation may be, there must first be a solidarity and a demonstrable bond with the legal system of the State of establishment. Corporations should not be left in a "no man's land" but must be situated in the legal sphere of a particular State. In a very broad sense, that "situation" is the alter ego of a corporation's nationality.

Since diplomatic and consular protection's axiomatic and *sine qua non* condition is that it will be extended only to "nationals" of that mission, it is necessary to know what corporate "nationality" is. No other means exist to determine whether a particular State may acknowledge the "nationality" of a corporation seeking its help in the form of diplomatic and consular protection. It may be necessary to acknowledge that corporations have peculiar characteristics not shared by physical persons but that do not affect in any way the need to endow corporations with a *"persona"* as a means of binding it to a particular legal system. The use of the same term, "nationality", in relation to both a physical and a legal person, to identity which State they are "nationals" of, is perhaps unfortunate but not per se a major hindrance to clarity, so long as everyone agrees that the term "nationality" has different definitions according to the nature, physical or moral, of the claimant. The problem is that, even in the countries where they are established, not every one does agree.

We therefore, somewhat reluctantly, share the opinion of BATTIFOL, namely, that it is not conceptually incorrect to use the notion of "nationality" for legal persons:

> "It does not so appear, so long as people remember that, although certain analogies to the national of physical persons exist, the nationality of corporations is a distinct concept.
>
> The similarity of terms has the inconvenience of veiling the distinction but the advantage is that it makes people aware of the analogies. The inconvenience is minimal, since, in fact, confusion is hardly possible." [118]

7.6.4. – *Corporate nationality theories*

Opposition to the concept of nationality for corporations likes to use terms such as "character" or "nature". That does not seem appropriate. Granting "nationality" to a legal person, in the circumscribed context of its application to a corporate entity, fulfils a real need on both the national and international levels. To declare the nationality of a legal person, to declare which State it is beholden to, to establish its local or foreign character are but the components of a single operation, that is to say the determination of what rules of law to apply to the corporation (cfr subparagraph 6.1). It is an accepted fact that a corporation's legal status depends upon its nationality, so long as it can be rationally determined, and the rules of international and domestic law which govern its actions and conduct are set.

---

[118] BATTIFOL, Henri, *Traité élémentaire de droit international privé*, Paris, Librairie générale de droit et de jurisprudence (LGDJ), 1955, p. 230.

The determination of a nationality for a corporation, on the basis of which legal bonds are created with a specific State, may be made on the basis of different criteria. VAN BOXSOM, for example, cites only two such factors, that of the corporate seat and that where it was incorporated:

> "According to the *'seat'* theory, the place where the management of the corporation is really conducted. Hence, the nationality of a corporation is where its principal 'seat' is."

> "According the *'incorporation'* theory, the nationality of a company is determined by the founders who, when it was constituted, declared that the company was established conforming to the laws of the State of their choice. The founders are those who select the legal system to which the corporation will be subject. If a corporation is incorporated in Britain, in accordance with applicable law, that corporation has British nationality and it is thereby incorporated within British corporate law." [119]

However, Western based concepts of justice and equity found that these two characteristics were insufficient to achieve the goal intended, that is, bind the corporation to a specific jurisdiction without stretching the meaning of the word "bind" to unacceptable exaggeration. Besides those two criteria, therefore, the nationality of a corporation has been found to be based on a third: that of *"control"* which need not necessarily be consistent with the other two. According to this idea, the company has the nationality of the State to which the majority shareholders belong and, thenceforth, in order to help it properly function, its nationality should be the same as that of the majority shareholders who take, almost as a sovereign, the corporation's important decisions. (cfr *infra*).

---

[119] VAN BOXSOM, G., *op. cit.*, p. 19, see footnote 116.

7.6.4.1. *Dominant Theory : Principal Seat*

At this time, therefore, there are three theories various States use to grant "nationality" to a legal person: Seat, incorporation and control.

The *SEAT* theory, adopted in most European countries (France, Germany, Luxemburg, Belgium and Italy, to name a few) where it is defended and vigorously applied. In Belgium, for instance, the law is not much different:

> "Every corporation which has its principal seat in Belgium is subject to Belgian law, even when it was established abroad". (article 197, Commercial Code)

Where the corporation's principal seat was established therefore has, in those countries, a decisive influence on its "nationality." Under the law, the Act constituting a corporation may have occurred abroad but wherever it is said that the principal seat is, the law of the seat applies. Thus, in Belgium,

> "Article 197, according to which a corporation established abroad but whose principal seat is in Belgium is subject to Belgian law, without exception, whether the corporation, established abroad, maintains its seat in Belgium since its establishment or one whose seat has been transferred to Belgium later. A corporation established abroad is subject to foreign law, in accordance with article 197, as long as its principal seat is set in the country where it was established : that corporation will become subject to Belgian law the moment its seat is transferred to Belgium." [120]

For the proper management of BIT's, it is interesting to note that Luxemburg applies the seat theory also. Most often, Luxemburg decides on a Luxembourger nationality when a company meets two mutually enhancing conditions, namely, that the corporation was established in Luxemburg and that its seat is there. This difference between Belgian and Luxemburger practice is not mentioned in the BIT's.

---

[120] VAN BOXSOM, G., *op. cit.*, p. 66, see footnote 116.

All of this begs the question : what does one mean by "principal seat"?

At least as to Belgium, jurisprudence has confirmed several times that the principal seat is where the seat of the corporation is *really* established (excluding phantom seats), serving as the management and authority centre :

> "In as much as the Board of Directors has held a greater number of its meetings in Roubaix, ...that the appellant has wrongly concluded that the Roubaix office had become the principal seat of the corporation, and that in fact more than two thirds of Board of Directors' meetings, in particular the last one prior to liquidation, were held in Brussels, that it is not otherwise unknown that General Meetings of shareholders have always met..., that the balance sheet was approved in Brussels, and that top management for the company's affairs was in that city..." [121]

The Brussels Court of Appeals held that the company was Belgian using the "real and principal seat" concept to support its decision. The principal seat may be different from the centre of production : whose location has no influence whatever on the corporation's nationality.

Doctrinal texts unanimously hold that the principal seat is where the centre of management of a Company is :

> "By principal establishment (seat), we understand the seat of its administration. The place where it has established its general accounting, where it keeps its archives and where its general meetings of shareholders are held, in a word where is concentrated its management activity, the centre of its interest and social affairs." [122]

In the "Novelles", the identical idea is stated :

> "Principal establishment means the place where the organisation's management impulses in company affairs start : jurisprudence has generally accepted this system, binding the principal establishment (principal seat) to the seat of administration, preferably where the seat and the principal commercial establishments are located in differ-

---

[121] VAN BOXSOM, G., *op. cit.*, p. 24, see footnote 116.
[122] *Répertoire pratique du droit belge*, *op. cit.*, n° 34, see footnote 9.

ent places : the factories and the marketing centres are but operating seats reference to which is made in Article 198." [123]

The "seat" criterion is dominant throughout Europe and even worldwide. However, different European and other BIT's formulate the theory differently, using terms such as head office, principal seat, social seat, registered office, etc. It seems evident to us that there ought to be be some consistency between the terms used in investment protection agreements and in the law. For instance, on their first negotiation or in a subsequent renegotiation, State BIT's could all use the term "principal seat". Protocols, annexed to the BIT's could give substance to the term by citing constituting elements such as management centre, Board of Directors meetings location, etc. ICSID's arbitral jurisprudence shows the concept is accepted by and large :

"The nationality concept (as adopted by the Convention) is a classical concept based on the law under which a moral person has been established, the place of its establishment and the place of its social seat." [124]

In the large majority of European BIT's, the "seat" theory has been adopted. LDC's, which are co-contracting Parties to these BIT's, follow it without problems. Here are a few examples :

"The term 'legal persons', with reference to either Contracting party, shall mean any entity *having its head office* in the territory of the Contracting Parties and recognised by it, such as public institutions, corporations, partnerships, foundations and associations, regardless of whether their liability is limited or otherwise." (BIT Italy/Nicaragua, 20 April 2004, article I) *(italics ours)*

"The term investor means : in respect of the Federal republic of Germany... any juridical person as well as any commercial or other company or association with or without legal personality *having its seat* in the territory of the federal Republic of Germany, irrespective of whether or not its activities are directed at profit." (BIT Germany/China, 11 november,2005, article 1) *(italics ours)*

---

[123] *Les Novelles, Corpus Juris Belgici*, Brussels, Larcier, 1931, Tome III, Sociétés commerciales, n° 5206.

[124] GAILLARD, Emmanuel, *op. cit.*, p. 70, see footnote 31.

Nonetheless, more recently, using the "seat" criterion as the sole test of a corporation's nationality is not as frequent as before. Combining corporate control and place of incorporation as joint criteria to determine corporate nationality is gaining ground.

7.6.4.2. *Place of Incorporation*

The place of incorporation of a company is the test which is often used for the definition of the nationality of a legal person. This theory is applied in Latin-American countries (ex. Peru, Brazil and Guatemala), as well as in the UK and the US. According to this theory, the nationality of a corporation is determined by the Act which founded it and the law on which this Act is based. Reincorporation or other corporate re-organisation in another State, and establishing the seat of a company in another State, may arguably change the corporate nationality. If the founders choose, in the incorporating documents, to apply the law of a particular State, the corporation will have the nationality of that State. The legal system in which the company was incorporated will govern its "life", from the moment of its creation to that of its liquidation:

> "If one keeps in mind that a legal person is always the creation of a legal system, that it cannot be born outside of a legal system, it is evident that the most logical solution is to determine the nationality of that legal person in accordance with the law to which it owes its creation." [125]

RABEL stresses that this system is also preferred in all countries which have adopted "common law" (usually interpreted to have at least some relation to English "common law"):

> "In all common law countries, a corporation lives under the law under which it has been created or "incorporated", the law from which in Westlake's expression, it "derives" its existence." [126]

---

[125] MAKAROV, A., "Conception du droit international privé d'après la doctrine et la pratique russes", The Hague Academy Collected Courses, La Haye, NIJHOFF Martinus, *Reports*, 1931, p. 523.

[126] RABEL, Ernst, *The conflicts of Law*, Chicago, Edition Wikipedia, 1958, p. 31.

Here are a few more examples of nationality related clauses in BIT's:

> "Investor means ... in respect of the United Kingdom, corporations, firms and associations incorporated or constituted under the law in force in any part of the United Kingdom..." (BIT UK/El Salvador, 1 December 2001, article 1)

> "company of a Contracting party means any kind of corporation, company, association, ownership, or other organisation, legally constituted under the laws and regulations of a Party or a political subdivision thereof whether or not organised for pecuniary gain, or privately or governmentally owned or controlled." (BIT US/Estonia, 19 April 1994, article 1, definitions)

7.6.4.3. Control Theory

This theory is based on the notion that corporate nationality depends upon the nationality of whoever controls the corporation. Thus, a Panamanian corporation controlled by Swiss shareholders would, if such theory is applied, be deemed to have Swiss nationality for the purposes of a BIT between Switzerland and Panama. This topic is addressed in further detail in Chapter VIII of this Work.

7.6.4.4. Combined Tests of Companies' Nationality

Previously a very clear distinction has been made between the "seat" theory and the incorporation theory. In his separate opinion in the "*Barcelona Traction*" case, Judge JESSUP articulated this distinction as follows:

> "There are two standards tests of the 'nationality' of a corporation. The place of corporation is the test generally favoured in the legal systems of the common law, while the 'siège social' is more generally accepted in the civil law systems."[127]

The concept used in conventions, either under the "seat" theory or the "incorporation" theory, do not correspond to

---

[127] *Barcelona Traction, Light and Power Company Limited*, op. cit., p. 183, see footnote 15.

current practice. The unique criterion approach with respect to corporate nationality is often abandoned in favour of a multiple approach, a combination of several criteria. In several BIT's, twin conditions are applied to determine whether an investor is protected or not: be incorporated under the law of one of the Contracting Parties and also have its seat on the territory of that Party:

> "Investor means... legal persons constituted in France conforming to the French law and having a Head office in France." (BIT France/Singapore, 18 October 1976, **Article 1**)

The concern, of course, is to avoid having a foreign company set up a "phantom" corporation on the territory of one of the Contracting Parties, in order to benefit from the protection of a BIT between the "Home State» and another State.

Another formula is to be found in the Belgo-Luxemburg BIT with Croatia dated 29 December 2003:

> "Investor means to either Contracting Party.... any legal person constituted or duly organised under the laws and regulations of one of the Contracting Parties, having its seat and economic activities on the territory of that Contracting Party and making investments on the territory of the other Contracting party." (article 1, 2, b)

Some BIT's bring all three corporate theories under one roof:

> "Investor shall mean.the companies, i.e. with respect to both Contracting Parties, a legal person constituted on the territory of one Contracting Party in accordance with the legislation of that Party having its head office on the territory of that Party, or controlled directly or indirectly by the nationals of one Contracting Party, or by legal persons having their head office in the territory of one Contacting Party and constituted in accordance with the legislation of that Party." (BIT UEBL/Philippines,6 March 1996, article 1)

Whether this "all-in-one" solution is desirable depends on the exact formulation, but, in any event, the "control" concept must be made explicit.

7.7. – ICSID VIEW ON NATIONALITY

7.7.1. – *ICSID' Nationality Conditions*

The Washington Convention of 18 March 1965 (ICSID) regarding the settlement of conflicts affecting investments and arising between States and nationals of other States is without any doubt one of the most important multinational conventions regarding international investments. This was an innovation in that for the very first time an international organisation was created to which private persons seeking an arbitration award regarding their conflicts with a foreign State had direct access. Probably under the pressure of States which had adopted the theory of control (USA, UK) a provision was inserted in this convention, opening the way for the application, under certain conditions, of this theory. In Article 25 of this Convention, it is stated that:

> "the Arbitration Centre has jurisdiction to decide cases arising between a Contracting State and the national of another Contracting State."

The conditions physical and legal persons must meet when filing an arbitration claim are described as follows:

> "A National of another State means:
>
> Any *natural* person who has the nationality of a Contracting State other than the State party to the dispute on the date on which the parties consented to submit such dispute to conciliation or arbitration as well as on the date on which the request was registered pursuant to paragraph (3) of article 28 or paragraph (3) of article 36, but does not include any person who on either date also had the nationality of the Contracting State party to the dispute; and
>
> Any *juridical* person which had the nationality of a Contracting State other than the State party to the dispute on the date on which the parties consented to submit such dispute to conciliation or arbitration and any juridical person which had the nationality of the Contracting State party to the dispute on that date and which, *because of foreign control, the parties have agreed, should be treated as a national of another Contracting State* for the purposes of this Convention."
> (*emphasis* ours)

As a matter of fact, this provision will be stimulating States to include in BIT's a provision similar to that in **Article 25(2)b** under which it is agreed to confer on legal persons the same nationality as that of foreign shareholders in one Contracting State who control the legal person in the Contracting State against which an arbitration claim has been filed. The local company, established according to the law of the State which is a party to the arbitration proceeding thereby does not lose its "legal" nationality. In addition, such nationality, to the extent it was conferred on the basis of the seat theory or the incorporation theory, is complemented by a conventional nationality. It is an *"ad hoc"* nationality which is valid only for the purposes of applying the ICSID convention, the BIT's and eventually any special agreement between host States and foreign investors. The attribution of the status of "other Contracting State company" to a domestic company because of its control by foreign partners is a special characteristic *"sui generis"*, with only temporary effectivity. The right of a domestic company to file a claim for arbitration by ICSID against the very State to which it belongs would cease to exist, should the foreign investors withdraw and foreign control thereby disappear.

7.7.2. – *"Functional and subsidiary nationality"*

Amadio uses the term "functional and subsidiary nationality":

> "A legal person of the nationality of a State which is a party to the issue may become a party to the procedure established by the Centre (ICSID) if the State in question agrees to deem it a national of another Contracting State on the ground of its control by foreign interests. This agreement confers to the legal person a kind of subsidiary nationality, functional only to the extent of the Centre's jurisdiction." [128]

---

[128] AMADIO, Mario, *Le contentieux international de l'investissement privé et la convention de la Banque Mondiale du 18 mars 1965*, Paris, Librairie générale de droit et de jurisprudence (LGDJ), 1967, p. 115.

The effective nationality of a corporation is therefore that which is attributed to it by its own State, on the basis of criteria provided for in that State's domestic law (seat, incorporation theories). The investor can only use his own functional and conventional nationality when he wishes to file an arbitration procedure, under the Washington Convention, for the settlement of a dispute relating to an investment covered by this Convention. A corporation's ability to file an arbitration procedure against his own national State is therefore an exception to the general rule. Normally, such a corporate investor is subject to the jurisdiction of the State of his own effective nationality. As a matter of fact, it is an instance of double nationality, created by means of a convention and for a specific and limited purpose.

7.7.3. – Origins of Article 25(2) b of the Washington Convention

We have already stated that this clause was inserted in the Convention at the behest of countries which apply the control theory. However, States hosting foreign investments have also contributed to the adoption of this system. In many developing countries, preference is given to foreign investments which use a locally established corporation. Developing countries have used this formula in order to give companies established and controlled by foreign interests access to ICSID.

The Congolese Investment Code (cfr *supra*) and the codes of other African countries include a provision requiring foreign investors to make their investments through a local corporation. Starting from this point, the writers of the ICSID Convention believed it was necessary to insert a special clause to protect foreign investors. It had become clear to them that developing countries considered that a procedure for the settlement of conflicts with private investors was an encroachment on their sovereignty. There was a real danger that such countries would try to limit the jurisdiction of IDSIC by arguing that procedures filed by domestic companies with the assistance of a foreign investor would be demurrable. A large portion of foreign investments in developing countries would then be outside of the application of ICSID:

> "There was a compelling reason for this last provision (**Article 25(2)b**. It is quite usual for host States to require that foreign investors to carry on their business within the territories through a company organised under the laws of the host country. If we admit that this makes the company technically a national of the host country, it becomes readily apparent there is a need for an exception. If no exception were made for foreign owned but locally incorporated companies, a large and important section of foreign investments would be outside the scope of the convention." [129]

7.7.4. – Scope and Interpretation of Article 25(2)b

ICSID's jurisdiction extends to conflicts relating to investments between States that are members of ICSID and individuals or legal persons having the nationality of a State bound by the convention. Private investors which have the nationality of a member State which has originated the conflict therefore cannot refer the matter to ICSID. As stressed above, and by way of an exception, **Article 25 (2)b** offers the possibility for legal persons having the nationality of a State originating the conflict and established on the territory of such State to file an arbitration claim with ICSID against their own State.

Demurrability is based on the fact that the legal person is controlled by foreign interests in the capital stock of the company. **Article 25(2)b** is not the best example of terminology, neither in the way it was written nor in its content.

Jurisprudence may help determine the exact scope of the provision reading: "...because of the foreign interests' control

---

[129] BROCHES, Aron, "The Convention on the Settlement of investment disputes between States and nationals of other States", The Hague Academy Collected Courses, Martinus NIJHOFF, 1972, volume 136, p. 358.

over the company." It will be analysed in the "Control" Chapter of this Work.

7.8. – MULTINATIONALS AND TRANSNATIONALS

Even medium sized and small independent companies do not hesitate, from time to time, to make international investments, although, admittedly, the large multinationals are the most active internationally and are the influences on local economies less developed countries have grown most to seek and fear:

> "A multinational enterprise is, in fact, an enterprise which includes several corporations, each established in different countries and each endowed with the nationality of the country of establishment." [130]

The United Nations Organisation defined multinational enterprises (MNE) as:

> "enterprises owning or controlling production or services facilities outside the country in which they are based. Multinational corporations are defined as 'enterprises having a network of wholly or partially (sometimes jointly with one or more foreign partners) owned affiliates producing, marketing or performing R&D in a number of countries.'" [131]

In legal doctrine, the term "transnational enterprise" is sometimes used. This is a reference to enterprises established in different States, under a single commercial name, each such enterprise having a different place of business, or "seat". A multinational, on the other hand, is composed of a parent company and affiliates connected to the parent by legal and economic ties. Within a transnational enterprise, affiliates may have a separate seat in the country where they are established but may have little economic connections with

---

[130] EYSKENS, Mark, *Economie van nu en straks*, Antwerp, De Nederlandse boekhandel (DNB), 1977, p. 295.

[131] ZEKOS, Georgios, "Finance and investment in globalization", *The Journal of World Investment*, Geneva, 2003, volume 4, n° 1, p. 85.

each other. Specific measures are therefore needed in order to assure optimal protection of the corporate identity of each affiliate.

The foregoing begs the questions : what is intended by "established", what is intended by "based", by "seat". Are there hybrids, making the entire topic of nationality as an indispensable basis for Bilateral Investment Treaties virtually impossible to study, the evidence of domicile/residence/establishment/base immaterial to the issues debated, possibly wholly irrelevant, and the debate itself a conversation of the deaf.

CHAPTER VIII
CONTROL

8.1. – Control Theory

According to this theory, the origin of the corporate capital and the invested capital since the corporation was first created must be considered. The corporation has the nationality of the legal or physical persons who, because of the importance of their participation in the capital, exert control over the company. In special cases (for instance, arbitration, diplomatic protection), the territoriality principle is not applied and the State on the territory of which the corporation was established does not consider the corporation to be its national. The proponents of this theory adopt an economic point of departure. According to them, foreign shareholders receive a great benefit from the importation of capital into the host country and it is therefore logical that the nationality of the corporation be the same as that of such persons who are responsible for its management and direction. However, the application of this theory is not self-evident.

The theory is rather exceptional, as has been made to appear in several arbitration awards:

> "The tribunal noted that the Washington Convention (ICSID) does not have a definition of 'nationality', as a result leaving to every State the right to define whether a corporation has or has not its nationality. Generally speaking, States, for this purpose, apply either the corporate seat or the incorporation theory. On the other hand, the nationality of shareholders of the control by foreigners other than by reason of their participation in the capital, is not normally a corporate nationality criterion, it being understood that the legislature may add these criteria for exceptional cases." [132]

---

[132] GAILLARD, Emmanuel, *op. cit.*, p. 38, see footnote 31.

In several countries exceptional legislation has been enacted after each World War in order to allow laws regarding asset sequestration to apply to corporations having a foreign and hostile character. The companies concerned were managed and controlled by shareholders whose States were at war with such countries.

The International Court of Justice (ICJ) has acknowledged that this was an exceptional situation:

> "With regard to the first enemy property, legislation was an instrument of economic warfare, aimed at denying the enemy the advantages to be derived from the anonymity and separate personality of corporations. Hence the lifting of the veil was regarded as justified 'ex necessitate' and was extended to all entities which were tainted with enemy character, even the nationals of the State enacting the legislation. The provisions of the peace treaties had a very specific function: to protect allied property and to seize and pool enemy-property with a view to covering reparation claims. Such provisions are basically different in their rationale from those normally applicable." [133]

No suggestion is made that this theory be applied wholesale today. In international practice, the use of the control criterion may lead to many difficulties. Thus, it is possible that conflicts arise between States regarding the interpretation of the "control" idea. What grounds will be used to claim that a corporation is effectively controlled by foreign shareholders? Are there any generally accepted grounds therefore?

Jurisprudence is negative on the concept:

> "There is no formula. It is of course obvious that the presence of a 100% foreign shareholder will lead to the conclusion control is foreign, no matter what the criteria will be, and the total absence of foreign shareholders would virtually prohibit a finding of such control. To know what is sufficient cannot be decided abstractly. Thus, when ICSID was negotiated, it was stated many times that interests sufficient powerful to block major changes in the company could determine what the control is, but that control could be acquired by persons owning as little as 25% of the stock, and even that 51% of share

---

[133] *Barcelona Traction, Light and Power Company, op. cit.*, p. 39, see footnote 15.

ownership could not be determinative of control, whereas in some cases as little as 15% would be sufficient." [134]

Arbitration institutions and tribunals will therefore examine not only the participation percentages but also other concrete elements such as a decisive influence on decisions taken within the corporation. If foreign majority shareholders are active only in the technical operations of a company and are not represented in the decision organisms thereof, it will be difficult for the judges or arbitrators to conclude that their nationality has been transferred to the corporation on the basis of the "control" theory.

Van Boxsom posits an extreme view that a corporation may have several nationalities and this by reason of the fact that it is necessary to examine if a corporation controlled by foreigners is or is not subject to certain areas of the law (private international law, foreigners' rights, etc.). He sees different kinds of nationalities awarded by a single State (in the example he used, Belgium) : one according to private international law, one according to the law regarding foreigners, yet another according to conventional law. The author believes that a company could, when this theory is applied, be deemed to be local in relation to its status within private international law and also foreign in relation to the application of foreigners' law. This idea has no support in the doctrine or in jurisprudence. A corporation is to be deemed a single legal entity and cannot have several nationalities foisted on it.

As validation for his idea, Van Boxsom analogises to diplomatic protection :

> "Let us observe that when a State undertakes diplomatic intercessions ('démarches' in diplomatic parlance) in favour of a company against which vexatious measures have been taken in another State, the interceding State deems that it is authorised to intercede on the ground of the 'interests' represented by the company (therefore pri-

---

[134] *Barcelona Traction, Light and Power Company, op. cit.*, p. 398, see footnote 15.

marily on the basis of the fact that a specific number of majority shareholders are nationals" of the interceding State), so that it is the bond between the shareholders and a specific State that governs and not the bond between the company, as a 'legal person' and such state." [135]

Incidentally, this example does not represent conventional practice in Van Boxsom's own country. Belgian official démarches do not seek validation based on the reasons cited in this example. In nationalisation agreements concluded since the end of the last world war, and in the BIT's, the seat theory is applied. Even if the company's capital includes important foreign holdings, a Belgian company may benefit from diplomatic intercessions. Very exceptionally (cfr *supra* "EBENSEE"), as in the agreement between Belgium and Czechoslovakia, which requested it, a provision mentioning the theory of control was inserted in the indemnification agreement (1962).

In this case, the ICJ also declared that the control theory could be exceptionally applied:

> "Also distinct are the various arrangements made in respect of compensation for the nationalisation of foreign property. Their rationale too, derived as it is from structural changes in a State's economy, differs from that of any normally applicable provisions. Specific agreements have been reached to meet specific situations and the terms have varied from case to case. Far from evidencing any norm as to the classes of beneficiaries of compensation, such arrangements are *"sui generis"* and provide no guide in the present case." [136]

8.2. – ANTECEDENTS OF "CONTROL"

Without a doubt, the most important antecedent to the theory of "control" is the decision rendered on 7 February 1970, as held by the International Court of Justice in

---
[135] VAN BOXSOM, *op. cit.*, p. 15, see footnote 116.
[136] *Barcelona Traction, Light and Power Company*, *op. cit.*, p. 40, see footnote 15.

The Hague in the *Barcelona Traction, Light and Power Company, Limited* case [137] (see also *supra* Chapter VI).

This case confirmed that the theory of control was not incorporated in international law and that therefore its application on an international level required a solid legal basis, namely an interstate convention. It is therefore not surprising that this celebrated case involving Spain, Canada and Belgium in 1970 gave special *impetus* to the development of the notion of "control" in bilateral investment treaties.

However, the context of the control theory is different in the BITs from that in the decision. The aim of BIT provisions concerning control is to include in the conventional investment protection system companies established in a third State and controlled by shareholders of one of the Contracting Parties. According to a special provision in the BITs, the controlling company established in the territory of one Contracting Party, and the controlled company, established on the territory of a third State (not a non-Contracting Party) are both considered investors of the Contracting Party.

In the Barcelona case, the main question was: has a State the right to extend its diplomatic protection in favour of such companies.

The practical implication of this decision was that it did not permit diplomatic protection of shareholders whose nationality was different from that of the country of incorporation of the company. According to this ruling, much foreign investment would have had to be made without the possibility of diplomatic protection of the home countries of the foreign investors. This was avoided by incorporating the notion of "control" into the definitions of "investment" or "investor". This approach renders the "Barcelona Traction" award inapplicable. Thus, assets indirectly owned or controlled by investors of the other contracting party are covered, regard-

---

[137] *Barcelona Traction, Light and Power Company, Limited, op. cit.*, see footnote 15.

less of the country in which the company directly owning the assets has been incorporated.[138]

It thus becomes necessary to enquire further and see whether the BITs provisions regarding control do in fact provide efficient protection.

In the Barcelona case, the link straddled three States: Belgium, the claimant and home State of the controlling shareholders; Canada, the state of incorporation of the controlled company, Barcelona Traction; and Spain, the expropriating State. In current terms, this type of investment has taken on the name of "triangular investment" to distinguish it from the formerly more common case of an investor from country A investing in country B. In more modern days, triangulation is no longer an anomaly.

8.3. – *Barcelona Traction* Triangulation

In the *Barcelona* case, the Belgian Government's petition with the Court of Justice in The Hague, exceptionally, invoked the theory of "control", because that was the only ground on which Belgium's intercession against Spain could be allowed. The facts may be succinctly stated as follows: The Belgian company (SIDO) held a majority share in a Canadian corporation, "Barcelona Traction Light and Power Company Limited" (BT). This corporation had held shares in the capital of various Spanish companies established by BT, according to Spanish law. The Spanish assets of BT were affected by various kinds of privative measures (expropriations, liquidations, etc.). Canada was not asking for compensation from the Spanish government.

Belgium's claim with the Court of Justice was in accordance with the wishes of Belgian shareholders of the Canadian company, in fact the indirect owners of the Spanish assets of

---

[138] UNCTAD, *Compendium International Investments*, Vol. III, p. 17.

that company. It has already been pointed out that a State has standing to assume the defence of private interests before this Court :

> "There was therefore no reason to question whether, when litigation commenced, a private interest had been affected, inasmuch as this is precisely what occurs in many conflicts between States." [139]

The actual issue in this lawsuit revolved around the nationality of the shareholders. A State's right to intervene in favour of private interests is based on the nationality of those persons for whom it intervenes. A State may only intervene validly (*locus standi*) if the beneficiaries of its intervention (physical or legal persons) are its nationals :

> "A State which puts forward a claim before a claims commission or other international tribunal must be in a position to show that it has '*locus standi*' for that purpose. The principal and almost exclusive factor creating that *locus standi* is the nationality of the claimant, and it may be stated as a general principle that, from the time of the occurrence of the injury until the making of the award, the claim must continuously and without interruption have belonged to a person or a series of persons having the nationality of the State by whom it is put forward, and not having the nationality of the State against whom it is put forward." [140]

This excerpt, parenthetically, shows how artificial the theory is. A company's shareholders change all the time as its shares are traded on various stock exchanges. It is not hard to imagine a company's majority shares changing hands several times while the case is winding its way month after month and year after year in the courts. The main question here was to determine whether the Belgian State could intervene in favour of Belgian majority shareholders of a Canadian corporation, on the basis that control was actually in Belgian hands.

The Court denied the petition on two grounds :

---

[139] Case *Nottebohm*, *op. cit.*, p. 24, see footnote 108.
[140] OPPENHEIM, L.F.L., *International Law*, Cambridge, Edition Cambridge University Press, 1967, p. 347, 1957, p. 347.

"Foreign shareholders of an affected company may be defended only by the State to which they belong; the Canadian company BT and its domestic and foreign shareholders therefore could only be defended by the Canadian State; Belgian control over the Canadian company has no bearing at all on its nationality and does not cause a change in its nationality : 'It follows from what we have said above that, when illegal acts have been committed against a foreign company, the general rule of international law gives the power to file an arbitration request only to the national State of that corporation.'" [141]

More fundamentally, the Court in the Barcelona case confirmed that Canada, and Canada only, had the right to intervene and protect the Canadian corporation, excluding therefore the foreign shareholders of the Canadian corporation. By *dictum*, the Court remarked that a simple but express agreement could have created a basis on which Belgium might have intervened on behalf of its shareholders :

"Here as elsewhere, a body of rules could only have developed with the consent of those concerned." [142]

Questions arise as to the scope of this statement. Are Canada and Belgium the only States affected? We try to answer these questions in sub-title 8.4.

8.4. – BIT's TRIANGULATION "LINK" BETWEEN STATES

In most any analogous situation, the "link" between the investor and the investment straddles three States, the State of the investor's nationality, the host State and a third State. On the latter's territory, the investor invested in a company which had holdings in the host State. What is needed therefore is to re-examine the definition of "investor" in order to adapt it to this particular situation. The definition of "Inves-

---

[141] *Barcelona Traction, Light and Power Company, Limited*, op. cit., pp. 46 and 47, see footnote 15.
[142] *Barcelona Traction, Light and Power Company, Limited*, op. cit., p. 47, see footnote 15.

tor" could, for instance, to the extent it included "any legal person not organised under the laws of one of the Contracting Parties but controlled by an investor, as hereinabove defined," be replaced by :

> "any legal person organised under the laws of a third State controlled by such investor".

The net effect is that there is a form of competition between States regarding the protection available to the investor. The Swedish formula would not be failure of proof. The third State, not bound by a BIT with the host State, could under this formula argue that the BIT between the host State and the investor (a national of the other Contracting State) is a *"res inter alios acta"*. It can, however invoke its right to diplomatic protection in favour of the company established on its territory even if such company is controlled by foreign investors.

In the absence of interstate conventions, the State of the nationality of the corporation is entitled to grant its diplomatic protection to such corporation. The ICJ has confirmed that this is an international law rule :

> "On the international plane, the Belgian Government has advanced the proposition that it is inadmissible to deny the shareholders' national State a right of diplomatic protection merely on the ground that another State possesses a correspondent right in respect of the company itself. In strict logic and law, this formulation of the Belgian claim to *'jus standi'* assumes the existence of the very right that requires demonstration. In fact, the Belgian Government has repeatedly stressed that there exists no rule of international law which would deny the national State of the shareholders the right of diplomatic protection for the purpose of seeking redress pursuant to unlawful acts committed by another State against the company in which they hold shares. This, by emphasising the absence of any express denial of the right, conversely implies the admission that there is no rule of international law which expressly confers such a right on the shareholders' national State" [143]

---

[143] *Barcelona Traction, Light and Power Company, Limited*, op. cit., p. 37, see footnote 15.

To avoid an interstate conflict in this connection, a formula would be beneficial which provides for diplomatic protection by one of the Contracting Parties in favour of persons who are its nationals, even though they may be shareholders of a company in a third State, in the event this third State refuses or neglects to provide diplomatic protection to a company established on its territory.

Actually, in the BT case, there was a triangular investment, that is, an investment by Belgian shareholders in Spanish companies through the middle ground of a Canadian company. Canada having refused or neglected to defend the Belgian shareholders Inspired by the negative outcome of the BT case, the Belgian government has, for the very first time, while negotiating with China, caused to be inserted in the Belgo-Chinese BIT a special clause regarding the protection of triangular investments :

> "In the application of **Article 4** of the agreement, in the case where investors of one of the contracting Parties are owners of capital shares of a foreign, non-Belgian, non-Luxembourger and non-Chinese, company, should the latter be the owner of shares in the capital of a corporation of the other Contracting Party, the latter will apply the rules of paragraphs 1 and 2 of **Article 4** to the said investors who are shareholders of the said foreign company. This provision shall apply only when the said corporation or State to which it belongs would not have the standing to file a claim for indemnisation or when such State would decline to file the indemnisation herein provided for." [144]

It is regrettable that this clause has not been used in other BIT's concluded since the BT case was decided. This is not a perfect formula. In this case also, the third State could claim that this clause of the convention is *"res inter alios acta"*. Conceivably judges or arbitrators called on to decide this matter will be able to overlook the third State's refusal to intervene and proceed in favour of an intervention by the first State in the investment chain.

---

[144] Belgian Federal Register dated 16 September 1986, p. 12522.

8.5. – NEED TO DEFINE "CONTROL" IN BIT's

8.5.1. – *Need for new Law*

It is odd that internationalisation of economics has not yet led to the creation of innovative law and to an acceptance on the international level of rules that acknowledges, in exceptional cases, the theory of control; this shortcoming may be remedied by conventional lawmaking:

> "That is why, *in the present state of the law*, shareholder protection arises from the adoption of conventions or special agreements concluded directly between the private interest and the State where the investment is made. Rules have evolved since the end of the Second World War regarding foreign investment protection and this evolution has manifested itself in the conclusion of bilateral or multilateral treaties between States or in agreements between States and companies. Sometimes companies become the holders of a direct right to defend their interests against States following a defined procedure. No such instrument is in effect between the Parties in this case." [145] (*emphasis* ours)

8.5.2. – *Legal Control Theory Changes after Barcelona case*

Since the BT decision was handed down, the law of conventions has much changed. Many States have entered into BIT's in which provisions have been included regarding the "control" concept. These provisions differ from one BIT to the other. Sometimes, the control element is that an investor from one of the Contracting Parties has over an investment linked to the territory of the other Contracting Party:

> "Investment of an investor of a Party means an investment owned or controlled directly or indirectly by an investor of such Party".
> (BIT Canada/ Peru.20 June 2007)

Italy uses a similar formula but the clause specifies that control must be over an asset in the territory of the other

---

[145] *Barcelona Traction, Light and Power Company, Limited*, pp. 46 and 47, see footnote 15.

Contracting Party:

> "The term 'investor' shall mean any natural or legal person of a Contracting party investing in the territory of the other Contracting party as well as any foreign subsidiaries, affiliates and branches controlled in any way by the above natural and legal persons." (BIT Italy/Nicaragua, 20 April 2004)

Some countries have tried to give greater substance to the concept of "control":

> "companies mean any corporations, firms and associations incorporated or constituted under the law in force in the territory of either Contracting party, or in a third country, if at least 51 % of the equity interests owned by investors of that Contracting Party, or in which investors of that Contracting party control at least 51 % of the voting rights in respect of shares owned by them." (BIT Sweden/India, 1 April 2001)

8.5.2.1. *Extension of BIT's scope to Non-Contracting Parties*

Switzerland, Sweden and the Netherlands do not limit their protection of their investors' investments, made on the territory of the other Contracting Party but, sometimes, these countries expressly state that investments made on the territory of a non-contracting Party are covered under the BIT's.

> "The term 'investor of a Contracting Party' shall mean:
> a) any natural person who is a national of that Contracting Party in accordance with its law, and
> b) any legal person or other organisation organised in accordance with the law applicable in that Contracting party, and
> c) any legal person not organised under the law of that Contracting Party but controlled by an investor as defined under a) or b)."
> (BIT Sweden/Guatemala, 12 February 2004, **Article 1**, Definitions)

A similar provision, may be found in the BIT between the Netherlands and Armenia (10 June 2005):

> "The term 'nationals' shall comprise with regard to either Contracting party the following subjects:
> (i) natural persons having the nationality of that Contracting party;
> (ii) legal persons constituted under the law of that Contracting party;

(iii) legal persons not constituted under the law of that Contracting Party but controlled, directly or indirectly, by natural persons as defined in (i) or by legal persons as define in (ii)."

Recently, triangular investments protection clauses, using the control theory as a basis, have appeared in various BITs. The following **Diagram 1** shows State A investors funding a State C subsidiary which, in turn finances a State B company. In this example, Company/A's interest in Company/C must be controlling. Note that Company/A has the power to protect its indirect investment in Company/B, stemming from the "BIT Agreement", between State A and B, if it includes appropriate language regarding "control". Company/A is thus cast as the protector of Company/C's interest.

"Capacity to defend" and Company/A's ability to "protect its interests" consist of the legal safeguards enshrined in the BIT. It would be futile to list all of the means of protection listed in various BITs, since BITs vary from time to time and country to country. Yet, many BITs have common features that can serve as a guide to the contents of other particular BITs. As examples, the right to fair and equitable treatment, investors' protection and security guarantees, the freedom to manage without State interference, respect for international law, most favoured nation treatment, the right to compensation and to transfer funds without restriction except in extraordinary circumstances, in other words an entire gamut of rules affecting the settlement of investment disputes appear with greater frequency in the more modern BITs. BITs may also provide alternatives for the investor's choice of modi of enforcement of rights that have been violated, and for fora which can dispense them. Not least institutions such as ICC and ISSID, but also, where appropriate, at the investor's choice, national courts and other means of adjudication, mediation or conciliation. For further details, see Chapters in this Work regarding various kinds of Protection, Nationality and Control, Fair and Equitable Treatment, Transfers, and Applicable Law, a non exhaustive List.

Diagram 1

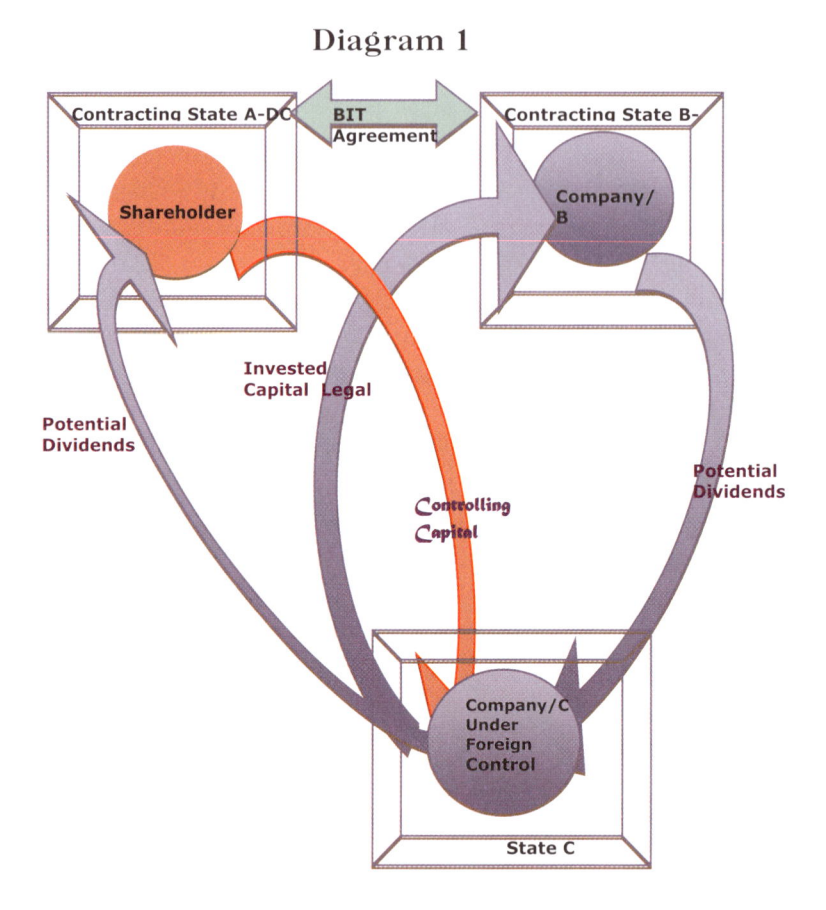

[Diagram showing BIT Agreement between Contracting State A-DC (containing Shareholder) and Contracting State B (containing Company/B), with flows of Invested Capital Legal, Controlling Capital, and Potential Dividends to Company/C Under Foreign Control in State C]

This example can work in reverse, Company/B switching places with Company/A and State B with State A. This is what the BIT's reciprocity format imply.

8.5.2.2. *Third State Protection*

The goal sought after is to protect, through the BIT, investments made by an investor from one of the Contracting Parties on the territory of the host State by an intermediary of a branch established in a third State. The legal person involved is therefore not established according to the law of any of the Contracting Parties but according to the law of a third State, not a participant to the BIT. The only condition is that the Contracting Party's investor controls or owns the foreign branch.

The goal is desirable because it helps ensure the protection of triangular investments, such as mentioned under subtitle 8.3 above. Nonetheless, we could ponder whether that goal will materialise in the protection structure engineered within the framework of some BITs. It is appropriate to recall that the International Court of Justice's decision in the 'Barcelona Traction' case (cnf *supra*) involved this kind of triangular construct.

The Court rejected Belgium's claim for compensation for damages flowing from Spain's expropriations and based its rejection on the lack of international law rules or conventions providing for the protection of shareholders, who, from a twice removed position, sought compensation for damages to their assets. Unfortunately, the Court did not specify which BIT could furnish a valid lgal basis for Belgium's intervention for the benefit of indirect investors. Would it have meant a BIT between Canada and Belgium, a BIT between Spain and Belgium, or some sort of agreement between the three Nations? So far, there are no precedent setting ICSID decisions approving triangular investment structures, even though the same is already provided for in some BITs (Netherlands, Sweden, Switzerland). Adherence to the *"res inter alios acta"* precept could prove to be an insurmountable obstacle to finding protection for triangular investments in any such BIT or agreement.

8.5.2.3. *Shareholders' rights*

There is yet another difficulty in the protection rights granted by convention to the shareholders of a Contracting State of a corporation established on the territory of a third State. According to international law, the management organisms of a company are those that have jurisdiction over the interests of such company. A State may also grant its diplomatic protection to the company as such and not to its shareholders. Shareholders have their own rights as against the company of which they are shareholders and therefore can file lawsuits against such organisms. Without any specific norm, shareholders of a foreign company may not by themselves defend the interests of that company :

> "Notwithstanding the separate corporate personality, a wrong done to the company frequently causes prejudice to its shareholders. But the mere fact that damage is sustained by both company and shareholder does not imply that both are entitled to claim compensation... No doubt, the interests of the aggrieved are affected, but not their rights. Thus whenever a shareholder's interests are harmed by an act done to the company, it is to the latter that he must look to institute appropriate action; for although two separate entities may have suffered from the same wrong, it is only one entity whose rights have been infringed." [146]

Even if there were a BIT, providing for triangular investments, doubts remain as to the practicality of the structure laid out in the preceding citation. In the Netherlands-Poland-Russia example (cnf 6.2.10.2), were Russia to expropriate assets of the Polish company's subsidiary, established on Russian territory, the parent Dutch company and the Dutch shareholders will not be able to file a claim on behalf of the Polish company they control, if both the Polish Government and the Polish company decline to support such claim or actively oppose it by alleging the issue to be governed by the principle of *"res inter alia acta"*.

---

[146] *Electronica Sicula S.p.A* (ELSI). *op. cit.*, p. 84., see footnote 86.

8.6. – NOTION OF CONTROL IN WASHINGTON CONVENTION (ICSID)

8.6.1. – *Corporations under Foreign Control*

According to the Washington Convention, the jurisdiction of the International Centre for Settlement of Investment Disputes shall extend only to disputes between a Contracting State and nationals (natural persons and corporations) of another Contracting State.

Article 25 (2)b provides for an exception to the general rule by stipulating that corporations of a Contracting State may be considered as "nationals of another State" under the following conditions :

"... Nationals of another Contracting State means any juridical person which had the nationality of the Contracting State party to the dispute ... and which ... because of foreign control, the parties have agreed should be treated as a national of another Contracting State for the purpose of this Convention".

Thus, the control theory may also apply to direct investments Company/A could make in Company/B. Assuming, that :

1. both parties are Convention members;
2. the applicable BIT contains all the necessary clauses needed to establish the consent of the parties to the control theory, in particular, Article 25(2)b of the Washington Convention;
3. both parties agree to allow Article 25(2)b to apply to any arbitrable dispute between them (*cfr.* 7.7.3), then, Company/A will be able to "protect" Company/B in an arbitration venue.

The following **Diagram 2** differs from **Diagram 1** in that it does not involve triangulation. It illustrates the relatively simple situation, where an investor in State A makes an investment in State B. It can work only if there is a BIT between the two States and if both States are members of the Convention.

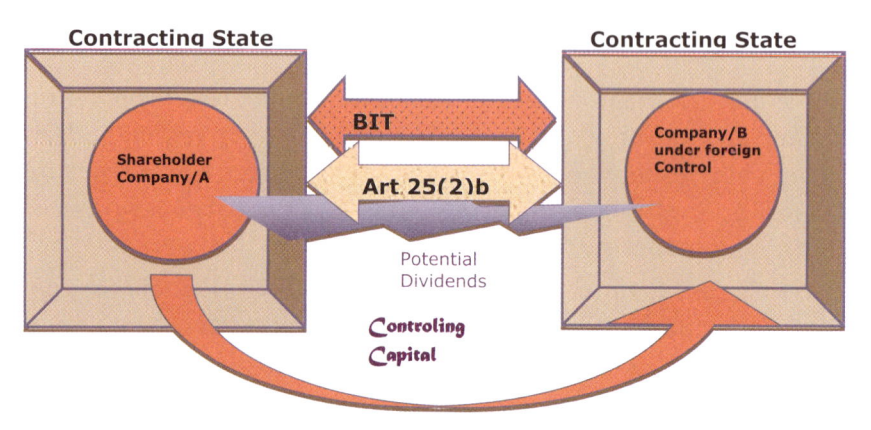

Diagram 2

Contracting State — Shareholder Company/A
Contracting State — Company/B under foreign Control
BIT
Art. 25(2)b
Potential Dividends
Controlling Capital

This example can work in reverse, Company/B switching places with Company/A and State B with State A. This is what the BITs reciprocity format imply.

8.6.2. – *Early ICSID decisions*

During ICSID's early period soon after its creation, many arbitration awards have been rendered on the basis of article 25(2)b. For instance, the 25 September 1983 decision regarding the conflict about an investment made on Indonesian territory is instructive. The investment codes of in many developing countries of Africa and Asia provide that an investment permit be generally required. An investment *convention* is often concluded between the investor and the host country.

Parties who wish to avoid the jurisdiction of domestic tribunals often include an arbitration clause in such conventions. This clause will allow the recognition of the jurisdiction of ICSID to handle eventual conflicts.

The control concept embodied in Article 25(2)b is *sui generis*. It affects only the Contracting States. Referring to Diagram 2, the underlying idea is to give Company/B, where State B is the host, the right to file an arbitration request against State B. This would be permitted only if this company were under control of State A investors (*cfr* Subtitle 16.8.3.4 infra). The *"ratio legis"* is that the respective States agree that a State B company, fully controlled by State A investors, will be deemed – for the purposes of arbitration – to have State A nationality. State B company has thus acquired a "foreign" nationality under State B law, thereby curing its disqualification from acting as plaintiff against State B.

8.6.3. – *AMCO Asia versus Indonesia*

8.6.3.1. *Case history – Application of Article 25(2)b*

In *AMCO Asia v. Indonesia* ICSID, a convention existed between the Indonesian State and an Indonesian company (PT Amco Indonesia), one of the petitioners to ICSID. The other two parties petitioner were American companies (Amco Asia Corporation and Pan American Development Limited, a company established under the laws of Hong Kong (at that time under the authority of the UK).

In substance, arbitration was asked regarding a conflict about a hotel investment. The Indonesian Government had cancelled the investment permit and had foreclosed on the hotel. The indemnification request was based on Article 25(2)b of the Convention in order to justify invoking the jurisdiction of ICSID

On her part, Indonesia was claiming that the arbitration clause of the investment convention (**Article IX**) reads:

> "In the event at a later date a conflict arises between the enterprise and the Government, this conflict will be submitted to the International Centre for the Settlement of Investment conflicts, an organisation of which Indonesia and the United States are members. Every decision taken on the basis of the above convention will bind the parties to the conflict (GAILLARD, *op. cit.*, p. 20)".

According to the Indonesian Government, PT Amco could not validly submit a petition in the absence of an arbitration clause explicitly referring to **Article 25(2)b** of the ICSID Convention. Consequently, no agreement existed between Indonesia and the domestic company that would allow consider PT Amco as a foreign company covered by such article, that is: "a national of another State because of the control over it by foreign interests." In any case, still according to Indonesia, the arbitration clause should also have mentioned – *expressis verbis* – *quod non* (and it didn't) – that American nationality had been cast upon PT Amco within the scope of the establishment convention and of the ICSID Convention. There also ought to have been a provision in the establishment convention regarding the identity and nationality of the foreign investors so controlling, and that point has somehow been lost during the negotiations by the Contracting Parties.

8.6.3.2. *Specific provision in BIT unnecessary?*

The tribunal rejected the Indonesian argument and decided that ICSID had jurisdiction over the conflict. According to the arbitrators, article 25 does not require the parties formally to acknowledge it in order to prove that the *domestic* company was in fact "foreign". An express provision in the establishment convention was therefore unnecessary:

> "Nothing in the convention and particularly in Article 25(2)b formally requires an express provision showing that the parties have decided to handle a company having legally the nationality of a Contracting State party to the conflict as having the nationality of another Contracting State because of the control to which she is subject."

The arbitration tribunal concluded that only two conditions had to be met to warrant the application of article 25.2b:

> "1. the corporation must have the nationality of the Contracting State party to the conflict;

2. the corporation must be under foreign control: the Contracting State must be made aware of this situation, that is, the parties in the conflict (Indonesia and PT Amco Indonesia) must have agreed that the local corporation was to be considered as a foreign legal person."

8.6.3.3. *Implied control*

According to the arbitrators, the first condition had been met:

> "There is no claim that, by reason of the place of its establishment, of the law under which it was organised and of the place of its seat, PT Amco did not have or does not still have Indonesian nationality."

The tribunal was also satisfied that the second condition had been met:

> "On the one hand, the First article of the petition for establishment states, as we have already mentioned, that the petitioner submits a request to invest *'in order to establish a foreign enterprise in Indonesia'*, and furthermore, article 3, paragraph 3 of the request for investment expressly states that *'all of the enterprise's capital is foreign capital.'*" *(emphasis* ours*)*

It therefore was clear that when it accepted the petition for establishment, the Government of Indonesia knew perfectly well that PT Amco would be under foreign control:

> "Knowing this express fact, the Government granted the request and the arbitration provision it contained; hence, it is perfectly clear that it agreed to treat PT Amco as the national of another State for the purposes of the Convention."[147]

Indonesia's argument that neither the foreign company's nationality nor that of the shareholders was mentioned in the arbitration clause was rejected by the Tribunal. According to the latter, such a requirement was not a condition of article 25.2b of the ICSID Convention:

> "First looking at the matter legally, and the contents of the agreement itself, the Tribunal sees, here too, that no provision of the Convention requires a formal acknowledgement in the arbitration agree-

---

[147] GAILLARD, Emmanuel, *op. cit.*, p. 23, see footnote 31.

ment itself of the nationality of the physical or legal persons controlling the legal person which has the nationality of one of the Contracting States party to the conflict."[148]

Furthermore, the Court observed that representations as to the identity of the "controlling corporation" and as to its American nationality had in any case been made in the request for investment, and the same were sufficient.

8.6.3.4. *Rights of other Petitioners*

8.6.3.4.1. *Amco Asia*

According to the arbitration tribunal, the two other parties who were petitioners in this case also had the right to intervene in the ICSID procedure. Indonesia claimed that Amco Asia as US company established in the State of Delaware could make no claim for arbitration because that company had not been explicitly mentioned in the arbitration provision of the investment contract. Consequent, Indonesia believed that the company had not met an important condition required by the Washington Convention, that is, the jurisdiction of ICSID had to be confirmed in writing by the investor. The tribunal rejected this approach. The investment contract which contained an arbitration clause represented proof enough in writing specified in **Article 25** of the Convention.

According to a principle of generally accepted international law, investment contracts must be interpreted in good faith, taking the wishes and the intentions of the parties into account :

> "The Tribunal refers to its previous statements regarding the method of interpretation of contracts relating to ICSID's arbitration : it must not be 'restrictive', nor 'extensive' because its purpose is to find from the documentation filed in the procedure a common inten-

---

[148] GAILLARD, Emmanuel, *op. cit.*, p. 23, see footnote 31.

tion among the parties and to give to this common intention the maximum effect." [149]

In fact, according to the arbitrators, Indonesia very well knew that Amco Asia was the foreign investor attributing to PT Amco the necessary capital and that she participated in the negotiation of the investment contract and in the wording of the arbitration clause. It is clear that both companies intended resorting to ICSID's arbitration. The purpose of the arbitration clause was, without any doubt, the protection of investments and specifically to show that no reasonable claim may be that the controlled company could benefit from the arbitration clause but the controlling company, that which supplied the funds, could not.

8.6.3.4.2. *Pan American's standing*

Insofar as the Pan American company was concerned, the reasons advanced by the arbitration tribunal deserve attention. This is the Hong Kong company to which Amco Asia had transferred its shares in PT Amco. This transfer was made with the explicit consent of *the Secretary General* of the Indonesian Ministry of Public Works and Energy. According to Indonesia, Pan American had no right to file a procedure with ICSID, with the cooperation of PT Amco and Amco Asia for mainly two reasons:

1. Article IX of the establishment contract does not mention Pan American and hence, there was no written consent regarding the jurisdiction of ICSID, such as that required by **Article 25** of the Washington Convention.
2. only a portion of the shares had been transferred, and, anyway, Amco Asia did not itself have a right to intervene in the ICSID procedure; how could a "claimed" right, which in fact did not exist, have been transferred by Amco Asia to the transferee?

---

[149] GAILLARD, Emmanuel, *op. cit.*, p. 29, see footnote 31.

The petitioner claimed that the written consent was evident from the official letter of the applicable Indonesian Ministry. Besides, Amco Asia had not lost its intervention right when it transferred part of its shares. Even as owner of a limited number of shares (after the transfer), Amco Asia could still invoke the ICSID clause, as an investor entitled to pursue its interests in PT Amco.

AMCO-ASIA, the original controlling company, had transferred its own right of intervention to PAN AMERICAN by assignment of a portion of its shares in PT AMCO. This is how PAN AMERICAN became a "controlling company", along with AMCO-ASIA. Together they represented the "foreign control", required by Article 25(2)b of PT AMCO.

8.6.3.5. ICSID Decision

The arbitration tribunal could not accept the Indonesian theory. The request to transfer shares in PT Amco to Pan American, submitted by AMCO ASIA had received official approval, according to the applicable Ministry's letter. This was a written consent as required by the Washington Convention. The arbitrators formally declared that Amco Asia had the right to invoke the clause, in the capacity of an investor which had subscribed to the clause and with Indonesia's agreement. This right could be transferred jointly with the shares so long as Indonesia approved the transfer. This agreement had been obtained in writing:

> "Consequently, the right to invoke the arbitration clause was transferred by Amco Asia with the shares she transferred, Amco Asia, however, not losing such right in her capacity as initial investor or partial investor to the extent she kept part of the shares she originally had. Consequently, the right to invoke the arbitration clause was transferred at the same time as the shares themselves, whether or not such transfer was a transfer of control, it being understood, we repeat, that for such a transfer of right to occur, the approval of the Government was indispensable." [150]

---

[150] GAILLARD, Emmanuel, op. cit., p. 30, see footnote 31.

8.6.3.6. *Evaluation of AMCO decision*

It would seem that the reason for the decision has no legal ground and that the decision itself may be weak. It may be true that article 25(1) requires only an approval to arbitrate. No words such as "à peine de déchéance" (failing which, a denial is required) appear in the section. It would follow that an agreement to arbitrate did not arise from a "solemn contract":

> "Consequently, although a consent to arbitrate through ICSID is indispensably required by **Article 25 (1)** of the Convention, such a written consent has not been solemnised in ritualistic and unique format." [151]

Any document therefore can serve to prove the wishes of the parties in order to submit an eventual conflict regarding their investment to arbitration. An investor's request for an establishment, followed by a permit and the conclusion of an investment contract (agreement), in which there is a provision for arbitration, meets the requirement of written consent. Insofar as the application of **Article 25(2)b** is concerned, the arbitration tribunal specified that a formal, written confirmation of nationality was not necessary ("Nothing in the agreement... cfr *supra*)." The arbitrators justified their positive decision regarding ICSID's jurisdiction on concrete data, that is, Indonesia's acceptance of the request for investment, and its knowledge of the controlling interest in the Indonesian corporation by a "foreign corporation."

It seems odd that ICSID and the arbitration tribunal accepted an arbitration request from three plaintiffs although Article 25(2)b is clear on the right a company established in the host State but under foreign control, is given to file such a request.

---

[151] GAILLARD, Emmanuel, *op. cit.*, p. 27, see footnote 31.

8.6.3.7. *Conventional Nationality*

The arbitrators' arguments may be debated. It is true that the wording "written consent" is not included in **Article 25(2)b**, but, nonetheless, one can draw the conclusion from a reading of article 25 on the whole, that ICSID jurisdiction required a "written consent". "Conventional" nationality is, without a doubt, an important exception to the general rule that ICSID is exclusively competent for *conflicts* between a Contracting State and a national of another contracting State. This exception may not be "presumed" but must be "expressly proven". The exception to the rule of written consent, mentioned in Article 25.1 must also be verified "in writing". Article 25(1)'s reliance on written consent lead us to believe that "consented to submit" and "have agreed to treat as a national of another Contracting State" equally apply to the terms mentioned in Article 25(2)b and require "a consent and agreement in writing". In order to protect investors' interests, a special provision is necessary by the terms of which the parties, the Contracting State and the domestic corporation expressly agree and in writing to deem such corporation as a "national of another Contracting State" because of the controlling interest of a foreign corporation over it.

8.6.3.8. *Morocco v. Holiday Inn*

In the case of *Morocco v Holiday Inn* (1973), the tribunal was inspired by this idea:

> "The question is, however, whether such a convention (regarding nationality) must be express or may be implicit. The solution such a convention is intended for is an exception to the general rule established by the convention and, hence, we should expect parties to express themselves clearly and explicitly upon a derogation to the rule. An implicit agreement would be acceptable only if particular circumstances excluded all other interpretation of the parties' intention. This is not the case in the present matter."[152]

---

[152] GAILLARD, Emmanuel, *op. cit.*, p. 63, see footnote 31.

8.6.3.9. *Comparison : Holiday Inn and Amco Asia*

In the *Holiday Inn v. Indonesia* case, the arbitration tribunal recused itself with respect to strictly local branch companies. As grounds, the tribunal cited the absence of an express convention allowing the local branches to be treated as "foreign" under the authority of Article 25(2)b. This tribunal held that a convention could not be implied from the facts. In the *AMCO Asia* case, a US corporation controlled the domestic Indonesian corporation, PT AMCO, but there was no express reference to "foreign control" had not been made in the establishment agreement. Thus, Article 25(2)b could not be used to sustain the tribunal's jurisdiction to hear an arbitration claim but the arbitrators nonetheless drew an implied agreement acknowledging the control theory.

Contrary to the arbitrators' interpretations in the Holiday Inn case, the arbitrators in AMCO accepted a broad interpretation of Article 25(2)b, holding that the Indonesian statement that "all of the capital was foreign" was sufficient to justify its jurisdiction.

8.6.3.10. *Explicit nationality wording unnecessary?*

To support its claim of absence of jurisdiction regarding Amco Asia, Indonesia wished to show, mainly, that neither the name nor the nationality of the American corporation had been mentioned in the arbitration clause. On the other hand, the arbitration tribunal adopted the theory of the petitioners and declared that Indonesia knew all it needed to know about the American company, by virtue of the negotiations and the documentation exchanged, hence, that explicit wording in the arbitration clause was no longer necessary :

> "Finally, this Tribunal does not believe that an objection based on the peremptory character of the clause may be drawn in this case, from the fact that the State from which the shareholders controlling PT Amco are nationals was not expressly mentioned in such a clause, nor from the fact, alleged by the defendant that it truly did not know what that State was. The Tribunal concludes, here again, that no pro-

vision of the Washington Convention requires formal identification in the arbitration clause of the nationality of foreign physical persons or corporations controlling the corporation having the nationality of the State against which the procedure has been filed." [153]

8.6.3.11. Difficulty of Proof

The reasoning of the Tribunal in this case is debatable. The text of Article 25 of the Convention specifies that the Centre's jurisdiction extends to conflicts relating to investments between a Contracting State and nationals of another Contracting State.

Exceptionally, the Centre is also competent to hear conflicts between a Contracting State and corporations of that same State if such corporation is under the control of foreign investors (article 25.2b). Foreign investors should be nationals of another State, member of the Washington Convention. This is confirmed in another decision of arbitrators (cfr *infra Soabi v. Senegal*):

> "The tribunal believes that the structure and purpose of the Convention requires that foreign interests which may serve as the basis for conferring 'alienage' to a domestic corporation must be nationals of Contracting States." [154]

Therefore, without an express reference of the company in the arbitration clause, proving that a local company is authorised to file a petition for arbitration against a State to which she belongs, it will be hard proving that the company has a foreign, conventional and subsidiary nationality. The legal force and application of **Article 25(2)b** require that the identity and nationality of the controlling company be mentioned in the arbitration clause.

---

[153] GAILLARD, Emmanuel, *op. cit.*, p. 23, see footnote 31.
[154] GAILLARD, Emmanuel, *op. cit.*, p. 39, see footnote 31.

8.6.3.12. *Jurisdiction over Pan American*

Insofar as Pan American (hereafter Panam), a Hong Kong corporation, Indonesia used the same arguments to contest ICSID's jurisdiction over it:

- There was no written consent regarding the jurisdiction of ICSID, since Panam was not even mentioned in the arbitration clause of the investment contract;
- Panam's right to intervene was wrongly considered to be an acquired right through the transfer of shares agreement Amco Asia/Panam, by which an important portion of the shares Amco Asia had was transferred to Panam.

The arbitration tribunal concluded that Panam had the right to file an arbitration proceeding with ICSID The tribunal's theory was not well supported. In fact, the investment was triangular. Economic relations between Panam and PT Amco rested on a threesome household, because it is by way of its participation on Amco Asia's capital that Panam could be considered as an investor in Indonesia. It was the Amco Asia corporation which should have undertaken the defense of its shareholders.

Shareholders, per se, do not have the right to substitute themselves in the place of the corporation in which they hold shares, no matter what their nationality may be.

8.6.3.13. *ICJ Position*

In a similar context, the International Court of Justice (cfr *supra*) decided that shareholders do not have a separate right of their own to file a judicial (or arbitral) proceeding against the will of the corporation in which they hold shares. The Court stressed that this right may arise by contract. In this case, the parties, the Indonesian Government, Panam and Amco Asia, should have included a special provision in the establishment contract and the investment contract, granting Panam, as shareholder of Amco Asia, the right to file an arbitration proceeding with ICSID, jointly with the American corporation Amco Asia.

8.6.3.14. *"Second level" of Control*

Furthermore, there is a "second level" of "control" PT Amco had to reckon with. The Indonesian Government thought it had found a good way to contest ICSID's jurisdiction analysing and referencing the "control" concept. It believed that the American company had lost effective control over PY Amco when it transferred shares. American control disappeared, according to Indonesia, by reason of the sale of a few shares by Amco Asia to Panam, the latter being controlled by a Dutch national. The tribunal rejected this theory properly. It is the nationality of the corporation that governs and not that of the shareholders of the controlling corporation:

> "To accept this argument, the Tribunal would have to admit from the very start that according to **Article 25 (b)2** of the Convention, it is not the legal nationality of the foreign corporation controlling the domestic company that counts but the nationality of physical or legal persons who control the controlling corporation. In other words, this would require we would have to be concerned about control in the second degree, possibly third and fourth or ninth degree."

It is therefore clear that the text of Article 25(2)b applies to a bilateral relationship only, wich involves an investor from one of the Contracting States and a company in the other Contracting State, in wich he has invested and which he controls. In the AMCO-ASIA case, control had been transferred to a Hong Kong corporation. The Tribunal interpreted the Washington Convention by taking its "control" concept to a next and, we submit, excessive level, never contemplated by the Convention's signers.

8.6.3.15. *Soabi v. Senegal*

In the *Soabi vs Senegal*[155] the arbitrators, wrongly, we think, took into account a second degree control. The Senegal corporation Soabi was considered a "legal person of a foreign State" because it was controlled by a Panamanian corporation, Flexa, which in turn was controlled by majority owners of Belgian nationality. At that time, Panama was not yet a member of the Washington Convention. According to the arbitration tribunal, ICSID had nonetheless jurisdiction to decide the Senegal/Flexa conflict. The tribunal's reasons were based on an extensive interpretation of **Article 25 (2)b**. The terminology "because of the control" appearing in this article referred, according to the arbitrators, to both direct and indirect control :

> "The nationality of this company (Flexa) which in 1975 held all of the subscribed shares of Soabi would be determinative of the nationality of foreign interests only if the Convention had to be interpreted as concerned with immediate control. But the Tribunal cannot accept such an interpretation which goes against the purpose of article 25 (2)b, in general. Belgian shareholders had, according to the arbitrators, direct control on the Flexa corporation and indirect control over (by way of Flexa) the Senegalese company Soabi. Senegalese authorities have the right to impose on foreign investors the duty to make their investment on Senegalese territory by way of a domestic corporation. Belgian investors, in turn, suppliers of invested capital, have the right to make their Senegal investments via a non-Belgian company.
>
> Yet, it is clear that, just as much for reasons arising in the host State, the legal form of this domestic corporation may be chosen by the entity making the investments, investors also, for reasons which are solely theirs, may be led to invest their funds through intermediaries, while keeping the same degree of control on the domestic corporation, even where they could, had they so wished, exercised direct control over it by owning shares in it. For the same reasons, the Tribunal has decided that the control over the Flexa corporation is, on the date that the investment contract was finalised, by nationals of Contracting States, namely the Kingdom of Belgium." [156]

---

[155] GAILLARD, Emmanuel, *op. cit.*, p. 24, see footnote 31.
[156] GAILLARD, Emmanuel, *op. cit.*, p. 40, see footnote 31.

This decision is important, particularly when viewed in the light of our remarks in subtitle 8.5.2.1 of this work, "Extension of BIT's Scope to non-contracting Parties". Belgium and Senegal had a BIT between them. However, Panama, was a non-contracting State and not even a member of the Washington Convention. With nary a thought on the conventional requirements for protection, the arbitration tribunal allowed the Belgian shareholders to intervene, even though their controlled company (FLEXA) was sited in a non-contracting State. We think the likelihood is low this decision will be precedent setting. Future ICSID arbitrators may well decide otherwise.

8.6.3.16. *Nationality Transferred by the Controlling Corporation*

The Tribunal's legal argument is not convincing. In order to grant to the Senegalese company Soabi a conventional and subsidiary nationality, based on the control theory, Flexa's nationality was of undeniable importance. It was the Panamanian company that signed the investment contract, including the ICSID clause. According to **Article 25(2)b**, it is the controlling corporation that transfers its nationality to the domestic corporation. The Senegalese Government was in agreement with this situation, since it signed the investment petition as well as the arbitration clause. The condition therefore is that the controlling corporation be a national of a Convention member. It is the nationality of the controlling corporation which determines the creation of a conventional nationality and not the nationality of the shareholders of the corporation. In this case, too, we have a triangular investment. In principle, (cfr *supra*), the right for shareholders to intervene could have been settled contractually, but Panama was not a member of the Convention at the time of the facts and the circumstances are therefore a problem.

8.6.3.17. *Advisability of Explicit Provisions as to Applicable Conventional Nationality*

Both investors and States which are members of the Convention should draw lessons from the development of ICSID's jurisprudence in as much as the latter is not always "uniform".

To achieve a safer legal background, concerned investors, domestic corporations and foreign "controlling" corporations should include in their investment contracts and establishment agreements clauses that are adapted to such jurisprudence. ICSID publishes "typical" clauses which can be adapted and amended according to the wishes of interested parties. In any case, in order to help ensure a proper application of **Article 25.1** and **25(2)b**, these provisions should include written proof that the domestic company is considered a "national" of another State, because of the application of the "control" theory, as well as a complete identification of the "controlling" corporation. In this way, States members of the Convention, having a network of BIT's at their disposal, should verify that the provisions of their contracts appropriately protect triangular investments.

8.7. – IMPRACTICABILITY OF UNIFORM REGULATION

Uniform regulation might seem to be preferable, in particular with respect to the criteria to be used to determine the "nationality" of a corporation. Those who support the idea of control as the rule apparently believe that the nationality of a company should be identical to that of the majority shareholders who have assumed the control and management of the company. If all of the majority shareholders have the same nationality, the company would then have that nationality too, at least for as long as the composition of the shareholders group's nationalities remained static. The general application of this theory would, without any doubt, result in virtually insurmountable inconvenience. It would be quite difficult to assign a nationality to a company when it is, in all practicality, impossible to know who or what group effectively controls the company at any one moment, as appears from the following comment:

> "We could expect other difficulties when the nationality of a corporation is to be determined on the basis of control. As everyone knows, transferring shares of stock from one individual to another is not a problem and occurs daily. As a result, there is constant change in the composition of the company's capital. If the control theory is to be applied, frequent changes in the nationality of the company would result. Those changes are incompatible with the need to assure the constancy of the legal status of the company. As an example, problems would arise in determining under whose diplomatic umbrella a company should seek protection [157].

Clearly, experts are unable to work up a uniform solution to determine a company's nationality. It might well be to everyone's advantage to abandon "control" as a critical determinant of the access of corporations to the benefits and protections of bilateral investment treaties. At the end of the day, what a foreign investor wants is maximum protection, the ability to choose between the jurisdictions he will submit to or take advantage of is critical. On the other hand, the possibility of manipulation should deter one from suggesting that a corporation has the nationality of whoever happens to control it at any one time but it would not be fair to "freeze" the nationality as that first proven to exist and saddle a corporation forever with a nationality based on that of its majority shareholders upon its foundation, even when they have been replaced by another set of different nationality or when the entire set of founders-incorporators, frequently the set of initial directors, have been replaced by an entirely different set. Yet, an unregulated ability to choose nationality, change it and choose again at will could be unfair. Clearly,

---

[157] SCHOKKAERT, Jan, *op. cit.*, p. 2262, see footnote 10.

some accommodation must be made with modern relativism or some investment will be discouraged.

The number of different doctrinal opinions and the precariousness of arbitral and judicial jurisprudence about the control theory lead us to suggest that it be used only under exceptional circumstances and be restricted to the scope of conditions clearly set forth in conventions. Perhaps the concept of "control" is past its prime and must be replaced. One thing is certain, however, the "nationality" of a corporation, whatever that is, is likely to remain a criterion governing the protection of international investments.

CHAPTER IX
PROTECTED INVESTMENTS DEFINITIONS

9.1. – Doctrinal Definition of Investments

Of course, economists and jurists will have differing opinions on the definition of the concept of "investment". There is no doctrinal unanimity on the definition of the word in international economic relations. These different interpretations occur also when the question is about which kind of investment deserve to be protected by means of a convention. Some authors believe that only direct contribution of capital to an enterprise can be considered an "investment", whereas portfolio investments cannot because they do not create an added value to the economic development of an enterprise. We believe it is wrong to infer, no matter how subtly, that it is important to protect direct investments and that indirect investments deserve little attention.

Other authors seem to wish to give to the word "investment" an even more limited scope. They approach the "investment" phenomenon on the basis of "development cooperation" and claim that only capital infusions and financial operations contributing to the growth of the host State's assets may be considered as "investments" : "In the same spirit, M. Georges Delaume has suggested we ought to limit investment to the idea of a nuanced contribution, even if not always efficient, to the economic development of the country in question." [158]

---

[158] DELAUME, Georges, "Droit de l'investissement : vers un droit international de l'investissement direct étranger?", *Journal de droit international*, Paris, 1982, n° 75, p. 801, (*International Law Journal*).

This review, however, covers the legal and *conventional* protection available for investments, made abroad by individuals or corporations, that are most common and regarding which there is a track record of jurisprudence, that is "so long as they are in the form of placements or contributions of capital, know how, management etc., or in the form of cash or equivalent in enterprises active in the economies of foreign states. In summary, they are participations in a foreign country's existing or potential trade or industry made for the purpose of production and profit".[159]

9.2. – Conventional Definition of Investments

9.2.1. – *Investments as defined in BIT's*

The definition which interests us most is that appearing in bilateral conventions regarding the promotion and the protection of foreign investments. It is not necessarily easy for the drafters of such conventions to develop a satisfactory definition. Unfortunately, existing legislation does not help us much in finding useable terms. In most countries, there is no legal definition of the term "investment". For instance, in Belgian economic legislation, emphasis is laid on investment possibilities, advantages granted to foreign investors, legal status of companies, etc. There are no commentaries on the content of the term "investment". The Belgian National Ducroire Office[160] (ONDD) has adopted a definition for the general conditions of its insurance contracts:

> "Investment: the contribution made by an insured in a local (foreign) company as described in the Special Conditions. Investment may take the form of a capital participation by means of which the insured can acquire ownership of participation securities or capital stock, or a loan or a security deposit."

---

[159] SCHOKKAERT, Jan, *op. cit.*, p. 328, see footnote 3.
[160] A Belgian State insurance organism against political risks.

That definition is not such as to allow it to be used "as is" in BIT's. Looking through documents written by various authors and negotiators of the Washington Convention relating to the settlement of conflicts regarding investments does not help much either. The text of the Convention contains absolutely no definition of the term and the problem has been deliberately avoided :

> "It was not found necessary to define the term 'investment' because the consent of the parties is already an essential condition and because of the mechanism by which the Contracting States may, if they so wish, list in advance the types of conflicts which they will or will not be prepared to submit to the Centre."

9.2.2. – *Typical flaws in Model Convention*

In the Belgian model convention, for example, the definition of "investment", which serves as a basis for the negotiation of new BIT's, is as follows :

> "For use in the present Agreement :
>
> The term 'investment' refers to any active element and any direct contribution in money, in kind or in services, invested or re-invested in any economic sector whatever.
>
> The following will be, non exclusively, considered investments under the present agreement :
>
> 1. all personal and real property as well as any real property rights such as mortgages, retention rights, privileges, pledges, usufructs and similar rights;
> 2. shares, social participations and other forms of participation, whether or not minority or indirect, in the capital of companies established on the territory of one of the Contracting Parties;
> 3. debt, credit and entitlements to any and all economically valuable actions;
> 4. authorship rights, industrial property rights, technical processes, brand names and commercial interests;
> 5. public law or contractual concessions, such as those regarding prospecting, cultivation, extraction or other exploitation of natural resources;

6. No change in the legal form in which assets and capital have been invested or re-invested will affect their qualification as investments under the present Agreement."

It suffers from multiple flaws:

Lien rights should be erased from the list. Bailment and lien rights are rights a temporary holder of another's goods may have to keep them and not to release them back to the owner, as long as the latter has not settled his obligations to the holder. These rights are acknowledged in many jurisdictions besides those that have adopted English common law, where a bailment is sometimes treated as a mere deposit:

"A deposit may be voluntary or involuntary, and for safekeeping or for exchange." (California Civil Code Sec. 1813 Kind)

It is, however, in such jurisdictions, viewed as a "right to exclusive possession", i.e. one of the rights in the bundle of rights which, together, constitutes a "property right." Bailment thus differs from liens in that a lien is merely

"...a charge imposed in some mode other than by a transfer in trust upon specific property by which it is made security for the performance of an act." (California Civil Code Section 2872 Definition)

Thus, although, liens may be accompanied by a transfer of possession, they can also exist without such transfer, whereas bailments require it. From the standpoint of investment protection, the practical application, internationally, of this difference may, however, be uncertain. Conceivably, upon a loan made to a company in a State party to a BIT, assets transferred by such company to secure the loan should be able to benefit from the BIT's mutual protection but devising conventional language that successfully extends BIT protection to mere liens, unaccompanied by a tangible transfer, may be quite difficult.

Intellectual property should be fully described. The text of the American model convention could be used as an example:

"Intellectual property, including copyrights and related rights in plant varieties, industrial design, trade secrets, including know-how and confidential business information, trade and service marks, trade names and rights conferred pursuant to law, such as licences and permits."

Protection of securities such as shares in the capital of an enterprise is not sufficiently guaranteed. Arbitration jurisprudence has not caught up with the fact that several developing countries still deny protection under their bilateral convention when an enterprise is established as a corporation under local law. The catch is that these countries require the invested enterprise to be established under such law.

In effect, these countries often claim that their legal basis for denying protection to such corporations is that they are nationals of those countries and therefore are not entitled to the protection of international law. When a conflict arises about the investment, they claim it is merely a conflict between one of the Contracting States and its national, to which local law only applies.

Using this argument, a few developing countries claim, among other things, that international arbitration does not apply to them. To help ensure efficient protection of majority investments, it is therefore important to specify that, when drafting the Bilateral Treaty, that the domestic company will be considered "foreign" in accordance with **Article 25(2)b** of the Washington Convention, if the foreign investor holds a majority participation (confirming his control over the local company) in the capital of companies established under the law of the other Contracting Parties.

The text of a model convention's definition of "investment" should therefore also include the following:

> "Shares of stock and all other participations, be they direct or indirect, majority or minority, in the capital of companies established by an investor of one of the Contracting Parties in the territory of the other Contracting Party."

Furthermore, regarding indirect investments, the model should include a clause covering triangular investments.

9.2.3. – *Other Conventional Definitions*

9.2.3.1. *Canada Definition (pre-2006)*

Before 2006, Canadian BIT's contained a definition for protected investments which resembled definitions used by other countries. It was an "asset based" definition and, by way of example, an illustrative, but not exclusive, definition was included. Article 1 of the bilateral agreement between Canada and Croatia, signed on 30 January 2001, read as follows:

"For the purpose of this agreement:
(a) 'enterprise' means:
   (i) any entity constituted or organised under applicable law, wether or not for profit, wether privately-owned or governmentally-owned, including any corporation, trust, partnership, sole proprietorship, joint venture or other association, and,
   (ii) a branch of any such entity;
(b) 'existing measure' means a measure existing at the time this Agreement enters into force;
(c) 'intellectual property rights' means copyright and related rights, trademark rights, patent rights, rights in lay out designs of semiconductor integrated circuits, trade secret rights, plant breeders' rights, rights in geographical indications and industrial design rights;
(d) 'investment' means any kind of asset owned or controlled either directly, or indirectly through an investor of a third State, by an investor of one Contracting Party in the territory of the other Contracting Party in accordance with the latter's laws and, in particular, though not exclusively, includes:
   • movable and immovable property and any related property rights, such as mortgages, liens or pledges;
   • shares, stock, bonds and debentures or any other form of participation in a company, business enterprise or joint venture;
   • money, claims to money, and claims to performance under contract having a financial value;
   • goodwill;
   • intellectual property rights;

- rights, conferred by law or under contract, to undertake any economic and commercial activity, including any rights to search for, cultivate, extract or exploit natural resources;
- but does not mean real estate or other property, tangible or intangible, not acquired in the expectation or used for the purpose of economic benefit or other business purposes.

For further certainty, an investment shall be considered to be controlled by an investor if the investor controls, directly or indirectly, the enterprise which owns the investment.

Any change in the form of an investment does not affect its character as an investment."

9.2.3.2. *North American Free Trade Agreement (NAFTA) style Definition (post 2006)*

From 2006 on, Canadian authorities adopted the NAFTA model. Its characteristic is that the list of protected investment is exhaustively defined. Furthermore, contrary to practice in other countries, Canada uses a negative approach, mentioning economic activities which are not considered investments and which, consequently, are not susceptible of being protected through the BIT:

"Investment means:
- an enterprise;

(II) an equity security of an enterprise;

(III) a debt security of an enterprise
  (i) where the enterprise is an affiliate of the investor, or
  (ii) where the original maturity of the debt security is at least three years,

  but does not include a debt security, regardless of original maturity, of a state enterprise;

(IV) a loan to an enterprise
  (i) where the enterprise is an affiliate of the investor, or
  (ii) where the original maturity of the loan is at least three years,

  but does not include a loan, regardless of original maturity, to a state enterprise;

(V) (i) notwithstanding subparagraphs (III) and (IV) above, a loan to or debt security issued by a financial institution is an investment only where the loan or debt security is treated as regulatory capital by the Party in whose territory the financial institution is located, and

(ii) a loan granted by or debt security owned by a financial institution, other than a loan to or debt security of a financial institution referred to in (i), is not an investment;

for greater certainty :

(iii) a loan to, or debt security issued by, a Party or a state enterprise thereof is not an investment; and

(iv) a loan granted by or debt security owned by a cross-border-financial service provider, other than a loan to or debt security issued by a financial institution, is an investment if such loan or debt security meets the criteria for investments set out elsewhere in this Article;

(VI) an interest in an enterprise that entitles the owner to share in income or profits of the enterprise;

(VII) an interest in an enterprise that entitles the owner to share in the assets of that enterprise on dissolution, other than a debt security or a loan excluded trom subparagraphs (III) (IV) or (V);

• real estate or other property, tangible or intangible, acquired in the expectation or used for the purpose of economie benefit or other business purposes; and

• interests arising from the commitment of capital or other resources in the territory of a Party to economie activity in such territory, such as under

(i) contracts involving the presence of an investor's property in the territory of the Party, including turnkey or construction contracts, or concessions, or

(ii) contracts where remuneration depends substantially on the production, revenues or profits of an enterprise."

9.2.3.3. AUSTRALIAN Definition

This negative approach has also been followed in Australia :

"For the purpose of this agreement : the term investment means...
But 'investment' does not mean :

(ix) a loan to an enterprise or a debt security of an enterprise where the original maturity of the loan or debt security is less than three yares (unless the enterprise is an affiliate of the Investor);

(x) a loan to, or a debt security from, a Contracting Party or a state enterprise, regardless of original maturity;

(xi) claims to money that arise solely from :
- commercial contracts for the sale of goods or services by a national or enterprise in the territory of a Contracting Party to an enterprise in the territory of another Contracting Party; or
- the extension of credit in connection with a commercial transaction, such as trade financing, other than a loan or other claim to money otherwise included within this definition of 'investment'; or...

(xii) any other claims to money that do not involve the kinds of interests set out in (i) through (viii) of this Article; (BIT Australia/Mexico, dated 23 August 2005)."

On the other hand, Australia did not adopt an exhaustive list of protected investments.

9.2.3.4. *USA Definition*

US practice has much changed over the years. Arguably, there have been three distinct periods during which the definition of protected investment had its own special characteristics :

1. BIT's which entered into force before 1994 defined investment as "every kind of investment," and set forth a list. It was not always clear if the list was drawn by way of example or if it was exhaustive. The term "non-exclusive" did not appear, such as, for instance, in the USA/Zaire BIT dated 28 July 1989 :

> "...
> (c) 'Investment' means every kind of investment, owned or controlled directly or indirectly, including equity, debt, and service and investment contracts; and includes :
> (i) tangible and intangible property, including all property rights, such as liens, mortgages, pledges, and real security;
> (ii) a company or shares of stock or other interests in a company or interests in the assets thereof;
> (iii) a claim to money or a claim to performance having economic value, and associated with an investment;

(iv) intellectual and industrial property rights, including rights with respect to copyrights, patents, trademarks, trade names, industrial designs, trade secrets and know how, and goodwill;

(v) licenses and permits issued pursuant to law, including those issued for manufacture and sale of products;

(vi) concessions granted under public law or under contract,

Including concessions to search for or utilise natural resources,

and rights to manufacture,use and sell products; and

returns which are reinvested."

This last point about reinvestments is quite useful. Many BIT's do not provide protection for reinvested revenue.

2. BIT's which entered into force on the basis of the 1994 model convention contain a similar provision. However, the reinvestment protection clause disappeared:

"...Investment of a national or company means every kind of investment owned or controlled directly or indirectly by that national or company, and includes investment consisting or taking the form of:

- a company;
- shares, stock, and other forms of equity participation, and bonds, debentures, and other forms of debt interests, in a company;
- contractual rights, such as under turnkey, construction or management contracts, production or revenue-sharing contracts, concessions, or other similar contracts;
- tangible property, including real property; and intangible property, including rights, such as leases, mortgages, liens and pledges;
- intellectual property, including:
  – copyrights and related rights, patents, rights in plant varieties, industrial designs, rights in semiconductor layout designs, trade secrets, including know-how and confidential business information, trade and service marks, and trade names; and
  – rights conferred pursuant to law, such as licenses and permits."

3. BIT's concluded on the basis of the 2004 Model Convention no longer use "investments" as the operative term but "assets". One unique aspect is the definition's explicit reference to characteristics of an activity or operation for the purpose of considering them as investments:

"'Investment' means every asset that an investor owns or controls, directly or indirectly, has the characteristics of an investment, including such characteristics as the commitment of capital or other resources, the expectation of gain or profit, or the assumption of risk. Forms that an investment may take include :

- an enterprise;
- shares, stock, and other forms of equity participation in an enterprise;
- bonds, debentures, other debt Instruments, and loans;[1]
- futures, options, and other derivatives;
- turnkey, construction, management, production, concession, revenue-sharing; and
- other similar contracts;
- intellectual property rights;
- licenses, authorisations, permits, and similar rights conferred pursuant to domestic law; and
- other tangible or intangible, movable or immovable property, and related property rights, such as leases, mortgages, liens and pledges."

9.2.4. – *Inclusive Enumeration*

It is important that BIT's include a definition of investment that is as inclusive as possible in order better to protect foreign investors :

> "The lack of an accepted terminology and the multifaced forms (contractual besides property) through which investments are currently carried out explain the care with which recent BIT's define investments, with a view to cover all types of transfers, and ownership in financial, tangible and intangible rights and claims of an economic value which represent or are connected with an investment in the economic sense." [161]

---

[161] SACERDOTI, Giorgio, "Bilateral treaties and multilateral agreements on investment protection", *Collected Courses of The Hague Academy of International law*, The Hague, 1997, p. 308.

Enumerating assets and operations which are considered as investments – specifying that the list is enumerative and not limitative – is one of the formulas used to reach the desired goal. It would be wrong to overestimate the protection that may stem from such a provision. You can expect difficult and long lasting arguments in cases when an "investment" is not expressly mentioned in the list. The host State will try to deny the conventional protection by arguing that the investor has not made an "investment" in the meaning of the Agreement. In case of conflict, the investor may be led to file for an arbitration proceeding in order to prevail.

It is therefore highly important that the list of covered investments be as exhaustive as possible, in order to foreclose any claim by the host State that the request for protection is demurrable, on the ground that the investment has not been expressly acknowledged to be among those covered.

9.2.5. – *Bills of Exchange qualify as "Investment"*

In *Fedax v. Venezuela*, the FEDAX company, established in the territory of Curaçao (Dutch Antilles), filed in 1997 a request for arbitration with ICSID, citing Venezuela as defendant. The topic of the conflict was the non-payment by Venezuela of bills of exchange issued by it and delivered to a Venezuelan company "Industrias Metallurgicas Van Dam CA" which assigned and endorsed them to S.A. Fedax.

A protection agreement had been entered into on 22 October 1991 between Venezuela and the Netherlands. The key question therefore was: was the purchase of Venezuelan bills of exchange by a foreign company to be deemed an "investment" or at least a financial operation bound to an investment? The answer thereto depended on the jurisdiction of ICSID.

Venezuela claimed that ICSID did not have jurisdiction because the FEDAX corporation had not effected a "direct investment" as the Washington convention (**Article 25**) required, and that elements of the term "investment" were lacking:

> "The Republic of Venezuela maintains on this topic that the possession by FEDAX of bills of exchange as specified below does not fall under the definition of 'investment', in that these circumstances do not constitute a direct foreign investment which implies a long term transfer of financial resources – a flow of capital – from one country to another (the recipient of the investment) in order to acquire an interest in a local company, an operation which normally includes risks for the potential investor." [162]

The arbitration tribunal rejected the motion for denial based on lack of jurisdiction as presented by Venezuela. It concluded that the contested event was to be considered an investment for the following reasons:

> The term "direct" in **Article 25** of the Washington convention refers to conflicts and not to investments; both direct and indirect investments are protected; a conflict which has a direct relation to a direct or indirect investment therefore may be adjudged by ICSID.

FEDAX is entitled to protection and is authorised to file for an arbitration proceeding on the basis of the provisions of the BIT:

> "litigation opposing one Contracting Party and the nationals of another Contracting Party, and concerning an obligation upon the first by virtue of this Agreement and in relation to an investment made by a national of the other State, will be submitted to the arbitration or conciliation procedure provided by ICSID (article 9.1). The term 'investments' includes all securities providing for a right to money, other goods or any other asset that has an 'economic value' (article 1a). Considering that the agreement of the Parties is binding for the definition of 'investment', ICSID has jurisdiction in the matter."

The bills of exchange were issued in US Dollars and therefore intended for international circulation; endorsement to a foreign company was therefore evident; without any doubt, there was a capital contribution, inasmuch as the Venezuelan

---

[162] GAILLARD, Emmanuel, *op. cit.*, p. 456, see footnote 31.

State could benefit from a credit until the maturity date of the bills; this credit could be used for public purposes; the "risk element" was also present; this risk was not bound to the proper functioning of the Venezuelan company but the possibility of non payment by the Venezuelan State; the purchase of bills of exchange, securities proving that a loan had been granted, should then be considered an "investment".

The investment *lists* therefore could be amended to include bills of exchange.

9.2.6. – *Investments may be evidenced by Accessory Contracts*

In *Salini Costrutorri S.p.A v. Morocco*, 2001, ICSID, two Italian companies, Salini Costrutione and Italstrade filed with ICSID, in 2001, an arbitration petition against the Kingdom of Morocco. They had concluded a contract with the "Société nationale des autoroutes de Maroc" (ADM), a public law corporation, for the purpose of building a section of the motorway Rabat/Fez. A conflict concerning the payment of an invoice arose and Salini/Italstrade claimed compensation for the damages they sustained.

A BIT had been concluded on 18 July 1990 between the Kingdom of Morocco and the Italian Republic, regarding the promotion and mutual protection of investments Could that contract be considered an "investment", to which the BIT as well as the Washington convention applied? Morocco believed it did not, the Italian investors claimed that it did. The respective positions of the Parties can be summarised as follows:

"Italy:

The enterprise contract falls under the BIT and must be considered as an investment

'in the sense of the present agreement, the term 'investment' includes, but not exclusively, all rights to any contractual performance having an economic value and all rights of an economic nature flowing from the law or a contract.' (Article 1. c) and e)) The right to indemnification is of an economic nature."

The BIT was violated and the conflict concerns a contract bound to an investment, so that ICSID has jurisdiction.

Morocco :

The 'contract' does not fall under the BIT definition clause cited by the plaintiffs but depends on the terms of Moroccan legislation, as the BIT provides : 'the term 'investment' covers all categories of goods invested by a physical or moral person including the Government of a Contracting Party, in accordance with the laws and regulations of such party.'

The provisions of the BIT have not been violated and the Washington Convention is therefore inapplicable; the objection for lack of jurisdiction is valid.

ICSID stated it had jurisdiction and denied the Moroccan objection. The decision was based both on the BIT and the Convention. This parallel condition is a constant in the ICSID jurisprudence. The Italian operation must be viewed as an "investment" in Morocco under both contractual instruments : the enterprise contract and the BIT.

Applying the bilateral agreement to the term "investment" :

The enterprise contract without any doubt has an economic character and created for the entrepreneur contractual rights which are also of an economic nature and therefore theirs was an investment in the sense intended by the BIT.

The BIT provision according which the investment must be made in conformity with the laws of the host State does not specify what activities are to be considered as 'investments'; this provision's purpose was to avoid illegal investments; the contract had received the approval of Moroccan authorities;

Disregard for contractual obligations (Moroccan refusal to pay) also fall under the BIT; article 8 of the protection agreement states that conflicts concerning the settlement of indemnification for nationalisation or analogous measures may be submitted to arbitration; this article must be interpreted very broadly; conflicts having a contractual character are not excluded from the application of this provision :

> "The terms of article 8 are very broad. The reference to expropriation and nationalisation measures, which depend on the unilateral will of State cannot be interpreted from the scope of this article in the sense of an exclusion of any grievance having a contractual origin." [163]

9.2.7. – ICSID's "JOY MINING MACHINERY v. Egypt" [164]

The arbitrators observed that objective conditions must be met for the ICSID jurisdiction to apply, in the sense that the conflict must be legal "in direct relation to an investment"; the arbitration tribunal decided that in this case the fundamental elements of an "investment" were present : the *infusion of capital* could not be denied (know how, delivery of production instruments to carry out the work, conclusion of loan contracts for financing the purchase of raw materials, etc.); the *time element* was also present : the *duration* of the work was fixed in the enterprise contract for 32 months; this meets the condition that the "operation be of long duration", such as that described in the doctrine (D. CARREAU, Th. LORY, F. JUILLARD). These authors believe that a duration of two years is sufficient to support a claim of an operation of "long duration"; the *risk element* was also present, several clauses of the contract referring to indemnities to be paid eventually by the Italian investors. (emphasis ours)

It is to be assumed that the fourth element, return or yield, was implicit.

---

[163] GAILLARD, Emmanuel, *op. cit.*, p. 635, see footnote 31.
[164] ICSID Case N° ARB/03/11, pp. 3 et suivantes, see website : www.worldbank.org/ICSID.

9.2.7.1. *Subject Matter of Dispute*

The dispute arose out of a contract between, on the one hand, a British company and, on the other, IMC, an Egyptian company and the State of Egypt which approved the contract. Within the framework of this contract, bank guarantees had been issued to the Egyption Contracting Party. A company named JMML wished to have the guarantees released. IMC would not comply with the British demand.

In substance, the dispute therefore concerned the need to know whether bank contractual guarantees could or could not be considered protected investments. The petitioner's position was stated as follows:

> "The company claims that the contract is an investment under this treaty (BIT) and that the decision by IMC and Egypt not to release these guarantees are in violation of the Treaty."

On the other hand, the defendant claimed:

> "That certain conditions required under articles 25 and 26 of the ICSID Convention and the Treaty are not fulfilled in this case, in particular the requirement of an investment".

9.2.7.2. *Bank Guarantees are not Investments (per ICSID)*

The tribunal's findings in respect of the existence of an investment was handled as follows:

First, the tribunal referred to the Washington Convention's lack of definition of the term "investment", stating:

> "The question that the Tribunal must answer is accordingly whether or not bank guarantees are to be considered an investment. It is an accepted fact that the ICSID Convention did not define an investment and that this was left to the consent of the parties, expressed by means of acontracts, national legislation or bilateral investment treaties, among other features."

However, the tribunal immediately added the absence of a definition on the Washington Convention did not at all imply that investors and the BIT's Contracting States could freely assume that any economic activity was an investment:

"The fact that the convention has not defined the term investment does not mean, however, that anything consented by the parties might qualify as an investment under the Convention."

It was necessary that the economic activity said to be a qualified investment effectively meet the principal characteristics of any investment:

"Summarising the elements that an activity must have in order to qualify as an investment, both the ICSID decisions mentioned above and the commentators thereon have indicated that the project in question should have a certain duration, a regularity of profit and return, an element of risk, a substantial commitment and that it should constitute a significant contribution to the host State's development."

Of course, this position binds only ICSID and has not necessarily been adopted by other arbitration institutions. The tribunal decided in this case that the bank guarantees in question could not be deemed "investments":

"The terms of the contract are entirely normal commercial terms, including those governing the bank guarantees. No reference to investment is anywhere made and no steps were taken to qualify it as an investment under the Egyptian mechanisms for the authorisation of foreign investments nor were any steps taken to take advantage of any of the many incentives offered by that country to foreign investors."

For the reasons discussed above, the Tribunal concluded that it lacked jurisdiction to consider this dispute because the claim fell outside both the Treaty and the Convention.

9.2.7.3. *Patrick Mitchell/Dem. Republic of the Congo* [165]

9.2.7.3.1. *Origins of the dispute*

The petitioner headed a lawyers' office in Kinshasa. By ordinance of the Military Court of the Congo, this office had been sealed on 5 March 1999 and Congolese authorities had

---
[165] ICSID Case N° ARB/99/7, pp. 2 et suivantes, see website: www.worldbank.org/ICSID.

seized documents and other materials (deemed "compromising"). According to the defendant, as a result of information provided by the lawyers' office to its client, SAKIMA SARL, the latter had been successful in having 99 tonnes of cassiterite seized by the South African tribunals which had jurisdiction over the matter. The SAKIMA company had been transferred to a company created by the Congolese Government and named SOMICO. The lawyers' office headed by MITCHELL had filed for arbitration, arguing that the privative measures undertaken with respect to an investment made on Congolese territory were in violation of the BIT.

9.2.7.3.2. *Parties' respective positions*

The defendant claimed that the ICSID had no jurisdiction to arbitrate the dispute mainly on three grounds:

"1. According to the Congolese Investment Code, there was no 'investment.'

In principle, an investment may be seen as the creation of a local enterprise or as a collection of contributions furnished by a promoter of such an enterprise... For an investment to be qualified as such, it must be made as an activity which is susceptible of contributing to the economic and social development of the host State, as appears from articles 1 to 6 of the Congolese Investment Code;

2. The BIT is a commercial agreement, lawyer services or the exercise of a similar liberal arts profession, such as the legal advice firnished by the Mitchell office are not to be deemed a commercial activity;

3. A lawyer's or legal counsel's activity does not correspond to the type of service to which reference is made in article 1, paragraph c, of the BIT and article 1 of the Investment Code. Defendant stresses that, in this connection, neither the foregoing provision of the BIT nor that of the Investment Code contain a definition of the term 'service'."

The petitioner claimed that:

"1. The materials and documents seized constituted an investment, within the terms of article 25 of the Washington Convention as well as under the BIT.

2. Article 1 of the BIT, defining 'investment' covers all activities having an economic value as well as contracts relating to services and to the investment."

9.2.7.3.3. *ICSID's Analysis and Decision*

The tribunal held that the concept of "protected investment" did not have to be based on the Congolese national Investment Code but that it had to be based on the international level in the light of the BIT. The BIT expressly states that contracts relative to services and activities having an economic value are "investments". The activities of the Mitchell office are therefore investments within the meaning of the BIT. Furthermore, the investments list is "illustrative" and not exclusive. Hence, even if there had been no express mention of service contracts, the Mitchell activity could be deemed an investment.

The tribunal held that the dispute qualified under the jurisdiction of the Centre. An indemnity was granted to the Mitchell office for damages sustained by an expropriation measure. This measure was not a formal expropriation since there had been no applicable legislation. Expropriation is an act by which the host State, acting in the public interest, deprives an investor of his rights with respect to goods and other assets affected by the measure. The concept of "expropriation" in this case is therefore of a material nature and the measures taken are equivalent to an expropriation.

9.2.7.3.4. *Annulment Hearing*

The Republic of the Congo filed a request for nullity with the *ad hoc* Committee having jurisdiction. The request was granted and the decision was annulled. In relation to the concept of "protected investment", which is the topic of the current Chapter of this Work, the ad hoc Committee justified its decision to annul as follows:

"The Committee believes that the Centre's decision is not properly grounded and does not comply with the rules set forth by article 52 of the Washington Convention reading :

Either Party may request the annulment of the award by an application in writing addressed to the Secretary General on one or more of the following grounds... that the award failed to state the reasons on which it is based."

The tribunal held that the term "investment" includes "services" and that the service concept must have a very large scope, including "any service furnished by a foreign investor". However, no explanation had been given why the Mitchell Office should be considered an investor. Furthermore, the BIT does not refer to "service". The Committee therefore held that a legal services office is an unusual activity for the purpose of investment. According to the Committee, that activity would first have to be considered as ontributing to economic development. There was no proof that the Mitchell Office had – through its activities – helped the Congolese State. The Centre's decision was held to be incomplete and obscure in that it considered different fragments of the lawyers' office operation as an investment.

9.2.7.3.5. *ICSID's Assertion of jurisdiction*

ICSID's assertion of jurisdiction in each of these cases confirms that the protected investments list appearing in BIT's must be as comprehensive and specific as possible. Anticipating issues, avoiding generalisations and eliminating doubt, are the best prescriptions for avoiding conflicts and the burden of arbitration proceedings. Heeding the ICSID decisions, the Italian and Belgian models' list, for instance, could, among other things, be improved by adding bills of exchange, enterprise contracts and service contracts to them.

The Contracting Parties may freely agree what "investments" are to be enumerated in the list, as current circumstances and the known intentions of prospective investors may dictate. They are bound by their choice and arbitrators will hold them to it. The list should also include the "new forms of investment" (NFI's) and mention "contractual rights". With respect to these rights, the US model convention meets this need:

> "...and includes investments consisting or taking the form of contractual rights, such as under turnkey, construction or management contracts, production of revenue-sharing contracts, concessions, or similar contracts."

So as not to risk omitting a reference to the jurisdiction of ICSID, a clause should be added that the rights intended to be covered are contractual and are those bound to the realisation of an investment ("in connection with an investment"). The ICSID Convention contains no definition of the term "investments", but the Centre has issued a number of decisions which interpret and clarify the concept. Consequently, it is useful to study some of those arbitral decisions.

Nonetheless, out of concern for the terms of the Washington Convention, whenever contracts are an issue, it would also be useful to specify that contracts must have a link to the investment. In fact, ICSID, as stated above, bases its jurisdiction mainly on two elements: there must be an "investment" in the sense intended by the BIT and the conflict it must decide on must be "in direct relation to an investment."

CHAPTER X
PROMOTION & ADMITTAL OF INVESTMENTS

10.1. – No Right to foreign Establishment

As a starting point, it is worth noting that international law does not require any State to admit foreign investments on its territory :

> "Under general international law, in the absence of treaty obligations and contractual commitments, States are free to regulate the admission of foreigners in their territory including the conditions and the extent of their carrying out economic activities, as a prerogative deriving from national sovereignty. No general obligations exist as to the movement (admission) of capital and the freedom for foreigners to carry out business and to establish themselves. Indeed, the policy of different groups of countries have been substantially at variance in this respect, depending upon the principles of their economic system." [166]

Prospective investors should carefully review local legislation of States where they wish to invest. Some States prohibit foreign investments in certain sectors of their economy because they wish to reserve those to domestic, sometimes politically well connected, investors. In the Colonia Protocol of the 23rd of March 2006, concluded among certain States of Latin America (Argentina, Paraguay, Brazil and Uruguay) regarding the reciprocal protection of investments on the territory of the "Common Market of the South/Mercado Comun del Sur", this principle has been stressed :

> "Each Contracting Party shall promote investments of investors of other Contracting States and shall admit them in its territory and

---
[166] SACERDOTI, G., *op. cit.*, p. 321, see footnote 161.

shall afford them a treatment not less favourable than the investments of its own investors or of the investments made by investors of third States, without prejudice for the right of each Party to maintain transitorily limited exceptions corresponding to sectors listed in the Annex."[167]

In the investment codes of some countries, there are provisions for the admission of only those investments which contribute to the industrial development of the country where they are admitted. Particularly in developing countries with an ambivalent attitude regarding the negotiation of BIT's, foreign investors, solely as a precaution, should not open themselves to expenses in preparation of an investment until they have ascertained the probable reception of proposals for such agreements. Short of firm contractual commitments, domestic legislation is usually the only one applied, leading to serious potential damages if it is not strictly observed, should there be a rejection or slowdown in cases where investment projects have already begun.

10.2. – STATE IS SOVEREIGN

The sovereignty principle in matters of international law regarding the power States have to reject or limit foreign investments is bound to the submittal to them of petitions for licences or permits to the appropriate local authorities:

"A national, company or State entity of a Contracting Party intending to make an investment in the territory of the other Contracting Party including collaboration arrangements on specific projects shall submit his or its proposal to a designated authority of the Party where the investment is sought to be made. Such proposals shall be examined expeditiously and soon after the proposal is approved, a letter of authorisation shall be issued and the investment shall be registered with the designated authority of the host State." (**Article 3**, reception of investments)[168]

---
[167] SACERDOTI, G., op. cit., p. 334, see footnote 161.
[168] SALEM, Mahmoud, op. cit., p. 602, see footnote 53.

10.3. – APPROVAL PROCESS

In most European BIT's, too little attention is given to the process of "approval of foreign investments". Developed countries usually emphasise provisions relating to the protection of investments. For the developing countries, bilateral accords are seen as a lever for growing the volume of foreign investments on their territory. Each side therefore has its own set of priorities which seldom match. Developing countries are loath to provide precise information regarding current procedures for the admission of foreign investors. In some cases, these procedures have not been consigned to writing but are matters of habit and suspicion of foreign intent buried deep in administrative layers.

Developing countries are led to conclude BIT's mainly for the economic benefits they expect from them:

> "In the final analysis, reciprocity of bilateral investment agreements draw their justification from an economic *quid pro quo*. Commitments by developing countries receiving investments from abroad may very simply stem from their quest to gain economic and social advantages that such investments may bring." [169]

After gaining independence, developing countries have wished to stress their sovereignty and have seized upon every opportunity to emphasise the importance of their domestic legislation, particularly when foreign interests were involved. Thus, where admission of a foreign interest was concerned, developing countries have wanted to reserve for themselves the right to apply, as much as possible, their own domestic laws.

In most BIT's, a very short provision is included whereby the Contracting Parties agree to encourage nationals of the other Contracting Party to invest on their territory and to admit them in conformity with domestic law.

---

[169] The American Law Institute, *Restatement of Foreign Relations Law of the United States*, Philadelphia, 1965, para. 165.2

BIT's are not written in order to confer to physical persons and corporations a "right" to make investments nor to declare an "open door policy" regarding foreign investments. It is mostly in order to recognise that developing countries have reservations whether the following classical and succinct formula ought to be included in BIT's:

> "Each Contracting Party encourages investors to settle on its territory and admits them in accordance with its own legislation and regulations."

10.4. – Formula for Approval

Model conventions usually use the same formula. For instance, in the Belgian model convention, under the title "Investment Promotion", the text of this formula is as follows:

> "Each of the Contracting Parties encourages investments on its territory by investors from the other Contracting Party and will admit their investments in accordance with its legislation.
>
> In particular, each contracting Party will authorise the conclusion and the execution of licence contracts and commercial, administrative or technical assistance accords, to the extent that such activities are related to the investments." (**Article 2**)

Solely referring to the application of domestic law regarding admission of investments without an added reference to the provisions of the BIT's is an error which may lead to difficulties. There is the risk that investments may be arbitrarily refused, in accordance with domestic law (on the ground, for example, that the project is not an investment according to local law). If there are no references to the provisions of the BIT, the filing of an arbitration proceeding could be imperiled.

French BIT's have sometimes used a different formula:

> "Each of the Contracting Parties will admit on its territory and maritime zone investments made by investors of the other Contracting Party in accordance with its legislation and encourages them to apply

the provisions of the present agreement." (Article 3. France/Mexico Agreement dated 12 November 1998)

This French formula is better than previous ones but still does not offer sufficient guarantees, since "admission" is severed from "promotion" (euphemistically called "encouragement") and the reference to BIT provisions is tied only to promotion.

This risk therefore continues to exist. It would be better to specify that both admission and promotion of investments are governed by local law as well as by the provisions of the BIT. The French negotiators have apparently realised the problem exists and an amended – and better – version has been inserted in the 11 February 1998 agreement with Slovenia:

> "Each of the Contracting Parties admits and encourages on its territory and maritime zone, in accordance with its legislation and the provisions of the present Agreement, investments made by nationals or companies of the other Contracting State."

Under these conditions, a refusal of an investment cannot occur on the ground of the local law's definition of "investments" in as much as the BIT definition will take precedence.

10.5. – Risk of arbitrary Change in Law

Developing countries, undeniably, do not hesitate to modify and improve their investment laws regularly, when they think that their interests will thereby be better served. In quite a few developing countries, investment codes change at an incredible rate. One may rightfully fear that sectors that are "open for admission" at the time of the conclusion of the BIT will be closed later to foreign investments on the ground of new laws.

The aforementioned classical, insufficient formula has been commonsensically corrected by the UK in its BIT with Lesotho, in 1981, where the following provision was inserted:

> "Each Contracting Party shall encourage and create favourable conditions for nationals or companies of the other Contracting State to invest capital in its territory and, subject to its right to exercise powers conferred by its laws existing when this agreement comes into force, shall admit such capital."

This, in effect, is a "stabilisation" clause. The purpose is to help assure investors that the conditions under which they make their investments will not be changed. Investments made after the conclusion of the BIT will not be retroactively affected by amendments to domestic law occurring after such investments are made. It is a preventative protection formula for future investments. Should the State in question modify its laws, it could still not escape its international responsibility.

10.6. – US Formula

The formula appearing in the 1994 US model convention enjoys a special position when compared to European or Asian alternatives. Regarding company establishment, it specifies that US investors must be treated the same as domestic investors as well as investors of the "most favoured nation":

> "With respect to the establishment, acquisition, expansion, management, conduct, operation and sale or other disposition of covered investments, each Party shall accord treatment no less favourable than that it accords, in like situations, to investments in its territory of its own nationals or companies (hereinafter 'national treatment') or to investments in its territory of nationals or companies of a third country (he hereinafter 'most favoured nation treatment') whichever is most favourable (hereinafter 'national and most favoured nation treatment')."

In European BIT's, there is an express reference to national legislation. In the US formula, this reference is indirect, in as much as it provides that national treatment is required. There is, however, an express reference to national legislation, insofar as investors' access rights to US territory are concerned:

> "Subject to its laws relating to the entry and sojourn of aliens, each Party shall permit to enter and to remain in its territory nationals of the other Party for the purpose of establishing, developing, administering or advising on the operation of an investment to which they, or a company of the other Party that employs them, have committed or are in the process of committing a substantial amount of capital and resources."

The right of the Contracting State to impose special duties when investments are made is confirmed by **Article 14** of the model convention:

> "This treaty shall not preclude a Part from prescribing special formalities in connection with covered investments such as a requirement that such investments be legally constituted under the laws and regulations of that Party, or a requirement that transfers of currency or other monetary instruments be reported, provided that such formalities shall not impair the substance of any of the rights set forth in this Treaty."

The US model ought not to be followed. The formula described in paragraph 10.5 above is preferable.

In the 2004 US model convention another formula appears. There is a specific reference to investment permits:

> "Investment authorisation means an authorisation that the foreign investment authority of a Party grants to a covered investment or an investor of the other Party." (article 1, Definitions)

Furthermore, a guarantee has been inserted in **articles 3 and 4** against discriminatory measures. The formula was used in the USA/Uruguay BIT (dated 4 November 2005). A commentator has expressed his view on this subject as follows:

> "National and Most Favoured Nation treatment (**Articles, 3, 4**): The treaty protects investors of a Party and the covered investments from discriminatory measures by the other Party during the full-life cycle of an investment, including the establishment phase, when investors are attempting to make an investment. Each Party commits to provide to investors of the other Party and to their covered investments treatment no less favourable that that which it provides, in like

circumstances, to its own investors or to investors from any third country and their investments."

10.7. – DEVELOPING COUNTRIES' FORMULA

Nearly all the investment codes published by developing countries require the filing of a petition to invest with the "appropriate authority". Yet, the conduct of these "appropriate authorities" is not always exemplary. Several investors have paid dearly while enduring long delays in the processing of their petitions. Permits are often issued with much delay. Some petitions remain unanswered. It is therefore past time for BIT's and Execution Protocols to provide guidelines for procedures of admission and agreement.

One can, for example, imagine that BIT's would include provisions requiring the "appropriate authorities" to take all necessary steps for the completion of petition review within a specified time from the petition filing date. Administrative schedules of listed formalities should likewise be fixed within specified limits and required to be observed by the competent authorities. Incidentally, it is rather surprising that few BIT's specify any particular procedure investors should follow in order to obtain permits to carry out their investments.

10.8. – ICSID AMCO/INDONESIA CASE [170]

10.8.1. – *Origins of the Dispute*

Arbitral decisions regarding the right of establishment and the authorisation to invest are few. The *Amco/Indonesia* case has been analysed from the "control" aspect in Chapter VIII. This paragraph is devoted to analysing the "admittal" aspect of foreign investments.

---

[170] ICSID, Case n° ARB/81/1, GAILLARD, *op. cit.*, pp. 140 and s.

In *Amco Asia v. Indonesia*, Amco Asia corporation, a company incorporated in the State of Delaware (USA) and two affiliate companies, Pan American Development Limited, a company incorporated in Hongkong, and P.T. Amco Indonesia, a company incorporated under the laws of Indonesia, instituted ICSID's arbitration proceedings against the Republic of Indonesia in January of 1981, in respect of a dispute arising from the implementation of an agreement for the construction and management of a hotel in Djakarta.[171]

Amco Asia had, on 22 April 1968, entered into a rental and management contract with PT Wisma, a corporation established under Indonesian law. PT Wisma was 100% controlled by an Indonesian cooperative, Inkopad, held in trust by the Indonesian Government. On 6 May 1968, the US company Amco Asia submitted to the Indonesian Government a request for admittal as an investor for the establishment of a domestic corporation, to be named PT Amco Indonesia. This request had been made under the terms of Indonesian Law no. 1 of 1967 regarding foreign investments. An investment permit was issued on 29 July 1968. Amco Asia then completed the construction of a hotel. Difficulties arose regarding the management method and the distribution of income. PT Amco Wisma then cancelled its contract with Amco Asia. Indonesian authorities in charge of investment audits revoked the investment permit granted to Amco Asia. Indonesian army and police installed PT Wisma – *manu militari* – as the hotel manager. Amco Asia, Panamerican and PT Amco Indonesia contested, before ICSID, the revocation of the permit.

---

[171] "ICSID Review", *Foreign Investment law journal*, p. 160.

10.8.2. – *Tribunal's decision regarding the Revocation of Investment Permit*[172]

First, the tribunal considered the Indonesian decision's compliance with the rules of Indonesian legislation. Article 6 of the decree of 1977 provided that the imposition of sanctions upon an investor which had not complied with his obligations should come only after the investor had been served with that a compliance demand. Rather bizarrely, this decree provided a maximum of three such demands be made each of which could be made only after the expiration of a delay next following a precedent demand (*sic*). No such demand having been sent to Amco Asia, the arbitrators concluded that the revocation was irregular, being contrary to Indonesian law. They also stated that the Indonesian measure was contrary to principles of international law, due process having been ignored. The decision to revoke had been taken during a meeting with Amco Asia which had lasted barely an hour.

The arbitrators then declared that the substantive grounds on which the revocation decision rested were insufficient to justify such a measure in reference to Indonesian and international law.

One of the grounds invoked was the transfer of the hotel's management to another company, named Aeropacific. This transfer would have occurred without the prior consent of the Indonesian Government. Amco Asia defended the transfer, claiming that it was merely a subcontract and that it, Amco Asia, a party to the main contract, remained responsible for the management. The arbitrators did not adopt the investor's position in this regard. They stated that the investment permit created a "*intuitu personae*" contract between investor and host State. The State relied on the qualifications of the investor. It was proper in principle, according to the tribunal, for it to conclude that the transfer of 100% of the execution of a contract with the host State, without the latter's con-

---

[172] GAILLARD, Emmanuel, *op. cit.*, pp. 146 and s., see footnote 31.

sent, constituted a violation of the investor's obligations and justified the revocation of the investment permit.

However, the arbitrators noted that PT Wisma had expressly accepted the subcontract and that the Indonesian Government knew of such acceptance and had not opposed it. Another ground for the revocation decision lay in the difference between, on the one hand, the amount of money Amco Asia had to invest, according to its request for an investment permit, and, on the other hand, the amount of capital actually invested. The tribunal concluded that the difference was too small to justify the revocation.

This decision again demonstrates how important it is to have properly written investment contracts. The modalities of management transfer, within the scope of subcontracts therefor, had not been addressed in the investment contract in this case. Had it been, the investor would have been better able to hold his ground. The 20 November 1984 decision was subsequently annulled. However, the *ad hoc* Committee annulled it on different grounds. The holding of the tribunal regarding the revocation was not contested.

CHAPTER XI

"FAIR AND EQUITABLE TREATMENT"

11.1. – No absolute Right to Invest

Foreign investors seeking to establish themselves in a host State do not necessarily have absolute and specific rights to invest. Just like domestic investors in the host State, they are subject to national legislation. An international investment necessarily implies that it is established in a foreign territory and is subject to the jurisdiction of the host State.

This is merely a recognition of the national sovereignty of the host State's and its agencies. The sovereignty principle is confirmed in several treaties and conventions. Thus in the Charter of States' Economic Rights and Duties of States[173], the following provision declares:

> "Every State has the right to regulate foreign investments within the limits of its national jurisdiction and to apply its authority over them in accordance with its own laws and regulations as well as in accordance with its priorities and national objectives." (**Article 2**)

It follows that a State that has passed a law excluding foreign investors from one or the other economic sector (for example, the mining sector) cannot be faulted for unfair or inequitable treatment of such investors.

When and under what conditions may it be concluded that the obligation of a State is based on international common law and why is it important? These are important issues because if an obligation is based on international common

---

[173] United Nations General Assembly Resolution, (UNGAOR) N° 3281, 29th Session, Supp. N° 31, 1974, p. 50.

law, the failure to observe would be viewed as a breach of the non-observing' State's responsibility.

11.2. – CHARACTER OF "FAIR AND EQUITABLE" TREATMENT OBLIGATION

According to doctrinal texts, an obligation becomes a rule of international law when a unanimous *"opinio juris"* has materialised, that is when the legal principle in question has been recognised in a whole gamut of international treaties and bilateral as well as multilateral conventions. The result then is that unanimous opinions and parallel conventional practice of States come into being, showing that they themselves are convinced they are bound in accordance with a duty imposed on them by international common law.

All authors believe that it is important to verify whether the duty to treat foreign investors fairly and equitably arises from international common law:

> "Another important issue of substance concerns the status of fair and equitable standard in customary international law. Of course, it is well established that in certain circumstances, the rules of a multilateral treaty may pass into the *'corpus'* of customary international law. When this occurs, the rule in the treaty becomes binding even on States that have not expressly accepted it. Also when a rule is set in a series of bilateral treaties, this may provide evidence that the particular rule has become a part of customary law."

However there is no unanimity in doctrinal texts about the international law character of fair and equitable treatment. Some authors claim that the duty to treat fairly and equitably is not a part of international common law. They recognise instead the existence of several multilateral agreements which impose this duty (Havana Chart, OCDE Treaty, UNCTAD, etc.) but state that it cannot be concluded therefrom there is a unanimous *"opinio juris"*, because several States which signed these treaties and conventions have not thereafter ratified them.

Another argument is that several developing countries regularly declare that they do not feel bound by international common law. Some developed countries stress their national sovereignty and declare their willingness to be bound conventionally only in exchange for the benefits they receive from BIT's or other treaties they have not abjured.

On the other hand, other authors believe that the duty of fair and equitable treatment does in fact arise from international common law. JUILLARD, for instance, a renowned French author confirms it :

> "The principle of fair and equitable treatment therefore represents an application, specific to investments, of the minimum standard required by international law stemming from custom."

11.3. – FAIR AND EQUITABLE TREATMENT OBLIGATION UNDER CUSTOMARY INTERNATIONAL LAW

The very fact there currently are an important number of multilateral conventions on the issue as well as an impressive network of bilateral conventions shows that developed as well as developing countries increasingly feel bound internationally to the duty.

States' obligation to provide to each other's investment "fair and equitable treatment" is mostly stated as being part of customary international law. Under this principle, foreign investors are entitled to a certain level of treatment, which may surpass the national treatment. Any treatment which is lower than the level required by international common law, called "international minimum standard", may give rise to international responsibility on the part of the State concerned :

> "The international minimum standard is a norm of international common law which governs the treatment of aliens, by providing for a mimimum set of principles which States, regardless of their domestic legislation and practices, must respect when dealing with foreign nationals and their property. While the principle of national treatment fore-

sees that aliens can only expect equality of treatment with nationals, the international minimum standard sets a number of basic rights established by international law that States must grant to aliens, independent of the treatment accorded to their own citizens. Violation of this norm engenders the international responsibility of the host State and may open the way for international action on behalf of the injured alien provided that the alien has exhausted local remedies." [174]

In the United States, the existence and obligatory application of an international minimum standard of treatment has been confirmed:

"The international standard of justice... is the standard required for the treatment of aliens by: a) the applicable principles of international law as established by international custom, judicial and arbitral decisions, and other recognised sources or in the absence of such applicable principles b) analogous principles of justice generally recognised by States that have reasonably developed legal systems." [175]

LIEBESKIND has confirmed the existence of a fundamental principle of international law regarding fair and equitable treatment:

"There are therefore, two levels of protection. The first, general, is the principle of fair and equitable treatment, a fundamental principle of public international law. This principle provides a safety net when more detailed guarantees have not been expressly formulated." [176]

The International Court of Justice (ICJ) has confirmed the duty to provide fair and equitable treatment to foreign investors. In the *"Barcelona Traction"* decision, the following *dictum* appears:

"As soon as a State admits foreign investments or foreign physical persons or corporations on its territory, it is bound to grant them the protection of the law and it assumes certain obligations regarding

---

[174] ROTH, Andreas Hans, *The minimum standard of international law applied to aliens*, The Hague, Edition Sijthoff, 1949, p. 127.

[175] The American Law Institute, *Restatement of Foreign Relations law of the United States*, Philadelphia, 1965, para. 165.2.

[176] LIEBESKIND, Christophe, "The Legal Framework of Swiss International Trade and Investment – Part I. Promotion", *The Journal of World Investment and Trade*, 2006, Vol. 7, n° 3, p. 339.

their treatment. These obligations are, however, not absolute nor without reservations."[177]

According to international law, it is therefore not enough for the host State to admit foreign investments. A necessary corollary follows that it has the duty to treat such investors well. However, since the right to invest is not absolute, the duty of fair treatment is likewise not absolute.[178]

Based on the foregoing observations, it may be concluded that a principle of international law exists imposing a duty on States to treat foreign investors and their investments fairly and equitably. Consequently, it seems to be clear that such an obligation binds every State, even those that have concluded no agreement regarding the protection of international investments as well as States which have not adopted such obligation in their domestic legislation.

11.4. – Content of fair treatment obligation

For some authors, the term *"just and equitable treatment"* by itself is sufficiently clear and its very mention *in a conventional text* is sufficient to guarantee investors a satisfactory protection. "Fairness" and "equity" are autonomous terms, having an independence which defines their content. It is not necessary to establish a standard to give the concept a clearer content. F.A. Mann especially defends this argument with enthusiasm:

> "For Mann, therefore, in ascertaining the content of the fair and equitable treatment standard, no other form of words is appropriate: for each dispute, the content of the standard is to be determined by inquiring whether 'in all circumstances the conduct in issue is fair and equitable or unfair and inequitable'. In effect, this amounts to the

---

[177] Barcelona Traction Light and Power Company Limited, *op. cit.*, para 33, see footnote 15.
[178] Vasciannie, Stephen, "The fair and equitable treatement standard in international investment law and pratice", *Britisch Yearbook of International Law*, 1999, p. 148.

application of the plain meaning of the terms 'fair and equitable treatment' in each individual case, independently of other standards. In practice too, this approach may also mean giving considerable discretion to the tribunal entrusted with determining whether a breach of the standard has occurred, bearing in mind the subjectivity inherent in the notions of fairness and equity."

However, the fact remains that the content of the "fair and equitable treatment" concept is not clear. International jurisprudence and doctrine may well be distilled, along with generally accepted principles regarding treatment of investments, *"pacta sunt servanda"*, respect for private property rights, duty to indemnify for expropriation damage, rights to defense, stare decisis, respect for judicial decisions, due process of law, execution of contract provisions etc. but to guarantee a correct application of this principle in the relations between host State and foreign investors, it is necessary that the duty of fair and equitable treatment be confirmed expressly in conventional international law. Already in 1970, the Court of International Justice observed that there were too few conventional rules regarding investments:

"Considering the important events that have occurred during the last 50 years, related to the development of foreign investments and the scope of activity undertaken by companies operating on a international scale, particularly holding companies which are multinational, and considering also the proliferation of State's economic interests, it may seem at first rather surprising that international law has not preceded these developments and that generallyaccepted rules have not crystallised on the international level." [179]

CIJ's recommendation did not fall on deaf ears and since then, conventional law regarding foreign investments has grown by leaps and bounds. In conclusion, it is safe to say that explicitly referring to the "fair and equitable" concept in bilateral conventions is extremely useful.

---

[179] Barcelona Traction Light and Power Company Limited, *op. cit.*, p. 89, see footnote 15.

It is also very useful in connection with the establishment of a correct arbitration procedure. In fact, where arbitrators are faced with a concrete case where an adequate fair and equitable treatment clause is lacking, a very broad freedom is given them to define the content of the treatment obligation.

11.5. – Other Standards of Treatment

11.5.1. – *National Treatment*

Some States sometimes believe that they have met the duty of fair and equitable treatment when they grant to foreign investors the same treatment as that granted to national investors. Yet, this does not mean that the State's international responsibility is automatically and fully disengaged. In fact, the international standard is a minimum. Where the national standard is significantly less favourable than the international minimum standard, investors made subject to the national standard could validly conclude that they have not been treated fairly and equitably. National treatment may not always be considered as a valid yardstick for the faur and equitable treatment to which foreign investors are entitled.

Statements made in conventions granting to foreign investors the same treatment as that granted by internal law and reserved to national investors certainly do not provide enough protection. According to principle of international law, national protection is not to be considered a limitation upon foreign investors. Quite possibly, national protection may not be apprpriate in regard to foreign investments unless it also conforms to principles and rules of international law :

"The important thing from the point of view of international law is not the equality of nationals and foreigners. It is the recognition and respect for principles. Were it to happen that a State should, for any reason, disregard them in relations with its own subjects, its international duty to observe them towards foreigners would continue to subsist in all its force." [180]

A reference to national treatment may, for some countries, be interesting in itself but other standards inserted in conventions should also be considered.

11.5.2. – *Most Favoured Nation Treatment (MFN)*

States also use as a measuring stick for "fair and equitable treatment", the treatment they grant to investors from third countries. Investors are then entitled to the treatment granted to the most favoured nation. Thus, mentioning only one standard is not enough. In general, conventional provisions include both standards, in the sense that an investor may demand a treatment that is at least as favourable as the national standard as well as the treatment reserved to the most favoured nation.

MFN clauses appearing in BITs are usually rather concise. For example, a BIT may state:

> "Neither Contracting Party shall subject investments and activities associated with such investments to treatment less favourable than that accorded to the investments and associated activities by the investors of any third State."

Sometimes, in a BIT, the MFN clause may be more specific. In individual cases where it is applied include: management, maintenance, use, enjoyment and sale of investments. However, there is some doubt as to the precise scope of the MFN clause. May it be invoked advantageously in the cases explicitly mentioned in the BIT or is its scope wider?

For example, to know, whether an investor may also claim the MFN clause when the arbitration formula in a third State's BIT is more favouyable than that appearing in his country's own BIT, could be very important.

---

[180] FRIEDMAN, Samy, *op. cit.*, p. 130, see footnote 30.

That very question has been raised in an ICSID arbitration procedure filed against the Argentine Republic by the Argentine company *TSA Spectrum de Argentina*, controlled by the Dutch TSI Corporation, and which led to the award dated 19 December 2008[181].

Article 10 of the Argentine/Netherlands BIT provided for three conditions precedent to the filing of an arbitration request with ICSID:

"1. Disputes regarding issued covered by the BIT should, if possible, be settled amicably;

2. If amicable settlement is not possible within three months from the date that such settlement has been requested, either party may submit the dispute to the administrative or judicial organs of the Contracting Party in the territory of which the investment has been made;

3. If, within eighteen months from the date of the submission of the dispute to the competent organs mentioned sub 2°, such organs have not rendered a final decision, or, if after a decision has been rendered, the parties are still in dispute, the investor concerned may resort to international arbitration (SCSID, UNCITRAL)."

In fact, the petitioners (ISA and TSI) had become aware of the existence of the arbitration formula provided for in the USA/Argentina BIT, which, according to the petioners, was more favourable than that in the Argentine/Netherlands BIT. The investors claimed that, therefore, because of the MFN clause, they were entitled to having the more favourable clause applied to them:

"More particularly, each Contracting Party shall accord to such investments the same security and protection as it accords either to those of its own investors or those of investors of any third State, whichever is more favourable to the investor concerned."

The US/Argentina BIT provided that an investment dispute between a Party and a national or company of the other Party, including a dispute involving an investment authorization or the interpretation of an investment agreement, may be submitted to international arbitration six months after the dispute arose. Exhaustion of local remedies was not required.

---

[181] Http://ita.law.uvic.ca/documents/TSA Award Eng.pdf.

The time lapse provided for recourse to arbitration being shorter and exhaustion of local remedies not being required, it was easy for the investors to show that the US/Argentina BIT formula was more favourable. Nonetheless, Argentina was arguing against such application, claiming that the clause related to the protection and security standard and did not include dispute resolution :

> "The intention of Argentina and the Netherlands was to add such protection to substantive issues and not to dispute resolution. This also appears from the wording of Article 3(2) which differs from the wording of MFN clauses. In some other bilateral investment treaties, which extent the protection to all matters governed by the treaty. Had it been the intention of the Argentine Republic and the Netherlands to include stipulations applicable to dispute resolution within the scope of the MFN clause, they would have included a phrase that allowed for such construction or general phrase referring to the whole BIT" [182]

The arbitration Tribunal has not rendered its decision on this matter, merely stating that in any event the investors were entitled to have recourse to ICSID arbitration. "However, we can draw an important point from the submittal of this very question to the arbitration tribunal. In most BIT's, the wording of the Most Favoured Nation clause is inadequate. Investors will be better protected if, in BIT and State Contract agreements, negotiators succeeded in getting MFN clauses written in, that very clearly define their scope. Thus, we suggest such clauses also specify that they apply to all questions raised in such agreements, expressly including, but not necessarily limited to, those relating to dispute settlement procedure."

11.6. – Specific reference to international law

In some protection conventions, there is an explicit reference to international law.

---

[182] Http://ita.law.uvic.ca/documents/TSA Award Eng.pdf, n° 71, page 24.

The advantage of mentioning international law is that, even though there is no doctrinal unanimity on the value or the legal scope of principles which govern the treatment and protection of international investments, most authors recognise that these principles really are an element of international common law and mentioning it avoids conflicting or alternative interpretations.

The reference to international law in a BIT has the advantage of transferring treatment and protection of international investments from domestic law concerning national treatment to the international level. The Contracting State which is guilty of an unfair or inequitable treatment will, in most cases, not be able to escape its international responsibility but some States, among the most powerful, are not always shy of flexing their muscle and declaring conventions outdated when their structures conflict with domestic or other international policies. However, in general, when a judicial or arbitration procedure is filed, this reference constitutes an excellent legal basis for the defence of investors' interests. This reference to international law is viewed in doctrinal texts as an absolute necessity for anyone wishing to give to the notion of "fair and equitable treatment" a concrete international content:

> "Another important issue regarding the fair and equitable treatment standard is whether it is tantamount to another standard or set of standards which form part of the traditional law on protection of nationals in foreign territory. On this issue, a number of sources, derived mainly but not exclusively from traditional capital-exporting perspectives, indicate that the fair and equitable treatment is, in fact, equivalent to the 'international minimum standard' which some countries believe constitutes a part of customary law." [183]

Within international institutions whose word is authoritative, the dominant opinion is that the concept of "fair and equitable treatment" must be tested by international law.

---
[183] VASCANNIE, Stephen, *op. cit.*, p. 139, see footnote 178.

The competent committee of the Organisation for Economic Development and Cooperation (OECD), in charge of preparing a multilateral model convention (MAI not approved) has stated, on this topic, as follows :

> "...that the concept of fair and equitable treatment *flowed from the 'well established principle of international law'* that a State is bound to respect and protect the property of nationals of other States".... (*emphasis* ours) [184]

In 1992, the World Bank published directives regarding the treatment of investments (Guidelines for the treatment of foreign direct investments) :

> "For the promotion of international economic cooperation through the means of private foreign investment, the constitution of this type of investment, its exploitation, its management, its control and the exercise of rights attached thereto as well as all other related activities that may be necessary or accessory thereto, are, subject to the principle of reciprocity and without prejudice to the provisions of applicable international instruments and the rules of common international law, dependent upon the following rules :
>
> Directives about the protection and security of the investors' persons, delivery of permits and licences of every kind, national treatment, most favoured nation treatment, adherence to schedules, issuance of work permits to foreign personnel, ease of reinvestment etc." [185]

The Swiss Foreign affairs Ministry has often recommended that BIT's include this reference and the recommendation has been adopted :

> "We are also referring to the classic principle of the Lex Gentium according to which States must place foreigners on their territory, and their assets, on the level of the 'international standard', that is to say to grant them a minimum of personal, procedural and economic rights." [186]

---

[184] VASCANNIE, Stephan, *op. cit.*, p. 140, see footnote 178.

[185] JUILLARD, Patrick, "investissements", *Annuaire français du droit international*, Paris, 1992, p. 803 (French annual Review of International Law).

[186] VASCANNIE, Stephan, *op. cit.*, p. 140, see footnote 178.

Reference to international law has therefore been confirmed as a useful tool for international venues. It is rather strange that a greater use of it is not made on a larger scale on the European level.

11.7. – CONVENTIONAL PROVISIONS ON FAIR AND EQUITABLE TREATMENT

We have stressed above that merely mentioning in conventions that investors have right on a fair and equitable treatment does not contain sufficient guarantees for the investors. It is necessary that a solid content be given to the notion of "fair and equitable treatment". This may be done by reference to standard treatment embodied in "national treatment", to standard treatment given to nationals of the most favoured nation and finally by reference to the standard of international law. The clarification of the normative content of these standards can be done in conventional provisions. The meaning given to the notion of "fair and equitable treatment" and the use of different standards is not the same in several treaties.

Here are some examples of conventional formulations.

11.7.1. – *Afro-Asian conventions*

Rather oddly, no mention at all is made in this model of the duty of fair and equitable treatment. Investors have only the right to be treated pretty much like how investors from the most favoured nation are treated:

> "Each Contracting Party shall accord in its territory to the investments or returns of nationals, companies or State entities of the other Contracting Party, treatment that is not less favourable than that it accords to the investments or returns of nationals, companies or State entities of any Third State." (article 4)

The content of the term "treatment" is further fleshed out:

"Each Contracting Party shall also ensure that the nationals, companies or State entities of the other Contracting Party are accorded treatment not less favourable than that it accords to nationals, companies or State entities of any third State in regard to management, use, enjoyment or disposal of their investment including management and control over business activities and other ancillary functions in respect of investments." (**Article 4**)

Sometimes a reference is made to national treatment in the sense that the host State (in this case an Asian country) agrees to extend to foreign investors a treatment which is at least equal to that extended to national investors. There is no reference to international law. It is striking that protection agreements between European and some Asian countries (Korea, Indonesia) include more extensive guarantees: application to investors of the most favoured clause and in addition a reference to the treatment offered by international law. Negotiators therefore should attend to the problem and try to obtain, when in Asia at least, guarantees in addition to those already contained in their model convention.

11.7.2. – *The US formula for Treatment*

11.7.2.1. *US prototype 1994*

The US formula is sufficiently favourable for investors. In the 1994 U.S. prototype bilateral investment treaty, mention is made of two standards: most favoured nation treatment and national treatment. In addition, it specifies that the investor may choose the treatment which appears most favourable to him:

"With respect to the establishment, acquisition, expansion, management, conduct, operation and sale or other disposition of covered investments, each Party shall accord treatment no less favourable than that it accords, in like situations, to investments in its territory of its own nationals or companies (hereinafter 'national treatment') or to investments in its territory of nationals or companies of a third country (hereinafter 'most favoured nation treatment'), whichever is most favourable (hereinafter 'national and most favoured nation treatment')."

Furthermore, the convention provides expressly for fair and equitable treatment and refers to international law standards:

> "Each party shall at all times accord to covered investments fair and equitable treatment and full protection and security, and shall in no case accord treatment les favourable than that required by international law."

More content is also expressly given to the concept of "fair and equitable": prohibition of unjustified and discriminatory measures apt to hinder the proper management of an enterprise (direction, production, sales, recognition of rights, submittal of claims, access to courts). Including "sales" is particularly important. Some developing countries impose on foreign investors obligations which jeopardise normal competition between domestic and foreign enterprises (requirement to purchase raw materials locally, prohibition against export to certain destinations, etc.). This negative provision, mentioning what may not be imposed to foreign investors gives more content to "fair and equitable treatment".

11.7.2.2. *US/Zaire*

There is an interesting formula in the US-Zaire accord of 28 July 1989, which provides that the investor may choose between national treatment and most favoured treatment whenever "new investments and *associated activities*" are involved.

Article II of the accord states:

> "Associated activities are:
> a) the establishment, control and maintenance of branches, agencies, offices, factories and other facilities for the conduct of business;
> b) the organisation of companies under the applicable national laws and regulations; the acquisition of companies or interests in companies; the management, control, maintenance, use and expansion, and the sale, liquidation and dissolution of companies organised or acquired;
> c) the making, performance and enforcement of contracts;

d) the acquisition (whether by purchase, lease or otherwise), possession with rights of ownership, and disposition (whether by sale, testament or otherwise) of property, both tangible and intangible;

e) the leasing of real property required for the conduct of the business;

f) the acquisition, maintenance, and protection of intellectual property rights, patents, trademarks, trade secrets, trade names, licences and

rights, patents, trademarks, trade secrets, trade names, licences and other approvals of products and manufacturing processes, and other industrial property rights; and

g) the borrowing of funds, the purchase and issuance of equity shares, and the purchase of foreign exchange for imports."

This is an important extension of the idea of "investments". The usefulness of such a clause has been shown in a preceding Chapter.

11.7.2.3. *US 2004 Model BIT*

The US formula has been considerably modified and improved. The new formula has already been used in the USA/Uruguay BIT. In view of the legal value of this formula, with reference to the three different standards already mentioned, it is cited in *haec verba* :

> "**Article 3** : National Treatment
>
> Each Party shall accord to investors of the other Party treatment no less favourable than that it accords, in like circumstances, to its own investors with respect to the establishment, acquisition, expansion, management, conduct, operation, and sale or other disposition of investments in its territory.
>
> Each Party shall accord to covered investments treatment no less favorable than that it accords, in like circumstances, to investments in its territory of its own investors with respect to the establishment, acquisition, expansion, management, conduct, operation, and sale or other disposition of investments.
>
> The treatment to be accorded by a Party under paragraphs 1 and 2 means, with respecttoa regional level of government, treatment no less favorable than the treatment accorded, in like circumstances, by that regional level of government to natural persons resident in and enterprises constituted under the laws of other regional levels of gov-

ernment of the Party of which it forms a part, and to their respective investments.

Article 4 : Most-Favored-Nation Treatment

Each Party shall accord to investors of the other Party treatment no less favorable than that it accords, in like circumstances, to investors of any non-Party with respect to the establishment, acquisition, expansion, management, conduct, operation, and sale or other disposition of investments in its territory.

Each Party shall accord to covered investments treatment no less favorable than that it accords, in like circumstances, to investments in ist territory of investors of any non-Party with respect to the establishment, acquisition, expansion, management, conduct, operation, and sale or other disposition of investments.

Article 5 : Minimum Standard of Treatment (cfr Annex A) :

Each Party shall accord to covered investments treatment in accordance with customary international law, including fair and equitable treatment and full protection and security."

For greater certainty, paragraph 1 prescribes the customary international law minimum Standard of Treatment of aliens as the minimum Standard of treatment to be afforded to covered investments. The concepts of "fair and equitable treatment" and "Minimum protection and security" do not require treatment in addition to or beyond that which is required by that Standard, and do not create additional substantive rights. The obligation in paragraph 1 to provide :

> "'fair and equitable treatment' includes the obligation not to deny justice in criminal, civil, or administrative adjudicatory proceedings in accordance with the principle of due process embodied in the principal legal systems of the world; and
>
> 'full protection and security' requires each Party to provide the level of police protection required under customary international law.
>
> A determination that there has been a breach of another provision of this Treaty, or of a separate international agreement, does not establish that there has been a breach of this Article.
>
> Notwithstanding **Article 14** [Non-Conforming Measures](5)(b) [subsidies andgrants], each Party shall accord to investors of the other Party, and to covered investments, non-discriminatory treatment with respect to measures it adopts or maintains relating to losses suf-

fered to by investments in its territory owing to armed conflict or civil strife.

Notwithstanding **paragraph 4**, if an investor of a Party, in the situations referred to in paragraph 4, suffers a loss in the territory of the other Party resulting from:

- requisitioning of its covered investment or part thereof by the latter's forces or authorities; or
- destruction of its covered investment or part thereof by the latter's forces or authorities, which was not required by the necessity of the situation;
- the latter Party shall provide the investor restitution, compensation, or both, as appropriate, for such loss. Any compensation shall be prompt, adequate, and effective in accordance with **Article 6** [Expropriation and Compensation]**(2)** through **(4)**, *mutatis mutandis*.

Paragraph 4 does not apply to existing measures relating to subsidies or grants that would be inconsistent with Article 3 [National Treatment] butfor Article 14 [Non-Conforming Measures] (5)(b) [subsidies and grants].

Annex A to the 2004 US BIT, entitled **International Common Law** provides as follows:

The Parties confirm their shared understanding that 'customary international law' generally and as specifically referenced in Article 5 [Minimum Standard of Treatment] and Annex B [Expropriation] results from a general and consistent practice of States that they follow from a sense of legal obligation. With regard to Article 5 [Minimum Standard of Treatment], the customary international law minimum standard of treatment of aliens refers to all customary international law principles that protect the economic rights and interests of aliens."

11.7.3. – *Australia*

In Australian BIT's, the protection formula is minimal:

"Investments of investors of either Party shall at all times be accorded fair and equitable treatment and shall, subject to the laws of the other Party:

a) enjoy full protection and security in the territory of the other Party end;

b) not be impaired in relation to management, maintenance, use, enjoyment or disposal by the other Party." (**Article 3**, BIT Australia/Sri Lanka, 12 November 2002)

There is no reference to the application of international law. On the contrary, there is an express reference to the application of national law: "subject to the laws of the other party". Australia and its co-contractors thus anchor the treatment of foreign investors within the scope of national law.

11.7.4. – *Belgium*

Under the heading "investment protection", the right to fair and equitable treatment is defined as follows:

> "1. All investments, whether direct or indirect, made by investors of one of the contracting Parties, shall enjoy fair and equitable treatment in the territory of the other Contracting Party.
>
> 2. Except for measures required to maintain *public order*, such investments shall enjoy continuous protection and security, i.e. excluding any unjustified or discriminatory measure which could hinder, either in law or in practice, the management, maintenance, use, possession or liquidation thereof." (article 3) (*emphasis* ours)

Under the sub-heading "National and Most Favoured Nation Treatment", the model states that investors have the right to be treated like national investors and like investors from a third Nation (the most favoured nation or MFP), except for benefits granted by reason of any agreement creating a customs union or a common market. However, unlike many other BIT's with less developed nations, a specific reference to international law is conspicuous by its absence in this particular model. A reference to international law has been provided for later.

As a first step, those who draft the model should either establish clearly the purpose of the *"public order"* qualification or delete it altogether. This clause is not present in the model conventions of three European countries which specialise in such conventions (France, Germany, and the UK). It entails a weakening of the guaranteed protection and opens the door to abuses. Furthermore, solid content should also be given in the model to the concept of "fair and equitable treatment" and a list of examples of inequitable acts should be set, as appears in the French model.

11.7.5. – *France*

The French formula is better than that generally used in other European conventions. The definition of fair and equitable treatment appears in the model convention is adopted in most Franch BIT's:

> "Each of the Contracting Parties commits itself to guarantee fair and equitable treatment, in accordance with principles of international law, to investments and investors of the other Contracting Party and do whatever is necessary so that the exercise of this recognised right shall not be hindered in law or in fact. In particularly, but not as a limitation, impediments in law or fact to fair and equitable treatment will be deemed to exist whenever a restriction exists limiting the purchase or the transport of raw materials and auxiliary energy or fuel supplies, as well as the means of production and exploitation of any kind, any impediment to the sale and transport within the host country and abroad, as well as any measures with analogous effect." (**Article 3**, BIT France/Guatemala, 27 May 1998)

There is a reference to international law; national treatment and most favoured nation treatment are also mentioned.

This formula provides investors with sufficient options to make them feel that they will benefit from a treatment suitable for their investments. Besides addressing the issue negatively (list of hindrances to proper treatment), the French text could be completed by the inclusion of "associated activities" such as the US model convention provides.

11.7.6. – *Germany*

Here too, the fair and equitable treatment clause is relatively short and has limited scope:

"Each Contracting Party shall in the territory in any case accord investments by investors of the Other Contracting Party fair and equitable treatment as well as full protection under the Treaty.

Neither Contracting State shall in any way impair by arbitrary or discriminatory measures the management, maintenance, use, enjoyment or disposal of investments in its territory of investors of the Other Contracting State." (article 2)

In the doctrine, the "Standard of Treatment" is defined as follows:

"As stated above the idea of concluding BIT's was motivated by the shortcomings of customary international law rules on the protection of aliens. With the dispute between international minimum standard and national treatment standard proponents still not solved today, it has become an important feature of BIT's to clarify the applicable law bilaterally... The various standards are complementary to each other and are necessary each on its own to overcome the shortcomings of customary international law. The fair and equitable treatment standard, although it is rather vague, can be considered at least as an incorporation of the international minimum standard." [187]

The mere mention of the duty to grant a fair and equitable treatment is therefore deemed to be an incorporation of the standard of international law in the BIT's. From a legal viewpoint, it is doubtful that such a formula is sufficient. To be legally safe, there ought to be an express reference to the standard of fair and equitable treatment as adopted by international law. The absence of such a reference results in the application ot two standards only, which are already rather vague by themselves:

"Neither Contracting State shall subject investments in its territory owned or controlled by investors of the other Contracting party to treatment less favouravble than it accords to investments of its own investors or to investments of investors of any third State." (article 3)

It would be necessary to complete the German text regarding treatment of investments by adding expressly the inter-

---

[187] FÜRACKER, Mathias, op. cit., p. 11, see footnote 52.

national standard and defining expressly and without limitation the content of this standard.

11.7.7. – *Netherlands*

The Netherlands use a characteristic formula, giving content of the duty of fair and equitable treatment : prohibition against unreasonable or discriminatory measures, national treatment, most favoured nation treatment, respect by the host State of contractual commitments with private investors. What actually distinguishes the Dutch text is mostly that the investor may choose, among these standards of treatment, which appears most favourable to him. This free choice is mentioned *expressis verbis*. He may choose national treatment or most favoured nation treatment. He may also choose the minimum international standard if he believes that it is more favourable than the other standards :

> "If the provisions of law of either Contracting Party or obligations under international law existing at present or established hereafter between the Contracting Parties in addition to the present Agreement contain a regulation, whether general or specific, entitling investments by nationals of the other Contracting Party to a treatment more favourable than is provided for by the present Agreement, such regulation shall, tot the extent that it is more favourable, prevail over the present agreement."

11.7.8. – *North American Free Trade Agreement (NAFTA) Formula*

This multilateral agreement (Canada, Mexico and the U.S.) mentions the three standards of treatment. First, there is a reference to national treatment :

> "Each Party shall accord to investors of another Party treatment no less favourable than that it accords, in like circumstances, to its own investors with respect to the establishment, acquisition, expansion, management conduct, operation, and sale or other disposition of investments." (article 1102)

A similar provision appears in **article 1103** applicable to investments. This distinction between investors and investments is particular to NAFTA. It is not to be found in other conventions, and, yet, this distinction is useful in that sometimes there are discussions between the Contracting Parties about what investment means and what are the companies or other legal entities entitled to the designation as "investors".

There is also a reference to the most favoured nation treatment. One of the characteristics here is the explicit statement that the host State is under the duty to grant to the investor the most favourable treatment, either on the national level or on the MFN level:

> "Each Party shall accord to investors of another Party and to investment of investors of another Party the better of the treatment required by **Articles 1102** and **1103**."

Finally, there is a reference to the minimum standard of international law:

> "Each Party shall accord to investments of investors of another Party treatment in accordance with international law, including fair and equitable treatment and full protection and security." (**Article 1105**)

11.7.9. – *General Appreciation of Treatment Formulas*

The US and NAFTA *formulae* certainly have great merit. All three standards are used. In addition, in the US text, the reference to the international standard mentions a few basic principles of international law whose application guarantees a fair and equitable treatment. A rather detailed content is therefore given to the notion of fair and equitable treatment. The list of what, under customary international law may be done and not done (discriminatory measures) could have been even more complete but, on the whole, the formula offers sufficient guarantees.

Other countries, both exporters and importers of capital, could commendably redraw their fair and equitable treatment clauses, emulating what has been done by NAFTA and the U.S., with the possibility of yet improving by an explicit reference to the three standards, showing a recommended list of the Contracting States' obligations and a negative list of acts which will be deemed unfair and inequitable.

11.8. – JURISPRUDENCE ON TREATMENT OF FOREIGN INVESTMENTS

In order to have an idea of the scope granted by judges and arbitrators of the duty of fair and equitable treatment, a few examples may be useful. They are examples but they give content to the concept.

11.8.1. – *ICSID Awards*

11.8.1.1. *American manufacturing & Trading Corp. v. Zaïre*

The dispute concerned damages sustained by reason of the action of the Zaire Army to the assets and installations of the Zaire industrial corporation (SINZA), owned 94% by AMT, a U.S. company. The Tribunal ruled against Zaire, holding that it had violated its duty of fair and equitable treatment and the guarantee of protection of foreign investors, stating:

> "The duty owed by the State of Zaire was an obligation to be vigilant so that Zaire, as a host State for the investments made by AMT, a US corporation, must take all necessary measures to ensure full enjoyment of the protection and security of its investment and could not validly draw upon its own legislation to argue that it can escape the consequences of its failure to uphold such duty."

The tribunal also referred to the rule of *"res ipsa loquitur"* in that no specific proof was required of AMT for the facts underlying the claim. It is noteworthy that the Tribunal rejected Zaire's argument based on the fact that its own nationals and the nationals of other countries, not parties to the agreement, had likewise not benefited from the special measures of protection, under similar circumstances. The arbitrators held that the failure to respect its duties regarding some other investor, even with respect to Zaire nationals, did not give Zaire the right to refuse its protection also to AMT. National treatment and that of the most favoured nation could not be invoked by Zaire to escape its obligation to grant "fair and equitable" treatment to AMT, obligation which applied also to other foreign investors.

11.8.1.2. *Metalclad v. Mexico*

Metalclad, a U.S. company, had been granted by the Federal Mexican authorities a permit to build a waste processing centre. When the centre was built, the Guadalcazar Commune claimed that a municipal permit was also required. Since such permit had not been obtained, the Commune prohibited Metalclad to operate the Centre. The area where the Centre had been sited was made into a natural preserve. Metalclad filed an arbitration request before ICSID.

The tribunal held the Mexican State liable, in particular by stating that the treatment reserved to the investor had not been fair or equitable... contrary to the international standard of treatment. There had, in fact, been a permit to build at the federal level and a dispute between the federal and municipal authorities regarding the need or not of a double permit to build, one by the federal authorities and the other by the municipal authorities.

The arbitrators interpreted the provision relating to the duty of fair and equitable treatment to be in conformity with international law, in the sense that this obligation included the duty to inform the investor rapidly and correctly about the legal conditions which would imposed so as to allow the investment project to come to fruition. Internationally, transparency was therefore an element of the minimum standard of international law :

"Each time that the authorities of the central Government of one of the Parties (whose international responsibility in this respect had been noted in the preceding section) are aware of the risk of a misunderstanding or confusion in this regard, it is their duty to determine rapidly what position to adopt and to enunciate it clearly so that the investors may proceed with their project with full knowledge of their conformance with the applicable rules of law."

11.8.1.3. Loewen v. U.S.

Solely on the ground of fair and equitable treatment of the investors, in accordance with international law, the investors wished to be indemnified for damages flowing from the judicial condemnation by a Mississippi tribunal. In order to appeal this decision, the investors had to deposit a very large security. They filed an arbitration procedure, based on two arguments:

"1. Obstruction to the appeal procedure;

2. Violation of the requirements of fair and equitable treatment owed to foreign investors, by virtue of article 1105 of NAFTA."

The Tribunal held that to assure "due process of law" to the investors was an element of international law's requirement of "fair and equitable treatment". The arbitrators acknowledged that the investors had been treated unfairly and inequitably by the lawyers for the other Party and by the jury and that, in particular, the rights of the petitioners in the case had been ignored:

"No matter what the evaluation criteria may have been, the judge in the lower court had denied Loewen the equitable process to which it was entitled, in order to reach the conclusion according to which the methods used by the jury and tolerated by the judge were antithetical to the adversary process. The tribunal 'admits that it is the State's responsibility in regard to international law', through the process of the different States' jurisdictions, to organise an equitable process in the business in which the foreign investor is engaged."

The arbitrators thereby recognised that customary international law held States to the duty to offer to foreigners a just and effective system of justice.

11.8.2. – *International Court of Justice decision in Electronica Sicula (ELSI) United States v. Italy*

Two separate principles may be drawn from this case with respect to fair and equitable treatment. First, in respect to seizure of an Italian corporation, which had failed and whose shareholders were U.S. nationals, the Court held that circumstances should dictate whether such a measure was contrary to the duty of fair and equitable treatment, conforming to national rules to which the Contracting State had committed:

> "The reference ...to 'constant protection and security' cannot be construed as the giving of a warranty that property shall never in any circumstances be occupied or disturbed... the protection provided by the authorities could not be regarded as falling below 'the full protection and security' required by international law, or indeed as less than the national or third State standards... The essential question is whether the local law, either in its terms or its application, has treated United States nationals less well than Italian nationals. This, in the opinion of the Chamber, has not been shown."

Second, the Court examined the investors' claim that the delays in the appeal procedure applicable to a seizure were too long and that the setting of such long delays were contrary to the concept of "due process of law." The judges noted that the standard of fair and equitable treatment of international law was a minimum standard. The United States had not proven that the contracting Parties had, as a complement to the international standard, agreed that the national standard and the Most Favoured Nation standard would have precedence, which might, for example, have provided for specific delays:

> "The primary standard laid down by article V is 'the full protection and security' required by international law; in short 'the protection and security' must conform to the minimum international standard. As noted above, this is supplemented by the criteria of national treatment and most favored nation treatment. The Chamber is here called upon to apply the provisions of a treaty which sets standards in addition to general international law which may go further in protecting

nationals of the High Contracting parties than general international law requires; but the United States has not suggested that these requirements do in this respect set higher standards than the international standard." [188]

11.9. – CONCLUSION

The foregoing observations and examples of the jurisprudence show how important a proper formulation of fair and equitable treatment clauses is. BIT's should mention all three standards, the international standard, the MFN standard and the national standard, while adding, by way of express agreement, content, as detailed as possible, to these standards.

---

[188] *Electronica Sicula, S.p.A* (Elsi), *op. cit.*, p. 66, see footnote 88.

CHAPTER XII
ENVIRONMENT

12.1. – Protection of the environment

Concerns about environmental protection first arose in organised fashion in the last decades of the twentieth century. This recent phenomenon led to measures to preserve the environment and combat its degradation from human activities at the national level. In many countries, laws were passed, regulations issued, affecting many economic sectors and creating constraints designed to protect the ambient conditions and set sanctions for violations of anti-pollution controls. Thanks to the affirmative actions of various non-governmental organisations, such as Green Peace, the problems flowing from environmental protection directives were translated from the national to the international theatre.

In 1992, the United Nations Conference on Environment and Development (UNCED), code named Earth Summit, was held in Rio de Janeiro and led to the conclusion of a basic convention urging the Contracting Parties to take the impact of the environmental policies into account:

> "...10,000 on-site journalists and heard by millions around the world. The message reflected the complexity of the problems facing us: that poverty as well as excessive consumption by affluent populations place damaging stress on the environment. Governments recognised the need to redirect international and national plans and policies to ensure that all economic decisions fully took into account any environmental impact. And the message has produced results, making eco-efficiency a guiding principle for business and governments alike".[189]

---

[189] Www.unced.org.

On 11 December 1997, the Kyoto Protocol to the United Nations Framework Convention on Climate Change was signed.

As of November 2007, 174 parties have ratified the protocol. Of these, 36 developed countries, (plus the EU as a party in its own right) are required to reduce greenhouse gas emissions to the levels specified for each of them in the treaty.... One hundred and thirty-seven (137) developing countries have ratified the protocol, including Brazil, China and India, but have no obligation beyond "monitoring and reporting emissions"[190]. The United States have not ratified the Protocol.

12.2. – NAFTA LINK BETWEEN ENVIRONMENT PROTECTION WITH INVESTMENT PROMOTION

Canada, the United States of America and Mexico entered into the North American Free Trade Agreement (NAFTA) on 17 December 1992. Those are the countries which, even before the entering into force of the aforesaid UN agreements on the environment, have provided for conventional conditions creating duties on this topic among the Contracting States. **Article 1114** of the agreement reads as follows:

> "Nothing in this Chapter shall be construed to prevent a Party from adopting, maintaining or enforcing any measure otherwise consistent with this Chapter that it considers appropriate to ensure that investment activity in its territory is undertaken in a manner sensitive to environmental concerns.
>
> The Parties recognise that it is inappropriate to encourage investment by relaxing domestic health, safety or environmental measures. Accordingly, a Party should not waive or otherwise derogate from, or offer to waive or otherwise derogate from, such measures as an encouragement for the establishment, acquisition, expansion or retention in its territory of an investment of an investor. If a Party considers that another Party has offered such an encouragement, it may

---

[190] Www. Kyoto protocol.org.

request consultations with the other Party and the two Parties shall consult with a view to avoiding any such encouragement." [191]

As a matter of fact, the Contracting Parties committed not to attract or promote foreign investments on their territory by softening legal and regulatory measures regarding the admission of such investments and the conditions of establishment.

12.3. – CANADIAN BIT'S ENVIRONMENTAL POSITION

As a member of NAFTA, Canada adopted a consistent attitude and the model convention adopted a specific provision:

"Health, Safety and Environmental measures

The Parties recognise that it is inappropriate to encourage investment by relaxing domestic health, safety or environmental measures. Accordingly, a Party should not waive or otherwise derogate from, or offer to waive or otherwise derogate from, such measures as an encouragement for the establishment, acquisition, expansion or retention in its territory of an investment of an investor. If a Party considers that the other Party has offered such an encouragement, it may request consultations with the other Party and the two Parties shall consult with a view to avoiding any such encouragement." (**Article 11**) [192]

The new model convention of Canada has been used since 2007. Before then, there was no mention of environmental measures in the Canadian BIT's. For the first time, an environmental clause appears in the BIT Canada/Peru of 20 June 2007. However, the intention of the Canadian Government is without any doubt to use the environmental clause in all its future BIT's as it appears from the following Governmental Notice of the Ministry of Foreign Affairs, published on 15 December 2007:

"DEPARTMENT OF FOREIGN AFFAIRS AND INTERNATIONAL TRADE

---

[191] Http://www.nafta-sec-alena.org.
[192] Http://www. Dfait-maeci.gc.ca/tna-nac/fipa-en.asp.

NOTICE OF INTENT TO CONDUCT A STRATEGIC ENVIRONMENTAL ASSESSMENT OF THE CANADA-KUWAIT FOREIGN INVESTMENT PROTECTION AND PROMOTION AGREEMENT

The Government of Canada will undertake a Strategic Environmental Assessment of the negotiations for a Canada-Kuwait Foreign Investment Promotion and Protection Agreement (FIPA). Comments are invited on any likely and significant environmental impacts of the negotiations on Canada.

The Government of Canada is committed to sustainable development. Mutually supportive trade and environmental policies can contribute to this objective. To this end, the Minister of International Trade, with the support of his Cabinet colleagues, has directed trade officials to improve their understanding of, and information based on, the relationship between trade and environmental issues at the earliest stages of decision making, and to do this through an open and inclusive process. Environmental assessments of trade negotiations are critical to this work." [193]

Co-Contracting Parties with Canada will therefore be henceforth confronted with a Canadian requirement to have an environment clause included in all BIT's.

12.4. – USA Formula

What applies to Canada is obviously also applicable to the USA since they are members of NAFTA. **Article 12** of the USA model BIT reads as follows:

"The Parties recognise that it is inappropriate to encourage investments by weakening or reducing the protections afforded in domestic environmental laws. Accordingly, each Party shall strive to ensure that it does not waive or otherwise derogate from, or offer to waive or otherwise derogate from, such laws in a manner that weakens or reduces the protections afforded in those laws as an encouragement for the establishment, acquisition, expansion, or retention of an investment in its territory. If a Party considers that the other Party has offered such an encouragement, it must request consultations with the

---

[193] Www.international.gc.ca/trade-agreements-accords-commerciaux/agr-acc/fipa-apie/index.aspx.

other Party and the two Parties shall consult with a view to avoiding such encouragement.

Nothing in this Treaty shall be construed to prevent a Party from adopting, maintaining, or enforcing any measure otherwise consistent with this Treaty that it considers appropriate to ensure that investment activity in its territory is undertaken in a manner sensitive to environmental concerns."

The US formula hardly deviates from the Canadian. It was first used in the USA/Uruguay BIT dated 4 November 2005, entering into force on 1 November 2006.

12.5. – ORGANISATION FOR ECONOMIC CO-OPERATION AND DEVELOPMENT (OECD)

OECD experts considered the relationship between the environment and the promotion and encouragement of international investments. They were of course aware of the NAFTA example, which may have made their research of environmental clauses consistent with the requirements of efficient protection of investments. However, their consideration did not lead to unanimous agreement. A tendency exists at OECD to link the environment not only with investment promotion but also with the working conditions of workers.

As an example, this is the text of a proposed clause which was included in the consolidated text of the Multilateral Agreement on Investment (MAI), which actually never came into being. This text has all the earmarks of the NAFTA model :

"The Parties recognise that it is inappropriate to encourage investment by relating health,safety or environmental measures.

Accordingly, a Contracting party shall accord to investors of another Contracting party and their investments treatment no more favourable than it accords to its own investors and their investments by waiving or otherwise derogating from, or offering to waive or otherwise derogate from health, safety, environmental measures with respect to the establishment, acquisition, expansion, operation, management, maintenance, use, enjoyment and sale or other disposition of investments.

In addition, a Contracting Party should not encourage investment by lowering its health, safety and environmental standards in general. If a Party considers that another Party has offered such an encouragement, it may request consultations with the other Party and the two Parties shall consult with a view to avoiding any such encouragement." [194]

12.6. – EUROPEAN BIT's CLAUSES RELATING TO THE ENVIRONMENT

Environment clauses in general are not included in European BIT's. Such a clause exeptionnally appears in the Norwegian and Belgian model conventions. That is not necessarily inappropriate since those are specific areas which, preferably, could, whenever individual circumstances show a need for them, be made the topic of separate bilateral conventions or specific multilateral agreements. The above mentioned NAFTA Agreement may have served as an inspiration for the Belgian model. Adopting this deviation from the usual conventional practice with respect to investment protection is not an encouragement – in fact, quite the contrary – it may discourage certain countries from concluding BIT's including such a clause. Nonetheless, the authors of the Belgian model chose to include it :

"ENVIRONMENT

1. Recognising the right of each Contracting Party to establish its own levels of domestic environmental protection and environmental development policies and priorities and to adopt or modify accordingly its environmental legislation, each Contracting Party shall strive to ensure that its legislation provide for high levels of environmental protection and shall strive to continue to improve its legislation;

2. The Contracting Parties recognise that it is inappropriate to encourage investment by relaxing domestic environmental legislation. Accordingly, each Contracting Party shall strive to ensure that it does

---

[194] Http://www1.oecd.org/daf/mai/introf.htm.

not waive or otherwise derogate from, or offer to waive or otherwise derogate from, such legislation as an encouragement for the establishment, maintenance or expansion in its territory of an investment;

3. The Contracting Parties reaffirm their commitments under the international environmental agreements, which they have accepted, they shall strive to ensure that such commitments are fully recognised and implemented by their domestic legislation;

4. The Contracting Parties recognise that co-operation between them provides enhanced opportunities to improve environmental protection standards. Upon request by either Contracting Party, the other Contracting Party shall accept to hold expert consultations on any matter falling under the purpose of this article."

The text is not obligatory, being instead of the kind known as "soft law". A further defect is that it offers no guarantee that the goal will be accomplished:

"Acknowledging that each of the Contracting Parties maintains the right to specify the level of environmental protection, to define its policies and priorities insofar as the environment and development are concerned, and to adopt or modify thereby its laws *ad hoc*, each of the Contracting Parties will see to it that its legislation will guarantee a high level of protection for the environment and will do all it can in order to improve steadily this legislation." (**Article 5(1)**)

It is not necessary to confirm by means of a convention that a State has the sovereign right to adopt laws and to modify them. It would seem entirely superfluous. It would have been preferable to include language recognising that "investments" are also subject to the States' rights to take environmental measures but the term has been ignored in this part of Article 5. Had the actual NAFTA text been used, the model would have been greatly improved. The NAFTA agreement confirms the right of each State to take measures to ensure that investments will be undertaken with due regard to the environment:

"...that investment activity is its territory is undertaken in a manner sensitive to environmental concerns." (**Article 1114**)

Instead, the model attempts to address environmental concerns as follows:

"The Contracting Parties reaffirm the commitments they have undertaken within the framework of international agreements regarding protection of the environment. They will see to it that such commitments will be fully respected and applied in their national legislation."

Respect for international conventions is an international duty, a specific application of international law's *"pacta sunt servanda"*. Hence, confirming in a BIT that obligations undertaken under another agreement will be followed seems quite unnecessary. This confirmation added nothing and did not enhance the force of obligations undertaken by reason of other international acts.

The Norwegian text advantageously provides that each Contracting State may request the initiation of consultations in the event that environmental concerns have been ignored or minimised by the other State. The following is the applicable text included in this model:

Article [11]. – Not Lowering Standards

The Parties recognize that it is inappropriate to encourage investment by relaxing domestic health, safety or environmental measures or core labour standards. Accordingly, a Party should not waive or otherwise derogate from, or offer to waive or otherwise derogate from, such measures as an encouragement for the establishment, acquisition, expansion or retention of an investment of an investor. If a Party considers that the other Party has offered such an encouragement, it may request consultations under Article [Joint Committee].

12.7. – ARBITRAL JURISPRUDENCE

There are very few arbitral decisions relating to the environment. This is hardly astonishing since very few investment protection treaties include provisions relating to the environment. However, the occasional holdings are not very favourable. In the ICSID case of *"Compania del Desarollo de Santa Elena (CDSE) v. Costa Rica"*, the arbitrators stressed that environmental protection could not transform an illegal act into a legal one:

"Although an expropriation or a measure taken for environmental reasons may be classified as measures in the general public interest, and hence legitimate, the fact that the asset was expropriated for that reason does not affect the nature nor the measure of indemnification due on account of the expropriation. In other words, the objective of environmental protection on account of which the asset was expropriated does not affect the legal character of the expropriation, on account of which an indemnity must be paid. Environmental expropriation measures, however laudable and beneficial to society they may be, are in this respect similar to other measures of expropriation a State may undertake to carry out its policies : when an asset is the target of an expropriation, even when the purpose is environmental protection, be it domestic or international, the State's duty to indemnify remains unchanged."

In the *Metalclad v. Federated States of Mexico* case, a dispute arose from the fact that Mexican authorities had first issued a construction permit for a waste disposal centre and subsequently this permit had been cancelled for ecological reasons. According to the arbitrators, the environmental protection motive could not justify the cancellation :

"The Commune's refusal to deliver a permit, motivated by considerations tied to the environmental impact for a project for the treatment of toxic waste was irregular, as would be any refusal by the Commune to deliver a permit for any reason other than those relating to the construction of physical defects of the site."

The future will show us whether the example of NAFTA members will be incorporated in European conventional practice and whether the large States, such as Germany, the United Kingdom, France, Italy, Spain, will include environmental clauses in their BIT's.

CHAPTER XIII
EXPROPRIATIONS AND NATIONALISATIONS

13.1. – Respect for Property Rights

Assets – and therefore investment of assets – situated in the territory of a State are generally protected by legal norms and regulations issued by the authorities having jurisdiction over them. In general, the Constitutions and associated documents of most democratic States explicitly guarantee property rights. For instance, Article 17 of France's Déclaration des Droits de l'Homme et du Citoyen dated 27 August 1789 (incorporated in the French Constitution) states unequivocally :

> "Private property, being a right that is sacred and inviolable, may not be stripped from anyone, except when public necessity, legally found to exist, evidently requires it, and on condition that it be fairly compensated in advance." [195]

Amendment 5 to the US Constitution recognises this principle and states, in part :

> "nor shall private property be taken for public use, without just compensation."

Article 42 (3) of the Italian Constitution states :

> "Private property, in cases determined by law and with compensation, may be expropriated for reasons of common interest."

Article 14 (3) of the German Constitution reads :

---

[195] Most citations in this Work are worded in English and are often translations of an original text in some other language. Where a citation is a translation, this fact will be indicated by an appropriate footnote, referring the reader to Appendix C of the Work, where the original text may be located by reference to the footnote number.

"Expropriation is permitted only in the public weal. It may take place only by or pursuant to law which provides for kind and extent of the compensation."

Article 11 of the Belgian Constitution states likewise:

"No one may be deprived of his property, except for reasons of public use and then only in cases and according to the procedure established by law and for the adequate and prior compensation."

Of course, the courts of each nation have interpreted these constitutional provisions according to their own culture, tradition and constraints, sometimes stretching the notion of public purpose beyond the limits accepted elsewhere and resulting in widely different outcomes for persons who are directly affected by an expropriatory measure which allowed a city to expropriate private property to accommodate the construction of modern improvements producing enhanced tax returns for the city [196]. Nonetheless, the underlying principle invoked is that rejecting any claim to the State's power to deprive its citizens of property except for a public purpose and upon due compensation.

These national guarantees are also applicable to foreign investors. On the other hand, *as* stressed in Chapter X, no State is bound to admit foreign investments on its territory:

"No one claims that international law requires a State to authorise foreign investment. In fact, many States prohibit them when they assume certain forms, such as ships or, more recently activities concerned with atomic energy. Outside of a treaty, there is no right of establishment." [197]

Sometimes, treaties define the right to making domestic investments. For example, in Latin America, Brazil, Argentina, Paraguay and Uruguay signed such a treaty on 26 March 1991:

---

[196] *Kelo v. City of New London* (2005), 545 *US.* 469.
[197] *The Hague Academy of International Law*, Collected Courses, The Hague, Edition Sijthoff, Leyden, 1961, p. 379.

"Each Contracting Party encourages investors from another Contracting Party to invest locally and shall admit them on its territory under conditions not less favourable than those allowed for investments made by its own investors and investors from other States, without prejudice, however, to the right of each Party to regulate, on an exceptional basis, restrictions on investments in the sectors mentioned in the said Protocol Annex." [198]

When States, however, have admitted foreign investors on their territory, they have an international obligation to protect them.

13.2. – STATES' FUNDAMENTAL RIGHT TO TAKE PRIVATE PROPERTY

As foreseen in international law, every State has the right to expropriate or nationalise private property. When a State wishes to change its economic structures and regulate the property rights of its nationals and companies, it has the right so to do. States have the same right as to foreign property. Among international institutions (UNO, UNCTAD, OECD) as well as in the doctrinal texts and international jurisprudence, such a right is generally acknowledged. Particularly since the decolonisation era and the birth of new independent States, individual property rights are no longer considered "sacred and inviolable". In quite a few international conventions, the right of expropriation is expressly recognised.

"Certainly, provisions contained in international conventions recognise, implicitly when not explicitly, the sovereign right of expropriation or nationalisation that every sovereign State possesses. It is hardly necessary to explain or justify the existence of such right, or to have recourse to constructs such as 'permanent sovereignty'. The State being the State, it can organise its economic self as it pleases and consequently define the rules which govern property rights." [199]

---

[198] Protocol de Colonia, signed on 17 January 1994 by Member States of Mercosur Brésil, Paraguay, Uruguay), article 2, not yet in force.
[199] JUILLARD, Patrick, *op. cit.*, p. 42, see footnote 41.

International law acknowledges States' rights of expropriation and nationalisation. In resolution 1803/XVII of 14 December 1962, adopted by the UN's General Assembly, the right of expropriation has been expressly underlined. Whether in national legal systems or in international law, it has been confirmed, on several occasions, that States have a fundamental right to nationalise or expropriate private property.

13.3. – Forms of Deprivation of private Property Rights

"Expropriation" is the generic term often used in doctrinal texts to refer to the various forms of property rights deprivation practised by States, whether against the private interests of its own nationals or those of foreign nationals.

Expropriation is actually a specific form of property right deprivation. It might be better to use some other term to designate deprivation of private property rights in general. The term "measures privative of property" or, more simply "privative measures" could be used better to encompass all forms of such deprivation. Property rights inhere to real and personal property goods and assets, but does not customarily include contractual rights emanating from agreements nor other rights that may arise from national law and regulation. An all encompassing if more cumbersome, term, such as "measures privative of acquired rights", could be used as a generic and would then include contractual rights.

The main forms of direct deprivation are expropriation, nationalisation, confiscation and requisition.

13.4. – Definitions of Forms of Deprivation

It is rather interesting that, in conventional practice regarding investment protection, a definition is not to be found for the two principal forms of deprivation, expropriation and nationalisation. Sometimes, authors treat nationalisation as a special form of expropriation :

> "There is no intention or desire to become involved in the controversy whether those expropriations which might be called 'nationalisations' should be accorded different treatment with respect to the requirement of compensation of aliens." [200]

Professor G. CHRISTIE also finds an assimilation and an equivalence of the two terms :

> "However, should the process (of nationalisation) involve the transference from private to public ownership of movable and immovable property, debts and intangible things of value, then it is one of expropriation and international law interests itself in the protection of foreign title-holders." [201]

Other authors had hazardly mix the terms "expropriation" and "nationalisation", as if there were no distinction between the two. Yet, those are indeed different forms of deprivation, whose goal and manner of proceeding have characteristics specific to each. Nationalisation stems from national economic measures, on a large scale, having the effect of transferring economic activity and operators active in key sectors of it to the State or to State organisms. This results in the creation of monopolies in favour of the State, depriving the former private property owners of all their rights in the assets taken.

> "Outright nationalisations in all economic sectors. These measures result in the termination of all foreign investment in a host country. They are usually motivated by policy considerations; the measures are intended to achieve complete State control of the economy and involve the takeover of all privately-owned means of production." [202]

---

[200] CHRISTIE, G., "What constitutes a taking of property under international law", *British yearbook international law*, Oxford at the Clarendon Press, 1962, p. 307.

[201] CHRISTIE, *op. cit.*, p. 769, see footnote 200.

[202] UNCTAD, *Taking of property*, UN 2000, see website : www.unctad.org/templates/Page.asp?int-ItemID = 2323&lang = .

Nationalisation results from legislative action. Expropriation is a private measure taken for reasons of public purpose in individual cases. Every physical person and corporation, whether national or foreign is subject to the adage *"salus patriae suprema lex"* on the territory of the State where it is domiciled or has a residence. Private property rights, therefore, may be annulled if the local authorities believe that such a measure is required to serve a public purpose (e.g. road construction, etc.). Differing from nationalisation, expropriation does not affect per se important investor groups Expropriation measures are generally taken within the framework of administrative measures, based upon an appropriately designed law.

Inasmuch as foreign investors may be affected both by expropriation and nationalisation measures, investment protection conventions must address at least both.

Confiscation is a privative measure which may be undertaken when penal law has been violated. Should, for instance, investors have engaged in illicit trade (drug traffic etc.), their goods and other assets may be confiscated. In most such cases, indemnification is unavailable.

Requisition is a privative measure which does not fundamentally affect ownership rights but is a temporary removal by the authorities who may be justified in so doing by reason of exceptional circumstances (f.i. war, rebellion, mob rule, etc.). Conceivably, possession and enjoyment of the requisitioned property may be restored after the commotion settles. Admittedly, confiscation measures may well be illegal and requisition measures may lose their temporary features and become expropriation measures.

Sequestration[203], in international law, is a form of seizure of an individual's property, sometimes by a belligerent power, and its appropriation by State organisms of such power. In some countries, sequestering merely means temporary, judi-

---

[203] *Webster New International Dictionary.*

cial supervision of the management of a private asset. Consequently, in order to provide investors with as wide a protection as possible, it may be wise to include such measure in investment protection treaties designed for the protection of private investors. So far, no BIT has mentioned the term "sequestration" and it is far from certain that negotiators of future BIT's will be able or willing to include it among measures against which explicit protection should sought.

13.5. – INDIRECT PRIVATIVE MEASURES

13.5.1. – *General Notion*

A nationalisation measure may well be indirect in the sense that investors from one State are damaged by a measure taken with respect to an enterprise they have created on the territory of another State, where such enterprise has assets on the territory of a third State. The nationalising State could consider itself as an indirect owner of assets situated on foreign territory by virtue of its nationalisation of a company situated on its territory. Such a measure would be contrary to a principle of international law regarding "extraterritoriality", that is, the principle holding that decisions taken by a competent State agency cannot have extraterritorial effect, i.e. outside the borders of such State.

Under this principle, measures privative of property, such as nationalisation, cannot have extraterritorial effect. For instance, the indemnification agreement concluded in 1952 between Belgium and Czechoslovakia remained a dead letter for several years (till 1976), held up until a decision was made regarding the extraterritorial effect or not of the nationalisation measures. Among the nationalised assets were found some of the Solvay Ebensee company, an Austrian subsidiary of the Czech parent in which Solvay Belgium had a majority participation. Austria blocked the implementation of this agreement for a long time, invoking the principle of non-extraterritoriality. In the opinion of Austrian authorities, Solvay Ebensee was not affected by the Czech nationalisation. The company was placed under Austrian administration. The case was finally settled by a special arrangement between Belgium and Austria.

13.5.2. – Use of the Term "indirect" in Conventions

However, the term "indirect" is not used in the same sense in investment protection treaties. These instruments consider indirect expropriation and nationalisation as measures which do not directly affect property rights but leave the property in the possession of the investor while depriving him completely or partially of the enjoyment of it. In doctrinal texts and in conventional practice, such measures are variously designated : "indirect expropriations", "measures having an effect equivalent to expropriation", "creeping expropriation", "measures tantamount to expropriation", etc. UNCTAD experts have defined "creeping expropriation" as follows :

> "This may be defined as the slow and incremental encroachment of one or more of the ownership rights of a foreign investor that diminishes the value of its investment. The legal title to the property remains invested in the foreign investor but the investor's rights of use of the property are diminished as a result of the interference by the State." [204]

The motto "what's in a name" seems appropriate since, although the name of the operation is different, the result is the same and, in reality, the measure so taken may, in its effects, be assimilated to a straight expropriation measure. Several judicial and arbitral decisions have highlighted the serious situation in which investors affected by such measures are placed :

> "The Norwegian Claims and the German interests in Polish Upper Silesia cases show that a State may expropriate property, where it interferes with it, even though the State expressly disclaims any such

---

[204] UNCTAD, *Taking of property, op. cit.*, p. 12, see footnote 202.

intention. More important, the two cases taken together illustrate that even though a State may not purport to interfere with rights to property, it may, by its actions, render those rights so useless that it will be deem to have expropriated them." [205]

In sum, indirect expropriation or nationalisation measures may be so called where the measures indirectly affect the investor but, in fact, are equivalent to direct measures when, because of a specific measure of action taken by the authorities, the investment may be considered as having been essentially expropriated and the rights of the investor, including the right of management, have been reduced to naught.

Examples are many : forced sale, excessive and illegal taxation, assumption of the enterprise by national administration, withdrawal of a licence. Even a temporary seizure may ripen into expropriation, if it seems that the measure acquires, after some years, a definite character.

13.6. – INTERNATIONAL LAW PRINCIPLES

13.6.1. – *Restrictions on use of Authority to expropriate and nationalise*

13.6.1.1. *"Public Purpose"*

There are important conditions which international law places on the validity of expropriating or restrictive measures. Among them is that measures must have been undertaken for a public purpose. Traditionally, according to doctrinal texts, jurisprudence and in the law applicable to conventions, the legality of measures taken by State authorities is based on their contribution to a public purpose. That requirement is a failsafe haven for States and their nationals who are often led to call on international conventions with other States which abuse the "public purpose" limitation to

---

[205] CHRISTIE, G., *op. cit.*, p. 312, see footnote 200.

shirk their treaty obligations and to justify the absence or inadequacy of the compensatory measures.

The first problem with this concept is that the term "public purpose" does not have a clear and concrete definition. It evolves with time and the venue where it is invoked:

> "What constitutes a public need is obviously not a static notion, but one which evolves according to the practice of nations. The building of highways and railroads, of military barracks and public cemeteries, the fulfilment of an international obligation, the secularisation of religious property, the mobilisation of commercial and industrial resources for the prosecution of a war are only some of the instances which international tribunals have accepted as clear cases of genuine public need."[206]

In any specific case, setting up a list of examples – similar to the investment list in BIT's – is not a solution. The "public purpose" concept is simply too broad and uncertain. That is why it is practically impossible to devise a more or less complete enumeration of measures qualifying for a "public purpose", and which are directly or indirectly responsible for depriving owners of their property.

Another problem consists in determining that the measures were taken under the cover of public purpose in order to conceal their true purpose for depriving owners of their property:

> "Public interest is generally held to be a necessary requirement of a lawful deprivation of property. It has been pointed out on the other hand that it is difficult to question the existence in specific instances of this requirement, except in the most evident cases of abuse since this would require appreciating a sovereign State policy and the motivation of its action."[207]

It is of course a bit delicate to question the "public purpose" character of measures taken by State authorities and to reveal proof that the State had other motives (political, retal-

---

[206] BIN CHENG, *General Principles of Law as applied by International Courts and Tribunals*, Cambridge, Edition Cambridge University Press, 2006, p. 33.

[207] SACERDOTI, Giorgio, *op. cit.*, p. 387, see footnote 159.

iatory, etc.). Was the general cancellation of rights to agricultural property (Indonesia, Congo) in the past really a "public purpose" measure involving structural reforms? Or was there not a concealed motive aimed at affecting the interests of former colonising powers?

It cannot be denied that the "public purpose" motive has been abused. The true motives of measures depriving owners of their property as well as other measures of similar scope are not easily detectable. International law does not provide criteria allowing affected investors to determine what is meant by "public purpose". Writes Charles DE VISSER:

> "Whatever the reasons for nationalisation may be, the sole judges thereof are the nationalising governments themselves. Nationalisation is an internal order often dictated more by political reasons than economic ones. Considered in principle, its legitimacy is governed by no international criteria." [208]

13.6.1.2. *Non-Discrimination*

A second condition that must be met according to international law in order to lend legality to such measures is the absence of discrimination. Discrimination may occur in international relations when a State takes such measures exclusively against persons who are nationals of a determined State.

The question is whether the "discrimination" issue should be raised in the context of the relationships between nationals and foreigners or in the relationship between a third State or its nationals and yet another third State or its nationals. International doctrine varies. BIN-CHENG stresses the applicability of national legislation with respect to nationals of the State as well as with respect to foreigners (including investors) residing on the territory of that State:

> "In application of a generally accepted principle, any person, taking up residence or investing capital in a foreign country, must assume

---

[208] SALEM, Mahmoud, *op. cit.*, p. 612, see footnote 53.

the concomitant risks and must submit, under reservation of any measures of discrimination against him as a foreigner, to all laws of that country." [209]

VERWEY and SCHRIJVER stress that international law prohibits any discrimination. According to international law norms, nothing but equal treatment of investors, when compared to treatment extended to nationals of the host State or a third State, is admissible. [210]

On the other hand, according to various world international organisations (UN and UNCCD, the "UN Commission for Commerce and Development"), some exceptions to the general prohibition against discrimination are acceptable. Insofar as expropriation is concerned, it is admitted that such measures affect only foreign investments, and not national investments, when economic reforms justify a deviation from the general rule. Furthermore, there is a tendency in these organisations to accept that international law does not conflict with discriminatory measures, whenever they reflect retaliatory action that may be justified. Where a State violates international law (for example, refusal to indemnify for nationalised assets), the State sustaining damage therefrom would be authorised to take measures which would exclusively affect the State or nationals of the State causing such damage.

13.6.1.3. *Due Process of law*

13.6.1.3.1. *Legal Basis Required*

It would be wrong to assume that, in every case, local courts are an impractical source of redress for an expropriation or other privative measures of property rights. Courts in some relatively less developed Nations do have an acceptable

---

[209] BIN CHENG, *op. cit.*, p. 36, see footnote 206.
[210] VERWEY, Delano R. & SCHRIJVER, Nico, "The taking of foreign property under international law: A new legal perspective?", *Netherlands Yearbook of International Law*, 1984, pp. 17-19.

level of expertise and impartiality to qualify as a resource for the redress of a wrong in the expropriation process. Besides, after all, BIT agreements are supposed to be "bilaterally" for the mutual benefit of developed Nations and less developed Nations alike. It is, therefore, quite possible, for a national of a less developed Nation to consider himself aggrieved by an expropriatory act of the developed Nation. In such a case, recourse to the expropriatory Nation's court system may well be the sensible course to take.

Nonetheless, in perhaps the majority of cases, the wrong committed will be alleged to have taken place in the less developed Nation, party to the dispute. The illegality question may arise more frequently in such a context. A third general principle would therefore be that nationalisation or expropriation measures may not be undertaken arbitrarily or without a legal basis. The mere lack of a legal basis may be grounds for an eventual arbitration award but in and of itself is not necessarily the same as lack of due process. Lack of due process is therefore not always an appropriate ground to allege. The nationalising State may have *properly* created legislation determining the goal of the nationalisation or expropriation measures and defining the procedure they are to follow. Thus, the "legal basis" may exist but it may still be invalid, on, for instance, constitutional, grounds. Property owners affected by nationalisation or expropriation laws must be able to evaluate the legality of the measures under local law.

Where legal basis is alleged to be lacking, however, the allegation is often tantamount to a claim of denial of due process of law. That may be enough to bring the dispute into the international order. However, if, for instance, the alleged illegality of the expropriation be based on a claim of discriminatory or confiscatory legislation, or on the improper exercise of the police power, local courts, when equipped impartially to entertain an attack on such legislation or police impropriety, may still be a practical forum for seeking redress.

Let us suppose, a claim be made by the host State that the party claiming compensation has forfeited any right to it because of, say, some alleged criminal act by such party. The latter may be able to claim, in a properly equipped local court, that the forfeiture is unconstitutional except upon named, specific grounds and that such grounds are lacking, and, furthermore, that substantive due process has been violated in the criminal proceeding itself. An arbitration forum may not always be the best venue for arguing such unconstitutionality or violation.

To evaluate the constitutionality of such basis, it is important that, in the negotiation of State Contracts, for example, a correct match be made so that Civil Law trained jurists be selected by the claimant for interfacing with their Civil Law trained opponents, and *vice versa*, that the skills and experience of Common Law jurists help guide negotiations with host States with a Common Law legacy. Failing to pay heed to such match will almost invariably introduce into the process elements of misunderstanding, that may not surface till the proceeding is well underway. A mismatch can manifest itself at the most inopportune moment, in the authentification of documents, the admissibility of hearsay or tainted evidence, or in many of the ways legal assumptions taken for granted by one or the other party are alien to or unknown to the other.

In matters of due process, Common Law jurists, when faced with challenges from authorities in jurisdictions with legal systems that are heir to British Common Law have an extremely broad resource by which to evaluate, in most any instance, whether due process of law has been respected or not. The issue is central to Common Law and its centrality offer jurists, when dealing with host States, formerly British colonies or possessions and retaining the colonial legal system, opportunities to pursue the interests of investors, backed by centuries of judicial interpretations and a truly immense jurisprudence. On the other hand, their task is made more problematic, in that they either have to work with equally trained, local jurists representing the interests of the host States, or, when working with States that have not adopted Common Law, they have to adapt their approach to issues based on a legal system with which they are not as familiar.

Civil Law jurists, on the other hand, when faced with challenges from authorities in host States that have adopted some form of Napoleonic Code, heir to the French Napoleonic Code, may feel that unforeseen procedural problems of a lower legal magnitude may have merely a de minimis effect and are only tardily made aware of their Common Law counterparts' concerns. Conversely, when dealing with former British colonies, for instance, Civil Law lawyers may be entering what is to them virgin territory which is elementary to their Common Law counterparts. Arbitration may then be viewed by either party as a minefield, precluding the smooth development of the proceeding.

If only because of the wealth of sources available to Common Law jurists on the due process of law issue, our analysis of the due process of law issue draws more from the prescriptions of Common Law than on perceived commonalities with the provisions of the Napoleonic-inspired codes of certain host States. Nonetheless, although stemming from different origins, it will be found that Civil Code provisions often parallel Common Law practices, thereby mitigating the problem.

For instance, it is sometimes argued that "due process of law" implies that the affected investors must have the means to contest, in local courts or other local venues, the modalities of indemnification for assets damaged by privative measures :

> "In large-scale nationalisations in the past, countries often expressly denied judicial review of compensation. The requirement that the compensation due to a foreign investor should be assessed by an independent host country tribunal is now found

in the takings provisions of many bilateral and some regional agreements."[211]

This is not always the view of Civil Law lawyers, although, without a doubt, adequate compensation, promptly paid is a very important, common demand by adherents of both systems of law. Denial of compensation may be viewed on either side of legal divide as a substantive denial of due process, based on this specific ground.

Unfortunately, this incidental commonality of views is sometimes lacking in connection with other measures, which the Common Law lawyer will almost immediately see as a violation of substantive due process. There are instances of due process of law violations which do not directly relate to compensation. Denial of compensation then becomes just one of the element of due process.

13.6.1.3.2. *Country Variations in Significance of Due Process*

Access to local tribunals may not always be sufficient to ensure investors will receive the benefit of adequate security and protection. Western oriented jurists may view this as a denial of due process of law but, as pointed out later in this Chapter, the notion of due process may vary from one country to another, even as between so-called "developed countries" in the Western world. In examining the process by which causes of action are treated by local tribunals, jurists can decide whether divergences from otherwise general accepted principles of Common Law with respect to due process, observable in the more developed States but lacking in some local legal systems, are serious enough to warrant their concluding that, according to their interpretation, substantive due process has been denied. With this conclusion, such jurists may well want to eschew the local legal system altogether or, if the divergences are merely procedural, protest

---

[211] UNCTAD, *op. cit.*, see footnote 202.

them for the record and reserve them for consideration in a later arbitration proceeding to have them considered in a separate matter dealing only with the due process issue, akin to an evidentiary hearing except that the only "evidence" reviewed is the substantiality of the due process objection. In rejecting the competence of local courts on this perceived ground, jurists from one or the other side of the legal divide may sometimes be doing themselves an injustice. Either a thorough research of the point involved or a pre-arbitration agreement excluding it from consideration will be the safer route to follow.

Caution should be exercised here, so that the selection of a local tribunal not be assimilated to a waiver of arbitration rights. It is better for investors to provide in their State Contracts or other agreement with the host State for the choice either to access the local tribunals or, should such access be denied or be patently contrary to established Common Law practice, to file an arbitration procedure with an international arbitration institution, where the violation of substantive due process may be challenged. Once such a choice is made, then, if the procedural violation has been fairly adjudicated in the local courts, the arbitrator may be justified in ignoring it any challenge to it during any arbitration proceeding in the same case.

Arbitrators may not necessarily be able to "cure" violations of substantive due process by taking it into account in their decision, whereas, with violations of procedural due process, they very well might. Hence, the earlier on that the due process issue is documented, the better and the greater the opportunity to defuse what could otherwise derail informal conciliatory talks. If the expropriating agency had, in a local proceeding by the claimant, the opportunity to extend substantive due process to the claimant, and failed to do so, it may have foreclosed itself from presenting evidentiary material and argument relating to its case, that would have been admissible, but for the failure.

13.6.1.3.3. *Admissibility of Evidence : Due Process Violation*

Admissibility of evidence is a matter that is commonly addressed in State Contracts and should not be overlooked. The admission of evidence, which the contract expressly excludes from being introduced in evidence, may be viewed as a procedural denial of due process, curable in the award. The denial of the presentation of evidence which contractually was admissible, may well be more serious. Depending on the nature of the evidence, its denial may have been crucial to the decision and an abuse of the arbitrators' discretion.

13.6.1.3.4. *Sine Qua Non Duty to Compensate : Element of Due Process*

With very few exceptions (f.i. former USSR and China), the duty to indemnify has generally been recognised by States which had undertaken to expropriate. The Fifth Amendment to the United States Constitution, for instance, provides :

> "No person shall be held to answer for any capital, or otherwise infamous crime, unless on a presentment or indictment of a Grand Jury, except in cases arising in the land or naval forces, or in the Militia, when in actual service in time of War or public danger; nor shall any person be subject for the same offence to be twice put in jeopardy of life or limb; nor shall be compelled in any criminal case to be a witness against himself, nor be deprived of life, liberty, or property, without due process of law; nor shall private property be taken for public use, without just compensation."

The Fourteenth Amendment, Section to the US Constitution provides :

> "**Section 1.** All persons born or naturalized in the United States, and subject to the jurisdiction thereof, are citizens of the United States and of the State wherein they reside. No State shall make or enforce any law which shall abridge the privileges or immunities of citizens of the United States; nor shall any State deprive any person of life, liberty, or property, without due process of law; nor deny to any person within its jurisdiction the equal protection of the laws."

Applicable portions of the English Bill of Rights (1691) provides a somewhat less categorical protection against privative measures but nonetheless the spirit against such measures without compensation appears from the following text:

> "the right of petition,
>
> an independent judiciary (the Sovereign was forbidden to establish his own courts or to act as a judge himself),
>
> freedom from *taxation* by royal (executive) prerogative, without agreement by Parliament (legislators),
>
> freedom from a peace-time standing army,
>
> freedom [for *Protestants*] to bear arms for their defence, as allowed by law,
>
> freedom to elect members of Parliament without interference from the Sovereign,
>
> freedom of speech in Parliament,
>
> freedom from cruel and unusual punishments and excessive *bail*, and
>
> freedom from fines and *forfeitures* without trial." [212]

Differing from the US Constitution, which addresses the basic rights of citizens as against the States and the Federal Government, "the English Bill of Rights" was intended to address the rights of citizens as represented by Parliament against the Crown. [213]

In its development in some Common Law countries, such as the United States (except Louisiana), and other former British Colonies, certain violations of due process are, almost by definition, considered substantive and therefore relatively safe from a res judicata challenge based on a local court decision. Among the most egregious of such violation is the failure adequately to compensate the party affected by a taking. In this respect, Common Law and Civil Law conveniently converge, though a Common Law Court might view it as a basic violation of a human right and the arbitration tribunal,

---

[212] See also http://www.fordham.edu/halsall/mod/1689billofrights.html.
[213] Wikipedia, "The English Bill of Rights".

depending on its composition, may view it as a violation of international law :

> "the due process clause has been interpreted as a limitation upon the legislative as well as the judicial and executive branches of the government, thus preventing arbitrary and unreasonable legislation. This aspect of the law is known as substantive due process to distinguish it from procedural due process." [214]

In jurisdictions that are heir to British Common Law, it may therefore be practical for the jurist faced with a condemnation or other privative measure to use the local court system to object to treatment, or even legislation, that violates substantive due process, before seeking arbitration relief. Thus, independently of international law, affirmative action in the local courts using Common Law as its system may be based on a violation of substantive due process. Just how far such action may go depends on how closely and impartially the local system adheres to Common Law, what adaptations may have been legislated which, on generally accepted Common Law grounds, validly modify it and what interpretations may have been given by local courts of review of such legislation. Inherent rights can easily be taken for granted by Common Law jurists in a variety of agreements, not least State Contracts and BITs, in one form or another. Nonetheless, access to local tribunals may not always be sufficient to ensure investors will receive the benefit of adequate security and protection. It is better for them to be able to have the choice either to access the local tribunal or to file an arbitration procedure with an international arbitration institution.

13.6.1.3.5. *Recognition of Duty to Compensate*

With very few exceptions (f.i. former USSR and China), the duty to indemnify has generally been recognised by States which had undertaken to expropriate. Indemnification agree-

---

[214] *Davidson v. New Orleans* (1877), 96 *US* 97, 24 *L. ed.* 616.

ments between European countries and members of the former Soviet bloc are numerous. They are the proof that those States felt obliged because of international law to indemnify other countries and the citizens thereof who had been damaged by State expropriation action. In doctrinal texts, the right to nationalise and the duty to compensate that follows are expressly acknowledged. Authors who claim that, when an expropriating State agrees to indemnify, this agreement is not pursuant to international law but freely as a sovereign State are very rare:

> "In the event that this or that State which effected nationalisation undertook an obligation to pay compensation to the nationals of another State in a bilateral treaty with that State, it was done not because the State was obliged to do so under the regulations of international law, but voluntarily and neither does the number of such bilateral treaties tend to constitute an international customary law, be it only 'status nascendi.'" (opinion of Professor KNAPP)[215]

In his book "Nationalisation and international law", the Russian author, VILKOV raises a question about the duty to indemnify:

> "In the second section regarding compensation for nationalised property, the author sets out his point of view regarding whether or not a State carrying out nationalisation is obliged to pay compensation to aliens for property nationalised. Vilkov agrees with authors who deny the existence in international law of rules regarding compensation in such cases. The author emphasises that in the 1952 General Assembly (UN) resolution regarding the right of free use and exploitation of natural wealth and resources, the Assembly recommended all members in implementing this right to have regard, consistently with their sovereignty, to the need for maintaining the flow of capital in conditions of security, mutual confidence and economic co-operation among nations. Thus the resolution contains only one condition that States should pay due regard to maintaining the need of flow of capital..."[216]

---

[215] LILLICH, Richard B. and WESTON, Burns H., *op. cit.*, p. 248, see fotonote 22.
[216] VILKOV, Anatoli, "Nationalisation and International Law", *Soviet Year-book of international law*, 1960, p. 67.

Despite these few exceptions in doctrinal texts, the majority supports the claim that international law imposes an obligation to indemnify. The International Court of Justice has, on several occasions, confirmed such obligation :

> "As to the first point, the Court holds that it is a principle of international law, that is, a general legal concept that any violation of a commitment carries with it the obligation to provide reparations. Already in its decision no. 8, holding it had jurisdiction on the basis of the Geneva Convention's Article 23, the Court has held that 'reparation is the indispensable complement for a failure to apply the law, there being no need for a specific reference thereto in the Convention itself.' The existence of the principle confirming the obligation to provide reparation, as an element of positive international law, has never been contested during the proceedings concerning the Chorzov case."

13.6.1.3.6. *Restitution in Kind or Financial compensation*

According to international law, the nationalising State's main duty is to compensate for the damages caused to the former owners. The duty to provide reparations or to indemnify applies to damage caused by property privative measures, when they fall within international law sanctioned acts, which in turn require certain conditions to be met (e.e. indemnification). That duty also exists for illegal acts, such as those that are contrary to a State's treaty commitments.

Just as with private law, in case of damages caused to an individual, one of international law's goals, in cases of deprivation measures, is *"restitutio in integrum,"* that is, to restore the person who has sustained damages to the position he held prior to the damaging measures.

It then follows that *"restitutio ad integrum"* must be structured and a measuring standard must be known. It may be said, for instance, that due process of law requires either the restitution in kind of the assets, a fairly well worn English Common Law principle. Unfortunately, that is not always possible. Restitution is a legal, not an equitable remedy. When no comparable item can be found or its remanufacture would be patently exorbitant, insisting on identical restitution would not be countenanced by a Court of Law. Portia would not have it in The Merchant of Venice and her logic still reigns.

The next question would be whether due process would allow, when restitution in kind is not possible, the alternative of monetary compensation. No one, so far as we know, has claimed, in jurisprudential records, that the claimant has the choice of one or the other.

In the *Chorzov* Case (*Germany v. Poland*), the Permanent International Court of Justice in the Hague, confirmed in 1928, and the principle is still valid, that restitution in kind is not always possible, and that monetary compensation, corresponding to the damages, is the most usual form of reparation :

> "The essential principle contained in the actual notion of an illegal act – a principle, which seems to be established by international practice and in particular by the decision of arbitral tribunals – is that reparation must as far as possible, wipe out all the consequences of the illegal act and re-establish the situation which would, in all probability, have existed, if that act had not been committed. Restitution in kind, or, if this is not possible, payment of a sum corresponding to the value which a restitution would bear, the award, if need be, of damages for loss sustained which would not be covered by restitution in kind or payment in place of it – such are the principles which would serve to determine the amount of compensation for an act contrary to international law." [217]

There have been cases on the international level where a restoration in kind was possible (for example, the restitution of a temple during the conflict between Cambodia and Thailand (CIJ). However, in nearly every other case, the only possible form of compensation for damages seems to be the payment of an indemnity.

---

[217] *Usine de Chorzov?* Permanent Court of International Justice (P.C.I.J), Série A, n° 17, 1928, p. 48.

ICSID's arbitral jurisprudence confirms that reparations in kind are impractical and that the payment of an indemnity, equal to the damages sustained, is the better formula:

> "The Tribunal acknowledges that reparation in kind is impractical and holds that LETCO's entitlement to damages includes *'lucrum cessans'* as well as *'lucrum emergens'*." (Emmanuel GAILLARD, *op. cit.*, p. 207).

Nonetheless, in another case, the arbitration tribunal allowed the State of Burundi another option. It gave Burundi the choice between an adequate and effective indemnification, based upon the compensable measure taken, or to terminate the measure. This dispute, however, stemmed from the cancellation of a Free Enterprise Zone certificate. The cancellation could be "cancelled" in turn and the investor restored to its former position. (see Emmanuel GAILLARD, *op. cit.*, p. 553).

13.6.1.3.7. *Indemnities must be "just", "adequate" and "effective"*

Nationalisation and expropriation measures are definitive, investors being unable to escape them. Hence, it is better for them to seek to obtain an adequate compensation than fight it otherwise or hope for restitution:

> "As far as public international law is concerned, the validity of a nationalisation is subject to a number of conditions. Of these conditions, the most important are that the nationalisation measure should not discriminate against foreign nationals per se, should not involve the commission of any irregularity on the part of the nationalising State, and should provide for the prompt payment of just, adequate and effective compensation. Since the nationalisation of foreign assets usually takes the form of a *'fait accompli'* and only the politically naïve would seriously pursue an action for restitution, the aspect of nationalisation receiving most attention is the form and amount of reparation due to the dispossessed foreign subject." [218]

---

[218] LABUSCHAGNE, J., "Compensation for expropriation in International law", *Speculum juris*, 1967, p. 5.

Indemnification is effective if their amount is established in the currency of the person entitled to it or in some other fully convertible currency. It would be contrary to the effectivity condition if the nationalising State were to fix the amount of indemnification in local currency or were to require they be paid into blocked accounts in the indemnitee's name. However, sometimes, indemnities may use blocked funds to purchase State guaranteed securities:

> "Often, regulations authorise owners of blocked accounts to use them for investment or deposits in the debtor country: they may, for instance be used to purchase shares in State Funds or even certain categories of industrial capital. Regulations may also allow a blocked account to be used for certain expenses in the debtor country, such as maintenance or repair of real estate, payment of taxes or bank costs." [219]

These restrictions on the use of indemnification does not meet the effectivity condition. The indemnitee must have full control over the disposition of indemnities that are due him. Indemnities must also be adequate, implying that they fully compensate the damages the dispossessed owners have sustained and that they cover the total value of the goods and assets nationalised or expropriated. Those are the "direct damages", corresponding to the actual value of nationalised or expropriated goods or assets. Indirect damages are not covered:

> "The reason is that indirect damages (for instance, insurance premium increases) always have an accessory character, resulting only as a consequence of the direct damage." [220]

In principle, therefore, indemnification must correspond to the total value of goods and assets expropriated or nationalised. However, as observed below, this may hardly be seen as an absolute requirement.

---

[219] SELLESLAGHS, François, *Pratique des paiements internationaux*, Presses Universitaires de Bruxelles, 1976, p. 111.

[220] DELBEZ, Louis, *op. cit.*, p. 162, see footnote 24.

13.6.1.3.8. *Notice and Opportunity to be Heard : fundamental to Due Process*

"Engrained in our concept of Due Process is the requirement of notice. Notice is sometimes essential so that the citizen has the chance to defend charges. Notice is required before property interests are disturbed, before assessments are made, before penalties are assessed. Notice is required in a myriad of situations where a penalty or forfeiture might be suffered by mere failure to act." [221]

The Notice requirement, however, is that the issue first be tried before a properly constituted judicial tribunal. A proceeding before an administrative officer or board, however, is adequate if the basic requirements of notice and opportunity for hearing are met:

The sufficiency of the notice and hearing is determined by considering the purpose of the procedure, its effects on the rights asserted and other circumstances [222] :

"The fundamental requirement of due process is an opportunity to be heard upon such notice and proceedings as are adequate to safeguard the right for which the constitutional protection is involved. It is necessary that the 'inexorable safeguard'... of a fair and open hearing be maintained in its integrity." [223]

The revocation by a city council of a permit to drill for oil, without notice or hearing is a violation of due process. [224] Legally competent evidence will ordinarily be required to sustain the determination of an administrative body. [225] This determination cannot be based on confidential reports or independent information received by the administrative board. [226]

---

[221] Witkin's, *ibid.*, p. 3598.
[222] Witkin's, *ibid.*, p. 3598.
[223] *Ohio Bell Tel. Co v. Public Utilities Com* (1939), 301 *US* 392, 81 *L.Ed* 1093, 1102.
[224] *Trans-Oceanic Oil Corp. v. Santa Barbara* (1948), 85 *C.A.* 2d776.
[225] *Consolidated Edison v. NLRB* (1928), 305 *US* 97.
[226] *Olive Proration etc. v. Agric. Prorate Com* (1941), 17 *C2d* 204, 210.

Due process requires fair warning and an opportunity to respond before penalties can be assessed :[227]

"Thus, sanctions cannot be imposed after an *ex parte* hearing and an order imposing sanctions must recite circumstances in justification."[228]

The absence of proper notice, even when statutorily not required, may constitute denial of the due process of law. Mitigating circumstances may sometimes make such lack of notice less damaging than may first appear. Though it is unlikely that all such owners will be individually notified, it is important that, at the very least, the host State officially publish the applicable law.

13.6.1.4. *Equal Protection*

Basic to Common Law systems is the concept of "equal protection." Thus, the 14th Amendment to the US Constitution forbids the denial, by any US State, to any person within such State's jurisdiction of the equal protection of the law. There is no equivalent equal protection right as against the US Government. Nonetheless, the federal Constitution requires uniformity in certain instances.[229]

Differing from the Due Process clause, the equal protection basic right does not guarantee a minimum protection. However, when taken together, the equal protection and due process rights are mutually inclusive, in that if the jurisprudence in a particular jurisdiction has set a standard for equal protection, then not applying it consistently may well be evidence of discrimination, a violation of due process. In other words, should the equal protection standard exceed that of due process, before application of the due process standard, then the equal protection standard will prevail. It goes hardly without saying that the reverse is true, that is, should

---

[227] TOKER, John A., *California Arbitration Practice Guide Sec.*, 5(d).
[228] *O'Brien v. Cseh* (1983), 148 *CA* 3d957.
[229] Art. I, section 8 US Constitution.

the due process standard exceed the equal protection standard, the due process standard will prevail. It also goes without saying that the sophistication and impartiality of the local fora, even when they claim to apply Common Law, can vary widely.

Equal protection means that persons similarly situated will be treated equally. Persons, physical or legal, may therefore be classified, so long as such classification is not arbitrary but based upon some trait common to a class and legitimate in itself. Legislation establishing such classes must have some relationship to the purpose distinguishing such class from other classes:

> "The courts must reach and determine the question whether the classifications drawn in a statute are reasonable in light of its purpose..."[230]

13.7. – JURISPRUDENCE

13.7.1. – *Arbitral jurisprudence*

In the arbitration awards of ICSID, the foregoing principles of international law are followed. In the case of *Letco v. Liberia*, the Liberian authorities had prematurely cancelled a concessionary contract that had a duration of 30 years. Liberia wished to justify the cancellation by arguing that Letco was guilty of non-compliance with contractual duties. ICSID denied the Liberian thesis but dwelt on a complementary examination of circumstances that could have justified the cancellation as a type of "nationalisation". The tribunal decided there was no nationalisation and explained its decision thus:

> "This would suppose that it could be established that it (the cancellation measure) has been taken in good faith and for a general public interest purpose, that it was not discriminatory and that it was

---

[230] *McLaughlin v. Florida* (1964) 379 US 184, 13 *L.Ed* 2d, 222.

accompanied by payment or at least an offer to pay of an adequate indemnification. None of these conditions were met in this case."[231]

None of these conditions having been met, the Tribunal held therefore that the measure could not be justified as a measure of nationalisation. The contract provisions should have been respected and their violation by Liberia opened the way to reparations.

The *Amco v. Indonesia* controversy, as arbitrated by ICSID in 1984 (cfr *supra*), concerned the cancellation of an investment permit for the construction of a hotel by the US company Amco Asia and the Pan American company, whose seat was in Hong Kong. The hotel's construction was financed by these two companies and the management was entrusted to two local Indonesian companies PT Amco and PT Wisma. Indonesian authorities had confiscated the hotel without payment of any indemnification. Furthermore a claim for damages and interest had been filed against the foreign investors. The property rights to the hotel had been transferred to the Indonesian company PT Wisma, which was already the owner of the land under construction.

The motive invoked by Indonesia was the violation of the investment convention. The arbitration tribunal decided that Indonesia was responsible, in that the Indonesian taking was contrary to Indonesia law and international law. A correct application of Indonesian law of 1967, governing foreign investments, forbade all measures of nationalisation regarding assets and interests of foreign investors unless such measures were taken for a public purpose. The arbitrators were of the opinion that such was not the case in this affair.

Insofar as the application of international law is concerned, it is interesting to note that the tribunal considered that expropriation, without the payment of an indemnity, was contrary to international law, even if the property rights had

---

[231] GAILLARD, Emmanuel, *op. cit.*, p. 206, see footnote 31.

not been acquired by the host State but had been transferred to one of its nationals:

> "It is also accepted in international law that an expropriation has occurred not only when a State grabs private property but also when the State transfers the property to another person or corporation. Thus, in international law, expropriation occurs when the State simply deprives the private owner of the protection of its jurisdictions by tacitly authorising the seizing of a seizer in possession to stay in possession of the asset seized, much like the *praetor romanus* would have in authorising the '*longi temporis prescriptio*'" [232]

The decision confirms that States have the right to nationalise under certain conditions, specifically for reasons of public purpose, and that even contractual rights may be subject to expropriation measures:

> "First all, the State is the natural protector of the public and social interest of the Nation. Consequently, except when States act as simple private persons might, using in no way its sovereign prerogatives, the State has the right to affect or suppress, whenever the general public interest justifies it, the situation or the relationship it has created by a precedent act, even if such act is the source of State commitments and obligations. This is a consequence of the fundamental principle of the right of sovereign States to proceed to nationalise or expropriate private property as well as contractual rights which may have been prior awarded by the State, even when such rights belong to foreigners." [233]

13.7.2. – *National Tribunals Jurisprudence*

Although arbitral legislation, treaties, procedure and jurisprudence have been the main topic of this Work, it would be a disservice to the readers not to mention the availability, in many countries, of national State tribunals. Unfortunately, as we have pointed out elsewhere, some countries, not limited to lesser developed countries, have, for historic and ideological reasons, not kept pace with the development of law to the extent promoted and appreciated in other, mostly, developed

---

[232] GAILLARD, *op. cit.*, p. 141, see footnote 31.
[233] GAILLARD, Emmanuel, *op. cit.*, p. 14, see footnote 31.

countries. As a result, complex issues, some of which call into question the fairness or competence of local government agencies responsible for the promotion and development of industry and commerce may, if filed in a local court, be subject to unusual requirements or outright discrimination, at odds with the standards of international arbitration and, possibly also, due process or equal protection.

Consequently, some investors are loath to entrust their grievances to local tribunals and seek international arbitration, because they believe international arbitration has a greater measure of consistency and fairness than what can be expected of some local tribunals. However, it is wrong to think that recourse to competent, sophisticated local justice is always ill advised. Where the envelope of constitutional, commercial and property law has been extended to dimensions not substantially less consistent with fairness or modernity than those used in international arbitration, national courts' dispensations of predictable awards and continuity of legal solutions may well outrank their counterparts in international arbitration. Some of these courts may use techniques reminiscent of international arbitration tribunals but have the advantage of appellate review, not available in international arbitration. Some, however, may view the possibility of appeal as a disadvantage.

Furthermore, judges on a number of national tribunals frequently have tenure. Records are kept of their competence. Experienced practitioners are aware of their philosophical persuasions. Many constitutional safeguards, not least due process and equal protection, are available to aliens as well as to nationals in equal measure. If local jurisprudence, whose records are public, convincingly shows fairness and sophistication, *stare decisis* continuity, and a reputation for impartiality and independence from other government agencies, local litigation may well be the more prudent course and not necessarily the less expeditious nor costlier alternative. Thus, the use of such tribunals should not be rejected out of hand, simply because they are national.

Another, not to be overlooked, consideration may arise when measures privative of private property rights occur in developed countries. As mentioned elsewhere in this Work, there is movement towards the negotiation of protective agreements between two less developed countries, as well as a similar phenomenon between developed countries. In State contracts, for example, between an investor from a developed country and a government from another developed country, chances are a choice of law clause will be included along with an arbitration clause, at least as an initial attempt to settle any dispute amicably and informally. Last but not least, these courts sometimes provide means of enforcement, such as pre-emptive attachment of assets that international arbitration tribunals are, as a matter of definition, unable to provide. These can become valuable for an investor dealing with a local State agency acting in.

In all of these situations, should they involve less developed countries, or not, prospective litigants should be aware of the historical origins of local law. These origins are often colonial, and may be roughly classified as heirs to Civil Law (Napoleonic Code) and British Common Law. These differences are sometimes reflected in the education of judges or arbitrators selected in any of these venues, be they ICSID, CCI, CCJ or any other. Litigants ignore such differences at their peril.

13.7.2.1. *Stare Decisis*

In areas of the world where the law is heir to British Common Law, a fundamental principle underlies the discipline which courts follow in the handing down of their decisions. The principle, whose roots are centuries old, is usually referred to as *"stare decisis"* and is based on "a doctrine that when a court has once laid down a principle of law, it will adhere to that principle and apply it to all future cases where the facts are substantially the same.[234]

Under this doctrine, a deliberate or solemn decision of court made after argument on questions of law fairly arising in the case, and necessary to its determination, is an authority or binding precedent in the same court or in other courts of equal or lower rank in subsequent cases where the very point is again in controversy."[235]

Common Law, as practised in such areas, may, therefore, be very reluctant to decide differently from precedent on the legal relationships arising from a similar set of facts between the same or other parties. "*Stare decisis*" is different from *res adjudicata* in that the latter is based on the law's unwillingness to readjudicate the same facts between the same parties. Since ideology on a number of topics changes over the decades, not infrequently, lip service only will be paid to the *stare decisis* principle, and a distinction will be found, sometimes barely visible to most, justifying departure from the law as laid down in a previous similar case. When acknowledged, *stare decisis* is more usually applied to decisions of appellate courts of equal rank, within the same jurisdiction, the decisions of appellate courts in other jurisdiction as well as those of lower courts being seen as advisory rather than obligatory.

Stare decisis is a judicial tool, sometimes seen as a right of the affected persons to the stable and consistent administration of justice. Some BITs (e.g. U.K.) may insist on the jurisdiction of national tribunals in cases of expropriation.

Judges trained in English Common Law will tend to apply the principle and be moved by analogies to previous cases as sources or inspiration for their decisions. Before them, Petitioners and defendants alike may be asked to show the factual differences, if any, warranting a deviation from the prec-

---

[234] *Moore v. City of Albany*, 98 *N.Y.* 396, 440. *Black's Law Dictionary*, WestPublishing Compant, 1951, St. Paul Minn.

[235] 128 *A.L.R.* 1506.

edent established in a previous case. Where such difference cannot be shown, petitioners should be prepared to present fairly strong countervailing arguments based on grounds more compelling than those underlying the previous case. Merely showing that good grounds exist for deciding the case differently from the previous case may not be sufficient to convince the tribunal that it should take such grounds into account to justify a different or contrary decision, or otherwise departing from the precedent.

The cogency of jurisprudence is therefore an element to be taken into consideration by the pleaders when a member of the tribunal is known to be a common law jurist. Conversely, since the *stare decisis* principle does not have as much cogency in the Civil Law, pleaders trained in the Common Law should be forewarned that their arguments must be accompanied by a great deal more than simple reliance on *stare decisis*.

13.7.2.2. *Due Process and Equal Protection Interdependence*

Jurisprudence uses these words often used in connection with the conduct of judicial or other authorities with respect to the rights of persons within their jurisdiction. As a jurisprudential issue, these rights are addressed together in Common Law jurisprudence mainly because they are mutually inclusive, and that, often, when judges speak of the one, the other seems inevitably to follow. That is, should equal protection fall short of due process, in assuring that fundamental rights of persons be respected, due process of law will make up the difference. Conversely, should equal protection in a jurisdiction provide rights superior to those guaranteed by due process, equal protection rights will have precedence. Unfortunately, in some jurisdictions, they amount to little more than a mantra inherited from a colonial past and lacking the substance given to it in places where a great deal of judicial thought has been given to their definition over the centuries :

"Due process of law in each particular case means such an exercise of the powers of government as the settled maxims of law permit and sanction and under such safeguards for the protection of individual rights as those maxims prescribe for the class of cases to which the one in question belongs."[236]

"Whatever difficulty may be experienced in giving to those terms a definition which will embrace every exertion of power affecting private rights and exclude such as is forbidden, there can be no doubt of their meaning when applied to judicial proceedings. They then mean a course of legal proceedings according to those rules and principles which have been established in the common law system of jurisprudence for the enforcement and protection of private rights."

Let us recall our citation earlier in this Chapter of the Fourteenth Amendment to the United States Constitution which, in substance provides that *"no state"* shall deprive any person of life, liberty, or property without due process of law. The Fifth Amendment to the US Constitution provides similar restrictions on the US Government. The origins of this declaration of rights are centuries old and, at that time, were indeed procedural.[237]

In the United States, due process has been interpreted in the jurisprudence as a limitation on the legislative process as well as the judicial and executive branches of government. Arbitrary legislation can therefore be reached by resorting to a due process argument, in effect shifting due process from "mere" procedure to actually substantive law (*Davidson v. New Orleans* (1877), 96 *US* 97, 24 *L.Ed.* 619. Cases where due process is invoked as substantive law frequently involve an excessive use of plice power but other government action (e.g. taxation) may also be attacked on that score alone.

It is important, therefore, where the choice of law in an arbitration agreement is the Law of a Common Law system, that petitioners and defendants be aware of the consequences resulting from the violation of due process and equal protec-

---

[236] *Cooley*, Const. Lim 441.
[237] Witkin, *ibid.*, p. 2569.

tion and not a mere procedural error. Insufficiency of proper notice, for example, may be a procedural defect, when promptly cured. Similarly, the exercise of jurisdiction over a person or subject matter over which the court or other authority did not have jurisdiction is viewed as a violation of procedural due process.

There are therefore many instances of denial of due process, too numerous to list here, falling the procedural category and which, conceivably could be curd by appropriate consideration later on in the proceeding. There are, however, categories of violations are not merely procedural and which cannot be so easily cured. Although due process of law is enshrined in the Constitutions of certain countries, including but not limited to the United States, or taken for granted in jurisdictions that have no written constitutions, its interpretations can vary from jurisdiction to jurisdiction. The meaning is generally clear and can hardly be denied, but it's application in jurisprudence may lead to different conclusions:

> "Due process of law implies the right of the person affected thereby to be present before the tribunal which pronounces judgment upon the question of life, liberty, or property, in its most comprehensive sense: to be heard, by testimony or otherwise, and to have the right of controverting, by proof, every material fact which bears on the question of right in the matter involved." [238]

The standard of due process of law has been incorporated in international agreements and in State Contracts, though it appears that often the meaning of the expression is little known or debated. Yet, in many State Contracts cases, the origins of disputes include different interpretations by opposing parties of the scope of the same principle when applied to the facts at hand. Contracts may be improved by the inclusion of appropriate language drawing the parties' attention to an element often taken for granted or deemed legalistic and

---

[238] *Black's Law Dictionary*, 590.

hollowed of its indispensable meaning. Because there is no exact equivalent in Civil Law, Common Law due process of law is sometimes taken by civil jurists to be strictly procedural, manifesting itself mainly in its violation and correctable by adequate consideration of the issue in any judgment or award. This is a common perception and it is a mistake.

13.7.2.3. *Stare Decisis as a function of Due Process of Law*

Due Process of Law is a fundamental right of Man, to be honoured by civilised Nations no less than the Basic Rights of Man[239]. It cannot be less than universal because ignoring it anywhere undermines it everywhere. Stare decisis may be subsumed under Due Process, as one of the bundle of lesser rights which are subject to change as circumstances fairly demand and the community of Nations fairly elects in the administration of equal justice within their borders.

13.7.2.4. *Civil Law and Common Law*

Stemming from different origins, it is not surprising that Civil Law and Common Law approach legal problems from different perspectives, Civil Law being more closely related to statutory law and Common Law to precedent setting decisions. Civil law does not officially recognise *stare decisis* but jurisprudence in that legal system plays an advisory role.

Nonetheless, in many countries that are categorised as Common Law countries, statutes frequently diverge, in their legal effect, from traditional Common Law. Where such statutes exist, a growing number of decisions interpreting the statutes is the basis for continuing, precedent setting jurisprudence. In the important process of arbitrator selection, litigants may prefer to select arbitrators whose legal training is more consistent with theirs.

---

[239] Déclaration universelle des Droits de l'Homme, ONU, 10 December 1958.

Where both sides of a controversy are from Common Law or Civil Law countries, adherence to basic principles specific to the parties' preferred legal system may be easier than when litigants are from countries with different legal systems. In either case, it would be unwise to expect that assumptions based on such principles will be taken for granted. Any such assumptions are preferably to be explicitly included in the parties' pre-arbitration agreement.

13.8. – Valuation issues

13.8.1. – *Notion of "Value"*

If the investor wishes to be compensated for the full or partial value of his investment, it must still be decided what value will be used to calculate the indemnity. There are several kinds of "value":

- the net accounting value, otherwise known as the balance sheet value, representing the difference between the assets and liabilities of the enterprise;
- the sales or market value:

    "This warrants the payment of market value, which normally means the price a willing buyer would pay a willing seller in a viable market. Usually this is based on previous sales pf similar enterprises or properties in the nationalising State."[240]

- the stock exchange value, namely, that obtained when the number of shares is multiplied by the price per share on the exchange;
- the yield value: obtained by capitalising profits which could have been made by the enterprise, had she not been nationalised (*"lucrum cessans"*) or by the capitalisation of profits made during a given number of years prior to nationalisation;

---

[240] LILLICH, Richard, *op. cit.*, p. 95, see footnote 22.

- the "real" value: equal to the objective value of goods and assets affected by the nationalisation or expropriation measure.

13.8.2. – *No international Compensation Standard*

International law does not provide a fixed standard of compensation. It speaks of adequate compensation, corresponding to the total value of the investment but does not specify what value to use. Doctrinal texts seem to recommend, not always to seek, a "full compensation" but that a reasonable indemnification should suffice according to circumstances:

> "If adequate compensation is taken to mean an amount equivalent to the full value of the property, it does not reflect the position or practice of a sufficient number of States to constitute a norm of customary international law. The standard of 'appropriate' compensation referred to in General Assembly resolution 1803, understood as an amount that is reasonable under all the circumstances, is probably the governing principle. Such a standard would permit a developing State which undertakes a general nationalisation program to pay aliens something less than the full value of their property or investment."[241]

There is therefore no uniformity of opinion. In the legislation of past nationalisations, there is a variety of bases for compensation: balance value of the enterprise (Bulgaria); net value of the assets taken over (Tanzania); actual purchase price plus the reasonable value of additions and improvements (Ceylon); book value (Chili); undepreciated part of the cost of the equipment and installations (Venezuela) etc.

13.8.3. – *Hull formula*

The legality of nationalisation and expropriation measures depends on the State's performance of its obligations (cfr *supra*). As we said earlier the most important State's obligation is indemnification. In international practice, reference is often made to the "*HULL*" formula, as shorthand for the for-

---

[241] LILLICH, Richard, *op. cit.*, p. 53, see footnote 22.

mula elaborated by US Secretary of State Cordell Hull. According to Hull, indemnification must correspond to the following guidelines:
- it must cover the total value of the affected investments;
- it must be paid without delay;
- it must be adequate, in the sense that it is adapted to the circumstances in which the assets were taken (public purpose);
- it must be effective so that the beneficiary of the indemnity will be able to have access to it without delay;
- it is paid in the currency of the beneficiary or in any other easily convertible currency.

This formula is generally recognised in Europe but even in some countries of Latin America, progress has been made towards the adoption of the formula compared to the attitude of these countries a few decades ago. The formula's principle has been included in the Protocol de Colonia, dated 26 March 1991, signed by Argentina, Brazil, Paraguay and Uruguay. The goal was to promote and protect investments made on the Common Market of the South (Mercado Comun del Sur – Mercosur).

The Contracting Parties agreed not to undertake measures of expropriation or nationalisation, nor measures with similar effect except when:

> "the said measures be taken for reasons of public utility, on a non-discriminatory basis and according to legal process. The measures will be accompanied by provisions for payment of prior, adequate and effective compensation." (article 4)

It would be difficult to maintain that the Hull formula is or ever has been applied consistently, for the purpose of "total value compensation". After the Second World War, nationalisation measures were undertaken massively in the Soviet dominated European bloc. Countries in Western Europe entered into global and lump sum indemnification agreements with the countries of the East bloc. The indemnities that were actually paid did not at all correspond to the Hull formula.

In general, the nationalising States were not concerned with rules of international law. Economic reasons – not legal reasons – underlay their interest in entering into those agreements. In more than one case, the indemnities were certainly not adequate and they were not established based on the objective value of the enterprises that were nationalised. Significant capital had been invested but only between 10 to 25% of the actual value was indemnified.[242]

The laws of some nations actually deviate from the Hull formula, for the alleged reason that the measures are taken for a public purpose to which a higher priority is given than compensation for private individuals. A partial compensation which covers only a reasonable fraction of the value of the assets and other nationalised rights is deemed to be "adequate":

> "The laws of most countries on the other hand give weight to the public interests and needs involved in case of lawful expropriations in the exercise of sovereignty for the public good.
>
> They admit some balancing criteria in order to avoid making these measures too burdensome.
>
> They may lead to provisions on compensation which, while being considered just, may in specific instances provide for less than full compensation for the private interests so sacrificed."[243]

In the decision of the European Court for the Rights of Man (*James* case), it was also stressed that compensation does not necessarily always have to be "full compensation":

> "...the payment of an amount reasonably proportional to the value of the expropriated property is adequate. According to the Court, Article 1 of the first Protocol does not guarantee in all cases the right to a full compensation, since legitimate objectives of public good, such as in cases of economic or social reforms, may justify a compensation which is less than the full commercial value."

---

[242] SCHOKKAERT, J., *op. cit.*, p. 438, see footnote 19.
[243] SACERDOTI, Giorgio, *op. cit.*, p. 396, see footnote 161.

13.8.4. – *Expropriations in Times of Financial Crises*

Evaluating nationalised goods and other assets in order to set a basis for the reckoning of indemnification is very much in the public eye these days. The current economic crisis and, in particular, the financial crisis have thrust banks and insurance companies in a very difficult position. Sorely needing the confidence of their customers, banks and insurance companies alike attempt to highlight the difference between the market value of their shares and the real value of their assets. These firms' managers claim that there is no reason to be overly concerned about the tanking of their share price because the companies' capital, that is its, realty and personalty assets are intact, and, therefore, the real, intrinsic value of their firms exceeds by far the share capitalisation.

They recognise, of course, that they have liquidity problems and that, currently, they find it hard to honour their debts and other financial obligations. Consequently, both in Europe and in the United States, some of these companies look to Government for financial help in meeting the challenges they are in.

There is therefore a perception that the eventual bankruptcy of these companies could be followed by a total collapse of these countries' economic systems. There follows a corresponding willingness to allow direct Government aid, under various forms, to floundering banks and insurance companies. In some cases, Governments have, in effect, nationalised partially or entirely some very large banking and insurance institutions. Nationalisation entails problems of indemnification, which in turn highlights the fundamental difference between the market value and the real value of the assets taken over. Calculating the indemnification on the basis of the market value would probably not meet the standard of "fair and adequate" compensation international law requires.

Today's measures occur in a context very different from that undertaken *en masse* after the Second World War by States in the East bloc. At that time, the goal in those States was to cancel out private property rights altogether and entrust the entire economy to the State. Today, instead, the goal is the extension of Government help to a few enterprises, it being clearly understood that the help is but temporary. The Governments involved in these nationalisations claim to do so with the intent of "reprivatising" the nationalised enterprises by the resale of their assets to national or foreign private parties.

Nonetheless, should this intention be honoured, there remains unaffected the problem of calculating the amount of the indemnification, the choice between market and real value and the inherent sub-problem of establishing what the real value is in each case. Legal problems are like unaffected, not least whether the nationalising Government will be the sole instrument and determinant in charge of the resale or will the former shareholders have a say-so in the operation and the distribution of the proceeds.

Most likely, nationalisation and re-privatisation operations will generate litigation. We have been informed that a Chinese investor in an important European bank will be seeking to recover just compensation under the terms of the applicable BITs concluded by China with several European countries.

How this litigation will unfold is unpredictable at this time but we can be relatively sure that valuation (market value or real value) will be one of the sticking points. Negotiations at various levels will most likely continue, not necessarily resulting in litigation. For the time being, in countries affected by such economic and financial crises, plain Government loans, to be repaid in an indeterminate future, do not seem to be the likeliest outcome. It is worth noting that this kind of aid is usually not allowed by international organisations to which such adhere (e.g. the European Union). A more widely favoured solution involves the partial or total takeover of shaky enterprises, followed by the sale of shares to the domestic or international private sector on terms that are yet to be formulated. Admittedly, this solution is akin to nationalisation or expropriation, entailing the usual valuation problems, but also involving the development of a new approach to the notion of "public interest" and the inevitable debates that will confront it.

13.9. – BIT Expropriation and Nationalisation Clauses

Provisions concerning nationalisation and expropriation rights and the conditions which must be met to ensure the validity of such measures must be included in BIT's, since they are the most appropriate instruments for the protection of international investments.

Version A of the Afro-Asiatic model convention contains, insofar as nationalisation and expropriation are concerned, provisions comparable to those already in place in European Bit's. On the other hand, version B is far more restrictive. Nationalisation rights are expressly confirmed but do not mention the conditions to be met, particularly in relation to public purpose. The fact that reference is made only to local law is worrisome. The payment of an adequate indemnity is mentioned but its principles are not set forth. Alternative formulas are reserved. The negotiators from Contracting States must therefore be quite attentive and try to negotiate provisions which will be more favourable than those set forth in this model version.

In European BIT's, the conditions which must be met by expropriating measures to be legally sufficient are usually set forth, according to international law (requirement of a public purpose, indemnity rights and prohibition against discrimination). However, a reference to international law is still often lacking, such as in the English and German texts. In some cases, it has been added that nationalisation must follow a legal process, as applicable in the expropriating State, and that it cannot be contrary to particular accords entered into between such State and investors. The US model convention contains identical provisions but does also contain a reference to international law:

> "Neither Party shall expropriate or otherwise nationalise a covered investment either directly or indirectly through measures tantamount to expropriation or nationalisation, except for a public purpose, in a non-discriminatory manner, upon payment of prompt, adequate and effective compensation, and in accordance with due process of law and the general principles of treatment provided for in Article II (3) (i.e. international law)." (article III)

13.9.1. – *Scope*

Investors should never be excluded from the benefits of a protection treaty. The nationalising State may argue that the privative measure which affects them is not covered by the treaty. For this very reason, the Contracting States have striven to provide an as wide a definition as possible of the kind of privative measures that are covered by the agreement. Here are a few examples which highlight this concern by sending States:

> "Investments of investors of each Contracting Party shall not be nationalised, expropriated or subjected to measures having effect equivalent to nationalisation or expropriation..." (**Article 5**, Danish Model Convention)

> "Neither Contracting Party shall expropriate or nationalise an investment either directly or indirectly through measures tantamount to expropriation or nationalisation..." (**Article 7** Australia/Mexico Agreement)

> "Neither Contracting Party shall take measures of expropriation or nationalisation or any other measure having the effect of dispossession, direct or indirect of nationals or companies..." (**Article 5**, France/Uganda Agreement)

> "No investment or any part of an investment of a national or a company of either Party shall be expropriated or nationalised by the

other Party or subjected to any other measure or series of measures, direct or indirect, tantamount to expropriation..." (USA/ Zaïre Agreement)

13.9.2. – *Bases of Compensation*

It is necessary that BIT's include a method for the calculation of the indemnification sum. There are two bases of calculation which are frequently, if not exclusively, categorised as "real" and "market value". There are exceptions to the rule : in some of its bilateral protection agreements, China chose "integral restitution" (*"restitutio ad integrum"*). In the Japan-China BIT of 1988, the following appears :

> "The compensation shall be such as to place nationals and companies in the same financial position as that in which nationals and companies would have been if expropriation, nationalisation or any other measure the effects of which similar to expropriation or nationalisation had not been taken." (**Article 5**)

This formula does not actually provide a basis for calculation and is therefore not satisfactory. The formula adopted in the Belgium-China BIT is not either :

> "Indemnities per **Article 4** of the Agreement will correspond to the value of the assets and other invested rights on the date immediately preceding the date of expropriation or on the date on which the expropriation was made public."

An investor would not know how the "value" which will serve as the basis for the indemnity will be calculated. Doctrinal texts do not always consider subjective value as a proper basis for calculation. As said before, the market value is defined as the price a seller could obtain under normal sales conditions. However, when nationalisations are contemplated, sellers are already operating under conditions which are not normal :

> "The fair market value concept is inadmissible because it purports to apply traditional commercial and property concepts in a situation which is not a normal commercial purchase, but more properly char-

acterised as the intervention of state power to restructure capital and the economy system."[244]

These are valid criticisms. If the value of a nationalised enterprise must be established on the basis of the stock market value (stock market quotes), the problem is even more delicate. A clause which defines the stock market value as that on the date preceding nationalisation or that on which the nationalisation has been made public provides no guarantee of adequate compensation. Stock market value is very fragile and is itself influenced by rumours of nationalisation even when no official declaration has been made. Besides, what developing country disposes of a reliable stock market to which reference could be made to determine true value?

BIT's have used several approaches to establish a basis for calculating the amount of indemnification. In most BIT's, the "real" value is chosen as the basis. In the German model convention, the term "value" is used, without any definition:

> "Such compensation shall be equivalent to the value of the expropriated investment immediately before the date on which the actual or threatened expropriation, nationalisation or comparable measure has become publicly known." (**Article 5**)

The English model uses "real value" it defines as follows:

> "such compensation shall amount to the *genuine value* of the investment expropriated..." (**Article 5**) (*emphasis* ours)

The Mercosur treaty also refers to the "real value" (article 4) In the US model convention, much is made of the "fair market value". In the NAFTA treaty, the US example has been followed:

> "compensation shall be equivalent to the fair market value and shall not reflect any change occurring because of the intended expropriation had become known earlier..." (**Article 1110**)

In doctrinal texts and in international practice, the general opinion is that BIT's should contain a more elaborate list of

---

[244] ANANTE, S.K., *Le Droit au développement*, S.C.A.D.L., 1980, p. 360.

the modalities of indemnification. It is not sufficient merely to state that the amount of indemnification shall correspond to the real or market value of the investments. The valuation criteria should be enumerated in order to establish the real or market value. In the "Guidelines established by the World Bank", this is how it is done:

> "Indemnification shall generally be deemed 'adequate' it is has been calculated from the true market value of expropriated asset such as it may be determined to be the value just before the expropriation or the publication of the decision to expropriate. The true market value is acceptable if it is determined by the host State on the basis of reasonable criteria as they relate to the market value of the investment, after taking into consideration the nature of the investment, of the circumstances under which it would have been exploited in the future as well as its particular characteristics, not least its age, the ratio of its tangible assets to the total investment, and other factors specific to the case. The evaluation shall be deemed reasonable if it is made according to one of the following methods:
> - the company involved is viable and its viability has been established on the basis of its value, as verified by its financial cash flow;
> - the company involved has proven that it is not viable if its value is based on being operated as in liquidation;
> - there are other active assets: on the basis of their replacement or book value if the latter has been recently established or determined on the day of expropriation and may therefore be considered a reasonable estimate of the replacement value." [245]

The NAFTA treaty also encourages the use of valuation criteria:

> "Compensation shall be equivalent to the market value. Valuation criteria shall include going concern, asset value including declared tax value of tangible property, and other criteria, as appropriate, to determine fair market value." (**Article 1110**)

All BIT's should expressly declare the valuation criteria to be used for investors. In the Protection Agreement between France and Guatemala dated 27 May 1998, it was agreed that

---

[245] JUILLARD, Patrick, "Investissements", *Annuaire français de droit international (AFDI)*, Paris, 1992, n° 38, p. 806.

the calculation of the real value should more properly take into account the economic circumstances which existed before the threat of expropriation had come into play:

> "Any measure leading to the deprivation of private property which could be undertaken must be promptly and adequately compensated in an amount equal to the real value of the investments in question, which must be calculated in relation to the economic situation prior to any threat of deprivation." (**Article 6(2)**)

This provision offers a better protection and allows the possibility of eliminating the negative influence on investments' value accompanying expropriation rumors. However, there is even a better formula in the bilateral accord between France and Mexico dated 12 November 1998:

> "Indemnification must be equivalent to the true market value, or, should this value be unavailable, then to the true value of the investment which was the object of the deprivation or nationalisation just before it occurred, and it cannot take into account any change in value arising from the fact that the deprivation measure was already a matter of public knowledge. Criteria for evaluation include the exploitation value, the asset value including the declared fiscal value for tangible assets, as well as other criteria, according to circumstances, allowing the determination of the fair market value."

This formulation is better than the others but it must be borne in mind that even terms as common as book value are seldom representative of true value. Book value may well be the original acquisition value, reduced by depreciation, amortisation or depletion. Some assets, carried at book value on the company's books, may in fact be worth nothing because of obsolescence. Replacement value is notoriously difficult to establish not only because many assets are unique in the area where the expropriation took place but even world wide. This assumes also a willing Seller and an able and willing Buyer who have no monopoly, theoretical or practical on the supply of certain types of assets. Giving the investor the choice among various criteria will nearly always result in a valuation that is on the high side, likely to be unpalatable to the indemnifying authorities.

In a very few cases, a decrease in the value of participation shares, resulting from the expropriation, has been taken into account :

> "When a Contracting party expropriates the assets of a company or an enterprise in its territory, which is incorporated or constituted under its law, and in which investors of the other Contracting party have an investment, including through shareholding, the provisions of this Article shall apply to ensure prompt, adequate and effective compensation for those investors for any impairment or diminishment of the fair market value of such investment resulting from the expropriation." (**Article 5**, Danish model convention)

The concept is valid but a question arises as to how shall the amount of the decrease in value resulting from the expropriation be calculated. The text does not address this point.

13.10. – INTEREST

After the Second World War, during the period when mass nationalisation was taking place, there was no possibility of adding interest to damages. This situation has changed since BIT's began to be adopted. BIT's now include a clause which allows the payment of interest. The importance of this issue is stressed in international doctrine :

> "Insofar as institutional interest is concerned, there are three views :
>
> When does interest begin to accrue – there is no uniform solution on this point. Arbitration decisions refer to three different moments in time : the date of the illegal act, the date when the claim for indemnification was filed, the date of the arbitration decision, if any.
>
> There is the same diversity of opinion in cases where, after an analysis of the '*dies a quo*', a question is raised about the '*dies ad quem*', that is when the running of interest ceases.
>
> Arbitration decisions sometimes allow the running of interest until the date of effective payment (eventually, full payment), sometimes until an arbitrary flat date which they fixed." [246]

---

[246] DELBEZ, Louis, *op. cit.*, p. 205, see footnote 24.

It is striking that in the German and British model conventions, only a *"dies ad quem"* is mentioned. This, of course creates a problem for judges and arbitrators who must resolve indemnification litigation. In the French BIT's, a *"dies a quo"* is not mentioned either:

> "Indemnification includes, until the date when it is paid (*'dies ad quem'*) interest calculated on the basis of a rate used in the applicable market (article 5, Agreement between France and Mexico dated 12 November 1998)."

Besides, starting the running of interest on the date the amount of the indemnities is established is very disadvantageous to the investor. This date is generally far removed from the actual date of expropriation. Negotiations having for their purpose the determination of indemnities may take months, sometimes years. Hence, an agreement providing for the start of the running of interest on the date indemnities are determined carries a definite risk.

In the US model convention, interest begins to run on the *"dies a quo"* which is the date of expropriation:

> "interest at a commercially reasonable rate for that freely usable currency, accrued from the date of expropriation until the date of payment."

In recent ICSID jurisprudence, arbitrators have also given preference to the date of expropriation:

> "Considering this deficiency (in domestic law), it is legitimate to apply logical and normal principles usually applied in matters of expropriation, that is, that the *'dies a quo'* is the date on which the deprivation took place, since is since then that the damage from the deprivation began. The jurisprudence of international tribunals supports this principle." [247]

The NAFTA Treaty provides that the arbitration tribunal may require the payment of interest:

---

[247] GAILLARD, Emmanuel, *op. cit.*, p. 376, see footnote 31.

"When a Tribunal makes a final award against a Party, the Tribunal may add separately or in combination only... (a) monetary damages and any applicable interest; (b) restitution of property in which case the award shall provide that the disputing Party may pay monetary damages and any applicable interest in lieu of restitution." (article 1135)

By applying this rule in the *Metalclad case against Mexico*, ICSID impose interest payments and on this occasion again confirmed that the *"dies a quo"* must be the date of expropriation or similar measure, such as the date on which a construction permit (previously granted) was withdrawn:

"The question is whether any interest is due on the indemnification amount."

Article 1135(1), provided for the Tribunal's authority to grant "pecuniary damages" and all applicable interest. NAFTA clearly foresaw the award of interest as part of an arbitration decision. After analysing confirmed doctrine, the Tribunal observed that:

"interest becomes an integral part of the compensation itself and that it must therefore begin to run from the moment when the host State's international responsibility arises... The Tribunal considers that, among the various possible dates when Mexico's responsibility first arose, it is reasonable to choose that on which the Commune of Guadalcazar rejected the permit to build Metalclad."[248]

Even this solution can be a problem. Not infrequently, privative measures are partial, a gradual erosion, at first apparently relatively benign but opening the way for later outright deprivation. Expropriation and other privative measures can be and are, of course, often directed at nationals of the expropriating State. Although the decision in a recent case in Ecuador did not involve the application of international law or any treaty, because no foreign investor was affected by it, the case could just as easily have devel-

---

[248] GAILLARD, Emmanuel, *op. cit.*, p. 679, see footnote 31.

oped in an international arena, had the investors been foreign.

The case involved a determination of squatters' rights. The local municipality initially acknowledged that a certain area of the investors' land had been occupied unlawfully by squatters, "legalised" the taking of a portion of the land and, as to the rest, would not allow its normal process of eviction to be initiated. Instead, it promised to "consider" the matter. It then delayed making a final decision, while the squatters' occupation over the entire property spread and became more permanent. It then redefined the boundaries of the squatted land, ignoring reality and continuing to deny relief for the investors' loss of use of property immediately adjacent to te officially expropriated land, even though the squatters' occupation severely restricted the owners' ability to farm any of the land and ultimately caused them to abandon farming altogether. This entire process was actually spread over a period of over twenty years. The investors claimed compensation for the land's value, interest and loss of profit.

During argument over the owners' entitlement to interest in addition to compensatory damages for the taking, the owners claimed that the date on which interest began to run was the very first day that squatting occurred and the refusal of the City to evict when its assistance was sought. The interest claimed was said to "refer back" to the earliest day of squatting. The City's demurrer was upheld. The matter is still pending on appeal.

Arguably, were foreign investors involved and recourse had to an international arbitration tribunal, the matter could have been decided faster. What can be learnt from that experience is that interest is always a touchy issue, perhaps because it is irritating and politically unpalatable for the expropriating authorities to have to admit, by allowing interest, that the taking of property was arbitrary *ab initio*. Sometimes, local law and custom (e.g. Sharia) may prohibit outright the payment of interest and some other justification must therefore be sought to recover for the loss of use.

13.11. – War Damages Specific Indemnification

Is there an obligation to indemnify for war damages? There is a diversity of opinion on the subject. According to some authors, there exists no obligation under international law to indemnify investors who sustained damages because of war but they stress the fact that the State which decides to indemnify voluntarily anyway must avoid discrimination:

> "Under general international law, the host State has no obligation to compensate the losses suffered thereby, partly from the obligation not to discriminate against foreign investors, in case of indemnification, provided that the requirements of minimum due protection have been complied with." [249]

The United States seem to think that no such obligation to indemnify exists under international law, unless the war damages are caused by military operations undertaken by the authorities while knowing they would be completely futile:

> "Each Party shall accord restitution or pay compensation... in the event that covered investments suffer losses in its territory, owing to war or other armed conflict, revolution, state of national emergency, insurrection, civil disturbance, or similar events, that results from:
> - requisitioning of all or part of such investments by the Party's forces or authorities; or
> - destruction of all or part of such investments by the Party's forces or authorities that was not required by the necessity of the situation."(**Article 4**, model convention)

Actually, the US position is such that the State involved is held to the duty to indemnify war damages when, in the absence of diligence to limit them, its international responsibility is established. Some authors agree with the US position:

---
[249] SACERDOTI, G., *op. cit.*, p. 406, see footnote 161.

"The principle of non-responsibility does not at all exclude a duty to exercise a certain degree of vigilance. Should a host State not be responsible for the revolutionary events themselves, it may nonetheless be responsible for whatever its authorities have done (??? of what was necessary) or omitted to do in order to mitigate their consequences to the extent possible." [250]

The Amerasinghe case reaches the same conclusion and specifies that simple negligence is sufficient to entail the international liability of the State:

"According to doctrine, a violation of international law entailing the responsibility of the host State must be deemed established when such State has just failed in its obligation of diligence. It is not necessary to prove malice or negligence." [251]

ICSID's jurisprudence has had a renewal effect on this subject. An important decision was rendered on 27 June 1990 in the AAPL case, *Asian Agricultural Products Ltd. v. Sri Lanka*. The company had its seat in Hong Kong and had created a domestic company. The installations of the local company were destroyed by rebels.

Sri Lanka claimed that, according to international law, the State was not responsible for damages caused to the investments as a result of revolt. The tribunal rejected this theory. Its motivation was interesting, in that the decision was based on international law and on the provisions of the BIT between Hong Kong and Sri Lanka:

"There exists a generally accepted rule in international law, clearly expressed by international arbitration decisions and the doctrine according to which

- a host State on whose territory an insurrection occurs, is not responsible for loss or damages sustained by a foreign investor unless it may be proven that the Government of such State has failed in its obligation to furnish the protection required under treaties or international law in the circumstances;

---

[250] BIN CHENG, *op. cit.*, p. 229, see footnote 206.
[251] GAILLARD, Emmanuel, *op. cit.*, p. 330, see footnote 31.

- the failure to furnish such protection creates the State's responsibility for losses sustained, independently of the question whether the damages occurred during a rebel offensive or as a result of a counterattack by government forces." [252]

The arbitrators' argument was based on the applicable BIT provision, assuring "full protection" and "security" to investors. Another ICSID decision, in the AMT case (American Manufacturing and Trading Corporation) against the Zaire State led to the same conclusion. The main Zaire argument to support the denial of indemnification to AMT was based on article IX of the US-Zaire BIT:

"This treaty shall not supersede, prejudice or otherwise derogate from:

all laws and regulations, administrative practices or international legal obligations."

According to Zaire, the Zaire ordinance no. 69-044 dated 1 October 1966, regarding damages caused by the troubles, declared that any motion based on the common law having as its purpose the payment by the State of indemnities for damages caused by riots or by insurrections was not justifiable. The tribunal, probably basing its decision on the precedence of international law, rejected the Zaire argument:

"The obligation (guarantee of protection and security for investments) incumbent upon the State of Zaire is an obligation of vigilance such that Zaire, as a welcoming State for investments made by AMT, a U.S. corporation, must take all necessary action to assure the full enjoyment of the protection and security of its investment and could not with any validity draw support from its own legislation in order to shirk the consequences of such obligations." [253]

In the light of this innovating jurisprudence, it would seem desirable for investors that such a provision be included in their country's BIT's, despite the special character of the

---

[252] GAILLARD, Emmanuel, *op. cit.*, p. 330.
[253] GAILLARD, *op. cit.*, p. 440, see footnote 31.

damages. However, as was done in the German and British model conventions, this provision should be the object of a separate article, using the appropriate title "Compensation for losses."

In actual fact, these cases are not properly dealt with as expropriations. It is rather astonishing that some European BIT's require no such duty to indemnify. Usually, BIT's provide that investors who have sustained war damages are entitled to the same treatment as national investors or those of the most favoured nation.

This formula offers no guarantee. It is quite probable that national investors will not be indemnified and that nationals of third States will likewise be denied. What can then be the use of a reference to national treatment or treatment granted to the most favoured nation? In addition, the particular character of the damages should be taken into account, indemnification being clearly distinguished from restitution. There is satisfactory text in the Afro-Asian model convention:

> "The nationals, companies or State entities of one Contracting Party who suffer losses in the territory of the other Contracting Party resulting from:
> - requisitioning of their property by its forces or authorities;
> - destruction of their property by its forces or authorities which was not caused in combat actions or was not required by the necessity of the situation;
> - shall be accorded restitution or adequate compensation." (**Article 8**)

The text in paragraph (b) above could yet be improved, were it to mention also "damages arising from revolution, national states of emergency or revolt", expressly exclude "states of war between States" and limit indemnification to internal conflicts. Yet, this could become a figurative minefield. Conflicts today include overt and covert interference by foreign States, e.g. Iraq, Iran, Syria, Lebanon, Israel, Burundi, Rwanda, Kenya, Kosovo, Serbia, Montenegro, and others, not to speak of multinational interferences (NATO,

"Coalition of the Willing", the UN or the EU) not amounting to an actual, official conflict between States as such but the outcome of which depends upon the assistance/intrusion vel non of a neighboring State or States".

CHAPTER XIV
TRANSFERS & SUBROGATIONS

14.1. – Transfers relating to investments

Ultimately, most every investment made in a foreign locale will involve some kind of transfer in or out of that locale, traditionally capital to and from the investment, but also in more modern times certain intangibles assets, such as know how, management, and other "new forms of investments" (cfr. *supra*). Transfers of money are anticipated not only when the investment is made but also when dividends are declared from the investment, interest, license fees, royalties, etc. are paid back to the parent, when assets are purchased or sold, when capital reductions or liquidations proceeds are repatriated. On a more personal level, expatriate employees of the investor may want to transfer back to their home State salaries and other emoluments earned while working abroad. Every time a transfer is made in or out, a fabric of commitments, sometimes conflicting, is used to facilitate, channel or regulate it, even though, in peaceful times, much of the fabric operates nearly invisibly to the author or recipient of the transfer.

Executing an investment abroad, using it fruitfully, managing it, requires a lot of international money and capital goods transfers. On this level, payments and machines initially go from *foreign investors* to host country. Getting started with investments on foreign territory usually requires important advance financing. Precisely at the moment when carrying out the investment project requires the construction of buildings, the location of installations, the recruiting of local personnel, etc., sizable sums must be paid to or into the host country. Likewise, reverse flows from the host country to the investment country, such as in the event of liquidation or sale may be very significant not only to the investor but to the host State, affecting its overall balance of payment with other States and its economy overall. Clearly, the interests affected by transfers can generate tensions which international relations, on many a level, are designed to defuse or minimise.

Transfers are the technique used for international payments :

> "Today, the great majority of international payments occur without any use of bills of exchange, drafts or cheques. Transfer is the simple and rapid technique which removes the need for these instruments.
>
> Transfers are bank orders, issued on the instruction of a bank client and handed to a correspondent of the bank in the foreign locale. The orders direct the correspondent to pay a set sum either directly to a specified person or to another bank on behalf of a designated person." [254]

14.2. – CONVENTIONAL RULES ON TRANSFERS

14.2.1. – *Freedom of Transfer v. State's Power to Regulate*

Foreign investors see maximum freedom to transfer as a key condition for making or managing their investments. Investors need to have the guarantee that the local authorities will not place obstacles in the way of payments they are required to make in connection with the local enterprise and the investors' management of their investment. They must be able freely to dispose of their reserves in currency and their assets in the bank.

On the other hand, it is hardly possible to ignore balance of payments difficulties which some host countries may eventually experience. They need to have the power sometimes to regulate "capital inflow" and "capital outflow".

---

[254] SELLESLAGS, François, *op. cit.*, p. 109, see footnote 219.

There is therefore the possibility of tension between investors' wishes to exercise a very broad freedom to transfer and the host countries' imperative need sometimes to master the movement of capital funds:

> "The most restrictive method consists in requiring 'non-residents' to obtain an authorisation from the local Currency Exchange Institute, each time they wish to dispose of in-country funds they own, whether they wish to use them locally or transfer them abroad. Authorisations are granted more or less liberally, in parallel with the condition of the deficit in the country's balance of payments and the impoverishment of the countries' foreign currency reserves."[255]

To help ensure that the principle of free transfer will be recognised in a constructive manner, it must therefore be expressly included in BIT's.

14.2.2. – *BIT's transfer clauses*

14.2.2.1. *Reference to Domestic Law*

Many BIT's concluded during the period 1975-1985 provide, that transfers be done in accordance with national laws and regulations.

For example, the Belgium/Malaysia BIT, 22 November 1979, provides as follows:

> "Subject to its laws and regulations, each Contracting party in whose territory investments have been made by nationals or companies of the other Contracting Party, shall without undue delay allow the free transfer of:
>
> a) interests, dividends, benefits and other current returns;
>
> b) amortisation and contractual repayment of foreign loans for which exchange control approval has been obtained;
>
> c) amounts assigned to cover expenses relating to the management of the investment;
>
> d) additional contribution of capital necessary for the maintenance of development of the investment;

---

[255] SELLESLAGHS, *op. cit.*, p. 109, see footnote 219.

e) royalties and other payments deriving from rights of licence and commercial, administrative or technical assistance." (**Article 5**)

Another such example appears in the US/Estonia BIT, dated 19 April 1994:

"Notwithstanding the provisions of paragraphs 1 and 2 (freedom of transfer), either Party may maintain laws and regulations (a) requiring reports of currency transfer; and (b) imposing income taxes by such means as a withholding tax applicable to dividends or other transfers." (**Article IV**)

Australia was initially also in favour of a reference to domestic law:

"A Contracting Party shall, subject to and to the extent permitted by its laws and policies applicable from time to time, when requested, permit all funds of a national of the other Contracting Party related to an investment and activities associated with an investment in its territory, and earnings of personnel engaged from abroad in connection with an investment, to be transferred freely and without unreasonable delay..." (**Article 9**, Australia/ Poland BIT, 4 May 1991)

Obviously, this type of provision substantially limit investors' protection level. Even when applicable law favours investors at the time of their investment, it could conceivably change afterwards. It is therefore important that, if possible, the principle of freely transferable assets be part of the BIT, without any reference to national legislation.

14.2.2.2. Freedom of Transfer without Restrictions

In a large number of BIT's, the freedom to transfer principle is acknowledged without any reference to its submission to national legislation or the host State's financial and monetary policy:

"These Contracting Parties shall guarantee that payments relating to an investment may be transferred. The transfers shall be made in a freely convertible currency, without restriction or delay. Such transfers include in particular though not exclusively:
a) profits, interests, dividends and other current income;
b) funds necessary:

i) for the acquisition of raw or ancillary materials, semi-fabricated or finished products, or

　　ii) to replace capital assets in order to safeguard the continuity of an investment;

c) additional funds necessary for the development of an investment;

d) funds in repayment of loans;

e) royalties or fees;

f) earnings of natural persons;

g) the proceeds of sale or liquidation of the investment;

h) payments arising under article 7.

(article 5, BIT Netherlands/Costa Rica, 1 July 2001)

The NAFTA treaty emphasises the freedom to transfer principle. The drafters have apparently found it useful to make it clear that this freedom is limitless, in the sense that it is the investor who decides, independently, what the transfer will be and cannot be either required by local authorities or penalised if he chooses not to transfer:

> "Each Party shall permit transfers relating to an investment of an investor of another Party in the territory of the Party to be made freely and without delay...
>
> No Party may require its investors to transfer, or penalise its investors that fail to transfer, the income..." (**Article 1109** NAFTA agreement)

Australia has revisited its initial position which required compliance with national legislation, and now prefers actually for the free transfer principle to be totally unrestricted:

> "Each Contracting Party shall permit all transfers related to an investment of an investor of the other Contracting Party in its territory, to be made freely and without unreasonable delay." (**Article 9** BIT Australia/Mexico 23 August 2005)

The USA have an interesting formula which appears in some of its BIT's, stipulating that free transfer shall apply to both "capital inflow" and "capital outflow":

> "Each Party shall permit all transfers relating to a covered investment to be made freely and without delay into and out of its territory..." (Article 7, US/Uruguay BIT, 4 November 2005)

Sweden also seems to favour unconditional freedom to transfer and refers expressly, among allowable transfers expenses connected with the management of the investment:

> "Each Contracting Party shall allow without delay the transfer in a freely convertible currency of payments in connection with an investment, and shall include in particular though not exclusively:
> a) the returns;
> b) the proceeds from a total or partial sale or liquidation of any investment by an investor of the other Contracting party;
> c) funds in repayment of loans;
> d) a compensation according to article 4;
> e) the earnings of individuals, not being its nationals, who are allowed to work in connection with an investment in its territory and other amounts appropriated for the coverage of expenses connected with the management of the investment..." (**Article 6**, BIT Sweden/Guatemala, 12 February 2004)

14.2.2.3. *Exceptions to Freedom of Transfer*

Many BIT's stress freedom to transfer but temper the freedom with exceptions. Should the host State be faced with balance of payment problems, prohibitions against and limitations of transfers could be imposed on investors:

> "As regards the investments made in its territory, each Contracting Party shall agree subject to its rights, in the event of balance of payments difficulties, to exercise temporarily, equitably, and in good faith powers conferred by its laws and regulations, and guarantee free transfer of their assets and in particular though not exclusively..." (Article 6, Belgium/Sri Lanka BIT, 5 April 1982)

Italy's BIT's sometimes condition freedom to transfer on the investor's fiscal compliance:

> "Each Contracting party shall ensure that all payments relating to investments in its territory by an investor of the other Contracting Party may be freely transferred into and out of its territory without undue delay after the fiscal obligations have been met. Such transfers shall include, in particular, but not exclusively..." (Article V, Italy/Nicaragua BIT, 20 April 2004)

A less helpful formula appears in the French model convention where the principle of free transfers is confirmed but it is also weakened by the addition of a clause making it possible to institute numerous restrictive measures:

> "In the event of serious imbalance of its balance of payments, each of the Contracting Parties may temporarily apply restrictions upon transfers, provided that the Contracting Party concerned shall establish measures or a programme consistent with the criteria of the International Monetary Fund. These restrictions are to be imposed on a equitable basis, non-discriminatorily and in good faith." (**Article 7**, France/Mexico Agreement dated 12 November 1998)

There has been substantial change in the position taken by the US. In the past, freedom to transfer was of prime importance, only a few minor exceptions being allowed:

> "Each Contracting Party shall, with respect to investments by nationals or companies of the other Contracting party: grant such nationals and companies the free transfer of...
>
> Notwithstanding the preceding paragraphs either Party may maintain laws and regulations: a) prescribing procedures to be followed with respect to the transfers carried out expeditiously and do not impair the substance of the rights set forth above in paragraphs 1 and 2; b) requiring reports of currency transfer and c) imposing income taxes by such means as a withholding tax applicable to dividends or other transfers. Furthermore either Party may protect the rights of creditors, or ensure the satisfaction of judgments in adjudicatory proceedings, through the equitable non-discriminatory and good faith application of its law." (**Article V**, US/Zaire BIT,3 August 1984)

Since their adoption of a new model convention in 1994, the US are clearly allowing in their BIT's prohibitions against transfers:

> "Notwithstanding paragraphs 1 through 3 (freedom of transfer), a Party may prevent a transfer through the equitable, non-discriminatory, and good faith application of its laws relating to:
>
> a) bankruptcy, insolvency, or the protection of the rights of creditors;
>
> b) issuing, trading, or dealing in securities, futures, options, or derivatives;
>
> c) criminal or penal offences;

d) financial reporting or record keeping of transfers when necessary to assist law enforcement or financial regulatory authorities; or

e) ensuring compliance with orders or judgments in judicial or administrative proceedings.

(Article 7, BIT US/Uruguay, 4 November 2005)

In the model Afro-Asian convention, a very restrictive formula appears:

> "Each Contracting Party shall ensure that the nationals, companies or State entities of the other Contracting Party are allowed full facilities in the matter of the right to repatriation of capital and return on his or its investments... subject also to the right of the host State to impose reasonable restrictions for temporary periods in accordance with its laws to meet exceptional financial and economic situations..."
>
> (**Article 6**)

This formula offers few guarantees to investors in as much as it is rather difficult to foresee what local authorities mean by "reasonable restrictions" and "exceptional financial and economic situations. When definitions are scarce, restrictions may be imposed in arbitrary fashion, leaving investors no discretion to oppose them efficiently. They could, for instance, agree that no restriction whatsoever apply to personal compensation transfers.

In conclusion, it seems that two types of transfer clauses are acceptable: unlimited freedom to transfer and freedom to transfer with exceptions. The latter formula, however, should be couched in terms of expressly defined exceptions such as balance of payment difficulties, execution of judicial decisions, etc. It should be acknowledged that the "transfer with exceptions" formula is more likely to bridge investors' requirements with local authorities' legitimate balance of payments concerns. States are sometimes required to adopt restrictive measures against transfers by reason of their obligations as members of the International Monetary Fund.

14.3. – SUBROGATION

14.3.1. – *Insurance against Political Risks*

Since most every investment involves a transfer or transfers of some kind and at various times, and since many BIT's foresee the possibility of restrictions on transfers, some countries have, for their own political or economic reasons, adopted extremely restrictive rules governing transfers. Most every person or company making foreign investments has an awareness of the inherent commercial risks. These risks are those inherent to most any industrial and commercial activities. Investors must and can be placed in a position such that they can best minimise the consequences flowing from these risks.

However, sometimes, foreign investors are exposed to extra political risks, that they could not reasonable anticipate or guard against, jeopardising their investments as well as any transfers from it.

Those political risks may range from measures privative of property rights, blocking bank assets, occasionally prohibiting transfers outright ("blocking" funds) or requiring them to be converted into a local currency the owners may not wish to hold, more generally, any kind of damage to the invested assets flowing from some specific government action or even armed attack. Industrialised States that wish to encourage foreign investments have created national guarantee systems which are designed to assure investors they will be given an indemnity (sometimes only partial) to compensate them for the damages sustained as a consequence of politico-economic measures taken against them. These insurance contracts provide for indemnifying the investor against such risks and, in turn, subrogating to the insurer the rights of the indemnified investors against the host State.

14.3.2. – *International Recognition of Subrogation*

Insurance contracts, providing subrogation and transfer of the rights of the indemnified investor to the national insurance agency of one Contacting Party, do not have per se international relevance. The subrogation should be explicit. International subrogation is not automatic. The first question that may be asked is whether a subrogee insurer qualifies as an "investor" under the Definitions provision of the treaty (see *infra* Para 12.6) Furthermore, payment by the insurer of indemnities provided by the insurance contract does not necessarily lead to a recognition by the host State of the validity of the subrogation. The insurance contract is a *"res inter alios acta"* for the host State. As a consequence, the host state may neither benefit from the advantages nor suffer the disadvantages flowing from a contract to which it was not a party: *"res inter alios acta, aliis nec nocet, nec prodest."*

The expropriating State therefore could not claim that because the investor is insured and has open to him a means of being indemnified, the State need not compensate damages which are compensable under the *insurance* agreement.

Official recognition of subrogation rights, however, may be acknowledged by way of a clause in the conventions. It would be sufficient for the States which are parties to the conventions – the host State and the investors' State – to agree mutually to recognise the right of subrogation in favour of an insurer which gave its guarantee to an investor investing on the territory of one of the Contracting Parties.

14.3.3. – *Multilateral Approach*

Some authors fear an substantial increase in interstate conflicts, should subrogation be allowed in favour of States or their official insurance agencies:

> "The issue of compensation is thus more likely to develop into an international dispute between the home State and the host State in case of subrogation. As a consequence, the conflict avoiding purpose

of the home State's national investment insurance scheme would be frustrated while the investment climate of the host State may be affected." [256]

States have tried to establish a multilateral international investment guarantee agency, which could be substituted for States and cover political risks which are inherent to international investments. There have been efforts for many years, under the aegis of OECD, for the purpose of creating such a multilateral system of investment guarantees. These efforts have not been very successful.

After many fruitless efforts by OECD, a multilateral convention was finally achieved on 11 October 1985, under the auspices of the World Bank (Multilateral Investment Guarantee Agency MIGA). Just like national law systems, MIGA's international activities are devised to promote foreign direct investments (FDI) in particular on the territories of less developed nations:

> "The objective of the multilateral investment guarantee agency shall be to encourage the flow of investments for productive purpose among member countries, and in particular to developing countries, to serve its objective, the Agency shall:
>
> issue guarantees, including coinsurance and reinsurance against non-commercial risks in respect of investments in a member country which flow from other member countries." (article 2)

Issuance of guarantees is subject to a few conditions: the contribution investments make to the development of the member host States, the consistency of the investments with local law, the agreement of the host States to grant sufficient legal protection to investors and their investments.

MIGA covers non-commercial risks: transfer restrictions, expropriations or similar measures, breach of contract, damages sustained by reason of military action or civil war. The guarantee does not cover the entirety of the claims. The added value that the MIGA convention brings, when com-

---

[256] SACERDOTI, G., *op. cit.*, p. 109, see footnote 161.

pared to national systems or BITS, should not be overestimated. One of the disadvantages of MIGA resides in the requirement for the host country's consent. The legal value of the Act is also affected by the rather weak formulation ("soft law") of some of its provisions. The grant of a fair and equitable treatment for investors is not seen as "a duty" on the part of the host States but as one of the conditions that are to be met for the grant to be made in the first place. It is therefore a kind of enabling clause only. How can it be proven that the member state fails to extend fair treatment to investors? The failure to respect enabling clauses does not result in international liability for the offending State and any judicial proceeding, be it through arbitration or otherwise, filed against such State, only had a meagre chance of success.

Consequently, it is preferable for investors who seek a financial guarantee against non-commercial risks, to conclude a contract with a national guarantee organism, so long as a bilateral agreement exists for investments with the host State. MIGA, therefore, may be less than what it may first appear and its guarantees are not eagerly sought after. For example, according to information provided by the office of the Secretary of MIGA, the number of local investors who have sought that agency's guarantee is insignificant. ONDD, the leading Belgian overseas credit insurance, "Ducroire-Del-Credere," participates with banks in the coverage of those risks but, so far, has not contracted with MIGA.

14.3.4. – Bilateral Approach

The NAFTA Treaty, does not contain a subrogation clause. As to bilateral relations, most BIT's address directly the issue of international recognition of subrogation and contain a subrogation clause recognising that the rights of the investor who has been indemnified, through the application of a guarantee or insurance contract, are transferred to the insurer.

However, subrogation clauses have greatly evolved in their formulation. In some agreements, the Contracting States used to be satisfied with a provision that contemplated subrogation without making it clear how the procedure for the settlement of litigation regarding the investments concerned would proceed. This is obviously an embarrassing shortcoming since, in the event of arbitration, for example, it is necessary to know whether the arbitration organism will acknowledge the insurer's subrogation rights. Such a clause appears in the Bleu/India BIT, dated 31 October 1997, among others:

> "Where one Contracting Party, or its designated Agency has guaranteed any indemnity against non-commercial risks in respect of an investment by any of its investors in the territory of the other Contracting Party and has made payment to such investors in respect of their claims under the Agreement, the other Contracting party agrees that the first Contracting party or its designated agency is entitled by virtue of subrogation to exercise the rights and assert the claims of those investors. The subrogated rights or claims shall not exceed the original rights or claims of such investors." (**Article 8**)

It is therefore not clear whether the Contracting States are in agreement as to whether the investor or the insurance agency may file for arbitration. Still, the said BIT expressly states that:

> "At any stage of the arbitration proceedings or of the execution of an arbitral award, none of the Contracting Parties involved in a dispute shall be entitled to raise as an objection the fact that the investor who is opposing party in the dispute has received compensation totally or partially covering his losses pursuant to an insurance policy or to the guarantee provided for in Article 8 of this Agreement."

A similar provision appears in the Netherlands/Laos BIT, dated 16 May 2003:

> "If the investments of a national of one Contracting Party are insured against non-commercial risks or otherwise give rise to payment of indemnification in respect of such investments under a system established by law, regulation or government contract, any subrogation of the insurer or re-insurer or Agency designated by one Contract-

ing party to the rights of the said national pursuant to the terms of such insurance or under any other indemnity given shall be recognised by the other Contracting Party" (**Article 8**)

On the other hand, the Bleu/Bangladesh BIT, dated 22 May 1981 includes a subrogation clause, providing *expressis verbis* for the investor's right to proceed in arbitration :

> "If either Contracting party or its designated Agency, makes payment, to its own nationals or companies, under a guarantee it has given in respect of an investment or any part thereof in the territory of the other Contracting Party, the latter Contracting Party shall recognise :
>
> a) the assignment, whether under law or pursuant to a legal transaction, of any right or claim from the party indemnified to the former Contracting party (or its designated Agency), and that the former Contracting party (or its designated Agency) is entitled by virtue of subrogation to exercise the rights and enforce the claims of such a party.
>
> Any such payment made by one Contracting Party, or any public institution of this Party, to its nationals in pursuance of this Agreement shall not affect the rights of the Nationals to take proceedings to the International Centre for Settlement of Investment Disputes in accordance with article 6 of this Agreement, nor shall it affect the right of the said nationals to carry on the proceedings until the dispute is settled."

14.3.5. – *Other Bilateral Formulas*

The USA deviate from the European practice. US BIT's do not contain any confirmation of subrogation. Under the topic, "settlement of indemnity, disputes," it states, however, that the payment of an indemnity paid in furtherance of a guarantee cannot have any influence on the character of an arbitration procedure filed :

> "In any proceeding involving an investment dispute, a Party shall not assert as a defence, counterclaim, right of set-off or for any other reason, that indemnification or other compensation for all or part of the alleged damages has been received or will be received pursuant to an insurance or guarantee contract (Article IX.7 US/Zaire, 3 August 1984)."

The motive for the U.S. strategy is probably inspired from the fact that the U.S. have concluded a great many separate guarantee agreements. In the event of a conflict, both the BIT's and these agreements will apply. Like the USA, France has concluded several separate agreements providing for financial guarantees for investments. However, the right of subrogation is recognised *"expressis verbis"* in its BIT's:

> "If one of the Contracting Parties or an agency qualified by such Party, by reason of an agreement of guarantee given for an investment made on the territory of the other Contracting Party, makes payment to an investor, such Party or agency will *ipso facto* be subrogated to the rights and actions of such investor, including the right to resort to international arbitration, in accordance with the provisions of article 8 of the present agreement." (Article 10 of the France/Guatemala Agreement dated 27 May 1998)

The validity of this provision is dubious insofar as it is not sure if it may be invoked in an ICSID arbitration procedure. According to **Article 25** of the Washington Convention, only litigation between a Contracting State and a national of another Contracting State may use the arbitration procedure. A government insurance organism is not a "national of another Contracting State" and therefore has no access to ICSID's arbitration (cfr *infra*).

Paragraph 1 and 2 of article 10 of the French BIT also include another significant inconvenience:

> "To the extent that legislation of one of the Contracting Parties provides a guarantee for investments made abroad, such Party may be granted such guarantee, within the scope of a case by case analysis, for investments made by such Party's investors in the territory of the other Contracting Party.
>
> Investments made by investors of one of the Contracting Parties in the territory of the other may obtain such guarantee only if they have received prior consent from the other Contracting Party."

This provision seems inspired by MIGA (cfr *supra*). However, it is difficult to see the usefulness of this requirement, unless it is the State itself that is the insurer. An organism providing Governmental insurance must be able, fully independently, to decide to accept or deny a guarantee request submitted by a national investor.

14.3.6. – *Link between Subrogation and Dispute Settlement Procedure*

As said above, the recognition of subrogation raises the question of the continuation and the operation of the dispute settlement procedure set out in the BIT provisions. It is not quite clear that the subrogated insurance agency of a Contracting Party, has jus standi, alone or with the investor, and may continue or introduce an arbitration procedure in relation to an investment affected by measures of expropriation or nationalisation.

Some BIT's contain no subrogation clause at all. They imply therefore no acknowledgment of the rights of the subrogated insurer. In such a case, the arbitration procedure between host State and investor, as provided for in the BIT's, is unproblematic. The investor himself will file the arbitration procedure in order to obtain indemnification for the damages he sustained. Should he obtain an award of indemnification, he should of course contact his insurer and reimburse him for what he has received, in as much as he cannot collect twice for the same damages, which would amount to unjust enrichment. Thus, insurance and subrogation constitute an internal matter between investor and insurer. It would be wise to include in the BIT a clause prohibiting the host State from indemnifying the investor, if he is already insured (US formula).

Some BIT's do contain a subrogation clause and an accompanying conventional acknowledgment of the insurer's rights but still are silent on the subrogated insurer's *jus standi*. However, in accordance with the applicable clauses of such BIT's, settlement of disputes by arbitration remains open to the investor. In such a case, the outcome will depend on the position taken by the arbitration institution selected by the investor. Should such institution be willing to recognise subrogation, the insurer will of course be able to file a procedure and even use the investor's help to pursue its interests. Should the investor be indemnified, the matter becomes a mere internal settlement between insured and insurer.

A more limited number of BIT's contain a clause providing for subrogation in favour of a State insurer, meaning that the *jus standi*, in an insurance case, is in effect transferred to the State of the investor:

> "If any of the Contracting Parties makes payment to any of its nationals or companies under a guarantee it has granted in respect of an investment made in the territory of another Contracting Party, the latter Contracting Party shall, without prejudice to the rights of the former Contracting Party under Article IX and X (dispute between the parties-arbitration) recognise the assignment of any right, title or claim of such national or company to the former Contracting Party and the subrogation of the former Contracting Party to any such right, title or claim. This however, does not necessarily imply a recognition on the part of the latter Contracting Party of the merits of any case or the amount of any claim arising therefrom." (Article VIII, Asian agreement, 15 December 1987)

Australia understands that such a formula could pose problems. She includes, in her BIT's, a subrogation clause which reserves to the investor jus standi with respect to the subrogated rights:

> "If a Contracting party or an agency of a Contracting Party makes a payment to an Investor of that Contracting Party under a guarantee, a contract of insurance or other form of indemnity it has granted in respect of an investment for non-commercial risks, the other Contracting Party shall recognise the subrogation or transfer of any right or title in respect of such investment. The subrogated or transferred right or claim shall not be greater than the original right or claim of the investor.
>
> Where such subrogation or transfer has occurred, only the following persons may pursue the subrogated or transferred rights or claims against the other Contracting Party:
>
> a) the Investor authorised to act on behalf of the Contracting Party or of the Agency of the Contracting party making the payment, or a corporation operating in accordance with commercial principles..."

The net result of this provision is that the *jus standi* will be claimed by the investor, as a private party, and that, in the arbitration procedure, the party opposing the host State will not be a "Contracting Party".

Canada uses a similar formula in its OECD based BIT's as well as in its NAFTA based BIT's:

"If a Contracting Party or any agency thereof makes a payment to any of its investors under a guarantee or insurance it has contracted in respect of an investment, the other Contracting Party shall recognise the validity of the subrogation in favour of the former Contracting Party or agency thereof to any right or title held by the investor.

A contracting party or an agency thereof which is subrogated in the rights of a investor in accordance with paragraph (1) of this article, shall be entitled in all circumstances to the same rights as those of the investor in respect of the investment concerned and its related returns.

Such rights may be exercised by the Contracting Party or any agency thereof or by the investor if the Contracting Party or any agency thereof so authorises." (Article VIII, BIT Canada/ Hungary, 21 November 1993)

It should be noted that the investor may act on his own in the arbitration procedure for the settlement of disputes relating to his investment. This provision may remove an obstacle to arbitration that would arise from a refusal by the arbitration organism to recognise subrogation.

14.3.7. – *Subrogation in the Washington Convention*

As previously said, subrogation is not acknowledged in the Washington Convention. **Article 25** regarding ICSID's jurisdiction does not mention it nor does it mention guarantee nor investment insurance.

However that article expressly provides that only litigation between one of the contracting States and a national of another Contracting State shall have standing before the tribunal. Legal essays published about the application of the Washington Convention confirm that public insurers may not be considered as "nationals of a Contracting State" and that consequently they may not be substituted for the investor himself whom they may have indemnified when an arbitration request is filed :

> "If the subrogee were a private insurer, 'a national of another Contracting state', there would appear to be no difficulty in it appearing as a party in ICSID proceedings in place of the investor;
>
> assuming that the host State has given its consent to the subrogation. However, when the subrogee is a governmental or an intergovernmental entity, it would appear that not being a 'national of another contracting state', such an entity could not avail itself of the investor's right to have recourse to ICSID arbitration against the host Contracting State." [257]

The point made is to avoid that ICSID become a forum for confrontation between States. In this respect, authors refer to the "depoliticisation" of the system of settlement of litigation relative to investments.

Hence, insofar as subrogation and *jus standi* in arbitration cases are concerned, several BIT's do not apply them but it seems the States concerned are not aware of this result. Were subrogation in favour of a State insurance agency to be acknowledged, and at the same time, were ICSID to be designated as the sole arbitration venue having jurisdiction, there would manifestly be a *"contradictio in terminis"*. In effect, ICSID does not recognise subrogation in favour of a Contracting State or of its State insurance agent.

An example of this embarrassing situation is the Bleu/ Morocco BIT, dated 13 April 1999. Subrogation in favour of the insurer, acting under a legal or contractual guarantee, is recognised. The BIT further states that investment related disputes are settled by arbitration before ICSID. Thus, in the case of the Belgian national insurance agency, the "Office du Ducroire" (OND), should it attempt to file an arbitration request with ICSID, it will be denied. And yet, in spite of the

---

[257] SACERDOTI, G., *op. cit.*, p. 409, see footnote 161.

non-acknowledgment by ICSID of subrogation in favour of a public insurer, the inclusion of a clause about it in the BIT's is still desirable for the following reasons :

"1. It is important that the Contracting Parties to a BIT be bound by such a clause since it cannot be excluded that a request will be filed in arbitration. In a first phase of litigation, the investor will perhaps prefer, in concert with his insurer, to seek a non-contentious arrangement with the host State which took measures privative of private property rights.

It may be to the investor's advantage to be *discreetly* assisted by his insurer during the negotiations with the host State, such assistance being provided, independently of the subrogation, by virtue of an agreement between them. Besides, it is possible that the insurer will be making provisory payments, with the proviso that the investor who has so been indemnified will exercise in his own name his right to have recourse to arbitration. In the event the investor were to choose ICSID as the arbitration tribunal, this initiative would be interesting, since the insurer could not then participate through subrogation in the ICSID proceeding.

2. According to most BIT's, the investor may choose the arbitration tribunal. He could therefore choose a tribunal which recognises subrogation. By choosing the International Chamber of Commerce as the arbitration tribunal, which, in principle, recognises subrogation, the insurer would be in a position to intervene, at least to the extent that domestic law or an international convention allows him to have his right of subrogation confirmed." [258]

---

[258] That would be the case for a Belgian investor who is insured : on the one hand the law of 31 August 1939 allows full subrogation in favour of the DelCredere institution, and on the other, provided the host State has recognised subrogation under the BIT, all conditions for the insurer's intervention would have been met.

14.3.8. – *State Insurance Agencies vs. ICSID's subrogation*

ICSID absolutely wants to avoid that investment related disputes, to be resolved by international arbitration by the Centre, ever become interstate disputes. The ICSID Convention's great innovation is that, for the very first time in the history of international arbitration, a private investor shall have direct access (without the intervention of the State of his nationality) to an international arbitration tribunal and thereby can sue a State.

Under these conditions, a State insurance agency will find itself in the impossible position of an inability to intervene in favour of the investor and before the ICSID Centre in an arbitration procedure, simply because a dispute between a State insurance agency and the host State is a State against State matter and ICSID will not hear it.

At first sight, and according to the above position strongly held by ICSID and legal authors, the answer to this problem is yes, that is, the insurer would be helpless, because of the non-recognition of subrogation. That situation bears a little more study. Because of the interests involved, all elements of the dispute should be looked at.

First, it is appropriate to note that subrogation in insurance law is a bit different from that in civil law. In the latter, a person who has paid a debtor's obligation due to a creditor usually steps into the shoes of the creditor, *pro rata* to the total amount of the debt. In insurance law, the insurer pays off his own debt to the insured and not that of a third party. The insurer's contract holds him to the payment of the indemnity. This situation does not exclude the possibility that the insured may obtain, in arbitration, an amount that is superior to the amount insured.

The payment of an indemnity therefore does not necessarily mean that the insured has lost his right to arbitration. There must also have been proven to exist, through a written agreement, the conditions under which the investor may exercise such a right in respect of the host State. In the event where the host State is held to be liable for the payment of a sum which exceeded the insured value, the investor must disgorge to the insurer a corresponding part of the indemnities he has received. He cannot lay claim to these indemnities because that would result in unjust enrichment. However, he is entitled to whatever is left over. Both the insurer and the insured therefore have an interest in filing an arbitration proceeding after the indemnities have been paid : the insurer wants to recover the indemnities paid and the insured wants to be compensated in full. In fact, it is current practice that the insurer will file a request for arbitration or a judicial complaint not in its own name but in that of the insured :

> "It is generally accepted that an insurer which has been subrogated to the rights of the insured, may file his claim in respect to third parties debtor, in the name of the insured and not in its own name. There is a tacit agreement, allowing the name swap between insured and insurer." [259]

The Belgian Supreme Court has confirmed the legitimacy of this practice in its decision of 21 October 1941 (Revue générale d'assurances – RGAR, 1979, p. 4499).

Normally, any arbitration proceeding, whether filed with ICSID or with any other institution, will be filed by the insured, in his own name and in *discreet* concert with the subrogated insurer. There may be a contract between the insured and the insurer providing for logistic support to be supplied by the insurer, an account then being required after indemnities have been determined by the arbitration tribunal, the settlement of costs, etc.

Even though such a contract may be *"res inter alios acta"* with respect to the ICSID and even though the arbitration request was filed by the investor and in his own name, there

---

[259] VANDEPUTTE, Robert, *Inleiding tot het Verzekeringsrecht*, Antwerpen, Edition De Standaard, 1978, p. 116.

is no reason for which the jurisdiction of the ICSID may be questioned. Besides, article 18 of the Washington Convention states:

> "Each party may be represented or assisted by agents, counselors or attorneys whose names and authority must be notified by such Party to the Secretary General, who will inform accordingly, without delay, the Tribunal and the other Contracting Party."

A member of the insurer's staff therefore could, in principle, assist the investor in his arbitration proceeding. In the event the investor does not want to have recourse to ICSID, dismayed perhaps by the eventual difficulties inherent in the procedure, then if he chooses another arbitration institution such as the CCI, the insurer who has been subrogated will probably want to be included explicitly to the procedure. The arbitration request could take the form of a joint request where the subrogated insurer as well as the investor are named as co plaintiffs. In this situation, it would also be indispensable that there be an agreement between the insured and the insurer so their legal relationships may be made clear within the framework of the arbitration method elected.

Another element to consider is the legal status of the State insurance agency involved. The question is whether a dispute between an insurance agency, created by one of the Contracting States but not managed by it must perforce be considered as a dispute between States.

Another point to check would be the interpretation by the arbitrators of **Article 25(1)** of the Washington Convention:

> "The jurisdiction of the Centre extends to conflicts of a legal nature between a Contracting State (or a public collective or organism so designed by such State to the centre) and the national of another Contracting state..."

To our knowledge, there is only one decision by ICSID, relatively recent (24 May 1999), addressing the interpretation of this provision. In the litigation between "Czechoslovakia Obchodni Bank", a privatised bank and the Slovakian

Republic, (Case ARB/97/4), one of the arguments of the Republic of Slovakia contesting the jurisdiction of ICSID was that article 15(l) of the Convention was violated because the plaintiff was not "a national of another Contracting state". The CSOB was, according to the opposing party "an agency of the Czechoslovakian State, the latter being the sole beneficiary of the solution of the litigation". It is useful to examine some of the reasons invoked by the Arbitration tribunal to deny this argument and re-assert its jurisdiction.

According to the arbitrators, the term "corporation", such as is used in **Article 25** does not require that it be in the hands of private parties. The State may well be the owner of a corporation

> "The legislative history of the Convention does provide some answers, however, that bear on the issues presented in this case. It indicates that the term 'juridical person,' as employed in Article 25, and, hence, the concept of national was not intended to be limited to privately owned companies, but to embrace also wholly or partially government owned companies. This interpretation has found general acceptance."

Thus, the fact that the "corporation" is under the control of the State does not per se deprive the insurer of the right to arbitrate before the ICSID:

> "For, as has been shown above, such ownership or control (of the State) alone will not disqualify a company under the here relevant test from filing a claim with the Centre as a 'national of another contracting State.'"

The tribunal then stressed that the fact that the corporation was acting under the orders of the State and in the interest of the State could not exclude the CSOB from the arbitration proceeding, as a "non-national of another Contracting State".

What is the deciding point is the fact that a State "corporation" is concerned with commercial activities and not governmental activities. It is therefore the nature of the activities that ought to be considered:

> "But in determining whether CSOB, in discharge of these functions, exercised governmental functions, the focus must be on the nature of these activities and not their purpose. While it cannot be doubted that in performing the above mentioned activities, CSOB was promoting the government policies or purposes of the State, the activities themselves were essentially commercial rather than governmental in nature." [260]

It is evident that this decision required an important evolution with respect to the very firm and negative attitude theretofore adopted by legal authors. The nature of the By-Laws of the insurer must therefore be studied in depth, with an eye to the grounds listed in the decision.

It would seem that the commercial nature of the activities of most insurance agencies of Contracting Parties can hardly be doubted. They are autonomous public bodies and their commercial decisions are not influenced by State orders. The Contracting State my not give orders to the designated agency for accepting some companies as clients.

Nonetheless, the right of the insurance agencies to be subrogated remains on delicate ground. In order to know for certain what the position of ICSID will be, an initiative should be undertaken by the authorities. Actually, **Article 25(2)b** provides for the duty to reveal to the Centre all "public collectivities or organisms (or agencies) depending from the State". We can conclude therefrom that member States may consult ICSID to determine whether an insurer is or is not to be considered as an organism or agency of the State. If it is yet not so designated, then a designation could be made.

It is, however, true that arbitration tribunals decide for themselves whether any case falls within their jurisdiction or not. In this case, it is not so much a request for its advice on the jurisdictional scope of ICSID but on the State nature of the insurance agencies. ICSID's jurisdiction is conditioned upon its attitude on this topic.

---

[260] Author's private archives.

CHAPTER XV
APPLICABLE LAW ON INVESTMENTS

15.1. – Basic principle: application of Domestic Law

Unless otherwise provided, the law applicable to investments made on the territory of any given State will be that State's domestic law. As stated in an earlier chapter, investments, as a general rule, made by national investors take on a national character and investments made by foreign investors bare a foreign character. However, investments made by non-nationals are not, by reason of their foreign status, given any relief from obligations imposed by legislation or regulation to which national investors are subject.

Thus, domestic law will be applied for investment permits and for any other aspect of the treatment reserved for investors and their investments, whether they are national or international. Investors have, in principle, no freedom to choose the law which will apply to their enterprises in the territory of the State where it is located.

That constraint is a logical application of the sovereignty principle. Immixture of foreign States, or their law, in the internal affaires of a host State is incompatible with the sovereignty of that State. When reference is made to *"territorial sovereignty,"* what is meant is that everything that happens on the territory of a given State falls under the authority of agencies of that State. When reference is made to *"personal sovereignty"*, on the other hand, what is meant is the dominion which a given State has over the nationals who belong to it or to which they owe allegiance. Each State determines in sovereign manner, on the basis of its legislation, who possesses its nationality. Investors, as a subset of a State's nationals, are deemed to have the nationality of the State of which they are nationals.

Of course, the constraint may also be seen as a right of which, barring discriminatory laws or regulations, foreign investors may avail themselves in connection with their relations with agencies of the host State.

15.2. – HOST STATES' POSITION

After gaining independence, less developed countries have forcefully rejected the immixture of other States in their internal politics, highlighting their entitlement to national sovereignty. They did not wish, within the scope of international conventions, to stray from the application of their domestic laws and jeopardise the jurisdiction of their national tribunals. UN resolutions regarding the right to nationalise private property, adopted at the behest of less developed countries typically demonstrate that attitude:

> "In any case, where the question of compensation gives rise to a controversy, it shall be settled under the domestic law of the nationalising State and by its tribunals, unless it is freely and mutually agreed by all States concerned that other peaceful means be sought on the basis of the sovereignty equality of States and in accordance with the principle of free choice of means." (**Article 2**. Charter of economic Rights and Duties of States, 1974)

During the last two decades, there has been a tendency, however, among less developed, "emerging", nations to temper, particularly when economic interests are involved, their expressions of sovereign will which, formerly, some foreign observers could have qualified as unnecessarily shrill. This softening is noticeable in the Seoul Declaration published by the ILA (International Law Association) in 1987, to which less developed countries have also agreed:

> "disputes on questions related to international economic relations have to be settled by peaceful means chosen by the parties concerned,

in particular by recourse to international adjudication, international or transnational arbitration, or other international procedures for the settlement of disputes. The principle of exhaustion of local remedies shall be observed where applicable." (Report of the 62nd Conference 1987)

Actually, even the requirement that local means of settling disputes, with recourse to local judicial or arbitration tribunals, be first exhausted, is no longer considered a requirement by most less developed countries. In BIT's, the requirement for the first exhaustion of local remedies is often adapted to meet a less restrictive standard.

15.3. – NEED FOR INTERNATIONAL RULES

In an investor's international relations with a host State, its nationals or other international investors in such State, the exclusive application of domestic law does not suffice to address questions which flow from the peculiar nature of their nationality and that of their investments. Unconditional application of domestic law may be weakened or limited when operating in an international context:

> "Territorial sovereignty of a State undeniably governs all foreign investments by its legislation, which is constrained only by pertinent rules of conventional or common international law." [261]

15.3.1. – *International Common Law*

It is a basic imperative that international investors must be able to enjoy the legal protection and security of international common law. Most countries are no longer opposed to this concept.

Using bilateral and multilateral conventions, the Contracting States may agree that, besides domestic law, other rules of law may be applied. In the BIT's, there are frequent ref-

---

[261] NGUYEN, Huu-Truu, "La suisse et les investissements", *Revue générale de droit international public*, juin 1988, pp. 654-657.

erences to the application of rules and principles of international law. These principles are applicable to international investments because of the precedence given international law over national law. Even when no express reference to international common law appears in a Treaty, investors should, in principle, be able to claim that it be applied :

> "JUILLARD, commenting on the draft OECD convention, notes that although its reference to fair and equitable treatment is blurry, there is no doubt about the fact that 'fair and equitable' treatment is a principle; that this principle is a general principle of international law; and that the general principle of international law exists independently of the conventional support expressing it." [262]

Nonetheless, it is extremely useful to be able to rely on conventional references which expressly make international common law applicable.

15.3.2. – *Importance of BIT's conventional rules*

The rather rudimentary character of international common law, in matters of international investments, make the entering into BIT's between industrialised States, exporters of capital, and host States, importers of capital, an important step. Conventional practice moves States' legal obligations regarding investors to the level of conventional international law :

> "One could say that a Bilateral Investment Treaty is an internationalisation vector, because it subjects to international law legal relationships, which, were they otherwise free of such constraint, would depend upon national law – be it the national law of the State of the investor's nationality or that of the territorial law applied where the investment is made." [263]

---

[262] Www.oecd.org/investment.
[263] JUILLARD, Patrick, "Symposium : treatment, protection and insurance of investments", *Droit et pratique du commerce international*, janvier 1987, pp. 9-63.

15.3.3. – Conflict of Law Rules: Domestic law v. BIT's

The possibility that the domestic law of a host State contains provisions which are, in certain respects, more favourable than the provisions of a BIT, cannot be excluded. Hence, it would be regrettable if, in such a case, the national law could not be applied. Effectively, the precedence of international law over national law must be respected but it is recommended that measures be undertaken so that domestic law provisions which are in fact more favourable to investors be not systematically disregarded.

Investors must consider not only the provisions of local law and of bilateral and multilateral conventions but also the rules of international common law as the overall legal climate within which they are constrained to operate. In the event of inconsistencies between national legislation and international acts, investors who look for maximum security for their investments must feel assured that the legal or conventional norms applied to them will be the most favourable. Yet, inexplicably, only a minority of BIT's address this particular topic. The US model convention speaks to it in the following fashion:

> "This Treaty shall not derogate from any of the following that entitle an investor of a Party or a covered investment to treatment more favorable than that accorded by this Treaty:
>
> 1. laws or regulations, administrative practices or procedures, or administrative or adjudicatory decisions of a Party;
> 2. international legal obligations (other BIT's) of a Party; or
> 3. obligations assumed by a Party, including those contained in an investment authorisation or an investment agreement."
> (**Article 16**, non-derogation)

The German model convention sees it another way:

> "If the legislation of either Contracting State or obligations under international law (other BIT's) existing at present or established hereafter between the Contracting States in addition to this Treaty contain a regulation, whether general or specific, entitling investments by

investors of the other Contracting State to a treatment more favourable than is provided for by this Treaty, such regulation shall to the extent that it is more favourable prevail over this Treaty." (**Article 8**)

Italy uses the same formula :

> "If a matter is governed both by this Agreement and another international Agreement to which both Contracting parties are signatories, and by general international law provision, the most favourable provision shall be applied to the Contracting parties and to their investors...
>
> Whenever the treatment accorded by one Contracting Party to the investors of the other Contracting party, according to its laws and regulations or other provisions or specific contract or investment authorisation or agreements, is more favourable than that provided for under this Agreement, the most favourable treatment shall apply." (Article XII)

It is the precedence of the most favoured nation rule that is stressed in these various provisions. However, the applicable law problem is not entirely resolved by these *formulae*. Problems of interpretation may arise between the host State and investors and involve the application of one or another legal rule. In order to avoid endless argumentation and provide the best guarantees to investors, they themselves must be able to choose the law which appears to them to be most favourable in any given context. Examples of such clauses follow :

> "In the event of any matter being provided as well in this Agreement as in an international agreement or in the national regulations of one of the Contracting Parties, no provision of this Agreement shall prevent a national or legal person of one of the Contracting parties who possesses investments, goods, rights or interests, in the territory of the other Contracting Party, from availing itself of the most favourable provisions." (**Article 7**, BIT Bleu/Korea, 20 December, 1974)

Another example appears in the Bleu/Uzbekistan BIT, of 17 April 1998 :

> "If an issue relating to investments is covered both by this Agreement and by the national legislation of one Contracting Party or by

international conventions, the investors of the other Contracting party shall be entitled to avail themselves of the provisions that are the most favourable to them." (Article 7)

The latter formulae, leaving to the investor the choice of applicable law are by far preferable.

15.4. – STATE CONTRACTS

15.4.1. – *General Concept*

Beside international treaties and agreements between States (so-called "Interstate Acts"), there are vehicles of international law, generally going under the name of "State Contracts", and consisting of contracts between a State, as one party, and a private contractor, as the other party, who may be a physical person or a corporation.

P. MAYER has analysed well the specificity of State Contracts:

> "What is involved is:
> - a contract between a sovereign State, that is, a State which is subject to international law, and a foreign firm, and
> - a contract that has been agreed on outside of the legal scope of the other Contracting State (this second characteristic derives from the first).

The primary characteristic of a State Contract is that it is entered into within the international legal order as a result of the fact that one of the Contracting Parties, is a State, acting "*Jure imperii*", in fully sovereign fashion, and therefore subject to international law. The legal nature of this kind of contract, its qualification as a "State Contract" is therefore determined by the legal capacity of one of the Contracting Parties. Many authors do not agree with this idea and do not see an international character to a transaction between a State and a private party. Nonetheless, State Contracts, in fact, do not necessarily have to be between parties that are subject to international law.

Plainly, should the private party be of the same nationality as that of the host State, it is harder to claim, credibly, that the contract's character is international, even though the State itself is an international construct. The State's internationality derives from its co-existence and relationship with other States but it does not necessarily follow that all of its transactions are international. The State necessarily has a "national" identity when dealing with its own nationals and, on occasion, its non-nationals residing on its territory. What allows a specific transaction to be potentially international is the foreign character of the private party as well as the foreign character of the transaction. A State Contract, involving a foreign investment by a foreign national has the requisite foreign character to make it international.

The thesis that a State Contract with a foreign national must be seen as a an international legal act is supported by well known jurists such as M. WEILL:

> "A State Contract is rooted in the international legal order, and, as such, must be seen as a proper international legal act. Being based in the international legal order, State Contracts are therefore in a separate category of international legal acts, on a level with other categories, such as those reserved for treaties, unilateral acts of States and international organisations, judicial acts and arbitral acts." [264]

There must be no confusion between State Contracts and *Administrative* Contracts. In both cases, a private individual or enterprise is the contractual partner of a State, but, administrative contracts are conventions (or concessions) by means of which competent local authorities grant to a private individual or enterprise the management of a public service (Underground railways, motorways, tolls etc.). As a contracting party of an Administrative Contract, the State acts *"jure gestionis"* just as a private individual seeking to further his

---

[264] KAMTO, Maurice, "La notion du contrat d'Etat", *Revue de l'arbitrage*, Paris, 2003, pp. 724-753.

own personal interests would. A distinction must therefore be made between State Contracts and Administrative Contracts.

The law applicable to Administrative Contracts is the State's private internal law. In the event of litigation, national tribunals will determine the outcome. The execution of these concessions is subject to specific contract provisions as well as various laws and regulations. In sum, the local authorities' decisional power is the leading factor:

> "Because the agency is responsible for the proper functioning of public services, it has a right of control, at the functional level, over the activities. The agency can take unilateral decisions for the purpose of protecting the public interest. Depriving the holder of a concession shall, in an appropriate case, entitle him to compensation. The agency may modify the conditions under which the holder of the concession may operate." [265]

In marked contrast, State Contracts are entered into outside of the internal legal order of a contracting State. The State acts as a public entity, subject to international law, on which sovereign powers *("jure imperii")* have been bestowed. These contracts contain specific clauses which create a quasi common legal level between the State and the private contractor. These are the so-called "compromissory" clauses allowing both parties the right to submit litigation to international arbitration, allowing stabilisation clauses, which shield the contract from subsequent multiple legislative changes, allowing intangibility clauses, which prohibit the State from modifying the contract unilaterally through legislation and, additionally, subjecting the State to applicable law which includes international law, in any litigation between the parties. The law applicable to State Contracts is international law. International tribunals or international arbitration institutions are the competent jurisdictional venues for State Contracts.

---

[265] MAST, André, *Belgisch Administratief Recht* (Belgian Administrative Law), Story-Scientia, Gent, 1981, p. 115.

15.4.2. – Investment State Contracts

Internationally, and in particular with respect to international investments, the conclusion of investment contracts between the host State and foreign investors has become common practice and has proven its worth since 1951. The oil industry gave it its first impulse and subsequently other sectors have joined it. BIT's mention these agreements under the title "Particular or specific Agreements". It is an anomaly that the term "State Contracts" appears nowhere in BIT's.

Investment State Contracts are entered into between host States and international investors. They determine the rights and obligations of the co-contracting parties within the framework of an investment project. When an investor agrees to contribute to the economic development of the host State by his investment contract, some authors use the term "Economic Development Contract", a euphemism. We prefer the term "State Contract" which untendentiously reveals the true and simple nature of the contract. Obviously, one could say that all investment contracts contribute to economic development and that, therefore, to distinguish between State Contracts and other international investment commitments on the basis of contribution vel non to economic development could be misleading, sycophantic nonsense.

The growing importance of contract adaptations between States and private foreign investors, when the aim is better to protect the foreign investors from the arbitrary exercise of the State's sovereign power, is clear for all observers with experience in these areas. The formula's success flows also from the establishment of investment codes in the less developed countries. These codes did not spring, Minerva-like, fully armed to distribute justice and wisdom but have evolved sometimes through bitter experience. Mainly their raison d'être, the driving force behind them, was the need by less developed states to promote as much as possible the growth of foreign investments on their territories. Less developed countries therefore have, through the means of individually tailored conventions, agreed to conclude contracts with private investors within the framework of their codes and adapt the sometimes fiercely nationalistic phraseology of these codes to the practical realities of investment.

Investors found this approach to be advantageous, since conventions offered them better protection. However, the multiplicity of contracts, notwithstanding the normalising effect of codes, sometimes led to unequal treatment among contractors.

Nonetheless, the State Contract is without a doubt an additional and useful protection instrument. This does not mean that such a contract offers absolute guarantees of safety. In theory, the Contracting Parties are on an equal basis but in actual practice, the investor is still the weaker of the two and runs heavy risks. It is only when the State is bound by a bilateral convention covering State contracts that the investor may better avoid the most egregiously discriminatory local measures, undermining with unilateral legerdemain the proper execution of an investment agreement.

Furthermore, not just local agencies but the State's national legislative arm may very well decide to meddle. The issuance of new fiscal laws, for instance, or of social, monetary and customs norms may fundamentally change the foreign investor's scenario. The right to unilateral change of a State contract, on the local authorities' initiative, is usually not expressly admitted in doctrinal texts but some authors believe that the State indeed has the right to change such contracts for reasons of public interest. The conclusion of a State Contract therefore is no guarantee per se of adequate protection. It is necessary, *through special provisions*, to provide expressly (for example : stabilisation clauses, (see *infra*) to remedy the inequality of the parties and restore equilibrium between the rights and obligations *of each contracting party*.

15.4.3. – *Special Protection Provisions in State Contracts : Stabilisation, Intangibility*

The question is which countervailing provisions may be included in a State Contract to assure the best protection of international investments. From the outset, it is clear that investors have an interest in not seeing the status of their investments change too drastically. WEIL suggests that such contracts include *"stabilisation clauses"* :

> "In the first case (legislative risks), the idea is to 'freeze' the national legislation of the host State in the condition where it was on the date the contract was executed, and thereby limit the power of the State to use its legislative function : those are 'stabilisation' clauses in the strictest of terms." [266]

There are a good many examples of stabilisation clauses in doctrinal texts of stabilisation clauses. The most frequently cited instance is that appearing in a State Contract entered into with Iran in 1954 :

> "No general or specific legislative or administrative measure or any other whatever, shall annul this agreement, amend or modify its provisions or prevent or hinder the due and effective performance of its terms. Such annulment, amendment or modification shall not take place except by agreement of the parties of this agreement." [267]

LDC negotiators may sometimes express the opinion that it is arrogant for a foreign firm or country to aspire to restrict the host State from legislating at will. On the other hand, investors, who are, as already said, in a weaker position as contracting party vis-à-vis the host State, must be able to defend themselves against a unilateral change of the State Contract by the host State. In order to accomplish this purpose, WEIL recommends that *"intangibility clauses"* be inserted in State contracts :

---

[266] WEIL, Prosper, "Les clauses de stabilisation ou d'intangibilité insérées dans les accords de développement économique", *Ecrits de droit international*, Paris, Edition Pedone, 1986, pp. 303-327 (Stabilisation or intangability clasues inserted in economic development agreements – International Law writings).

[267] WEIL, Prosper, *op. cit.*, p. 309, see footnote 266.

> "In the second case (contract amendment), the remedy is to protect investors from the exorbitant exercise of host State powers drawn from the State's domestic laws regarding its contracting parties: these are 'intangibility clauses.'" [268]

An example of an intangibility clause appears in an agreement between Greece and Péchiney (1960):

> "The provisions of the present convention may not be abrogated or modified unless by agreement between the parties, any legislative provision to the contrary being inapplicable to the extent it conflicts with the provisions hereof." [269]

Stabilisation clauses purport to prohibit new *legislation* that would affect the agreement. Intangibility clauses insulate the agreement from any contrary legislation whereas stabilisation clauses would merely restrict the State's *power* to the effect it shall not exercise it exorbitantly. Nonetheless, a distinction between the two clauses is not always made. Often referral is made only to stabilisation clauses, adding that such term is to be interpreted broadly. This idea is defensible since, actually, in both cases, the issue is stabilisation, either of legislation or of the State Contract:

> "In order better to appreciate their import, we shall keep to the broadest definition of stability, meaning thereby any provision in a contract signed between a State or a national corporation, on the one hand, and a person who does not in fact have the nationality of that State or of that national corporation, on the other hand, and by reason of which the partner commits itself in favour of its foreign contracting party not unilaterally modify the contract itself or rules applicable to it. This commitment may of course be undertaken under various forms and affect various domains." [270]

Conceivably, only one such clause might be sufficient in a State Contract, labeled "protection clause", so long as such a clause have the detail necessary to demonstrate that guaran-

---

[268] WEIL, Prosper, *op. cit.*, pp. 303-327.
[269] WEIL, Prosper, *op. cit.*, p. 309.
[270] DAVID, Nicolas, "Les clauses de stabilité dans les contrats pétroliers", *Journal de Droit international*, Editions techniques, Paris, 1986, no. 1.

teed stabilisation means both a commitment not to change the contract terms nor appplicable legislation

15.4.4. – *Sovereign State's Right to accept Stabilisation Clauses*

The particular character of the contractual relationships between the parties to an Investment State Contract cannot be underestimated. On occasion, the private party may actually have greater economic clout than its State partner because he brings the capital the State badly needs. On the other hand, the State is a sovereign, wielding wide powers regarding investments located in its territory. State contracts are inherently subject to a sovereignty risk, where the contracting State may, at least in principle, take legislative and regulatory measures modifying the legal context in which the contract is to be carried out. Investors therefore will want to protect themselves against eventual abuses of power by their State contracting partner, which, in turn, can be very protective of its prerogatives as a sovereign:

> "It is in hopes of minimising this sovereignty risk which they fear so much, that investors more and more frequently demand that their State Contract include protection clauses by virtue of which the State commits itself expressly not to use its legislative or contractual prerogatives flowing from its sovereignty. This is how they hope secure the stability of the legal environment. 'Intangibility' of their contractual rights is the means they value the most." [271]

The question therefore is that one must well understand the legal value of the State commitment and to know whether the State may validly abandon, by way of the State Contract, any of its sovereign powers.

One might well ask whether the State, which, supposedly, is concerned with the public interest, has the right and the jurisdiction to agree to clauses of stabilisation or intangibility. On this topic, doctrinal texts are not unanimous. Those

---

[271] WEIL,Prosper, *op. cit.*, p. 303, see footnote 266.

that are hostile to this type of provision say that the sovereign power of a state cannot be alienated. It cannot, they say, by contract, abandon, its sovereign powers. Any renunciation of the attributes of sovereign power cannot, according to these authors, have any legal validity. It is void *ab initio*.

Those who favour such clauses – and they are more numerous – have no objection to State Contracts containing stabilisation clauses. The State, they say, has the jurisdiction to conclude interstate treaties and conventions (*"jus tractatus"*). The State also has jurisdiction to conclude contracts with private persons, in its capacity as guardian of the public interest. This in no way affects the State's sovereignty. On the contrary, the jurisdiction to conclude State contracts is a manifestation of the sovereign power:

> "In line with the quasi unanimity within the doctrine, the Tribunal accepts the notion that the conclusion of contracts is an instance of the exercise of the State's sovereignty and that stabilisation clauses, even if they constrain considerably the State's freedom to decide, do not reach the level of an injury to, a better term being wanting, what can be called the public international system. When other conditions to sovereignty are considered, this particular instance is probably of equal validity. The Tribunal clearly believes in the sovereignty principle." [272]

Those who favour this clause seem to be on firmer ground. To our knowledge, there are no compelling legal argument sufficient to disqualify the State's jurisdiction. In general, State legislation specifically provides for the conclusion of State Contracts with private interests or governmental entities acting as private interests.

The State's sovereign decision to commit or not by a convention and to abstain from exercising any portion of its powers is precisely a very convincing manifestation of its retention of sovereignty.

---

[272] KAHN, Philippe, "Contrats d'Etat et nationalisation", *Journal du droit international*, Editions techniques, Paris, 1982, n° 4, p. 857.

15.4.5. – *Validity and Effect of Stabilisation clauses*

When the concept is accepted that States have the competence to enter into State Contracts for international investments, and that they can also abstain from exercising certain sovereign powers, there is still an open issue as to whether stabilisation clauses have a real and durable effect on the legal status of protected investments. In other words, is the State held indefinitely to the respect of such clauses or may it breach its contractual commitment, with impunity, changing the status of the investment anyway by the simple invocation of motives of public interest?

Authors are divided on this point, the validity or the invalidity of intangibility clauses remaining a stumbling block. In legal theory, several arguments may be made to justify the validity or invalidity of such clauses.

On the one hand, it may be argued that these contracts, whether or not they include a stabilisation clause, must be respected absolutely and unconditionally ("sanctity of contracts"). The contract represents the law as between the parties and the protection clauses which it includes must be applied, like any other provision of the contract. According to this view, the contract trumps sovereignty and could not be affected by new laws passed after the signature of the investment contract. This thesis has been offered several times before the Court of International Justice. It has been confirmed that it applies to investment contracts:

> "The principle '*pacta sunt servanda*' applies not only to agreements between States but also to those between a State and foreign nationals." [273]

By its arbitration award dated 19 January 1977 and when ruling on the interpretation of a State contract between

---

[273] BERLIN, Dominique, "Les contrats d'Etats et la protection des investissements internationaux", *Droit et pratique du commerce international* (DPCI), Paris, 1987 p. 211.

Lybia and the Texaco Company, this principle has been stressed :

> "It is incontestable that the maxim *'pacta sunt servanda'* represents a general principle of law : it is an essential foundation of international law. No international jurisdiction, anywhere, has ever expressed the slightest doubt as to the existence, in international law, of the rule *'pacta sunt servanda.'*"[274]

Carried to its extreme, such a theory would make stabilisation clauses supernumerary in documents already quite complex in their nature. On the other hand, it is legally possible to waive the incontrovertible character of contracts and claim that State contracts may be amended by the State unilaterally, since, contrary to a private contractual partner, the State has the implied right to reserve, *a priori*, the public interest. The question then is : can the stabilisation clauses be an actual contractual obstacle, depriving the State which is a party to the contract from the right to use its State power to impose amendments and modifications to its private contractual partner? The answer to this question is not uniform, either in the doctrinal texts or in the arbitration jurisprudence (cfr *infra*).

15.4.6. – *Legal Order of State-Contracts with Stabilisation Clauses*

For an in-depth examination of the scope and value of stabilisation clauses in State contracts to be persuasive, there must first be there exists a commitment to the legal order to which these contracts belong.

There are two theories :

Either the State Contract belongs to the internal legal order of the contracting State; in this case, national legislation will apply and constitutes the legal basis to determine the validity or invalidity of stabilisation clauses, or

---

[274] BERLIN, Dominique, *op. cit.*, p. 212, see footnote 273.

State contracts belong to the international legal order and in this case, principles and rules of international law will apply.

Private international law has rules of reference and rules governing conflict of laws. The rules usually refer to the legislation of a specific State. This legislation will then be applied to resolve a conflict of laws on the international level. The conflict is tied to a specific legal system (domestic law) because of the way in which it is settled. This is done on the basis of factors which tie the cause or parties to a specific place. In a conflict of laws involving personal rights, this basis could be the parties' nationality. In a conflict of laws involving property rights, the law of the place where the property is located could well be the law to be applied to the litigation (*lex rei sitae*).

In public international law, by definition, there are no specific reference or appeal rules, that is, no specific rules under the terms of which a cause may be sent back (*"remand"*) for examination by a judge or commission for further determination of facts or other aspects of the case, or forwarded to a higher court for redetermination of matters of law. Besides appeals, which must follow rigorous rules to be allowed to proceed, British common law, for instance, as interpreted in jurisdictions which are heir to British law, has crafted various other means, sometimes called "writs", for the re-examination of the facts or the law of a case.

In private international law, legal relations between States are governed by treaties and conventions about international common law and the principles and rules of international law. Hence, in contractual relations between a host State and a private party (State contract) the contracting parties should be able freely to choose, at the outset, what law will be applicable to their contract (*lex contractus*). This is no longer contested, neither in the doctrinal texts nor in judicial jurisprudence :

"We shall not debate here once again the right of the parties to choose what law will be applicable to their contract, including international law." [275]

When a State concludes a contract with a private party, both contractual partners will therefore have to choose and determine under what legal order the contract falls. It is obvious that they can agree to place their contract under a mixed regimen, both domestic and international, whether or not this mixture poses eventual questions of conflict of laws.

15.4.7. – *State Contracts rooted in Domestic Law*

When negotiating with each other, the parties may therefore choose the applicable law and record their intention expressly in the terms of the contract. If the contracting parties agree on the sole application of domestic law, the validity of stabilisation clauses will hinge on domestic legislation and regulations of the contracting State. There is a hierarchical question between the obligation undertaken under the State Contract and the domestic law of the host State. It is mainly in that situation that the effect of stabilisation clauses may pose a problem. As we know, less developed countries believe it is very important to them to have the supremacy and primacy of their sovereign rights recognised. When national legislation exists, which states that a new law takes precedence over contractual obligations, these countries do not hesitate to rely on such legislation.

More often than not, developing countries tend to amend consummated contracts alleging reasons of public utility. What could, in such a case, be the effect of a stabilisation clause?

If the contracting parties have chosen domestic law, it will apply in its entirety and stabilisation clauses do not escape its scope. If a new law is passed, changing the legal status of investments and agreements relating thereto, that law will

---

[275] DAVID, Nicolas, *op. cit.*, p. 83, see footnote 270.

apply. The value then of stabilisation clauses will depend on what the new law says:

> "Just as domestic law may authorise a new law to apply and enable the State to modify or dissolve the contractual bonds, the State also has the right to determine if the stabilisation clause can freeze or crystallise those bonds or if it is convenient instead to consider it was never written." [276]

It is generally recognised, as a matter of judicial principle that the contract represents the law between the parties. However, a contract should not violate existing law. The only tenable position is that, in the hierarchy of norms, domestic law takes precedence over contract provisions:

> "Legislation voiding stabilisation or intangibility clauses would, of course, violate contract provisions. Legislation modifying an existing contract would be no lesser violation, but, because contracts are hierarchically on a level inferior to legislation, it is not at all clear that, for those who wish to insist of such hierarchy, such avoidance or modification would be illegal." [277]

It seems evident that international investors and the States to which they belong would want to avoid having only domestic law apply, since it could conceivably negate every expectation of the contractor and deny him the fairness of review. Choosing domestic law as the applicable law *(lex contractus)* entails the application of that law to determine the fate of the State contract, no matter how arbitrary that law may be or become. Efficient defenses against States' disavowal or brazen ignorance of stabilisation clauses in such a case simply vanish. In the event the litigation were to be submitted to the judgments of national courts, they would have no choice but to apply domestic law and the contractors' procedure would therefore most likely fail. Chances are the same could then be said about any putative diplomatic immunity, making diplomatic demarches moot.

---

[276] WEIL, Prosper, *op. cit.*, p. 317, see footnote 266.
[277] DAVID, Nicolas, *op. cit.*, p. 95, see footnote 270.

On the other hand, it is also true that, *on the international level*, the non-recognition of contractual obligations is fundamentally an illegal act with consequences involving the responsibility of the State committing it. How persuasive such a truth may be in the local venues is a matter of opinion. However, if domestic law has been selected, the investor would have no access to international courts. His only recourse would be to the protection of his own State, petitioning it to file a complaint adopting the facts and legal position of its national. Unfortunately, his own State is unlikely to do so, knowing that it will most probably not prevail. Any legal basis it may advance for its arbitration request would likely be futile, in as much as any new tribunal it chooses to argue its case with would have to apply the domestic law of the host State, so long as the legal order chosen is the domestic law.

International investors therefore have an interest in seeing to it that their contracts specify that they will be subject to international law or eventually a mixed regimen of domestic and international law.

15.4.8. – *"Internationalisation" of State Contracts*

International investors are therefore ill protected if the State Contract they underwrite is subject only to the domestic law of the host State, even where stabilisation clauses have been included:

> "Submitting a stabilisation clause to the domestic law of the host State provides the foreign investor only a very limited guarantee. In order to invigorate such a clause, it is indispensable that the contract also be expressly subject to international law." [278]

Authors and arbitrators who believe that State contracts ought to be "internationalised", are essentially right, as a

---

[278] DAVID, Nicolas, *op. cit.*, p. 105, see footnote 270.

matter of necessity, as any failure to be so qualified will prevent them from being subject to international law :

"Since the very start of this study, it has been acknowledged that investment contracts containing a stabilisation clause need to be internationalised, lest such a clause's full validity and real effect be negated."[279]

"Internationalisation" means therefore that the State contract is anchored in the international legal order, even though one of the parties may not be subject to international law. An "internationalisation" clause in the investment contract does not automatically exclude the application of domestic law. It has already been stated that the contracting parties may choose the applicable law. It is therefore perfectly possible that their choice rests upon several legal systems and that applicable rules of law may overlap. This was highlighted by the Institute of International Law :

"Contracts between a State and a private foreign person are subject to the law chosen by the parties, or, should such a choice not have been made, to the rules of law with which the contract implies the closest bond. The parties may for instance choose as the law applicable to the contract one or more internal laws, or principles common to all of these, or general principles of law, or principles applied in international economic relations, or just international law or a combination of these various sources of law."[280]

DAVID argues that a reference in an international investment contract – in our parlance, a State Contract – to the application of national law implies automatically a reference to the principles of international law. This is an unwarranted stretch of logic, open to serious contestation. In order to avoid problems, the choice of international law should be made *"expressis verbis"*. Investors have no interest in relying on the very wide discretion granted to an arbitration tribunal in the hope that it will decide that the international character of any contract subject to national law will be sufficient to require the application of international law.

---
[279] DAVID, Nicolas, *op. cit.*, p. 109.
[280] DAVID, Nicolas, *op. cit.*, p. 107, see footnote 270.

It has become an axiom that, international public law does not have conflicts of laws rules. International law applies to a State Contract when the parties so choose. Basically, one should not need conflict of laws rules if a contract is properly written but it is possible that the parties simply fail to choose expressly what the applicable law will be and that they then agree that the arbitrator will apply the law specified by the rules of international private law. The Washington Convention has foreseen the possibility of the lack of designation of applicable law by the parties:

> "Lacking an agreement between the parties, the Tribunal applies the law of the Contracting State, a party to the dispute... including rules relative to conflicts of laws as well as principles of international law on the issue." (**Article 42**)

A mere reference to the conflict of laws rules of international private law in BIT's or in investment contracts is insufficient. To the contrary, *it is in fact quite possible that the presence of such a reference will complicate matters* for the arbitrator rather than help him. Even without any reference to conflict of laws rules, arbitrators are free to choose the applicable law, where none has been specified.

In this situation, "internationalisation" is the key. WEIL correctly says that the State which contracts with a private person and signs a State Contract containing a stabilisation clause, is bound to apply the national legislation that was in force at the time the contract was signed:

> "The mandatory character of the stabilisation clause therefore seems difficult to gainsay. If this clause is ignored in the name of the inalienability of legislative jurisdiction... which we repeat remains intact because it is foreign to an internationalised contract... the host State commits itself not only as to the individual investor but also as to the State of which he is a national."[281]

---

[281] WEIL, Prosper, "Les clauses de Stabilisation ou d'intangibilité insérées dans les accords de développement économique", *Mélanges offerts à Charles Rousseau*, Paris, Edition Pedone, 1974, p. 221.

In essence, the State hasn't given up any of its legislative power which remains intact but it only agreed not to apply new legislation to an internationalised State contract *with stabilisation clause*.

15.4.9. – *Validity of "Intangibility" Clauses*

A similar question arises as to "intangibility" clauses. In substance, they document the host State's agreement to set aside explicitly its power unilaterally to amend or terminate a State contract. The State which gives its assent to such a clause is *ipso facto* showing its assent to the idea that every State has the power to modify and terminate a State Contract, at least under certain conditions and within certain limits. Like stabilisation clauses, intangibility clauses are part of the State's conventions and override the principle of absolute sovereignty, whenever the State Contract is "internationalised".

There is no unanimity among writers on this topic nor in the arbitration or judicial jurisprudence. Opposing theorists remain convinced that the State must be able to take, under any circumstance, the measures that are deemed necessary in the public interest. In law, the demands of public utility may justify the modification of State contracts, which, in general order, are beneficial to the private interests involved in such contracts. The State, according to some, may not bind itself, by way of a convention, not to modify or terminate State contracts to which it is a party.

The invalidity of clauses of intangibility has been argued as follows:

> "For certain authors, intangibility clauses are devoid of any value at all and must be deemed simply non written, to the point that no distinction need be made between a contract which includes such a clause and that which does not. To support this thesis, proponents invoke the theory of inalienable State sovereignty, in that the State cannot waive any of its prerogatives aiming at any moment to safe-

guard public interests of which it has been entrusted the protection." [282]

These arguments are hardly compelling. The contracting State, when it accepts such a clause, does so precisely in the exercise of its sovereignty, as it considers it appropriate, when the State Contract is signed, for the purposes of a public utility. The concern it has over the spread of private investments in its territory is a motive of public utility which can justify contractual commitments of this type.

Not every arbitration decision is favourable to the insertion of these specific protection clauses in State contracts. However, the verdict in *Lybia v. Texaco* gives a good example of their opinion about that validity:

> "There is no doubt that in the exercise of its sovereignty a State has the power to make international commitments. There is no value to dwell at any great length on the existence and value of the principle under which a State may, within the framework of its sovereignty, undertake international commitments with respect to a private party. This rule results from the discretionary competence of the State in this area. The result is that a State cannot invoke its sovereignty to disregard commitments freely undertaken through the exercise of this same sovereignty, and cannot through measures belonging to its internal order make null and void the rights of the contracting party which has performed its various obligations under the contract." [283]

The conclusion of State Contracts in which protection clauses of stabilisation or intangibility have been inserted is a manifestation of the independence of the State's will. Furthermore, the obligation to carry out agreements in good faith is a generally accepted principle of international law. There is no doubt that the State which grants freely, by way of a convention, advantages to international investors could be accused of bad faith in the event it cancel such contracts unilaterally.

---

[282] WEIL, Prosper, *op. cit.*, p. 323, see footnote 281.
[283] WAELDE, Thomas, "Stabilizing international investment commitments", *Texas International Law Journal*, Spring 1996, no. 2, p. 245.

There are, of course, more than a few ways to cancel or modify a contract. Some of these ways do not amount to a "unilateral" cancellation or modification but is the result of subtle and imaginative measures and navigation between the reefs of good and bad faith, to the point where some foreign investors may welcome the cancellation or modification of their contract because the State's measures or casuistry make it more desirable to cancel or modify than to continue operating under the old guide rules. Investors may well have had a solid right to exploit the property in which they invested but found it impossible to obtain State or local support in day to day operations. Local political pressure on State officials may force the hand of the investors to the point where, lacking their cooperation, they are in effect maneuvered into entering into a modification of their investment contract. Some investors may try to initiate a modification in order to gain an advantage over other investors in the same sector of the host State's economy. This may be despite the fact that the State was bound by the investment contract to provide cooperation in the successful exploitation of the investment. If this ploy were successful, other, likewise situated investors, might, by alleging that one modification deserves another, start a cascade of State Contract modifications. Finally, simple inertia, rather than outright bad faith, can be just as deadly to investors' expectations.

Our conclusion is that international investors would benefit from the insertion in State Contracts they are parties to, of internationalised clauses of stabilisation and intangibility. BIT negotiators should also try to obtain the insertion of a clause by which the contracting Parties agree to respect the clauses of intangibility and stabilisation. In spite of divergent opinions in the doctrine and among arbitrators about clauses of this type, their insertion gives to investors more efficient means to have their rights enforced, particularly during an arbitration procedure.

15.4.10. – *Validity of Non-Nationalisation Clauses*

When a State has contractually agreed not to nationalise, it may be argued that this is merely a special modality of protection. How solid is the guarantee that international investors who have obtained such clauses be inserted in their contracts actually have that their investments not be nationalised?

It has already been stated that domestic law provisions do not offer sufficient guarantees. How domestic law may affect "internationalisation" may be seen by the following example of Congolese investment code legislation:

> "Private or collective property rights of an investors are guaranteed by the Constitution of the Democratic Republic of the Congo. An investment may not be directly or indirectly, in whole or in part, nationalised or expropriated by a new law and/or by a decision of a local authority having the same effect, except for reasons of public utility and provide that compensation of a fair and equitable indemnity is paid." (**Article 26**, Investment Code)

Experience has shown that this guarantee is not satisfactory because, before the Code was legislated, the Congolese Constitution already contained provisions of that type and this did not stop property privative measures from being undertaken. There are many examples showing that States invoke rather lightly claims of public utility in order to escape their legal and contractual obligations to protect investments. In the event a State contract is concluded which is exclusively governed by the domestic law of the host State, investments will not be satisfactorily protected. In order to gain added security, the international investor will therefore have to try to gain additional guarantees. In any case, the State contract must be "internationalised" so that it is governed by international law.

15.4.11. – *Scope of Guarantee in State Contracts with Non-Nationalisation Clause*

Is a contractual commitment by a State safer for the investor when such commitment is a part of an "internationalised" investment contract provision, not to take nationalisation measures? Just as with stabilisation and intangibility clauses, the validity of a clause of non-nationalisation depends of the emphasis given to the notion of State's sovereignty. May a State validly limit by way of a convention, its right to nationalize.

There are also two trains of thought: some plead their validity and others the opposite. A few arbitration awards have formally supported the concept that the right to nationalise has no limits and therefore no contractual limits may be placed on it. According to this thesis, the local authorities must serve the public interest (eventually by taking measures of nationalisation) and this goal takes precedence, even when contractual rights will be violated. An arbitration award in the case of *Amco v Indonesia* (5 June 1990) is an example of this concept:

> "This is the fundamental principle of the right of a sovereign State to nationalise or expropriate property. Including contractual rights previously granted by itself, even if they belong to aliens, by now clearly admitted in national legal systems as well as in the international law." [284]

The argument of the arbitration tribunal rests on poor grounds. When a State limits contractually its right to nationalise, it has not alienated its sovereignty but, quite to the contrary, it has proven that its sovereignty persists. Those who favour this position claim, arguably quite correctly that the opposing argument, if adopted, would lead to the total practical inability of a State to enter into any lasting contract.

---

[284] BERLIN, Dominique, *op. cit.*, p. 212, see footnote 273.

On the other hand, to claim that international law fundamentally acknowledges the right to nationalise, in the face of an existent commitment not to do so, is an overstatement.

In doctrinal texts and several arbitration awards, much is made of the fact that contractual commitments of non-nationalisation do not per se affect the right of the State to nationalise. There is only a limitation of the right to nationalise in respect of the investor with whom the State concluded a contract containing a non-nationalisation clause. The State retains the right to conclude agreements (*"jus tractatus"*) not only with other States but also with other investors in State Contracts or even with the same investor in connection with a different contract. Provisions which have been freely adopted by the State as contracting Party, not least non-nationalisation clauses, should be acknowledged as valid and given respect.

The approach taken by LALIVE is the better solution. According to it, international law obligates States to respect, under international law, State contracts containing non-nationalisation agreements:

> "Nationalisation should not prevail against an international contract containing stabilisation measures between a State and a foreign enterprise. In other words, this rule is clear, resulting from the universally accepted principle of *'pacta sunt servanda'*; when a State commits itself in advance and contractually to guarantee to its foreign contractor that his enterprise or the activities which are the contract's object shall not be nationalised, the State merely exercises freely its sovereignty rights. This conclusion is consistent with the practice and the teachings of international law." [285]

---

[285] LALIVE, Jean Flavien, "Un grand arbitrage pétrolier entre un Gouvernement et deux sociétés privées étrangères : Arbitrage Texaco Calasiatie c. Gouvernement Lybien", *Journal de droit international (JDI)*, 1977, volume 104, n° 2, p. 342.

15.4.12. – Arbitral Approach of Non-Nationalisation Clauses

In the arbitration decision dated 19 January 1977, issued in the case of *Texaco/Calasiatic v. Libya*, the arbitrators held that public international law contains no rule of law prohibiting contracting States dealing with private parties from inserting in their contracts clauses of non-nationalisation :

> "Also on the level of public international law, claims have been made that permanent sovereignty over natural resources has become an imperative rule of '*jus cogens*' (mandatory law), preventing States from granting, by contract or treaty, guarantees of any nature regarding the exercise of public authority in connection with natural resources. These claims are baseless. Even if some of their provisions (ONU Resolution) may be seen as codifying rules which reflect international practice, it would not be possible to conclude that a rule exists in international law prohibiting a State to commit itself not to undertake a nationalisation during a limited period. In fact, it may be most useful for host States to be able to commit themselves not to nationalise a foreign enterprise within a limited period. No rule of international law stops them." [286]

The Tribunal expressly confirmed that a State may, in a State Contract, commit itself not to nationalise an investment, precisely because States, differently from its co-contracting private party, has sovereignty prerogatives :

> "In reliance on the quasi unanimity of doctrinal texts, the Tribunal accepts the concept that entering into contracts is a way to exercise sovereignty, and that stabilisation clauses, even when they significantly restrict the State's freedom of action do not offend what is, for want of a better term, referred to as the international public order. ...The Tribunal also admits that in the exercise of its sovereignty, a State may even renounce its right to nationalise. However, this does not mean that a non-nationalisation commitment results automatically from the tenor of an ordinary stabilisation clause." [287]

In order to secure the maximum protection, investors should attempt to have a stabilisation clause included in their

---

[286] KAHN, Philippe, *op. cit.*, p. 893, see footnote 272.
[287] DAVID, Nicolas, *op. cit.*, p. 858, see footnote 270.

contract, limiting the State's power to modify or void a State Contract through legislation and expressly specifying a non-nationalisation commitment. VERHOEVEN approved of the arbitrators' decision in the *Texaco* case, referring to a holding by the Permanent Court of International Justice in the "*Wimbledon*" case, stating:

> "In effect internationalising the contract, the arbitrator paraphrased the holding of the International Court of Justice in the '*Wimbledon*' case [288] '...like a Treaty, an 'international' concession contract is not tantamount to an alienation of sovereignty but instead shows its exercise. This is notwithstanding the terms of any stabilisation clause, where the rights granted may be limited in terms of time and scope.'" [289]

This does not mean that this very clear and formal position taken by the arbitration tribunal in the *Texaco* case solves all the problems. In another case, *Letco v. Liberia* (award dated 31 March 1986), a somewhat less bold position was adopted:

> "The arbitration tribunal in the *Letco* case crafted in fine a limitation on the integrity of the stabilisation clause by allowing its violation when the violation is in good faith, in the general public interest, is not discriminatory and is accompanied by an adequate offer to indemnify. This decision begs the question as to the exact scope of any stabilisation_clause." [290]

15.4.13. – *Limited Validity Period for Stabilisation Clauses*

The validity of the clause conditioning the commitment for a "limited" period is defensible because investment contracts are generally concluded for a limited period (for example 30 years). In some cases, State Contracts contain a clause envisaging a commitment by the contracting State to renego-

---

[288] *SS. Wimbledon Case, by France, Italy, Britain, Japan and Poland v. Germany*, Permanent Court of International Justice (PCIJ). Série A, n° 101, 1923, for refusal to allow steamship through Kirl Canal in violation of Versailles Treaty. The Court held "But the right of entering into international engagements is an attribute of State foreignty".

[289] VERHOEVEN, Jos, "Droit international des contrats et droit des gens", *Revue belge de droit international*, janvier 1978, p. 223.

[290] GAILLARD, Emmanuel, *op. cit.*, p. 215, see footnote 31.

tiate, by mutual consent, if circumstances justify it. This formula has certain advantages. It conforms to the principle of *"pacta sunt servanda"*, which in turn is modified by the principle of *"rebus sic stantibus"*. In the event of a fundamental change is the circumstances which obtained at the time of the signature of the investment contract, a renegotiation can be quite useful.

In spite of the uncertainty which surrounds the validity of particular clauses (stabilisation, intangibility, non-nationalisation), the international investor has an interest in asking that they be inserted in the State Contract. It may be feared that less developed countries will not always accept that these clauses be inserted but if the investor's negotiating position allows it, he should insist on their use in order to obtain greater protection.

15.4.14. – *Internationalisation of State Contracts under "Umbrella" Agreements*

The foregoing examples of and remarks about stabilisation, intangibility, non-nationalisation and conflict clauses help show how important it is to be thorough in the drafting of a complete and clearly understandable text to be inserted in State Contracts.

Furthermore, the need to "internationalise" State Contracts should no longer be subject to question. The ideal internationalisation of such contracts would be their placement under the umbrella of a specific international convention, namely that of a bilateral investment treaty (BIT).

When a State Contract is placed under the aegis of a BIT and when it includes the special protection clauses of stabilisation, intangibility, non-nationalisation, the validity of these clauses will only be questioned with difficulty. Under these conditions, their validity derives from an international convention. The State signing a State Contract is responsible for adhering to it in good faith, both in regards to the other, private, contracting Party but also in regards to the other Contracting State. This approach is confirmed in several ICSID awards. Consequently, clauses which wrap stabilisation, intangibility and non-nationalisation in the BIT's are often referred to in doctrinal texts and arbitration jurisprudence as *"umbrella"* agreements or "covering treaties":

> "According to SGS, this clause has the effect of transforming possible violations of contracts by the host State into violation of the basic Treaty of Protection. The host State shall have undertaken a double commitment, first, directly to the investor and second to the other Contracting State under the BIT, for the general benefit of investors who are nationals of such State. This is why the clause is often described as the 'umbrella' clause or 'covering' clause because it places the State contract under the protection of the BIT. It is sometimes called a 'mirror' clause because it reflects commitments undertaken at the level of the BIT."[291]

When there is between the host State, a party to a State Contract, and the State of the co-contracting private party, a bilateral protection treaty, the commitment to carry out the State Contract is *ipso facto* become an international obligation. The BIT requires the host State to respect its commitments, as expressed in the State Contract. The contracting State thenceforth must respect both its contracts with private parties (State Contracts) and its contracts with other States. It cannot invoke principles of sovereignty to escape its contractual commitments. This principle has also been accepted by the Permanent Court of International Justice:

> "The Court declines to see in the conclusion of any Treaty by which a State undertakes to perform or refrain from performing a particular act an abandonment of its sovereignty. No doubt any convention creating an obligation of this kind places a restriction upon the exercice of the sovereign rights of the State, in the sense that it requires them to be exercised in a certain way. But the right of entering into international engagements is an attribute of State sovereignty."[292]

---

[291] GAILLARD, Emmanuel, *op. cit.*, p. 833, see footnote 30.
[292] Permanent Court of International Justice (PCIJ), Judgement of 17 august 1923 on *S.S. Wimbledon* (steamship), Serie A, Collection of judgements, n° 101, p. 25.

In the event that a State, party to a State Contract, fails to honor its commitments in such contract, its international liability is triggered. In doctrinal texts, an important group of authors (F. Mann, Prosper Weil, E. Gaillard, etc.) have emphasised the importance of umbrella clauses. SHIHATA, for instance, says:

> "Treaties (BIT's) may furthermore elevate contractual undertakings into international law obligations, by stipulating that breach by one State of a contract with a private party (State Contract) from the other State will also constitute a breach of a Treaty between the two States." [293]

15.4.15. – *Umbrella clauses in Model Conventions*

In the US model convention, there is no specific provision regarding State Contracts. State Contracts are addressed only in the definition of the types of litigation which may be submitted to arbitration:

> "For purposes of this treaty, an investment dispute between a party and a national or company of the other party arising out or relating to an investment authorisation, an investment agreement or an alleged breach of any right conferred, created or recognised by this treaty with respect to a covered investment." (**Article IX**)

The German model convention contains the following provision:

> "Each contracting Party shall observe any other obligation it has assumed with regards to investments on its territory by investors of the other contracting State."

FUERACKER states:

> "By virtue of this clause, any contractual obligation of the host State towards an investor is brought under the 'umbrella' of the BIT. This clause protects the investor's contractual rights against any interference which might be caused by either a simple breach of contract or by administrative or legislative acts of the host State'. [294]

---

[293] SHIHATA, John, "Applicable law in international arbitration", *The World bank in a changing World, Selected essays and issues*, Vol. II, Leiden, 1995, p. 601.
[294] FÜRACKER, Matthias, *op. cit.*, p. 15, see footnote 52.

It must be borne in mind that this result will obtain only if the State Contract contains a stabilisation clause. The French model convention contains an unusual provision entitled "Specific Commitment":

> "Investments which are subject to a specific commitment of one of the Contracting Parties towards investors from the other Contracting Party are, irrespectively of the provisions of the current Agreement, governed by the terms of such commitment to the extent the same includes provisions that are more favourable than those in the present Agreement. The provisions of Article 8 of the present Agreement (Arbitration) are applicable, even in the case of a specific commitment waiving international arbitration or designating a venue that is different from that mentioned in Article 8 of the present Agreement."
> (**Article 10**)

It is therefore clear that investment status is governed by the parallel application of the State Contract and the BIT. However, the State Contract has precedence, when it includes provisions which are more favourable than those contained in the BIT. Nonetheless, insofar as the settlement of investment disputes is concerned, the BIT takes precedence. Thus, even when the State Contract does not provide for arbitration or contains a formula which deviates from the BIT in such regard, the BIT provisions will have priority.

Under the title "Specific Agreements", the Belgian convention states:

> "Investments made pursuant to a specific agreement concluded between one Contracting Party and investors of the other Party shall be covered by the provisions of this agreement and by those of the specific agreement.
>
> Each Contracting Parties undertakes to ensure at all times that the commitments it has entered into vis-à-vis investors of the other Contracting party shall be observed."

Under the title "**Promotion and Protection of Investments**", the British model convention states:

> "Each Contracting Party shall observe any obligation it may have entered into with regard to investments of nationals or companies of the other Contracting party."

In most model conventions, the terms of the umbrella clause are virtually identical:

> "Each Contracting Party shall observe any obligation it has entered into with investors of the other Contracting Party, with regard to their investments." (Netherlands, Sweden, Switzerland, Denmark, etc.).

15.4.16. – *Inconsistency of Rules in BIT's Umbrella Clauses*

There is a difficult and delicate problem inherent to the relationship between the BIT provisions and those of a State Contract. In the event of a parallel application of a BIT and a State Contract, provisions in each may contradict each other, requiring that an election be made as to the legal value of a State Contract when confronted with an incompatible BIT. The solution rests in the manner in which the umbrella clauses have been formulated. Actual BIT's deviate frequently from the models and are surprisingly diverse. Some BIT's limit themselves to stating that the Contracting Parties must respect commitments undertaken vis-à-vis foreign investors. Australia, for instance, uses a minimalist formula, under the title "Undertakings given to investors":

> "A Contracting Party shall, subject to its laws, do all in its power to ensure that a written undertaking given by a competent authority to a national of the other Contracting Party with regard to an investment is respected." (**Article 10**, Australia/Poland, 7 May 1991)

This formula provides insufficient protection to investors. It is silent on the selection of the State Contract or the BIT in the event of conflicts between the provisions of each.

In its BIT's, France frequently deviates from its own model. In most French BIT's, a separate article is included for State Contracts under the title "Specific commitments". This is how the following text in the bilateral Guatemala/France convention, dated 27 May 1998, was structured:

> "Investments which are subject to a special commitment by one of the contracting parties in respect to investments made by the other

contracting party are governed, without prejudice to any other provisions of this agreement, by the terms of that commitment to the extent such commitment includes provisions that are more favourable than those which may be part of the present agreement." (**Article 11**)

This article provides for the application of both State Contract and the BIT but the manner in which it is formulated may give rise to misinterpretations. Actually, insofar as special commitments (i.e. State Contracts) are concerned, it is stipulated that the provisions of the contract take precedence over those of the BIT, so long as the provisions of the State Contract are more favourable. What is the meaning and the import of such wording? When the BIT requires an arbitration procedure through ICSID, but the State Contract foresees only a recourse to the competence of the domestic courts as well as arbitration, which of the two provisions is the most favourable?

The answer to this question will depend on the circumstances and in particular how justice is administered in the host State. The text does not say who will decide and what the choice of law will be. It is therefore not obvious that the contracting Parties will find any basis for agreement if litigation ensues. Had the model convention formula been followed, there would have been no problems since the model's text clearly establishes the precedence of ther BIT in arbitration matters. In the bilateral protection convention between France and Tunisia (20 October 1997), it is stated that, in an appropriate case, only those provisions appearing in the State Contract will be applied:

> "Investments ruled by a particular commitment of one of the parties, either towards the other party or towards nationals, physical persons or companies of the latter, shall be governed exclusively by the terms of this commitment." (article 5)

This formula is clearer but presents a significant disadvantage, that is, its failure to address internationalisation. The parallel application of the State contract and the BIT is preferable, so long as it is also stated that the investor will have the right to choose which of the provisions he deems most favourable to himself.

In some of its BIT's, Germany has realised the problem that could result from conflicting provisions between the BIT and the State Contract. In the Germany/India BIT (1995), it is stated :

> "Each Contracting Party shall observe any other obligation it has assumed with regard to investments in its territory by investors of the other Contracting party, which dispute arising from such obligations being only redressed under the terms of the contracts underlying the obligations." (**Article 13**)

It is regrettable that the problem addressed is solely that regarding the settlement of disputes between host States and investors. There could very well be other contradictions between the BIT and the State Contract. For the moment at least, as regards dispute settlement, the solution is quite clear : the State Contract provisions take precedence.

Switzerland, in its BIT's, chooses to apply the most favourable legal solution :

> "If provisions of the legislation of a Contracting State or obligations of international law, current or future and binding the Contracting States, contain, besides the present Agreement, general or special rules which grant to investments made by investors from the other Contracting State a treatment that is more favourable than that provided for under the present Agreement, then those more favourable provisions will take precedence over the present Agreement to the extent such provisions are in fact more favourable." (**Article 12**, Kuwait-Switzerland BIT, 31 October 1998)

It is clear that the same problem affects this formula, namely the risk of divergent interpretations of what constitutes the "most favourable rule".

In some BIT's, Belgium uses the following formula :

> "Applicable regulations : If an issue relating to investments is covered both by this Agreement and by the national legislation of one Contracting Party or by international conventions, existing or to be subscribed to by the Contracting parties in the future, the investors

> of the other Contracting party shall be entitled to avail themselves of the provisions that are the most favourable to them."
>
> "Specific agreements: Investments made pursuant to a specific agreement concluded between one Contracting party and investors of the other Contracting Party shall be covered by the provisions of this Agreement and by those of the specific agreement. Specific agreement means an agreement between a Contracting party and an investor of the other Contracting party concerning a concrete investment in the territory of the former Contracting party." (**Articles 7** and **9**, Bleu/Kazakhstan BIT, 16 April 1998)

This formula evidently has the advantage of providing a definition of the specific investment contract but it is regrettable that a more consistent term such as "State Contract" was not used. In the India/Bleu BIT, dated 1 October 1997, there appears another formula, quite unfortunate for investors:

> "Other commitments: Each Contracting Party shall observe any obligation it may have entered into with regard to an investment of an investor of the other Contracting Party. In relation to such obligations, dispute resolution under article 9 shall however only apply in the absence of normal local judicial remedies being available." (Article 14)

Again here, terms are used ("normal remedies") whose content are not defined.

15.4.17. – Need for Amendments in BIT's Umbrella Clauses

An evaluation of umbrella clauses contained in all BIT's is well beyond the scope of this Work. It seems that it is necessary to amend the text *of* these clauses to avoid being driven into an impasse. The inclusion of a confirmation, in *expressis verbis*, is required, that each of the Contracting Parties is committed to respect the contractual obligations entered into within the scope of State Contracts with investors, including clauses of stabilisation, intangibility and eventually non-nationalisation. That is not merely an acknowledgement of the primacy of a duty based on international law but also an express confirmation of such duty, helping avoid the question, often made, about the validity of special protection clauses.

The legal consequences and advantages for investors are evident since, in the event such obligations are not respected, then, after the realisation of investments, the State in question will not be able to avoid liability under international law. Eventual conflicts will be submitted to arbitration, where the arbitrators will not be able to deny the express contractual obligations of the State concerned. In addition, the applicable law problem must also be resolved, in the event where the respective texts of the BIT and the State Contract contradict each other. The text should expressly state that it is the investor who has the right to choose the law most favourable to him, either as stated in the specific State contract or in the BIT. In general, the investor's choice is respected in many BIT's because developing countries see it as an encouragement to future international investors.

Insofar as national treatment or most favoured nation treatment is concerned, BIT's must also provide that the investor has the right to choose that which he deems most favourable to him. Thus, in the same BLEU/Kazakhstan BIT mentioned above, it is stated :

> "If an issue relating to investments is covered both by this Agreement and by the national legislation of one Contracting Party or by international conventions, existing or to be subscribed to by the Contracting Parties in the future, the investors of the other Contracting party shall be entitled to avail themselves of the provisions that are the most favourable to them."

It would also be useful to include a clause providing explicitly that litigation concerning the execution of State Contracts may be submitted to arbitration. For this purpose, the convention does not single out the host State and private persons, but it should confirm that the terms "any disagreement regarding contract execution" include disagreements about the execution of State Contracts referred to in the BIT's.

France has solved the problem by specifying that the arbitration formula provided for in the BIT is applicable, even in cases of "specific commitments (State Contracts) which waive international arbitration. An alternative formula could provide that investors have the right to choose between the dispute settlement procedures provided for in the BIT or the State Contract.

Hence, if international investors wish to protect their investment best, they should see to it that their contracts with the host State include selected clauses of protection and must also ensure that a bilateral protection convention, *with an umbrella clause*, exists between the State to which they belong and the host State.

CHAPTER XVI

JURISDICTION
SETTLEMENT OF INVESTMENT DISPUTES THROUGH ARBITRATION

16.1. – ELEMENTS OF INTERNATIONAL INVESTMENT DISPUTE RESOLUTION

Relations between international investors and host State authorities are not always ideal. Even though most developed countries are strongly motivated to attract and keep international investment, litigation between them and investors is frequent. Circumstances can change, requiring adjustments. For good relations to survive change, host States and investors alike have an interest in crafting legal instruments plainly and unambiguously setting forth their respective rights and obligations. Their agreements must reflect their expectations that their rights will be honoured. They need to anticipate differences and agree as to the means and place where they, and the facts surrounding them, will be honestly presented and fairly resolved.

In actual practice, before venturing into any commitment in the host State, investors should ask whether the host State has a structured legal system *(lex rei sitae)*, there is a legal forum sufficiently efficient and neutral in the determination of litigation relative to the investments and, above all, if, internationally, there are alternative possibilities for finding solutions to eventual disputes, such as arbitration. The existence of legislation which opens the door to arbitration is of capital importance.

Candidate investors should check the host State's policy in regards to international investment. In particular, they should check whether domestic law allows for the conclusion of State contracts, and if, in actual practice, the host State uses this solution and allows that arbitration clauses be inserted in the State contract.

On the one hand, investors should check on the existence of a bilateral convention for the protection of investments (BIT) and of its content. It is important that the investor has the freedom to file an arbitration procedure for the settlement of eventual conflicts. On the other hand, they should verify that the States which are a party to the convention have given their consent to a recourse to arbitration in the case of conflicts.

Where arbitration clauses are missing from legislation or contracts with the host State, investors have grounds to fear that the host State may take measures (through legislation, for instance) to anchor the conflicts in its local legal system and give its local courts exclusive jurisdiction. Furthermore, not only do less developed countries favour the jurisdiction of their local courts but they question the authority of any other.

For many years, foreign investors have wanted to avoid being subject to local tribunals' jurisdiction. In State Contracts, arbitration clauses had become the norm. As the years went by, it became apparent that arbitration clauses had to be backed up, whenever possible, by intangibility clauses (cfr. Subtitle 15.4.1).

In State Contracts, such clauses protect investors against the possible cancellation of arbitration clauses by legislative action of the host State. The Permanent Court of International Justice (PCIJ) met the issue in the *Losinger case*. On March 2nd 1929, a contract was entered into between the autonomous district Pozarevac of Yugoslavia and a US company "American Oriental Construction Syndicate". The goal of the contract was the planning, constructing and financing of railways in that Yugoslavian district.

Difficculties arose between the original parties. As a result, the contract was novated without any substantial amendments between the Yugoslav State and Losinger & Cie, a Swiss company. The contract contained an arbitration clause:

> "Any differences of opinion or disputes which may arise between the contracting Parties in connection with the carrying out or interpretation of the clauses and conditions of this contract shall be settled by compulsory arbitration, if a friendly settlement cannot be reached by the contracting Parties." (Article XVI).

Further disagreements arose. Despite the contract's arbitration clause, the Yugoslav Government refused to have the issues arbitrated, claiming under a law dated 19 July 1934, and alleging as follows:

> "Article 24 of said law specifies that any and all actions against the Yugoslav State may be adjudicated only by the State's regular tribunals. These requirements are procedural public law; every person, physical or moral, Yugoslav nationals or not, are subject to them, when they negotiate contracts with the State, for any litigation in connection with such contracts."

The Swiss Government assumed the defence of the Losinger company and filed a request with the Permanent Court of International Justice (PCIJ).[295] In its request, the Swiss State asked the Court to reject the Yugoslav objection to its jurisdiction and to the validity of the arbitration clause. The Court accepted the Swiss request and ordered Yugoslavia to honour the international law rule of «*pacta sunt servanda*» which compelled the execution of the contractual commitment regarding arbitration. A contract may not be cancelled by a subsequent law.

Clearly, had there been an intangibility clause in the Losinger contract, Switzerland would have been in an even better position. It is evident that intangibility clauses meet a real

---

[295] Cour Permanente de Justice Internationale (CPIJ), Judicial Year 1936, *The Lösinger & Co Case*, Série C, number 78.

need. Accordingly, to help reinforce investors' security, arbitration clauses in their contracts should be appropriately drafted.

16.2. – What constitutes international arbitration

Arbitration in the context of bilateral conventions is not internal arbitration, that is, it is not arbitration of litigation between persons and enterprises having the same nationality and reflecting no externality. On the national level, local legislation also provides sometimes for recourse to arbitration, under certain conditions, for the settlement of litigation:

> "Every litigation that arises or could arise from a specific legal relationship subject to resolution by settlement, may be submitted to arbitration, when the same is allowed under local legislation." [296]

In the current study, we have analysed international arbitration, and more particularly that relating to conflicts between host States and the nationals of another State, within the scope of bilateral protection agreements (BIT's) or of State Contracts which contain an arbitration clause. However, in many national legislative systems, there are no definitions for arbitration. Definitions may, however, be found in doctrinal texts:

> "Arbitration is a technique aiming to achieving the resolution, by the decision of one or more other persons, of a question affecting the relationship between two or more persons." [297]

Some authors define arbitration in limited and banal fashion:

> "Arbitration is the settlement of litigation by arbitrators designated by the parties." [298]

---

[296] Belgian Judicial Code, Article 1676.
[297] DAVID, René, *L'arbitrage dans le commerce international*, Economica, Paris, 1982, p. 9.
[298] VAN HECKE, G., *Internationaal Privaatrecht*, Gent, Edition Story Scientia, 1989, p. 393.

Actually, the arbitrator is a private judge, chosen by the litigating parties. He must have professional competence, just as much as that required of a State judge to determine the outcome of litigation. The jurisdiction of the arbitrator or of the arbitration tribunal to decide on litigation in obligatory and final fashion (that is, in nearly all the cases where his decision is not appealable) finds its legal basis most frequently in a contract between the parties. The legislatures of some States, has found that certain lawsuits may not proceed through the regular courts unless they have first been submitted to arbitration, whether the parties like it or not and whether they agreed so to do or not. However, arbitration of international litigation against an independent State is universally considered to have a contractual basis.

Insofar as international investments are concerned, such contracts may have various forms, either a written contract between the host State and the investor (State Contracts), with an arbitration clause, or a separate arbitration convention annexed to an investment contract, or still an arbitration clause in a State to State convention for protection of investments (BIT). The settlement of conflicts through arbitration rests on two pedestals: the arbitration convention and the arbitral character of litigation arising between the parties.

In the arbitration convention, the parties freely agree to submit to the jurisdiction which will take the arbitration decision and to acknowledge the fact that such decision will finalise the litigation.

Arbitration is not the proper procedure for all conflicts. By their very nature, some conflicts cannot be arbitrated and another choice must therefore be made. For domestic arbitration, this selection is usually done by the legislature determining the conditions that must be met before arbitration may be considered:

> "The conditions under which litigation is subject to arbitration by a private judge is a matter for the exclusive determination of each

State's legislators. By declaring that a certain type of litigation is subject to arbitration, the legal system authorises the parties to avoid the jurisdiction of local tribunals which normally exercise the power to judge. Normally a State will adopt such legislation only when it believes that private interest litigation may best be settled by private action." [299]

For international litigation, the selection of proper areas to be subject to arbitrations is done by the contracting States (cfr BIT's) or by the host State and its contractual partner in State contracts. The definition of the term "investment" in the BIT's has a direct effect on the volume of investment litigation subject to arbitration : the more numerous the activities considered to be investments according to the BIT, the more litigation of investments subject to arbitration will there be. Some conflicts are resolved through conciliation.

Based on all of the foregoing, international arbitration may be defined as follows:

"Arbitration is a legal system for the settlement of specific international conflicts, through which jurisdiction is granted to arbitrators selected by the parties to the litigation, so they may render, through their award, a final and mandatory decision regarding such conflicts without recourse to the established judicial system."

The arbitrator is a private judge and therefore not a State judge. Important legal differences flow from this distinction. In most cases, a judgment rendered or an order issued by a State judge is *ipso facto* executory, no additional measure being, as a rule, required in most jurisdictions, to make them executory. By way of contrast, an arbitral award does not include a formula for execution. In principle, the victorious party must file with a State judge a request that the award be made executory so that the arbitration award may be carried out.

---

[299] SCHOKKAERT, Jan, *Rechtskundig Weekblad*, (Legal Weekly), Antwerpen, Edition Intersentia, 1999/2000, no. 38, 20 May 2000, p. 1304.

16.3. – Types of arbitration

There are two arbitration modalities: *ad hoc* arbitration and *institutional arbitration*.

In *ad hoc* arbitration, the arbitration procedure to be followed is determined by the parties themselves. The arbitration convention then contains rules for the notice of request for arbitration to comply with, for the designation of the arbitrators, the place of arbitration, the use of languages, the determination of schedules, applicable law, the structure of the award, etc.

Drawing up an arbitration convention is not an easy task. This is a task specifically "tailored" for the occasion because for each of the particulars mentioned above, it is necessary to establish clear and complete rules. The United Nations Organisation (UN) is aware of the problems companies and private individuals may encounter and has therefore taken the initiative to encourage and facilitate arbitration *ad hoc*. The United Nations Commission on International Trade (UNCITRAL) has developed a set of rules for arbitration *ad hoc*.

The UN General Assembly approved this set of rules by resolution 31/98, adopted on 15 December 1971:

> "...recommends the application of the Arbitration Rules of UNCITRAL for the settlement of conflicts in commercial international relations, particularly through the reference to the arbitration rules in commercial contracts."

Although this text is intended for commercial contracts, it is evident it may be used *"mutatis mutandis"* for investment contracts also. We should, however, note that UNCITRAL is not concerned with individual cases. Since it is not an arbitration institution, it does not administer arbitration files. This type of settlement for arbitration may inspire international investors who wish to agree upon a State Contract regarding an investment to be made in a less developed country and specifying arbitration as the means for settling disputes.

Next to arbitration *ad hoc*, there is *institutional arbitration*, a framework, entrusted to one of the arbitration institutions which specialise in this matter. They are spread all over the world (Chamber of Commerce for Arbitration in Paris (CCI), African Business Law Harmonisation Organisation (OHADA), London Court of International Arbitration (LCIA), the American Arbitration Association (AAA) etc.

International investors must therefore choose between one of these two formulas. When they conclude a State Contract, they naturally are not alone in that choice. As has been stressed before, less developed countries are very eager to protect their sovereignty. In many cases, they have expressed a preference for arbitration *ad hoc*. This allows them, even as they are inspired by the model UNCITRAL convention, to try to negotiate its terms:

> "Less developed countries have an even greater freedom of choice in *ad hoc* arbitration because they believe they can detect in existing institutional arbitration a tendency to discriminate, essentially based on the fact they did not participate in the establishment of these institutions and would not have accepted the arbitration settlement rules on which they are based, if they had. They therefore find the administration *ad hoc* alternative more favourable to them. They more and more require that the arbitration of State Contracts be modeled after the arbitration settlement procedure developed within the framework of UNCITRAL."[300]

However, it seems to us that arbitration *ad hoc* has a greater number of negatives and more risks for international investors than institutional arbitration. When arguing for arbitration *ad hoc*, it is often said that, in a State Contract, contract partners are on an equal footing and that they together can agree to measures that distribute respective rights and obligations fairly and equitably. Actually, that is not true. In the event the international investor should agree

---

[300] BERLIN, Dominique, *op. cit.*, p. 253, see footnote 273.

to arbitration *ad hoc*, he himself will have to negotiate with a presumably stronger partner the terms of the clause designed to regulate compromises. He will have to see to it that this clause contains sufficient legal fail-safe provisions to protect him efficiently against eventual bad faith of the host State and avoid that the procedure be frozen pursuant to the tactics of that State. International arbitration institutions indubitably have experience and know-how with respect to their arbitration rules and these rules contain clauses that have withstood the test of time for the maximum protection of the rights of either party. The fact that these institutions take charge of all administrative matters required for the filing of an arbitration request is a definite advantage for investors and equally respect the rights of host States.

The arbitration centre manages the arbitration file and keeps the parties informed during its development:

> "The security of institutional arbitration rests on the existence of a set of arbitration rules and on the material and institutional support the institution can afford to grant during the progress of the proceeding. Thus, the rules provide for difficulties that may arise during the course of the proceeding. Security also rests on the fact that the arbitration centre will see to it that the tribunal is established, that arrangements for costs and fees have been paid, that schedules are respected and, generally, that the proceeding unfolds correctly." [301]

16.4. – Advantages and disadvantages of arbitration

16.4.1. – *Impartiability and freedom from undue choice*

In doctrinal texts, there is a tendency to consider private arbitration as an excellent means for solving international disputes relating to investments, whereby a private enterprise can best confront a host State. It is hard to deny that this

---

[301] MEYER, Pierre, *Droit de l'arbitrage*, Brussels, Bruylant, 2002, p. 32.

alternative method for the settlement of disputes offers important benefits. For the international investor, arbitration generally provides a guarantee of neutrality and impartiality. In many countries, the principle of separation of powers is barely acknowledged and the political pressure applied to judges cannot be underestimated. :

> "When the host State it itself party to the dispute, the local judiciary may not always be relied upon as being independent from the political power. Furthermore, in the past, judicial systems in many countries were not sophisticated enough to handle such disputes and did not guarantee impartiality towards foreigners."[302]

Of course, what may be seen as an advantage for an investor may be seen in the reverse light by a host State. However, an advantage to the investor is not necessarily a disadvantage for the host State. Likewise, a disadvantage for the investor is not necessarily an advantage for the host State. Some features are advantages to both sides and some are disadvantages for both sides, though not always in the same measure.

One can readily see that a host State might see some of the features investors prefer as distinct disadvantages and, particularly in State Contracts where their negotiating power may be greatest, States might resist agreements which, in their view, limit their exercise of discretion or sovereignty. Yet, not every advantage to investors has such a mirror image of a disadvantage to host States. The following is a list of features of arbitration, arguably, advantages for investors or disadvantages for host States:

> "arbitrators are not allowed to be nationals of either party to the dispute and are not subject to the authority of hierarchical supervisors; they need not be concerned about having sanctions applied to them and harming their careers."

---

[302] SACERDOTI, Giorgio, *op. cit.*, 414, see footnote 161.

16.4.2. – *Choice of Law*

In the large international arbitration institutions (f.i. ICSID, CCI), the parties have great freedom to act: they may choose the law applicable to the substance of the dispute and determine the place of arbitration. Insofar as arbitration procedure is concerned, the parties may choose the procedure adopted by the institution but they may also choose another (cfr *infra* for examples of ICSID action):

> "...neither the parties nor the arbitrators are required to follow any specific state law governing procedural points likely to arise during the proceeding. They may be quite satisfied... by a reference to a private arbitration procedure rule, as may be proposed in advance by an arbitration centre... They may just as freely have recourse to transnational rules stemming from comparative law analyses or from their observation of arbitration jurisprudence..."[303]

If they choose that a State law be applied, obviously then its obligatory legal provisions must be used by the arbitrators (for instance, those of public order).

The confidentiality which surrounds the entire procedure can likewise be an advantage. Many business people like to settle their differences with a minimum of notoriety: the arbitration tribunal sessions are not public and awards are not published, unless the parties have given their express consent to publication. It follows that the commercial relations between the parties are not disturbed after the award is issued. There is therefore probably not quite the same poignancy in the sense of winning or losing after an arbitration award, as there would normally be in a judicial proceeding in a public venue. On the other hand, some may complain that there is not enough of the transparency that 21st century mores, private or public, personal or commercial, seem to require.

---

[303] FOUCHARD, Philippe, *Traité de l'arbitage commercial international*, LIEC, Paris, 1996, p. 649.

The freedom to choose arbitrators is an incontestable asset. The parties may choose in advance arbitrators who are already experts in the matter to be decided.

State judges are bound by very strict procedure rules whereas private arbitrate may choose among them. Furthermore, parties to the litigation may select the direction in which their problems will be solved, when they choose freely the applicable law:

> "The international negotiator may 'invent' his own judge when he initiates an arbitration proceeding. This is not exactly a new concept, since it existed already in Plato's time, when the solution of litigation could be entrusted to neighbours who had a better acquaintance with the parties and the nature of their conflict, likely to lead to conciliation and, should this fail, to decide. This kind of private justice with a contractual basis validated the regulatory power of the 'contracting parties'. If they could invent their applicable law, they could likewise invent the applicable law and their competent judge will then use and apply it." [304]

16.4.3. – Greater Jurisdictional Scope

The international investor who is a party to a State contract has the ability, subject to the host State's consent, to cause to be included a clause of "amiable compromise" in the contract. In such a case, arbitrators have a greater scope of jurisdiction than state judges. They have the special mission of having to examine the substance of the litigation not only on a legal basis but also on an equitable basis and for the common best interest of the parties. This implies, that insofar as needed, arbitrators may weaken the strict effect of investment contract provisions. In practice, the arbitrators will be creating an amiable arrangement of the dispute under the format of a final and mandatory award:

> "The amiable composition clause amounts to a conventional renunciation of the effects and benefits of the rules of law, the parties agree-

---

[304] BLANCO, Dominique, *Négocier et rédiger un contrat international*, Paris, Dunod, 2002, p. 653.

ing to waive the requirements deriving from the strict application of the law and arbitrators using correspondingly the power to moderate the consequences flowing from contractual stipulations whenever equity or the common interest of the parties suggests it." [305]

This does not at all mean that the arbitrators in an "amiable compromise" situation may overlook rules of law. They continue to apply the rules of law, although they are allowed to consider other sources of law, mostly in equitable fashion, and to weaken or amend, eventually, contractual provisions, whenever the parties will have expanded their jurisdiction in that regard. The "amiable compromise" mission cannot be presumed and must be mentioned *expressis verbis* in the arbitration convention. Not acknowledging the existence of the amiable compromise clause may be cause for the cancellation of an award, on the ground of abuse of the scope of the arbitrators' powers:

> "Abuse of power may well reside in the arbitrator's failure to apply rules set forth in the compromise agreement or in the application of other rules. That may occur when the arbitrator (such as arbitrator Barge in the *Orinoco* case) applying local law rules, although the compromise agreement allowed him to decide the case... 'on the basis of equity alone'... regardless of local provisions of law or *vice versa*, if he issues a decision based on equity whereas he is held to decide based on the law." (BIT's Canada/US case decision of 10 January 1831 regarding the border between the two countries) [306]

In passing, it is worth mentioning that national legislation does not always refer to the term "amiable compromise". For instance, Belgian legislation does not mention it. The eventuality of an amiable compromise may be deduced, by arguing *a contrario*, from the text of the judicial code:

> "Except as may be otherwise provided later than the notice to which reference is made in article 1683, arbitrators will base their decision on rules of law." (**Article 1700**)

---

[305] BLANCO, Dominique, *op. cit.*, p. 645, see footnote 304.
[306] GAILLARD, Emmanuel, *op. cit.*, p. 165, see footnote 31.

There is therefore a contractual ground on which to base an arbitration decision as well as an equitable basis if the parties so choose. It is surprising also that the French term "amiable composition" has not been translated widely in the doctrinal texts nor in other national legislations. Generally, the French term is used "as is" in such legislations. The Dutch judicial code is an exception :

> "The arbitration tribunal will decide according to rules of law. It will decide as 'equitable good men' if the parties have granted them such a power in their contract." (**Article 1054**)

In the Belgian doctrinal texts, two terminologies are used "amiable compositors" and "equitable good men". No effort has been made to find a more suitable translation :

> "On the one hand, there is arbitration 'in law' : arbitrators receive from the parties the mission of deciding the litigation according to rules of law. On the other hand, there is the 'amiable composition' type of arbitration, where arbitrators have received from the parties the right to decide based 'on law and equity'. They decide as 'amiable compositors' would." [307]

It is clear from the usage of such term that what is at stake is an arbitration award (and therefore a final and mandatory decision) based in law and equity. Furthermore, we suggest that this formula be clearly set forth in the arbitration convention.

16.4.4. – *Pratical Benefits*

It can hardly be questioned that, for investors, there are some very valuable benefits to arbitration. Conversely, less developed host States may see some of these features as inimical to their interests. In particular, they may see the use of institutional arbitration fora, such as ICSID, as Western conceived and created, too Western oriented, using arbitrators trained in Western law and traditions, imbued with Western

---

[307] VAN HOUTTE, Hans, "De 'amiable composition én de nieuwe arbitragewet", *Rechtskundig Weekblad*, 36th jaargang, 1972, no. 16, p. 739.

values difficult for even the most impartial of men to divorce themselves from in the circumstances of the cases before them. They may, of course, select arbitrators with a different background, more closely allied to their mindset and traditions. Being required, for instance, to select arbitrators not of the nationality of the parties may seem discriminatory to them, even as to investors, it may appear to be fundamental justice. Yet, for investors and host States alike, some of arbitration's features have to be viewed with caveats that can hardly be ignored :

Speedy disposition. It is said that justice delayed is justice denied. The procedure is far from speedy. Investors are naturally interested in a speedy disposition of the dispute. The host State, on the other hand, for political or economic reasons, may view the delay less unfavourably. The success and development of arbitration during the last few decades have occasionally resulted in the failure to meet established schedules. In 1974, ICSID registered 5 registration petitions, compared to 2003 when the number was 30. This growth is due mainly to the increasing number of bilateral protection conventions. At the present, there are more than 2000 bilateral conventions in the entire world and most of them contain an ICSDI clause. The International Chamber of Commerce (CCI) annually file hundreds of requests for arbitration. It is therefore understandable that the speed of the procedures has been slowed due to the increase in the number of files to be handled.

Cost. Theoretically, the cost of arbitration was to be less than a judicial proceeding before the courts. In fact, the cost of an arbitration proceeding should not be underestimated, inasmuch as the administrative costs for the management of files in an arbitration proceeding by an international institution may be quite high.

As an example, we can refer to the price list of "costs" of the Court of Arbitration of the International chamber of Commerce (CCI).

A. Administrative expenses

Sum in dispute (in US Dollars)				Administrative expenses*
up to	50 000			$2500
from	50 001	to	100 000	4.30%
from	100 001	to	200 000	2.30%
from	200 001	to	500 000	1.90%
from	500 001	to	1 000 000	1.37%
from	1 000 001	to	2 000 000	0.86%
from	2 000 001	to	5 000 000	0.41%
from	5 000 001	to	10 000 000	0.22%
from	10 000 001	to	30 000 000	0.09%
from	30 000 001	to	50 000 000	0.08%
from	50 000 001	to	80 000 000	0.01%
over	80 000 000			$88 800

For illustrative purposes only, the table on the following page indicates the resulting administrative expenses in US$ when the proper calculations have been made.

B. Arbitrator's fees

Sum in disput (in US Dollars)				minimum	maximum
up to	50 000			$2500	17.000%
from	50 001	to	100 000	2.5000%	12.800%
from	100 001	to	200 000	1.3500%	7.250%
from	200 001	to	500 000	1.2900%	6.450%
from	500 001	to	1 000 000	0.9000%	3.800%
from	1 000 001	to	2 000 000	0.6500%	3.400%
from	2 000 001	to	5 000 000	0.3500%	1.300%
from	5 000 001	to	10 000 000	0.1200%	0.850%
from	10 000 001	to	30 000 000	0.0600%	0.225%
from	30 000 001	to	50 000 000	0.0560%	0.215%
from	50 000 001	to	80 000 000	0.0310%	0.152%
from	80 000 001	to	100 000 000	0.0200%	0.112%
over	100 000 000			0.0100%	0.056%

Hence, costs may be quite high. They may be kept under some control if only one arbitrator is selected but it may be difficult for parties with fundamentally different mindsets and traditions to agree on any one individual.

Nonetheless, on balance, arbitration is the best formula for the settlement of investment disputes. Particularly at the international level, institutional arbitration is a good formula for the resolution of disputes. Host States may find that agreeing to arbitrating disputes institutionally is an indispensable element of their development strategy and that excessive resistance to investors' demands in this respect may cause them to invest elsewhere. The role ICSID has played in framing the theatre within which the resolution of international disputes between investors and host States has played out cannot be underestimated. We leave to investors and host States alike the task of evaluating, from the following examples of ICSID action, the advantages and disasdvantages of international arbitration.

16.5. – BITs Reference to International Arbitration Institutions

One could say that, at the present time, all BITs contain arbitration clauses for the settlement of disputes regarding international investments. In the past, the jurisdiction of local tribunals for the resolution of this type of litigation had precedence over all others. This situation has changed during the last few years. BITs seldom refer to the jurisdiction of tribunals. In the large majority of cases, investors are free to choose directly for the submission of disputes to arbitration. Furthermore, investors may, generally, choose arbitration institutions mentioned in their agreement. Sometimes, only the "Centre for the Settlement of Investment Disputes" (ICSID) is the only institution mentioned in the BITs, although more frequently investors can choose between ICSID and ICC's International Court of Arbitration.

16.5.1. – *Exhaustion of Local Remedies*

Litigators in these international arenas are conscious of the "exhaustion of local remedies" requirement. Obviously, the investor's "standing", allowing him to file directly an arbitration request against the State where his investment is located, would be seriously limited, if he were to exhaust all available internal remedies, before proceeding with his request. The Washington Convention negotiators knew how important that question was. Article 26 of the Convention reads as follows :

> "Consent of the parties to arbitration under this convention shall, unless otherwise stated, be deemed consent to such arbitration to the exclusion of any other remedy. A contracting state may require the exhaustion of local remedies as a condition of its consent to arbitration under this convention."

In actual practice, most of the States negotiating BITs show that they are satisfied in granting their consent to arbitration, without expressly waiving prior exhaustion of redress through internal recourse. Their consent imply the waiver of any requirement that the rule about exhaustion of remedies be met.

However, to avoid any misunderstanding, we believe it is better that the Contracting States include in their BITs an express waiver of the exhaustion of local remedies rule. The Belgian model convention includes such a clause :

> "To this end, each contracting party agrees in advance and irrevocably to the settlement of any dispute by this type of arbitratuion. Such consent implies that both parties waive the right to demand that all domestic administrative or judiciary remedies be exhausted."

This clause, or its equivalent, is very valuable to investors. BITs and State Contracts should preferably include it.

16.6. – THE ICC INTERNATIONAL COURT OF ARBITRATION

16.6.1. – *Origin and Description*

The International Chamber of Commerce (ICC) is an association subject to French law, created in Paris in 1919. Representative national committees have spread the world over. In 1923, the ICC established, under its own roof, an international Court of Arbitration. The creation of the ICC's International Court of Arbitration was intended to promote commerce and investment of an international character:

> "The arbitration mechanism has been developed primarily to further the ICC's purpose of facilitating international trade, not to raise revenue. The settlement and prevention of disputes is a natural part of any effort to remove barriers to transnational commerce and investment." [308]

The ICC International Court of Arbitration is the world's foremost institution in the resolution of international business disputes. While most arbitration institutions are regional or national in scope, the ICC Court is truly international. Composed of members from over 80 countries, the ICC Court is the world's most widely representative dispute resolution institution.

The ICC Court is not a "court" in the ordinary sense. As the ICC arbitration body, the ICC Court ensures the application of the Rules of Arbitration of the International Chamber of Commerce. Although its members do not decide the matters submitted to ICC arbitration – this is the task of the arbitrators appointed under the ICC Rules – the Court oversees the ICC arbitration process and, among other things, is responsible for: appointing arbitrators; confirming, as the case may be, arbitrators nominated by the parties; deciding upon challenges of arbitrators; scrutinising and approving all

---

[308] CRAIG, W. Laurence, PARK, William W., PAULSSON, Jan, *International Chamber of commerce arbitration*, New York, Oceana publications, 1990, p. 27.

arbitral Awards; and fixing the arbitrators' fees. In exercising its functions, the Court is able to draw upon the collective experience of distinguished jurists from a diversity of backgrounds and legal cultures as varied as that of the participants in the arbitral process.[309]

16.6.2. – Jurisdiction and Scope

Article 1 of the ICC arbitration rules reads as follows:

> "The function of the Court is to provide for the settlement by arbitration of business disputes of an international character in accordance with the rules of arbitration of the International Chamber of commerce."

It has already been stated that the Court does not settle litigation. It only takes whatever measures are necessary so that the designated arbitrators may render a decision settling the dispute in conformity with the arbitration rules of the ICC.

The jurisdiction of the arbitration court is therefore not altogether clear. The key word of course is "jurisdiction: business nature". Nowhere in the ICC documents does one find a definition of this type of disputes. The expression is so broad and generic that an initial impression might be that there are very few limitations to the Court's jurisdiction. However, disputes involving family law, succession, labour law are obviously excluded because they have no relationship with commerce.

16.6.3. – Jurisdiction over International Investment Disputes

A not very well known fact is that the ICC's International Court of Arbitration was, before ICSID was created, very active in the resolution if disputes relating to international investments:

---

[309] Cfr http://www.iccwbo.org/court/arbitration/id 4399/index.html.

"On the one hand, the late awakening of the ICSID arbitration during the nineties, in part because of the more or less recent execution of some 2000 bilateral investment treaties, is now notorious. Before 1990, ICC arbitration an *ad hoc* arbitration, in particular that organised under the rules for arbitration of the CNUDCI, gave to private investors and States host to international investments, two systems for the resolution of disputes that were most likely to be used."[310]

Litigation relating to international investments are therefore open to arbitration. This may be justified on the basis of statutes, inasmuch litigation is most frequently characterised by their commercial contractual nature. Investors as well as States may become parties to arbitration proceedings with respect to international investments:

"As noted above, a substantial number of cases submitted to ICC arbitration concerned governments or governmental entities directly. This fact reflects one particularly salient feature of the ICC process: it is frequently chosen as part of the contractual framework of large investment projects involving the local government and in which neither side is willing to accept the jurisdiction of the other's national courts."[311]

The decision rendered in a dispute between, on the one hand, the Arab Republic of Egypt and "Egoth", a general Egyptian company for tourism and hotels and, on the other hand the SPP (Middle East) companies and Southern Pacific Properties SPP/Hong Kong, exemplifies this development. Leaving aside the main theme of this decision, a question was raised about the jurisdiction of the ICC Court of International Arbitration. An arbitration clause, providing arbitration by the Court had been inserted in one of the conventions entered into between the parties relating to a tourist village on the Pyramids plateau. This clause stated:

---

[310] ROMERO, Eduardo Silva, "Quelquels brèves observations du point de vue de la Cour Internationale d'arbitrage, de la Chambre de Commerce Internationale", *Revue du Centre de documentation et de recherches de la Cour Internationale d'arbitrage, de la Chambre de Commerce Internationale (CCI)*, 2006, p. 332.

[311] CRAIG, Laurence, *op. cit.*, p. 10, see footnote 308.

"Any dispute relating to this Agreement shall be referred to the arbitration of the International Chamber of commerce in Paris, France."

In spite of the fact that the arbitration clause appeared only in one of the conventions, and could therefore be the subject to valid criticism, the Arbitration Tribunal decided that it had jurisdiction over the issue:

"We accept the principle that acceptance of an arbitration clause should be clear and unequivocal : However, in the December Agreement we see no element of ambiguity. The Government, in becoming a party to that agreement, could not have reasonably doubted that it would be bound by the arbitration clause contained in it. It follows that any disputes relating to the extent of the Government's obligations assumed by its signature and as to whether there has been any breach of those obligations is within the scope of the arbitration clause. We therefore consider that the disputes submitted to us and referred to in the Terms of Reference are within the scope of that submission."[312]

16.6.4. – Link between State Contracts and BIT's

ROMERO stresses that references to ICSID have produced a reduction in the number of arbitration proceedings submitted to ICC. However, it must be realised that there are more and more arbitration clauses in the BIT's providing that the investor may choose among several other arbitration institutions. Mainly, a double reference to both ICC and ICSID has become a rather current practice for many European countries. It is therefore not impossible that, in the future, the number of cases submitted to ICC and ICSID will become even.

Sometimes, a BIT exists between, say, an African State and a State of which the investor is a national, and such investor has entered into a State Contract with the host State. In principle, the investor may therefore claim the pro-

---

[312] JARVIN Sigvard, DERAINS Yves, *Collection of arbitral awards*, Paris, Kluwer, 1998, p. 129.

tection guaranteed by the BIT as well as that provided for in the State Contract. That is the effect of the "umbrella clause" in the BIT which expressly places the State Contracts under the umbrella protection of the BIT. However, insofar as arbitration is concerned, it could also be that the BIT contains a reference to ICSID and the State Contract contains a reference to ICC. In that situation, ICC will take precedence over ICSID and its jurisdiction must therefore apply. The host State will have difficulty contesting a move by the investor to have the ICC's Court take over the case.

In BIT's, there is often a clause whereby contracting States commit themselves to respect the commitments appearing in State Contracts. This includes obviously the State Contract's arbitration provisions in accordance with the principle of *"generalia specialibus non derogant"* which is recognised under international law. The State Contract then becomes a *"lex specialis"*. Were the host State to apply to ICSID, disregarding the provisions of the State Contract, the General Secretary of the Centre should refuse registration of the application, because of its manifest contradiction with the provisions of the Washington Convention, whose article 26 states:

> "Consent of the parties to arbitration under this convention shall, unless otherwise stated, be deemed consent to such arbitration to the exclusion of any other remedy."

The arbitration clause in a State Contract must therefore be considered as a contrary stipulation and implies its precedence in the determination of the proceeding's venue.

A question arises when an investor, after incurring an unfavourable decision by the ICC, could then again go to ICSID, hoping perhaps to get a better deal there. In such a case, an investor would therefore have a kind of appeal or reconsideration right with ICSID for a decision rendered in the same case by ICC. ROMERO favours this result, citing *SGS v. Pakistan*.[313] He reaches the following conclusion:

---

[313] GAILLARD, Emmanuel, *op. cit.*, p. 816, see footnote 31.

> "If our interpretation of these decisions is correct, an ICSID tribunal could 'reconsider' on the basis of international law a decision of an arbitration tribunal such as an ICC arbitration settlement rendered in accordance with the provisions of the State Contract." [314]

The answer to this question is a little more complex. ICSID's and ICC's dual jurisdictions have different goals:

> "The fact that we see, in the SGS case, a clause providing for local arbitration rather than host State jurisdiction does not change at all the nature of the problem, in as much as the parties have, in each of these hypotheses, taken care to designate the magistrate capable of coexisting with the magistrate designated by the BIT." [315]

There are, therefore, two separate procedures, following the rules of each institution, and not a reconsideration issue. Obviously the State Contract must fall under the protection of the BIT. The State Contract must expressly be placed under the jurisdiction of the BIT, in conformity with the said clause (sometimes called the "lift" clause) which elevates the State Contract's commitments to the level of international law. In order to increase their legal security, States which are parties to BIT's should expressly stipulate that the State's commitments are international obligations and that their violation is assimilated to a violation of the applicable BIT:

> "As Prosper WEIL has observed treaties may furthermore elevate contractual undertakings into international law obligations, by stipulating that breach by one State of a contract with a private party from the other State will also constitute a breach of the treaty between the two States." [316]

The jurisdictional dualism may therefore stem from the fact that the judge reviewing the contract will examine the State's violation of its contractual duties and will decide on the contractual responsibility of the State, whereas the judge designated in the BIT will examine the host State's violations of the contract conditions elevated to the level of interna-

---

[314] ROMERO, Edoardo Silva, *op. cit.*, p. 342, see footnote 310.
[315] GAILLARD, Emmanuel, *op. cit.*, p. 832, see footnote 311.
[316] GAILLARD, Emmanuel, *op. cit.*, p. 833, see footnote 31.

tional commitments and he will then deduce the international responsibility of the State. There are therefore two distinct procedures, one before the judge reviewing the contract only and the other before a judge concerned with the BIT.

Eventual jurisdictional problems could also be resolved if the BIT contains an arbitration clause granting jurisdiction to ICSID and the investor manages to have included, in his State Contract, a clause providing for the same jurisdiction. In such a case, the investor could submit to ICSID any and all disputes regarding the investment contract.

In the event that the State Contract shows ICC as the competent arbitration tribunal and the BIT shows ICSID, there would likewise be no problem, if, in the State Contract, there is then a "fork-in-the-road" clause stating that the investor has a choice between various fora (local tribunal, international arbitration) but that, once he has chosen among these possibilities, his choice is final. The investor then could not go shopping for another forum if the forum he chose still has jurisdiction or has reached a decision.

16.6.5. – *Prerequisite for ICC Arbitration*

The principle of consent which governs in international arbitration is also a fundamental principle of the arbitration rules of the ICC's International Court of Arbitration. If the parties cannot prove the existence of an arbitration agreement, the Court will not initiate the procedure and will not go about assembling an arbitration tribunal.

A dispute may be submitted to arbitration by means of an arbitration clause contained in a contract. It is generally recognised that the arbitration clause, and thus the arbitration agreement, are to be deemed separate and independent from the main contract. The result therefrom is that the arbitration clause is still valid, even when the main contract should be declared void.

16.6.6. – *Arbitrators as "Amiable Compositeur"*

As a general rule, the arbitration tribunal hearing a dispute will render its decision based on the terms of the contract and applicable law :

> "The parties shall be free to agree upon the rules of law to be applied by the arbitral tribunal to the merits of the dispute. In the absence of any such agreement, the Arbitral Tribunal shall apply the rules of law which it determines to be appropriate." (**Article 17**)

There is a question whether the arbitrators will be able to consider outside factors in order to come to an easier solution for the dispute submitted to them. This is indeed possible, provided that the parties themselves entrust to the arbitrators the specific duty so to do, that is, the power to render a decision as "amiable compositors", an expression derived from the French usage.

This specific power cannot be presumed. There must be an express mention of it in the arbitration clause or agreement. **Article 17.3** reads as follows :

> "The arbitral tribunal shall assume the powers of an amiable compositeur or decide *ex aequo et bono* only if the parties have agreed to give it such powers."

"Amiable compositors" cannot avoid applicable law but they have the power to interpret such law and the contract which is the subject matter of the dispute, taking into consideration equity (*ex aequo et bono*), general legal principles and *"lex mercatoria"* as well as their own consciences. However, their power is not unlimited. Thus, if national law is shown to be that applicable to the contract, as if often the case, amiable compositors may not disregard such legal rules, inasmuch as they are a matter of public order, such as the rule that the contract is the parties' law :

> "Considering that, even in their capacity as amiable compositors, as conferred upon them by Article 3 of the Rules of the Arbitration Court, arbitrators do not have the power to craft a new contractual equilibrium and to substitute themselves to the parties who failed to

renegotiate their contract. It is not within their jurisdiction to proceed to revise the contract in the manner requested by..."[317]

16.7. – OHADA's Common Court of Justice and Arbitration (CCJA)[318]

Until now, European countries have not yet referred, in their arbitration clauses, to arbitration institutions other than ICSID and ICC's International Court of Arbitration. Looking to the future, however, it may be worthwhile to mention briefly CCJA, a well organised arbitration institution in Africa.

16.7.1. – *Origins*

The Organisation for the harmonisation in Africa of Business Rights (OHADA) was created by the multilateral Treaty of 17 October 1993. Within OHADA, a Common Court of Justice (CCJA) and arbitration has been installed. This court has jurisdiction over judicial affairs and may, among other things, rule on decisions rendered by the appellate courts of the Contracting States. The Court may also be consulted by Contracting States. Finally, the Court has competence for the organisation of arbitral procedures :

> "In applying a arbitration clause or an out of court settlement, any party to a contract may, either because it has its domicile or its usual residence in one of the Contracting States, or if the contract is enforced or to be enforced in its entirely or partially on the territory of one or several contracting States, refer a contract litigation to the arbitration procedure provided in this section.
>
> The Common Court of Justice and Arbitration does not itself settle such disagreements. It shall name and confirm the arbitrators, be informed of the progress of the proceedings, and examine decisions, in accordance with **Article 24**." (**Article 21** Treaty)

---

[317] JARVIN, Sigvard, *op. cit.*, p. 32, see footnote 312.
[318] Www.Juriscope.org.

16.7.2. – Scope

The international character of CCJI arbitration cannot be compared to ICSID arbitration. To begin with, the number of adherent States is rather limited.[319]

In a material sense, recourse to CCJI arbitration is limited to contractual disputes. This provision is obviously an important limitation in the scope of arbitration recourse. Furthermore, there must be a link between the private contractor and the member State. The private person who is a party to the dispute must have his domicile or customary residence on the territory of a member State and the contract has been or will signed on the territory of one or more of the member States.

The term "investment" does not appear in the Treaty, nor in the arbitration rules. This does not necessarily imply that international investments are excluded, as long as there is in fact an investment contract. Regarding jurisdictional immunity, private parties may benefit from a favourable provision, in the sense that the host State may not invoke its own national legislation to claim immunity :

> "Any person, physical or moral, may have recourse to arbitration of the rights to which he is entitled.
>
> The States and other public agencies in the territory as well as other Public Establishments may also be parties to an arbitration proceeding, without, however, invoking their own right to contest the arbitrability of the dispute, their ability to enter into compromises, or the validity of the arbitration agreement." (**Article 2** of the Uniform Arbitration Law)

Some authors see in this provision a promotional incentive for international investments :

> "This provision is particularly interesting for foreign investors who are generally forced to establish a 'joint venture' with a public agency

---

[319] To day : Benin, Burkina Faso, Cameroon, Central African Republic, Comores, Congo Republic, Ivory Coast Gabon, Guinea, Mali, Niger, Senegal, Chad, Togo.

or establishment, to the extent that this construct prevents the latter from invoking jurisdictional immunity."[320]

However, it appears that revisions to the arbitration system are required in order to allow OHADA CCJI to become an arbitration institution adapted to the needs of international investors, as with ICSID in Washington. Contractually, that is by referring expressly to OHADA CCJI in the BIT's, the arbitration procedure could be harmonised with the interests of international investors and thereby be "internationalised" further.

16.7.3. – *CCJA as Arbitration Centre*

The Common Court of Justice and Arbitration does not itself pass upon jurisdictional questions. The CCJA has administrative functions and organises arbitration: composition of the arbitration Tribunal by nominating arbitrators, recusal of arbitrators, examination of proposed decisions. The Court does not review the substance of the dispute. It may only make purely formal proposals. Decisions are not appealable. As with ICSID decisions, they may be subject to procedures challenging their validity. This procedure is comparable to the annulment procedure of ICSID. As an exception to its customary administrative role, the CCJI, in its power to render decisions on the recourse submitted to it, has, at least jurisdiction over such recourse.

The seat of the CCJI is in Abidjan (Ivory Coast) and its Secretary General is also its Recorder.

---

[320] MARTOR, Boris, PILKINGTON, Nanette, *Le droit uniforme africain des affaires issu de l'OHADA*, Paris, Litec, 2004, p. 253.

16.8. – ICSID THE INTERNATIONAL CENTRE FOR SETTLEMENT OF INVESTMENT DISPUTES

16.8.1. – *Enabling Legislation*

ICSID was created as an autonomous international institution under the auspices of the World Bank. It was the object of a multilateral convention entitled "Convention for the Settlement of Investment Disputes between States and nationals of other States" signed in Washington, D.C. on 18 March 1965 and opened for signature by other States. This multilateral convention entered into force on 14 October 1966, several States having delayed their adherence significantly. Today, most of the world's States are members of this important convention. There are over one hundred and forty member States.

The number of arbitration petitions submitted to the Centre has increased notably since 1997. ICSID was created as an impartial international forum providing facilities for the resolution of legal disputes between eligible parties, through conciliation or arbitration. The Centre is not an international court but an administrative institution, offering aid and logistic assistance for the establishment of arbitration tribunals and commissions. It does not itself render decisions. The Arbitral Tribunal, constituted in accordance with the arbitration rules decides on the disputes.

The parties signatory to the Convention have innovated in the sense that they created the possibility for private parties (*in casu*, international investors) to file for an arbitration procedure against States. Till then, only States could submit their disputes with other States to an international Court. Evidently, the ability for a private investor to cause an arbitration procedure to be initiated between him and a State is a very valuable asset to him, arguably a significant restraint on the host State:

> "This summary description will suffice to bring out the principal feature of the Convention, namely that it provides procedures on the

international level for adjudicating disputes between states and private Parties... this capacity of individuals to appear with States on a footing of equality before international conciliation commissions and arbitral tribunals is a further recognition of the status of the individual as a subject of international law." [321]

As evidenced by its large membership, considerable caseload, and by the numerous references to its arbitration facilities in investment treaties and laws, ICSID plays an important role in the field of international investment and economic development. [322]

16.8.2. – ICSID has Limited Jurisdiction

ICSID's jurisdiction does not extend to any and all disputes. **Article 25(1)** of the Convention defines the Centre's jurisdiction as follows:

> "The jurisdiction of the Centre extend to disputes of a legal nature between a Contracting State (or such public collective or other organism dependent upon such State and designated as such by it to the Centre) and the national of another Contracting State, provided that such disputes are directly related to an investment and, in accordance with the parties' written consent, are to be submitted to the Centre. When the parties have given their consent, none of them may unilaterally withdraw it."

Essentially, the Centre's limited jurisdiction is based on three constraints or rules:

1. capacity of the parties;
2. the nature of the dispute;
3. the consent of the parties involved to submit their dispute to the Centre.

These three rules are interdependent. How case law and international law practice have fashioned their interpretation to promote foreign investment and help less developed countries craft public policies encouraging economic development

---
[321] Private archives.
[322] Www.worldbank.org/icsid.

and sound, modern commercial practices will be addressed in detail in the chapters that follow.

16.8.3. – *Identifying Potential Parties and their Capacity for having Access to ICSID*

16.8.3.1. *Exclusions of ICSID Competence*

Interstate disputes may not be submitted to ICSID arbitration. Such disputes may eventually be submitted to the International Court of Justice and the International Court of Arbitration (under certain conditions). States may also consider a diplomatic solution and sometimes arbitration *ad hoc*.

Governmental institutions or agencies providing insurance for foreign investments against political risks (see, for instance, *supra* **ONDD**) are assimilated to States for the purpose of determining capacity and hence also lack capacity and may not be parties claimant in an ICSID arbitration procedure filed against a host State. After indemnifying the investor, these institutions may well be subrogated to the investor's rights but that does not mean that they can become parties to an ICSID procedure filed by a private party against a host State.

When the Convention was in the process of negotiation, some States suggested that public insurance institutions might become parties to ICSID procedures in their capacities as subrogees, but the idea was never acted upon:

> "While there was general agreement from the outset that private versus private and State *versus* State disputes should be excluded from the jurisdiction of the Centre, a number of Governments felt that an exception should be made permitting a State or public international institution which had been subrogated to the claim of an eligible investor, to be substituted for that investor in proceedings under the auspices of the Centre. This view was urged principally by the governments of capital exporting countries and was accepted by some

developing countries. However, other developing countries opposed it vigorously, and in the end, it was dropped."[323]

In perfect symmetry with the State v. State disqualification, where the dispute is solely between private parties, for instance between an international investor and a lawfirm of the host State, the disputes of such parties, are likewise disqualified under the Convention, because a "State" is missing. The missing element makes the parties ineligible to the use of the Centre's procedure because neither of the parties is a member State. Analogously, investors who lack capacity are at liberty to choose a national tribunal having jurisdiction over the matter of their dispute, or they could have recourse to commercial international arbitration (f.i. the International Chamber of Commerce).

Where the litigation is between a Contracting State and one of its own nationals, the parties are likewise not eligible to use the jurisdiction of ICSID, because the investor may not have the nationality of the State on whole territory the investment has been effected. Capacity is based upon a "diversity" of nationalities. In the aforementioned cases, the litigants are excluded from ICSID arbitration and must choose another forum.

16.8.3.2. *Contracting States as Disputing Parties*

Under the regimen of the Washington Convention, one of the parties must be a State member of the Convention, or any constituent subdivision or agency of a Contracting State. The Secretariat of ICSID can easily verify if a State which is a party to a dispute is a member of the Convention. All members are registered.

There is a bit of a problem when the Secretary must verify that a party to the dispute is indeed a constituent subdivision or agency of a Contracting State. In order to avoid conflicts

---

[323] BROCHES, Aron, *op. cit.*, p. 265, see footnote 71.

on this issue, the Convention's negotiators have wisely decided that it was the Contracting State's burden to notify the ICSID the names of the entities to be considered as State subdivisions or agencies.

Investors who commit to a State agency should nonetheless take care that their co-contracting party is indeed registered with ICSID. If not, the arbitration clause would be ineffective inasmuch as a non registered subdivision cannot be assimilated to a Contracting State and cannot participate in an arbitration proceeding.

For many years, States applied the principle of sovereignty. There was double immunity in that they were jurisdictionally immune as well as immune from being required to perform :

> "Sovereign immunity is a principle of international law under which States are exempted from the jurisdiction of foreign States A sovereign State cannot be impleaded in the municipal courts of another State... As a concomitant to this rule, the courts accorded absolute immunity from execution to States. Execution on State property was seen as an encroachment upon the smooth conduct of governmental affairs and a threat to the comity of nations." [324]

It should be noted that the application of the sovereignty principle has weakened over the years. Currently, it is believed that it is no longer applicable absolutely and that, in particular with respect to the commercial activity of States, immunity is no longer accepted :

> The restrictive theory of immunity grants immunity to public acts of States (i.e. acta jure imperii) but denies immunity to their private acts (i.e. acta jure gestionis). Under this theory a State loses its immunity whenever it engages in commercial activities."

In any case, there is no immunity for States within ICSID. States are free to waive their immunity, conventionally. Investors who benefit from an arbitration clause or agreement signed by a State registered with ICSID need not fear

---

[324] CHUKWUMERIJE, Okezie, "ICSID Arbitration sovereign immunity", Anglo-American Law review, volume 19/1990, p. 170.

that the dispute submitted to the arbitration Tribunal will thereafter be transferred to a national Tribunal:

> "Under the ICSID regime, however, consent to arbitration is exclusive of all other types of remedies. ICSID arbitration is, to a considerable extent, freed from contact with the municipal court system. A municipal court in a country that ratified the ICSID convention is obliged to decline jurisdiction if a dispute is brought to it in contravention of an ICSID arbitration clause"[325]

In any event, **Article 26** of the Washington Convention expressly confirms this rule:

> "Consent of the parties to arbitration under this Convention shall, unless otherwise stated, be deemed consent to such arbitration to the exclusion of any other remedy."

16.8.3.3. *Investors Nationals of another Contracting State*

Being a "national" of a member State is a key element of an investor's capacity but being of a nationality different from that of the opposing State is just as indispensable for the claimant's standing to file. Thus, *diversity of nationality* is another precondition of an investor's *capacity* entitling him *to have acces to ICSID* arbitration procedure.

In international practice, continuity of nationality is often required in order to validate the standing of a claimant. The Washington Convention also has this requirement for nationals of another Contracting State:

> "National of another Contracting State means: any natural person who had the nationality of a Contracting State other than the State party to the dispute on the date on which the parties consented to submit such dispute to conciliation or arbitration, as well as on the date on which the request was registered... but does not include any person who on either date also had the nationality of the Contracting State party to the dispute..." (**Article 25(2) a)**)

Although it is not so said expressly, this provision may well excludes people who have a double nationality on one of the

---

[325] CHUKWUMERIJE, Okezie, *op. cit.*, p. 174, see footnote 324.

aforesaid dates, should one of these nationalities be that of the host State.

16.8.3.4. *The Corporate Exception*

The term "national of another Contracting State" applies to both natural and legal persons. Whether the investor is a private individual or a corporation, he or it must have the nationality of another Contracting State in order to gain access to ICSID arbitration. Physical and legal persons which have the nationality of the host State are therefore excluded.

However, the Convention's capacity provisions create an important exception available only to corporations parties to a dispute with the State where they have invested as nationals thereof (see also Chapter VII).

This exception is not available to physical persons who, as already stated, must be an eligible "national", that is, having the nationality of a Contracting State other than the State which is a party to the dispute. **Article 25.b** broadens the definition of eligible nationals to qualify not only corporations which clearly have a nationality of a Contracting State other than the Contracting State party to the dispute on the date on which the parties consented to submit the dispute to arbitration, but also:

> "any legal person which had the nationality of the contracting State, party to the dispute, on that date and which, because of foreign control, the parties have agreed should be treated as a national of another Contracting State for the purposes of this Convention."

We have already seen that the quality of nationality for a corporation is different from that of a physical person, but here again use is made of the term "nationality" as if the corporate quality were the same as the individual's. References are therefore made to corporate "nationals" and physical person "nationals" with as little practical discomfort as is with the mismatch of corporation nationality and physical person nationality.

JURISDICTION 527

The Washington Convention and international practice allow the parties to the dispute to agree to consider that a corporation sharing the nationality of the host State is nonetheless a corporate national of another State if it *is* under *foreign control*. As a result, any such corporate "person" is an eligible "national" of a State other than the host State and may submit therefore an investment dispute to ICSID.

A problem therefore could arise when ownership of the share capital of a corporation changes and foreign control is lost after the date of consent to arbitration. The host State cannot change the nationality of a physical person but it could invoke the loss of foreign control of a legal person. For this reason, the term "national of another Contracting State" has been formulated differently for legal persons than for physical persons. The requirement of continuity of nationality does not apply to legal persons. They must, however, have the nationality of a Contracting State other than that of the State which is a party to the dispute but only on the date on which the parties consented to submit such dispute to arbitration and not on the date on which the request for arbitration was registered.

The *"ratio legis"* of this provision is clear. If the loss of foreign control, occurring between these two dates were a valid cause for invalidating ICSID's jurisdiction, a risk arises that the host State will itself take measures to terminate the foreign control and thus escape arbitration. Initially, there were doubts and some thought that, notwithstanding **Article 25(2)b** regarding "continuity of control", it was reasonable to admit that foreign control had to exist on both dates. Today, however, there is no doubt. Many decisions of ICSID have confirmed that foreign control need exist only on the date of consent to arbitration:

> "It is mostly the reason for being of the distinction, as very clearly enunciated in the decision, *Vaccum Salt v. Ghana*, which carries that conviction. If the loss of a local company's foreign control were sufficient to remove compliance with the Center's jurisdictional require-

ments, all that the host State would have to do would be to expropriate the investor's local company and thereby escape the Center's jurisdiction. For physical persons, a risk that the host State undertake measures, in the time between the dates of consent and that of the arbitration request, resulting in the investor's loss of the benefit of the required nationality does not exist. It is quite understandable, in these conditions, that for legal persons, the condition of foreign nationality, stemming from the nationality of the party having foreign control upon the local company, will only be required at the time consents are exchanged."[326]

International investors and States should keep well in mind this special provision, concerning the influence of control on corporate nationality when negotiating with each other. As a valuable exception, investors should seek to "nail it down" in their State contracts. Conversely, States that are jealous of their judicial sovereignty should resist it or use it as a lever to extract concessions from the investors. As we shall see from a review of case law, the exception, though frequently invoked by investors is just as frequently challenged by States. The matter is of capital importance to both.

16.8.3.5. *How the issue arises*

Investment codes in several less developed countries require investors to make their investments through a domestic corporation. This is part of the host States' strategy for maintaining exclusive legal control over entities operating in their territories. Furthermore, in their view, diversity of nationality will be lacking and ICSID jurisdiction would be denied. Here is how, for example, the Congolese code handles the situation:

> "Investors (foreign) are admissible to the application of the present law under the following conditions... be an economic entity established under Congolese law." (**Article 8**)

Some codes appear to acknowledge expressly the intrinsic foreign character of an investment;

---

[326] GAILLARD, Emmanuel, *op. cit.*, p. 404, see footnote 31.

> "A direct foreign investment (IED) is any investment whose foreign participation in the capital of an enterprise in which the investment made is at least 10%." (**Article 2.e** Congolese Code)

But this does not exclude the possibility that the host State may still claim the enterprise is not, for the purposes of ICSID, a diverse national. The code provision may, at most, allow the host State, when it suits its purposes, to claim ICSID is the proper place for the enterprise to file a claim. But there is no obligation, when it is not stipulated expressly that the local company has the "nationality of the other Contracting party" as follows out of the foreign control on the local corporation.

The Rwanda investment code requires that the foreign capital meet a minimum of the total invested in order to qualify for foreign national status:

> "Foreign investor: a physical person, a commercial company, or a corporation, whose investment is at least equal to one hundred thousand US dollars of foreign capital in an enterprise to which the present law applies and which is a commercial corporation established in accordance with Rwandese law in which more than half of the shares or capital participations are held by persons which do not possess Rwandese nationality nor the nationality of any State which is a member of the Common Market of the States of Southern and Eastern Africa." (**Article 1. f.iii**)

This, again, establishes a minimum but does not exclude the possibility that a local enterprise with foreign capitalisation exceeding the minimum will not be challenged. If it files with ICSID, then if it has not been stipulated that it is under foreign control, it fails the test. These codes therefore are examples how less developed States overtly grant to international investors the possibility to justify their participation majority or minority, when measures that are privative of private property rights are taken with respect to a local corporation in which they invested, but covertly reserve for themselves the chance of a counterargument, saying that the measures are taken against a national company. It would therefore be imprudent for an international investor to rely solely on these code provisions.

In actual practice, it has turned out that some Contracting States, most notably from the African continent, have attempted to exclude international investors from having recourse to ICSID arbitration. These States have taken the position that the litigation does not concern any foreign investor and are solely between a Contracting State and a local company sharing its nationality.

As already said, it would seem appropriate that foreign investors be particularly attentive to the requirements of **Article 25(2)b** of the ICSID Convention. Whenever a State contract is about to be concluded with a host State, the foreign party should see to it that a clause be inserted in the contract, acknowledging that a local company will be considered as a national of another State, because of the control exercised over that *local company by a foreign investor, national or corporation*. This will help undercut any host State claim to the contrary. **Article 25(2)b** attributes a subsidiary or functional nationality to a domestic corporation, precisely in order not to limit ICSID's jurisdiction unduly. Negotiators for less developed States should be aware of the reason for most investors' insistence on this point and design their conventional and legislative strategy accordingly.

BROCHES showed that this exception served a real need:

> "There was a compelling reason for this last provision (**Article 25(2)b** . It is quite usual for host States to require that foreign investors carry on their business within their territories through a company organised under the laws of the host country. If we admit that this makes the company technically a national of the host country, it becomes readily apparent that there is a need for an exception. If no exception were made for foreign owned but locally incorporated companies, a large and important sector of foreign investment would be outside the scope of the Convention."[327]

---

[327] BROCHES, Aron, *The Hague Academy Collected Courses*, 1975, p. 358.

16.8.3.6. *Mere diversity is not enough: there must be "control"*

As previously stated, ICSID provides that a corporation, party to the dispute, of the contracting State, may be considered as a "national of another State" by virtue of "the *control* exercised" on it by foreign interests. The Washington Convention's text does not make clear what percentage determines what a sufficient controlling interest is. The ICSID jurisprudence offers little help in establishing this percentage:

> "The tribunal has noted and confirmed that foreign control in the sense of the second provision of **Article 25(2)b** neither requires nor implies any specific percentage of capital shares. Every case under which this question arises under such provision must be considered within its own context on the basis of facts and circumstances. There is no 'formula'. It is self-evident, of course, that a shareholding that is 100% foreign would lead almost certainly to the conclusion that foreign control exists, no matter what criteria are used, and that a total absence of foreign shareholders would virtually prevent reaching a conclusion of foreign control. How to know what is 'sufficient' cannot be decided in the abstract. Thus, during the negotiation of the Convention, on several occasions it was pointed out that 'interests sufficiently important to block major changes in the company' would be a characteristic of 'control', that 'control' could be established by persons holding as little as 25% of the capital and even that 51% of the shares would not necessarily characterise control but that as little as 15% might, in other cases, be sufficient." [328]

What precautionary measures does such a holding lead an international investor to adopt? First of all, investors must insist on the execution of an explicit State Contract which recognises their investment and the nationality thereof. The foregoing shows that it is not necessary to specify a percentage of the investors' participation but it is necessary that the parties expressly agree on the subsidiary nationality and not leave it to implication only. For political and other reasons, neither party may wish to document the percentage of control. Besides, shares may be sold, traded or otherwise alien-

---

[328] GAILLARD, Emmanuel, *op. cit.*, p. 398, see footnote 31.

ated, bringing about a change in the percentage. The investor, at least, may not want to see its status as a "foreign national" jeopardised by share transfers over which it has little to say.

In the case of *Holiday Inn*, *Amco* and *Klöckner*, the ICSID arbitrators studied the modalities of application of **Article 25(2)b**. The parties in the dispute (host State and foreign investor) had not expressly mentioned that the domestic company had to be considered a foreign company because of the control of foreign interests. ICSID's jurisdiction was found to exist on the ground that the investment contract as well as the request for an investment licence referred to a "foreign company".

This would seem to be weak evidence indeed. An express contract provision making it clear in writing that the domestic company was to be considered foreign would have been highly desirable. Even where a convention does follow a precise model, text in the State contract that evidences that "the parties agreed" to the investor's foreign nationality should be unmistakable. Explicit provisions are the rule, since the burden is on the filing party to show ICSID's jurisdiction. In his commentary on the Holiday Inn award, LALIVE argued indirectly for an explicit and written contract provision:

> "A question arises, however, about the need for an express provision in the agreement or whether the issue may be implicit. The solution which such a agreement is intended to achieve uses an exception to the general rule established by the Convention. The parties may therefore be expected to express themselves clearly and explicitly when they diverge from the rule. An implicit commitment would be acceptable only if unusual circumstances excluded any other interpretation regarding the parties' intent. This is not what we have before us in this case." [329]

---

[329] GAILLARD, Emmanuel, *op. cit.*, p. 63, see footnote 31.

It cannot be denied that arbitrators are not unanimous regarding their interpretation of **Article 25(2)b** of the Washington Convention and the need, *vel non*, of an express agreement of the parties regarding the meaning of the term "national of another State, because of the control exercised on the domestic corporation by foreign interests". Some ICSID arbitrators have given a broad interpretation to that article and did not require a specific, written provision.

Here is another example of this relaxed attitude: In the case *Letco v. Liberia*, an award was made on 31 March 1986, despite the opposition of Liberia to ICSID's jurisdiction on the ground that there was no written express provision regarding the application of article 25(2)b. That award confirmed ICSID's jurisdiction on the ground that Liberia had signed with Letco a State investment contract containing a ICSID arbitration clause. The arbitrators stressed that ICSID's jurisdiction could be deduced from the Liberian authorities' consent to ICSID arbitration. Through this consent, Liberia had indirectly but implicitly agreed – according to the arbitrators – that Letco, despite the absence of a reference to article **25(2)b** was to be "considered as a 'foreign company'". The issue of "control" seems to have been ignored.

As a matter of fact, according to the Washington Convention, ICSID is uniquely competent to hear claims by investors who are "nationals of another State". According to the arbitrators, consenting to ICSID arbitration was therefore sufficient to allow the inference of a consent to the foreign nationality of Letco:

> "When a Contracting State signs an investment agreement containing a ICSID arbitration clause with a corporation of the same nationality as the Contracting State but under foreign control, and when such State does so in full awareness that the agreement may be submitted for arbitration within the jurisdiction of ICSID, it accepts that such corporation shall be treated as a national of another Contracting State. Such State may be deemed having given its assent simply from the fact that it has consented to the ICSID arbitration clause. That

is particularly true when the law of such State requires that foreign investors establish a domestic corporation when they make their investment."[330]

Nonetheless, international investors should not rely too much on a broad interpretation of the arbitrators' reliance on an "implicit agreement". It is far better that they see to it, for the sake of legal safety, that the home State's BIT as well as their State Contract include an explicit nationality clause. ICSID has made forms of such a clause available for the use of investors.

16.8.4. – Nature of Dispute

16.8.4.1. Dispute must be about a point of law

Only those legal disputes which relate to an investment may, according to the Washington Convention, be submitted to ICSID's arbitration. The term "any legal dispute", as used in Article 25 regarding ICSID's jurisdiction implies that the disputes must relate to the rights and obligations of the parties to the dispute. That means that only such disputes that have arisen from rules of positive law law as incorporated in an agreement, (principles of international law as generally accepted) or as may stem from the investment contracts themselves are acceptable. When one of these rules of law is violated, disputes relating to it may be submitted to an arbitration tribunal established according to ICSID's rules. There are many examples: a BIT's interpretation, the failure to respect or perform contractual commitments (stabilisation clauses, f.i.), requests for compensation of damages, violation of BIT conventional rules regarding national treatment and MFN treatment, etc.)

Mere conflicts of interest are not susceptible of being arbitrated. If, for example, after a State contract has been signed, the investor wanted to renegotiate it but the host

---
[330] GAILLARD, Emmanuel, *op. cit.*, p. 202, see footnote 31.

State opposed such a renegotiation, that dispute could not be submitted to ICSID's arbitration since no specific violation of a rule of law relating to a right of the investor was involved.

In the *Barcelona Traction* case, another example has been provided:

> "Creditors do not have any right to claim compensation from a person who, by wronging their debtor, causes them loss. In such cases, no doubt, the interests of the aggrieved are affected, but not their rights. Thus whenever a shareholders' interests are harmed by an act done to the company, it is to the latter that he must look to institute appropriate action; for although two separate entities may have suffered from the same wrong, it is only one entity whose rights have been infringed." [331]

16.8.4.2. *Dispute must be directly related*

Furthermore, the Washington Convention specifies that the dispute must relate directly to an investment. Purely commercial transactions fall outside the scope of application of the Convention. However, since the Convention does not provide a definition of the term "investment", doctrinal texts saw this absence as a source of difficulty insofar as the scope of ICSID's jurisdiction was concerned. Later, it appeared this concern was ill founded. ICSID's jurisprudence shows that the jurisdiction of ICSID's tribunals has not been circumscribed by such absence.

ICSID's arbitrators have had a tendency to widen the scope of their jurisdiction by interpreting the term "investment" quite broadly. For example, in the *Holiday Inn v. Morocco* case (1972), where a basic investment contract had been followed by annexed agreements which referred to the basic agreement and defined the financing and execution conditions, Morocco objected to ICSID's jurisdiction. Morocco claimed that these annexed agreements could not be consid-

---

[331] *Barcelona Traction Light and Power Company Limited*, op. cit., p. 35, see footnote 15.

ered an "investment" and that disputes tied to their execution were not "relative to an investment".

Morocco's position was rejected by ICSID arbitrators on the ground that investments cannot be seen as isolated transactions but rather within the context of a global operation which included all kinds of secondary activities:

> "But, in very concise manner, the arbitration tribunal has also extended its reasoning much further, by insisting on the global character of the contractual bonds typing the parties to each other, and by invoking, for the very first time and in order to justify its step, the notion of unicity of the investment operation considered by the parties. The arbitrators have noted that it was well known that an investment is achieved through a number of legal acts of all kinds. Therefore, neither economic reality nor the will of the parties would be acknowledged, if we were to analyse each of the acts in complete isolation from any of the other. It was particularly important for the tribunal to determine, within the framework of such analysis, the act which constituted the basis for the investment and from which the other acts derived, as the means to carry it out." [332]

16.8.4.3. "Services" as "investment"

In the case of *Mitchel v. the Democratic Republic of the Congo* (2004), a U.S. lawyer had filed an indemnity claim based on damages sustained as a result of the sequestration of his assets by the Congolese Army. The Republic of the Congo denied ICSID's jurisdiction, claiming that a lawfirm, including its furniture and files, could not be considered an "investment" under the Washington Convention. The arbitration tribunal rejected the Congolese argument, notably on the basis of an ICSID report which expressed a preference for a very broad definition of the notion:

> "It appears to the Tribunal that, absent any indication that particular activities which could be considered to be services are excluded from the scope of the Treaty (BIT), this notion must be viewed broadly and include any and all services furnished by a foreign inves-

---

[332] OUAKRAT, Philippe, "The ICSID Practice", *Droit et Pratique du Commerce International (DPCI)*, 1987, Tome 13, n° 2, p. 289.

tor on the territory of the host State. In this respect, the notion of 'service' is one that is specific to the BIT. There is no other indication by reason of which this notion should be interpreted in accordance with other agreements defining the notion of service, such as those agreed on within the scope of GATT or OMC... Therefore, services normally furnished by a lawfirm, such as they were furnished by the office of the claimant, are covered by the notion of service as specified in the BIT." [333]

The dissident opinion of arbitrator Yawovi Agboyibo is interesting. According to him, the tribunal confused the notion of "investments" with that of "activities relating to an investment". An investor, he says, must first of all invest capital and thereafter may conduct activities which support his initial investment without necessarily resulting in seeing those activities as investment in themselves. Such activities, according to him, cannot be the legal basis for ICSID jurisdiction:

> "One should not confuse 'goods or services invested for the purpose of production' with 'goods or services produced'. In this case, services furnished to third parties by the claimant in the Republic of the Congo and the fees billed or set off are products of the investment. It would only be different if these fees had been reinvested." [334]

When analysing ICSID's jurisdiction, one can see that arbitrators, when confronted with the notion of "investment" define it on the ground of international law as well as the provisions of the applicable BIT. In some cases, they also consider the terms of the content of an investment contract. *Some model conventions* which includes such a definition, could advantageously be amended as follows:

> "The term 'investment' refers to any active element and any cash, kind or service contribution, direct or indirect, invested or reinvested in any economic sector whatever." (**Article 1, 2**)
>
> "The following investments have been but are not necessarily the one kind of activity that are included in the definition of the term:

---

[333] ICSID, Case no. ARB/99/7, decision dated 26 January 2004, p. 13.
[334] ICSID, Case no. ARB/99/7, decision dated 26 January 2004, p. 3.

a) ...;

f) activity and supply of services of any nature, including the contracts relative to such services."

16.8.4.4. *Need for Special Provision*

In most cases, there is no conflict about the notion of "investment." However, as stated in Chapter I under the topic "New Investments", many new kinds of investments have come about. Technology and know-how transfers are examples.

There is an obvious interest in making certain that the investor will see his investment treated by the host State as a foreign investment, susceptible to arbitration by ICSID. Arbitration clauses and agreements usually limit themselves to specify that disputes relating to investments are susceptible of being arbitrated. The result is that the host State may well, later, attempt to avoid arbitration, by arguing that the investment made by the claimant does not appear in the list of investments appearing under the topic "Investments" in the BIT.

Therefore, investors should see to it they follow the suggestion made in the "model clauses" of ICSID:

> "In order to eliminate any ambiguity, the parties should state expressly in the instrument recording their consent that the particular transaction between them constitutes an investment for the purpose of the Convention."

It would be useful to add to this clause by stating expressly that the investment regarding which consent to arbitration has been registered as an investment in the sense of **Article 25(2)b** of the Washington Convention regarding jurisdiction. Delaume believes that a separate written confirmation would be a good alternative:

> "Another alternative might be for the private party to secure a statement from the Host State that it considers the transaction involved as an investment, and that in the event of a dispute the State would raise no objection to the jurisdiction of an ICSID arbitral

tribunal, on the ground that the nature of the dispute would not relate to an investment within the meaning of the Convention."[335]

16.8.5. – *Consent of Parties*

16.8.5.1. *Evidence of Acceptable Consent*

The settlement of disputes through an arbitration procedure is based on the consent of the parties. This consent is all-important in any arbitration procedure, namely that the arbitrator shall have jurisdiction, that it shall be contractually provided for, even in cases of arbitration *ad hoc*, that it might be institutional and that it may also be commercial and international. A World Bank activity report, issued by its administrators stresses that, in ICSID arbitration,

"Consent of the parties is the touchstone of the Centre's jurisdiction."

Therefore, evidence that consent has been given must be adduced. According to the Washington Convention, this consent is given in writing, both by the host State and the investor, whether a physical person or a corporation. However, an arbitration agreement selecting ICSID as the arbitrator between a member State and an investor who is national of a non-member State can have no possible effect. There may be consent but it is not of the acceptable kind. It is self evident that BIT's as well as State contracts may foresee recourse to other international arbitration institutions (International Chamber of Commerce etc.).

Most practitioners realise that the "exhaustion of local remedies" rule is not always followed but is important in regards to the parties' consent. Obviously, the investor's standing, when filing his request for arbitration against the host State would be seriously limited if he were compelled to exhaust internal remedies first. The Washington Convention

---

[335] DELAUME, Georges, *op. cit.*, p. 119, see footnote 158.

negotiators know how important this question was and drafted Article 26 accordingly :

> "Consent of the parties to arbitration under this Convention shall, unless otherwise stated, be deemed consent to such arbitration to the exclusion of any other remedy. A Contracting State may require the exhaustion of local remedies or judicial remedies as a cndition to its consent to arbitration under this Convention."

In actual practice, most of the States negotiating BITs accept mentioning their consent to arbitraion without explicitly state that they waive recourse to local remedies as a prerequisite for the disputing investor. In fact, Article 26 of the Washington Convention states that an explicit clause is required to demonstrate that the State extends its consent to arbitration only when local remedies have been exhausted. Their consent therefore implies a waiver of the «exhaustion of remedies' rule.

To avoid a misunderstanding, it seems preferable to mention expressly, in the BITs, that the State party to the BIT has waived the rule. Such a clause appears in the Belgian model convention :

> "To this end, each Contracting Party agrees in advance and irrevocably to the settlement of any dispute by this type of arbitration. Such consent implies that both Parties waive the right to demand that all domestic administrative or judiciary remedies be exhausted."

Such a clause is in the interest of investors. It would be helpful if both BITs and State Contracts made by investors, mention it expressly.

16.8.5.2. *Anticipatory consent*

According to current practice, a member State gives its anticipated consent to ICSID arbitration by concluding a bilateral agreement (BIT) with another member State. This implies that BIT's are made effective through the application of international law rules. However, just the signature of the BIT by the Contracting States is not enough. The BIT must have become effective law in accordance with instruments of legislative ratification exchanged between the signatory States.

Mutual ratification of the BIT is a requirement but it is not self-executory for disputes to be eligible for submission to ICSID. A request for arbitration issuing from one of the contracting States or one of its nationals, sent to the Secretary General of ICSID must contain all required information regarding the nature of the dispute and the consent of the parties. When a petition for arbitration is submitted, the investor must not only refer to the BIT in order to establish the anticipatory consent of the host State but most also specify his own consent.

When a State Contract is signed, involving an investment, it is in the investor's interest to ask for the express insertion of a provision stating that the contract is under the protection of the BIT (cfr *supra* : umbrella clause). Such a clause will not be cancellable by a domestic law or administrative decree of the host State. The consent to arbitrating as specified in the BIT cannot be withdrawn.

Any State which is a party to a BIT may inform ICSID about the categories of disputes which it considers subject to the Centre's jurisdiction. However, this notification must be made when the Washington convention itself is ratified. After this ratification, a State may not revoke or qualify its consent :

> "With this ratification, it is self evident that a host State may not subsequently be allowed to retract it in order to avoid having a dispute arbitrated by ICSID for the type of dispute such State has accepted ICSID arbitration by the use of a appropriate and valid compromissorial clause. It is therefore quite proper that ICSID arbitrators, when deciding the *Alcoa Minerals of Jamaica v. Jamaica*, determined that they had jurisdiction to consider that, notwithstanding Jamaica's notice, given to ICSID by the Jamaican Government one month before an increase in the royalties due by the investors, a dispute relating to a mining investment in Jamaica and involving differences between the parties as to the nature of raw material and nat-

ural resources, did not fall outside the Center's jurisdiction, because the said notice was given significantly after Jamaica's adhesion to the Washington convention..."[336]

16.8.5.3. Revocation of Consent – Implied Consent

Sometimes, the text of the Washington Convention is not always sufficiently clear. This is indeed the case with respect to the matter of the parties' consent. Other than requiring that consents be in writing, nothing has been provided with respect to the formalities nor the dates of the parties' consent. The text of **Article 25(2)b** of the Convention (that is "disputes... that the parties have consented in writing to submit to the Centre") may, since it does not provide a definition as to date of consent, be interpreted to mean that each party may give such consent on a different date. Thus, consent to arbitration need not be evidenced by a single document, for example, an arbitration convention contemporaneously signed by both parties. The arbitration petition (cfr *supra*) must, of course, state the date on which both consents have become effective.

In international practice, two different systems have been used for that purpose. If a specific contract (State Contract) has been signed between the host State and an investor, mutual consent is desirably to be expressly included and dated in such contract. Some LDC's, however, which may see arbitration as an encouragement for foreign investments on their territory, have included specific arbitration clauses in their investment codes. The Congolese Code specifies that:

> "If the parties do not reach an amiable settlement of their dispute within three months from the first written notice demanding that negotiation be initiated, the dispute shall be settled, on the request of the aggrieved party, in accordance with an arbitration procedure governed by:
>
> i. the Washington Convention of 18 March 1965 for the Settlement of Disputes regarding Investments between States and nationals of

---

[336] SCHMIDT, J.T., *Harvard International Law Journal*, 1979, p. 103.

other States (ICSID Convention, ratified by the Democratic Republic of the Congo on 29 April 1970, or

ii. the Arbitration Rules of the International chamber of Commerce in Paris (article 38 of the Code)."

The Rwanda law no. 14/1998 dated 18 December 1998, referring to the creation of the Office for the Promotion of Investments, provides as follows:

i. "Litigation between a foreign investor and the Rwandan Office or State regarding a registered enterprise, which has not been settled through negotiation, may be submitted to arbitration, in accordance with the following methods and the parties' mutual agreement:
ii. ...;
iii. either within the framework of a bilateral or multilateral agreement regarding the protection of investments, to which the State and the State of which the investor is a national;
iv. in accordance with any other international procedure for the settlement of litigation involving investments, in particular the Convention of 18 March 1965 regarding the settlement of litigation relating to investments between States and nationals of other States, as agreed upon under the aegis of the International Reconstruction and Redevelopment Bank, as ratified by the Rwandan Republic by decree dated 16 July 1079." (**Article 40** of the Rwandese code)

Do these provisions protect sufficiently the interests of international investors?

The answer to that question is no. When the consent of the host State is not specified in the BIT, the availability of arbitration may be limited by a new law or a new ministerial decree canceling those provisions. The best is the consent of the contracting Parties to arbitrate within the scope of the BIT (cfr *infra*). The contracting State which is a member of the Washington Convention is deemed to have signaled its anticipatory and irrevocable consent to a specific arbitration clause. When the dispute arises, an investor can then extend his own consent and mention that he did in his petition for arbitration.

As a matter of law, this is nothing but a process of mutual consents following the time tested laws of offer and demand. The host State provides its consent through the bilateral convention or according to a domestic law and the investor (usually the petitioner) uses the option to accept the written State offer.

Such a process is not altogether new in as much as the occurrence of consents at different dates is usually recognised and practised on the international level. When dealing with commercial international arbitration, the most widespread opinion is that written evidence serves only as proof (*ad probationem sed non ad validitatem*) and that most any document could be used to the same effect. Several countries have followed the very broad idea which took hold among UN members and which had been transcribed as follows in the UNCITRAL form law about commercial international arbitration:

> "The arbitration agreement must be in written form. An agreement is in written form if it is contained in a document signed by the parties or in an exchange of letters, of telex communications, of telegrams or any other means of telecommunication which shows its existence, or even in the exchange of a conclusion being offered and a conclusion responding to it, in which the existence of such an agreement is alleged by one party and not contested by the other." [337]

16.8.5.4. *ICSID's Jurisprudence on ICSID's Jurisdiction*

Several ICSID awards have centred on disputes regarding a denial of jurisdiction based on absence of consent. In the case of *Hong Kong (Southern Pacific Middle East Ltd – PPP) v. Egypt*, a most important arbitration decision was precisely regarding the topic of ICSID's jurisdiction and consent to arbitrate. The party plaintiff claimed that Egypt had given its consent to arbitrate as a result of article 8 of Egyptian law no. 43 of 1974, enabling ICSID arbitration. This law provided as follows:

---

[337] SHOKKAERT, Jan & KANGULUMBU, Vincent, "L'arbitrage en droit comparé", *Revue de droit africain (RDJA)*, Jodoigne, Belgique, 2004, no. 31, p. 253.

"Contests relating to investments and concerning the execution of provisions of the present law are settled by the means agreed upon with the investors, or within the framework of conventions in effect between the Arab Republic of Egypt and the State of the investors, or within the framework of the Washington Convention for the Settlement of Investment Contests between the State and citizens of other States, to which the ARE has adhered by virtue of Law no. 90 of 1971, provided the said Convention is applicable thereto."

Egypt denied the claim, arguing that a simple mention in domestic law about ICSID's jurisdiction was insufficient to establish consent and that a separate express consent was required for the current dispute. For Egypt, the law was not compulsory but only provided for discrete settlement possibilities of disputes.

The tribunal first confirmed that a State which is a member of the Washington Convention was authorised to give its anticipatory consent to arbitrate through ICSID, and this by virtue of a provision in its domestic law (cfr *supra*):

Furthermore, the tribunal stressed that the Egyptian law is self-executory, as it appears from the term "shall be settled" included in it. Of the three possibilities for arbitration offered by the Egyptian law, only ICSID arbitration was realistically possible because no convention had been concluded with the investor (formula no. 1), no bilateral accord including an arbitration clause had been signed between Egypt and Hong Kong (formula no. 2).

From that observation, the arbitrators established their jurisdiction in the following terms:

"Regarding which method of dispute settlement should be given priority under article 8, the various methods mentioned and the order in which they are mentioned show a hierarchical relationship among them. These methods are listed in the order of the most specific – first an agreement between the parties regarding how a dispute will be resolved, second a more general, bilateral agreement between the investor's State and Egypt, and third the most general method of all for the settlement of a dispute, to wit, the multilateral Washington Convention. **Article 8** reflects the adage *"generalia specialibus non derogant"* a principle which has been recognised by writers since Grotius and which appears in the jurisprudence of the Permanent International Court of Justice."[338]

A rather important number of awards by ICSDI have been rendered regarding the parties' consent. Arbitrators – who can decide on their own whether or not they have jurisdiction – rarely abandon their authority and are apt to interpret **Article 25(2)b** of the Washington Convention very broadly.

In two cases, host States denied ICSID's competence stating that involved private parties either had not signed the arbitration agreement or were not clearly designated in the relevant arbitration clauses.

In the *Holiday Inns v. Morocco* case, the State had attempted to refuse to honour the jurisdiction of ICSID by saying that the two US companies (Holiday Inn and O.P.C.) had not signed the convention providing for arbitration and that the signature of their subsidiaries in Morocco was insufficient. The arbitration tribunal rejected Morocco's arguments:

> "The Tribunal also apparently refused to be swayed by formalistic arguments when it was clear that the parties had both at the time of signing and thereafter, reasonably contemplated ICSID's jurisdiction over all principal parties to the dispute. This portion of the Holiday Inns jurisdictional ruling is significant as a precedent for the extension of jurisdiction over unnamed parties not signatories to the agreement containing the arbitration clause."[339]

The circumstances here are not clear in that the Tribunal denied jurisdiction in part (cfr *supra*, subtitle 8.6.2.9), absent an express consent to the application of Article 25(2)b. This case, however, is of little significance since, ultimately, the parties settled.

---

[338] GAILLARD, Emmanuel, *op. cit.*, p. 355, see footnote 31.
[339] RAND, William, "ICSID's emerging jurisprudence", *Journal of international law and politics*, vol. 19, 1986, p. 57.

In another case, *Amco v. Indonesia*, this State attempted to refuse ICSID's jurisdiction by arguing the fact that the foreign investor Amco Asia, which controlled the Indonesian company had not been expressly designated in the arbitration clause. The Tribunal rejected the Indonesian thesis, stating that the arbitration clause was not to be interpreted restrictively nor liberally or inclusionarily. The arbitration clause and the arbitration agreement must be interpreted in a manner leading to the discovery of the parties' real intentions. If the terms of conventional acts show that both the local investor and the foreign investor had opted for arbitration, then this common will had to be respected:

> "In reaching its conclusion, the Tribunal reasoned that the arbitration clause must have been intended to protect the investor. The Tribunal asked: 'How could such protection be insured, if Amco Asia (the 'foreign investor') would be refused the benefit of the clause.. which benefit P.T. Amco the local subsidiary possesses... because of the foreign control under which it is placed: would it not be fully illogical to grant this protection to the controlled entity but not to the controlling one?'"[340]

In any event, the ICSID jurisprudence can only encourage international investors to follow a rule along the lines of what we suggested (cfr *supra*, p. 141) and that is to conclude, whenever possible, a specific investment contract (State Contract) with the host State. In such a contract, the parties can explicitly agree about what an "investment" is as well as on the modalities of the consent to arbitrate. As a *"lex specialis"*, this specific contract will then have to be applied, as a priority, by the arbitrators.

16.8.6. – *Execution of Awards*

The Washington Convention created an autonomous international jurisdictional system, free and independent of any state intervention. Decisions rendered by ICSID's arbitration

---

[340] RAND, William, *op. cit.*, p. 58, see footnote 339.

tribunals bind the parties. The host State cannot escape the execution of a decision with an invocation of its sovereign immunity or public order. Each contracting State commits itself to abide by the decisions:

> "Each Contracting State shall recognise an award rendered pursuant to this Convention as binding and enforce the pecuniary obligations imposed by that award within its territories as if it were a final judgment of a Court in that State" (**Article 54**)

There is, however, an exception to the non-intervention rule for the issues and tribunals of States involved in a case. In the event where execution measures, such as seizure of assets would be necessary on the territory of the State in question, national procedure must be followed.

Authors are unanimous in recognising that honoring the execution of arbitration awards has not been a problem:

> "What makes arbitration a reliable tool, is that the parties submit themselves to the award and do not take measures intended to escape the execution of the arbitration award. Observers of this part of the process are very positive, most of the awards being spontaneously executed, in the large majority of cases. This is certainly true for awards given out by permanent centers of arbitration."[341]

Several model conventions and BIT's addresses the topic and do mention that arbitration awards shall be final and mandatory for the parties to the dispute and that the Contracting Parties agree to carry out the awards in accordance with its national legislation. Nonetheless, the *"exequatur"* of awards, at the international level, did exceptionally encounter problems in certain States and, as a result, a multilateral convention has been signed, entitled "Treaty for the Acknowledgement and Execution of Foreign Arbitration Awards", done in New York on 10 June 1958.[342]

---

[341] BERNARD, A, *L'arbitrage volontaire en droit privé*, Bruxelles, Bruylant, 1937, p. 213.
[342] Belgium ratified the Treaty by law dated 10 June 1958 (Belgian Federal Register dated 15 November 1975).

To date, nearly all of the UN member nations are parties to this multilateral Treaty. The touchstone of this convention is the recognition of arbitration conventions and arbitration awards:

> "Each Contracting State acknowledges the written Convention by reason of which the parties commit to submit to the decisions of the arbitrators all or some disputes arising between them or which could arise between them about a legal contractual relationship or not, relative to a dispute susceptible of being arbitrated." (**Article 2.1**)

> "Each Contracting State shall recognise, under the terms of the provisions set forth in the articles or thereafter, *(that)* arbitration awards are obligatory, and executory, in accordance with procedural form in force on the territory where such award is relied on..." (Article 3) *(parenthetical "that" supplied by authors)*

Considering that most of the countries, having concluded BIT's, are also members of the New York Convention, a specific reference to this Convention would be desirable. Such a reference is already included in the US model convention:

> "Each party hereby consents to the submission of any investment dispute for settlement by binding arbitration, in accordance with the choice of the national or company. This consent and the submission of the dispute shall satisfy the requirement of:
> a. **Article 11** of the United Nations Convention on the recognition and enforcement of foreign arbitral awards, done at New York, June 15, 1958 for an 'agreement in writing'.
> b. Any arbitration shall be held in a State that is a Party to the United Nations Convention on the Recognition and Enforcement of Foreign Arbitral Awards, done at New York, June 10, 1958 (paragraph 4.b and 5)."

16.8.7. – *Interpretation disputes of the Washington Convention between Contracting States*

In the event of disputes regarding the interpretation or application of the Washington Convention, preference is to be given to a negotiated solution. If the interstate negotiation does not succeed to resolve the dispute, the most diligent party will be able to submit the case to the International Court of Justice. It is unfortunate that, in an international arbitration convention, the Contracting States have accepted to abandon that formula for the solution of disputes and have opted for an extremely heavy procedure. Article 64 of the Washington Convention reads as follows :

> "Any dispute arising between Contracting States concerning the interpretation or application of this Convention which is not settled by negotiation shall be referred to the International Court of Justice by the application of any party to the dispute, unless the States concerned agree to another method of settlement."

Conciliation and arbitration are therefore not completely excluded. One has to fear, however, that if negotiation of the dispute does not succeed, then negotiation of a method of settlement other than recourse to the CIJ will not succeed either. It would have been preferable if, after the failure of a negotiation, the Contracting States were committed to submit the dispute to arbitration conforming to the rules of UNCITRAL.

16.8.8. – Annulment of the awards

The lack of appealability from arbitral decisions shows that the contracting States unquestionably wanted to avoid any intervention by national State courts. Even writs of execution ("*exequatur*") to check on and carry out compliance with decisions by the courts where such compliance is to take place are lacking. In accordance with **Article 53** of the Washington Convention, every decision was to be[49] final and immune from any re-examination.

An Appeal having been intentionally excluded, the Convention's negotiators nonetheless thought that, in exceptional cases and in the interest of justice, an internal system had to be established, affording to parties the opportunity to defend themselves against a manifestly unjust decision. According article 52 of the Convention, the parties may file a request for annulment with the Secretary Genertal of ICSID. To emphasise that the purpose sought was to make decisions rendered as final as possible, the conditions precedent to an annulment are listed to the exclusion of any other:

(a) the arbitration tribunal was not properly selected;

(b) the Tribunal has manifestly exceeded its powers;

(c) there was corruption on the part of a member of the Tribunal;

(d) there has been a serious departure from a fundamental rule of procedure;

(e) the award has failed to state the reasons on which it is based (failure of grounds).

A specific organism, an *ad hoc* Committee, established by the Secretary General decides the issue. In doctrinal texts, some authors favour and some are against this internal system of control of decision integrity:

> "Annulment of an arbitral decision should not be seen as harmful per se. On the contrary, it is sound policy that arbitrators, knowing their powers are limited by a consistent system, not be tempted to yield to a drunkenness of power which might lead to suppression of any kind of control. The need for such limits is particularly clear in the ICSID arbitration system where any state control of the decisions reaching the writ of execution stage has already been wholly cancelled." [343]

Other authors are not so kind to the annulment procedure. It is mostly the grounds for annulment that are criticised, and in particular, the ground specified under paragraph (c) above. These authors believe that this particular exception should have been limited to the absence of adequate jurisdiction. The rule does not include the term "jurisdiction" and hence the phraseology "...has manifestly exceeded its powers..." may include defects other than jurisdiction. In the *Kloeckner* case, for example, the annulment committee decided that the non-application by the arbitration tribunal of local law was a manifest excess of the use of power.[344]

---

[343] GAILLARD, Emmanuel, *op. cit.*, p. 189, see footnote 31.
[344] GAILLARD, Emmanuel, *op. cit.*, p. 192, see footnote 30.

Opponents of annulment mostly fear that members of the *ad hoc* Committee might want to re-examine the substance of the dispute and that such re-examination is to be avoided. In the *Amco v. Indonesia* case, the *ad hoc* Commmittee had annulled the decision partially, based on the fact that the arbitral Tribunal had not properly calculated the amount of indemnification owed and that, as a result, it had manifestly exceeded its powers:

> "Even more than in the *Kloeckner* case, the *ad hoc* Committee has, in order to annul, indulged in actually passing judgment on the legal competence of the arbitral Tribunal, thus transforming the annulment mechanism into a Supreme Court form of certiorari, very different indeed from the scope of exceptional and limited recourse envisaged by the authors of the Washington Convention."[345]

If the award is annuled the dispute shall, at the request of either-party be submitted to an *ad hoc* Committee.

16.8.9. – *ICSID's additional facility rules outside of the Convention*

The reader may incidentally be interested in the existence of a particular ICSID power, arising from sources outside of the Washington Convention. Additional rules have been formulated:

"The Administrative Council of the Centre has adopted Additional Facility Rules authorising the Secretariat of ICSID to administer certain categories of proceedings between States and nationals of other States that fall outside the scope of the ICSID Convention. The Secretariat of the Centre is hereby authorised to administer, subject to and in accordance with these Rules, proceedings between a State (or a constituent subdivision or agency of a State) and a national of another State, falling within the following categories:

(a) Conciliation and arbitration proceedings for the settlement of legal disputes arising directly out of an investment

---

[345] OUAKRAT, Philippe, *op. cit.*, p. 308, see footnote 33.

which are not within the jurisdiction of the Centre because either the State party to the dispute or the State whose national is a party to the dispute is not a Contracting State;

(b) Conciliation and arbitration proceedings for the settlement of legal disputes which are not within the jurisdiction of the Centre because they do not arise directly out of an investment, provided that either the State party to the dispute or the State whose national is a party to the dispute is a Contracting State; and

(c) Fact-finding proceedings.

The administration of proceedings authorised by these Rules is hereinafter referred to as the Additional Facility."[346]

The additional facility rules are not addressed in this book.

16.9. – LONDON COURT OF INTERNATIONAL ARBITRATION (LCIA)

16.9.1. – *Origin and Description*

As stated on the London Court of International Arbitration (LCIA) website[347], this organisation is one of the long established institutions for commercial dispute resolution. Established in London, UK, based in London, it is an international body, providing impartial quality administration of dispute resolution proceedings for all parties regardless of their location. It operates under a three-tier structure, including the company itself, the Arbitration Court and the Secretariat.

In 1975, the Institute of Arbitrators joined the organisation, the Director of the London Court of Arbitration becoming the Registrar of the Court. In 1981, it was renamed "The London Court of International Arbitration."

---

[346] Www.worldbank.org/icsid.
[347] Http://www.lcia-arbitration.com.

The LCIA is largely made up of various councils, designed to specialise in specific activities. Thus, its current "users" Councils are :

> The European Users' Council
> The Arab Users' Council
> The North American Users' Council
> The Latin-American and Caribbean Users' Council
> The Asia-Pacific Users' Council, and
> The African Users' Council.

As of March 2008, the LCIA Users' Councils had more than 1600 members from 83 countries.

16.9.2. – *LCIA Jurisdiction*

Stemming from a decision by the Court of Common Council of the City of London formed in 1883, the original intent was to limit its jurisdiction to the arbitration of domestic as well as "trans-national" commercial disputes "arising within the ambit of the City." At its inauguration a few years later, the hope was expressed that :

> "This Chamber is to have all the virtues which the law lacks. It is to be expeditious when the law is slow, where the law is costly, simple where the law is technical, a peacemaker instead of a stirrer-up f strife." [348]

Nonetheless, it did not actually see the light of day until the passage by Parliament of the Arbitration Act of 1889 when the scheme for its composition and membership was adopted and it was given its formal name of The City of London Chamber of Arbitration. In 1903, it was renamed the London Court of Arbitration and was to sit at Guildhall under the direction of a committee made up of members of the London Chamber and the City Corporation.

Some may misconstrue the name of this institution. It is not a "Court" in the sense of the word usually given by legal

---
[348] Law Quarterly Review.

practititioners, nor is it any kind of tribunal within Britain's judicial system. It is, instead, an independent institutional arbitration centre, as emphasised in the following except from an LCIA brochure:

> "Arbitration is now the first-choice method of binding dispute resolution in the widest range of international commercial contracts. It is a private process requiring the agreement of the parties, which is usually given by way of an arbitration clause in their contract, but may also be entered into once a dispute has arisen" (LCIA, brochure "Arbitration-Mediation", London, 2002, p. 1).

LCIA's jurisdiction includes investment litigation. Key words are "disputes" and "contracts". What counts is that the parties have agreed to having their disputes arbitrated. When this consent exists, LCIA decides whether or not it has jurisdiction.

Consequently, including LCIA as one of the arbitration organisations that parties to an investment dispute may choose for the submittal of an arbitration request, would be enough. Furthermore, LCIA may also administer arbitration procedures which, if the parties agree, will conform to UNCITRAL rules.

16.9.3. – *LCIA Rules*[349]

The Court's Rules are published on its website. They cover the exercise of the Court's powers, the details of the procedure, the powers of the arbitrators themselves. Article 1 of the Rules, for example, provides as follows:

16.9.3.1. *Request for Arbitration*

> 1.1 Any party wishing to commence an arbitration under these Rules (the "Claimant") shall send to the Registrar of the LCIA Court (the "Registrar") a written request for arbitration ("Arbitration Request", containing or accompanied by:

---

[349] Brochure LCIA "Arbitration Rules", 1998, London.

the names, addresses, telephone, facsimile, telex and e-mail number (if known) of the parties to the arbitration and of their legal representatives;

a copy of the written arbitration clauses or separate written arbitration agreement invoked by the Claimant (the "Arbitration Agreement") together with a copy of the contractual documentation in which the arbitration clause is contained or in respect of which the arbitration arises;

a brief statement describing the nature and circumstances of the dispute, and specifying the claims advanced by the Claimant against another party to the arbitration (the "Respondent");

a statement of any matters (such as the seat or language(s) of the arbitration, or the number of arbitrators or their qualifications or identities) on which the parties have already agreed in writing for the arbitration or in respect of which the Claimant wishes to make a proposal;

if the Arbitration Agreement calls for party nomination of arbitrators, the name, address, telephone, facsimile, telex and e-mail numbers (if known) of the Claimant's nominee;

the fee prescribed in the Schedule of Costs (without which the Request shall be treated as not having been received by the Registrar and the arbitration as not having been commenced);

confirmation by the Registrar that copies of the Request (including all accompanying documents) shall be submitted simultaneously on all other parties to the arbitration by one or more means of service to be identified in such confirmation.

16.9.3.2. *Admissibility of Evidence*

The arbitrator, on his motion, can decide to apply or not strict rules of evidence regarding admissibility, relevance or weight. He may require third persons to be joined to the litigation, on the application of one of the parties and with the consent of the third person. As in many other arbitration contexts, the LCIA arbitrators' decision is deemed final and binding. Parties agreeing to LCIA arbitration agree to abide by the decision and make restitution or provide compensation without delay. Should a losing party fail to comply, enforcement will be easier than if reliance on a national court's decision were the only basis. A successful party will be able to rely on the provisions of the 1988 New York Convention on the Recognition and Enforcement of Foreign Arbitral Awards. It is therefore recommendable that arbitration take place under LCIA rules in a State which adheres to the Convention and that the enforcement is against assets of the losing party located in another Convention State.

16.9.3.3. *Dies a quo*

Rule 1.2 provides that the date of receipt by the Registrar shall be treated as the Date on which the arbitration has commenced for all purposes, The Request (including all accompanying documents) should be submitted to the Registrar in two copies where a sole arbitrator should be appointed, or, if the parties have agreed or the Claimant considers that three arbitrators should be appointed in four copies. However, Rule 4.2 provides:

> "For the purpose of calculating a period time under these Rules, such period shall begin to run on the day following the day when a notice or other communication is received. There are naturally extensions for holidays."

16.9.3.4. *Dies ad quem*

Rule 4.6. states that, if the last day of a period within which an event is to occur for the purpose of determining compliance with a time limit falls on a Sunday or holiday, the period is extended to the next business day.

16.9.3.5. *Response*

Per Rule 2.1, the response (the "Response"), to be served on Claimant by the Respondent within 30 days (or such lesser period fixed by the LCIA Court), shall be sent to the Registrar together with confirmation or denial of all or part of the claims advanced by the Claimant in the Request, a brief statement of the nature and circumstances, as advanced by the Respondent, comments as to statements in the Request relating to the conduct of the arbitration, and confirmation to the Registrar that all copies of the Response and accompanying documents are being served on the Claimant. The Response must be submitted to the Registrar in two or four copies depending on the number of arbitrators selected.

So far, the procedure is quite typical of most Common Law jurisdictions practice. However, departing from such practice, if the Response is untimely, and the Arbitration Agreement calls for such nominations, the Respondent may still deny the claim and advance counterclaims but shall be deemed to have waived irrevocably his opportunity to nominate an arbitrator. The same waiver applies if the Respondent fails to file a Response or Answer. There is no corresponding penalty on the Claimant, should he fail to nominate an arbitrator. Arguably, since Rule 1.1 requires the claimant to submit the names of the parties to the arbitration, simple equity might require the claimant to nominate one or more arbitrators in timely fashion or be deemed to have waived his right to do so. In the alternative, the Registrar could claim that the entire paperwork submitted by Claimant is defective in that a requirement – the nomination of the arbitrator – is missing. Depending on what substantive rules the parties may have agreed in respect of the bar of the Statute of Limitations, failure to attend to what is basically a back office calendar maintenance may be costly to the Claimant.

This requirement therefore seems harsh, unless the Arbitrator ultimately selected has the power to cure the late fling by mutual written agreement of the parties. Parties, however, must keep in mind that arbitration is not the equivalent of a judicial proceeding, that it simplifies and can be far more flexible in the course of the hearings, and that, hence, adherence to sensible rules of business is not necessarily an inequitable demand on the parties. Besides, if need be, and time is of the essence, the parties may reach a compromise in that regard, allowing the Arbitrator to exercise greater discretion.

16.9.4. – *Nature of services*

The LCIA is not a Court in the usually accepted sense of the word. It is not linked or associated with the government of any jurisdiction. It is not, despite its name, emphasising services to the UK business community, in that some 70% of all the cases referred to it involve no UK parties at all. The members of the various councils play no part in the governance nor in the administration of disputes referred to the LCIA. No one must actually be a member of LCIA to draw upon its resources. The parties' contract is the vehicle by which the parties agree to refer their disputes to the LCIA as an independent body. Should the contract so provide, the LCIA will assume jurisdiction. In particular, the LCIA is empowered and does actually conduct cases under the UNCITRAL Arbitration Rules. A sole arbitrator will be appointed unless the parties agree otherwise. Rule 5.6 states:

> "In the case of a three-member Arbitral Tribunal, the Chairman (who will not be a party-nominated arbitrator) shall be appointed by the LCIA Court."

16.9.5. – *Court Membership*

The Court is made up of up to 35 members who provide a balance of leading practitioners in commercial arbitration, of whom no more than 6 may be of UK nationality.

16.9.6. – *Nationality of Arbitrators*

Where the parties are of different nationalities, a sole arbitrator or Chairman of the Arbitral Tribunal shall not have the same nationality of any party unless all the parties who are not of the same nationality as the proposed appointee agree in writing otherwise. The nationality of the parties shall be understood to include that of controlling shareholders or interests.

An interesting provision for double nationality parties is prescribed by Art.6.3:

"For the purposes of this Article (Art. 6), a person which is a citizen of two or more states shall be treated as a national of each state; and citizens of the European Union shall be treated as nationals of its different Member States and shall not be treated as having the same nationality."

This provision may be seen as a means to expedite the selection of arbitrators but in addition, the Rules provide that any party may petition the court.

16.9.7. – *Three or more Parties*

Where the arbitration agreement entitled each party to nominate an arbitrator, the parties number more than two and such parties have not all agreed in writing that the disputant parties represent two separate sides, then, in exceptional circumstances, any party may request that a new or replacement arbitrator be appointed by the Arbitral Tribunal. LCIA Court shall appoint the Arbitral Tribunal without regard to any party's nomination.

An arbitrator may, for instance, persistently refuse to participation in the deliberation of the Tribunal, the two remaining members of the Tribunal are authorised to continue the arbitration, including any decision, notwithstanding the absence or non-cooperation of the third arbitrator.

Arbitrators may be replaced on a number of different grounds, besides resignation. Thus, a party may claim that justifiable doubts have arisen as an arbitrator's impartiality, so long as such reasons became apparent only after the challenged arbitrator's appointment. However, if two arbitrators find that they will not continue to work with the third, after proper notification, to all parties and the LCIA Court, the latter will consider the revocation of the third arbitrator's commission and the replacement of all three arbitrators.

16.9.8. – *Confidentiality*

In general, all communications shall be made through the Registrar, with copies to the parties, unless and until the Registrar determines otherwise.

No one not a party to a case of arbitration over which the LCIA has assumed jurisdiction may obtain information about any pending or completed case. Awards are not published. However, once a request for arbitration has been filed, the LCIA will provide the parties in dispute a list of the names of available arbitrators. On application for arbitration, the parties list their key criteria for the selection of arbitrators. The LCIA then determines which of their panelled arbitrators are best matched to the claimants' criteria and the parties are then notified.

Per Art. 30, the parties agree to hold all awards, together with all materials relating thereto in confidentiality, except to the extent a party may show he has the legal duty, or must divulge the arbitrations proceedings or part thereof in order to protect a right, enforce or challenge the *bona fide* legal proceedings before a State court.

16.9.9. – *Two Tiers of Submittals*

Similarly to usual practice in Courts world wide applying Common Law, unless the parties agree differently, or unless the Arbitrator otherwise orders, two stages of argumentation are contemplated. Within 30 days of receipt of the Request, the Claimant may treat the Request as his Statement of the Case and will stipulate as to which grounds and facts are to be deemed admitted and what contentions of law are relied on. Should there be any counterclaims, the counterclaimant will follow the same procedure and submit them together with this Statement of Defence.

The Claimant then has 30 days to reply to the Statement of Defence and counterclaims, and will, at the same time, submit his defence thereto. It is not clear from the Rules when this exchange of charges, defences and counter charges actually ends, but clearly at some point before the hearing, all defences and claims should have been filed.

16.9.10. – *Majority Vote*

Where the three arbitrators fail to reach agreement, the two remaining arbitrators, if they agree, render the decision. The award is then delivered to the LCIA Court

16.9.11. – *Arbitrators' Questions*

In advance of any hearing, arbitrators may submit questions to the parties. This power appears to present an opportunity to be exercised therefore fairly early in the proceeding, before expert and factual witnesses have been sworn and testify. The parties may require that any witness upon whose written testimony a party relies shall be made available for cross-examination. If the witness does not appear, the Arbitrator has the discretion to exclude the witnesses' written testimony altogether. It appears from Rule 20.7, that any party may depose any witness prior to the hearing.

The second tier of submittal is therefore the hearing where any party has the right to be heard orally on the merits, unless the parties have agreed before hand to limit argumentation and evidence to the documentation. All meetings are private and their time table is set by the Arbitrators.

16.9.12. – *Currency and Interest*

The award may be expressed in any currency and an order that simple or compound interest shall be paid on it is within the Tribunal's discretion, without being bound by any State Court decision about the issue.

16.9.13. – *Enforcement of Awards*

According to Rule 23.1, the Arbitral Tribunal has the power to rule on its own jurisdiction, even if the arbitration clause relied on was intended for another agreement. Just how this clause will be viewed in the light of a *res inter alios acta* objection will be interesting. *Vice versa*, a decision that the arbitration agreement is invalid does not *ipso iure* entail the invalidity of the arbitration clause itself.

Rule 32 merely provides that:

> "In all matters not expressly provided for in these Rules, the LCIA Court, the arbitral Tribunal and the parties shall act in the spirit of these Rules and shall make every reasonable effort to ensure that an award is legally enforceable."

16.9.14. – *LCIA Court Decisions*

The LCIA Court hears matters relating to the arbitration. Its decisions are final, reasons therefore not being required. As for decisions of the Arbitral Tribunal the parties are deemed to have waived appeal and review.

All awards are final and binding. The parties shall have agreed not to pursue review or appeal, recourse to any other Court, State or otherwise. Should a respondent claim that the Arbitral Tribunal does not have jurisdiction, he must raise it again in the Statement of Defence or be deemed to have waived it. Likewise a claim of exceeding its authority will be treated as waiver by the Tribunal unless the claim is promptly made again after the Tribunal indicates it is ready to render a decision.

Furthermore, when agreeing to arbitration, the parties automatically exclude themselves from the jurisdiction of any other Court (or judicial authority) unless the parties agree or the Arbitral Tribunal authorises. Once the award is made, stating the reasons on which it is made, the date of the award and the seat of the tribunal, the other arbitrators may proceed in an arbitrator's absence if it is shown that he failed to comply with the mandatory provisions of any applicable law; the remaining assenting tribunal members then sign.

16.9.15. – *Powers of Arbitrators*

Arbitrators under the LCIA have very wide powers to allow any party to amend his claim, counterclaim or defence, extend or abbreviate time schedules and take the initiative in identifying issues and ascertaining the relevant facts and laws appropriate to the litigation. He may order any party to make property under its control available to the other parties, produce documentation in their custody or power. In this regard, the arbitrator's powers go beyond those normally exercised by a Common Law Court and, unless discretion is closely monitored, engage in "fishing expeditions" without necessarily being bound by the traditional rules of evidence.

16.10. – SUI GENERIS UNITED STATES COURT: UNITED STATES COURT OF INTERNATIONAL TRADE (USCIT)

16.10.1. – *Foreword*

Expropriation or condemnation, and *a fortiori*, nationalisation are blunt instruments. Nations who use it to resolve local political or economic problems tend to cut themselves off from future private investment, News travel fast, carefully planned investments are quickly put on hold. Reactivation requires the re-establishment of trust which may take years, changes in administration, competitive pressures from other candidate investors. Litigation usually follows, either under neutral supervision or, where assets of the expropriating nation are seized, in adversarial fashion.

Some nations have gradually come to the realisation that there are less stressful ways of achieving their expropriation ends. In an earlier chapter, we have addressed "creeping expropriation" syndrome, where the taking is gradual and the relationship with the victimised investor is not totally jeopardized at the outset. There are, thus, other ways, which are more subtle than piecemeal takings, but which tend to achieve similar results. One of these is fiscal policy which includes customs and other entry obstacles.

For example, if a cold drink plant in a host State becomes a runaway success, local cold drink producers will want a part of the market. With access to governmental agencies that have oversight over imports, the delivery of raw materials in the form of specially formulated powder may gradually be shut off or at least reduced by the imposition of duties. Sometimes, imports of the raw materials may be conditioned upon a corresponding export of other or the same product.

These fiscal measures, applied across the board in order to avoid the appearance of discrimination but most deeply felt by the foreign investor, may make it difficult, even impossible to manage companies established in the host State by capital originating in a foreign developed country.

Generally speaking, BITs are designed to protect against such measures, using specific language:

> "Except for measures required to maintain public order, such investments shall enjoy continuous protection and security i.e. excluding any unjustified or discriminatory measure which could hinder, either in law or in practice, the management, maintenance, use, possession or liquidation thereof."

This is an example but it should be kept in mind that the BITs reciprocity principles may not mitigate the restrictive measures, because investments made by a less developed country's investor in a developed country are rare. This is why we have previously explained that reciprocity in BITs is a legal issue mostly.

16.10.2. – *Anti-Dumping and Countervailing Duties*

It is, however, an established fact that many developed countries impose, for instance, impose so-called anti-dumping and countervailing duties when they find that domestic industries are injured by less expensive imports of similar materials. An anti-dumping duty surcharge might be imposed when it is found that an item is imported at less than cost or fair value. A countervailing duty might be imposed when it is found that the exporter (from a developing country) has benefited from subsidies (in his country). In either case, discrimination is seen as an unjust enrichment. These extraordinary duties are then applied to the imported product on the request of a party who alleges he and members of his class have been injured by it (if it is one that qualifies for the anti-dumping or countervailing duty). It can readily be seen that abuses may creep into the process.

16.10.3. – *USCIT is a United State Federal State Court and not an arbitration institution*

The U.S. Court of International Trade is a State Court forum (where "State" means the US Federal Government) which, among other things, reviews determinations by agencies closer to the offending imports such as Customs, the Office of International Trade or the International Trade Commission, but it also reviews determinations by other agencies including the distribution of monies flowing from the surcharges by, f.i., the Department of Agriculture. A detailed exposition of the operations of these agencies is beyond the scope of this Work.

16.10.4. – *USCIT Jurisdiction over Investment Disputes*

In matters of jurisdiction, it may be axiomatic that, for issues of investment protection to be raised, there must first be an investment. At first glance, one might wonder the relevance of remarks about the USCIT jurisdiction. After all, in a great number of cases, the exporter's goods enter the country on the basis of discrete trade transactions rather than investment. It should come as no surprise that where an issue arising out of straight commerce, not accompanied by an "investment", the jurisdiction of institutions such as the ICSID and other arbitration organisms may not extend, whereas that of the USCIT may. In BITs, strictly commercial acts are excluded by a detailed definition of 'investments' on which the agreement is applicable.

Sometimes, commercial acts are explicitly excluded:

> "Investment means... but does not include... claims arising only from commercial contracts or from the grant of credits for a commercial operation." (Canada Model Convention)

However, as we have seen in an earlier chapter, new forms of "investment" are constantly being developed, refined, and redefined. The most obvious tie behind the raison d'être of arbitral resolution of investment conflicts and judicial resolution of dumping and countervailing duties is discrimination. Conceivably, discrimination may also be achieved by other means than those that are most blatant.

16.10.5. – *Anti-Dumping and Countervailing Duties*

In a price dumping or countervailing situation, the imposition of penalising duties is legally, politically and perhaps morally justified on the basis that price dumping and export subsidies unfairly discriminate against domestic producers who may have greater overhead and production costs than the foreign importer. The mere existence of a difference between such costs may not be enough to warrant penalising duties but where it is found, for instance, that the foreign manufacturer flouts his own domestic laws with impunity, or deliberately underprices his exports in order to gain market share or destroy that of domestic competitors, manufacturers in the importing country may have a legitimate grievance and right to claim unlawful discrimination.

These circumstances do not automatically exclude arbitral organisations from assuming juricdiction. If a commercial operation is directly tied to an investment or if it falls within a category of "new investment", we can readily conceive that arbitral organisations will retain their jurisdiction over the matter.

16.10.6. – *The Long Hand of the Law*

On the other hand, foreign investors thwarted by property privative measures in their exploitation of a lawfully established manufacturing or mining base in the host State may discover that other foreign manufacturers in such State are not affected similarly. Those investors likewise have a grievance sounding in discrimination. Discrimination thus is the common element to both situations. Hence, it is appropriate to study how claims of discrimination are dealt within a non-arbitral context or venue, even though the discrimination is not necessarily the direct result of an explicit property privative measure.

Arguably, host State discrimination may be seen as an advantage granted to some well established entrepreneurs in the host State and denied the newcomer, a form of favouritism, allowing the favoured entrepreneurs to export at lesser prices than the newcomer. If the export is to the US, query whether a properly worded complaint by the newcomer filed with the USCIT, resulting in a countervailing duty against the exporters who benefit from such favouritism, is an appropriate means of defence.

Imaginative entrepreneurs may try to sidestep the problem by establishing companies in the host State, assigning to them segments of their operations. These segments may, in extreme cases, be nothing more than a liaison office, in other cases may actually participate in the finishing, packing for distribution, and even distributing the product. In such a case, domestic competitors in the host State who have access to compliant government agencies may try to throttle the import of the foreign investor's raw materials. Lest an inference be drawn that such underhanded practices are solely to be found in undeveloped countries, we remind the reader that developed countries are just as eager to protect their own industries and frequently just as compliant. In the United States, the US Court of International Trade is what stands between proper use and abuse in these respects.

An example of the reciprocity principles of BITs comes to mind when raw materials and semi-finished products are exported to a developed country, where they are finished and distributed at prices far below those of developed countries' producers of the same product. The aggrieved producers first seek the assistance of various government agencies, not infrequently Customs or the Commerce Departments or Ministries of such countries in order to block entry to more favourably priced goods. Where the foreign exporter establishes a company in the developed country, thus making an "investment" there, it becomes easier to see a scenario for filing arbitration requests based on discrimination.

Earlier, we mentioned that reciprocity was more of a legal concept than a business one, mainly because the normal flow of investments is from developed countries to less developed countries, but the USCIT scenario shows this is not always the case. A developed country's investors may invest in a non-developed country precisely to obtain a more advantageous manufacturing base from which to export at more competitive prices to their home country or to other countries. When anti-dumping or countervailing measures are taken, our sympathies may not necessarily lie with the investors but with others who played no part in the outsourcing but are nevertheless affected by the measures. Each case is different. The USCIT is a forum where the legitimacy of a complaint either against discriminatory measures or the failure to have them applied or applied sufficiently.

Precisely how the USCIT's jurisdiction intersects with the jurisdiction of arbitration tribunals dedicated to the protection of foreign investments is unclear. Many factors, the language used in applicable BITs, if any, the familiarity of the companies with the remedies provided by the BITs, the litigation cost and delays, all play a role in the selection of the forum.

16.10.7. – *Choice of Forum*

At least for US investors and those of any country disposing of a tribunal with jurisdiction similar to the USCIT, there seems to be a choice to be made between resorting to the USCIT or equivalent and an arbitration forum. It is more than likely that investors from countries that have no such Court will opt for the remedies provided in their countries' BIT with the LDC, if any. Even for US investors, where the adverse measures are taken by a host country party to a BIT with the US, chances are the US investors will also opt for the BIT remedies.

In a USCIT context, it is not clear just how persuasive a claim of immunity by the foreign State will be but even if it is honoured, the host country's expectations of a return on its own investment in the industry established locally by the foreign investor may well be defeated unless it joins in the US litigation. Claiming sovereign immunity may well prevent it from showing mitigating evidence. Whether the USCIT forum then is worse or better for the host State than an arbitration forum, that choice, for the host State at least, will depend on the details and an expert analysis of the advantages and perils of each forum.

On the other hand, for a US importer (say, a subsidiary of the host State exporter), and for any importer situated in a country with a Court similar to the USCIT, the choice may be out of his hands. If, on importing the goods in question, he is hit by an anti-dumping or countervailing duty, he must either pay it or fight it in the USCIT. If he loses, the question then arises whether he can raise the question again in an arbitral situation, where he might show he has been unfairly discriminated against by the US Government. Even if *stare decisis* were considered by the arbitration tribunal, it is highly unlikely that it could apply because the causes of action are different in the USIT from an ICSID tribunal. *A fortiori, res judicata* should not be a concern.

The real question is whether the UCSID arbitration tribunal will dare to tread where angels fear to go, namely where another lawfully established Court has already disposed of a related conflict between the same parties.

16.10.8. – *Relative Importance of the USCIT in International Commerce and Investment*

We have already mentioned that a US investor investing in an LDC for the purpose of exporting to a DC such as the US may be forced to choose the USCIT, or its equivalent if any in the DC of which he is a national, because that may well be the only safe place to go to get adequate redress against an anti-dumping or similar discriminatory levy. Waiting to file a claim with arbitration tribunal may be a risk he is unwilling to take, though he might do so if he thinks his chances there are better.

It is therefore appropriate to evaluate the importance of that Court in relation to other venues. Repetitive trade can easily turn into an investment or a "new form" of investment. The Court is located in New York, N.Y. It is no longer an open secret but an admitted fact that international trade is more important than ever to the American economy. Upon a thriving international trade of goods coming in and going out of the United States depend not only millions of jobs and many trillions of Dollars in the country's continental homeland but an equal or even greater number of jobs and amount of capital abroad. Much of the country's currency is used and exchanged strictly outside the borders of the United States, thereby creating a separate but dependent US dollar economy in itself. on which research, development, capital creation, transportation of foods and people, in short, the very lives of many people hinge. Treaties, alliances, coalitions may wax and wane on the political scene but all the while, even among enemies of the United States and enemies of each other, nations vie for a share of the resources generated by this economy.

People die of starvation or violence when much needed goods, paid for one way or another in US Dollars, do not reach their destination, overt and covert transfers are made, emergency loans are extended or denied, weapons procured and shipped, armies maintained, scientific research vital to the wellbeing of the planet and its inhabitants timely conducted. Despite the emergence of competing currencies such as the Euro, the US Dollar remains, for now at least, the medium not only of trade but a giant machine for global civilised conduct. The current global economic crisis may well confirm it.

These circumstances entail trade morphing into development as trade volume increases. The United States responsibility for maintaining the dollar machine is immense. Much has been written about the incompetence of US agencies, even their irrelevance, even in seeing to it that sand does not get into the gears of world exchanges. However true or exaggerated these accusations may be, the fact remains that, notwithstanding some movement away from the dollar, the US and the rest of the world remain attached to it like an umbilical cord. There may be signs that this dependency encourages mismanagement and exploitation by government agencies and capital interests the world over, with both short term and long term effects. Nonetheless, these exchanges continue and grow. All of them, except perhaps a miniscule portion distracted from the flow by criminal activities, rest on investment under some kind of agreement, oral, written, implied, express, clear, confused but in any case relied on by the parties to such agreement to achieve their respective ends.

At some point in time, some of these contracts remain unfulfilled or poorly fulfilled, unpaid or undelivered. For the parties bearing the harm from such failures, the trillion dollar flow around them is of scant importance: they look for redress from any place in the world most likely not only to recognise their right to have redress but actually give it to them in a reasonably enforceable manner. When their capital or lives are at stake and all manner of friendly resolution seems unavailable, they turn to the judicial or arbitral venues of this or that Nation as a last resort short of armed conflict. They naturally ask which one? Which one has more clout than another?

16.10.9. – *Choice between State Courts and Arbitration*

Arbitration institutions have been established in many of the leading world countries, designed to resolve the disputes in a predictable manner. Thus, for example, the International Chamber of Commerce and the International Centre for the Settlement of Investment Disputes often refer to arbitration, under their auspices, of disputes between investors and the States where they invest. State Courts, such as USCIT, have a more circumscribed radius of action in that it is primarily geared towards the resolution trade disputes as distinguished from investment disputes.

It is on that basis that the choice must be made. Where the measures complained of affect strictly limited commercial trade interests, State Courts are usually the better medium but where investments depend for their survival on those trade interests, courts such as the USCIT may be candidates equal to or superior to arbitral tribunals. So far, perhaps, the circumstances militating in favour of such a State Court as the USCIT may be exceptional but it would be imprudent to think the Court will not want to broaden its footprint, such as when trade and investment overlap, and therefore it would be imprudent to ignore such Courts' decisions. The sheer magnitude of the interests they serve in highly developed countries should, it seems to us, make it wise to consider them as appropriate candidates for deciding issues that are increasingly global in character.

16.10.10. – *Discriminatory Protection of Domestic Producers*

Some of the requests for settlement of disputes by arbitration are based upon local company claims of discrimination measures taken by the host State's agencies. Not infrequently, in some countries, exorbitant import or export taxes are imposed on local companies controlled by foreign interests. These measures favour local companies that are locally owned and operated, enabling them better to compete with foreign investors.

In such cases, a superficial analysis may lead the aggrieved party to select international arbitration. Before launching into this avenue of redress, an investor may want to check other options, if any, where arbitration may not be the sole remedy. For instance, not infrequently, this discrimination is in the form of health and quality standards applicable to everyone similarly situated but applied selectively. When these protectionist tools are insufficient, some countries do not hesitate to apply special tariffs to imports by a local company from a location also controlled by the local company's foreign shareholders.

Proving discrimination, in either an arbitration or a judicial context, can be complex. A mere showing that anti-dumping duties have been levied, making the foreign imports non-competitive with local products may not be sufficient. Proof that a local court has been confronted with the issue and decided in favour of the taxing agency does not, in and of itself, necessarily preclude the petitioner from raising the issue in an arbitration venue. In this context, violations of due process (cfr Subtitle 13.6.1.3 *supra*).

When discriminatory measures have been debated before the USCIT in such circumstances, there could very well a problem if the importer loses the case. Of course, he can still have recourse to the US Court of Appeals and the US Supreme Court perhaps but the higher he goes and persistently loses, the greater will the reluctance be for any arbitral tribunal to reconsider the case. It is not a matter of *stare decisis*, since we already know that argument does not usually carry much weight in many arbitration deliberations. Arbitration is not to serve as an additional appeal avenue. The ICSID Convention provides that:

> "consent of the parties to arbitration shall... unless otherwise stated be deemed consent to such arbitration to the exclusion of any other remedy..."

Some might question whether this prohibition is anticipative or postoperative but tribunals, in general, arbitration or State, are usually reluctant reverse the decisions of their brethren, except under exceptional circumstances.

However, some BITs provide explicitly that other means of internal law redress must be exhausted before arbitrage may be initiated. In such a case, may it not be argued that, having exhausted, and lost, his recourse to the USCIT, and the in-country appellate procedure thereafter, the plaintiff is now in rights to have an arbitration tribunal reconsider? How would justice benefit from denying such rights? Unlike the situation where the plaintiff first chooses arbitration, where he explicitly consents not to seek redress elsewhere, there is no USCIT rule that prohibits a disappointed petitioner, after exhausting his first recourse, from looking to the USCIT for redress.

A showing that local precedents have determined the specific customs surcharges were unlawful may already exist in decisions rendered by the local court. Arguments made in such venues, if accepted by them, could play a role in convincing an arbitration tribunal of the petitioner's rights against the host State. The problem here is that the local tribunals might not have had the jurisdiction to rule against the host State, no matter how sympathetic they may have been to the plaintiff's plight. An investor-exporter could, conceivably, through its corporate subsidiary in the taxing State, file a request for arbitration if the parties consent and the venues' rules are met.

16.10.11. – *United States Customs Court Act of 1980*

With the Customs Courts Act of 1980, the U.S. Congress

> "equipped the federal judicial system to deal effectively and efficiently with the increasingly complex problems arising from international trade litigation. In essence, the Act clarified and expanded the status, jurisdiction, and powers of the former United States Customs Court and changed the name of the court to the United States Court of International Trade. The new name more accurately describes the court's expanded jurisdiction and its increased judicial functions relating to international trade disputes."[350]

The work of this Court has been described as follows:

> "Utilizing the nationwide jurisdiction of the United States Court of International Trade, the Act, as described by President Jimmy Carter, 'creates a comprehensive system for judicial review of civil actions arising out of import transactions and federal statutes affecting international trade.' The Act also ensures expeditious procedures, avoids jurisdictional conflicts among federal courts, and provides uniformity in the judicial decision-making process for import transactions as required under Article I, section 8, of the Constitution of the United States."

Though not part of arbitral jurisprudence, USCIT cases are a valuable source of factual and legal histories which can, quite arguably, be replicated in an arbitral context. Antidumping determinations and tariff applications may conceivably be argued, when the facts sustain it, as a discriminatory measure violating the provisions of a BIT. What criteria the USCIT uses to determine whether Customs has applied the proper classification to a specific product depends on the nature of the product as interpreted by the Court, upon advice of adversary counsel and its own research staff. Though they may not be used as precedents, they provide a technical mine for either side of an arbitration proceeding to

---
[350] Http://www.cit.uscourts.gov/inform.

use in order legally to justify and prosecute their claims or defend against them. The world benchmarks Customs agencies of various countries use to determine whether a product is dumped or not are equally relevant in an anti-dumping action as in an arbitration case based on discrimination. The USCIT's interpretation of these benchmarks can make the difference between allowed and disallowed discrimination.[351]

16.10.12. – *History*

In 1926, the outmoded Board of General Appraisers that had, until then, handled importation cases, was replaced by the US Customs Court. Thirty years later, the court was declared to be one established under the Constitution, an important change in status. Its responsibilities changed little till 1980, when its name and function were changed for the purpose of offering to the international trade community, domestic interest groups, labour organisations an improved, affordable forum for judicial review. Judges are appointed for life, their courtrooms are in New York.

16.10.13. – *Jurisdiction*

The Court's geographical jurisdiction extends throughout the United States but the court "can and does hear and decide cases which arise anywhere in the Nation and is also authorised to hold hearings in foreign countries."[352]

The court's subject matter jurisdiction includes the jurisdiction previously granted to the Customs court but also a residual authority to decide any civil action against the United States, its officers or its agencies arising out of any law pertaining to international trade. The Act makes it clear the Court has the complete powers in law and equity or as conferred upon other US Courts by statute, including but not limited to money judgments, writs of mandamus, preliminary

---

[351] *Home Products International v. US USCIT Case*, n° 07-00103 (7 April 2008).
[352] *Ibidem*.

and permanent injunctions. Furthermore, the Court has exclusive jurisdictions over actions brought by the United States under the laws governing import transactions as well as any third party actions relating to claims pending in the court. Appeals from final decisions of the USCIT may be taken to the US Court of Appeals for the Federal Circuit and ultimately to the US Supreme Court.

16.10.14. – *Residual Jurisdiction of USCIT*

Just as investors may run risks of expropriation and nationalisation measures in the country where they have invested, they also run risks of discrimination when the products of their foreign investment are exported back to their country of origin or another developed country. Besides measures dictated by the developed country's ongoing legislation for the protection of its citizens, investors run the risk of discrimination in the form of anti-dumping legislation and countervailing duties to the point where their foreign investment is rendered worthless. This risk may arise at the point of entry of raw materials into the LDC or at the point of entry in a developed country of goods finished in the LDC.

16.10.15. – *Rules*

Rule 2 of the USCIT is to confirm the concept that there is only one form of action. Like many other Common Law jurisdictions, differences between equity and common law have been erased, at least on paper, yielding the conclusion that the same court may hear causes of action that sound in law as well as those that sound in equity. Tradition, as well as constitutional limitations on ordinary courts, continues to keep alive procedural distinctions between law and equity in many venues.

The USCIT extends that concept and, like arbitration tribunals, uses the judge or a panel of judges both to try and find the facts and to determine the law. However, when dealing with matters determined to be "of law", a litigant may insist on having a jury be the trier of facts.

An action in the USCIT is commenced by filing a summons and a complaint, much like in all other United States courts, and paying the required fees. Under Rule 3.1, however, an action may be transferred to the USCIT from a Bi-national Panel or Committee pursuant to Code section 16 (a(g)(12)(B) or (D). A copy of the request for transfer must be filed with the Court and with the U.S. Secretary. Notice is to be given all parties involved. In such a transfer, any person who files a Notice of Appearance under NAFTA Article 1904 or NAFTA Extraordinary Challenge Committee Rule 40 will be treated as Intervenor, if he otherwise meets the requirements of USCIT Rule 24. Rule 3.1 is quite specific as to time requirements for notice and filing, as well as plaintiff's right to file an amended complaint when an intervention has been filed. Proposed judicial protective orders may be requested.

Rules 4 and 5 governs service of complaints and summons while Rule 4.1 governs the service of other papers in the action. Rules 6 through 25 concern the pleadings, who can be parties, who can be joined and substituted. Rules 26 through 37 cover discovery and penalties for failure to comply, Rules 38 through 53 concern trial, including jury trial on matters of law, Rules 54 through 63 concern judgments and rules 64 through 69 concern execution of judgments (e.g. property seizure).

The Court publishes a Handbook that takes the practitioner from the moment of filing up to but excluding appeal.

16.10.16. – *USCIT Jurisprudence*

Decisions of the USCIT more frequently seem to affirm the lower Panel's determinations,[353] but, nonetheless. The USCIT has overruled and sent back for remand numerous determi-

---

[353] E.g. *Husteel v. US*, 23 Dec. 2008, Case n° 8-139.

nations by the lower panels.[354][355] The Court may review appeals or requests for redetermination of decisions made, for example, by the U.S. Customs, the International Trade Commission, the Office of the US Trade Representative. The Court's actions are far from automatically supportive of the decision of such agencies and are frequently highly detailed in their analysis of the facts and applicable law. The Court can and has also determined that facts were insufficient to support the order sought and remanded for further evaluation.[356]

16.10.17. – *Tjianjin v. US* – Customs Duties Discrimination

Tjianjin Magnesium Inc. (TMI) v. US. and US Magnesium, Case 8.01, (2008) decided on 8 January 2008 is an interesting case where a civilian private intervener joined with the US to dismiss the plaintiff's contest of an order by the US Department of Commerce to rescind the deferral of the Department's administrative review. Plaintiff TMI sought to enjoin the ongoing administrative review of the Department's entries, invoking the Court of International Trade's residual jurisdiction under 28 U.S.C., §1581(i) (20001). The Court in this case admitted that the plaintiff had not exhausted all of its remedies. In a very complex opinion, where the parties' respective motions and requests for extension were discussed in detail, the Court concluded that it did not have jurisdiction because the plaintiff had not exhausted all of its remedies. The case is an example of the thoroughness of the Court's analysis but serves also as a reminder that exporters,

---

[354] E.g. *Allied Pacific v. US*, 22 Dec. 2008, Case n° 8-138 where the Court determined that the Department's surrogate value for the goods imported was not properly calculated and remanded the case for further calculation.

[355] *P.S. Chez Sydney LLC v. US International Trade Commission and US Customs Service*, Court Case n° 02-00365, 24 January 2008.

[356] E.g. *Volkswagen of America, Inc. v. U.S.*, 18 Dec. 2008, Case n° 8-137. This case had apparently been appealed to the District Court of Appeals for the Federal District where the party aggrieved prevailed.

whether of raw materials or reprocessed goods, face a difficult road when confronted with discrimination based on alleged dumping. The decision did not actually find there was dumping nor that there was discrimination but clearly the litigation had been long and the result negative for the plaintiff. The result was proportionately favourable for the home industry, raising the possibility that its intervention was motivated by a desire to squelch the foreign competition. In a case such as this, a remand is equivalent to a loss by the exporter and a gain by the home industry, merely because of the passage of time and the intervening fluctuation of prices.

The exporter apparently did not choose to seek relief under any applicable BIT, although its main basis for the claim it did seek in the USCIT was discrimination. A cause of action under a BIT requires the presence of an investment.

It is frequent practice for exporters to test the foreign market and, if the test is successful, establish a subsidiary company in that market to handle a variety of tasks, such as the processing of raw materials into finished products, advertising and distribution. The imposition of a sentence which effectively prohibited the exporter from gaining a foothold in the foreign market might be viewed as a precursor of discrimination against such a subsidiary. It requires but little imagination to see that the foreign exporter might then be dissuaded from establishing the subsidiary and licensing the same to process the raw materials exported. New forms of investments, such as licensing, could be structured along those lines. It should not matter that the subsidiary had not yet been established if the intent to do so existed and initial steps, such as exporting had been taken. Local industry's possibly easier access to the taxing authorities may easily result in a pre-emptive strike against the imports.

If the *Tjianjin case* could have been viewed in that light, the possibility was deftly sidelined by the court's finding that the claimant's petition was premature. Query whether the prior establishment of a processing subsidiary might have laid the basis for an arbitration request on the basis of discrimination and avoided the jurisdiction of the USCIT altogether.

16.10.18. – *Mittal Steel v. U.S* [357]

In *Mittal Steel v. U.S*, slip opinion 8-03, another anti-dumping case, the Court confirmed the scope of the international Trade Commission duties as follows:

> "In anti-dumping proceedings, the ITC is charged with determining whether an industry in the United States has suffered or is threatened with material injury by reason of imports, citing U.S.C. section 1673d(b)."

When such a determination is made, and anti-dumpimg duties are applied, the implication is that there has been no objectionable discrimination. In the case where the imports are imported by a subsidiary of the foreign exporter, it may logically be argued that the anti-dumping measures do not violate the anti-discrimination provisions of any BIT between the exporter's and the importer's countries.

In Ames True Temper v. US,), decided on 18 January 2008, the Court held that:

> "When reviewing a final anti-dumping determination from Commerce, the court 'shall hold unlawful any determination, finding, or conclusion found'... to be unsupported by substantial evidence on the record, ..."

A contrario, the Court may well find that a determination, finding or conclusion which is supported by substantial evidence, is perfectly lawful. Whether it is or it is not a discrimination is then moot. Many developing countries complain that anti-dumping actions on their products, as well as illegal dumping in their countries, affect their economies disproportionately. Yet, at the same time, investors from some of the developed countries actively pursue opportunities for cost-effective sourcing in the less developed countries. According

---
[357] USCIT Consolidated Case n° 06-00173.

to the NAFTA Article 1904 Panel Rules (Rules of Procedure for Article 1904 Binational Panel Reviews), an investor[358] caught in this tug-of-war may try to intervene in the determination of the panel. If there is a BIT between the less developed country where he invested and the developed country, then, when the latter imposes unpredictable anti-dumping measures, the investor may want to have the dispute arbitrated by the arbitration venue selectable under the BIT. Yet, he cannot stand idle in the face of an Article 1904 Panel ruling and abandon lodging an appeal with the USCIT, for, by not participating in the appeal, he may run the risk of being held to have waived his claim.

At this time, NAFTA's membership is limited to the United States of Mexico, the United States of America and the Commonwealth of Canada. Proposals have been made for extending NAFTA to other Western Hemisphere countries. The circumstances under which current and future USCIT's jurisdiction interact or will interact with NAFTA are not all easily predictable and in any event are beyond the scope of this Work, but, clearly, investors, in particular those active in "new investment forms" as described earlier in this Work, have an interest in knowing what part the USCIT may play in their plans for foreign investments.

16.10.19. – *Other Hostile Measures*

Anti-dumping measures and the like are not the only ways by which a host State may try, under cover of law, to exclude products imported by the investor's local company. Examples of such measures are many: revocation of broker's licence[359],

---

[358] As an "interested person," defined as follows: "interested person" means a person who, pursuant to the laws of the country in which a final determination was made, would be entitled to appear and be represented in review of the final determination; (*personne intéressée*) (*persona interesada*).

[359] *Sherri N. Boynton v. US*, USCIT Case 06-00095, decided on 23 January 2008.

misclassification of the imported goods, revocation of previous tariff classification.[360][361]

In *Royal Thai Government v. U.S.*,[362] the US objection to certain Thai imports was based on alleged Thai subsidies given the exporter.[363] The Court confirmed that:

> "Commerce can impose countervailing duties on foreign products that are imported, sold, or likely to be sold in the United States, if a foreign government has directly or indirectly subsidized its manufacture, production, or export. See 19 *U.S.C.* 1671(a); accord *Allegheny Ludlum Corp. v. United States*, 24 *USCIT* 452, 112 *F. Supp.* 2d 1141 (2000). These duties are intended 'to offset the unfair competitive advantage that foreign producers would otherwise enjoy from export subsidies paid by their governments.' *British Steel PLC v. United States*, 20 *CIT* 663, 699, 929 *F. Supp.* 426, 445 (1996) (citing *Zenith Radio Corp. v. United States*, 437 *U.S.* 443, 456 (1978)."

NSK Corporation v. Fag Italia, Consol Court No.06-334, (2008) dated 15 February 2008 is unremarkable except for the claim that an Intervener could expand the scope of the litigation to include imports of the same products from countries other than that whose imports were being taxed. The court denied the intervener's plea, stating quite clearly:

> "one of the most usual procedural rules is that an intervener is admitted to the proceeding as it stands, and in respect of the pending issues, but is not permitted to enlarge those issues or compel an alteration of the nature of the proceeding."

In *Alloy Piping Products Inc. v. US and Ta Chen Stainless Steel Pipe*, Defendant-Intervener, (2008) decided on 13 March 2008 is interesting in that it shows that the ability third parties have to intervene (or bringing in third parties as interveners) in a USCIT action can be used to benefit the plaintiff.

---

[360] *International Custom Products v. US*, USCIT Case n° 07-00318 dated 31 March 2008.

[361] *US Steel v. US*, USCIT Case n° 07-00271 dated 5 August 2008.

[362] Note how a State is brought into the USCIT's jurisdiction by the bias of having chosen to "appeal" another US agency's action.

[363] *Royal Thai Government, Sahavirya Industries v. US Consolidated USCIT*, Case 02-00026 dated 32 January 2008.

In this case, plaintiff sought to have some 37 additional companies named as affiliates of the main defendant (who already had identified 12 affiliates). The more usual scenario is for plaintiff to resist allowing extra parties to intervene. Ta Chen, the exporter, was operating through its US subsidiary. Plaintiff, a domestic producer of pipe, challenged the Commerce Department's determination, declining to apply available adverse facts in its anti-dumping analysis.

The plaintiff's strategy was not successful, the Court denying plaintiff's Motion for Judgment on the Record. The Court's grounds for the denial appears to be based on the facts of the case. However, we see no logical basis for such a legal strategy to be unavailable in that Court if facts had been different, and further posit that a similar strategy could well be used in an arbitration case. The USCIT court rested part of its decision on the following definition of "affiliated parties":

> "Section 1677(33) defines 'affiliated' or 'affiliated persons' as those who are:
>
> (A) Members of a family, including brothers and sisters (whether by whole or half blood), spouse, ancestors, and lineal descendants;
>
> (B) Any officer or director of an organization and such organization;
>
> (C) Partners;
>
> (D) Employer and employee;
>
> (E) Any person directly or indirectly owning, controlling, or holding with power to vote, 5 percent or more of the outstanding voting stock or shares of any organization and such organization;
>
> (F) Two or more persons directly or indirectly controlling, controlled by, or under common control with, any person; and
>
> (G) Any person who controls any other person and such other person.
>
> *Id.* In addition, 'a person shall be considered to control another person if the person is legally or operationally in a position to exercise restraint or direction over the other person'." ...

The regulations further provide that in determining whether control over another person exists. The Court further commented :

> "[Commerce] will consider the following factors, among others :
> corporate or family groupings;
> franchise or joint venture agreements; debt financing; and close supplier relationships. [Commerce] will not find that control exists on the basis of these factors unless the relationship has the potential to impact decisions concerning the production, pricing, or cost of the subject merchandise or foreign like product."

It seems to us that this rather expansive attitude towards control cannot help but resonate in an arbitration proceeding, where, for instance, an individual corporate subsidiary in the host country claims that it has been the subject of discrimination. It is an example of the Pandora's box type of situation that can result when intervention becomes an accepted arbitration feature. There may be argument as to whether "affiliation" with other companies amounts to control, allowing that company to claim the benefit of Art 25(2)b of the Washington Convention but a defence based upon the above definition of affiliation and control, when the facts support it, cannot be excluded. Global companies today enter into a plethora of agreements with their subsidiaries and affiliates, making such companies vulnerable to being joined as parties cross-defendants in an arbitration proceeding. The precise line between mere affiliation and control appears to be irrelevant in a USCIT context and has not yet, so far as we know, been set in an arbitration context.

Elkem Metals etc. v. US. USCIT Case no. 99-00628 (2008) dated 5 September 2008 is another interesting case where the alleged dumping had injured domestic industry but it was found that an unlawful price fixing arrangement had existed between the domestic manufacturers. After an exhaustive analysis of the periods during which this conspiracy existed, the Court held that the lower price imports did not contribute to any injury to the domestic industry.

16.10.20. – Stare Decisis, Res Judicata

The USCIT's attitude towards Stare Decisis and Res Judicata appears to be more flexible than in other US Courts. In *Warner Lambert v. US USCIT Consolidated* Case no. 02-00520 (2008) dated 14 March 2008, the Court held that neither *res judicata* nor *stare decisis* requires the Court to find in favor of the Plaintiff. It cited that United States Supreme Court's holding "long ago" that res judicata did not apply to customs classification cases. See *United States v. Stone & Downer Co.*, 274 Court No. 02-00520, p. 5, *U.S.* 225, 233-37 (1927); *DaimlerChrysler Corp. v. United States*, 442 *F.3d* 1313, 1321 (Fed. Cir. U.S. 225, 233-37, 1927); *Avenues in Leather, Inc. v. United States*, 317 *F.3d* 1399 (Fed. Cir., 2003); *Schott Optical Glass, Inc. v. United States*, 750 *F.2d* 62, 64 (Fed. Cir., 1984).

Moreover, the USCIT confirmed that "the doctrine of *stare decisis* applies to only legal issues and not issues of fact[.]" *Avenues in Leather, Inc. v. United States*, 423 *F.3d* 1326, 1331 (Fed. Cir., 2005).

There is nonetheless a question as whether *stare decisis* or *res judicata* may be the basis for valid objections raised against the plaintiff or petitioner. Courts, arbitral or otherwise, are loath to allow themselves to be used for the prosecution of a multiplicity of actions based on the same facts and the same law. Arbitral courts do not see themselves as endowed with appellate jurisdiction. Normal strategy would therefore not often contemplate trying the matter in State courts and subsequently attempting to have it retried in an arbitral context in hopes of a better outcome.

16.10.21. Estoppel

It is, however, conceivable that, when a cause is shaky, and the failure in state courts is not excluded, that may well be the time to formulate the state court action in a manner such so that a difference can be claimed in a subsequent arbitration action. The pleader may then hope that any *res judicata* objection might be overruled if such a difference exists and is found. Success at this stage is not necessarily dispositive. Defence can simultaneously or in sequence claim that plaintiff's claim is barred by collateral estoppel. There are several types of estoppel.

One type of estoppel objection, the most likely to be sustained, when facts and law are substantially similar, is "estoppel by judgment." Parties to a proceeding cannot generally question the conclusiveness of a judgment as to matters already litigated or litigable.[364] To overcome this objection, the difference must be such that the prior action did not rule on the issue and, *in extremis*, that it could not have been presented based on the same facts.

"Promissory estoppel" is where one makes a promise on which another justifiably relies : the promisor may be denied the opportunity to claim he did not originally get paid. If the defence did not raise this objection in the State Court action, he is not foreclosed from raising it in arbitration.

"Estoppel in pais" or "equitable estoppel" prevents a party from contradicting a statement he intentionally made, leading another to act on it, believing it was true. It is a defence in equity but is not infrequently made inoperative by an imprudent waiver, express or implied. Generally speaking, equitable estoppel will not bar another remedy (i.e. one inconsistent with the first remedy sought) unless the plaintiff is estopped because of reliance and change of position of the defendant. If the facts pleaded are different (though related), or if another party joins in, pleading facts supporting his individual grievance, neither *res judicata* nor estoppel wll help the defendant against this other plaintiff or petitioner.

Clearly, after having litigated in State Court and lost, or not won sufficiently, the risk of a rejection in arbitration is not negligible, but, with careful navigation, that risk may be

---

[364] 46 Am. Jur. 2d, *Judgements*, sec. 379, 394.

minimized. Common Law has numerous cases on record where estoppel of one kind or another was allowed or disallowed. Even good cases may be lost in State Court. Ergo, those losses should not deter an imaginative claimant from seeking relief in an arbitration context if he can formulate his claim, or have it independently claimed by another, so that the legal and factual footprint will be different and so that the claim remain within commonsensical principles of absence of fraud, reliance and fair conduct. The mere possibility of continuing litigation in another forum may lead the parties to settle.

16.10.22. – Sufficiency of Evidence

The Zhejiang Native Produce etc. v. US. Case no. 06-0234 (2008) dated 16 June 2008 is informative in that it sets forth a standard for the sufficiency of substantial evidence that could equally be applied to arbitration cases:

> "The court reviews the Final Results under the substantial evidence and in accordance with law standard set forth in 19 *U.S.C.*, §1516a(b)(1)(B)(i). ('The court shall hold unlawful any determination, finding, or conclusion found... to be unsupported by substantial evidence on the record, or otherwise not in accordance with law...')."

In Huaiyin Foreign Trade Corp. (30) v. United States, 322 *F.3d* 1369, 1374 (Fed. Cir., 2003) (quoting *Consol. Edison Co. v. NLRB*, 305 *U.S.* 197, 229 (1938)) "substantial evidence" was descrbed as follows:

> "'Such relevant evidence as a reasonable mind might accept as adequate to support a conclusion.' It 'requires more than a mere scintilla, but is satisfied by something less than the weight of the evidence', quoting *Altx, Inc. v. United States*, 370 *F.3d* 1108, 1116 (Fed. Cir., 2004 (quotations and citations omitted). The existence of substantial evidence is determined 'by considering the record as a whole, including evidence that supports as well as evidence that 'fairly detracts from the substantiality of the evidence.'" (quoting *Atl. Sugar, Ltd. v. United States*, 744 *F.2d* 1556, 1562 (Fed. Cir., 1984)"

The possibility of drawing two equally justifiable, yet inconsistent conclusions from the record does not prevent the agency's determination from being supported by substantial evidence. See *Consol v. Fed. Mar. Comm'n*, 383 *U.S.* 607, 620 (1966); *Altx, Inc., op. cit.* at 1116 1116.

16.10.23. – *Compliance with International Treaties*

In *ThyssenKruppAcciai etc. v. US* (2008) USCIT, Case no. - 00390 dated 1 July 2008, the Court deferred to provisions of the WTO Dispute Settlement Body which found the US Department of Commerce decision inconsistent with US obligations under WTO Agreements. The Uruguay Round Agreements Act (19 *U.S.C.* 3538), on request of the Office of the US Trade Representative, was obliged to bring its determination in line with WTO decisions. The Court found for the plaintiff and denied the US Government's motion to dismiss plaintiff's complaints.

16.10.24. – *Equal Protection and Standing*

Occasionally, plaintiffs rest their argument or parts thereof on novel grounds. In *Totes-Isotoner v. US*, USCIT case no. 07-0001 (2008) dated 3 July 2008, plaintiff claimed that by classifying men's gloves and other gloves differently, the Customs determination violated the Equal Protection Clause of the US Constitution. Some may have found this claim far fetched but the US Government seized on it by claiming that, besides lacking standing, Plaintiff was relying on unacceptable gender differences, could not file a claim that was "political" and therefore non-justiciable. Quoting *Japan Whaling Ass'n v. Am. Cetacean Society*, 478 *US* 221, 230 (1986), the Court held that:

> "The political question doctrine excludes from judicial review those controversies which revolve around policy choices and value determinations constitutionally committed for resolution to the halls of Congress or the confines of the Executive Branch. The Judiciary is particularly ill suited to make such decisions, as 'courts are

fundamentally underequipped to formulate national policies or develop standards for matters not legal in nature.'" (quoting *United States ex rel. Joseph v. Cannon*, 642 *F.2d* 1373, 1379 (1981) (footnote omitted), cert. denied, 455 *U.S.* 999 (1982))).

The Court further held that the Supreme Court's admonition in the Japan Whaling holding was directly applicable.

As to constitutional "standing", the Court held in *Lujan v. Defenders of Wildlife*, 504 *U.S.* 555, 560-61 (1992) ("Defenders of Wildlife")(citations omitted):

> "To establish a sufficient stake for purposes of Article III standing, plaintiffs must demonstrate: (1) that they have suffered some injury-in-fact; (2) that there is a causal connection between the defendant's conduct and this injury-in-fact; and (3) that this injury is redressable by the court."

As to "prudential" standing, the Court held that:

> "[T]he interest sought to be protected by the complainant [must be] arguably within the zone of interests to be protected or regulated by the statute or constitutional guarantee in question." (quoting *Ass'n of Data Processing Serv. Org., Inc. v. Camp*, 397 *U.S.* 150, 153 (1970)),

and that:

> "the zone of interest test only 'denies a right of review if the plaintiff's interests are [] marginally related to or inconsistent with the purposes implicit in the statute...' *Clarke*, 479 *U.S.* at 399."

16.10.25. – *Punitive Damages*

Pam v. US, USCIT Case no.04-00082, (2008) coming for reconsideration on 9 September 2008 addresses an issue on which common law and civil law jurists often differ. Plaintiffs cited the earlier USCIT opinion in the case, dated 9 July 2008, in which the Court, by way of dictum, stated that the 45.49 % anti-dumping penalty might be considered as "punitive damages" against the violating plaintiff.

During reconsideration, plaintiff claimed that an intervening decision of the US Supreme Court undermined the preceding Ta Chen decision, specifically referring to the *Exxon*

Shipping Company v. Baker, 128 *S.Ct.* 2605, (2008), as a basis for claiming that the earlier Ta Chen decision was "manifestly in error." In the Exxon case, the jury had awarded plaintiffs 287 million dollars in compensatory damages and 5 billion dollars in punitive damages. The US Court of Appeals reduced the punitive damages to 2.5 billion but the US. Supreme Court held that even the reduced amount was against maritime common law and therefore should be no higher than the compensatory damages. The US Supreme Court pegged the amount of allowable punitive damages to no more than 1.1 times the compensatory.

The Pam Court refused to accept the plaintiff's claim that the Exxon case undermined the earlier Ta Chen decision, holding that the facts were fundamentally different. We mention this case here to show that precedents in the USCIT jurisprudence can be useful in helping arbitration tribunals decide on adequate compensation for an aggrieved plaintiff, and that, besides international common law, *lex mercatoria* and established usage, maritime common law is yet another source of information for petitioners and defendants alike in the argumentation of an arbitration cause. Where the award appears to be out of line with the damage sustained, the issue of covert punitive damages may be raised in opposition. Proof of the moderation of courts which allow punitive damages is another tool available to defendants in any context or venue.

16.11. – APPLICABLE LAW ON INVESTMENT DISPUTES

16.11.1. – *European Conventions*

European model conventions do not always address the rules of law to be applied by arbitrators of the disputes. It is generally accepted that the Contracting States (in the BITs) and investors (in State Contracts) may specify the applicable law and that, if they do not, the arbitrators may themselves decide the issue :

> "If the parties have selected an applicable law, arbitrators, mostly and justifiably, feel bound thereby. On this point, there should therefore be no uncertainty. On the other hand, where the will of the parties regarding applicable law is not manifest, that law will be determined by the arbitrators." [365]

This position is confirmed by ICSID jurisprudence :

> "The decision concludes that the parties had not had the opportunity to express their choice regarding the rules applicable to the substance of the dispute in their arbitration agreement. It is, however, to be noted that it is not inconceivable that a treaty for the protection of investments includes provisions specific to applicable law. Such provisions would commit the host State signing the bilateral investment treaty, as well as the investor, claiming under the treaty, to their intent to submit to them. When confronted with an absence of initial choice, the majority (of arbitrators) has deemed that, from the parties' documentation, it could be seen that the parties had indeed reached agreement on the applicability of the bilateral treaty itself to the case." [366]

In the *Amco/Indonesia* case, the following was held :

> "Regarding applicable law, the tribunal found that, absent a choice of law by the parties, it was appropriate, on the basis of **Article 42(1)** of the Washington Convention, to apply Indonesian law as well as principles of international law to the issues in question." [367]

The arbitrators' power to select the applicable law, in the event no choice has been made by the parties to the dispute, is not an innovation created by ICSID. This is an ancient principle, by which the arbitrator himself may do so. This is quite logical in that arbitrators should not be able to deny jurisdiction simply because the parties have not expressly selected an applicable law.

During the few first years after its passage, when the Washington Convention was just beginning to exist, an arbi-

---

[365] MARTOR, Boris, *op. cit.*, p. 210, see footnote 320.
[366] GAILLARD, Emmanuel, *op. cit.*, p. 337.
[367] GAILLARD, Emmanuel, *op. cit.*, pp. 336 and 337.

tration award was issued in the *Revere* case. Absent consent on the choice of law by the parties and reference to domestic law, the arbitrator decided that international law would be applied. The issue before them concerned the execution of an investment contract, signed in 1967 between the Jamaican Company Revere Copper and Brass (subsidiary of the US Company Revere) and the investment insurer "Overseas Private Investment Corporation (OPIC)". Arbitration was a possibility contemplated in the insurance contract which covered political risks.

A majority of the arbitrators decided that international law was applicable:

> "Whereas one member of the Tribunal held that only American law was applicable for the determination of OPIC's liability, the majority correctly relied on the law which governed the investment contract. This contract, however, did not contain a clause on the applicable law. The tribunal's majority nevertheless held international law applicable. This view was based on three grounds:
> a. the tribunal referred to precedents;
> b. the Tribunal classified the investment contract as an international development agreement, which was subject per se to rules of international law and
> c. the Tribunal was of the view that the contract was 'internationalised' by the fact that the United States and Jamaïca had concluded an agreement regarding the subrogation of a claim from the investor to the United States in cases of OPIC's liability." [368]

At the time, the grounds used by the tribunal were roundly criticised. In any event, the decision shows again how extensive the power of arbitrators is regarding what law shall be applied. Both the contracting States and investors have an interest in specifying what law shall be applied to their disputes, as such a provision will then bind the arbitrators. Because of the international character of disputes regarding international investments, the list of legal rules to be applied

---

[368] KOHLHAMMER, *Zeitschrift für ausländisches öffentliches recht und völkerrecht*, Band 42, p. 507.

must be as exhaustive as possible. The list may include the domestic law of the host State. Furthermore, international law should always include: treaties, common international law rules and generally accepted principles of international law.

It would also be useful to specify that arbitrators must, eventually, consider the norms that have been developed in internal law practice, such as the *"lex mercatoria"* :

> "What is involved here are private rules, which do not reflect the national law of any particular State and which have been developed by international commerce operators. In its original sense, the "lex mercatoria" consisted essentially of codified usages (such as, for example, incoterms or rules and usages of documentary credit), customary clauses, types of contracts and (mostly) known arbitration jurisprudence."

The parties may also want to have it clearly stated that the rules of equity shall be observed subsidiarily.

16.11.2. – *Clauses in BIT's*

BIT's do not always refer to applicable law. When, because of a provision in a BIT, investors may choose the arbitration institution, applicable law then hinges on what the particular institution chosen may have provided in its rules. The ICSID arbitration rules confirm free choice of law as a matter of principle:

> "The tribunal shall render its decision based on rules of law adopted by the parties". (**Article 42)(1)**)

The parties of course have to prove the choice. Should the State Contract, for instance, provide for choosing the applicable law, showing documentary proof will be easy.

Should ICSID be made aware? It is rather surprising that the ICSID Convention does not expressly require the parties to send a copy of the State contract to the Centre, nor to inform the Centre about the applicable law chosen by the parties (cfr **Article 36**).

Submittal of this information should be mandatory. It could be submitted when the petition for arbitration is filed, based on the arbitration rules:

> "The petition may furthermore list all other provisions relating to... as well as all of the provisions which have been agreed upon regarding the settlement of the dispute." (**Article 3** Filing instructions)

Amending the BIT provisions regarding individual agreements would be another solution. Each of the contracting Parties could agree to send to ICSID or any other arbitration institution a copy of the applicable contracts when filing the arbitration petition. Should the parties not have chosen an applicable law, the ICSID convention provides as follows:

> "Absent an agreement between the parties, the tribunal shall apply the law of the State which is a party to the dispute – including rules as to conflicts of laws – as well as the principles of international law in the matter. ... The provisions of the foregoing paragraphs do not affect the Tribunal's power, if the parties are in agreement, to render a decision *ex aequo et bono*". (**Article 42**)

For reasons already explained in this analysis, we believe that it would be best to avoid the use of conflicts of laws rules, since the parties may resolve the problem in their agreement. How has the applicable law question been resolved in the rules of other institutions of international arbitration? In the rules of procedure of the International Chamber of Commerce, there is the following provision:

> "The parties are free to choose the rules of law the Tribunal is to apply as to the substance of the dispute. In the event of the parties' failure to specify applicable law, the arbitrator will apply the law which he deems appropriate. In all cases, the arbitral Tribunal will take into consideration the provisions of the contract as wel as the pertinent usages of international commerce." (**Article 17**)

If investors were to choose the International Chamber of Commerce as its arbitration institution, it would be appropriate for them to agree with the other party to the dispute that international law has to be included in the definition of applicable law. The text of the ICC provision has, nonetheless, an important flaw in that arbitrators have discretion to apply international law if they consider that this law is a part of "appropriate rules of law" but are not bound to do so if they do not so consider. It is therefore better not to have any doubt in this area and explicitly require that international law be applied.

In the rules of other international arbitration institutions, no provision can be found to govern the application of specific rules of law to the dispute (e.g. LCIA, CEPINA). The arbitration rules of the Dutch Institute for Arbitration (NAI) contains a provision similar to ICC's:

> "Applicable law: if the parties have chosen an applicable law, the arbitration tribunal will render its decision in conformity therewith. If no choice of law has been made, the tribunal will decide on the rules of law it considers appropriate (**Article 46).** In any case, the tribunal will respect applicable commercial usage." (**Article 47**).

The Belgian model convention, to the credit of its drafters, does contain a provision regarding applicable law:

> "The arbitration tribunal shall render its decision in conformity with rules of the domestic law, including the rules of conflicts of laws of the Contracting State which is a party to the dispute and on whose territory the investment was made, as well as on the basis of provisions in this convention, provisions contained in the particular contract relating to the investment and principles of international law." (article 12)

This provision does not appear in all the Belgian BIT's but it has been used, for instance, in the BIT with the Republic of Khazakstan (Federal Register dated 15 March 2005, at p. 9295).

The mere enumeration of applicable law rules is both too restrictive and too broad. It is not complete enough in that commercial usage and equity should also be mentioned. It is too broad in that the application of rules of conflicts of law should not have been mentioned since mentioning such rules in the Convention may be responsible for creating a "dispute within a dispute" regarding what law is applicable to the main issue.

Among practitioners of international arbitration, it is generally accepted that application of the domestic law regarding conflicts of law (reference) should be avoided :

> "When there is a reference to the national law of a State, it may be admitted that all of the legal rules of substantive and procedural law have been considered, excluding the rules of appeal under private international law. Furthermore, when the parties do select national law as applicable law, such selection must be understood to mean, unless otherwise provided, rules of substantive law and not its conflict of law rules, so that a transfer of a case to another tribunal is, for all intents and purposes, not available." [369]

As we have already stressed, the Washington Convention, somewhat unexpectedly, provides for the application of rules of conflicts of law. This reference has probably been adopted at the request of Asian and African host States. This does not exclude the parties from agreeing not to be bound by such rules when they negotiate bilateral protection conventions. Such agreement will then take precedence over the provisions of the multilateral convention as a *"lex specialis"*.

Some of the BIT's, as signed by Spain, also contain an applicable law provision. Thus in Spain's BIT's with Nigeria and Macedonia, it is stated that the arbitrators must decide on the basis of the BITs provisions, the host State's national law, including conflicts of law rules, as well as generally recognised rules of international law.

---

[369] POUDRET, J.F., *Droit comparé de l'arbitrage international*, Bruxelles, Bruylant, 2002, p. 614.

16.12. – EXAMPLES OF ARBITRATION CLAUSES TO BE INSERTED IN STATE CONTRACTS

16.12.1. – *ICSID* [370]

Under the Washington Convention, consent may be given in advance, with respect to a defined class of future disputes. Clauses relating to future disputes are a common feature of investment agreements between Contracting States and investors who are nationals of other Contracting States.

Clause 1

A. The [Government]/[name of constituent subdivision or agency] of *name of Contracting State* (hereinafter the "Host State") and *name of investor* (hereinafter the "Investor") hereby consent to submit to the International Centre for Settlement of Investment Disputes (hereinafter the "Centre") any[6] dispute arising out of or relating to this agreement for settlement by [conciliation]/[arbitration]/[conciliation], followed, if the dispute remains unresolved within *time limit* of the communication of the report of the Conciliation Commission to the parties, by arbitration pursuant to the Convention on the Settlement of Investment Disputes between States and Nationals of Other States (hereinafter the "Convention").

B. Consent in Respect of Existing Disputes.

Consent may also be given in respect of a particular, existing dispute.

Clause 2

The [Government]/[name of constituent subdivision or agency] of *name of Contracting State* (hereinafter the "Host State") and *name of investor* (hereinafter the "Investor") hereby consent to submit to the International Centre for Settlement of Investment Disputes (hereinafter the "Centre") for settlement by [conciliation]/[arbitration]/[conciliation followed, if the dispute remains unresolved within *time limit* of the communication of the report of the Conciliation Commission to the parties, by arbitration] pursuant to the Convention on the Settlement of Investment Disputes between States and Nationals of Other States, the following dispute arising out of the investment described below : ...

---

[370] Www.worldbank.org/icsid.

16.12.2. – ICC clauses [371]

In the ICC rules of arbitration appears the following standard consent clause :

> "All disputes arising out of or in connection with the present contract shall be finally settled under the rules of arbitration of the International Chamber of Commerce by one or more arbitrators appointed in accordance with the said rules."

16.13. – INVESTMENT DISPUTES RESOLUTION SYSTEM AND ARBITRATION CLAUSES IN BIT's

Every BIT will include an article concerning the procedure to follow in the event that a dispute arises betwen a host State and an investor from another Contracting State. The most complete provision in this regard appears in the Danish model convention. For this reason, the text of article 9 of this convention is quoted here *in extenso* :

> "1. Any dispute concerning an investment between an investor of one Contracting Party and the other Contracting party shall, if possible, be settled amicably.
>
> 2. If any such dispute cannot be settled within six months following the date on which the dispute has been raised by the investor through written notification to the Contracting Party, each Contracting Party hereby consents to the submission of the dispute, at the investor's choice, for resolution by international arbitration to one of the following fora :
>
> The International Centre for Settlement of Investment Disputes (ICSID) for settlement by arbitration under the Washington Convention of 18 March 1965 on the Settlement of Investment Disputes between States and Nationals of Other States provided both Contracting Parties are parties to the said Convention; or
>
> • the Additional Facility of the Centre, if the Centre is not available under the Convention; or
>
> • an *ad hoc* tribunal set up under Arbitration Rules of the United Nations Commission on International Trade Law (UNCITRAL).

---

[371] Www.iccarbitration.org.

JURISDICTION

The appointing authority under the said rules shall be the Secretary General of ICSID; or
- by arbitration In accordance with the Rules of Arbitration of the International Chamber of Commerce (ICC).

3. For the purpose of this Article and **Article 25(2)b** of the said Washington Convention, any legal person which is constituted in accordance with the legislation of one Contracting Party and which, before a dispute arises, was controlled by an investor of the other Contracting Party, shall be treated as a national of the other Contracting Party.

Any arbitration under paragraph **2 b) – d)** of this **Article** shall, at the request of either party to the dispute, be held in a state that is a party to the United Nations Convention on the Recognition and Enforcement of Foreign Arbitral Awards, done at New York, June 10, 1958 (the New York Convention).

The consent given by each Contracting Party in paragraph (2) and the submission of the dispute by an investor under the said paragraph shall constitute the written consent and written agreement of the parties to the dispute to its submission for settlement for the purposes of, **Chapter 11** of the Washington Convention (Jurisdiction of the Centre) and for the purpose of the Additional Facility Rules, Article l of the UNCITRAL Arbitration Rules, the Rules of Arbitration of the ICC and Article 11 of the New York Convention.

In any proceeding involving an investment dispute, a Contracting Party shall not assert, as a defence, counterclaim or for any other reason, that indemnification or other compensation for all or part of the alleged damages has been received pursuant to an insurance or guarantee contract.

7. Any arbitral award rendered pursuant to this Article shall be final and binding on the parties to the dispute. Each Contracting Party shall carry out without delay the provisions of any such award and provide in its territory for the enforcement of such award."

The following clause concerning the settlement of disputes between a Contracting Party and an investor of the other Contracting Party is distinct from clauses generally found in European conventions. It offers extensive guarantees to investors :

"Each of the Contracting States consents in advance and grants the investor the right to submit his eventual dispute to one of the following fora : ICSID, the International Centre for the Settlement of

Investment Disputes; the Additional Facility of the Centre, if the Centre is not available under the Convention; an *ad hoc* Tribunal set up arbitration rules of the United Nations Commission on Inbternational Trade Law (UNCITRAL); the International Chamber of Commerce (ICC).

The appointing authority under the UNCITRAL rules shall be the Secretary general of ICSID. This is a good formula. It is one of these rare conventions which expressly provides recourse to the potential 'Additional Facility' hosted by ICSID. The clause also refers to the control exercised by an investor in a local company, the latter being considered a 'national of another State' because of such control. It is further provided that the arbitral proceeding will take place in a State which is a party to the United Nations Convention on the Recognition and Enforcement of Foreign Arbitral Awards, done in New York on 10 June 1948 (the 'New York Convention')."

Finally, the Danish convention also states that the anticipatory consent provided therein is that corresponding to article 25 of the Washington Convention.

The reference to ICSID and ICC furthermore allows the subrogation of a parastatal insurance agency to the investor's rights. Thus, when ICSID refuses to recognise subrogation, ICC will accept it. There are therefore more options for the submittal of an eventual dispute to arbitration. Nonetheless, it may be suggested that a "fork-in-the-road" clause and an applicable law clause could be advantageously added.

CHAPTER XVII
INTER-STATE DISPUTES REGARDING BIT'S' INTERPRETATION

17.1. – COMMON INTERPRETATION OF THE WASHINGTON CONVENTION

According to the Washington Convention:

> "Every dispute arising between the Contracting States regarding the interpretation or application of the present convention and which has not been amiably resolved will be submitted to the International Court of Justice on request of any party to the dispute, unless the States parties thereto shall agree to another form of settlement." (**Article 64**)

We already know that disputes between a Contracting State and an international investor regarding the interpretation or application of a State contract or of BIT's are within the scope of ICSID's jurisdiction. and as the case may be, of other international arbitration institutions. Such disputes may on request of the investor, first be dealt through diplomatic démarches but as soon as an arbitration request is filed, such demarches are excluded. However, inter-state disputes regarding the Washington Convention must be submitted to the International Court of Justice.

17.2. – COMMON INTERPRETATION PROBLEMS OF BIT'S

Disputes between Contracting States regarding the interpretation or application of a BIT cannot be submitted to ICSID, since it does not have jurisdiction over disputes involving two States. Such disputes do happen. For example, profound changes in the capital transfer policy of a Contracting State often leads to bitter arguments between Contracting States. International investors who generally benefit from the freedom of capital transfer provisions under BIT's could be affected by a sudden change in the host State's policy towards capital transfers and encounter severe difficulties in this regard. BIT's also provide for the free transfer of salaries of foreign personnel or at least a substantial portion of such salaries. A host State could suddenly block such transfers also. Sometimes, the BIT's do refer to an unbalanced posture of the host State's balance of payments that may justify a change in capital transfer policy. Contracting States may differently interpret the realities of the difficulties that may surround international payments and thereby contest a host State's blockage. There is little doubt that blocked accounts will damage international investors' interests:

> "The existence of blocked accounts creates problems when currency exchange rates change. If, originally, the debt had been expressed in terms of the currency of the 'non-resident' creditor or in a third party currency, or if the currency of the debtor country sustains an after-the-fact devaluation, the creditor will surely wish to have a recourse against the original debtor. The latter, however, will consider that his payment to the bank agreed upon has validly freed him of his obligation, particularly if this payment was one required of him by the laws of his State."[372]

Contracting States – as well as investors – therefore have an interest in seeing to it that an efficient settlement procedure be established in order to settle inter-State conflicts. The procedures for settlement between States are largely outside the scope of this Work. However, sometimes, as when an interstate conflict affects private interests, recourse may be had to the applicable BIT, so long as investors are involved.

---

[372] SELLESLAGS, François, *op. cit.*, p. 110, see footnote 254.

17.3. – CLASSICAL SETTLEMENT FORMULA

In most BIT's, the settlement procedure for disputes consists of two phases. Usually, it is first expected that the contestant States will try to resolve the problem by diplomacy. If those démarches are not successful, each of the Contracting Parties must then assume the initiative and have recourse to arbitration. This procedure will lead to an arbitration award which will be mandatory and irrevocable.

As an example of the classical formula, **Article 9** of the Swedish model convention is quoted here:

"1. Any dispute between the Contracting Parties concerning the interpretation or application of this Agreement shall, if possible, be settled by negotiations between the Governments of the two Contracting Parties.

2. If the dispute cannot thus be settled within six months following the date on which such negotiations were requested by either Contracting Party, it shall at the request of either Contracting Party be submitted to an arbitration tribunal.

3. The arbitration tribunal shall be set up from case to case, each Contracting Party appointing one member. These two members shall then agree upon a national of a third State as their chairman, to be appointed by the Governments of the two Contracting Parties. The members shall be appointed within two months, and the chairman within four months, from the date either Contracting Party, has advised the other Contracting Party of its wish to submit the dispute to an arbitration tribunal.

4. If the time limits referred to in Paragraph (3) of this Article have not been complied with, either Contracting Party may, in the absence of any other relevant arrangement, invite the President of the International Court of Justice to make the necessary appointments.

5. If the President of the International Court of Justice is prevented from discharging the function provided for in Paragraph (4) of this Article or is a national of either Contracting Party, the Vice-President shall be invited to make the necessary appointments. If the Vice-President is prevented from discharging the said function or is a national of either Contracting Party, the most senior member of the Court who is not incapacitated or a national of either Con-

tracting Party shall be invited to make the necessary appointments.

6. The arbitration tribunal shall reach its decision by a majority of votes, the decision being final and binding on the Contracting Parties. Each Contracting Party shall bear the costs of the member appointed by that Contracting Party as well as the costs for its representation in the arbitration proceedings; the cost of the chairman as well as any other costs shall be borne in equal parts by the two Contracting Parties. The arbitration tribunal may, however, in its decision direct that a higher proportion of costs shall be borne by one of the Contracting Parties. In all other respects, the procedure of the arbitration tribunal shall be determined by the tribunal itself."

The classical formula, such as is shown in the quotation, has disadvantages. Contrary to the procedure for the settlement of Investor/State disputes, the classical formula for the settlement of State to State disputes is not particularly innovative. An *ad hoc* arbitration procedure has been set up but, except in a few particulars, it does not incorporate the settlement rules of UNITRAL. A procedure for the nomination of arbitrators, for example, would have been useful. Normally the parties submit nominations but in the event of disagreement, either party may petition the Secretary General of the International Court of Justice in the Hague. Lodging an appeal with the President of the Court of International Justice, for the appointment of arbitrators, is not an efficient formula. There could still be a better formula. The ICSID's Secretary General would be better qualified to make the nominations.

The Contracting Parties could have provided for institutional arbitration proceedings, for instance, before the Arbitration tribunal of the International Chamber of Commerce (ICC). Nonetheless, several European BIT's contain the classical formula (Belgium, Denmark, France, Germany, Italy, the Netherlands, Spain, United Kingdom etc.)

17.4. – SOME COUNTRIES DEVIATE FROM THE CLASSICAL FORMULA

17.4.1. – *Australia*

Australia has adopted rather innovative rules. Disputes may be submitted to an *ad hoc* arbitral tribunal, whose membership is set by the BIT rules. However, recourse to any other international arbitration tribunal is expressly allowed:

> "...it (dispute) shall be submitted at the request of either contracting Party to an arbitral tribunal established in accordance with the provisions of this article or, by agreement, to any other international tribunal."

The contracting States could then agree to have eventual recourse to institutional arbitration, such as the ICC in Paris. Insofar as the arbitrators' nominations are concerned, it is provided that they must be third party nationals and be residents or domiciled in such third party State, if it has relations with the host State and the complainant's State. It specifies that arbitration proceedings shall be instituted upon notice being given through diplomatic channels by the Contracting party instituting such proceedings to the other Contracting Party. Even during the proceedings, the Parties may always propose an amicable settlement. It is confirmed that the arbitral tribunal decides itself all questions relating to its competence. This is a very useful precaution as it helps avoid disputes on the dispute, that is a dispute on the jurisdiction of the Tribunal to pass judgment on the dispute relating to application or interpretation.

17.4.2. – *Afro-Asian model convention*

Article 11 of the Afro-Asian model convention reads as follows:

> "(i) Disputes or differences between the Contracting Parties concerning interpretation or application of this Agreement shall be settled through negotiations.

(ii) If such disputes and differences cannot thus be settled, the same shall upon request of either Contracting Party be submitted to an arbitral tribunal.

(iii) An arbitral tribunal shall be composed of three members Each Contracting Party shall nominate one member within a period of two months of the receipt of the request for arbitration. The third member, who shall be the Chairman of the Tribunal shall be appointed by agreement of the Contracting Parties. If a Contracting Party has failed to nominate its arbitrator or where agreement has not been reached in regard to the appointment of the Chairman of the tribunal, within a period of three months, either contracting party may approach the President of the International Court of Justice to make the appointment. The Chairman so appointed shall not be a national of either Contracting Party.

(iv) The arbitral tribunal shall reach its decision by majority of votes. Such decision shall be binding on both the Contracting Parties. The tribunal shall determine its own procedure and give directions in regard to the costs of the proceedings."

This formula has disadvantages. Procedural schedules are not at all or not clearly mentioned. The duration of negotiations and consultations is not set, causing uncertainty as when the arbitration request must be filed. The *"dies a quo"* for a two month delay, to be used for the nomination of an arbitrator by each of the Contracting Parties is the date the petition for arbitration is received. However, a more diligent Party, namely the one which starts the arbitration process, is of course not the one which receives the petition but the one who sends it to the other contracting State. The question arises: when does the two month delay begin for the sender State?

The problem could be resolved quickly by specifying that the two month delay starts from the date the sending State delivers an appropriate note to that effect through diplomatic channels.

On the other hand, no *"dies a quo"* is specified for the three month delay provided for in *Article 11* within which an appeal to the President of the International court of Justice is to be lodged. Since there is no *"dies a quo"*, it follows, there is no *"dies ad quem"* and the expiration of the delay cannot be known with certainty.

17.4.3. – *Belgium*

The Belgian model convention, in accordance with usage, stresses that contracting States should try to resolve their differences through diplomatic channels. If an amiable settlement is not possible, then the convention provides that:

> "Should settlement through diplomatic channels fail, the dispute shall be submitted to a mixed Commission, composed of representatives of each party. The commission will meet upon the request of the most diligent party and without unjustifiable delay." (**Article 13.2**)

This provision is superfluous and is not found in any other BIT. A superficial reading of this section yields the impression that there are two phases in the preliminary process, first the diplomatic level and then the commission. Actually, in both cases, the same representatives for each Party are usually the actors, but in the case where they are not, the representatives' negotiation instructions are apt to be the same. If the diplomatic channel cannot resolve the differences, it is hard to see how the Commission could.

Besides, the provision lacks several important elements. How many members shall the commission have? Within what time must it meet? Within what time must it render a decision? The duration of diplomatic negotiations has not been set and the commission's meeting schedule is therefore unknown. A Contracting Party could therefore delay negotiations and prevent that the commission shall convene without undue delay, as required in the Convention.

These flaws affect the arbitration proceeding adversely. Since the parties may not begin the arbitration proceeding itself before the commission has rendered its decision, and if it has not been able to resolve the issue, when and how will their failure to do so be effective? In the classical formula, as used by the UK and Germany, there are set delays, so that the start of the arbitration period and the period during which arbitrators must be nominated are relatively well known.

Thus, the "commission" phase should be deleted from the Belgian text. Just as with the settlement of disputes between a host State and an investor, a written notice of the dispute should be sent, together with a memorandum of the grounds. The text should also articulate the power for each Party to have recourse to arbitration in the event where diplomatic demarches and negotiations fail within two months from receipt of the notification.

Using the office of the President of the International Court of Justice as a "nomination authority" for the arbitrators is an unwieldy and impractical formula. The Belgian convention should, just as the US model convention does, select the ICSID Secretary General.

17.4.4. – Denmark

Denmark closely follows the classical formula. However, the Danish formula is different from that of other European countries in its applicable law clause :

> "The arbitral tribunal shall reach its decision on the basis of the present agreement and applicable rules of international law."

Such a provision is really necessary. Disputes on the application and interpretation of an international convention can only be resolved on the basis of the principles and rules of international law.

17.4.5. – France

French BIT's generally use the classical formula for the settlement of disputes regarding interpretation of the BIT. There are nonetheless certain differences.

Thus, they do not provide for an appeal to the President of the International Court of Justice but instead appoint the Secretary General of the United Nations Organisation as the person who shall make the nominations. Obviously, this change does not simplify the classical formula. French negotiators have realised the need for simplification. In the French BIT with Slovenia (11 February 1998), the Chairman of the International Chamber of commerce has been indicated as appointing authority. This is naturally a very good formula.

A second very useful derogation appears in the BIT France/Mexico, dated 12 November 1990, which prohibits the simultaneous filing of parallel arbitration procedures: one with ICSID for a dispute between the contracting State and an investor, on the basis of the dispute settlement State/investor, and the other for the same dispute, on the basis of the article concerning the interpretation and application dispute settlement State/State:

> "Neither of the Contracting Parties may initiate a procedure under the present article on the basis of a dispute regarding the failure to respect investors' rights, as submitted by an investor subject to the procedure required under **Article 9**, unless the other Contracting Party has failed to comply with the award made on the dispute." **(Article 11.6)**

This avoids the rendering of double awards to resolve basically the same dispute. Should one of these awards contradict the other, a problem would arise since, as has already been shown, each award is mandatory and final.

17.4.6. – *Germany*

Like other European countries, Germany requires Contracting States to seek an amiable solution to every dispute concerning the interpretation or application of the BIT's. If a dispute cannot thus be settled, it shall upon the request of either Contracting State be submitted to an arbitral tribunal.

FUERACKER derives from this text the conclusion that, even if, originally, the dispute existed between a Contracting State and an investor, such a dispute may result in an interstate dispute and be subject to the arbitration proceeding provided for in the State-to-State dispute settlement procedure:

"In connection with the so-called umbrella clause, even disputes that originate from the relationship between an investor and the host country may thus come under the dispute settlement provided for in **Article 10**. By virtue of the umbrella clause, contractual obligations between an investor and the host State are transferred to obligations covered by the BIT."[373]

It is not evident that such a result will necessarily occur. One of the conditions that must first be met is that the State Contract contain an arbitration clause for the resolution of disputes. Furthermore, the State of the investor must then accept that an interstate procedure be filed. There could very well be political objections preventing such acceptance. There is also the matter of costs. In a State v. investor procedure, the investor's own State does not share in the costs.

FUERACKER's interpretation shows that the text of arbitration clauses for the settlement of disputes between States should be modified and completed. Just as for France, the contracting States should agree that an interstate procedure may not be filed if the investor requires that the arbitration procedure specified in the State Contract be used..

The interstate arbitration formula is sometimes improved in the German BIT's. Thus, in the Germany/Nicaragua BIT, dated 6 May 1996, it was agreed that a dispute between an investor and the host State, which was in conformity with **Article 25(b)2** of the Washington Convention, could not allow the filing of a State to State settlement by arbitration.

17.4.7. – *Italy*

Italy has also opted for an *ad hoc* arbitration. Rules concerning the composition of the tribunal's membership are set in the clause entitled "Settlement of Disputes between the Contracting Parties." Regarding the conditions of nationality of the arbitrators, most of the Contracting States provide that each Contracting State must choose its own arbitrator

---

[373] FÜRACKER, Mathias, *op. cit.*, p. 16, see footnote 52.

and that the President of the tribunal is then nominated by the two arbitrators so selected, and must have a third State nationality. The three-month time allowed for the nomination, i.e. from the date on which the other two members, is too long. Other countries should also provide for shorter delays. Most agree that the speediness of an arbitration proceeding is a definite advantage, and, hence, long delays for the nomination of arbitrators should be avoided.

17.4.8. – *Norway*

Norway has adopted in its model convention a very special formula in the form of a mixed commission:

> "The Parties hereby establish a joint committee composed of representatives of the Parties. The joint committee shall meet whenever necessary. Each Party may request at any time through a notice in writing to the other Party, that a meeting of the joint committee be held. The request shall provide sufficient information to understand the basis for the request, including, where relevant, identification of issues in dispute. Such a meeting shall take place within 60 days of receipt of the request, unless the Parties agree otherwise."

This commission cannot be compared to that provided for in the Belgian model convention, because its statutes are very different. The joint committee has very broad powers, including even a modification of the Bit's. If the parties cannot agree on a solution of the dispute, the most diligent party may file an arbitration procedure in accordance with the Permanent Court of Arbitration's optional rules for arbitrating disputes between two States, as in effect on the date of this Agreement.

Norway is the only country that has declined to adopt arbitration *ad hoc* and which instead insists on institutional arbitration. It is interesting to note that Norway's arbitration procedure must concern a dispute arising from the violation by one of the Contracting States of the provisions of the Convention. This may in fact avoid parallel arbitration procedure, filed on the basis of the BIT and the State Contract.

17.4.9. – United States

The US model convention also gives precedence to amiable settlement through consultations and diplomatic negotiations. Only when an amiable arrangement cannot be reached may the parties then have recourse to arbitration.

However, in the arbitration process, the US convention deviates in several respects from the classical formula. The US convention provides that the proceeding will be held in accordance with the UNCITRAL arbitration rules, unless the parties are opposed to it. Furthermore, the parties may amend and adapt those rules as they see fit by mutual consent. For the selection of arbitrators, unless the disputing parties otherwise agree, the tribunal shall comprise three arbitrators, one arbitrator appointed by each of the disputing parties and the third, who shall be the presiding arbitrator, appointed by agreement of the disputing parties. There are no nationality requirements.

The power to nominate (in the event the parties have not addressed the issue) rests with the Secretary General of ICSID. However, the parties may also confer this power upon another person or institution. Thus, in the model convention, ICSID's Secretary General is invited to nominate if the parties cannot agree on arbitrators within the required delay. This is considerable progress because the ICSID Secretary General is more approachable that his counterpart at the UN, the Permanent Court of Arbitration or the International Court of Justice.

Section C of the 2004 US model convention makes no reference to the form and effect of arbitration awards. Actually, it would be superfluous to mention them since the UNCITRAL rules are already quite clear in the matter:

> "The award is issued in writing. It is not appealable to another arbitration tribunal. The parties agree that they shall execute the award without delay. The tribunal will validate its decision, unless the parties shall have agreed that this is not required." (article 32, Arbitration settlement UNCITRAL/CNUDCI)

INTER-STATE DISPUTES ON BIT'S' INTERPRETATION   615

It is also worthy of note that provisions relating to *"Amicus Curiae"* and "Governing Law" are applicable, *mutatis mutandis*, to the interstate arbitration procedure.

17.5. – INTERPRETATION PROBLEMS

17.5.1. – *Applicable multilateral conventions*

The International Law Commission (ILC), created in 1948 with the United Nations Organisation had, as one of its tasks, the preparation of treaties in the realm of international law. The activities of this Commission have led, among other things, to the signature on 23 May 1969 of the Vienna Convention on the law of treaties. This multilateral law came into force on 27 January 1980. The Vienna Convention contains rules governing the interpretation of international conventions and treaties, but its preamble warns that the Convention has no claim to be complete and that the rules of international common law remain in force :

> "Affirming that the rules of customary international law will continue to govern questions not regulated by the provisions of the present Convention, article 31 provides :
>
> A treaty shall be interpreted in good faith, in accordance with the ordinary meaning to be given to the terms of the treaty in their context and in the light of the object and purpose."

Good faith is a general principle whose content has not been defined. Authors often reach the conclusion that its interpreters must most of all seek to discover the real intention of the parties. If an individual party claims there is a defect in the formulation of a commitment, even though the intendment of the provision is clear, such a party will be in bad faith. The side notes of the negotiations which have led to an agreement sometimes prove the true meaning of commitments, even when the terms actually used are inadequate.

Arbitrators must also interpret the terms of a convention in their ordinary sense, that is, giving them the significance given to such terms in ordinary parlance. Unusual and exceptional significances are to be avoided. This also implies that texts must be interpreted in such a way that they do have a meaning and that interpretations which lead to nonsense about the terms of an agreement are to be shunned.

Of course, the context surrounding the conventions must also be considered. The goal of bilateral agreements is the security and protection of international investments made in the framework of the agreement. An interpretation making the goal of the conventions moot should not be adopted.

Other agreements entered into and having the same goal by the contracting parties with a third party state may also have an importance and lead to a good interpretation of the parties' intentions. Positions adopted by other Contracting States may sometimes provide guidelines for good interpretation.

Finally, the convention stresses that the interpretation of conventional texts of conventions must adhere to international law rules. This reference not only covers international common law but also principles of international law, such as *"pacta sunt servanda"* and *"de specialibus generalia non derogant."*

17.5.2. – *ICSID's jurisprudence*

There are not too many ICSID decisions regarding interpretation problems of BIT's. In the *Metalclad v Mexico* case, the arbitration tribunal referred to the provisions of the Treaty of Vienna, even though there was actually no clause in the BIT regarding applicable law. It is interesting to note that the arbitrators stressed the point that a State that is a party to a Treaty may not invoke the provisions of its domestic law in order to justify a violation of the BIT:

> "Article 31 (1) of the Treaty of Vienna concerning the Law of Treaties provides that a treaty must be interpreted in good faith in accordance with the ordinary meaning to be given to the terms of the treaty, within the context and in the light of the goal and purpose of the Treaty. In order to interpret the treaty, the context includes, besides

its preamble and its appendices, any agreement having a relationship to the treaty and which occurred between all the parties at the time the treaty was entered into. Consideration shall also be given to any pertinent rule of international law... A State, which is a party to a treaty, may not invoke the provisions of its domestic law to justify its failure to execute the treaty."[374]

GAILLARD stresses that a good interpretation of a treaty must aim to discover the common intentions of the parties:

"Like any other convention, an arbitration Convention must not be interpreted restrictively, nor extensively or liberally. It must be interpreted in a manner such as to produce and respect the common intention of the parties: such a method of interpretation is nothing other than the application of the fundamental principle *'pacta sunt servanda'*, common to all systems of domestic and international law."[375]

17.5.3. – *Need for Special Provisions*

It is rather surprising that there is no express reference to the Vienna Convention in the BIT's. In a strict legal sense, it is not necessary do so, because this Act is a part of international law and its application produces no problems. Nonetheless, an express clause in the articles of the BIT's regarding State to State disputes settlement is to be recommended. International public law includes various components: treaties and conventions, international common law, the general principles of international law, the decisions of international organisations, and the *jus cogens*. The latter includes the rules of international law which are mandatory for every State, to the extent they have been accepted by every State.

An express clause regarding applicable law certainly could be advantageous and could read as follows:

"The arbitral tribunal shall interpret the provisions of the BIT on the basis of international law and in particular in accordance with the international method selected by the Treaty of Vienna on the Law of Treaties, dated 23 May 1969."

---

[374] GAILLARD, Emmanuel, *op. cit.*, p. 672, see footnote 31.
[375] GAILLARD, Emmanuel, *op. cit.*, p. 45, see footnote 31.

CHAPTER XVIII
SCOPE OF BILATERAL INVESTMENT TREATIES

18.1. – Objective and personal scope of BIT's

The goal of BIT's is to protect and encourage international investments. It is also the BIT's main topic. Chapter I listed a number of investment types which are governed by the terms of BIT's. Those are mere examples. BIT's can apply to other economic transactions bringing capital into an industrial or commercial enterprise. Any operation that does not involve a durable investment, say, a sale, is excluded from the scope of BIT's.

Regarding the capacities of persons who may benefit from the terms of BIT's, Chapters VII and VIII have set forth the conditions they must meet in order to protect their investments. Concepts of "control" and "nationality" are important elements of this functionality.

18.2. – Geographic Scope

Quite a few BIT's are silent of the matter of territoriality. South Korea and Egypt have entered into some BIT's which have no territorial clause. However, such a clause appears in most other BIT's, such as, for instance the Australia/Mexico BIT :

> "The term territory means : the territory of either of the Contracting parties, as defined by their respective laws and regulations, including the territorial sea, maritime area or continental shelf adjacent to the coast of the Contracting Party concerned, where such Contracting Party exercises sovereignty, sovereign rights or jurisdiction in accordance with international law."

Such a formula is frequently used in European BIT's. Sometimes, an express reference is made to the Convention on the Law of the Sea. India has used this formula several times:

> "Territory means:
> i) in respect of India the territory of the Republic of India including its territorial waters and the airspace above and other maritime zones including Exclusive Economic Zone and continental shelf over which the Republic of India has sovereignty, sovereign rights or jurisdiction in accordance with its laws in force and international law, including the 1982 United Nations Convention on the Law of the Sea;
> ii) in respect of Australia the territory of Australia included the territorial sea, maritime Zone, Exclusive Economic Zone or continental shelf where Australia exercises its sovereignty, sovereign rights or jurisdiction in accordance with international law." (BIT Australia/India)

The Canadian formula, as it appears in its model Convention, is very broad and even refers to artificial islands:

> "Territory means:
> insofar as Canada is concerned
> The terrestrial territory, the airspace, waters of the territorial interior and the sea of Canada;
> Zones, including exclusive economic zones and sea bottoms, including their subjacent grounds, regarding which Canada exercises or has, in accordance with international, sovereign rights or jurisdiction with respect to exploration and exploitation of natural resources; and artificial islands, structures and installations built in the exclusive economic zone or on the continental shelf with respect to which Canada has jurisdiction by reason of its coastal geography."

In its BIT's, the United Kingdom provides that the contracting States may agree on territorial definition by exchanging separate notes:

> "Territorial extension: At the time of (signature) (entry into force)(ratification) of this Agreement, or at any time thereafter, the provisions of this agreement may be extended to such territories for whose international relations the Government of the United Kingdom

are responsible as may be agreed between the Contracting parties in an exchange of Notes."

Denmark has used yet another formula, showing that the BIT is not applicable to some territories but could be made applicable to them through an exchange of notes:

> "Territorial extension : This agreement shall not apply to the Faroer Islands and Greenland. The provisions of this agreement may be extended to the Faroer Islands and Greenland as may be agreed between the Contracting parties in an exchange of Notes."

In their model Convention, the Netherlands have used a formula which should allow the BIT's application to overseas territories. They have used this formula in their agreement with Costa Rica:

> "As regards the Kingdom of the Netherlands, the present Agreement shall apply to the part of the Kingdom in Europe, to the Netherlands Antilles and to Aruba, unless the notification provided for in **Article 14 (1)** provides otherwise." (**Article 13**)

18.3. – TEMPORAL SCOPE

18.3.1. – *Prior investments*

On the date of entry into force of a BIT, national investors of a contracting State other than the host State may already have made investments. The question then is whether such investments are covered by a BIT dated after their entry on the host territory. In other words, are investments existing on the date of entry into force of a BIT covered by it?

Domestic law and international law adhere to the principle of non-retroactivity. Treaties and international conventions do not have retroactive effect, unless otherwise stipulated. This principle was acknowledged in the Treaty of Vienna. The Afro-Asian model convention provides as follows:

> "The provisions of this Agreement shall apply to investments made after the coming into force of this Agreement and the investments previously made which are approved and registered by the host State, in

accordance with its laws, within a period of... from the date of entry into force of this Agreement."

This text confirms the non-retroactivity principle. The application of the convention to pre-existing investment is tied to unwieldy conditions. There is, actually, a specific reference to the investment codes. An investor, who is already established on the territory of the host State, would have to file a new request for investment approval and registration. Such a provision is not in the interest of investors, quite to the contrary. However, the principle of non-retroactivity is not sacred. Exceptions apply whether under domestic or international law.

It therefore would be useful to specify in any new convention or an amendment to existing conventions that investments made prior to its effective date are also covered. There are many examples of clauses providing application of the BIT's to both future investments and already existing investments at the date of entry into force of the BIT:

> "The present Agreement shall also apply to investments made, before it became effective, by investors of any of the Contracting Parties on the territory of any other Contracting Party in compliance with the laws and regulations of the latter." (Belgian model convention)
>
> "The provisions of this Agreement shall apply to all investments made by investors of one Contracting party in the territory of the other Contracting party, prior to or after the entry into force of the Agreement. It shall, however, not be applicable to divergences or disputes which have arisen prior to its entry into force." (Danish model convention)
>
> "The provisions of this Agreement shall, from the date of entry into force thereof also apply to investments, which have been made before that date." (Dutch model convention)

The French model convention also provides for retroactivity but stresses at the same time the need for investments to conform with the host State's national legislation. Such a rule also appears in their BIT's and is better formulated than any of the foregoing excerpts. For instance, Article 2 of the France/Slovenia agreement, dated 11 February 1998 states:

> "The present Agreement applies
> a) in the territory...;
> b) to investments which have already been made or which could be made after the entry into effect of this Agreement, in compliance with the legislation of the Contracting Party in such territory or in the maritime zone in which the investment is made."

Protection for pre-existing investments is therefore not unconditional in the French BIT's. The convention notes that pre-existing investments, are protected on the ground that they conformed to existing domestic law applicable on the date of their realisation. Thus protection could be refused on the ground that existing investments have not been made in compliance with the legislation of the host State. However, it would be better if the convention stated that pre-existing investments also benefit from the protection of the convention, thereby achieving retroactive and unconditional effect by way of a convention.

The Danish and Dutch formulae therefore offer greater guarantees that there will be fewer conflicts in regards to existing investments. Just like Denmark, some other countries state in the BIT's that the convention is not applicable to investments made before the date of entry into force of the BIT. This appears to be logical with respect to disputes which have already reached the judicial or arbitral procedure level but not for other investments. The Conventions texts should be amended accordingly.

18.3.2. – *Usual Duration of BIT's*

The duration of the validity of protection conventions is usually 10 years. At the end of such period, most BIT's provide that the convention is tacitly extended for an unspecified duration. The conventions could be cancelled at any moment after a six month notice.

Some BIT's provide for a longer delay after cancellation of the BIT :

"In respect of investments made before the date of the termination of the present agreement, the foregoing articles shall continue to be effective for a further period of fifteen years from that date." (Dutch model convention)

The German model convention provides for a 20 year duration

"In respect of investments made prior to the date of termination of this Treaty, the provisions of the preceding Articles shall continue to be effective for a further period of twenty years from the date of termination of this Treaty."

Ten years is too short a period. Usually, during the first few years, the yield on investments made is low, as this is when work just gets started. It would be better that this sunset provision be extended to 20 or 30 years minimum. Most corporations are created to last at least 30 years. Since local investment codes sometimes require that investments be made under the form of a corporation, and that such corporation must be locally created, the duration of the effectivity of the BIT's should be adapted to be consistent with the requirements of local codes.

A 30 year duration would therefore be preferable. Furthermore, it would be useful to provide that cancellation is not allowed during the first duration period. Investors would be without conventional protection too soon if the BIT could be cancelled too quickly after its entry into force (for instance, 5 years).

Germany has adopted a formula which avoids this problem :

"After the expiry of the period of ten years (first period of validity) this Treaty may be denounced at any time by either Contracting State giving twelve months notice."

18.3.3. – *Amendments*

The content of treaties and international conventions must from time to time be adapted to evolving rules of law as the years go by. This need also affects bilateral conventions for investments. Investment codes do not stay up to date for ever, are themselves frequently amended and added to. The interpretation of rules and principles of international law, in judicial and arbitration jurisprudence is also an important source of changes in the law. Particularly, the ICSID and CCI awards are sometimes quite innovative. The legal context in which international investments are made changes continually *("perpetuum mobile")*. Hence, eventually, bilateral protection conventions must be updated. Though the Treaty of Vienna may well direct that international conventions are, in principle, inalterable, deviations from this principle are appropriate in certain circumstances:

- the existence of such circumstances was an essential element of the consent of the parties bound by the treaty, and
- the change causes a radical transformation of the scope of the obligations still to be performed by virtue of such treaty." (**Article 62/1 Treaty of Vienna**):

"A fundamental change of circumstances, happening in relation to those which existed at the time a treaty was concluded and which had not been foreseen by the Parties, may not be invoked as a valid reason to terminate a treaty or to withdraw therefrom unless:

The need to renegotiate a BIT has already been observed several times. A specific provision in the BIT's should enable renegotiation. The Contracting Parties could, for instance, agree to hold talks on this issue, say, every five years. A specific provision could be added to BIT's and could read:

"The Contracting Parties agree to consult with each other at the request of the most diligent party about the opportune timing for renegotiations of the BIT, whenever such renegotiation appears to be useful to improve and reinforce the reciprocal protection of investments, in the light of changes in the legal and economic circumstances in which such investments were made."[376]

---

[376] Private archives.

CHAPTER XIX
FUTURE EXPECTATIONS

19.1. – Economic Value

No one has any doubts about the economic value of investments made abroad. It is generally accepted that both host States (production capacity, employment creation, growth of local consumption, etc.) and businesses who create the investments (export promotion, etc.) benefit from foreign investment.

The United Nations Conference on Trade and Development (UNCTAD) and the Organisation for Economic Cooperation and Development (OECD) have often stressed the beneficial effect of international investments. OECD publishes regularly statistics that demonstrate the importance and impact of investments on economic growth.[377] Obviously, it cannot be denied that developing countries particularly need foreign investments on their territory. These investments are of vital interest for their economic growth. Less developed countries realise this need and undertake measures to make such investments attractive to foreign investors.

Usually, local capital is insufficient to undertake the necessary investments for growth. The actual cost of investing is extremely high, their yield often low when local capital only is used. Direct investments by foreign companies having sizeable financial means available to them and the necessary industrial and commercial expertise on an international level are welcome by the less developing countries.

---

[377] www.oecd.org/investment.

It is also clear that the promotion and protection of international investments are an indispensable element of the public policy of cooperation and development.

19.2. – Bringing the model conventions and BIT's up to date

Regular modification of the model conventions is necessary and frequently urgent. Many of the existing BIT's, based on the model conventions, will have to be renegotiated. The existing model conventions and bilateral investment treaties will meet the needs of international investors only if a sagacious choice is made between the several alternatives that have been proposed here and elsewhere. The authors suggest that a conference be organised, where the competent authorities, the delegates of enterprises and their representative organisations should make proposals for improvement of conventional protection of international investors and their investments abroad. The text of the investment treaties needs to be adapted to the arbitral jurisprudence of the last decade. Principally, the decisions of ICSID in Washington are sometimes very innovative. It would be appropriate to take into account the principles of international law applied in these decisions for the renovation of the text of international investment agreements.

19.3. – Changing Circumstances

A new fact in the realm of conventional protection of international investments must be taken in account. Since the end of the colonisation era and the attainment of independence by many African and Asian countries, entering into bilateral agreements for the protection of international investments was a privilege reserved for industrial States and initiated by them. This development was the result of a reaction to waves of measures privative or restrictive of property rights that the newly independent but less developed countries had undertaken with respect to the investments made on their territory by foreigners.

What is new is that, in the recent past, the LDC's have begun to enter into such investment protection agreements with each other. Investments made on the territory of an LDC by another LDC are being protected conventionally. Some LDC's have likewise redacted model convention texts paralleling those authored by industrialised countries. The question then is, whether, in the future, bilateral investment protection conventions may be entered into between industrialised countries also.

It cannot be ignored that, in the past few years, measures restrictive of property rights have been undertaken by industrialised States with respect to investments coming from other industrialised States. These measures have sometimes resulted in the total liquidation of such investments, even though the foreign investors had benefited from financial aid and support from the very State on which their investments had been made.

Entering into investment State contracts between industrialised States may bring a solution to the problems posed by this development, although this practice is not yet widespread. Nonetheless, it would be worthwhile to study whether the international responsibility of the States of which the investors are nationals should not be regulated by means of a convention, in particular with respect to compensation for such States' financial aid.

APPENDIX I
BURUNDI CASE NOTES
Restrictions on State Sovereignty – Jus Standi of Shareholders

In this study, we have considered the fundamental right of host States to expropriate, nationalise or otherwise deprive owners of their property. We have seen how this right is circumscribed in that it can lawfully only be exercised provided its exercise meets certain conditions.

Like many other aspects of international law, arbitration tribunals have created case law showing how a host State's right to deprivation of the property rights of international investors is restricted. Domestic courts and internal laws may also provide rules limiting the right of the State, agencies thereof or municipality to expropriate. As a general rule, BIT's include, or should include, provisions which prohibit preferential treatment to national investors. On the basis of such BIT's, or as a matter of international law, international investors therefore should be able to take advantage of the local forum to vindicate their claims for compensation or restitution if their property has been expropriated or nationalised.

APP. I.1. – ICSID CASE: "*GOETZ V. BURUNDI*" [378]

However, sometimes, the local forum is not suitable. It may not have the resources nor the political freedom to handle such matters. Its docket may be overloaded, inhibiting

---

[378] Http://icsid.worldbank.org/ICSID/Index.jsp, ICSID Case ARB/95/3 number 35.

the prompt resolution of disputes. The host State's nationalisation laws may still be in gestation. In such cases, international investors look to international fora. *Goetz v. Burundi* (an independent Republic, formerly a UN mandate under Belgian authority) can serve as an encapsulation of several principles of law limiting the right of deprivation, a case study of sorts where many of the principles enunciated in individual chapters can be seen applied in a single example. ICSID decided it on or about 10 February 1999. It is a good source for the drafting of improvements to model convention provisions relating to such restrictions. The "Belgium/Burundi" BIT, to which the tribunal made reference to reach its conclusions, is based on the Belgian model convention.

App. I.2. – Case Background – Factual Findings

On 22 December 1992, a limited liability company was established according to notarial law, with its seat in Bujumbura. The firm was to refine metals and was named, in abbreviated fashion, "Affimet".

Affimet's capital consisted of one thousand shares distributed among six Belgian investors, including Mr. Antoine Goetz and relatives. On 3 February 1993, the local Ministry of Commerce and Industry delivered to Affimet its "free enterprise" certificate authorising the firm to exercise its activities in a free zone that had been specially created for such activities. After substantial investments had been made by the company, the same Ministry sent it a letter, dated 9 July 1993, claiming disputes of interpretation of the documents governing the company's activities.

Following a temporary suspension of the certificate, the Ministry of Foreign Commerce, using the services of an international consultant (Amex International, Washington) informed Affimet, on 29 May 1995, that its activities regarding the said minerals was no longer eligible for the free zone treatment. Affimet protested and attempted, in vain, to resolve the matter amiably. Lacking a solution, the Belgian shareholders, acting in their capacity as founders of the company, filed for an arbitration procedure with ICSID, based on the Belgium/Burundi BIT.

App. I.3. – Applicable provisions of the model convention and actual BIT's

Article 7 of this Belgian model entitled "Privative and restrictive measures affecting property", is set forth *in extenso* :

"1. Each of the Contracting Parties is committed to undertake no expropriation or nationalisation action nor any other measure whose effect is to dispossess directly or indirectly investors of the other Contracting Party from investments which are located in its territory and belong to them.

2. In the event that requirements of public utility or of security or national interest justify a failure to respect the provisions of article 1, the following conditions must first be met :

f) the measures in question shall have been taken in accordance with law;

g) they shall be neither discriminatory, nor contrary to specific commitments;

h) they will be accompanied with provisions for the payment of an adequate and effective indemnity.

3. The amount of the indemnities will correspond to the real value of the investments in question on the day before the day when such measures are taken or made public. Indemnities will be settled in the currency of the State the investor is a national of or in any other convertible currency. They will be paid promptly and freely transferable. They will bear interest at the normal commercial rate as set from the date their amount has been determined until that of payment.

4. Investors from either Contracting Party whose investments may have been damaged as a result of war or any other kind of armed conflict, revolution, state of national emergency or revolt occurring on the territory of the other Contracting State will be granted by the latter a treatment that is at least equal to that granted to the most favoured

nation regarding restitutions, indemnifications, compensations or other damage awards.

5. In regards to questions addressed in this Article, each of the Contracting Parties shall grant to investors of the other Contracting Party a treatment which is at least equal to that benefiting investors from the most favoured nation and in no event less favourable than that acknowledged by international law."

For the settlement of investment disputes, a special provision provided for submission to arbitration by ICSID.

APP. I.4. – COMPARATIVE DEFINITIONS OF PROPERTY PRIVATIVE MEASURES.

For comparison, in the French model convention, paragraph 2 of **Article 6** determines property privative measures as follows:

"The Contracting Parties do not take measures of expropriation or nationalisation nor any other measure whose effect is to dispossess directly or indirectly investors of the other Contracting Party from investments which are located in its territory and belong to them..."

Generally in BIT's, terms such as "expropriation and nationalisation" are used indiscriminately. The term "dispossession" is also used, but rarely. In civil property law, there is, of course, a great deal of difference between "property" and "possession," and thus between "expropriation" and "dispossession."

France has paid heed to this distinction in the text of its own BIT's, in accordance with the formula used in its model convention:

"None of the contracting Parties shall take measures, be they direct or indirect, to dispossess or nationalise, or any other measure having an equivalent effect on investments." (**Article 5** of the Franco-Mexican agreement of 15 November 1998)

In that context, is there a difference between expropriation and nationalisation? In doctrinal texts, it is usually admitted that expropriation is a privative measure affecting property rights on an individual basis and on a small scale (for instance, the construction of a public right of way), whereas nationalisation is a privative measure of vast scope done within the scope of economic restructuring affecting an important group of owners (investors):

> "By expropriation is meant the coercitive appropriation by the State of private property, usually by means of individual administrative measures. Nationalisations do not differ in substance from expropriations except that they are statutorily based and have a wide coverage. They have been the instruments of widespread political and economic policy changes by the State, with a view to subjecting specific sectors of the entire process of production and distribution to the ownership of and management by the State, excluding private economic initiatives."[379]

Actually, privative and restrictive measures against private property rights may be classified as follows:

- nationalisations: direct measures, usually country-wide, depriving owners active in a specific industry of their property rights and having an economic goal (cfr *supra*);
- expropriations: direct measures, usually selective, privative of property rights, undertaken on the basis of an administrative or individual purpose (cfr *supra*);
- "*de facto*" expropriations: indirect measures, allowing for a property theoretically to remain with the original owners but nonetheless depriving them of important elements of their rights (for example, the "*ius fruendi*": enjoyment of proceeds; the "*ius utendi*": use or disposition of the property through sale or lease);
- disguised expropriations: indirect measures having a similar deprivation effect, denying the owner the right to manage or use his enterprise under normal conditions (for example, abusive cancellation of a use or construction permit).

---

[379] SACERDOTI, Giorgio, *op. cit.*, p. 379.

App. I.5. – De iure vs. de facto ("Creeping") Deprivation

The difference between measures of indirect expropriation can be very subtle. So that *de facto* and disguised expropriations, for instance, are not inadvertently excluded from the protection of BIT's and State Contracts, it would be opportune to amend the model to help investors make a better case for the presentation of their claims for indemnification, in accordance with international law, thus:

> "Each of the contracting Parties agrees to abstain from taking any measure privative of property rights, direct or indirect, such as nationalisations, expropriations, dispossessions, confiscations, requisitions, '*de facto*' expropriations, disguised expropriations, or any other type of measure having a similar effect privative of property rights affecting the investments of investors from the other Contracting Party."

When discussing disguised expropriations, doctrinal texts speak of "rampant" or "creeping" expropriations. This is where property rights are left supposedly intact but the owner may not exercise them under normal conditions. The value of his investment, the usefulness of his property decrease slowly (in a "creeping" manner") over time incrementally, gradually restricting the owner's freedom to operate, until, for all practical purposes, he is left with a bundle of obligations but no rights.

In international doctrine, there is unanimity of agreement regarding the right to indemnification in any such cases. Investors may and should be able to claim compensation for the damages they sustain. On the other hand, opinions diverge regarding the criteria to be used in order to show that an expropriation is of the "creeping" kind. The following examples have been submitted: arbitrary taxation, illicit interference in the property's management, cancellation of a construction permit, absolute prohibition against exports or imports. Generally, these measures end up with the liquidation of the investment.

Authors agree that measures of this kind may be assimilated to regular, open expropriation measures:

> "Creeping are the so-called indirect expropriations, namely measures which even if they are not aimed at transferring property rights, imply an interference with the exercise of property rights equivalent to that of a measure of expropriation."

In the *USA/Iran* case in 1981, the *ad hoc* tribunal's dictum as to the duty to indemnify in the event of creeping expropriation has been keenly emphasised:

> "An interference by a State in the use of property or with the enjoyment of its benefits is a deprivation or taking of that property, even where legal title to the property is not affected. Compensation under international law is warranted whenever events demonstrate that the owner was deprived of fundamental rights of ownership and it appears that the deprivation is not merely ephemeral." [380]

A typical measure of "creeping expropriation" occurred during the period immediately following the Congo's independence. Belgian colonials, owners of a house on Congolese territory were expelled by force of arms from their property. In theory, they still had property rights but the Congolese State was in charge of renting the property and collecting the proceeds. The owners received a few rental payments but for many years they received nothing. In principle, they are still the registered owners of the property today, but, for all practical purposes, their assets have been made worthless and useless. Reference is made to a legal analysis one of the authors of this work, Jan SCHOKKAERT, made about these measures.[381] (cfr *infra*).

---

[380] SACERDOTI, Giorgio, *op. cit.*, p. 384, see footnote 161.

[381] SCHOKKAERT, Jan, "Analyse juridique de l'accord belgo zaïrois du 1ᵉʳ juillet 1985, sur le transfert de propriété visant des biens d'habitation situés au Zaïre", *Revue de droit international et de droit comparé*, June 2002, p. 348, ("Legal analysis of the Belgium-Zaire Agreement of 1 July 1985, regarding transfer of property rights in habitable ????? located in Zaire").

APP. I.6. – APPLICATION TO *GOETZ V. BURUNDI*

With respect to "creeping expropriation", ICSID's award in the *Goetz v. Burundi* case is very instructive. Recall that it is generally accepted that a serious affront to private property rights has the same effect as a privative measure and that a State's international duty compels it to compensate the damaged party. The arbitrators confirmed that the withdrawal of the free zone certificate was to be deemed an indirect expropriation measure, thus a measure having a similar effect as an outright expropriation. In principle, this measure did not affect the property right but made the company's management of the property impossible:

> "In as much as, according to the data given the Tribunal by the petitioners, the revocation of the free zone certificate forced them to cease all further activity as from 13 August 1996, which is the date of the last export, and in as much as this event has cancelled any use of the investments made and has stripped the petitioning investors of the benefit they could expect from their investment, we conclude that the litigious measure may be considered have an effect similar to 'a property privative and restrictive measure in the sense of article 4 of the investment convention.'"[382]

The arbitration tribunal decided that the Republic of Burundi had to indemnify AFFIMET, on the ground of the illegality of the measure undertaken against in and by virtue of international law (*cfr. infra*). The measure was viewed as "creeping expropriation." On the other hand, the tribunal confirmed that the measure was not illegal under Burundi law.

The Tribunal's rejection of the petitioners' "established rights" theory bears watching in the future. The arbitrators decided that the Burundese authorities had the right to change the list of enterprises admitted to the free zone. There were no "established rights" to the continuation of a regula-

---

[382] GAILLARD, Emmanuel, *op. cit.*, p. 550, see footnote 31.

tion wich the regulatory authorities were entitled (as stated in the regulation) to modify or abrogate.

App. I.7. – Do shareholders have "*IUS STANDI*"?

The decision contains language which is quite remarkable in regards to the nature of appropriation, but, besides showcasing the facts as an example of "creeping expropriation", there are other aspects of the arbitration award that merit attention. Thus, the first problem encountered by the tribunal was whether the arbitration request was demurrable. Did the shareholders, as distinguished from the company, have standing to file a ICSID procedure (*jus standi*) when the measure complained of affected only their company, Affimet, a domestic corporation ?

It is rather strange that, in an administrative procedure, filed before the ICSID procedure, Affimet had filed a request in its own name and that, when before ICSID, petitioners had filed the same request in the name of the shareholders of Affimet. In effect, in the presence of the arbitrators, the shareholders claimed that Affimet could not file under the ICSID Convention because one of the shareholders did not have Belgian nationality. This claim was not convincing and was in fact groundless because the majority of the shareholders possessed Belgian nationality and thereby controlled the company. The tribunal decided that it had jurisdiction. It first pointed out that the Affimet Corporation could have filed directly. **Article 25(2)b** of the Convention defines ICSID's jurisdiction, stating that a local corporation controlled by a foreign corporation is deemed to be "foreign" (national of another State) when the parties have consented thereto.

The arbitrators' reasoning here leaves much to be desired. The Burundi Government certainly did not consent but did not raise the point. Had Affimet chosen to file, the filing should not have been entertained. There is absolutely no doubt about AFFIMET's capacity as a corporation established under Burundi law and that the company could not be considered as a "national of another Contracting State". An arbitration request filed by AFFIMET could not have been accepted by ICSID. In fact, the arbitration request had been filed by investors themselves (the Belgian stockholders of Affimet). Could it be said that they, in their once removed position from the affected asset, had standing?

Whatever the answer to that question may be, the Tribunal decided that the shareholders did have *ius standi* and that a demurrer to the request on that ground was not valid:

> "No matter what may be the motives which led the Belgian shareholders to act as such rather than file a petition in the name of the Affimet company, the Tribunal observes that prior ICSID jurisprudence does not limit the capacity to file only to moral persons directly affected by litigious measures but extends it also to shareholders of such persons, since they are the true investors..." [383]

Referencing certain previous ICSID decisions where foreign corporations controlling the local corporation had been deemed to have standing, the tribunal decided that the request in the name of the shareholders was *"receivable"* and that the demurrer thereto should be denied. The arbitrators apparently believed that physical persons controlling a local corporation likewise had *"ius standi"*:

> "What is true for a foreign corporate investor controlling a domestic company should also be true of a foreign physical person controlling a local company. The tribunal decided that the filing by the six Belgian shareholders who controlled the Burundi local company Affimet was receivable." [384]

The grounds used by the tribunal for its decision are dubious in that the arbitrators apparently wanted to emphasise that the filing of an arbitration petition by AFFIMET, a Burundi corporation and not a corporation of another Con-

---

[383] Http://worldbank.org/ICSID/Index.jsp, p. 496.
[384] GAILLARD, Emmanuel, *op. cit.*, p. 539.

tracting State would nonetheless have been accepted as well as a petition filed by the foreign shareholders in their own name, using the control theory as their means to reach such conclusion.

Article 25(2)b is concerned with corporations, physical persons not being mentioned at all. "Juridical persons which had the nationality of a Contracting State other than the State party to the dispute..." and "... any juridical person which had the nationality of the Contracting State party to the dispute ... because of foreign control, the parties have agreed should be treated as a national of another Contracting State..." AFFIMET is not included in the first category because it is a Burundi corporation and, hence, has the nationality of the State which is a party to the dispute. In turn, what AFFIMET might not do, neither might its shareholders when acting in the name of the Burundi corporation. AFFIMET is not in the first category in that it is a Burundi corporation, therefore having the nationality of the State, which is a party to the dispute. Hence, the shareholders should not have been able to file an arbitration request in the name of the Burundi corporation.

Furthermore, in the ICSID cases to which the Tribunal refers, the controlling shareholders had invoked Article 25(b)2, stating and proving that control was real and that the Contracting State had impliedly consented to the application of Article 25(b)2 by recognising the "foreign" character of the enterprise. The outcome in this case was different because of, in this case, there was a problem of proof: Burundi's consent regarding the application of Article 25(2)b was not convincingly proven. The issue therefore stays open: did the Belgian and Luxemburgian shareholders have the right to file an arbitration request on the basis of Article 25(2)a or 25.2(b) of the Washington? There was therefore no legal basis to justify granting standing to private persons who file an arbitration request complaint alleging that they exercise control along the lines of Article 25 and confirming that the Contracting Parties anticipatively agree to the filing of an arbitration procedure by corporations as well as physical persons controlling a domestic corporation.

It would then follow that "foreign interests control" mentioned by Article 25(2)b also include physical persons. We should need not lose sight of the fact that "investment" includes both minority and majority shareholding in foreign corporations. When faced with arbitration, less developed countries have frequently tried to avoid such a procedure, basing their argument that only a domestic corporation is involved. For that very reason, we think that a provision inspired by the Burundi case tribunal's decision would be useful.

The extraordinary nature of this decision may also be brought out by the fact that, under the law of many developed countries, shareholders are not given the *ius standi* to file an arbitration request complaint for a wrong sustained by their corporation, except under extraordinary circumstances. The cause of action for a wrong sustained by the corporation is one that the corporation has exclusive right to file an arbitration request complaint for and cannot discretionarily delegate to the shareholders the right to do so in its place. Had there been any domestic shareholders in Burundi, an arbitration request complaint filed by them domestic shareholders of a Burundi corporation, alleging a cause of action arising from a wrong to the corporation, not controlled by foreign interests, would not, presumably under Burundi law, withstand a demurrer. The legal systems of newly independent countries, former colonies of developed countries but still in the process of development, are often influenced by the legal system in force when they were colonies. Their national legislation often is very restrictive and does not provide for arbitration of investment disputes. Chances are corporation and shareholders would not be able to show *ius standi* and withstand a demurrer. Enlarging the scope of Article 25(2)b to include foreign physical persons as well as corporations within the "control" exception should be an improvement to the text of the Washington Convention. A good solution could be found by completing the model conventions and the BITs which require the Contracting States to accept the application of Article 25(2)b of the Washington Convention. We recommend the inclusion of Article 25.2.b of the Washington Convention because LDC's regularly attempt to avoid arbitration and investors just as regularly favour it. LDC's argue that it is for the local company to defend the interests of the foreign investors.

In any event, we should not overlook the fact that natural persons having a Contracting State's nationality other than that of the other Contracting Party to the dispute and who do not control the domestic company may also file an arbitration request pursuant to Article 25(2)a, if both Contracting States consent. Normally, most small shareholders would be deterred from filing, unless they join forces to begin an action.

App. I.8. – The deprivation must be illegal

The second problem to be solved by the arbitration tribunal was the legality of the measure in the light of Burundi's domestic law as well as international law. The Protection Convention between Belgium and Burundi dated 13 April 1989 (effective 13 September 1993) included an Applicable Law clause. It was therefore necessary to elect between, on the one hand, Burundi domestic law and, on the other, the principles and rules of international law. This analysis was necessary because the legality of a measure undertaken in regards to an investor could be interpreted differently depending on the choice:

> "It is appropriate to note that the question of the legality of the host State's acts need not necessarily be given the same answer, whether domestic or international law is used to reach it. In the case of *Elsi and Italy*, the International Court of Justice declared that an act by a public agency may be deemed to have been illegitimate under

domestic law without entailing its illegitimacy, in international law, as a violation of a treaty, for example, or otherwise. *Vice versa*, an act that is legitimate under internal law may well be illegitimate under international law."[385]

Was the suspension of the Free Zone certificate legal under Burundi law? According to the tribunal, the answer to this question was yes. Burundi authorities had the right to modify the list of sectors eligible for Free Zone treatment. Amendment and modification of the list were measures foreseen in the ministerial ordinance.

Was the measure legal under international law? According to the arbitrators, there had been no discrimination, Affimet's investors not having been treated any worse than other investors. On the other hand, the arbitrators believed that the suspension of the certificate could be considered as a measure similar to a measure privative of property rights. The revocation of a Free Zone certificate had nullified the usefulness of the investments and caused the spoliation for the investors of the revenue they reasonably expected. Without actually using the word, the arbitrators acknowledged that there was in fact a *"creeping expropriation"*.

Three, out of four, conditions of international law had been met for the protection of the BIT to be invoked: a public purpose (promotion of foreign investments in the interest of the national economy), a legal procedure, and absence of discrimination. But the main condition, the duty to indemnify had not been met. The tribunal adopted a particular attitude, deviating from its usual practice. The Republic of Burundi had a choice: either pay an indemnity, or revisit the revocation decision and restore the Free Zone certificate. This is one of the rare examples where a tribunal decides that the *"restitutio ad integrum"* could resolve an international conflict. The Burundi government could escape the burden of an

---

[385] GAILLARD, Emmanuel, *op. cit.*, p. 543.

indemnity if it restored the damaged party to its former position.

It also decided that the arbitration procedure could be started up again if Burundi did not conform to its decision:

> "If, within four months from the date of notification of the present decision, the Republic of Burundi shall not have taken either of the decisions defined in the foregoing paragraph, her conduct would constitute an internationally illegal act, because, such act would be contrary both to the duty she assumed to abstain from taking, in respect of the investors, any measure which would have an effect similar to a privative measure or one that restricts the exercise of property rights, *and* to the duty she assumed to guarantee to Belgian investments on her territory constant security and protection.
>
> It would behove the parties then to return before this Tribunal in order to determine the amount and the terms of the compensation due..."[386]

APP. I.9. – THE VALUATION ISSUE

In Belgian and other European BIT's, one finds sometimes a reference to the real value and sometimes one to the market value without further comment. There ought to be consistency between the versions, the real value being the criterion that, preferentially, ought to be selected. Besides, valuation criteria to be used to determine the real and the market value should be mentioned.

In summary, the text of the model conventions should be amended and completed. The "real value" criterion may be kept but the valuation of this real value should be established in reference to the economic circumstances existing before the threat of expropriation arose. It should also consider the choices an investor should be able to make among various valuation criteria, such as market value, book value, replacement value etc.

---

[386] GAILLARD, Emmanuel, *op. cit.*, p. 553, see footnote 31.

App. I.10. – Interest

The importance of setting a time during which interest accrues is also evident from the *Goetz* decision. In some BIT's, either the beginning date or the ending date are not specified. In the *Goetz* decision, Burundi was_required to follow the terms of the certificate. Normally, interest is payable from the date the privative measure takes effect till the date the indemnification is paid.

In *some* Belgian BIT's, both *"dies ad quem"* and *"dies a quo"* are to be found :

> "Indemnities will bear interest at the normal commercial rate from the date their amount has been determined till that of their payment." (**Paragraph 3, Article 3**)

In this convention, the time when interest begins does not follow international law. The *"dies a quo"* is the date on which the obligation of the expropriating State begins. Interest therefore begins to run on the date privative measures have occurred. This is a date certain and cannot create any doubt. Usually the date of effect of privative measures is published in the country's Official Register. **Paragraph 3 of Article 5** of the Belgian model convention and other model conventions and BIT's should state that *"dies a quo"* is the date of occurrence of measures privatives of private property rights. In fact, calculating the amount of the indemnification may take place a long time after the nationalisation or expropriation measure has been undertaken.

App. I.11. – Duty to respect national and international law

Burundi claimed in *Goetz* that the measure undertaken with respect to Affimet was legal, inasmuch as a sovereign State has the power to take measures that conform to domestic legislation and Burundese regulation. The Tribunal, in its response, stated that Burundi had to respect both its domestic legislation and its international obligations:

> "In the present case, therefore, the Burundi Republic's obligation to respect not only domestic law but also the provisions of the Convention it entered into with Belgium is nothing other than the expression of its State sovereignty in the full sense of the term. It is appropriate to recall the famous dictum from the International Court of Justice in the *Wimbledon Steamboat* case:
>
> The Court does not see that any treaty whereby the State commits itself to do or not do anything constitutes an abandonment of its sovereignty."

By entering into a BIT with Belgium, Burundi manifested its will to place Belgian investments on its territory under international protection:

> "On a general level, the existence of a bilateral promotion and protection agreement for investments show the will of host States to place foreign investments made on their territory by nationals of another State under the guarantee of interstate relations and international law. It is not happenstance that a clause providing this double protection is often called an 'umbrella' agreement.
>
> As has already been stated by the Tribunal, one of the essential characteristics of this case has been the existence of an international treaty, sometimes called a 'covering' treaty in the Belgium-Burundi BIT, for the protection of investments and defining the rights and obligations of the parties. However commanding the control the State of Burundi may draw from its sovereignty, it is held, by reason of this very sovereignty, to respect its international commitments."[387]

APP. I.12. – DOES THE BURUNDI CASE SET A PRECEDENT?

It is arguable whether Burundi will be a precedent for foreign shareholders who are physical persons to have *ius standi* to file for arbitration in their own names. It is just as likely that the case will be considered *sui generis*, sustainable only

---

[387] GAILLARD, Emmanuel, *op. cit.*, p. 549, see footnote 31.

when the particular circumstances of a future case may be found to be identical to those surrounding Burundi.

It is not at all certain that the shareholders' *ius standi* in arbitration proceedings before ICSID will be recognised in every ICSID procedure. Some arbitrators, no doubt, will conclude that the local company which is the victim of a measure by the State to which it belongs must file such a request and that the foreign shareholders should not. Yet, a Burundese company cannot, in principle, proceed at law against its own State. As said above, shareholders could claim the application of Article 25.2(b) for filing an arbitration procedure. This conclusion, however, would not necessarily preclude the filing of an arbitration proceeding in some other venue, such as the International Chamber of Commerce.

One of the Washington Convention's characteristics, in fact, is that an arbitration procedure is possible only by a State which is a party to the dispute and an investor from one of the other Contracting States. The ICC has no such constraint. States that become parties to BIT's would be well advised not to rely too much on Goetz as a precedent. In the interest of foreign investors, they should try to include in their BIT's a clause which confirms the application of article 25.2(b) of the Washington Convention, adding that when a corporation in the host State is controlled by an investor from one of the other Contracting States, this investor may file a joint petition with ICSID.

APPENDIX II

ZAIRE CASE NOTES

Investments in the Democratic Republic of Congo (formerly known as Zaire)

App. II.1. – Background

Formerly the Belgian colony of the Belgian Congo, the country's post-independence name was the Republic of the Congo until August 1, 1964, when its name was changed to Democratic Republic of the Congo (to distinguish it from the neighbouring Republic of the Congo, a former French colony). In 1971 the country was renamed *Zaire*. Following the First Congo War in 1997, the country was renamed Democratic Republic of the Congo. From 1998 to 2003, the country suffered greatly from the devastating Second Congo War (sometimes referred to as the African World War), the world's deadliest conflict since World War II.

Belgium's long history of colonisation in the region, as well as the Belgian development and exploitation of Congolese resources helped usher in a period of close collaboration between the two countries. The end of the colonial status and the attainment of independence in 1960 were followed by the confiscation of considerable property owned by Belgian nationals and companies. Immediately after independence, Belgian tenants and owners of quite a few residences located in Kinshasa and suburbs were expelled *"manu militari"* from their lodgings and properties. The problems resulting from these measures, in particular the indemnification problems, have never been settled. The measures taken were typical examples of "creeping expropriation" because, in theory, the rights in the fee of the property had been left intact but the owners had been denied the right of management and the right to alienate their properties. The indemnification problems were finally made the object of an agreement between Belgium and Zaire but to this day, this agreement remains unperformed.

Belgian enterprises continued to make important investments on the Congolese territory. Their worst experience was the "Zairianisation" promulgation of 1977. An interdepartmental decree by the then Zaire government organised the carrying out of measures of "Zairianisation", which were merely prototypes of indirect measures of nationalisation, even though the term does not appear anywhere in the regulatory texts. Foreign investors were forced to sell their properties to Zaire nationals.

App. II.2. – Indemnification of "Zairianised" assets – Valuation of Assets

Somewhat bizarrely, in 1976, two agreements were concluded in parallel between Belgium and Zaire. On 28 March 1976, the "Protocol between the Kingdom of Belgium and the Republic of Zaire, regarding the mutual Promotion of Investments, was entered into. On the same date, in Kinshasa, the "Protocol between the Kingdom of Belgium and the Republic of Zaire, regarding the settlement of Zairianised assets belonging to Belgian physical persons", was signed. The control theory was applied, in as much as moral persons, stock companies, were also to be covered by such measures in the event 50% or more of the capital was in the hands of Belgian physical persons.

In most cases, a "Record of Takings and Returns" was established between the new Zaire owner and the previous Belgian owner. If no agreement could be reached on the value of the property, a valuation process was entrusted to representatives of buyer and seller, chosen by common agreement.

Actually, such representatives were experts in commercial transactions, operating from similar assets. The transfer price was to be paid in Zaire currency. The Indemnification Protocol contained no provision regarding the currency exchange rate to be used. By merely exchanging letters, the value in Belgian francs as set at 45.25 Francs per Zaire unit. The Contracting States would agree on a payment system spread over ten years and based on the compensation for indemnification allowed and the sums to be paid within the framework of development cooperation.

Investors were therefore harmed in two ways, first by a defective valuation of their loss and second by the subsequent devaluation of the Congolese currency (the "zaire").

One might say this is not altogether unusual. Drastic devaluations have occurred in many developing countries and insidious devaluation is still going on in several developed countries. Carrying out the said Protocol has given rise to many difficulties. Belgian parties entitled to compensation wanted to receive the difference between the calculated indemnities on the basis of the currency exchange rate in effect on the date of "taking" and "Return", which oscillated at about eighty Belgian francs for 1 Zaire. They successfully filed lawsuits against the Belgian State.

This turn of events shows how important it is to mention in the BIT's and in the indemnification agreements the bases for valuation, the dies a quo and the *dies ad quem* for the payment of interest and for the exchange rate to apply.

App. II.3. – National Protection of international investments in the DRC

The Congolese governments that have succeeded the initial years of self-governance have without a doubt tried hard to create a favourable climate for international investments. The several Investment Codes which have been legislated have given investors a foretaste of the new order.

App. II.3.1. – *New Investment Code*
(*see also Chapter III*)

On 21 February 2002, Congolese authorities realised the need for a course correction and enacted a new Investment Code. It is still in force today. The Report on the new law approving the code recognises the economic impact of investments and the need for efficient and adequate protection :

> "Investments have been shown to be the primary factor for economic growth and development in that it improves the dimensions of the economy. The State must play the role of organiser and catalyst of living forces by taking control of infrastructures and basic industrial investment and by establishing an institutional and legal framework assuring the protection of people and their assets."

The new Congolese investment code is a positive element in itself, because it gives investors a legal basis for structuring their claims and requests. This does not mean, however, that the protection that has been offered is adequate in all respects. Without a doubt, the law could stand some amending in order to be complete and more effective.

App. II.3.2. – *Discriminatory exclusions*

The text of the Code is still objectionable in the sense that important economic sectors fell outside the code's field of application. This would be understandable and admissible in the military sector but foreign investors are also excluded from the Congolese banking and mining sectors. This was certainly not a good omen for the encouragement of foreign investments in other sectors. The mining production (cobalt, diamonds, copper) was for many years and worldwide one of the most important segment of investment. Meanwhile, a recession has hit this sector. The exclusion of foreign investors from these sectors was a poor decision because it was precisely those sectors that required an intensive use of capital, locally scarce, and, hence, foreign assistance would have been useful. Instead of an absolute prohibition, it would have been better to devise a partnership formula (e.g. "joint venture") for these important sectors. Admittedly, the authorities' position in this area is mercurial, some permits being exceptionally granted. The affected sectors are governed by special laws which make it possible to find exceptions to the general rule.

App. II.3.3. – *Licit Character of Investment is a Normal Rule*

The Congolese law furthermore specifies that its application and the securing of specific benefits hangs on the "licit" character of the investment ("All investors, whether domestic or foreign, who conduct a licit activity."). Investors who might, when they first made their investments, violated local legislation and have conducted inadmissible activities (whether punishable or not) are denied protection from Congolese authorities' decisions. Investors who received a licence (*"Agrément"*) for making an investment and who, under the cover of this licence, actually conducted illicit operations (f.i. illicit banking activities) are deemed to have placed themselves outside of the umbrella of the code. This principle is generally admitted and was already applicable under Roman Law : *"nullum commodum capere de sua propria iniuria potest et ex delicto non oritur actio"* – no one may benefit from his own illicit activity nor file an action originating in delictual activity').

Nonetheless, in actuality, some activities were declared illicit simply because they had not been listed in a previous agreement, not necessarily because they were contrary to morals or known legislation.

App. II.3.4. – *Investment*

The Congolese legislators actually did a better job than the lawyers who wrote the international convention creating the International Centre for Settlement of Investment Disputes (ICSID, Washington). The Convention's authors gave up on the difficult issue of an adequate definition of the term "investment":

> "Considering the difficulties in defining universally what an investment is, the choice made during negotiations of the Convention was to leave to the Parties the right to agree among themselves on the definition." [388]

The Congolese code's definition of the term "investment" is rather complex:

> "All investments under the present law, when considered by a new enterprise or an existing one aiming to establish a new capability or to increase an existing capability to produce goods or services, broaden the spectrum of manufactured products or services offered, increase the productivity of enterprises or improve the quality of goods or services." (**Article 2**)

Article 3 of the Code mentions the economic sectors to which the legislation does not apply. Unfortunately, no list has been established of economic activities and assets which are to be considered as investments, such as could have followed the example of the BIT's. On the basis of his residence abroad, a person of Congolese nationality is considered "a foreign investor". This statement was neither in accordance with domestic Congolese law nor international law.

App. II.3.5. – *Misleading nationality concept*

In Article 2 of the Congolese Investment Code, there is another bizarre and unusual definition of the term: "direct foreign investor" (translation):

> "Any individual who does not have Congolese nationality or having the Congolese nationality but residing abroad and any public or private corporation having its principal place of business outside of Congolese territory, and making a direct investment in the RDC."

States may apply different criteria for the acquisition of nationality by individuals. This conforms to international law, each State having the right to decide what person carries

---

[388] *Review Foreign Investment Law Journal* (FIJL), 1996, pp. 355-358.

its nationality on the basis of its own legislation. In this case, the Congolese State was creating a double nationality on the basis of two domestic laws, which are contradictory.

The investment code provides that a Congolese investor with residence abroad is considered a "foreign investor" (thus not having the Congolese nationality). The same investor has Congolese nationality and is qualified as a "Congolese national" by virtue of Law no. 197 of 2 February 1999 concerning nationality. The duality of nationality, where a Congolese investor is concerned, is contrary to Congolese legislation and also in contradiction with international law which states, for reasons of legal security, that a State may bestow only a single nationality upon its nationals.

App. II.3.6. – *Territoriality*

On the other hand, Article 2 of the Congolese Investment Code directly conflicted with international law's principle of "territoriality". Decisions taken by a competent State organisation cannot have extraterritorial effect.

State power may be validly exercised only within the State's jurisdiction, that is, its territorial borders. This affects all measures taken by public authorities. Measures privative of property, such as nationalisation, cannot have extraterritorial effect.

The same principle has been used to block state intervention in arbitration proceedings introduced abroad:

> "As a matter of public international law, the Bangladesh legislator cannot validly interfere with arbitral proceedings which are pending in a foreign country to which its territorial jurisdiction does not extend."[389]

It is clear that the Republic of Congo cannot exercise power over the territory of a foreign State. Nevertheless, this is precisely what the Congolese legislator did, the investment

---

[389] *Recueil des Sentences arbitrales de la Chambre de Commerce International de Paris (CCI)*, Kluwer, 1974/85, p. 325.

code granting (implicitly) the nationality of the State of residence to a Congolese national. **Article 2** of the Code should therefore be amended to avoid practical and legal difficulties. The goal sought, when considering a Congolese national residing abroad, is not clear. It could not be to enable investments since a Congolese national residing abroad can evidently make investments in his own country.

App. II.3.7. – *Internal inconsistency*

Neither was this article even consistent with other Congolese contract practice. In the bilateral Agreement of 3 August 1984 between the USA and the Republic of Congo (RDC), the following definition was inserted:

> "'National' of a Party means any natural person who is a national of that Party in conformity with its laws."

Consequently, an individual with Congolese nationality by virtue of the Congolese legislation on nationality carries this nationality abroad with him. His residence in a foreign country does not at all annul his Congolese nationality. In this context, it may be convenient to refer to the Convention for the Settlement of Investment Disputes between States and nationals of other States, which was signed in Washington on 18 March 1965 (ICSID Convention) and which came in force on 14 October 1966.

Let us suppose that a Congolese national, residing in Florida files an ICSID procedure against the Congo State. The USA should certainly not countenance such a filing and should claim that the RDC/USA BIT, providing for arbitration, is not applicable to Congolese nationals, in an action against his own State... It is not clear whether the Congolese State should or would give its consent to such filing against it. However, on the improbable assumption that it would, it is certain that the Arbitration centre ICSID would declare itself incompetent on the basis of the Convention and also by application of the aforesaid BIT on investment disputes between a Contracting State and a national of another State.

A dispute between Congolese investors, residing abroad but having invested in the territory of the Congo, may not be submitted to an ICSID tribunal.

App. II.3.8. – *Divided authority*

An important part of the new Congolese investment code related to the creation of a national agency for the promotion of investments (ANAPI: National Agency for the Promotion of Investments). The Congolese authorities intended to offer guarantees to foreign investors so their investment requests could be examined objectively. They also wanted to reduce administrative impediments.

Unfortunately, these objectives could not be achieved. First, the very structure of the agency may be put into question. A semi-public statute would have been more appropriate, as it would have given the agency the necessary jurisdiction over final and independent decisions concerning licences to foreign investors.

The designation of a supervising Ministry, in charge of budget control only, would have been a better choice, but the Congolese legislation has not placed ANAPI under the wing of just one Ministry but instead under the authority of several Ministries. Legal rules governing the distribution of jurisdictional issues are unclear. Article 4 of the investment code reads :

> "A national agency for the promotion of investments is hereby established. ANAPI, as its monogram is placed under the authority of Ministries having the Plan and its portfolio among their jurisdictional competence. ANAPI is a welcoming organisation, charged, on the one hand, with the receipt of projects to be agreed on, to inform them and to decide on their acceptance..."

In actual practice, ANAPI is only in charge of the preparation of the decisions concerning the granting of investment licences. In addition, Article 6 provides that the Ministry of Finance is also to give its advice on the approval of foreign investments. Consequently, the Ministerial decree, including the approval of and agreement for investment projects must be signed off by at least three Ministries. On this ground alone, the chosen structure is far from functional and requires streamlining.

That is not to say that ANAPI has not done good work. It has but its efficiency could be improved if relatively slight structural reforms were enacted.

App. II.3.9. – *Turf disputes*

The efficient operation of ANAPI was not assured at the ministerial level and, moreover, there were many obstacles on the administrative level. Disputes concerning discrete jurisdictions were frequent, as each agency naturally wanted to meddle with the files handled by other agencies. In addition, the legislature itself had created a mix of jurisdictions and consequently brought about an interdependence between several administrative offices. The result was a decisional process which is very slow and inefficient with respect to requests for investment approval. ANAPI did not have the power to grant authorisations which were subject to outside agreement on the realisation of the projects. The Ministry of Employment had to issue Work Permits, subject to long delays in the actual issuance of the decision to approve the investment due to opposition by contesting interests. Likewise, power and water supply depended on a favourable decision by the Energy agency.

Thus, if a request for a licence was expected to be granted within a reasonable time after its filing, there had to be a certain willingness on the part of all parties. Every candidate investor was not always prepared to display that willingness to collaborate.

App. II.3.10. – *Future Adaptations*

As mentioned several times already, entering into State Contracts should be more frequently practiced, particularly where important investment projects are involved. These contracts must include an adequate clause regarding the possibility of submittal of disputes relating to investments to ICSID's arbitration or other arbitration venues.

The Belgium/Democratic Republic of Congo BIT, signed on 15 February 2005, should be renegotiated to adapt it to evolving protection of international investments. Every contractual arrangement regarding investments should fall under the protection of the BIT, including the right to arbitrate.

ANNEX

NORWEGIAN MODEL CONVENTION

Agreement between
the Kingdom of Norway
and
....
for the promotion and protection
of investments

The Kingdom of Norway and the................................, hereinafter referred to as the "Parties";

Desiring to develop the economic cooperation between the Parties;

Desiring to encourage, create and maintain stable, equitable, favourable and transparent conditions for investors of one Party and their investments in the territory of the other Party on the basis of equality and mutual benefit;

Desiring to achieve these objectives in a manner consistent with the protection of health, safety, and the environment, and the promotion of internationally recognized labour rights;

Desiring to contribute to a stable framework for investment in order to maximize effective and sustainable utilization of economic resources and improve living standards;

Conscious that the promotion and reciprocal protection of investments in accordance with this Agreement will stimulate the business initiative;

Emphasising the importance of corporate social responsibility;

Recognising that the development of economic and business ties can promote respect for internationally recognised labour rights;

Reaffirming their commitment to democracy, the rule of law, human rights and fundamental freedoms in accordance with their obligations under international law, including the principles set out in the United Nations Charter and the Universal Declaration of Human Rights;

Recognising that the promotion of sustainable investments is critical for the further development of national and global economies as well as for the pursuit of national and global objectives for sustainable development, and understanding that the promotion of such investments requires cooperative efforts of investors, host governments and home governments;

Recognising that the provisions of this agreement and provisions of international agreements relating to the environment shall be interpreted in a mutually supportive manner;

Determined to prevent and combat corruption, including bribery, in international trade and investment;

Recognising the basic principles of transparency, accountability and legitimacy for all participants in foreign investment processes;

Have agreed as follows:

SECTION 1. – SCOPE AND APPLICATION [390]

Article [1]
Scope

1. This Agreement applies to measures adopted or maintained by a Party, after the entry into force of this Agreement, relating to investors of the other Party or to investments of investors of the other Party. The Section [Dispute Settlement Provisions] does not apply to disputes arising out of events that have occurred before the entry into force of this Agreement, cf. Article ["Non-Retroactive Application"].

2. This Agreement applies to investments made prior to or after its entry into force.

3. This Agreement shall apply to the land territory, internal waters, and the territorial sea of a Party, and the airspace above the territory in accordance with international law.

4. This Agreement shall not apply to Svalbard, i.e. the land territory of the Archipelago, internal waters and the territorial sea of the Archipelago.

Article [2]
Definitions

1. "Investor" means:

(i) a natural person having the nationality of, or permanent residence in, a Party in accordance with its applicable law; or

(ii) any entity established in accordance with, and recognised as a legal person by the law of a Party, and engaged in substantive business operations in the territory of that Party, such as companies, firms, associa-

---

[390] In an EFTA Free Trade Agreement the geographical scope will be addressed under the horizontal part of the Agreement. The Article [Scope] and other provisions may also be amended to reflect that services is addressed in another part of the Agreement and for other technical purposes e.g. "another Party" instead of "the other Party" etc.

tions, development finance institutions, foundations or similar entities irrespective of whether their liabilities are limited and whether or not their activities are directed at profit.

2. "Investment" means:

Every kind of asset owned or controlled, directly or indirectly, by an investor of a Party, including, but not limited to:

(i) any entity established in accordance with, and recognised as a legal person by the law of a Party, whether or not their activities are directed at profit;
(ii) shares, stocks or other forms of equity participation in an enterprise, and rights derived therefrom;
(iii) bonds, debentures, loans and other forms of debt, and rights derived therefrom;
(iv) rights under contracts, including turnkey, construction, management, production or revenue-sharing;
(v) contracts;
(vi) claims to money and claims to performance;
(vii) intellectual property rights;
(viii) rights conferred pursuant to law or contract such as concessions, licenses, authorisations, and permits;
(ix) any other tangible and intangible, movable and immovable property, and any related property rights, such as leases, mortgages, liens and pledges.

In order to qualify as an investment under this Agreement, an asset must have the characteristics of an investment, such as the commitment of capital or other resources, the expectation of gain or profit, or the assumption of risk.

SECTION 2. – TREATMENT AND PROTECTION
OF INVESTORS AND INVESTMENTS

Article [3]
National Treatment

1. Each Party shall accord to investors of the other Party and to their investments, treatment no less favourable than the treatment it accords in like circumstances[391] to its own investors and their investments, in relation

---

[391] The Parties agree/are of the understanding that a measure applied by a government in pursuance of legitimate policy objectives of public interest such as the protection of public health, safety and the environment, although having a different effect on an investment or investor of another Party, is not inconsistent with

to the establishment, acquisition, expansion, management, conduct, operation and disposal of investments.

2. National treatment shall not apply to the reservations set out in Annex [A].

Article [4]
Most-Favoured-Nation Treatment

1. Each Party shall accord to investors of the other Party and to their investments, treatment no less favourable than the treatment it accords in like circumstances [392] to investors and their investments of any other State, subject to the country-specific reservations set out in Annex [B], in relation to the establishment, acquisition, expansion, management, conduct, operation and disposal of investments. [393]

2. If a Party accords more favourable treatment to investors of any other State or their investments by virtue of a free trade agreement, customs union [or similar agreement that also provides for substantial liberalisation of investments] or by a labour market integration agreements, it shall not be obliged to accord such treatment to investors of the other Party or their investments. However, upon request from another Party, it shall afford adequate opportunity to negotiate the benefits granted therein.

3. For greater certainty, treatment referred to in paragraph [1] does not encompass dispute resolution mechanisms provided for in this Agreement or other International Agreements.

Article [5]
General Treatment and Protection

Each Party shall accord to investors of the other Party, and their investments treatment in accordance with customary international law, including fair and equitable treatment and full protection and security.

Article [6]
Expropriation

1. A Party shall not expropriate or nationalise an investment of an investor of the other Party except in the public interest and subject to the

---

national treatment and most favoured nation treatment when justified by showing that it bears a reasonable relationship to rational policies not motivated by preference of domestic over foreign owned investment.

[392] See footnote 2.
[393] ???

conditions provided for by law and by the general principles of international law.

2. The preceding provision shall not, however, in any way impair the right of a Party to enforce such laws as it deems necessary to control the use of property in accordance with the general interest or to secure the payment of taxes or other contributions or penalties.

Article [7]
Compensation for losses

1. Investors whose investments have suffered losses due to armed conflict or civil strife, shall benefit from treatment in accordance with Article [National treatment] and Article [MFN] as regards restitution, indemnification, compensation or any other settlement it adopts or maintains relating to such losses.

2. [Without prejudice to paragraph 1 of this Article, an investor of a Party who, in any of the situations referred to in that paragraph, suffers a loss in the area of another Party resulting from

(i) requisitioning of its investment or part thereof by the latter's forces or authorities,

or

(ii) destruction of its investment or part thereof by the latter's forces or authorities,

which was not required by the necessity of the situation, shall be accorded restitution or compensation.][394]

Article [8]
Performance Requirements

1. No Party may impose or enforce any of the following requirements, or enforce any commitment or undertaking in connection with the establishment, acquisition, expansion, management, conduct or operation of an investment of an investor of the other Party:

(i) [to export a given level or percentage of goods or services;]
(ii) [to achieve a given level or percentage of domestic content;]
(iii) [to purchase, use or accord a preference to goods produced or services provided in its territory, or to purchase goods or services from persons in its territory;]

---

[394] Kan være aktuell i forhandlinger med enkelte land.

(iv) [to relate in any way the volume or value of imports to the volume or value of exports or to the amount of foreign exchange inflows associated with such investment;]

(v) [to restrict sales of goods or services in its territory that such investment produces or provides by relating such sales to the volume or value of its exports or foreign exchange earnings;]

(vi) [to transfer technology, a production process or other proprietary knowledge to a natural or legal person in its territory, except when the requirement]

 (a) is imposed or the commitment or undertaking is enforced by a court, administrative tribunal or competition authority to remedy an alleged violation of competition laws, or

 (b) concerns the transfer of intellectual property and is undertaken in a manner not inconsistent with the TRIPS Agreement;]

(vii) [to locate its headquarters for a specific region or the world market in the territory of that Party;]

(viii) [to supply one or more of the goods that it produces or the services that it provides to a specific region or the world market exclusively from the territory of that Party;]

(ix) [to achieve a given level or value of research and development in its territory;]

(x) [to hire a given level of nationals;]

(xi) [to achieve a minimum level of domestic equity participation other than nominal qualifying shares for directors or incorporators of corporations.]

2. A measure that requires an investment to use a technology to meet generally applicable health, safety or environmental requirements shall not be construed to be inconsistent with paragraph 1.

3. Performance requirements, other than those referred to in paragraph 1, shall only be applied in the public interest and shall be set forth in the national legislation of the Party imposing the requirement and published in the official gazette or otherwise be publicly available according to Article [Transparency] so that investors may become acquainted with them before the investment decision is made. All performance requirements shall be applied against all investors and their investments in a non-discriminatory, transparent and objective manner.

4. A Party may not apply new performance requirements to existing investments, or amend existing performance requirements in a manner restricting the commercial freedom of the investor, except where such requirements are at the same time made applicable to all other investors in that Party.

Article [9]
Transfer

1. Each Party shall ensure that all payment relating to an investment of an investor of another Party may be freely transferred into and out of its territory without delay. Such transfers shall include, in particular, though not exclusively:

(i) the initial capital and additional amounts to maintain or increase an investment;

(ii) profits, interest, dividends, capital gains, royalties, fees and returns in kind;

(iii) payments made under a contract including a loan agreement;

(iv) proceeds from the sale or liquidation of all or any part of an investment;

(v) earnings and other remuneration of personnel engaged from abroad in connection with an investment.

2. Each Party shall further ensure that such transfers may be made in a freely convertible currency. Freely convertible currency means a currency that is widely traded in international foreign exchange markets and widely used in international transactions. Transfers shall be made at the market rate of exchange prevailing on the date of transfer.

3. It is understood that paragraphs 1 and 2 are without prejudice to the equitable, non-discriminatory and good faith application of measures:

(i) to protect the rights of creditors,

(ii) relating to or ensuring compliance with laws and regulations

   (a) on the issuing, trading and dealing in securities, futures and derivatives,

   (b) concerning reports or records of transfers, or

   (c) concerning the payment of contributions or penalties,

   (d) concerning financial security or any other equivalent regarding the prevention and remedying of environmental damage,

(iii) in connection with criminal offences and orders or judgments in administrative and adjudicatory proceedings.

Article [10]
Key Personnel

1. Each Party shall, subject to its laws and regulations relating to the entry, stay and work of natural persons, grant natural persons of the other Party, and key personnel who are employed by natural or juridical persons of the other Party, temporary entry and stay in its territory in order to

engage in activities connected with an investment, including the provision of advice or key technical services.

2. Each Party shall, subject to its laws and regulations, permit natural or legal/juridical persons of another Party to employ, in connection with an investment, any key personnel of the natural or legal/juridical person's choice provided that such key personnel has been permitted to enter, stay and work in its territory and that the employment concerned conforms to the terms, conditions and time limits of the permission granted to such key personnel.

3. The Parties shall, subject to their laws and regulations, grant temporary entry and stay and provide any necessary confirming documentation to the spouse and minor children of a natural person who has been granted temporary entry, stay and authorisation to work in accordance with paragraphs 1 and 2. The spouse and minor children shall be admitted for the period of the stay of that person.

Article [11]
Not Lowering Standards

1. The Parties recognize that it is inappropriate to encourage investment by relaxing domestic health, safety or environmental measures or core labour standards. Accordingly, a Party should not waive or otherwise derogate from, or offer to waive or otherwise derogate from, such measures as an encouragement for the establishment, acquisition, expansion or retention of an investment of an investor.

2. If a Party considers that the other Party has offered such an encouragement, it may request consultations under Article [Joint Committee].

Article [12]
Right to regulate

Nothing in this Agreement shall be construed to prevent a Party from adopting, maintaining or enforcing any measure otherwise consistent with this Agreement that it considers appropriate to ensure that investment activity is undertaken in a manner sensitive to health, safety or environmental concerns.

SECTION 3. – DISPUTE SETTLEMENT PROVISIONS

Article [13]
Non-Retroactive Application

This Section does not apply to disputes arising out of events that have occurred before the entry into force of this Agreement.

Article [14]
Governing Law

1. A Tribunal established under this Section shall make its award based on the provisions of this Agreement interpreted and applied in accordance with the rules of interpretation of international law.

2. An interpretation by the Joint Committee of a provision of this Agreement shall be binding on a Tribunal established under this Section.

A. – *disputes between a party and an investor of the other party*

Article [15]
Disputes between a Party and an Investor of the other Party

1. This Article applies to legal disputes between a Party and an investor of the other Party arising directly out of an investment of the latter that falls under the jurisdiction of the former. The dispute must be based on a claim that the Party has breached an obligation under this Agreement and that the investor of the other Party has incurred loss or damage by that breach.

2. Any dispute under this Article shall, if possible, be settled amicably. The Party and an investor of the other Party should initially seek to resolve the dispute through consultation.

3. If any such dispute should arise and either

(i) agreement cannot be reached between the parties to this dispute within 36 months from its submission to a local court for the purpose of pursuing local remedies, after having exhausted any administrative remedies; or

(ii) there are no reasonably available local remedies to provide effective redress of this dispute, or the local remedies provide no reasonable possibility of such redress;

[and,

(iii) the investor has provided a clear and unequivocal waiver of any right to pursue the matter before local courts,]

then each Party hereby consents to the submission of such dispute to arbitration under the Convention on the Settlement of Investment Disputes between States and Nationals of Other States opened for signature at Washington on 18 March 1965 (ICSID Convention) in accordance with the provisions of this Article. The consent and the submission of the dispute by an investor under this Article shall be considered to satisfy the requirements of Article 25 of the ICSID Convention [ICSID Additional Facility

Rules, with the approval of the Agreement by the Secretary General to ICSID].

4. [An investor may not submit a dispute for resolution according to paragraph [3] if more than ten years have elapsed from the date the investor first acquired knowledge of the events giving rise to the claim.]

5. Each request for arbitration shall include information sufficient to present clearly the issues in dispute so as to allow the Parties and the public to become acquainted with them. All requests for arbitration shall be made publicly available by the Parties and by ICSID.

Article [16]
Additional Procedural Issues

The Tribunal shall, as appropriate, take into account the principles of *res judicata* and *lis pendens*, in accordance with international law, to hinder abuse of rights under this agreement, as well as otherwise exercising sound judicial economy. If all parties to the dispute so agree, the Tribunal may consolidate claims.

Article [17]
The Award

1. Any arbitral award rendered pursuant to Article [Disputes between a Party and an Investor of the other Party], shall be final and binding on the Parties to the dispute.

2. Where a Tribunal makes an award against a Party pursuant to Article [Disputes between a Party and an Investor of the other Party], the Tribunal may only award monetary damages, including applicable interest, as well as costs in accordance with the applicable arbitration rules.

3. All awards and substantive decisions of the Tribunal shall be made publicly available.

4. The costs of arbitration shall in principle be borne by the unsuccessful Party. However, the Tribunal may apportion such costs between the Parties if it determines that apportionment is reasonable, taking into account the circumstances of the case.

Article [18]
Participation in the proceedings

1. The Party complained against shall, within 30 days after receiving a request for arbitration, notify the other Party in writing and transmit a copy of the request.

2. The Tribunal shall give the other Party the opportunity to:

(i) be present at the substantive meetings of the Tribunal with the parties to the dispute preceding, except for portions of such meetings when confidential information designated as such by the Party that submitted it is discussed;

(ii) make a written submission prior to the first oral hearing; and

(iii) make an oral presentation to the Tribunal at the first oral hearing,

provided that it has informed the Tribunal no later than [30 days] after the establishment of the Tribunal of its desire to participate in the proceedings.

3. The Tribunal shall have the authority to accept and consider written *amicus curiae* submissions from a person or entity that is not a disputing Party, provided that the Tribunal has determined that they are directly relevant to the factual and legal issues under consideration. The Tribunal shall ensure an opportunity for the parties to the dispute, and to the other Party, to submit comments on the written *amicus curiae* observations.

4. The Tribunal shall reflect submissions from the other Party and from *amicus curiae* in its report.

Article [19]
Transparency of Proceedings

1. All documents submitted to, or issued by, the Tribunal shall immediately be made publicly available by the Tribunal.

2. When submitting information to the Tribunal, a Party to the dispute may designate specific information as confidential if the information

(i) is not generally known or accessible to the public, and

(ii) if disclosed would cause or threaten to cause prejudice to an essential interest of any individual or entity, or to the interest of a Party.

Such information shall be treated as confidential and shall only be made available to the parties to the dispute and to the other Party.

3. If another Party objects to the designation of information as confidential, the Tribunal shall decide if the designation meets the above mentioned criteria. If the Tribunal considers that the information does not meet the criteria, the Party submitting the information may

(i) withdraw the information, or

(ii) withdraw the designation of the information as confidential.

4. The Tribunal shall conduct hearings open to the public and shall determine, in consultation with the disputing parties, the appropriate logistical arrangements.

B. – *Disputes Between the Parties*

Article [20]
Disputes between the Parties

1. Any dispute between the Parties concerning the interpretation or application of this Agreement shall, whenever possible, be settled amicably through consultations in the Joint Committee.

2. If the Parties are unable to reach a mutually satisfactory resolution of a matter through consultations, they may have recourse to good offices or to mediation or conciliation under such rules and procedures as they may agree.

3. A Party may not initiate arbitration against the other Party under paragraph 4 of this Article unless the former Party has requested consultations and has afforded the other Party a consultation period of no less than 60 days after the date of the receipt of the request.

4. Either Party that has complied with the consultation requirement of paragraphs 2 and 3 of this Article, may submit a dispute between them as to whether one of them has acted in contravention of this Agreement to final and binding arbitration in accordance with the Permanent Court of Arbitration Optional Rules for Arbitrating Disputes between Two States, as in effect on the date of this Agreement.

5. The place of the arbitration proceedings shall be The Hague, The Netherlands.

6. The language to be used in the arbitral proceedings shall be English.

7. The appointing authority shall be the Secretary General of the Permanent Court of Arbitration.

8. Nothing in the present Article impairs the right of the Parties to agree at any time to settle a dispute between them concerning the interpretation or application of this Agreement by any peaceful means of their own choice.

Article [21]
Transparency of Proceedings

1. All documents submitted to, or issued by, the Tribunal shall be made publicly available by the International Bureau of the Permanent Court of Arbitrations, except for confidential information contained therein.

2. The Tribunal shall conduct hearings open to the public and shall determine, in consultation with the disputing parties, the appropriate logistical arrangements. The arbitral tribunal, after hearing the parties, may decide to close the hearings wholly or partially.

3. The Tribunal shall have the authority to accept and consider written *amicus curiae* submissions from a person or entity that is not a disputing Party, provided that the tribunal has determined that they are directly relevant to the factual and legal issues under consideration.

4. When submitting information to the Tribunal, a Party may designate specific information as confidential if the information

(i) is not generally known or accessible to the public, and

(ii) if disclosed would cause or threaten to cause [serious] prejudice to an essential interest of any individual or entity [lawfully in control of the information].

Such information shall not be disclosed and be treated in accordance with procedures to be established by the Tribunal for each particular case.

5. If another Party objects to the designation of information as confidential, the Tribunal shall decide if the designation meets the above mentioned criteria. If the Tribunal considers that the information does not meet the criteria, the Party submitting the information may

(i) withdraw the information, or

(ii) withdraw the designation of the information as confidential.

C. – *Subrogation*

Article [22]
Subrogation

1. If the investments of an investor are insured against non-commercial risks, any subrogation of the claims of the investor pursuant to this Agreement, shall be recognized by the other Party.

2. Disputes between a Party and an insurer shall be settled in accordance with the provisions of [Annex C] of this Agreement.

SECTION 4. – INSTITUTIONAL PROVISIONS

Article [23]
The Joint Committee

1. The Parties hereby establish a Joint Committee composed of representatives of the Parties.

2. The Joint Committee shall meet whenever necessary. Each Party may request at any time, through a notice in writing to the other Party, that a meeting of the Joint Committee be held. The request shall provide sufficient information to understand the basis for the request, including, where

relevant, identification of issues in dispute. Such a meeting shall take place within 60 days of receipt of the request, unless the Parties agree otherwise.

3. The Joint Committee shall:

(i) supervise the implementation of this Agreement;

(ii) in accordance with Article [Disputes between the Parties], endeavour to resolve disputes that may arise regarding the interpretation or application of this Agreement;

(iii) review the possibility of further removal of barriers to investment;

(iv) where relevant, suggest to the Parties ways to enhance and promote investment action;

(v) review investments covered by this Agreement;

(vi) review case-law of investment arbitration tribunals relevant to the implementation of this Agreement;

(vii) oversee the further elaboration of this Agreement;

(viii) where relevant, discuss issues related to corporate social responsibility, the preservation of the environment, public health and safety, the goal of sustainable development, anticorruption, employment and human rights; and

(ix) consider any other matter that may affect the operation of this Agreement.

Where appropriate, the Joint Committee may:

(i) decide to amend the Agreement, as set forth in Article [Amendments]; and

(ii) interpret this Agreement, bearing in mind that this competence shall not be used to undermine the amendment provisions of Article [Amendments]. The Joint Committee should refrain from adopting interpretations of provisions already submitted to a Tribunal in a dispute between a Party and an Investor of the other Party.

5. The Joint Committee may take decisions as provided for in this Agreement. On other matters the Joint Committee may make recommendations. Decisions and recommendations shall be made by consensus.

6. The Joint Committee shall establish its rules of procedure.

SECTION 5. – EXCEPTIONS

Article [24]
General Exceptions

Subject to the requirement that such measures are not applied in a manner which would constitute a means of arbitrary or unjustifiable discrimination between investments or between investors, or a disguised restriction on international [trade or] investment, nothing in this Agreement shall be construed to prevent a Party from adopting or enforcing measures necessary [395]:

(i) to protect public morals or to maintain public order; [396]
(ii) to protect human, animal or plant life or health;
(iii) to secure compliance with laws and regulations that are not inconsistent with the provisions of this Agreement;
(iv) for the protection of national treasures of artistic, historic or archaeological value; or
(v) for the protection of the environment.

Article [25]
Prudential Regulation

Notwithstanding any other provisions of this Agreement, a Party shall not be prevented from taking measures for prudential reasons, including for the protection of investors, depositors, policy holders or persons to whom a fiduciary duty is owed by a financial service supplier, to ensure the integrity and stability of the financial system, or to enhance market competition, including ownership control and limitation.

Where such measures do not conform with the provisions of the Agreement, they shall not be used as a means of avoiding the Party's commitments or obligations under the Agreement.

Article [26]
Security Exceptions

Nothing in this Agreement shall be construed:

(i) to require any Party to furnish any information, the disclosure of which it considers contrary to its essential security interests; or
(ii) to prevent any Party from taking any action which it considers necessary for the protection of its essential security interests:
   (a) relating to investment in defence and security sector[s];
   (b) relating to fissionable and fusionable materials or the materials from which they are derived;

---

[395] For greater certainty, the concept of "necessity" in this Article shall include measures taken by a Party as provided for by the precautionary principle, including the principle of precautionary action.

[396] The public order exception may be invoked only where a genuine and sufficiently serious threat is posed to one of the fundamental interests of society.

(c) taken in time of war or other emergency in international relations; or

(iii) to prevent any Party from taking any action in pursuance of its obligations for the maintenance of international peace and security, including under the United Nations Charter.

Article [27]
Cultural Exceptions

The provisions of this Agreement shall not apply to a Party's laws and measures specifically designed to preserve and promote linguistic and cultural diversity, cultural and audiovisual policy, as well as rights and obligations of the Parties under international agreements and national laws and measures relating to copyright and related rights.

Article [28]
Taxation

1. Nothing in this Agreement shall affect the imposition, enforcement or collection of direct or indirect taxes imposed by a Party.

2. Nothing in this Agreement shall create any right to any benefit under an agreement for the avoidance of double taxation concluded by a Party.

3. Any dispute as to whether paragraphs 1 and 2 apply, may only be brought before the Competent Tax Authorities of the Parties according to the procedure of Article [The Joint Committee] or the national courts or appeal organs of a Party, and shall not be covered by Section [Dispute Settlement Provisions] of this Agreement.

4. If the Competent Tax Authority of one of the Parties, after the procedure of Article [The Joint Committee] has been completed, does not agree that paragraph 1 above apply, but takes the position that the case should be considered under Article [Expropriation], then the dispute shall be covered by [Section [Dispute Settlement Provisions] of this Agreement.]

SECTION 6. – FINAL PROVISIONS

Article [29]
Relation to Other International Agreements

The provisions of this Agreement shall be without prejudice to the rights and obligations of the Parties under other international agreements.

Article [30]
Regional and Local Government

Each Party is fully responsible for the observance of all obligations and commitments under this Agreement by its respective regional and local governments and authorities, and by non-governmental bodies in the exercise of governmental powers delegated to them by central, regional and local governments or authorities.

Article [31]
Transparency

1. The Parties shall publish their laws, or otherwise make publicly available their laws, regulations and administrative rulings and judicial decisions of general application–as well as their respective international agreements that may affect the operation of this Agreement.

2. The Parties shall promptly respond to specific questions and provide, upon request, information to each other on matters referred to in paragraph 1.

Article [32]
Corporate Social Responsibility

The Parties agree to encourage investors to conduct their investment activities in compliance with the OECD Guidelines for Multinational Enterprises and to participate in the United Nations Global Compact.

Article [33]
Amendments

1. Amendments to this Agreement, decided by the Joint Committee in accordance with Article [Joint Committee], shall be subject to ratification, acceptance or approval by the Parties.

2. Amendments shall enter into force on the first day of the third month following the date of receipt of the last notification by a Party informing the other Party that its internal constitutional requirements have been fulfilled.

Article [34]
Entry into Force

1. This Agreement is subject to ratification, acceptance or approval.

2. This Agreement shall enter into force on the first day of the third month following the receipt of the last notification informing the other Party that the internal constitutional requirements have been fulfilled.

Article [35]
Duration and Termination

1. Each Party to this Agreement may, by means of a written notification to the other Party, terminate this Agreement. The termination shall take effect on the first day of the [X] month after the date on which the notification was received by the other Party.

2. In respect of investments made prior to the date of termination of this Agreement, the provisions of this Agreement shall remain in force for a further period of fifteen years from that date.

IN WITNESS WHEREOF the undersigned, being duly authorised thereto, have signed this Agreement.

Done at ...., this .... of .... 200x in duplicate [in the English, Norwegian and [XXX] languages, all texts being equally authentic. In case of divergence of interpretation, the English text shall prevail.

For the
Kingdom of Norway

For the

Annex A
Reservations/Exceptions from National Treatment

1. A Party may, at any time, remove in whole or in part its reservations set out in this Annex by written notification to the other Party.

2. A Party may, at any time, incorporate a new reservation into this Annex, or amend an existing reservation, provided that the Party has offered compensatory adjustments that maintain the overall level of commitments of that Party under this Agreement as it existed immediately prior to the modification:

(i) A Party shall notify its intent to modify its list of reservations to the other Party and at the same time suggest appropriate compensatory adjustments. The Joint Committee shall immediately be seized of the matter. Where the Joint Committee approves the modifications, they shall enter into force [3 months] after the decision by the Joint Committee.

(ii) Where the Joint Committee has not made a decision within [6 months] of receipt of the notification by the modifying Party, the modification shall take effect. In such circumstances, the other Party may withdraw concessions equivalent to the modification within [6 months] thereafter.

3. A modification pursuant to this Article may not impose on an investor a requirement to sell or otherwise dispose of an investment in the territory of the Party.

Annex B
Exceptions/Reservations from Most Favoured Nation Treatment

1. Article [Most-Favoured-Nations] shall not apply to treatment accorded under bilateral agreements signed by Norway prior to 1997 nor to treatment accorded under the EFTA-Singapore Free Trade Agreement signed 26 June 2002.

[Procedures for amendments/modification must be prepared]

Annex C
Disputes between a Contracting Party
and an insurer in accordance with Article [Subrogation]
of this Agreement

1. This Annex applies to legal disputes between an insurer and a Contracting Party, based on Article [Subrogation] of this Agreement, provided

that the insurer does not have legal standing under Article 25(1) of the ICSID Convention.

2. Each Party hereby consents to the submission by an insurer of a dispute, in accordance with Article [Subrogation] of this Agreement and Paragraph 1 of this Annex, to international arbitration under the UNCITRAL Arbitration Rules ("UNCITRAL").

3. The consent under Paragraph 2 and the submission of the dispute by an insurer shall be considered to satisfy the requirements of Article 1 of UNCITRAL.

4. Any arbitral award rendered pursuant to this Annex, shall be final and binding on the parties to the dispute and will be recognised and enforced in accordance with the Convention on the Recognition and Enforcement of Foreign Arbitral Awards, done in New York on 10 June 1958.

5. Articles [alle som gjelder for investor-stat-tvisteløsning] of this Agreement and the procedural rules of ICSID shall apply to disputes under this Annex *mutatis mutandis*.

TABLE OF AUTHORITIES
BIBLIOGRAPHY

I. – Books [*][**]

AMADEO, Mario, «Le Contentieux international de l'investissement privé et la convention de la Banque Mondiale du 18 mars 1965», Paris, 1967 : **128/251**

BATTIFOL, Henri, «Traité élémentaire du droit international privé», Paris, Librairie générale de droit et de jurisprudence (LGDJ), 1955 : **118/242**

Black's Law Dictionary, Bryan A. GARNER, Henry Campbell Black, Minnesota, St Paul MN : Thomson West, 2006 : **238/400**

BERNARD, A., «L'arbitrage volontaire en droit privé», Bruxelles, Bruylant, 1937, p. 41, obs. J. VERKEST; C.E., *Bourgeois et autres*, n° 189.815 du 27 janvier 2009). En revanche, le fait que l'assiette de la voirie resterait propriété privée p. 213 (Consensual arbitration in private law) : **341/548**

BIN CHENG, "General Principles of Law as applied by International Courts and Tribunals", Cambridge, Edition Cambridge University Press', 2006 : **206/374**

BLANCO, Dominique, «Négocier et rédiger un contrat international», Dunod, Paris, 2002 (Draft and negotiate an international contract) : **304/502**

CARREAU, Jean, «Droit international économique», Librairie générale de droit et de jurisprudence (LDGJ), Paris, 1980 (Economic International Law) : **4/8**

Centre des Nations Unies sur les Sociétés Transnationales, New York, 1989 (United Nations Centre for Transnational Corporations) : **51/70**

COOLEY, Thomas, «A Treatise on the Constitutional Limitations which rest upon de Legislative Power of the States of the American Union», p. 441 : **236/399**

DAVID, René «L'arbitrage dans le commerce international», Economica, Paris, 1982 : **297/494**

---

* Translation of titles is for convenience only.

** Numbers following authors' names refer to footnotes and to pages of this work : f.i. : Amadeo, 128 = number of footnote ; 251 = number of page of this Work.

DELBEZ, Louis, «Les principes généraux du contentieux international», Librairie générale de droit et de jurisprudence (LGDJ), Paris, 1962 : **24/30**

DILLEMANS, Roger, «Wegwijs recht», Davidsfonds, Leuven 2000 (Legal Manual, Belgium, 2000) : **13/17**

EYSKENS, Mark, «Economie van nu en straks», *De Nederlandse Boekhandel (DNB)*, Antwerpen, 1977 (Economy today and tomorrow, Belgium, 1977) **130/254**

FOUCHARD, Philippe, «L'OHADA et le perspectives de l'arbitrage en Afrique», Bruylant, Brussels, Belgium, 2000 : **303/501**

FRIEDMAN, Samy, "Expropriation in International Law", London, Stevens and Sons, 1953 : **30/40**

GAILLARD, Emmanuel, «La jurisprudence du CIRDI», Pedone, Paris, 2004 (ICSID jurisprudence) : **31/44**

JARVIN Sigvard, DERAINS Yves, «Collection of arbitral awards», Paris, Kluwer, 1998 : **312/512**

LILLICH, Richard and WESTON, Burns, "International claims ; Their settlement by Lump Sum Agreements", Charlottesville, University Press of Virginia, 1975 : **22/28**

MARTOR, Boris, «Le droit uniforme africain des affaires issu de l'OHADA», LITEC, Paris, 2004 (OHADA case based African Common Law) : **320/519**

MAST, André, «Belgisch administratief recht», Story-Scientia, Gent, 1981 (Belgian Administrative Law) : **265/457**

MEYER, Pierre, «Droit de l'arbitrage», Brussels, Bruylant, 2002, p. 32 (Arbitration Law) : **301/499**

OMAN, Charles, «Les nouvelles formes d'investissement», Organisation de coopération et de développement économique (OECD), Paris, 1984 (New forms of investment, Organisation for Economic Cooperation and Development) : **8/11**

OPPENHEIM, L.F.L., "International Law", Edition Lauterpacht, Cambridge University Press, Cambridge, 1967 : **140/263**

POUDRET, J.F., «Droit comparé de l'arbitrage international», Bruxelles, Bruylant, 2002, p. 614 (International Arbitration Comparative Law) : **369/598**

RABEL, Ernst, "The conflicts of Law", Chicago, Edition Wikipedia, 1958 : **126/247**

Recueil de sentences arbitrales de la Chambre de Commerce International de Paris, Kluwer, 1974/1985 : **389/655**

Roth, Andreas Hans, "The minimum standard of international law as applied to aliens", The Hague, Edition Sijthoff, 1949 : **174/330**

Sacerdoti, Giorgio, "Bilateral treaties and multilateral agreements on investment protection", Academy of International Law, The Hague, Netherlands, 1997 : **161/303**

Selleslags, François, «Pratique des paiements internationaux», Presses Universitaires de Bruxelles, Bruxelles, 1976 (International Payments Practice, Brussels, Belgium) : **219/389**

Sornarajah, M, "The international Law on foreign investments", Cambridge University Press, 2004 : **44/66**

Toker, Joh, A., California Arbitration Practice Guide, San Francisco, Lawpress Corporation Westport Comm., 1997 : **227/391**

Van Boxsom, «Rechtsvergelijkende studie over de nationaliteit van vennootschappen», Brussels, Bruylant, 1994 (Comparative Law Study regarding Corporate Nationality, Brussels, Belgium) : **116/237**

Vandeputte, Robert, «Inleiding tot het verzekeringsrecht», Standaard, Antwerpen, 1978 (Introduction to Insurance Law) : **259/444**

Van Hecke, G., «Internationaal privaatrecht», Story-scientia, 1989 (International Private Law, Ghent, Belgium) : **298/494**

Vranken, André, «Hedendaags consulair recht», Cockaert, Lier, 1989 (Consular Law Today, Lier, Belgium) : **16/21**

Wikipedia, "The English Bill of Rights" : **213/383**

Witkin, B.E : Summary of California Law, Westlaw edition, 2005-2008 : **221/390**

Webster International Dictionnary : **203/370**

Wolff, Joël, M., "Private International Law", London, Clarendon Press Oxford, 1950 : **117/239**

II. – Citations of legal reviews [*]

1/5 *Répertoire de droit international*, Dalloz, Paris, 1969, p. 190 (Repertory of International Law)

2/8 IMF Committee on balance of Payments Statistics and OECD Workshop on International Investment Statistics, DITEG# 3 : Indirect Investment, defining the Scope of the Direct Investment Relationship

---

* Reference numbers are to footnotes and to pages of this work

The first number refers to the footnotes and de second number to pages of this work : f.i. 1/5 Répertoire de droit international; 1 = number of footnote; 5 = number of page of this work.

prepared by Marie MONTANJEES, *IMF Statistics Department*, April 2004, p. 2

3/8 SCHOKKAERT, Jan, "La pratique conventionnelle européenne en matière de protection juridique des investissements privés, effectués à l'étranger", *Revue de droit international et de droit comparé*, Bruylant, Brussels, June 2003, p. 328 (Conventional European Practice regarding legal Protection for private investments made abroad, International and Comparative Law Review, Bruylant, Brussels, June 2003) p. 328

5/9 OGUTÇU, Mehmet, "Foreign direct investment and regional development", *The journal of world investment*, June 2003, Geneva, p. 493

9/15 *Le Répertoire pratique de droit belge*, Corporations, Brussels, Bruylant, 2007, n° 34 Corporations (Practical Repertory of Belgian Law)

10/15 SCHOKKAERT, Jan, "Verdragsrechtelijke schadeloosstelling van in het buitenland benadeelde particuliere bezittingen", *Rechtskundig weekblad*, 1974, n° 36, p. 2262 ("Conventional Indemnification of private assets, affected on foreign territory", *Legal Weekly*)

12/17 Comité européen de coopération juridique, *Conseil de l'Europe*, «Questionnaire relatif à la notion de résidence et à la notion de domicile», Paris, 1975, p. 3 (European Committee for Legal Cooperation, *European Council*, Paris, 1975)

14/19 Commission de droit international (CDI) de l'organisation des Nations Unies, «Rapport 2000», New York, 2000, p. 425 (International Law Commission Report)

15/20 *Barcelona Traction, Light and Power Company Limited*, Judgment International Court of Justice (ICJ), *Reports*, 1970, p. 45

18/26 KNOEPFLER, François, "L'immunité d'éxécution contre les Etats", *Revue de l'arbitrage*, Paris, juillet, 2003, n° 3, p. 1018 (States' Immunity from Execution, Arbitration Review, Paris, July 2003)

19/26 SCHOKKAERT, Jan, "Pratique contractuelle de la Belgique en matière d'indemnisation des avoirs privés lésés à l'étranger", *Revue belge de droit international (RBDI)*, Université de Bruxelles, Septembre 1974, p. 435 (Belgian Conventional Practice regarding Indemnification for affected Private Assets abroad, University of Brussels, September 1974)

23/29 LEBEN, Charles, "L'évolution de la notion de Contrat d'Etat", *Revue de l'arbitrage*, LITEC, Paris, 3/3003, p. 641

25/32 International Law Association, Report Toronto Conference 2006, p. 355

27/36 Code des investissements congolais, Loi n° 004/2002, du 21 février 2002, portent Code des investissements, *Journal Officiel* n° 6 du 15 mars 2002, Exposé des matifs, p. 1

28/36 Paths out of Poverty, International Finance Corporation (IFC), Washington D.C., 2000

41/66 JUILLARD, Patrick, «Les conventions bilatérales d'investissement conclues par la France : A la recherche d'un droit perdu ?", *Droit et pratique du commerce international*, Editions scientifiques internationales, Paris, 1987, Tome 13, n° 1, p. 9 ("Bilateral Investment Conventions with France : Looking for lost rights ?", *International Commercial Law and Practice*, Paris, 1987)

42/66 VAN DE VOORDE Willem, "Belgian bilateral treaties as a means for promoting and protecting foreign investments", *Studia Diplomatica*, Editions Royal Institute for international relations, Brussels, 1991, volume XLIV, n° 1, p. 109

43/66 SCHACHTER, Oscar, "Compensation for expropriation", *American Journal of International Law*, 1984, p. 121

48/69 PETERSON, Luke, Eric, *BIT's and Development policy making*, Winnipeg, Manitoba, International institute for sustainable development, 2003, n° 1, p. 9

49/69 VAN DE VELDE, Kenneth, "The economics of bilateral investment treaties", *Harvard International Law Journal (HILJ)*, Cambridge, 2000, n° 121, p. 488.

52/71 FÜRACKER, Mathias, "Relevance and Structure of Bilateral Investment Treaties", *German arbitration journal*, Petersberger Schiedstage, Petersberg, March 2006, pag. 4

53/72 SALEM, Mahmoud, "Le développement de la protection conventionnelle des investissements à l'étranger", *Journal de droit international JDI*, Editions techniques, Paris, June 1981, n° 3, p. 582 ("Development of conventional Protection for foreign Investments", *International Law Journal*, Paris, June 1981)

54/73 MANN, F.A., "British Treaties : Promotion and Protection of Investments", *British Yearbook of International Law (BYIL)*, 1981, p. 241

55/73 LAUTERPACHT, Eli, "The Drafting of Treaties for the Protection of Investment", *British Institution of International law and comparative law quarterly*, London, 1962, n° 3, p. 27

60/86 International Law Commission (UNO New York), *Yearbook of the International Law Commission* (ILC), 1975, vol. ii, p. 61

62/88 Eduardo JIMENEZ DE ARÉCHAGA, *International law in the past Third of a century*, Academy of International Law, The Hague, Netherlands, *Collected Courses*, 1978, p. 159-1

65/114 KOHONA, Palitha, "Investment Protection Agreements : An Australian Perspective", *Journal of World Trade Law*, 1987, n° 79, p. 82

71/123 BROCHES, Aron, "The Convention on the Settlement of Investment Disputes : Some Observations on Jurisdiction", *The Columbia Journal of Transnational Law*, vol. 5, n° 1, 1966, p. 272

75/134 STERN, Brigitte, "Un petit pas de plus : L'installation de la société civile dans l'arbitrage CIRDI entre Etat et investisseur", *Revue de l'arbitrage*, LITEC, Paris, n° 1/2007, page 10

83/149 Commission du droit international (CDI) de l'organisation des Nations Unies, *Rapport de l'Assemblée générale*, 53° session, supplément n° 10, A 56/10, p. 87

92/189 LIEBESKIND, Jean-Christophe, "The legal Framework of Swiss International Trade and Investments, Part II Protection", *The Journal of World Investment and Trade*, Geneva, 2006, Vol. 7, n° 4, p. 491

123/246 *Les Novelles, Corpus Juris Belgici*, Brussels, Larcier, 1931, Tome III, Sociétés commerciales, n° 5208

125/247 MAKAROV, A, «Conception du droit international privé d'après la doctrine et la pratique russes», The Hague Academy Collected Courses, La Haye, NIJHOFF Martinus, *Reports*, 1931, p. 523

129/253 BROCHES, Aron, "The convention on the settlement of investment disputes between States and nationals of other States", The Hague Academy Collected Courses, Martinus NYHOFF, 1972, volume 136, p. 358

131/254 ZEKOS, Georgios I., "Finance and Investment in Globalization", *The Journal of World Investment*, Geneva, February 2003, vol. 4, n° 1, p. 85

158/293 DELAUME, Georges, «Droit de l'investissement : vers un droit international de l'investissement direct étranger», *Journal de Droit International*, Paris, 1982, n° 75, p. 801 (International Law Journal)

161/303 SACERDOTI Giorgio, "Bilateral treaties and multilateral agreements on investment protection", Collected Courses of the Hague Academy of International Law, The Hague, 1997, p. 308

175/330 The American Law Institute, "Restatement of Foreign Relations Law of the United States", Philadelphia, 1965, para 165.2

176/330 LIEBESKIND, Christophe, "The Legal Framework of Swiss International Trade and Investments, Part I Promotion", *The Journal of World Investment & Trade*, 2006, vol. 7, n° 3, p. 339

178/331 VASCANNIE, Stephen, "The fair and equitable Treatment Standard in International Investment Law and Practice", *British Yearbook of International Law*, 1999, p. 139

185/338 JUILLIARD, Patrick, "Investissements", *Annuaire français du droit international*, Paris, 1992, p. 803 (French annual Review of International Law)

197/366 The Hague Academy Collected Courses, The Hague, Edition Sijthoff, Leyden, 1961, p. 379 (Courses Reports, Academy of International Law, The Hague, Netherlands) p. 379

200/369 CHRISTIE, G, "What constitutes a taking of property under international law", *British yearbook international law*, 1962, p. 307

210/376 VERWEY, Delano R. & SCHRIJVER, Nico, The taking of foreign property under international law: A new legal perspective?", *Netherlands Yearbook of International Law*, 1984, pp. 17-19

216/385 VILKOW, Anatoli, "Nationalisation and International Law", *Soviet Yearbook of International Law*, 1960, p. 67

218/388 LABUSCHAGNE, J, "Compensation for Expropriation in International law", *Speculum juris*, 1967, p. 5

245/412 JUILLARD, Patrick, "Investissements", *Annuaire français de droit international (AFDI)*, Paris, 1992, n° 38, pp. 806

261/451 NGUYEN, Huu-Truu, "La Suisse et les Investissements", *Revue générale de droit international public*, june 1988, pp. 654-657

264/456 KAMTO, Maurice, "La notion du contrat d'Etat", *Revue de l'arbitrage*, Paris, Janvier 2003, pp. 720-753 ("The concept of a State contract", *Arbitration Review*)

266/460 WEIL, Prosper, "Les clauses de stabilisation ou d'intangibilité insérées dans les accords de développement économique", *Ecrits de droit international*, Paris, Pedone, 1986, pp. 303-327 ("Stabilisation or Intangibility Clauses inserted in Economic Development Agreements", *International Law writings*)

270/461 DAVID, Nicolas, "Les clauses de stabilité dans les contrats pétroliers", *Journal de Droit international*, Editions techniques, Paris, 1986, n° 1. (Stability Clauses in Oil Contracts, International Law Journal, Technical editions)

272/463 KAHN, Philippe, "Contrats d'Etat et nationalisation", *Journal du droit international*, Editions techniques, Paris, 1982, n° 4, p. 857 (State Contracts and Nationalisation, International Law Journal, Technical Editions)

273/464 BERLIN, Dominique, "Les contrats d'Etats et la protection des investissements internationaux", *Droit et pratique du commerce international* (DPCI), Paris, 1987, p. 211 (State Contracts and International Investment Protection, Law of International Practice)

283/473 WAELDE, Thomas, "Stabilizing international investment commitments", *Texas International Law Journal*, Spring 1996, n° 2, p. 245

285/477 LALIVE, Jean Flavien, «Un grand arbitrage pétrolier entre un Gouvernement et deux sociétés privées étrangères: *Arbitrage Texaco*

Calasiatic c/ Gouvernement Lybien», *Journal de droit international (JDI)*, 1977, volume 104, n° 2, p. 342

289/479 VERHOEVEN, Jos, Journal de "Droit international des contrats et Droit des gens", *Revue belge de droit international*, January 1978, p. 223 (*Belgian Review of International Law*, January 1978)

293/482 SHIHATA, John, "Applicable Law in international Arbitration", *The World Bank in a changing World, Selected Essays and Issues*, Vol. II, Leiden, 1995, p. 601

297/494 DAVID, René, *L'arbitrage dans le commerce international*, Economica, Paris, 1982, p. 9 (Arbitration in International Commerce)

299/496 SCHOKKAERT, Jan, *Rechtskundig Weekblad* (Legal Weekly), Antwerpen, Uitgeverij Intersentia, 1999/2000, n° 38, 20 May 2000, p. 1304

307/504 VAN HOUTTE, Hans, "De 'amiable composition' en de nieuwe arbitragewet", *Rechtskundig Weekblad*, 36ste jaargang, 1972, n° 16, p. 739 ("Amiable Composition" and "the new Arbitration Law", *Legal Weekly*).

308/509 CRAIG, W. Laurence, PARK, William W., PAULSSON, Jan, *International Chamber of commerce arbitration*, New York, Oceana publications, 1990, p. 27

310/511 ROMERO, Eduardo Silva, "Quelques brèves observations du point de vue de la Cour Internationale d'arbitrage de la Chambre de Commerce internationale", *Centre de documentation et de recherches de la Cour Internationale d'arbitrage de la Chambre de Commerce International (CCI)*, 2006, p. 332 (International arbitration Court – Litigation regarding Investments)

324/524 CHUKWUMERIJE, Okezie, "ICSID Arbitration sovereign immunity", *Anglo-American Law review*, volume 19/1990, p. 170

327/530 BROCHES, Aron, The Hague Academy Collected Courses, 1975, p. 358 (Courses Reports, Academy of International Law, 1975)

332/536 OUAKRAT, Philippe, "La pratique du CIRDI", *Droit et pratique du commerce international*, Tome 13, n° 2, 1987, p. 308 (ICSID Practice, International Commercial Law and Practice)

336/542 SCHMIDT, J.T., *Harvard International Law Journal*, 1979, p. 103

337/544 SCHOKKAERT, Jan & KANGULUMBU, Vincent, "L'arbitrage en droit comparé", *Revue de droit africain*, Editions Recherches et Documentation Juridiques Africaines, (R.D.J.A), Jodoigne, Belgique, n° 31, 2004, p. 253 (African Law Review, Jodoigne, Belgium, 2004)

338/546 RAND, William, "ICSID's emerging jurisprudence", *Journal of International Law and Politics*, vol. 19, 1986, p. 57

368/594 KOHLHAMMER, *Zeitschrift für ausländisches öffentliches recht und Völkerrecht*, Band 42, p. 507 (Review of Foreign Public Law and Private Law)

381/637 SCHOKKAERT, Jan, "Analyse juridique de l'accord belgo zaïrois du 1er juillet 1985, sur le transfert de propriété visant des biens d'habitation situés au Zaïre", *Revue de droit international et de droit comparé*, June 2002, p. 348 (Legal Analysis of the Belgium-Zaïre Agreement of 1 July 1985, regarding the Transfer of Property Rights in habitable Assets located in Zaïre)

III. – WEBSITES [*]

Selected per Country/Organisation :

Australia : www.austlii.edu.au/cgi-in/sinodisp/au/other/dfat/treaties/2007/20.html : Page **109**

Belgium : www.diplobel.fgov.be/nl/default.asp : page **117**

Canada : www.international.gc.ca/trade-agreements-accords-commerciaux/menu.asp, www.dfait-maeci.gc.ca/tna-nac/other/invest-en-asp **72/126**

Congo (RDC) : www.anapi.org/8_raisons.html : **29/39**

Egypt : www.gafinet.net : **33/45**

Germany : www.bmwi.de/BMWI/Navigation/aussenwirtschaft,did=194058.html : Page **153**

ICA /ICC (International Court of arbitration of the International Chamber of Commerce) www.iccwbo.org/court/arbitration/id 4399/index.html : **309/510**

ICJ (International Court of Justice) www.icj-cij.org/docket/index.php : **15/20**

ICSID : www. worldbank.org/icsid/Index.jsp : **59/83**

Italy : www.esteri.it : page **161**

LCIA (London Court of arbitration) : www. Lcia-arbitration.com : **347/553**

NAFTA (North American Free Trade Agreement) : NAFTA (North American Free Trade Agreement) : www.nafta-se-alena.org **191/357**

Netherlands : http ://www.ez.nl/content.jsp?objectid=147333&rid=151340 : page **167**

Sweden : www.sida.jsp?d = 108& language=en_US

UNCTAD (United Nations Commission for Trade and development) : www.unctadxi.org/templates/Docsearch_779.aspx : **64/105**

---

[*] Numbers refer to footnotes and to numbers of the pages of this work :
f.i. Canada : 72 = number of footnote; 126 = number of page of this work

IV. – Cases

	pages
Aguas de Tunari v. Bolivia, ICSID (2002)	134
Allegheny Ludlum Corp v. United States, 24 USCIT 452, 112 F. Supp. 2d 1141 (2000)	584
Allied Pacific v. US, 22 Dec. 2008, Case no. 8-138	580
Alloy Piping Products Inc. v. US and Ta Chen Stainless Steel Pipe, Defendant-Intervener (2008)	584
Altx, Inc. v. United States, 370 F.3d 1108, 1116 (Fed. Cir. 2004)	590
Amco Asia v. Indonesia (1981) ICSID	323/275
American Manufacturing & Trading Corporation (AMT) v. Republic of Congo	44
Ames True Temper v. US, USCIT Case no. 5-00581, (2008)	582
Ass'n of Data Processing Serv. Org., *Inc. v. Camp*, 397 U.S. 150, 153 (1970)	591
Atl. Sugar, *Ltd. v. United States*, 744 F.2d 1556, 1562 (Fed. Cir. 1984)	589
Avenues in Leather, Inc. v. United States, 317 F.3d 1399 (Fed. Cir. 2003)	587
Barcelona Traction, Light and Power Company Limited, Judgment I.C.J. Reports 1970	20
British Steel PLC v. United States, 20 CIT 663, 699, 929 F. Supp. 426, 445 (1996)	584
Clarke, 479 U.S. at 399	591
Compania del Desarollo de Santa Elena (CDSE) v. Costa Rica, ICSD ARB96/1	362
Consol. v. Fed. Mar. Comm'n, 383 U.S. 607, 620 (1966)	590
Consol. Edison Co. v. NLRB, 305 U.S. 197, 229 (1938)	589
Consol. Edison Co. v. NLRB, 305 U.S. 97 (1928)	390
DaimlerChrysler Corp. v. United States, 442 F.3d 1313, 1321 (Fed. Cir. U.S. 225, 233-37 (1927)	587
Davidson v. New Orleans (1877) 96 US 97, 24 L.Ed 616	384
Electronica Sicula, S.p.A (Elsi), Judgment I.C.J. Reports (1989), p. 66	169, 272, 353
Elkem Metals etc. v. U.S., USCIT Case no. 99-00628 (2008)	586
Exxon Shipping Company v. Baker, 128 S.Ct.2605 (2008)	592
Fedax v. Venezuela (1997) ICSID	304

TABLE OF AUTHORITIES 691

FLEXA v. SENEGAL (1988) ICSID	287
GOETZ v. Burundi	631
Home Products International v. US, USCIT Case no. 07-00103 (7 April 2008)...	577
Huaiyin Foreign Trade Corp. (30) v. United States, 322 F.3d 1369, 1374 (Fed. Cir. 2003)	589
Husteel v. US, 23 Dec. 2008, Case no. 8-139	579
ICSID, Case no. ARB/03/11, p. 3 and subs....................	308
ICSID, Case no. ARB/81/1	322
ICSID, Case no. ARB/99/7 537,	310
International Custom Products v. US, USCIT Case no. 07-00318 ...	584
Japan Whaling Ass'n v. Am. Cetacean Society, 478 US 221, 230 (1986)...	590
Joy Mining Machinery v. Egypt (2003) ICSID	308
Kelo v. City of New London, (2005) 545 U.S. 469...............	366
Lichtenstein v. Guatemala, (ICJ) 1955, Nottebohm case...........	228
Loewen v. U.S.	352
Lösinger & C° Case, Cour Permanente de Justice Internationale (CPSI), 1936, Série C, number 78	493
Lujan v. Defenders of Wildlife, 504 U.S. 555, 560-61 (1992).......	591
Malaysian Historical Salvors Sdn v. Malaysia (ARB 05/10) ICSID	83
McLaughlin v. Florida (1964) 379 US 184, 13 L.Ed2d, 222	392
METALCLAD Company v. Mexico, ICSID (2000)	351
Mitchell v. Democratic Republic of the Congo, ICSID (2000).......	310
Mittal Steel v. U.S. slip opinion 8-03.........................	582
Moore v. City of Albany 98 N.Y. 396, 440 Black's Law Dictionary, West Publishing Company, 1951, St. Paul Minn	397
Morocco v. HOLIDAY INN (1973) ICSID	282
NSK Corporation v. Fag Italia, Consol Court No. 06-334 (2008)...	584
O'Brien v. Cseh (1983) 148CA3d957	391
Ohio Bell Tel. Co v. Public Utilities Com (1939) 301 US392, 81 L.Ed 1093, 1102...	390
Olive Proration etc. v. Agric. Prorate Com (1941) 17 C2d 204, 210 .	390
P.S. Chez Sydney LLC v. US International Trade Commission and US Customs Service, Court Case no. 02-00365, 24 January 2008	580
Pam v. US, USCIT Case no. 04-00082, (2008)...................	591

Panevezis/Saldutiskis Railway Case, Permanent International Court of Justice, (PCIJ), Judgment of 28 february 1939, série A/B, Fascicule no. 75.	23
Republic Ins. Co. v. Cunningham, Tex. Civ. App. 62 S.W. 2d 339, 343	220
Revere Copper and Brass (subsidiary of the US Company) and the investment insurer "Overseas Private Investment Corporation (OPIC)"	594
Royal Thai Government, Sahavirya Industries v. US Consolidated, USCIT Case 02-00026	584
SALINI Costruttori S.p.A. v. Morocco (2001) ICSID	91, 306
Schott Optical Glass, Inc. v. United States, 750 F.2d 62, 64 (Fed. Cir. 1984)	587
Sherri N. Boynton. v. US, USCIT Case 06-00095	583
Soabi v. Senegal (1984), ICSID	287
Texaco/Calasiatic v. Libya (1977), ICSID	478
ThyssenKruppAcciai etc. v. US (2008) USCIT, Case no. 07-00390	590
Tjianjin Magnesium Inc. (TMI) v. US. and US Magnesium, Case 8.01, (2008)	580
Totes-Isotoner v. US, USCIT case no. 07-0001 (2008)	590
Trans-Oceanic Oil Corp. v. Santa Barbara (1948) 85 C.A. 2d776	390
United States ex rel. Joseph v. Cannon, 642 F.2d 1373	591
United States v. Stone & Downer Co., 274 Court no. 02-00520 Page 5, U.S. 225, 233-37 (1927)	587
U.S. Steel v. U.S., USCIT Case no. 07-00271 (2008)	584
Volkswagen of America, Inc. v. U.S., 18 Dec. 2008, Case no. 8-137.	580
Warner Lambert v. U.S., USCIT Consolidated Case no. 02-00520 (2008)	587
Wimbledon Case, by France, Italy, Britain, Japan and Poland against Germany, per PCIJ, Ser. A., No. 1, 1923	479
Zhejiang Native Products etc. v. U.S., Case no. 06-0234 (2008)	589

INDEX (*)

A

AALCC : 106
Abidjan
  CCJI : 519
abuse
  of power : 503
ACP : 81-82, 84
acquisition of capital goods : 5
ad hoc
  arbitration : 145, 165-166, 177, 184, 203, 207, 497-498, 511, 606, 612
  conventional settlements : 119
ad probationem sed non ad validitatem : 544
additional facility rules : 552
  consent : 601
ADM : 306
administration
  expenses : 506
Administrative Contracts : 456
administrative decree
  cancellation : 541
Admissibility of Evidence : 382
adversary fashion : 42
Aeropacific : 324
Affimet : 639
affinity : 236
Africa : 2, 35, 48-49, 116, 274, 517
African : 28, 37, 57, 80-81, 106, 109, 125, 252, 498, 512, 518, 530, 598, 628, 649
Afro-Asiatic Model : 106
Agboyibo : 537
agreements
  international : 59, 61

(*) References are to page numbers.

Particular : 458
Specific : 458
Agrément : 41, 653
Agricultural Products Ltd : 419
Aguas Argentinas et Aguas de Santa Fe : 135
Aguas de Tunari v. Bolivia : 134
Alcoa : 541
ALENA : 85
Algeria : 195
Alloy Piping Products Inc. v. US : 584
Amadio : 251
AMCO ASIA : 275, 278, 323, 393, 547
Amerasinghe case : 419
American : 12, 48-49, 76, 85, 103, 121, 123-124, 126, 137, 140, 142, 151, 173, 200, 206, 208, 219, 230, 240, 275, 278, 286, 296, 299, 330, 350, 498, 524
  law : 594
American Law Institute, The : 330
American Manufacturing & Trading Corporation : 44, 420
Ames True Temper v. US : 582
Amex International : 632
amiable
  compositeur : 516
  composition : 120, 502, 504
  compositors : 516
Amiable compositeur : 516
Amiable composition : 504
amiable settlement for disputes : 145
amici curiae : 134-138
AMT : 44-45, 350, 420
ANAPI : 37-38, 657
annulled
  calculation of indemnification : 552
annulment : 312, 550-551
anticipatory
  consent : 3, 46, 53, 62, 93, 102, 109, 120, 145-146, 149, 166, 176, 182-184, 188, 204, 207, 541, 545, 602
anti-dumping : 565-567, 569
Antwerp : 3, 17, 254
appeal : 395, 583
  appointment of arbitrators : 606

CCJA : 519
compensation : 417
condemnation : 352
delay : 608
France : 610
ICSID decision : 513
intentional exclusion : 550
nationality : 30, 60, 102, 199, 222
public international law : 466
rules : 598
applicable law : 29, 92, 200, 347, 449, 467, 470-471, 488, 497, 602
avoidance of domestic law : 468
Belgian model convention : 597
choice : 501
Denmark : 610
interpretation : 454
parties' choice : 502
selection : 593
approval : 22, 74, 100, 280-281, 307, 317, 425, 622, 657-658
Arab Republic of Egypt : 45-46, 511, 545
Arab Users' Council : 554
arbitral
  jurisprudence : 2, 6, 246, 628
  procedures : 3
arbitration
  ad hoc dispute resolution : 522
  arbitration tribunal
    abuse of power : 551
    confidentiality : 501
  benefits : 504
  clause interpretation : 547
  consent : 539
  cost : 505
  definition : 496
  discriminatory : 505
  Institute of the Chamber of Commerce in Stockholm : 183
  institutional : 498
  international : 62
  nationality : 494
  of Civil and Commercial Issues : 46

proceedings : 3, 102, 141, 154, 313, 323, 435, 511, 648, 655
  scope : 153, 512
  specific violation : 535
  subsidiaries : 546
  tribunal : 13, 45-46, 62, 115, 122, 134, 165, 175-178, 207, 218, 276, 278-280, 283, 305, 308, 393, 415, 417, 442-444, 451, 470, 476, 479, 495, 515, 534, 536, 631, 643
  types : 497
  waiver : 558
arbitrator
  as private judge : 495
  jurisdiction : 495
  nationality : 505
  nationals : 500
  replacement : 560
Argentina : 111
Armenia : 268
article 25(1) : 177, 445
article 25(2)b : 43, 45, 149, 202, 207-208, 253, 274, 276, 281, 297, 437, 447, 527, 530-533, 538, 542, 546, 639, 648
article 25(a) : 525
ASEAN : 99-100, 102
Asia : 2, 35, 116, 125, 274
Asian : 37, 57, 80, 109, 320, 339, 430, 598, 628
Asian-African Consultative Committee : 106
Asia-Pacific Users Council : 554
associated activities : 5, 341, 346
Australia : 109, 118, 300-301, 426-427, 439, 484, 620
Austria : 230
Austrian : 230, 371
awards
  exequatur : 548

B

balance of payments : 1, 8, 39, 424-425, 428-430, 604
Balance of Payments Compilation Guide : 8
bankruptcy : 406
Barcelona Traction : 20, 119, 168, 185, 187, 196, 248, 258, 260-262, 264-265, 267, 330, 332, 535
Barge : 503

INDEX 697

Battifol : 242
Belgian : 2, 66, 85, 185, 195-196, 262, 265-266, 287, 295, 441-442, 494, 632, 640
    francs : 651
Belgium : 17, 21, 23, 85, 116, 122, 148, 187, 196, 223, 244, 261-262, 425, 486, 548, 606
Belgo-Luxemburg Economic Union : 72, 117
benchmarks
    discrimination : 577
benefits : 39, 55, 61-62, 165, 206, 228-229
    corporation : 219
    fiscal : 39
    naturalisation : 236
    physical persons : 90, 219
Benin : 518
Berlin : 464, 476, 498
Bernard : 548
bilateral investment treaty : 14, 16, 60, 79, 85, 197, 208
bills of exchange : 304-306, 313, 424
Bi-national Panel : 579
Bin-Cheng : 375-376
birth : 232, 236, 367
    nationality : 230
BIT : 79
BITs : 2, 16, 69, 89, 103, 195, 303, 427-428, 548
    Argentine-Uruguay : 93
    Australia-Argentina : 82, 117
    Australia-China : 110
    Australia-Mexico : 109, 111-112, 409, 619
    Australia-Poland : 110, 117, 426, 484
    Australia-Sri Lanka : 110, 113, 345
    Belgium-Burundi : 643, 647
    Belgium-China : 143, 170, 266, 410
    Belgium-Congo : 659
    Belgium-Croatia : 124, 249
    Belgium-India : 487
    Belgium-Kazakhstan : 487
    Belgium-Khazakstan : 597
    Belgium-Malaysia : 425
    Belgium-Montenegro : 124
    Belgium-Uruguay : 3, 80, 85, 124
    Belgium-Burundi : 632

Bleu-Korea : 454
Bleu-Uzbekistan : 454
Canada-Croatia : 298
Canada-Hungary : 440
Canada-Mexico : 123
Canada-Peru : 128-129, 154, 228, 357
Canada-Poland : 227
Canada-US : 503
China-Czech Republic : 144, 146
China-Japan : 2-3, 16, 46-47, 50, 69, 80, 83, 85, 104, 113, 116, 127-128, 135, 142, 148, 158, 162, 184, 191, 212, 222, 227, 240, 268, 295, 329, 363, 410, 429, 438, 488, 604
China-Netherlands : 146
China-US : 581
Cyprus-Russia : 184
Egypt-Russia : 184
France-Cambodia : 151
France-Guatemala : 151, 346, 412, 437
France-Mexico : 151, 319, 413, 611, 634
France-Nicaragua : 151
France-Singapore : 249
France-Slovenia : 151, 319, 611, 623
France-Tunisia : 485
France-Uganda : 148, 409
Germany-China : 246
Germany-India : 486
Germany-Nicaragua : 612
Germany-Russia : 182
Guatemala-France : 484
Hong Kong-Sri Lanka : 419
Hungary-Russia : 181
India-Australia : 620
Italy-Nicaragua : 221, 246, 428
Morocco-Belgium : 224
Netherlands-Algeria : 167
Netherlands-Armenia : 167
Netherlands-Bahrein : 167
Netherlands-Bolivia : 135
Netherlands-Cambodia : 167
Netherlands-China : 142

INDEX 699

    Netherlands-Costa Rica : 221, 621
    Netherlands-Laos : 435
    Netherlands-Russia : 183
    Norway-Russia : 181
    Russia-Egypt : 180
    Russian Federation-Cyprus : 180
    Serbia-Switzerland : 192
    Spain-Nigeria : 598
    Sweden-India : 268
    Switzerland-Algeria : 191
    Switzerland-Azerbaidjan : 191
    Switzerland-Guatemala : 190
    Switzerland-Kuwait : 486
    Switzerland-Lithuania : 194
    Switzerland-Malaysia : 190
    Switzerland-Montenegro : 192
    Switzerland-Panama : 248
    UEBL-Bangladesh : 436
    UEBL-Philippines : 249
    UEBL-Uruguay : 213
    UK-Lesotho : 319
    UK-Salvador : 248
    USA-Congo : 656
    USA-Uruguay : 213, 321, 342, 359, 430
    USA-Zaire : 205, 410
    US-Estonia : 248, 426
    US-Uruguay : 427
    US-Zaire : 341, 429, 436
    US-Zaire BIT : 420
Blanco : 502
BLEU : 72, 117, 435-436, 441, 487-488
block
    capital outflow : 604
Board members
    majority : 129
Board of General Appraisers : 577
BOCG : 8
bonds : 9-10, 58, 188, 202, 220, 229, 233-234, 243, 298, 302-303, 468, 536
    naturalisation : 235
Brazil : 79, 91, 247, 315, 356, 366, 404

British Common Law : 384, 396-397
Broches : 123, 253, 523, 530
Brunei : 99
Bulgaria : 403
Burkina Faso : 148, 518
Burns : 28, 226, 385
Burundi : 49, 421, 633, 640, 646-647
business enterprise : 5, 52, 298

C

Cairo Regional Center for International Commercial Arbitration : 46
calculation of indemnities : 56
calculation of interest : 42, 172
California : 2, 17, 240, 296
CAMCA : 121
Cameroon : 518
Canada : 57, 85, 90, 95, 110, 116, 118, 123, 125-126, 128, 154, 156, 185, 187, 189, 196, 209, 261-262, 264, 266-267, 299, 348, 356-357, 440, 620
cancellation
  covert : 474
capital
  inflow : 1-2, 5-6, 8-13, 15, 18, 35-36, 39, 44, 48, 51, 54, 56, 58, 65, 73-76, 83, 94-96, 101, 112-113, 125, 162, 169, 174, 184, 210, 253, 257, 260, 262, 266, 277, 279, 285, 287, 290, 293-297, 300, 303, 305, 308, 315, 320-321, 325, 337, 350, 375, 385, 389, 405, 411, 423-424, 427, 452, 462, 522, 527, 529, 531, 537, 604, 619, 632, 650, 652
  outflow : 65, 116, 424, 430
Carreau : 8, 16, 308
case law : 521, 528
  review : 178
CCI : 125, 158, 445, 498, 501, 505, 625, 655
  applicable law : 596
  costs : 505
CCJA : 125, 517
Centre for Arbitration and Mediation : 125
CEPINA : 125, 597
Ceskoslovakia Obchodni Bank : 445
Ceylon : 403
Chad : 518

Chamber
  of Arbitration London : 554
Charter of Economic Rights and Duties of States : 450
Chile : 79
China : 72, 80, 116, 142, 200, 220, 266, 356, 382, 384, 410
Chinese : 142, 266
choice
  between State Courts and Arbitration : 573
  of Forum USCIT : 570
  of law : 396, 594
Christie : 369
Chukwumerije : 525
citizens : 27, 109, 219-220, 330, 366, 385, 545
Civil
  Code : 379
  Law : 378-379
  Status Registry : 17
claim : 11, 23, 25, 27-28, 30, 52, 91, 106, 132-133, 138, 165, 182, 196-198, 201, 215-216, 226, 234, 236, 253, 258, 262-263, 266, 278, 297, 301, 308, 366, 372, 414, 436, 439, 444, 465, 518, 536
  filing : 446
  legal : 176
  nationality : 226
  reasonable : 279
Claims : 28
clean hands : 30
Climate Change, Convention : 356
CNUDCI : 511, 614
Coalition of the Willing : 422
codified usages : 595
Colonia Protocol : 315
COMESA : 48-50
Comité européen de coopération juridique : 17
commercial
  arbitration : 539
  corporation : 529
  terms : 310
commercial agreement : 311
Commercial Arbitration and Mediation Center for the Americas : 121

Common
    Council Court : 554
    Court of Arbitration and Justice : 125
    Court of Justice and Arbitration : 517, 519
    Law : 247, 378-380, 384, 397, 420
    Market of the South : 315, 404
    Market of the States of Southern and Eastern Africa : 529
Common Court of Justice and Arbitration : 517
common law : 247
Commoros : 49
Commune of Guadalcazar : 87, 416
Compania del Desarollo de Santa Elena (CDSE) : 362
compensation : 28, 52-53, 60, 96-98, 101, 107, 119, 145, 164, 171, 181-184, 188, 194, 198, 202, 213, 226, 260, 262, 272, 306, 344, 365, 410, 428, 430, 432, 436, 450, 475, 601, 631, 636, 645
    adequate : 51, 101, 365-366, 369, 379, 385, 388, 403
    interpretation : 534
    standard : 403
compensation
    adequate : 379
concession contract : 479
conciliation : 98-99, 102, 108, 120, 122, 183, 188, 195, 199, 250, 305, 496, 520-521, 525, 552, 599
Conciliation Commission : 121, 599
Confiscation : 370
conflicts
    interests only : 534
    international public law : 471
    interstate : 67, 110, 115, 158, 170, 187, 233, 247, 250, 252-253, 258, 263, 275, 282, 284, 295, 305, 307-308, 421, 432, 445, 488, 492, 494, 523, 596
    of laws
        interstate : 597
    of laws, rules : 471
conflicts
    interstate : 274
Congo : 37-38, 41, 49, 375, 475, 518, 536, 637
Congolese : 30, 37-41, 43-45, 252, 475, 528-529, 536, 542
consanguinity : 236
Conseil de l'Europe : 17

INDEX 703

consent
  acceptable : 539
  arbitration : 525
  of the parties : 540
  to arbitration : 508
conservation of depleting natural resources : 131
constraints
  environmental : 355
  legal : 7, 214
  public purpose : 366
  transport : 155
consular : 19-21, 24-25, 28, 30-31, 65, 196, 222, 241
Consulate : 18
content
  good faith : 615
  remedies : 487
  treatment : 54, 71, 80, 89, 113, 117, 130-131, 156, 253, 294, 331-333, 337, 339, 341, 346, 348-350, 537, 624
contracts
  administrative : 456
  law between parties : 468
  State : 456
control : 8, 10, 15-16, 18, 24, 29, 43, 49-50, 58, 90, 96, 99, 101, 105, 112-113, 129, 135, 154-155, 163, 185, 189-192, 202-206, 209, 215, 238, 243-244, 249-250, 253, 257-260, 262-264, 267, 286, 288-290, 322, 341, 526-528, 533, 602, 619, 650
  corporate : 261, 290
  corporate nationality : 529
  foreign : 547
  interaction with nationality : 105
  percentage : 531
  request for annulment : 551
  second degree : 287
  theory : 261
  voting rights : 113
control
  corporate : 261, 291
convention : 2, 20, 24, 44, 103-104, 108, 126, 143, 188, 190, 208, 217, 224, 234, 253, 257, 275, 314, 338, 355, 429, 433, 483, 497, 546, 634
  draft : 79, 105
  intangibility : 461

jurisdiction : 495
multilateral : 433, 520
State Contracts : 459
World Bank : 251
Convention on the Settlement of Investment Disputes between States : 93
Convention on the Settlement of Investment Disputes between States and Nationals of Other States : 599
conventional international law : 137
convertible currency : 51-52, 172, 181, 213, 389, 404, 426, 428, 633
corporate exception
nationality : 236, 526
Costa Rica : 221, 362, 427, 621
Cotonou Convention : 81-82
scope : 82
Cotonou Protocol
applicable law : 94
Countervailing Duties : 565
Court
for the Rights of Man : 405
of International Trade : 564, 566
courts
international : 30
Craig : 509, 511
creeping : 636
creeping expropriation : 114, 372, 636, 644, 649
CSOB : 446-447
Curaçao : 304
currencies
general : 572
currency : 1, 95, 171, 213, 321, 389, 404, 415, 424, 426, 429, 431, 604, 633, 651
currency
convertible : 562
customary international law : 114, 328
customary law : 234
Customs : 39
Customs Court : 576
Cyprus : 180
Czechoslovakia
subrogation : 445

INDEX 705

D

damages : 20, 25, 28, 60-61, 85, 98, 107, 118, 205, 215, 306, 312, 316, 350, 352, 389, 393, 414, 418, 431, 601, 636
- interpretation : 534
- legal services : 536
- pecuniary : 416
- punitive : 591-592

Danish : 409, 623
Darussalam : 99
David : 461, 467, 469-470, 478
David, René : 494
de facto : 635-636
- associatons : 154

dealership contracts : 12
Déclaration des Droits de l'Homme et du Citoyen : 365
defense statement : 561
Definitions : 37, 48, 91, 94, 106, 126, 142, 154, 159, 161, 167, 174, 179, 184, 200, 204, 209, 321, 368, 432, 634
- Canada : 92, 126, 200, 227-228, 430
- China : 142
- investments : 294, 654
- legislative systems : 494
- Sweden : 184
- Switzerland : 189

Delcredere : 434
Delaume : 293, 538-539
Delaware, USA : 323
delays : 42, 322, 353, 613, 658
- diplomatic channels : 609

Delbez : 30, 389
Democratic Republic of the Congo : 649
denial of benefits : 16, 22, 38-41, 51, 54, 56, 61, 63, 75, 90, 96, 116, 125, 163, 214-215, 236, 290, 329, 345, 409, 637
Denmark : 484, 606, 610, 621
Derains : 512
derivatives : 303
developing countries : 1, 9, 68-69, 73, 103, 105, 118, 125, 204-205, 208-209, 252, 274, 297, 316-317, 319, 322, 329, 341, 356, 433, 467, 488, 523, 651
developing States : 72

development cooperation : 11, 82, 205, 209, 293, 651
dictum : 264, 330, 637, 647
dies a quo : 42, 53, 172, 181, 216-218, 414, 416, 608, 646, 651
dies ad quem : 172, 181, 414-415, 646, 651
Dillemans : 17
diplomatic : 15, 19-25, 28, 30-31, 65, 195, 198, 259
  channels : 198
    institutional arbitration : 607
  démarches : 603
  intervention : 185, 195
  interventions : 133
  negotiations US : 614
  protection : 163, 186, 222, 265
    Canada : 138
    refusal of protection : 23, 133, 138-139, 169, 195, 198, 222, 236, 240, 257, 261, 265-266
  umbrella : 290
diplomatic protection
  refusal of protection : 196-197, 235-236, 265
direct foreign investor : 7, 9, 38, 68, 304, 654
direct investment
  foreign : 8-9
discrimination : 24, 26, 75, 78, 96, 213, 375-376, 408, 418, 644
discriminatory : 24, 52, 69, 79, 81, 101, 130, 171, 180-181, 214, 237, 321, 341, 345, 347-349, 392, 429
  laws : 450
  legislative : 459
  local measures : 459
disguised : 635-636
dispossess : 633-634
dispossession : 53, 409
dispute : 25, 27, 43, 53, 119, 121, 132-133, 137, 139, 167, 195, 204, 208, 211, 215, 217, 436, 491, 518, 535
  amiable settlement : 542
  amiable solution : 611
  conciliation : 98, 108, 116
  conflicts of law : 597
  decision : 511
  diplomatic solution : 522
  disqualification : 523

economic reality : 536
investment : 138
nationality : 250
nature of : 541
New York Convention : 549
notification : 43
origins : 310
outside factors : 516
permit : 363
point of law : 534
resolution : 121
speed in disposition : 505
verification : 523
when not subject to arbitration : 535
distinguished from nationals : 449
diversity
nationality : 179, 414, 418, 510, 523, 525, 528
doctrinal texts : 13, 328, 337, 367, 372-373, 385-386, 411, 459-460, 462, 465-466, 477-478, 481-482, 494, 499, 504, 535, 551, 634
doctrine : 5, 30, 73, 83, 86-87, 106, 136, 195, 197, 225-226, 245, 254, 259, 293, 308, 332, 375, 397, 403, 410, 414, 416, 419, 463, 474, 590, 636
clean hands : 30
standard of treatment : 347
domestic investors : 320, 327
domestic law : 62, 107, 139, 158, 318, 415, 426, 449
applicable : 451
cancellation : 541
interstate conflicts : 598
State Contracts : 467
domicile : 17-18, 56, 219, 229, 231, 238, 255, 517-518
dominant
interest : 190
nationality : 128, 226-227
double nationality : 38, 105, 203, 223, 252, 655
draft convention : 79
Draft Convention on the Protection of Foreign Property : 78
Droit et pratique du commerce : 65, 147, 452, 464
Ducroire : 434
subrogation : 441
due process : 114, 324, 343, 377-378, 398

due process
  discrimination : 391
  hearing : 390
  of law : 144, 181, 332, 352, 379, 409
  of law
    definition : 400
    denial : 377
  procedural : 380, 399
  substantiality : 381
  substantive : 381, 383
dumping : 581
duration : 7, 10, 83-84, 308, 310, 392, 608-609, 623-624
Dutch : 144, 167, 169, 286, 348, 504, 597, 623
Dutch Antilles : 304
Dutch Institute for Arbitration : 597
Duty to Compensate : 382

E

Earth Summit : 355
East bloc : 404
Eastern bloc : 226
Ebensee : 371
economic : 1-2, 5, 9-10, 13, 22, 35, 37-38, 40, 58, 68-69, 83, 94, 125, 185, 189, 258, 537
  activities : 249, 315
  cooperation : 338, 385
  development : 35-36, 82-84
    ICSID : 521
    State Contracts : 458
  entities : 142
  entity : 528
  legislation : 294
  measures : 431
  nationalisations : 369
  partnership : 84
  quid pro quo : 317
  relations : 75, 293
  rights : 338
  sectors : 327

INDEX 709

   strategy : 36, 77
   surveys : 68
   traditional : 6
   warfare : 119
Ecrits de droit : 460
effective nationality : 227, 231, 252
Egypt : 45-46, 49, 220, 309, 544-545, 619
Electronica Sicula : 169, 272, 353-354
Elkem Metals etc. v. US : 586
ELSI : 169, 272, 353, 643
Embassy : 18, 21
emergency : 60, 418, 421, 633
Emerson : 126
enforcement
   Arbitral Tribunal : 563
   modi : 269
   New York Convention : 556-557
   private rights : 399
English Bill of Rights : 383
enterprises
   national : 24
environment : 1, 40, 118, 124, 173, 178-179, 189, 355-356
environmental protection : 124
equal protection : 391, 395, 398, 590
   definition : 392
equal treatment : 115
Eritrea : 49
establishment : 17, 52, 58, 76, 89, 123, 130, 132, 156, 200, 203, 241, 244-246, 254-255, 276, 281, 289, 320-321, 323, 356, 359, 361, 366, 458, 498, 519
Estonia : 248, 426
estoppel : 587-588
   by judgment : 588
   equitable : 588
   promissory : 588
Ethiopia : 49
EU : 142, 356, 422
Europe : 38, 105, 173
European : 9, 14, 22, 24, 43, 60, 65, 80, 87, 109, 176, 205, 405, 606
European
   countries : 244

formula : 173
practice : 141, 151, 159, 174, 179, 204, 209, 221, 436
Union : 79, 81, 222
Users Council : 554
evidence
    admissibility : 382, 556
ex aequo et bono : 516, 596
exchange control : 425
executive
    position : 90
    positions : 128, 212
executive positions : 128
exeption
    national procedure : 548
exhaustion
    of local remedies : 508, 539, 575
experts : 7, 42, 55, 80, 135, 185, 211, 240, 359, 372, 502, 651
Expropriation : 344, 368
expropriation : 40-42, 47, 52, 101, 107, 144, 147, 160-161, 164-165, 171, 180-183, 187, 194, 213, 312, 344, 363, 366, 368, 370, 408, 475, 631
extraterritoriality : 371
Exxon Shipping Company v. Baker : 592
Eyskens : 254

F

fair and equitable treatment : 41, 114, 328
    content : 331
fair warning : 391
false documents : 30
family law : 510
FCN : 109, 113-114, 207
FEDAX : 304
Federal Register : 23, 85, 266, 548
    Belgium : 597
fees
    arbitrator : 506
Fifth Amendment : 382
Financial Crises : 406
FIPA : 125-126, 139, 358

fishing expeditions : 564
Flexa : 287
foreign
  currency : 1, 48, 56, 425
  direct investments : 13
    guidelines : 338
  Investment Promotion and Protection Agreements : 125
  law : 449
foreword : 1
forfeiture : 378
fork-in-the-road : 515, 602
Fouchard : 501
Fourteenth Amendment : 382
France : 21, 65, 244, 249, 345, 363, 365, 415, 429, 437, 484, 489, 606, 612
Free Trade
  Agreements : 126
  Commission : 139
freedom from fines : 383
French : 17, 21, 85, 146, 149-150, 152, 249, 318, 329, 346, 365, 415, 429, 437, 483-484, 504, 516, 610, 634, 649
  law : 509
Friedman : 40
Friendship Treaties for Commerce and Navigation : 109
FTC : 140
full protection and security : 114
Füracker : 482, 611-612
futures : 303

G

Gabon : 518
Gaillard : 47, 83, 87-88, 136, 155, 246, 279-282, 479, 482, 513-514, 528, 551, 593, 617, 638, 644
GATT
  services : 537
generalia specialibus non derogant : 513, 545
German : 71, 229, 238, 365, 372, 408, 415, 421, 612
Germans : 221
Germany : 154, 221, 244, 246, 345, 363, 486, 606, 609, 611
Ghana : 527

Goetz : 631-632
Government : 23, 50-53, 74, 83, 86-87, 92, 95, 127, 138, 142, 170, 185, 262, 265, 275, 277, 280, 285, 307, 311, 323-324, 352, 357, 419, 437, 541, 620, 639
government agencies : 572
Government
  as a party : 512
  consent : 599
Grand-Duchy of Luxemburg : 143
Grotius : 546
growth : 1, 9-11, 35-36, 96, 293, 458, 505, 627
Guadalajara : 17
Guadalcazar : 351
guarantees : 2, 29-30, 38, 41, 45-47, 59, 67, 150, 160, 309, 430, 433
  bank : 309
  banks : 310
  minimum : 62
Guatemala : 190-191, 193, 228, 232, 234, 247, 268, 346, 412, 428, 437
Guggenheim : 235
Guinea : 518

H

Havana Chart : 328
health : 86, 123, 131, 173, 178, 356-357, 359
Heckscher : 2
Holiday Inn : 282, 532, 535, 546
Holiday Inns v. Morocco : 546
Hong Kong : 80, 125, 275, 279, 285, 393, 419, 511, 544-545
Hong Kong International Arbitration Centre : 125
host State : 2, 11, 19-21, 24-26, 28-29, 45-46, 62-63, 65, 67, 69, 80-84, 90, 95-98, 104, 107-108, 116, 119, 122, 139, 144, 152, 160, 163, 172-173, 175-176, 180, 183-184, 192, 194, 197-198, 203, 207, 210, 223-224, 264-265, 287, 293, 304, 310, 327, 331, 348, 394, 412, 416, 419, 424, 426, 428, 430-432, 442, 458, 466, 500, 526, 541
  ratification : 541
  restraint : 520
  restrictions on : 460
host States : 58, 67, 116, 155, 433
HULL formula : 403-404
Hungary : 182-183, 440

INDEX 713

I

ICC
  prerequisites : 515
  scope : 509
ICJ : 20, 185, 258, 260, 265, 285, 330
ICSID : 2-3, 27, 43-45, 83, 87, 93, 102, 108, 116, 120, 122-123, 132, 134-135, 137, 145-146, 149, 157-158, 176-177, 182, 194, 197, 208, 218, 225, 250, 252, 258, 275, 278, 281, 285-286, 288-289, 304, 308, 310, 314, 322-323, 350-351, 392-393, 415-416, 420, 437, 440-441, 447, 485, 504, 507, 510, 513, 515, 517-521, 524, 529-530, 532, 535-538, 541, 545-547, 551, 602, 628, 631-632, 634, 639-640, 648, 653, 656, 659
  constraints : 521
  exclusion : 522
  role : 507
  Secretariat : 523
illegal : 19, 30, 169, 264, 307, 414, 643, 645
  act : 387
  acts : 362
  avoidance : 468
  confiscation : 370
  non-recognition of contracts : 469
  taxation : 373
illicit banking activities : 41, 653
IMC : 309
IMF : 8
immunity : 25, 114, 518, 524
  diplomacy : 468
  double : 524
  sovereignty : 524
  theory : 524
implied control : 277
indemnification : 20, 22-23, 28-29, 47, 56, 60-61, 97, 107, 119, 131, 144, 160, 165, 172, 175, 181, 183, 202, 225, 231, 260, 275, 363, 370, 379, 410, 552, 601, 646, 649
  Belgium-Czechoslovakia : 371
indemnity : 22, 41-42, 165, 172, 312, 431, 435, 443, 475, 536, 644
India : 85, 126, 159, 268, 356, 435, 486-487, 620
Indian law : 159
individual property rights : 41, 367
Indonesia
  annulment : 552
  control : 547

public purpose : 99, 275-281, 283, 285-286, 322-323, 340, 375, 393, 476

Industrias Metallurgicas Van Dam CA : 304

Inkopad : 323

Institute of International Law : 470

institutional arbitration : 183-184, 497-499, 507, 606-607, 613

insurance : 38, 84, 86, 172, 177, 220, 294, 389, 431-432, 436-437, 441, 452, 522, 594, 601

insurer : 123, 172, 177, 431-432, 434-435, 437, 442-444, 594

intangibility : 460

 example : 461

 invalidity : 472

 voided clause : 468

interest : 8, 11, 21, 52, 58, 97, 107, 133, 137, 140-141, 159, 171-172, 181, 213, 263, 281, 300, 305, 363, 365, 393, 414-416, 423, 464, 633, 644, 646, 651

 payment : 60

internal law : 67

internal law practice : 595

international : 1-3, 5, 7-9, 11-14, 16, 19, 23-24, 26-30, 36, 40, 57, 60, 65-66, 72-73, 86, 120, 125, 147, 149, 169, 183, 231, 251, 258-259, 293, 338, 355, 358, 369, 385, 418, 433, 443, 449, 451-452, 458, 460-461, 463-464, 466, 470, 473, 477, 479, 482, 494-495, 501-502, 542, 546, 595, 598, 637

 agreement : 74

  most favourable treatment : 454

 arbitral tribunal : 182

 arbitration : 93, 101, 297

  Australia : 115

 arbitration institutions : 120

 Arbitration London Court : 553

 Centre for the Settlement of International Disputes : 2, 87

 Chamber of Commerce : 3, 125, 203, 442, 505, 509, 523, 539, 573, 596, 600, 648

  rules : 509

  rules of arbitration : 601

 common law : 13, 87, 212, 327-328, 337, 451, 615-617

  application : 452

  conventions : 466

  rudimentary : 452

 convention : 442

 conventions

  scope : 450

 Court of Arbitration : 509

Court of Justice : 20, 26, 28, 70, 136, 168, 175, 185, 196, 228, 258, 285, 330, 353, 386, 479, 481, 522, 546, 550, 603, 608, 643, 647
Dispute Resolution Centre : 121
economic relations : 470
fora : 84
institutions : 337
investments : 13
investor : 108
judiciary tribunal : 195
law : 47, 60, 67, 70, 76, 87, 158, 233, 264-265, 297, 315-316, 324, 336-337, 376, 384, 420, 452, 537
   customary : 343
   environment : 362
   foundation : 465
   general principles : 452
   minimum standard : 93
   mixed regimen : 467
   practice : 113
   principle : 331, 524
   right to choose : 467
   rule : 328
   rules : 107, 161, 278
   standards : 341
   State Contracts : 486
Law Association : 450
Law Commission : 149, 615
legal order : 455
minimum standard : 329-330, 333, 347, 349
Monetary Fund : 8, 429-430
practice : 94, 411, 521, 527
procedure : 53
public law
   axiom : 471
public order : 478
Reconstruction and Redevelopment Bank : 543
relations : 1, 65, 133, 149, 196, 375, 424, 497, 620
responsibility : 98, 127, 148, 320, 330, 333, 337
rules : 451
standard : 338
trade law : 184

treaties : 455, 590
internationalisation : 67, 180, 267
  domestic law : 470
  effect of BITs : 452
  ideal : 480
  in parallel wih State Contracts : 485
  key clause : 471
  questionable protection : 475
  significance : 470
internationalised
  indispensability : 475
interpretation : 14, 43, 88, 106, 138-139, 153, 158-159, 175-176, 178-179, 183, 190, 233, 258, 278, 282, 287, 445, 464, 514, 521, 532, 534, 549, 605, 607, 610, 615-616, 625, 632
Interstate Acts : 455
interveners : 584
intervention : 20-23, 26, 28, 134, 136, 222, 263, 280, 411, 442-443, 655
  by national courts : 550
  exception for execution measures : 548
intuitu personae : 324
invest : 2, 35, 57, 128, 277, 287
investment
  amount
    minimum : 38
  Code : 37, 39, 41, 252, 311-312, 475, 652, 654
  codes : 13, 35, 37, 57, 62, 71, 274, 316, 319, 322, 458, 542, 622, 624
  direct : 70
  licence : 38, 50, 129, 532
  limitation : 96
  promotion Agency : 50
  volume : 69
investments : 1-3, 5-11, 13-14, 16, 18, 24, 28-30, 35, 37-38, 41, 57, 59, 61, 66, 68, 70, 73, 80, 85, 95, 107, 125, 154, 173, 182, 193, 202, 215, 300-301, 314-315, 404, 423, 429, 433, 441, 452, 522, 654, 657
  admittal : 322
  applicable law : 449
  definition : 6
  direct : 68
  foreign : 6, 59-61, 127
  international : 65

INDEX 717

   list : 454
   new forms : 538
   other : 39
   private : 5
   promotion : 518
   public utility : 39
   scope : 111
   Ukraine : 58
   World Bank : 338
investors : 1-3, 6, 8, 10-11, 13, 16, 19, 27, 35, 37, 40, 42, 52-53, 61, 79-80, 85, 96, 101, 113, 116, 120, 125, 154, 192-193, 214-215, 220, 261, 303, 308, 352, 388, 427-428, 430, 432, 454, 458, 483, 487, 543, 547, 632
   basic imperative : 451
   conventions : 453
   defined : 57
   definition : 48, 91, 221
   domestic : 40
   exclusion : 327
   foreign : 56, 58-60, 62-63, 66, 70, 114
   lack of capacity : 523
   local law : 453
   majority : 268
   minimum level of safety : 114
   nationality : 105, 452, 523
   private : 117
   security : 338
IPA : 54, 116
Iran : 421, 637
   State Contracts : 460
Iraq : 421
ISA Spectrum de Argentina : 335
Israel : 421
Italstrade : 306
Italy : 83, 161, 163, 165-166, 221, 244, 267-268, 306, 313, 353, 363, 365, 428, 454, 606, 612, 643
ius soli : 237
Ivory Coast : 519

J

Jamaica : 541, 594
James case : 405
Japan Whaling Ass'n : 590
Jarvin : 512, 517
Jessup : 248
Jimenez de Aréchaga : 88
JMML : 309
Joint Committee : 178
joint venture : 12, 204, 208, 210, 298, 518, 653
joint ventures : 11, 58
Joseph v. Cannon : 591
Journal
  de droit : 72, 293, 477
  of World Investment : 254
Judges
  procedure : 502
judicial
  procedure : 25, 98, 127, 146
  tribunals : 23, 116
judicial procedure : 98
Juillard : 65, 147, 338, 452
jure gestionis : 456, 524
jure imperii : 457, 524
juridical person : 250
jurisdiction : 19, 25, 43-46, 53, 60-61, 75, 86, 97, 99, 108, 116, 120, 122, 133-134, 136, 145, 160-161, 164-165, 169, 175, 183, 188, 195, 197-198, 207, 211, 229, 234, 239, 250-252, 271, 274, 278, 282, 287, 312, 314, 327, 365, 386, 440-441, 445-446, 450, 463, 492, 495, 502-503, 513-515, 530, 533, 535, 541, 546-547, 619, 639, 655
  consent : 539
  denial : 544
  dispute directly related : 535
  exemption : 524
  ICC : 511
  ICSID : 304, 532
  ICSID limitation : 521
  immunity : 519
  lack of : 305, 307, 310-311
  legislative : 471

local : 109, 127
nationality : 225
point of law : 534
stabilisation : 462
jus cogens : 478, 617
jus standi : 265, 438-439, 441, 631, 639
Australia : 439
justiciable claim : 105

K

Kahn : 463
Kangulumbu : 544
Kenya : 49, 421
Key Personnel : 175
Klaesstad : 233
Klöckner : 532
Kloeckner : 551-552
Knapp : 385
Knoepfler : 26
know-how : 308
Kohlhammer : 594
Kohona : 114
Korea : 340, 619
Kosovo : 421
Kyoto Protocol : 356

L

labour : 54, 118, 124, 173, 510
Lalive : 477, 532
Latin-American and Caribbean Users Council : 554
Lauterpacht : 73, 76
law : 2-3, 6, 13-14, 19, 23-24, 26-28, 39-41, 45, 47, 49-50, 52-55, 57, 59-60, 73, 86, 88, 123, 141, 161, 201, 203, 221, 247, 259, 268-269, 298-299, 323, 330, 347, 369, 385, 388, 429-430, 433, 453, 455, 482, 503, 546, 548, 594-595, 644, 654
choice of : 455
civil : 443
Egypt : 47
general principle : 465

insurance : 443
international : 25, 27, 40
mixed regimen : 469
municipal : 68
national : 29
notarial : 632
of Treaties : 211
penal : 370
renunciation : 502
rules of conflict : 453
succession : 510
tax : 31
LCIA : 121, 125, 158, 498, 555, 559, 597
   Rules : 555
LDCs : 1-2, 9, 24, 35, 37, 116, 124, 131, 246, 529, 542, 629
   arbitration : 504
least developed countries : 1
Lebanon : 421
legal status : 3, 15, 140, 242, 290, 294, 445
   investments : 467
   stabilisation : 464
legal systems
   national : 47
legislative : 25, 59, 74, 88, 149
   action : 370
   history : 446
   intangibility : 461
LETCO : 533
Letco v. Liberia : 392, 479, 533
lex contractus : 466, 468
lex Gentium : 338
lex mercatoria : 516
   private rules : 595
lex rei sitae : 466, 491
lex specialis : 513, 547, 598
Liberia : 392-393, 533
Libya : 49, 478
licensing : 12
Lichtenstein : 228, 231, 233
licit activity : 41, 653

Liebeskind : 189, 196-197, 330
lift clause
   State Contract : 514
Lillich : 28, 226
limitation : 78, 86, 100, 147-148, 175, 193, 211, 346, 518
   right to nationalise : 477
   stabilisation : 479
limited period
   stabilisation clause : 479
liquidations : 262, 423
litigation
   basis : 495
local law : 319, 408
local tribunals : 25, 46, 60-61, 75, 97, 108-109, 119, 123, 144-146, 160-161, 165, 176, 181, 207, 380, 496
Loewen v. U.S. : 88, 352
Lomé Convention : 81
London
   Court of International Arbitration : 125, 498, 553
   Inter-Bank Offered Rate : 61
longi temporis prescriptio : 394
Lybia v. Texaco : 473

M

Madagascar : 49
MAI : 76, 79-80, 338, 359
majority : 8, 11, 15, 44, 202-203, 259-260, 262-263
   participation : 154
Makarov : 247
Malawi : 49
Malaysia : 99, 425
Malaysian Historical Salvors Sdn v. Malaysia : 83
Mali : 518
management contracts : 12, 302, 314
Mann : 331, 482
manu militari : 323, 649
maritime zone : 147, 318-319, 623
market value : 42, 101, 144, 164-165, 181, 213, 410, 645
Martor : 519

Mauritius : 49
Mayer : 455
means of enforcement
  courts : 396
Mélanges : 471
Mercado Comun del Sur : 315, 404
MERCOSUR : 91, 411
Metalclad : 87, 351, 363, 416, 616
Metalclad v. Federated : 363
Mexican : 87, 351
Mexico : 17, 85, 87, 111, 223, 319, 348, 356, 363, 409, 413, 415, 427, 429, 611, 616, 619
Meyer : 499
Meyers : 211
MFN : 96, 153-154, 171, 193, 212-213, 349
  interpretation : 534
MFP : 345
MIGA : 433-434, 437
Military Court of the Congo : 310
minimum protection : 343
minority : 11, 187, 202
  participation : 154
minority participations : 194
misclassification : 584
Mittal Steel v. U.S. : 582
model convention : 126
  Afro-Asian : 421, 430, 607, 621
  Afro-Asiatic : 408
  Australia : 109
  Belgium : 118, 318, 360, 597, 609, 613, 622, 646
  Canada : 126, 130, 138
  China : 145
  Denmark : 409, 414, 600, 622
  France : 146, 622, 634
  Germany : 153, 182, 411, 453, 482, 624
  India : 159
  Italy : 161
  Netherlands : 167, 622, 624
  Norway : 173, 176, 613
  source : 632

Sweden : 184, 605
Switzerland : 189
UK : 200, 483
United States : 204, 208
US : 409, 411, 415, 453, 482, 549, 610, 614

model conventions : 103

models : 106

modification
  bad faith : 474

monopoly : 81, 413

Montanjees : 8

Montenegro : 124, 195, 421

moral persons : 41, 49, 55, 95, 159, 167-168, 179, 185, 190-191, 220, 640, 650

Morocco : 23, 83, 223-224, 282, 307, 441, 535, 546

mortgages : 303

most favoured
  nation : 59, 78, 93, 96, 100, 107, 109, 115, 118, 131, 143, 154, 170, 174, 201, 214, 320, 334, 338-340, 345-346, 348-349, 421, 488, 634
    precedence : 454
  nation clause : 100, 174, 201
  nation treatment : 334

Motion for Judgment on the Record : 585

multilateral : 75-77, 79, 94, 187, 303, 328-329, 360, 433, 517
  agreement : 348
  agreements : 543
  conventions : 451
  model convention : 338
  treaties : 267
  treaty
    New York Convention : 549
  Washington Convention : 2

Multilateralism : 75

multinational enterprise : 205, 254

multinationals : 71, 254

N

NAFTA : 76, 85, 87-88, 121, 124, 126, 129, 137, 139, 142, 156, 209, 211, 299, 348, 356, 411, 415, 427, 434, 440
  scope : 85, 88

NAI : 597

Napoleonic
  Code : 379, 396

national : 1-2, 9, 13, 16, 19, 21, 23-26, 37, 44, 56, 62, 95, 109, 121, 128, 133, 151, 208-209, 224, 252, 301, 327, 426-427, 432-433, 437, 445-446, 449, 471, 644
  argentine : 93
  content : 131
  courts : 269
  emergency : 118
  foreign : 527
  identity : 456
  investments : 13
  law : 67, 71, 165, 345
    inconsistencies with international : 453
  legislation : 69, 107
  protection : 333
  Register : 43
  resources : 130
  sovereignty : 327, 329
  sub-national : 127
  treatment : 59, 100, 212, 214, 329, 339, 346
  tribunals
    developing nations : 450

nationalisation : 22, 28, 42-43, 56, 101, 105, 107-108, 115, 175, 202, 225, 229, 260, 307-308, 367-368, 385, 392, 408, 438, 463, 475, 478, 480, 632, 655

nationalised : 41-42, 60, 371, 376, 409, 475, 631

nationalities
  multiple : 14

nationality : 6, 14-16, 18, 23-24, 37-39, 42, 48-50, 61, 90-91, 95, 101, 104, 128, 154-155, 162, 167, 185, 189, 191-192, 200-201, 203, 219, 221-223, 226, 247, 250, 257, 259, 261, 263-264, 268, 276-278, 284, 287, 291, 443, 450, 525-529, 619, 654
  acquisition : 223
  change : 223
  continuity : 525
  control : 526
  conventional : 282
  corporate : 14, 239, 257, 533
  corporate exception : 526
  corporations : 220
  definition : 257

    diversity : 529
    double : 14, 41, 49, 54, 92, 105-106, 111, 127-129, 167, 220-224
    effective : 226
    exclusion : 224
    explicit : 283, 534
    foreign : 41
    functional : 251
    investors capacity : 525
    Italy : 612
    legal : 286
    original : 223
    personal rights : 466
    precautionary measures : 531
    requirements : 614
    residence : 130
    Rwanda : 49
    subsidiary : 530
nationality (Overseas) : 219
nationals : 2, 19-24, 26-27, 30, 55, 78, 95, 115, 185, 189, 196, 209, 221, 258, 260, 266, 284, 319, 375, 409, 428-430, 449
    corporations : 526
    defined : 28, 35, 40, 46, 55
    foreign : 55
NATO : 421
natural person : 91, 95, 106, 110-111, 128, 184, 209, 221, 227, 250, 268, 525, 656
naturalisation
    honesty : 223-224, 228, 232-236
negotiation : 2, 31, 43, 66, 75, 105, 108, 184, 200, 215-216, 279, 295, 316, 522, 531, 542-543, 550, 609
Netherlands : 161, 167, 181, 221, 268, 304, 348, 376, 427, 435, 484, 606, 621
new form of investment : 571
new forms of investments : 581
new law : 475
New York Convention : 158, 188, 207, 549, 601
NFI : 314
NGO : 134
Nguyen : 451
Nicaragua : 246, 268
Nicolas : 467-470, 478
Niger : 518

no interest, no standing : 133
non-discriminatory : 343, 404
non-governmental organisations : 57, 134, 355
non-nationalisation : 477
   maximum protection : 479
   stabilisation : 478
   validity : 476
non-nationalisation inclusion in State Contract : 480
non-nationals : 449
non-retroactivity principle : 622
North America : 105
North American Agreement on environmental cooperation : 124
North American Users Council : 554
Norway : 173, 179, 613
Norwegian : 173, 176, 372, 661
not less favourable treatment : 340
notice
   sufficiency : 390
Nottebohm : 228-229, 231, 233-234
Novelles : 245-246
NSK Corporation v. Fag Italia : 584
nullity : 312
nullum commodum capere de sua propria iniuria potest et ex delicto non oritur actio : 41, 653

O

O.P.C. : 546
OECD : 7-8, 65, 76, 78-80, 103, 115, 126, 221, 338, 359, 367, 433, 440, 452, 627
Office of the US Trade Representative : 590
Ogutçu : 9
OHADA : 125, 498, 517, 519
   origins : 517
Oman : 11-12
OMC : 537
ONU Resolution
   international law practice : 478
OPIC : 594
Oppenheim : 263
options : 303

Organisation for African Harmonisation of Business Rights : 125
Organisation for Economic Cooperation and Development : 7, 76, 78, 627
Organisation of the Islamic Conference : 94
origins : 252
Orinoco : 503
other hostile measures : 583
Ouakrat :536
outsourcing : 12
Overseas Private Investment Corporation : 594

P

pacta sunt servanda : 29, 124, 332, 362, 464-465, 477, 480, 616-617
Pam v. U.S. : 591
Pan American : 275, 279, 285, 323, 393
Panevezys/Saldutiskis Railway case : 23
Paraguay : 91, 315, 366, 404
Park : 509
participation
  majority : 371
participations : 18, 113, 187, 202, 294-295, 529
partnership : 48-49, 99, 204, 208, 210, 298, 652
Paulsson : 509
PCIJ : 23
peace treaties : 118-119, 258
percentage
  control : 531
performance requirements : 89, 130, 156, 175, 209, 212-214
Permanent Court of International Justice : 23, 27, 479
permanent resident
  Australia : 14, 57, 91-93, 109-111
  Canada : 127
Peru : 128-129, 154, 156, 228, 247, 267
Peruvian : 129
petition to invest : 322
phantom
  companies : 90
  corporations : 90, 245, 249
Philippines : 99

physical persons : 8, 55, 57-58, 91, 95, 117, 167, 175, 180, 190-191, 219, 236, 241-242, 257, 284, 330, 485, 526-527, 640, 650
  protection : 220
Pilkington : 519
place
  of incorporation : 95, 180, 189, 247
  of residence : 16-17
pledges : 303
Poland : 169, 484
Polish : 169-170, 372
political : 1, 5, 20, 22, 69-70, 73, 75, 77, 104, 196, 232, 239, 248, 294, 374, 431, 474, 505, 531, 594, 612, 631
  judges : 500
  ONDD : 522
Pope case : 211
portfolio investments : 10, 38
Poudret : 598
precedence : 62, 67, 107, 160, 319, 353, 420, 483, 507, 513
  amicable settlement : 614
  BIT over multilateral convention : 598
  contract rights : 476
  domestic law : 468
  international law : 452-453
  most faboured nation : 454
  national law : 452
  new law : 467
price dumping : 567
principal business : 15
principle of international law : 66, 148, 452
private international law : 466
  appeals : 598
privileges : 55, 59, 61, 295
procedural due process : 400
proceeding
  adversary : 42
promotion : 1, 9, 35, 37, 48, 50, 54, 65, 69, 71, 73, 82, 84, 99, 106, 118, 173, 294, 306, 319, 356, 627-628, 644, 647
protection : 2, 6, 8, 10-11, 13, 15, 18-21, 23, 25, 28, 30, 40-41, 56, 59, 66, 72-73, 78, 85, 89, 93, 104, 114, 134, 157, 159, 163, 215, 219, 259, 303-304, 345, 429, 452, 459, 464, 644

conventional : 294
diplomatic : 468
directives : 338
environment : 361
freeze : 460
intellectual property : 342
legal : 451
stabilisation : 459
State Contracts : 459

protection clause : 461
Protocol between the Kingdom of Belgium and the Republic of Zaire, regarding the mutual Promotion of Investments : 650
Protocol de Colonia : 367, 404
Protocol of Cotonou
 natural person : 93
prototype BIT : 340
PT AMCO : 275-277
PT AMCO INDONESIA : 275, 277, 323
public establishments : 518
public interest : 47, 51, 56, 96, 141, 144, 164, 171, 175, 181, 196, 312, 374, 392, 459, 462-463
 intangibility clause : 472
public international law : 330, 466, 478
public international system : 463
public law : 81
public law corporation : 306
public purpose : 164, 366, 370, 373, 404-405, 408, 644
 Indonesia : 393
public training : 86
public utility
 bad faith : 475
 investments : 473

R

Rabel : 247
Rand : 546
ratification
 legislative : 541
 mutual : 541

RDC : 37, 41, 654
Read : 233, 234, 235
real value : 42, 181, 411, 633, 645
rebus sic stantibus : 480
Rechtskundig Weekblad : 496
reciprocity : 72-73, 317, 338, 569
reconsideration
  rules : 514
reference
  international law : 471
Répertoire : 5, 245
re-privatisation : 407
Republic Ins. Co. v. Cunningham : 220
Republic of Slovakia : 446
requisition : 370
res adjudicata
  stare decisis distinguished : 397
res inter alios acta : 169, 186-187, 206, 222, 265, 432, 444, 563
res inter alios acta, aliis nec nocet, nec prodest : 432
res ipsa loquitur : 350
res judicata : 571, 587
residence : 17
Residual Jurisdiction of USCIT : 578
residual jurisdiction of USCIT : 578
restitutio ad integrum : 410, 644
restitution : 119, 344, 388, 410, 416, 418, 421, 631
Revere case : 594
Revere Copper and Brass : 594
revocation : 584
revolt : 419, 421, 633
revolution : 118, 418, 421, 633
Revue belge de droit : 26, 479
Reyntjens : 3
Rio de Janeiro : 355
RIPA : 50, 53
risk : 2, 7, 10, 14, 24, 53, 69, 77, 84, 97, 102, 144, 169, 174, 199, 210, 235, 303, 306, 308, 310, 314, 318, 352, 415, 486, 527
  legislative : 460
  sovereignty : 462
Romero : 511-514

Rousseau : 471
Royal Thai Government v. U.S. : 584
royalties : 423, 426-427, 541
rules
   NAFTA : 583
Russia : 169, 182, 184, 200
Russian : 170, 179, 385
Rwanda : 36, 48-50, 52-53, 421, 529, 543
Rwandan : 48-51, 53

S

safety
   MAI : 65, 114, 123, 173, 178, 330, 356-357, 359, 459, 534
SAKIMA : 311
Salem : 72
Salem : 72, 316, 375
Salini case : 83
Salini Costrutione : 306
Salini v. Morocco : 306
salus patriae suprema lex : 370
Schachter : 66
Schmidt : 542
Schokkaert : 2, 8, 15, 26-27, 290, 637
Schrijver : 376
scope : 5, 7-8, 11, 14, 16, 20, 42, 67, 74, 85, 100, 137, 141, 173-174, 185, 193, 210-211, 253, 268, 276, 293, 313, 325, 337, 346, 350, 375, 409, 437, 476, 619
   abuse : 503
   CCJI : 518
   commerce excluded : 619
   legal : 455
   limited recourse : 552
   obligations : 625
   of application of Convention : 535
   services : 536
   stabilisation : 479
   stabilisation clauses : 465
   State Contracts : 467
   subrogation : 447
   Washington Convention : 530

seat : 37-38, 99, 142, 162, 179-180, 185, 189-191, 201, 243, 248, 251, 255, 257, 260, 277, 393, 632

secretariat
  additional facility rules : 552

Secretary General : 606
  consent : 601
  request for annulment : 550

Secretary General ICSID : 614

Selleslags : 424, 604

Senegal : 287, 518

Seoul Declaration : 450

sequestration
  assets : 119, 258, 536

Serbia : 192, 195, 421

services : 6, 9, 12, 38, 40, 48, 81, 86, 89, 112, 136, 156, 164, 215, 254, 295, 301, 311-313, 538, 654
  for production : 537
  included in BIT : 536
  produced : 537

settlement of disputes : 3, 69, 92, 116, 144, 148-151, 160, 192, 197, 203, 438, 440, 486, 500, 507, 539, 610, 612
  scope : 105

Seychelles : 49

SGS : 481, 513-514

SGS v. Pakistan : 513

shareholders
  majority : 43, 45, 107, 113, 238, 287, 289, 529, 639
  minority : 101, 529

shares : 9-10, 15, 21, 44-45, 49-50, 58, 95, 101, 112, 130, 154-155, 164, 185, 188, 194, 202-203, 238, 262, 265-266, 268, 279-280, 285, 290, 295, 298, 301-302, 342, 389, 402, 414, 531, 632

shares of stock : 303

Shihata : 482

Singapore : 99

SINZA : 44, 350

Slovakian Republic : 446

Slovenia : 623

SOABI : 287

Soabi : 284, 287

Soabi vs Senegal : 287

social interest : 47, 394
Société industrielle zaïroise : 44
Société nationale des autoroutes de Maroc : 306
soft law : 124, 234, 361, 434
Solvay : 371
Solvay-Ebensee : 260
SOMICO : 311
Sornarajah : 66
South African : 311
Southern Pacific Middle East Ltd : 544
sovereign : 25, 47, 97, 114, 240, 243, 361, 374, 385, 394, 449, 524, 646
    alienation of power : 463
sovereignty : 21, 24, 47, 149, 252, 315-317, 367, 385, 405, 450, 524, 619-620, 647
    abstention : 464
    alienation : 476
    developing countries : 450, 498
    immunity : 548
    inalienability : 472
    judicial : 528
    national : 450
    non-nationalisation clauses : 476
    permanent : 478
    personal : 449
    primacy : 467
    retention : 463
    right to abandon : 462
    territorial : 449, 451
Soviet Year-book : 385
Spain : 187, 196, 261-262, 363, 598, 606
Specific Agreements : 483
spouses : 55
squatters : 417
Sri Lanka : 419, 428
stabilisation : 59, 165, 320, 460
    domestic law : 467
    expression of sovereignty : 472
    legal effect : 464
    limitation : 479
    mandatory : 471
    protection clause : 460

validity : 467
voided clause : 468
stability of the financial sector : 131
stabilization
  examples : 460
  interpretation : 534
standard treatment : 212
Standing : 590
Standing
  constitutional : 591
  prudential : 591
stare decisis : 396-397, 587
State : 14, 16, 18-19, 22-25, 29-30, 37-39, 489
  contract responsibility : 469
  host : 453
  international responsibility : 515
  legislative measures : 462
State agencies : 149
State Contract : 7, 29, 45, 149, 160, 455-456, 458, 461, 494, 497, 512, 515, 531, 542, 595, 612, 636, 658
  characteristic : 455
  countervailing clauses : 460
  internal legal order : 465
  international legal order : 466
  lex contractus : 466
  nationality : 534
  reference in BIT : 480
  unilateral change : 460
State Court : 566
State interest : 137
States : 1-3, 6, 18-19, 21-29, 45, 49, 76, 80, 83-85, 93, 101, 114, 142, 156, 197, 208-209, 263-264, 267, 330, 356, 367, 421, 432, 514, 612, 627
  industrialised : 452, 629
Stern : 134
stock exchange : 10, 42
stock market : 10
Subrogation : 177-178, 431, 438, 440
  Ducroire : 441
  State agency : 602
subsidiaries : 1, 12, 58, 161, 205, 268

subsidiary : 581
subsidiary nationality : 226, 251, 531
subsidies : 566
substantive due process : 399
Sudan : 49
Sufficiency of Evidence : 589
Swaziland : 49
Sweden : 162, 184, 188, 268, 428, 484
Swiss : 185, 188, 190, 193, 195, 197, 248, 338
Switzerland : 161, 184, 189, 191, 193-194, 197-198, 268, 484, 486
Syria : 421

T

Ta Chen Stainless Steel Pipe : 584
Ta Chen v. US : 591
taking : 9, 52, 196, 278, 314, 369, 375, 383, 393, 412, 417, 476, 636-637, 645, 651
Talbot case : 211
Tanzania : 403
technology : 9, 11-12, 89, 125, 156, 175, 214
territoriality : 257, 619, 655
territory : 12, 14-15, 19, 21, 24, 30, 38, 41, 55, 85, 90, 104, 118, 140, 154, 156, 162-163, 166, 174, 180, 187, 189, 215, 246, 249, 287, 298, 300-301, 315, 356, 359, 361, 427-428, 436, 439, 473, 518, 549
    domestic law : 449
Texaco/Calasiatic case: 478
Texas International Law Journal : 473
Thailand : 54-56, 99
The African Users' Council : 554
third State : 26, 143, 154-155, 162-163, 168-169, 174, 180, 185, 191-192, 201, 208, 214, 262, 264-266, 270-271, 298, 339, 347, 353, 371, 375-376, 605, 613
ThyssenKruppAcciai : 590
Tjianjin case : 581
Tjianjin v. US : 580
Togo : 518
Totes-Isotoner : 590
trade transactions : 566
traditional protection law : 337
transfer : 1, 12, 56, 89, 95, 156, 175, 182, 211, 213-214, 279-280, 285, 296, 305, 324-325, 423, 425-433, 439, 598, 604, 651

international payments : 424
transnational enterprise : 254
transparency : 80, 131, 134, 136, 139, 141-142, 351
treaties : 2, 7, 19, 26, 28-29, 62, 65-66, 73, 78, 80, 85, 211, 303, 385, 463, 514, 624
  environment : 362
  international : 66
  multilateral : 66
  private international law : 466
treatment : 3, 24, 29, 40-41, 59, 76, 78, 83, 93, 100, 105, 109, 113, 127, 143, 149, 154-155, 163, 165, 169-171, 174, 180, 201-202, 211, 220, 316, 331, 346, 452-453, 459
  free zone : 633, 644
  interpretation : 534
  minimum standard : 114
  more favourable : 454, 486
  national : 63, 488
  non-discriminatory : 81
Treaty
  concerning conflicts of nationality : 233
  for the acknowledgement and execution of foreign arbitration awards : 548
  of Vienna : 19, 175, 211, 616, 621, 625
Treaty of Vienna : 19, 625
triangular investments : 266, 269, 271, 289
triangular transactions : 186
triangulation : 262
TSI Corporation : 335
turnkey : 12, 300, 302-303, 314

U

U.S. Customs : 580
Uganda Model Convention : 148
UK : 21, 200-202, 247-248, 250, 275, 319, 345, 609
Ukraine : 57, 59-60
Ukrainian : 57-58
umbrella : 41, 160, 290, 480-482, 484, 487, 489, 513, 541, 647, 653
  model conventions : 484
umbrella clause : 612
UN : 166, 356, 368-369, 376, 385, 422, 450, 497, 544, 549, 614, 632
UN Commission for Commerce and Development : 376
UNCCD : 376

INDEX 737

UNCED : 355
UNCITRAL : 102, 108, 115, 146, 165-167, 177, 184, 188, 203-204, 207, 215, 497, 544, 550, 559, 600, 614
UNCTAD : 70, 185, 211, 328, 367, 369, 372, 627
unemployment : 1, 237
unfair discrimination
  US Government : 570
United Kingdom : 200, 219, 248, 363, 606, 620
United Nations : 47, 70, 87, 184, 203, 254, 355-356, 497, 549, 601, 615, 620
  arbitration rules : 600
  Secretary General : 610
United Nations Conference on Environment and Development : 355
United States : 95, 116, 204, 237, 594
United States Constitution : 382, 399
United States Customs Court : 576
United States of America : 219
Universal Declaration of Human Rights : 236
unjust enrichment : 566
Upper Silesia : 372
Uruguay Round Agreements Act : 590
US : 38, 48-49, 82, 85, 114, 116, 136, 142, 173, 204-205, 208-209, 230, 239-240, 247, 301, 314, 320, 404, 420, 429, 436, 482, 549, 594, 610, 614
US Department of State : 205
US formula for treatment : 340
USA : 21, 45, 123, 160, 200, 250, 301, 358, 427, 437, 637
usages of international commerce : 596
USCIT : 564, 568, 573
  in International Commerce : 571
  Rules : 579
USSR : 180, 182, 382, 384

V

Vaccum Salt v. Ghana : 527
value
  acquisition : 413
  actual : 405
  added : 433
  asset : 412
  balance sheet : 402

basis : 412
book : 403, 645
commercial : 405
economic : 303, 305, 312, 627
exploitation : 413
fair market : 164, 411
fiscal : 413
full : 403
genuine : 160, 411
insured : 444
legal : 342, 434
legal total : 462
market : 402, 410
net : 403
net accounting : 402
objective : 403, 405
partial : 402
real : 403
replacement : 413, 645
stock exchange : 402
stock market : 411
subjective : 410
tax : 412
total : 3, 9-10, 39, 42, 51-52, 57, 60, 66, 89, 122, 144, 156, 165, 171, 181, 193, 293, 298, 301, 305-306, 337, 369, 372, 389, 404-405, 465
true : 411
true market : 412
yield : 402

Van Boxsom : 237, 243-245, 259
Van De Voorde : 66, 68
Vandeputte : 444
Van Hecke : 494
Van Houtte : 504
Vascannie : 338
Venezuela : 304, 403
Venezuelan : 304
Verhoeven : 479
Verwey : 376
Vienna Convention on the law of treaties : 615
Vilkov : 385

Visser : 375

W

Waelde : 473
waiver : 540
War : 28, 35, 258, 267, 404, 414, 418, 649
Warner Lambert v. US : 587
Washington Convention : 27, 103, 108, 135-136, 188, 192, 198, 202-203, 250, 252, 278, 309, 437, 445, 471, 513, 523, 527, 531, 533, 552, 602
  conflicts : 598
Weil : 67, 456, 460-462, 468, 471, 482, 514
Westlake : 247
Wimbledon : 479
Wimbledon Steamboat : 647
Wisma : 323, 325, 393
Wolff : 239
World Bank : 338, 412, 433, 520, 539
writs : 466, 550
WTO : 590

Y

Yearbook of International Law : 337, 376

Z

Zaire : 21, 44-45, 301, 420, 429, 649, 651
Zaire currency : 651
Zairianisation : 650
Zambia : 49
Zekos : 254
Zhejiang : 589
Zimbabwe : 49

IMPRIMÉ EN BELGIQUE

Etablissements Emile Bruylant, société anonyme, Bruxelles
Prés.-Dir. gén. : Jean Vandeveld, av. W. Churchill, 221, 1180 Bruxelles